SIR HALLEY STEWART TRUST PUBLICATIONS

ELIZABETHAN
NONCONFORMIST TEXTS
Volume III

THE WRITINGS OF
HENRY BARROW

1587-1590

THE WRITINGS OF

HENRY BARROW

1587-1590

Edited by

LELAND H. CARLSON

PH. D.

Published for
THE SIR HALLEY STEWART TRUST

GEORGE ALLEN AND UNWIN LTD
RUSKIN HOUSE
MUSEUM STREET LONDON

PREFACE

THIS and its companion are the third and fourth volumes in the series on "Elizabethan Nonconformist Texts." Volume I was issued in 1951 with the title, *Cartwrightiana*. Volume II was issued in 1953, *The Writings of Robert Harrison and Robert Browne*. I had hoped that Volumes III and IV would have been ready for the printer by 1957, but this hope proved illusory. During the past five years I have served as president of Rockford College in Rockford, Illinois. The problems connected with the transition from a women's college to a coeducational institution, with the establishment of Rockford Men's College, and Rockford Evening College, with the constant need for fund-raising and friend-raising, with the insistent demands for speeches, committee meetings, conferences, with the care and feeding of trustees, counselors, faculty, students, alumnae, alumni, parents, donors, friends, critics, and Monday morning academic quarterbacks, have been legion. Correspondence has been heavy, crises have been numerous, trips have been frequent, and the months have been replete with inaugurations, workshops, educational sessions, programme planning, board meetings, interviews, complaints and suggestions. In short, the centrifugal pulls of the president's office have not been conducive to centripetal research. This book has been prepared in the early hours of the morning, late evenings, snatches of time the summer "vacations." It has been a labour of love and a very present help in times of trouble. I have learned from hard experience why most administrators are compelled to abandon research.

Volumes III and IV present for the first time the collected works of Henry Barrow and John Greenwood, for the period 1587-1590. There are forty items, of which sixteen are by Barrow, six by Greenwood, and five by both men, in addition to thirteen related Barrowist items in the Appendix. In later

volumes, *The Writings of Henry Barrow and John Greenwood*
for the period 1591-1593, there will be approximately twenty-
five items, many of which are made available to the general
reader for the first time. It is deplorable that the basic
writings of these two founding fathers of Separatism are not
widely known, even to scholars. The reasons are not far to
seek. Some of the documents exist in manuscripts difficult to
locate, read, and understand. Others exist in rare tracts and
books. There are only two copies of *A Plaine Refutation*
(1591). There are about a half a dozen copies of *A Brief
Discoverie of the False Church*. There are two copies of the
first edition of *A True Description out of the Worde of God, of
the Visible Church*, wrongly catalogued, unlisted in the *Short-
Title Catalogue*, and competing with other " first " editions
incorrectly listed. Some of the material has been made available in esoteric publications with a limited circulation, and
some of it has been published with incorrect attributions of
authorship. The harvest truly is plenteous, but the labourers
have been few, and the consequent crop has been small. There
have been about six research specialists in this field during the
last sixty years — for an average of one each decade. Certain
it is that the origins of Separatism, Independency, and Congregationalism are deserving of serious study, and my hope is
that the publication of the basic documents in conveniently
accessible books will further this study. Separatism strengthened the Lutheran doctrine of the priesthood of all believers.
It promoted the spirit of individualism. It re-enforced the
emphasis on freedom of inquiry. And in insisting upon the
spiritual principle of a direct, immediate, and intimate relationship between the infinite God of love and the finite man in
quest of sanctity and dignity, against the powerful opposition
of state and church, even at the cost of imprisonment and loss
of life, Separatism and Separatists became the benefactors of
true religion and spiritually-minded men by aiding the process
of the recovery of the innate rights of man.

There are thirteen entries for Barrow in the *Short-Title
Catalogue*. Number 1520 should be dated about 1680-1.

Preface

Number 1521 is not by Barrow, and therefore numbers 1522 and 1522a are also wrongly attributed to him. Number 1526 is not a first edition, and the Harmsworth copy at the Folger Shakespeare Library is not a first edition, but probably a third edition. Number 1527 is not a second edition, and the copy at the British Museum is identical with the Harmsworth copy. For Greenwood the *Short-Title Catalogue* has four entries. The first item (number 12339) is correct, but the second entry (12340) should be dated 1603. The British Museum copy (3475 b. 20) is not a 1590 edition but a re-issue of the first edition, with the addition of Greenwood's *A Fewe Observations*, and with the date 1603 (A i *recto* — A iv *verso*), although the date 1590 has been reprinted on the title page. The third entry (12341) is correct, but the book may have been printed in England. The fourth item (12342) wrongly attributes *M. Some Laid Open in His Coulers* to Greenwood, on the basis of the initials I. G. It is certain that Greenwood could not have written this book, which is somewhat Presbyterian in viewpoint and somewhat like Martin Marprelate's pen in style. The probable author is Job Throkmorton.

A statement needs to be made about the principles and rules followed in editing documents. In the first two volumes of this series, an attempt was made to reproduce the documents *literatim*, with superior letters, abbreviations, indications of omission of " er " and " re," of " m " and " n," and with slavish accuracy in the reproduction of " i " and " j," " u " and " v." Dr. Albert Peel wanted to resist the temptation to modernize the text, but I have concluded that the literal reproduction is expensive to print, slow to read, and difficult to justify in these days when microfilm and photostats are available. Consequently I have reduced superior letters, extended abbreviations, regularized the use of " i " and " j," " u " and " v." I have not altered spellings, except that " then " becomes " than," yᵉ becomes " the " and yᵗ becomes " that." If capitalization and punctuation occasionally needed adjustment, I felt free to make changes. I have tried to retain the spelling, tone, flavour, and vocabulary of the period, but

I have also tried to assist the general reader who dislikes interruptions to his reading and thinking. Some idea of the differences involved in the two philosophies of editing may be seen in the following example:

Y^e otħ goûnm^t y^t attēds uppō ye BB. & patrones curtesie, wch o^r Saui^{or} X. cōdēns wth no ûᴓtain voyse, & wch like a silû tōge is oppꝑssed wth a ḿvailous heat, we haue ꝓued more dāgerous then sī & ꝓtēse. but yor mīisters pphane ye L. table wth whorem^{rs}, usur^{rs}, & otħ. O^r god is a ielous god.

The other government that attends uppon the bishops' and patrones' curtesie, which our saviour Christ condemns with no uncertain voyse, and which like a silver tongue is oppressed with a marvailous heat, we have proved more dangerous than sin and pretense. But your ministers prophane the Lord's table with whoremasters, usurers, and others. Our God is a jelous God.

Since England continued to use the Julian calendar after 1582, all dates are given in Old Style. If a date falls between January 1 and March 24, it is given in Old Style for the month and day, but the year is given both in Old and New Style. Therefore, we shall find December 31, 1592, and January 1, 1592/3, March 24, 1592/3, and March 25, 1593.

I owe a special debt of gratitude to the officials and staff of the Folger Shakespeare Library, where I have done much of my research. I am deeply grateful to Dr. Louis B. Wright for three Folger fellowships which have made possible prolonged periods of study and writing. To the staff of the Library of Congress, the New York Public Library, the Union Theological Seminary Library, the Sterling Memorial Library at Yale University, the Boston Public Library, the Houghton Library in Harvard, the Newberry Library in Chicago, Northwestern University Library, University of Chicago Library, and the Henry E. Huntington Library, I express my thanks. Likewise, to the officials and friends in the British Museum, the Public Record Office, the Lambeth Palace Library, Dr. Williams's Library, the Bodleian Library, the University Library and the Trinity College Library, Cambridge, I wish to record my appreciation.

Preface

To my former colleagues and friends at Northwestern University I feel grateful, especially to Dr. Gray C. Boyce, Dean Simeon E. Leland, Dean Moody E. Prior, and Dr. Arthur R. Tebbutt, as well as to the Committee on Research of the Graduate School of Northwestern University.

To those who have aided me in making the transition from heavily revised handwritten sheets to typed pages and galley proof, I tender my sincere thanks — especially to my secretary, Miss Rosie Johansen, the printers, George Allen and Unwin Ltd., and to the trustees of the Sir Halley Stewart Trust.

LELAND H. CARLSON.

April 25, 1959.

Southern California School of Theology
Claremont Graduate School
Claremont, California

CONTENTS

PREFACE   vi

INTRODUCTION   1

THE WRITINGS OF HENRY BARROW   47

1587

I.   Four Causes of Separation   49

II.   Profes of Aparant Churche   67

III.   A Breefe Sum of Our Profession   81

IV.   Barrow's First Examination, November 19, 1587   86

V.   Barrow's Second Examination, November 27, 1587   101

VI.   A Pastoral Letter from Prison   106

1588

VII.   A Brief Summe of the Causes of Our Seperation,   118
       and of Our Purposes in Practise

VIII. Reply to Dr. Some's *A Godly Treatise*   151

1589

IX.   Barrow's Third Examination, January 1, 1588/9   170

CONTENTS

X. Barrow's Fourth Examination, March 18, 1588/9   173

XI. Barrow's Fifth Examination, March 24, 1588/9   190
(Barrow's Version)

XII. Barrow's Fifth Examination, March 24, 1588/9   203
(Register's Version)

XIII. A True Description out of the Worde of God,   208
of the Visible Church

1590

XIV. The First Part of the Platforme   224

XV. Letter to Mr. Fisher   250

XVI. A Brief Discoverie of the False Church   259

Index   674

INTRODUCTION

Four Causes of Separation

This is the earliest known writing of Henry Barrow. It is a clear call to the truly devoted and spiritual believers, who profess Christ as Lord and Master, to forsake the Church of England, to separate themselves from the parish assemblies which are a motley, confused, disordered aggregation of non-believers as well as of nominal Christians. These assemblies are a repudiation of the New Testament model established in the first century by the apostles and their contemporaries. They are an abrogation of the will and testament of Christ, a repudiation of Christ as king, priest, and prophet, and an exaltation of antichrist who reigneth in the temple of God.

The first cause of separation is that the Anglican churches worship the true God in a false manner. By this allegation the Separatists charge that the worship service is based on the *Book of Common Prayer*. This book is uncharitably termed a piece of swine's flesh, Dagon's stump, a device of men, a human invention, a false idol, a mark of the beast, an abominable sacrifice unto the Lord.

A second cause for separating from the established parish assemblies is that the principle of membership is wrong. The parish churches are geographical and ecclesiastical units. Membership is legal, comprehensive, required, and automatic. Consequently, churches are a spiritual hodge-podge, composed of unwilling and ungodly persons, comprised of the profane and secular, of the indifferent and the hostile, of cool disbelievers and luke-warm Laodiceans. As in the Roman Catholic Church, all are baptized and made automatic members, regardless of profession, practice, or protest. Baptism is general, and the sacrament of the Lord's Supper is almost

1

general, since only a few egregious persons are excluded, and since the power of excommunication is exercised by the hierarchical courts rather than by the minister and the congregation.

The third cause for separation is that the ministry of the Church of England is antichristian, false, and unscriptural, in reference to the calling of clergymen, to the method of selection, and to the mode of financial support. The ministers have not been rightly called by God, and therefore their entrance into the sheepfold of Christ is not in accordance with the laws and ordinances of the Scripture. Their selection has not been made by the congregation, but by the bishop or the patron, who has imposed them upon the people, and therefore is a violation of the true canons of ministerial election. Since they are supported by tithes, endowments, and wages, instead of by the free-will offerings of the faithful members, their subjection to the Old Testament system of Hebrew tithes instead of to the New Testament dispensation of voluntary support is disgraceful and discreditable.

The fourth cause of separation is the system of discipline, the method of governing the churches through an episcopal system, including the hated spiritual courts that exercise a secular and profitable jurisdiction. The true head of the church is Christ, not the Queen. Prince and parliament are not the source of ecclesiastical law, and their regulations do not take priority over the commands of God Himself. Reformation must proceed without tarrying for any permission from the magistrate, and progress is not effected by petitions to legislatures or suits to parliament. The apostles planted the gospel without the sanction of governments, and the christian church developed in the face of opposition and bitter persecution. The prince or magistrate or lord or commoner is subject to the law of Christ, and the kings of men are subservient to the King of Kings, who yields not his sceptre to any man. God's ways are not man's ways, God's law is higher than man's laws, and God's thoughts transcend the ideas of men. Christ endowed his government with divine power and majesty. No minister can serve two masters, and if man-made government imposes itself upon the servants of Christ, they are enjoined to resist it and to serve Christ only. The government of Christ's church is revealed in the New Testament, consists of pastors and doctors, elders and deacons, and is permanent, perpetual, and prescriptive. If Christ cannot rule through his own officers, he is dethroned, and antichrist rules in his stead. Christian liberty is a precious legacy, subject to no restrictions, and is to be defended unto death. Christ's government is the guardian of that liberty, is immutable, all-embracing, and divinely sanctioned.

Profes of Aparant Churche

This essay is a series of reasons why the parish churches of England are not the true, visible, apparant churches of Christ. It is a comprehensive and polemical challenge to the people to forsake the false church and join in building the new Mount Sion.

The true kingdom is the church of Christ, not the whole world. As an integral part of this kingdom, the New Testament pattern of church government is essential. Those who tarry for the magistrate, and who compromise their stand, previously admitted that the true government of the church was lacking. Now they assert that because they preach the word they need not be concerned with polity. Therefore they are not the apparant church.

It is clear to all that ecclesiastical jurisdiction is exercised by lordly archbishops and bishops, deans and archdeacons, chancellors and commissaries. Government has been forfeited to usurpers who continue the papal system, and the rightful government by pastors and teachers, elders and deacons, and the entire congregation, is thwarted. Since the usurpers do not constitute the true rulers of Christ's kingdom, their assemblies are not the apparant church.

In the true and rightly gathered assembly, any member may " tell the church," and may seek correction of abuses and transgressions. This right does not exist in the English churches, since the bishops and their courts have preempted this jurisdiction. Therefore they are not the apparant church. The commissaries and their courts have usurped the keys of the kingdom of Christ, and have deprived the congregation of the power to bind and loose. No true subject, entrusted with an office by his monarch, would overthrow that office without incurring the charge of being a traitor to his king. But the tolerating preachers have abdicated their disciplinary office to the bishop and commissary, and therefore are traitors to their heavenly king. Therefore they are not the true visible church.

The Anglican parsons have been called by a bishop or a patron. They in turn proceed to gather the good and the bad indiscriminately. But a true minister receives his calling from God and is selected by the consent of godly Christians without any admixture of profane multitudes, and he is called to keep separate the wheat and the chaff. Although men are fallible and sinful, and their secret sins cannot be fully known, the retention and toleration of open wickedness and gross pollutions constitute a blot against the church. Even if a teacher is joined with an Anglican parson, the latter is frequently an idol shepherd, a time-server, a dumb dog who cannot preach. Since the teacher lacks the authority of a true pastor or doctor, he cannot minister to a select company of gathered saints. The maintenance of this intolerable system proves that the present assemblies are not the apparant church of Christ.

The use of the magistrate's sword to enforce wicked ceremonies, punish those who seek to maintain a good conscience, impose read prayers, persecute the saints, and prevent the spiritual worship of God, is sufficient proof that the ecclesiastical establishment is not the apparant church. Furthermore, this false establishment not only continues its falsity, but it prevents the true church from developing. The false ministers not only refuse to reform the crying abuses but even

4

submit willingly and cravenly to their taskmasters who have usurped the functions of God's chosen vessels. Their great concern is for their own wages and stipends, rather than for the heavenly pattern of the church. During his ministry Christ instructed his disciples, and after his resurrection he spent forty days with the apostles, teaching them how to build the church according to his divine plan. The Anglican church is a refutation of this beautiful pattern. Not only is it deficient in small details of pins and curtains, which is inexcusable, but it lacks the chief pillars and walls, which is intolerable. Therefore, it is not the true apparant visible church of Christ.

A Breefe Sum of Our Profession

This manifesto of one page is a brief statement of the purposes of the Separatists and a presentation of the four reasons why they have forsaken the parish assemblies in England. The Separatists intend to seek the protection and peace of Almighty God, and to further the kingdom of Christ on earth. This general purpose is applicable to any christian sect, but different groups will place their own interpretation on the meaning and structure of Christ's kingdom. Specifically, the Separatists intend to establish a church with a covenant, with faithful and obedient Christians as members, and with officers chosen by the members. This church will be guided and governed by the laws of Christ, without alteration of, omission from, or addition to the pattern set forth in the New Testament. In this faith and order they will lead their lives, despite persecution and even deprivation of life. By these intentions, realized in a true church, they will repudiate the false worship, profane membership, the antichristian ministry, and unscriptural polity of the Church of England.

Barrow's First Examination, November 19, 1587

This examination does not provide us with ideas or teachings, but it affords us biographical details of Barrow's life. We learn that Barrow and a Mr. Hul visited Greenwood in the

Clink on November 19, 1587, just six weeks after the arrest of the Separatists. It is clear that the authorities had been searching for Barrow, since Mr. Shepherd, the keeper of the prison, arrested Barrow without a warrant, and Watson, the pursuivant, said he had sought Barrow for a long time. We learn of Barrow's presence at Cambridge University and Gray's Inn. It becomes clear from Barrow's testimony that he had been indicted for non-attendance at church, having violated the statute of 23 Elizabeth, *caput* 1. Barrow also testified that he did not live in London, that his father, Thomas, was still living in Norfolk, from which we may conjecture that both father and son were living in Shipdam in East Anglia.

The appearance of Barrow at Lambeth Palace before Archbishop Whitgift, Archdeacon Mullins, and Richard Cosin, vicar-general of the Province of Canterbury, gives us a fascinating insight into the character of two defiant men, Archbishop Whitgift and Barrow. The archbishop has a reputation among Puritans and Separatists for displaying " choler," and his temper rises above the surface occasionally. He was irritated because Barrow refused to accept and read the pursuivant's letter which emanated from Lambeth. He labelled Barrow a Donatist and a schismatic, accused him of pride and sedition, and threatened to arraign him as a heretic. He and Dr. Cosin accused Barrow of being clamorous, derided him for his memory, and gloated that his divinity was like his law.

The resistance of the Separatists to the *ex-officio* oath is depicted in this examination. Barrow believes that an oath is lawful, in proper circumstances, but he refuses to swear an oath before Whitgift. He irritates the archbishop by refusing to swear by the Bible or with hand on the Bible. He will not place his hand on the table or in the hand of the archbishop, and although he admits that it is not amiss to hold his hand towards heaven and swear, he will not do so under pressure or requirements ; but will use his liberty. He tells the archbishop bluntly that he will not swear before he knows the substance of the accusations against him. When Whitgift charges him with non-attendance at church, with disobedience to the queen, and with asserting that the Church of England is a false church, Barrow replies that since these are mere reports, he will not deign to answer until witnesses are produced. An impasse is reached, and when Barrow refuses to be bound to attend the Church of England service, although he is willing to enter bond with surety for his good behaviour, he is imprisoned in the Gatehouse.

Barrow's Second Examination, November 27, 1587

This examination was held eight days after the first one, at Lambeth Palace, before the Court of High Commission. When Barrow refused to take an oath until he knew the charges against him, the archbishop relented and caused a bill of objections to be read. The indictment summarized allegations against the Church of England, its false worship, ministry, membership, and polity. It charged Barrow with saying that the archbishop and bishops were antichrists, that elders were really bishops, that ministers and preachers were secret hypocrites, that Calvin and Beza were in error, and that catechisms were idolatrous. Archbishop Whitgift caustically remarked that Barrow in his impartiality regarded all of his enemies as equally reprehensible.

Having satisfied Barrow's humour by informing him of the matter of the bill, the archbishop expected immediate compliance from Barrow in taking the oath. Barrow irritated the archbishop by replying that the form of the bill was false. When Whitgift demanded a direct answer to his question of taking the oath, Barrow threw caution to the winds, refused to swear, and bluntly retorted that there was more reason for demanding that the archbishop take an oath. Whitgift exploded, peremptorily ordered Barrow into close imprisonment, and forbade him to have any visitors. Whitgift boastfully prophecied that Barrow would tell another tale before the archbishop had finished with him, but he was completely wrong. Barrow yielded not an inch, amplified his tale through his books, and remained in prison, defying the archbishop even by his death in 1593.

A Pastoral Letter from Prison

Shortly after his arrest, imprisonment, and appearance before the Court of High Commission, Barrow wrote a letter to the Separatists, who appear to have organized themselves into an assembly of believers. This assembly seems to have been an informal one, an incipient Separatist congregation. Evidently many people were engaged in a serious soul-searching as to what they should do. Was it better to continue in their parish assemblies, remain obedient to the ecclesiastical law and hierarchy, and hope that religious conditions would improve? Should they heed the advice of those who said that it was better to bear the burdens for a time until the Lord's pleasure ordained otherwise? Was it honest principle or only expedient policy to hope for the best in the meantime and to use prayer and such liberty as they possessed to bring in the kingdom of God? In short, what was God's will in the critical issues which these radical Puritans confronted?

Barrow warns his friends of three prevailing conditions or factors. One was the prevailing conditions of materialism and indifference. The times were evil, people were preoccupied with worldly cares, and the Lord's field was untilled and even unattended. A second factor was the negligence of the preachers, those false husbandmen, those incompetent and lazy builders, those deceitful labourers. They have planted good seed in poor soil, and they have sown unsound seed in the Lord's field. They have been building an ecclesiastical edifice for the last twenty-eight years (1559-1587), but the foundation is still lacking and not even one stone is rightfully placed. They have pretended to do the Lord's work, but they are deceiving themselves and others, and labour in vain. These false preachers are unwilling to preach a true gospel of repentance, but as false prophets they purchase peace with the world. Also, that ancient enemy, Satan, remains as watchful, as envious, and as malicious as ever.

Introduction

Because of the adverse *Zeitgeist*, Barrow exhorts his brethren to separate themselves, to avoid the wicked, and to refuse fellowship with the throng of iniquity. He reminds his readers that they are a chosen generation, a light set on a hill, a holy nation, a people set at liberty, a royal priesthood. He urges them to avoid vacillation, and, remembering the warning given to the lukewarm Laodiceans, to be either hot or cold. Since the Lord abhorreth a double-minded man, Barrow warns them not to halt between two opinions or two courses of life, not to sit on the religious fence, not to forsake the society of Christ's servants. Christ has ordained that beautiful order and pattern of government for his church, and it is worthy of all the suffering it entails.

Barrow concludes his pastoral letter by describing his experience before the Court of High Commission. It is a pontifical court of bishops and well-fed silken priests, who show forth neither equity, charity, nor conscience. He relates his refusal to take an oath, his promise to answer truly and directly, and his defiance of the archbishop, who loses his temper and orders Barrow committed to close imprisonment.

A Brief Summe of the Causes of Our Seperation, and of Our Purposes in Practise

The first portion of this treatise is a repetition of " A Breefe Sum of Our Profession," and needs no restatement or further summary. The rest of the treatise is George Gifford's answer to each article and to the four principal transgressions. Barrow disclaims any purpose of meddling with the reformation of the state, and even insists that the Separatists do not seek the repair of the ruins of Jericho or the reformation of the Babylonish deformities in the Anglican church. The sole purpose is to establish a church in conformance with the laws and ordinances of Christ's Testament, and if that is done, the decline and fall of the Anglican church may safely be left to the Lord's visitation and judgment, which was exemplified in the destruction of Sodom and Babylon.

To the first purpose, that of seeking the peace and protection of the most High, and of seeking the kingdom of Jesus Christ, Gifford agrees that this is a purpose for all Christians, but he objects to the identification of the kingdom with separation and a new form of church discipline. The kingdom is inward and spiritual, not partial and disciplinary. To the second purpose, that of worshipping God aright, Gifford offers no objection or qualification. To the third purpose, that of organizing a church of believers only, bound together by a covenant, and of electing a group of church officers, Gifford asserts that such an action is pure Donatism. To the fourth purpose, that of establishing and obeying the laws of ecclesiastical polity as prescribed in the New Testament, Gifford replies that this is not the function of private individuals who have no lawful calling. To the fifth purpose, that of standing firm in faith and polity, even unto death, Gifford applauds the spirit of the martyrs, but points out that those who stand firm in error are guilty of great obstinacy, as Anabaptists and heretics have demonstrated in the past. To the sixth article, which is a transitional statement introducing the four principal transgressions, and which affirms the English churches to be heinously faulty and wilfully obstinate, Gifford indignantly answers that such an affirmation reveals intolerable pride and presumption by private men who have intruded themselves into God's judgment seat.

The first principal transgression charged is that the Anglican worship is the invention of man, even of antichrist. Gifford contends that the Anglican worship is the embracing of the Holy Bible and that many English ministers approve the *Book of Common Prayer* only to the extent that they believe it is consonant with the Scripture. The charge is made in the second principal transgression that the profane and ungodly are received without exception into the membership of English churches. Gifford counters with six observations. First, some pastors refuse to admit sinful persons to the sacrament. Secondly, the *Book of Common Prayer* expressly commands that those who lead ungodly lives shall not be admitted.

Thirdly, some individuals have been justly excommunicated. Fourthly, the worship of the faithful is not polluted by the presence of profane persons. Fifthly, worship in the Jewish Temple was practised by mixed multitudes. Sixthly, private men have no authority to reform the worship in temples or churches.

The third principal transgression alleged is that the Anglican ministry is false and antichristian. Gifford refutes this sweeping assertion by appealing to the judgment of learned and famous theologians in many churches, men who have approved of the Church of England. Is not such a church the true church, rather than a Separatist assembly, comprised of uncharitable members, closely resembling the churches of Anabaptists and Donatists? Why are English clergymen false and antichristian? He wisely asks for specific criteria by which ministers may be approved or condemned.

The fourth transgression charged against the English churches is that they are ruled by an ungodly, unchristian, and unscriptural ecclesiastical hierarchy. In keeping with his latent Presbyterian beliefs, Gifford is compelled to admit that there is an antichristian yoke under which the Church of England labours, but despite this weakness and handicap, the church is still the spouse of Christ.

Reply to Dr. Some's *A GODLY TREATISE*

Dr. Some's treatise consists of 37 pages, but we have Barrow's interleaved notes only through page 12. Since his comments answer various phrases, clauses, and sentences, they are necessarily brief and unsystematic, but they provide us nevertheless with some of his beliefs.

For Barrow the unpreaching ministers, those " dumb dogs " —to use the phrase of the prophet Isaiah (56: 10)—are unlawful clergymen. Since the preaching and expounding of the word are essential, since faith cometh by the hearing of the word, the unpreaching minister is failing to fulfill his true function.

Furthermore, a true calling is given by a particular congregation, not by the bishop or the patron. A double-beneficed clergyman and an unpreaching minister were not permitted by the teaching of Augustine or Calvin, and Scripture is against such abuses. Hence such ecclesiastical officials are not true ministers of Christ. Therefore, they cannot truly administer the sacraments. Likewise, the sacraments administered by the Roman Catholic priests are false, because the church itself is false.

The maintenance of ministers should not be by endowments, Jewish tithes, or mercenary wages. The Old Testament dispensation has been superseded by that of the New Testament, and the law has been abrogated by Christ. Too many Anglican clergymen, especially the roving ministers, mercenary chaplains, and collegiate divines, live in idleness and irresponsibility. The lordly prelates are the worst violators, and their princely palaces, worldly splendour, large revenues, and fat livings are in striking contrast to the simplicity of the gospel and the poverty of the disciples and apostles. The true minister of Christ lives by the free contributions of the faithful members, in accordance with need. They do not require the endowments of the past to maintain their work. Inasmuch as university endowments and church livings have the same popish origin as the abbeys, Elizabeth should confiscate them, even as her father, Henry VIII, seized the monastic establishments. Tithes, glebe lands, impropriations, benefices, prebends, and temporalities should redound to the prince and commonwealth, not to sychophantic parsons and lordly prelates and collegiate idle bellies.

Barrow is caustic in his criticism of the false ministers. He is equally scathing in his criticism of Dr. Robert Some and the Church of England. He derides Dr. Some's title, doctor of divinity, and declares that there is but one Doctor, even Christ, in whom the divine godhead dwelleth bodily. Dr. Some and his companions are proud Pharisees and counterfeit scribes. The Church of England, which Dr. Some equates with the commonwealth, as later, Edmund Burke also did, is a portion, a small part, a remnant, but it is not the visible church of Christ.

Barrow's views on the powers of the magistrate to enforce religion are blunt, terse, and lacking in toleration as understood to-day. The magistrate may set up true religion, may abolish false religion, and he may compel people to hear the word of God and participate in prayers. Thus, he may enforce external worship upon all his subjects. Open impenitent offenders cannot be made members without true faith and repentance. In asserting that such profane persons who participate in external worship and sacraments actually pollute the services and compromise the believers, Barrow seems to be inconsistent. If the magistrate can compel attendance for all, he seems guilty of compelling pollution, which results from such attendance. If the magistrate fails to do his duty, or if he establishes false worship—in violence of Scriptural standards—the only course open to the faithful is to reject such false worship and to suffer the penalties imposed. Barrow admits the right of the magistrate to coerce, and by his imprisonment demonstrates his willingness to suffer.

The magistrate may not select ministers to teach and preach God's word. This is the function of the individual gathered churches, of which the magistrate is but one member. The magistrate may assist the churches with the civil sword, even as the civil power of the Jewish monarchy assisted the Levites. But he may not encroach on the jurisdiction of the believers in calling their own minister. Faith cometh by the hearing of the word, and the people must always be careful in selecting true teachers and promoting right doctrine, and in rejecting false ministers and wrong teaching. In effect, Barrow transfers some of the ecclesiastical prerogatives of Queen Elizabeth to the individual congregations, and permits the crown to enforce what the congregations decide. Such a permission and such a transference were unpalatable to the queen, her government, her church, and her subjects, and consequently were rejected.

Henry Barrow

Barrow's Third Examination, January 1, 1588/9

This brief and incomplete examination provides us with a minimum of general information and with one Barrowist teaching. We learn that the lords of the Privy Council had ordered Richard Young and Dr. Robert Some to interrogate Barrow about some marginal writings in Dr. Some's book, *A Godly Treatise Containing and Deciding Certaine Questions, Moved of Late in London and Other Places, Touching the Ministerie, Sacraments, and Church*. The examination occurred on Tuesday, January 1, 1588/9, in the Fleet prison, where Barrow was a close prisoner, the warden being present. It is evident that the handwriting was not that of Barrow, but whether Greenwood or some other Separatist served as an amanuensis, we do not know. It is likely that the book had been seized in one of the prison chambers, and it is almost certain that Barrow knew who had made the marginal notations. When Barrow answered: " I know not what may be in the booke," he may be saying that he doesn't remember all the points discussed therein, or he may mean that he doesn't recall all the marginal notes added to the book.

The one doctrine manifested in this collection of marginal notes is the Separatist belief that the church has one head, even Christ. Therefore, Henry VIII was wrong in assuming the title of " only supreme head in earth of the Church of England, called *anglicana ecclesia*," and Elizabeth erred in taking a modified title of " the supreme governor . . . in all spiritual or ecclesiastical things or causes." Only a false church could have two heads, but in the Separatist church, Christ was the head, the magistrate was a humble member, the pastor was the leader of the particular church, and the congregation was the ultimate source of discipline. No wonder there " began a great discourse of the majestrate's power " !

Barrow's Fourth Examination, March 18, 1588/9

This examination before the Privy Councillors was one of the most important events in Barrow's prison life. It affords some biographical details, indicates two or three beliefs, and reveals the temper and spirit of Barrow, as well as the impression of him by his judges.

From this examination we learn that Barrow was imprisoned in the Gatehouse prison for about six months. The reasons for his incarceration were that he refused to take the oath *ex officio*, had refused to enter bond and to promise attendance at his parish assembly, and had defied and irritated the archbishop. But Whitgift said that he imprisoned Barrow because he was a sower of errors. Barrow challenged the archbishop to prove any errors, and when the archbishop indicated that he had matters of heresy to be charged against Barrow, the latter replied that he might err, but that by the grace of God he would never be a heretic. In complaining of injustice, Barrow contended that he had been imprisoned without due trial. When confronted with his admission that he had been found guilty of violating the statute of 23 Elizabeth, *c.* 1, Barrow replied that this statute was intended for papal recusants, not Protestants. When asked by Lord Burghley if Barrow had been allowed any conference, Bishop Aylmer and Dr. Some and Justice Young spoke of two conferences and of Barrow's mocking, arrogant, and unreverend speeches.

Barrow's beliefs emerge from his answers to questions. He recites the familiar four charges against the Church of England, and when both Bishop Aylmer and Lord Burghley asked wherein the worship of the Anglican churches was idolatrous, Barrow replied that there was nothing else in the *Book of Common Prayer*, that the commemorating of the saints in the church violated the first commandment, that the sanctifying of eaves and the observing of fasts was idolatrous, and that worship should be directed to God and not to any creature, even a saint. He dislikes the practice of naming days after saints, and, as the Quakers in the next century, he urges that Sunday, Monday, Tuesday, etc., be called the first, second and third days. Challenged because he had referred to Sunday as the Lord's day, Barrow quickly replied that so the Holy Ghost

15

had termed it in Revelation 1: 10. Asked what was wrong with the prayers in the *Book of Common Prayer*, Barrow answered that prayers should not be stereotyped and stinted, nor should they be tied to place, manner, time, or form. Lord Burghley was much interested in Barrow's view that Parliament could not provide tithes for clergymen, since tithes were a part of the Jewish law that had been abrogated by Christ. How then should the clergy be supported? Barrow contended that the profane and worldly people should not be taxed to pay the salaries of God's servants. Rather, let those who had been taught in the word—the faithful believers—support their minister by free-will offerings, by clear alms.

Barrow's high spirit is revealed in his unbridled tongue. After sixteen months of misery and lingering close imprisonment, after living with daily thoughts of injustice, unfairness, illegality, religious decay, spiritual cowardice, it is not surprising that Barrow spoke sharply, defied his questioners, threw caution to the winds. He did not believe in compromise, and he feared no man. He never learned that a soft answer turns away wrath, and that there are two sides to many disputed questions. Consequently, his temper flared upon provocation. He corrected the Bishop of London in a Scriptural quotation. He took issue with the Lord Chancellor, contradicted Lord Burghley, and irritated Lord Buckhurst. He bluntly told Archbishop Whitgift and Bishop Aylmer that they were devoid of all true learning and godliness. He probably amused Lord Burghley by describing the archbishop as a monster, a miserable compound neither ecclesiastical nor civil, that second beast, that man of sin, that son of perdition. Lord Burghley slyly asked for the Scriptural proofs of these labels. No wonder that Whitgift gnashed his teeth, spoke " in great choller," and very peremptorily denied Barrow's request for a conference.

Barrow's character and manner are partly revealed by the impressions made on his judges. Lord Buckhurst characterized Barrow as a proud presumptuous spirit, as one out of his wits, as a man who delighted to hear himself speak, and yet he complimented Barrow for his denial of heresy. Lord Chancellor Hatton declared that he never heard such stuff before in all his life. Lord Burghley perceived that Barrow was a fantastical fellow, who took delight in being the author of a new religion, who was possessed of a hot brain, who seemed to have a troubled conscience, and who took the Lord's name often in vain. The Bishop of London asserted that Barrow had mocked those who questioned him in prison, and Justice Young accused Barrow of arrogant and unreverend speeches against Archbishop Whitgift.

These criticisms give us an idea of the impression that Barrow made on others, but the fact that Barrow himself is the source of all these strictures on himself gives us a deeper insight into an honest soul.

Barrow's Fifth Examination, March 24, 1588/9.
  Barrow's Version

In the examination of March 18, 1588/9, Archbishop Whitgift said he had matter to call Barrow before him as a heretic. Although Barrow denied any charge of heresy, he was summoned six days later to appear before a special Commission appointed by the queen. This commission consisted of Sir Christopher Wray, Lord Chief Justice of the Queen's Bench ; Sir Edmund Anderson, Lord Chief Justice of the Court of Common Pleas ; Sir Roger Manwood, Lord Chief Baron of the Exchequer ; Sir Gilbert Gerard, Master of the Rolls ; Baron Thomas Gent, of the Court of the Exchequer ; Archbishop John Whitgift, Bishop John Aylmer, and Bishop Thomas Cooper ; and also chancellors, civil doctors, registrars and scribes.

The atmosphere of the examination was somewhat different from that of March 18, 1588/9. Although Barrow refused to take an oath, the Lord Chief Justice Wray did not berate him,

17

and Whitgift behaved with restraint. Accepting Barrow's statement that he would answer nothing but the truth, the archbishop concluded that a christian man's word was as true as his oath, and began the examination. In the course of the examination the bishops accused Barrow of evasion, said the papists answered more directly, and interrupted the interrogation with slanders and untruths. But Lord Chief Justice Wray complimented Barrow by saying he answered directly and compendiously and that he spoke well. He even stated that if Barrow had doubts on an answer it should not be recorded.

The examination consisted of twelve main questions besides those which were prompted by Barrow's answers. The questions were based on material which Dr. Some had obtained from conferences and reading, and also on confessions made by Clement Gambell, John Dove, and Mr. Love. Material had been taken from manuscript treatises found in the possession of Quintin Smith and Roger Jackson. Much of this material may be seen in " Certain Wicked Sects and Opinions," conveniently summarized in " The Assertions of the Conventicles Lately Apprehended." Barrow explained his view on the Lord's Prayer, saying it was a foundation for all prayer but that it was not prescribed as a substitute for individual prayer. He denounced read prayers and prescribed liturgies, and characterized the *Book of Common Prayer* as popish and idolatrous. Although he believed that sacraments were not rightly administered in the Church of England, he concluded that those who had been baptized in Queen Elizabeth's reign needed not and ought not to be rebaptized. He characterized the ecclesiastical laws, courts, and governors as unlawful and unchristian. On the touchy question of the queen's prerogative in ecclesiastical matters, Barrow acknowledged the queen as supreme governor of the realm and church, but denied to the queen or to the church itself any power to make laws for the church other than those found in the word of God. He was somewhat hesitant about the prince's extent of power to alter the law of Moses, and concluded that the moral law must be upheld but that the ceremonial law had been abrogated by Christ and therefore could be altered by the prince. Barrow denied the right of private men to reform the state in a public reformation if the prince neglected his duty, but no man should consent to any unlawful action commanded by the prince. Barrow had previously answered that the prince could not make laws for the church, and when he was asked if each church or parish should have a presbytery, he replied that each congregation to the utmost of its power should seek to establish an eldership.

At the conclusion of his examination, Barrow was taken back to prison while his brethren were examined. Then he was brought back again before his examiners, and Archbishop Whitgift asked if Barrow would take an oath in accordance with the Act of Supremacy. He protested his loyalty as a subject to the queen and against her enemies, but said he could not swear loyalty to a successor whom he knew not and who might be a papist. Then the archbishop asked two more pointed questions. If the prince neglected his duty or failed to correct abuses, not in the state but in the church, could the church reform without tarrying for the prince. Barrow said the church could do so, and ought to do so, even though the prince prohibited the same and threatened death to violators. Then the archbishop asked if the church could excommunicate the prince, and who would pronounce the same. Barrow did not flinch or hedge, but replied that with the church of Christ there was no respect of persons, that if anyone persisted in sin he should be excommunicated, the prince included, for the sake of his own salvation, and that the pastor should pronounce the excommunication.

Barrow's Fifth Examination, March 24, 1588/89.
      Register's Version

This examination is the record made by the register of Barrow's answers. It is substantially the same set of questions and answers, but the register's record is briefer and less interesting than Barrow's version. In the register's version, one question on the judicial law of Moses is omitted because the bishops ordered that the question and the answer be blotted out, evidently on the suggestion of Lord Chief Justice Wray. There are two questions on baptism in the register's version, but Barrow has omitted the one that pertained to infant baptism.

If we compare the questions and answers in the two versions, we notice that in Barrow's version the answer to the first question is slightly longer and includes a question on the meaning of *Pater Noster*. The second, third and fourth questions and answers are basically the same. In the fifth answer (Barrow's seventh), Barrow's version is longer, and includes disagreements and exceptions made by Bishop Aylmer and Judge Anderson. In one version the archbishop seems to be asking the question, but Barrow says Judge Anderson caused the question to be moved. In the sixth question (Barrow's fifth), the answers vary, and it seems that Barrow may have confused the answer he made. Part of his answer includes material in reply to the tenth question in the register's version. In the seventh question (Barrow's sixth), the register has shortened the question and has omitted Barrow's statement that persons once baptized need not and ought not to be baptized again. In the register's version, the eighth question pertains to infant baptism, but Barrow has omitted it, perhaps because he had already included a question and answer on baptism in general. In the register's ninth question (Barrow's eighth), the two versions agree, but Barrow includes the reactions of the bishops, their slanders and evil speeches, his reprimanding the Bishop of London, and Judge Wray's compliment. The tenth question and answer in the register's version agree with Barrow's fifth question and answer. In the eleventh question, both versions have presbytery in the question, but in the answer Barrow has " eldership " and the register has " presbytery " again. The register's twelfth answer pertains to the touchy matter of the queen's possible excommunication. Barrow's version is three times as long. In the thirteenth and final question (Barrow's tenth and twelfth), the register has omitted

Barrow's statement that private men should not intrude into
the office of the prince.

The register has omitted some of the interesting aspects,
such as the refusal to swear, the questions of the Bishop of
Winchester and Judge Anderson, the statements of Judge
Wray, the quibbling exceptions, the inquiry whether Barrow
would take an oath according to the Act of Supremacy, and
the archbishop's refusal to provide Barrow with a written copy
of his answers.

A True Description out of the Worde of God, of the Visible Church

In all ages men have described the church in various ways.
They have spoken of the Church Intellectual, with Augustine,
Jerome, and Thomas Aquinas in mind. They have spoken of
the Church Militant, under the leadership of Gregory the Great,
Innocent III, and Boniface VIII. They have responded to the
Church Spiritual, with inspiration from Francis of Assisi,
Catherine of Siena, and Bernard of Clairvaux. They have
marvelled at the Church Architectural, as they gazed upon
St. Peter's Cathedral, Notre Dame, and Beauvais. And in
times of corruption and worldliness, they have dreamed of the
Church Invisible which transcended the limitations of sinful
men.

For Barrow the Church Invisible did not exist either in the
New Testament or in real life. There was no Platonic spiritual
archetype which had actual existence, but there was an Aris-
totelian nominalistic concept which did exist as an ideal. This
ideal was the Church Visible, which was realizable, cognizable,
and meaningful in daily affairs and localized in true visible
churches, which collectively comprised the Church Visible,
spiritually unified but geographically diverse.

Since the word of God was the last will and testament of
Christ, its authority was absolute and unerring. Since the
Scripture contained the laws and ordinances of Christ, its

21

regulations were final. And since Christ had prescribed the infallible ordinances of His church, since He had stamped once for all His beautiful pattern, since He had established an unalterable model, and since He had effected through the disciples and apostles the New Testament church, men were bound to accept it. The development of the Roman and Anglican churches has been a deviation from the true course. The map was in the New Testament. All that was necessary was a re-examination of the New Testament and a description of the church as found in its pages. This Barrow proceeded to do.

His description of the true church is a masterpiece of brevity, beauty, and simplicity. It is a skillful weaving together of Biblical language ; it is succinct, comprehensive, and christian. It begins with an affirmation of the oneness of God, the supremacy of Christ, the singleness of truth, the unity of faith, the uniqueness of the church, the solitary hope, the sole way, the pure salvation, the one rule—the word of God. This church is then defined as a fellowship of believers, rightly gathered out of the world, truly worshipping God aright, correctly governed by laws and officers of Christ. It is described by similes taken from the Old and New Testament. The church is a temple, a chosen generation, a vineyard, a sister, a spouse, a queen, the joy of the whole earth, the kingdom of Christ united by a covenant and strengthened by the presence and power of God.

The officers of the church are elected by the faithful members, who have an interest not only in the selection but also in the ordination and administration of their officers. The pastor must be a true shepherd of the flock, patient, watchful, loving, and wise. The doctor or teacher must be able to divide the word of God aright, apt to teach, and able to edify his hearers. The elders or ancients are the presbyters, the governors of the church. Their task is to assist the pastor and teacher, to enforce the laws and ordinances, to prevent and redress evils, and to maintain order and decorum. The deacons are responsible for collecting and distributing money and goods, for attending to the needs of the poor, and for providing proper maintenance to the officers of the church. The relievers or widows are women, of a minimum age of sixty years, whose task is to minister to the sick, to bring comfort to the weary, and to set a christian example for the younger women. These officers are all members of one body, whose head is Christ, and if any office is not filled, lameness, injury, and deformity ensue.

The visible church through each member possesses the keys of the kingdom of heaven to bind and to loose. Discipline is a necessary practice, and is not left to the discretion and arbitrary desires of persons who may neglect their duties and vacillate in their censures. The church has power to cast down Satan like lightning, to overthrow strongholds, to rebuke anyone who exalteth himself against God, to excommunicate anyone—even queens and kings. Methods are prescribed for dealing with private and public offences, but great care must be used in admonishing, rebuking, and excommunicating weak and sinful members.

The tract, *A True Description out of the Worde of God, of the Visible Church*, is less a creed, as Williston Walker has suggested, and more a constitution for the true church of Christ. It consists of a preamble, a description of the church, a definition of the church, a specification of officers, a summary of the duties of each office, and a prescription for disciplining and excommunicating erring brethren. It closes with a kind of malediction on those who are outside the church.

Thus, the structure of the true visible church, in conformity with the New Testament model, is seven-tiered : Jesus Christ, the pastor, the teacher, the elders, the deacons, the relievers, and the members of the congregation. To all of the people belongs the power of election, calling, ordination, administration, disciplining and excommunicating, in accordance with the laws of Christ and the examples of the apostles, as revealed in the Scriptures.

The First Part of the Platforme

Barrow and Greenwood were examined by Lord Burghley and others in March, 1588/9. Burghley was sharp and caustic in his statements, and showed neither patience nor sympathy, but the Separatist leaders continued to hope that the Lord Treasurer would aid their cause. In April, 1590, fifty-nine Separatists in prison addressed a petition to Lord Burghley, and in 1591 Barrow and Greenwood addressed their " Epistle Dedicatory " of *A Plaine Refutation* to William Cecil, Baron of Burghley. On September 13, 1590, Barrow and Greenwood wrote a letter to Lord Burghley, and also sent him a treatise, *The First Part of the Platforme*. They had desired to send this work to the queen or the privy council, but Burghley had suggested that it be sent to him. When he received it, he made known his displeasure immediately. Thereupon, with heavy hearts, Barrow and Greenwood wrote a second letter on September 18, 1590, in which they craved his pardon for any possible offence, and urged as a last request that they were ever likely to make that they " be allowed some peaceable and christian conference, in loving and sober maner, where these hie and weighty matters in controversy may by the worde of God be discussed and decided." Unfortunately, Lord Burghley was unwilling to accede to their petition, despite the pitiful, almost abject, tenor of the letter, and Barrow and Greenwood remained in jail. The second part of the platform was never written.

The *First Part of the Platforme* contains four main ideas. The first recommendation which Barrow makes is that the entire Anglican hierarchy, with its attendant courts and officials, should be abolished. This means that the offices of archbishops, bishops, archdeacons, deans, sub-deans, prebends, stipendiary lecturers, vicars, and curates should be eliminated. Likewise, archiepiscopal courts, diocesan courts, and archidiaconal courts should be abolished. A second emphasis is that the revenues of these officials should be appropriated by the queen. Church endowments, glebe lands, temporalities, tithes, advowsons, fees and fines should be converted to civil uses, at the discretion of the monarch. A third recommendation is that the true ministers of God should be supported not by the taxes imposed upon the rank and file of the people but by the free-will offerings and loving benevolences of faithful Christians who really believe in the New Testament and its pattern of church government and maintenance. A fourth suggestion is that the prince should promote the true preaching and practice of the gospel of Christ. What is also recommended is that the prince should forbid and extirpate all other religions within the realm. In other words, Barrow is suggesting that there is only one true form of religion, found in the pages of the New Testament, that men can ascertain and agree upon that form, that divergent views should be eliminated, that intolerance should prevail, and that Anglicanism, Catholicism, Judaism, and Anabaptism should be extirpated.

How this millenium is to be ushered in is not always clear. Barrow assigns the task to the prince and rulers, and denies to private subjects the right to usurp the office of the magistrate and to use force. What shall be done if the magistrate neglects his duties, or if public abuses prevail? Then is it the duty of Christians to protest, to pray, to exhort, to propagandize, and to use all other peaceable methods to influence the prince. If this avails not, the true Christian must accept suffering and imprisonment as the price of his ineffectual protest.

Barrow concludes his treatises by replying to objections to his platform. The main arguments which he seeks to refute are that intolerable innovation, dangerous alteration, and subversion of the state will follow. He denies that those who wish to change the ecclesiastical *status quo* are enemies of the realm. He found it necessary to repudiate the charge that learning would decay, ignorance and barbarism would flourish, and democracy and anarchy would replace monarchy. And he feels called upon to suggest that if his ideas are taken seriously, it will not be difficult to make certain adjustments. Such ecclesiastical functions as performing marriages, proving wills

B*

and testaments, adjudicating cases of adultery, can and should
be handled by the civil magistrate. And those who will lose
their positions, such as civilians in the courts, priests, and
bishops, should follow some lawful calling, such as teaching
and preaching, provided they have faith and gifts unto edification.

Letter to Mr. Fisher

This is one of the more interesting letters of Barrow, and is
valuable for the insights it provides of Barrow's private life
and thought. Barrow rejoices that a Supplication or petition
has been delivered to the queen personally, and he is sustained
by the hope that her majesty will search out the truth of the
Separatists' cause. There is a kind of naivete in Barrow's
vain hope that the queen or Lord Burghley will somehow discover the tyrannous behaviour of the bishops and correct this
abuse. Throughout his five and a half years in prison Barrow
maintained the belief that if an impartial conference could be
held, the Separatists would justify their cause, and understanding and harmony would prevail.

This letter gives us additional and corroborating information
about the arrest and treatment of Separatists. Since October,
1587, about 82 had been imprisoned. By April, 1590, there are
59 in prison, and by December, 1590, about 50 still remain in
various jails. Evidently Archbishop Whitgift is sensitive to
the charge of having caused needless deaths of prisoners, and
allegedly is courting the favour of jailers to mitigate the
reports from the various prison wardens. Barrow cites the
cases of Richard Jackson, Margaret Maynerd, Alice Row, and
Nicholas Crane as examples of persons who have died without
a proper inquest. In fact, he states that Bishop Aylmer had
ordered that no *post-mortem* be held. Barrow states that when
the venerable clergyman, Nicholas Crane, died, the authorities
forbade the carrying of his body into the city through Newgate,
lest the people learn of the cruelties of the bishops. He speaks
of the barbaric treatment of John Purdye, who was beaten with

a club and put into that torture hole, " Little Ease." He is bitter in his denunciation of Dr. Edward Stanhope, chancellor to the Bishop of London, for putting a young man, about seventeen years old, Roger Waterer, into the dungeon, ladened with irons for a whole year.

Barrow denounces Archbishop Whitgift unmercifully. He castigates his policy of indiscriminate and wholesale arrests of christian believers, of cruelly punishing innocent wives and children, of devouring Christ's poor sheep, rending their flesh, and breaking their bones. Is not this a christian bishop ?— he ironically asks. He represents the archbishop as seeking to alter or suppress the reports of the jailers, of cleverly turning over cases to the civil magistrates and Quarter Sessions to avoid criticism. And Barrow is convinced that the Archbishop of Canterbury is determined to inflict death upon him and Greenwood.

Barrow's close imprisonment must have been close indeed. He has seen no visitors. Only one person has access to his cell—a " poore simple creature," perhaps a maidservant, char-woman, or an employee who brings food to his chamber. Barrow does not know what to do, has concluded that he dare not appeal to Lord Burghley again (since his rebuke in Sep-tember, 1590), and asks for counsel and advice. It is an abject picture indeed.

A Brief Discoverie of the False Church

This is Barrow's main work. It is certainly a " discoverie," or disclosure or unmasking of the false church, but it is not brief. In the original printed edition, it required about 270 pages of close print, and in typescript with notes it is about 410 pages long. Although it is not his first writing, it is his first full-length book. It is also the work from which extracts were taken by his accusers. Because of this book, he was accused of violating the statute of 1581, was arraigned, indicted, and executed. It is interesting, therefore, to inquire what

Barrow's motives were in writing this volume, which seeks to expose, reprove, and cast down the false church.

Barrow was constrained by the love of Christ and zeal for the glory of God. He was deeply committed to the Bible as the word of God, as the infallible book whose admonitions, injunctions, and examples must be heeded at all costs. His patriotic love of England, his concern for the salvation of sinners, his conviction that his friends and kinsfolk were spiritually dying, his conviction that men were afraid to speak the truth, and his conclusions that the Elizabethan Settlement of 1559-1589 was a half-way programme of reform, a lackadaisical acquiescence in the *status quo*, an obsequious deference by the church to the state, and a dangerous compromise with Roman Catholicism—these were some of the ideas that agitated his restless spirit and led him to express his thoughts in militant and crusading fashion. He makes no claim to a beautiful or literary style, but desires to speak in words taught not by human wisdom but by the Holy Ghost. In fact, he apologizes for his weakened memory, and reminds his readers that he has written this book in prison, one sheet at a time. Without a library or even reference works, without an opportunity to revise his chapters, without the privilege of reading proof, Barrow has produced a remarkable book which reveals a vital and vibrant spirit in its pages. There is a moving eloquence in his direct and impassioned style, despite its obvious faults.

Barrow begins by examining the foundation stones of the Church of England. It was established in 1559 by Parliamentary decree and a blast of Queen Elizabeth's trumpet. Alas, the entire realm does not become a church by the promulgation of the magistrate, without a trial, examination, and true confession of christian faith. This church rests upon the authority of Calvin, not of Scripture. Even by the criteria of Calvin, who said that the true marks of a church were manifest when the word was rightly taught and when the sacraments were rightly administered, the Church of England is deficient, since it lacked both requirements. No true church may retain the unfaithful and profane in its membership, and no true church may dispense with the power to chastise, correct, and cast out offenders. There must be a faithful people gathered by the word of Christ, governed by a New Testament discipline, and possessed of the power to censure and redress sins and sinners.

Barrow is sharply critical of the ministry of England, which he divides into three categories. The governing officials include the archbishops, bishops, archdeacons, chancellors, commissaries, high commissioners, civil doctors, registers, scribes, proctors, summoners, and pursuivants. The serving ministry includes parsons, vicars, curates, lecturers, preachers, house priests, chaplains, half-priests or deacons, churchwardens, sidesmen, questmen, and parish clerks. In the third category of the collegiate ministry he includes deans, and sub-deans, prebendaries, canons, petty canons, gospellers, pistellers, vergers, and sextons. Most of these officers, he asserts, are unscriptural. They had their origin in antichrist, and they developed further in the popish church. They emerged from the smoke of the bottomless pit, and are like unto the monstruous, crowned, horned, poisonous locusts that issued therefrom. Satan is their general, Apollyon is their lieutenant-general, and they are the captains of the hosts of evil.

Barrow is equally critical of the educational preparation of the clergy. The colleges are like cages of unclean birds, like the seminaries of the pope, and not unlike the Turkish seraglios with their captive Janizaries. The colleges are comprised of boys and young men who lead lives of idleness and revelry. Their study of Greek and Latin is based on the writings of lascivious poets and heathenish philosophers. The study of logic is formal and barren ; rhetoric is superficial and stilted ; philosophy is devoid of true theological doctrine. Aristotle and Cicero are the chief mentors. Furthermore, the study of divinity is dependent on men's writings rather than on the word of God. When students for degrees issue their bills of challenge and post them on the doors of the colleges, they dispute in Latin to give a semblance of learning, but they neither edify nor are edified, and they prove the obvious and disprove that which men already generally disbelieve.

Once they have completed their degrees, these young divines are not called by a congregation of christian believers, but they must rely upon a patron, even though he be a glutton, an absentee lord, or an atheist. Once settled in his parish or church, the new minister will present and observe the injunctions, read the *Book of Common Prayer*, administer the sacraments, visit the sick, and church women. But preaching the word will be conspicuously absent from his duties. Nonresidency is possible by using a vicar, and moving to a better living is achieved without the permission of his parishioners. In these services he will be maintained not by the benevolences of the faithful, but by the Jewish tithes of the profane, by the offerings, fees, and mortuaries of the poor.

In the public administration of the church, the *Book of Common Prayer* is their pattern and guide. Here is a calendar to regulate the services of each week. Here are given their stinted prayers and prescribed liturgies. Provision is made for their Jewish and popish feasts, in keeping with ceremonial law, and they are celebrated with riot and gluttony, with May games and laughter. Their worship of saints deceased is unscriptural, and their fasts are hypocritical. Regarding the observance of fasts, the magistrate may not make a positive law. Even the church itself should never prescribe fasts as a matter of course, but use them only for urgent and special occasions.

Barrow boldly states that the queen may not forbid her subjects to eat flesh on special days or seasons—as a religious measure. This right is a gift of God and is in the liberty of each individual. If the queen wishes to promulgate a secular measure to increase the supply of meat, to aid the fishmongers, or to provide for the needs of the navy, she may, but she may not regulate the conscience of men. Dr. Some, following Calvin, contended that the queen's law did not bind the conscience but only the outward action. To this argument, Barrow replied that the distinction between the external court and the court of conscience was a subtle and false one, and therefore sophistry. Any law affecting the public actions of the church, any prescription for worship, prayer, or fasting, was a matter of conscience. If a person conformed in outward action, but not in conscience, he would set the stage for a struggle between mind and heart, for a warfare between right and wrong. Actions must be in accord with conscience or else they become hypocritical expressions of a divided soul.

In evaluating the sacraments of the Church of England, Barrow specified three criteria which must be satisfied. There must be a lawful ministry, a faithful people, and a correctness in outward elements and forms. Since these are lacking in the Church of England, with its Romish antichristian ministry, its profane and confused people, and its trifling ceremony, the consequent administration of the sacraments is false and adulterated. Barrow is critical of the sacrament of baptism because its administration includes a hallowed font and water, use of gossips, godfathers and godmothers, and a pretty dialogue between the priest, parish clerk, and attendants. He is also critical of the second baptism, known as bishoping or confirmation. He is scornful of the third kind of baptism—the hasty baptism by a midwife of a child that is in danger of death, and he regards as useless the fourth kind of baptism, one in which the priest repeats the baptism if he is in doubt about the efficacy of the midwife's action—a baptism by supposition.

The subject of baptism was a touchy issue. Many of the Anglican bishops had been baptized in the Roman Catholic faith. Were they truly baptized ? Dr. Some entered into this discussion by asserting that the baptism of the Roman Catholic Church was a true sacrament. Dr. Fulke contended that the Roman Catholic Church was a false church, and therefore its sacraments were not valid. If this latter position was correct, then the queen was not properly baptized, since she had received the sacrament of baptism from John Stokesley, Bishop of London, on September 10, 1533, when England was still a Catholic nation. Into the fray jumped the clerk of Oxford, the friend and defender of John Penry. This was probably Job Throkmorton, who wrote a book called *M. Some Laid Open in His Coulers*. Because this work carried the initials "J.G.", it has been ascribed to John Greenwood, and is so listed in the *Short-Title Catalogue* (12342). This is an error, inasmuch as the ideas and style are not those of Greenwood. Greenwood was in prison, and he would not invite the strong criticism which came from his intimate fellow-prisoner, Henry Barrow. But the ideas and style are very close to those of Job Throkmorton, who was an Oxford graduate and a friend of Penry and a critic of Dr. Some. Throkmorton, or "J.G.", argued that the Roman church was a false church, but it did not follow that the queen was in need of rebaptism. She was persuaded in her conscience that she was baptized, and therefore gave proof that she had received the inward grace and did not need the outward sign or seal of God's covenant.

Barrow departed from his disclosure of the false church to resolve this problem. He attacks the position of Dr. Some that the Roman Catholic Church is a true church. If this is true, then the popish priests were true ministers, their sacraments were valid, and the Church of England is in schism from the Roman Church. Then Dr. Some is also a schismatic. Barrow agrees with Dr. Fulke that the Roman Catholic Church is a false church and that its priests are false ministers. From this position Dr. Fulke proceeded to the conclusion that the sacraments were false, that those who were baptized in the Roman church up to 1559 were not truly baptized, and—by implication—the queen was not truly baptized. With this latter conclusion Barrow disagreed. But Barrow reserves his deepest scorn for the argument of Throkmorton, or "J.G." To suggest that the queen is truly baptized because she is persuaded in her conscience that it is so is to give away the whole case to the bishops. Then anyone is truly baptized who is persuaded in his conscience by an easy mental legerdemain. Then the Archbishop of Canterbury and the Bishop of London and the Bishop of Winchester are right because the queen is persuaded in her conscience that this is so. Then subjective thought replaces objective action, and relativity replaces objectivity. It is of no avail to bring unchristian flattery or imaginary comfort to the queen. Such delicate handling of the queen's baptism is insincere sychophancy, poor logic, pure sophistry, and terrible theology. Furthermore, it is dangerous doctrine. If the queen takes comfort in illegality and unrighteousness, may she continue in sin ? If a papist takes comfort in his shrines and relics, may he perpetrate superstitition ?

How to cut Gordian knot ? How to steer between the rocks of popery and the quicksands of Anabaptistry ? This is the problem which Barrow seeks to resolve. He concludes that Calvin is wrong in stating that the church of Rome is a church, though corrupted. He asserts that Dr. Some is in error and schism in holding the sacraments of the Roman church to be valid. He repudiates the doctrine of Throkmorton or " J.G." that one may dispense with the outward sign or action of God's covenant by taking comfort in a persuaded conscience. He accepts Dr. Fulke's belief that the Roman church is a false church, with false sacraments, but rejects the implication that baptism must be repeated.

To solve the problem Barrow goes to the Old Testament. The ordinances and promises of God stand firm and unchanged. In the times of Hezekiah, Josiah, Ezra, and Nehemiah, the Israelites were guilty of apostasy and schism. Yet when they forsook their false worship and returned to the true temple to worship God aright, they were not required to be circumcised anew. God's covenant in this seal was nullified when the Israelites practised false worship, but it was renewed when they returned to faith and obedience. Even so, baptism, though it be wrongly performed, need not be repeated if the faults of incorrect baptism are purged by repentance and faith. God in his wisdom and mercy does not require the outward action to be repeated for those who forsake their apostasy, rely upon the ordinances of God through faith, and give evidence of a new baptism of God's spirit in the inward man by true worship, christian conduct, and heartfelt repentance.

The administration of the Lord's Supper, or Eucharist, he finds trifling and superstitious. It is performed publicly in the churches, or privately in the homes as a communion for the sick. All is done according to the *Book of Common Prayer*, in popish manner, with special ceremony.

The sacrament of penance as practised in the Church of England and in the Church of Rome is an assumption of power that belongs to God. The power of binding and loosing was given to Peter, but also to the twelve apostles and to the seventy disciples. It was given to the whole church, and any member may bring comfort and peace to an erring sinner who has confessed his wrongs to God in true repentance. The word of God, believed and apprehended by faith, frees or looses anyone from his sins through the blood of Christ. The word of God, rejected or transgressed, binds or enslaves a person in his sin until he comes to the judgment seat of Christ.

In the sacrament of marriage, the ceremony was performed usually on a Sunday morning by the priest. The ring was placed upon the *Book of Common Prayer*, and thus hallowed. Some priests regarded the ring as an idolatrous relic, and refused to use it. In so doing, said Barrow, they violated their oath of canonical obedience, since the use of the ring was enjoined by the service book and the bishop. Furthermore, such a mild protest was insufficient. What was needed was a frank recognition that marriage was properly a civil action, not an ecclesiastical function. Boaz and Ruth were married in a civil ceremony, without a priest or religious ceremony. Marriage is an ordinance of the second table, and should be arranged by parents, performed in private houses, in the presence of witnesses, without a priest.

Barrow is even more caustic in his remarks about the

method of burying the dead. Why should the corpse be covered with holy cloth and linen crosses ? Why should a rich man be given preferential treatment by burial in the church, where he may remain high and dry ? Is it necessary that the grave be cut east and west that he may rise with his face towards the east ? Are the common people right in thinking that if burial be not in the church or churchyard, with priest, pomp, ceremony, dirges, heralds, mourners, then are the dead buried like dogs ? Why should rich men have their tombs embellished with exquisite sculpture, engraved with arms, decorated with images, garnished with figures ? Why all the hypocritical preaching and oratorical nonsense ? Will rhetoric make a dead man a better Christian in the grave than he was in life ? Will the recitation of excellent virtues convert a corpse into a god-fearing Christian, though in life he was an atheist, a glutton, a worldling, and an extortioner ? And why should all the mourners, arrayed in black, with hoods, caps, and crosses, be gathered together after a solemn funeral in a costly and sumptuous banquet ? " Is not this jolly Christian mourning ? Who would not mourne thus everie day in the yeare ? "

Barrow is scornful of the behaviour of priests at weddings and funerals. He is even more vexed at the way they preach the gospel or fail to preach the word. By their oath of canonical obedience, they have sold their birthright as free men. They have promised to observe whatever is or shall be commanded by the bishop. They are subject to discipline, censure, fine, suspension, deposition, or prison. Their licence to preach, what to preach, where to preach, how long to preach, when to preach, depends upon episcopal grant. They are sworn not to speak against anything by public authority enjoined or hereafter to be enjoined, and they are required to exhort their parishioners unto obedience to injunctions, be they right or wrong. They are required to use vestments which are too nice, curious, and affected.

Their numbers are legion. Some are collegiate priests,

35

others are roving mercenary ministers, and some are parsons and vicars. There are non-residents, plurified parsons, dumb ministers who cannot and will not preach, sychophants who insinuate themselves into a nobleman's household, where they are well fed and safe from all storms. There they lead lives of luxury and idleness. As cunning physicians of the soul, they prescribe medicine according to the inclinations of their rich patients, they cater to the prejudices of their host, and they demonstrate by their fawning and obsequious behaviour that expediency rather than principle is the best policy, that the word of their lord is more to be heeded than the word of the Lord. They neglect preaching, to their shame, and they wrongfully seek to confine the exercise of prophesying to themselves. Prophesying, as the expounding and interpretation of the Scriptures, is a prerogative of the entire membership of the church. The Apostle Paul, I Corinthians 14: 20-40, declares that this right belongs to all the believers. To deny the faithful the privilege of hearing and speaking, of publicly teaching and exhorting in the church, is a potent denial of a Scriptural injunction.

As a final criticism of the Church of England, Barrow asserts that its government and ordinances are not in conformity with the pattern and canons of the New Testament. The Bishop of Winchester, Thomas Cooper, in his book, *An Admonition to the People of England* (1589), had presented the Anglican view that Christ's kingdom was not perpetual, that history and circumstances altered the original pattern, that growth and expansion necessitated changes, that Christ left to the discretion of his followers the right to effect changes, and that the widespread differences observed in the many nations proved the flexibility of the pattern, as altered by the will of man. Therefore, the pattern as it existed in England was fitting and proper, and any attempt to copy the old model was fraught with dangerous consequences for the government, the courts, the civilians, and the clergy. To this argument, later revised and supplemented by Thomas Bilson and Richard Hooker, Barrow replied that the Church of Christ in all things must conform to the prescriptions specified by God himself, and that the canons and ordinances of the New Testament were necessary, inviolable, and perpetual, subject to no changes by the will and whim of man. Therefore, the rule by bishops, who governed hundreds of churches in their dioceses, was false. Therefore, the evolution of a system of ecclesiastical courts, such as the Prerogative Court of Canterbury, the Court of High Commission, the Court of Faculties, of Delegates, of Arches, was unscriptural, with no prototypes in the New Testament, and therefore false. These courts represented the extension of power of one man—the bishop, but Christ gave the power of censure not to one individual but to the entire church. Consequently, the plan of the Reformists or Presbyterians, who wished to establish a hierarchy of courts such as the presbyteries, classes, councils, and synods, was also unscriptural and false. The new presbyter or elder was but old bishop writ large.

Barrow directs his hardest blow against the Court of High Commission. This monstrous engine of injustice is the very throne of the beast. Its power is abolute and final. Who can stand against it ? Its jurisdiction is as wide as the land itself. Its writ runneth wherever it listeth, and its pursuivants invade whatever homes and places they please. Its warrants are general and indefinite, and its summoners may command any of the queen's subjects or officers to serve and attend, to watch and to ride, by day or by night. The actions of this Court of High Commission are a threat to the royal prerogative, to the common law courts, to the liberty of all subjects, yea, to Magna Carta itself. It has invaded the precincts of the civil courts and has not even hesitated to intercept causes belonging to the High Court of Parliament. In its arrogance and power, it even stops the course of God's word and of his church.

Among the most heinous of the Spanish arts practised by this court is the insistence upon taking the oath *ex officio* by a defendant before he knows either his accusers or accusations. He must place his hand or three fingers upon the Bible, swear by God and the contents of the Scripture, to answer truly unto such questions as are presented to him, even though he be driven to incriminate and accuse himself and his friends. If he refuses to take the oath, the defendant is committed to close prison, there to remain until he yield or die. If he takes the oath, he is subject to the decision of the court, which can impose, depose, determine, judge, censure, and punish, without any control or contradiction or review by a higher court.

For Barrow the English Court of High Commission had usurped absolute power over all laws, causes, persons, and estates. It had become a filthy sink from which flowed all the errors and abuses, disorders and poisons, of church and commonwealth. It represented the Romish Spanish Inquisition transplanted in English soil, and every true-blooded liberty-loving Englishman should seek to extirpate it. With a canny prescience, Barrow predicted that God, who disclosed all secrets, would reveal the sneaking practices of the inquisitorial bishops and make them as odious as they were now honorable. A half-century later, in 1640-42, his predictions were fulfilled. Not only did the Court of High Commission fall, but episcopacy collapsed, and what Barrow would have called the false church toppled.

Crop

Fragment of a Letter

This letter is dated 1587, and is the earliest one that we have from John Greenwood. It is valuable because it gives us the early views of the Separatists and of one of their critics. A prisoner in the Clink, Greenwood had received money from one of his critics. This good deed, tempered by criticism, evoked a reply which is characterized by a rare spirit of gratitude, amity, forbearance, and honest disagreement.

Greenwood's critic had suggested that inasmuch as King David had been forbidden to build the temple, therefore the Separatists erred in seeking to establish a church until the Lord commanded it. Greenwood alleged the familiar thesis of Robert Browne that Christians should proceed with reformation without tarrying for any. No probibition had been given by God to Queen Elizabeth. Furthermore, the task of building a true church belonged to the whole body of Christians, of whom the queen was only one member ; her royal power was civil, not ecclesiastical.

Greenwood had criticized those who had translated the prayers and collects of the Catholic liturgy and had incorporated them into the *Book of Common Prayer*. His critic asserted that the martyrs were good men, not antichrists. Greenwood replied that men such as Cranmer, Ridley, and Latimer were good men, but they were guilty of the sin of ignorance. It was necessary to make a distinction between good men and bad actions. God was aware of the special sins of Noah, Isaac, Jacob, the patriarchs, Aaron, Miriam, the princes, King David, and Peter, but in his mercy he had pardoned them. Even so, he had pardoned Cranmer for his work in translating and patching the ancient prayers and for his sin of accepting the unscriptural office of archbishop or metropolitan.

Again, he had charged that a formalized reading of prayers was a quenching of God's spirit. Since his critic disagreed, Greenwood contended that there was a warfare between the flesh and the spirit. The flesh persuaded the worshipper to use book prayers. The flesh intimated that since extemporaneous prayer resulted in poorly conceived words and ideas, the use of book prayers was preferable. But the spirit urged man not to yield to the promptings of the flesh. God looks not to form, ritual, beautiful words, or mechanical reading. The prayers of a righteous man, uttered in simple terms with a contrite spirit, availed much. The poor publican asking for mercy, the holy women falling at Christ's feet, did not use book prayers but poured out their spiritual feelings. Some book prayers, such as those of Calvin and other good men, but not those in the *Book of Common Prayer*, were good for meditation and education. They revealed how others prayed and felt, and they made readers more fervent in their own prayer life. They should be read in the same way that other books were read for edification and spiritual instruction, but they should not be a substitute for prayers conceived in our own hearts and minds. God never despised a contrite heart or a troubled spirit. If book prayers were used, the worshipper failed to use the spirit. This practice resulted in mental atrophy and effectual quenching of the spirit.

One special criticism called forth a strong reply by Greenwood. His critic had asked what the small incipient struggling church of the Separatists amounted to in comparison with the Church of Geneva. Greenwood replied with a passionate plea for the poor persecuted church. It had the same God and Father, the same Lord, the same faith, the same baptism, and the same spirit. It preached the same gospel. It exercised the same discipline enacted in the New Testament. It had the same officers, such as pastors, teachers or doctors, elders, deacons, and widows or relievers. But it did not tolerate known hypocrites in the membership of the church, and it did not observe the superstitious feasts at Easter and Whitsuntide.

Reasons against Read Prayer

This is one of the earlier writings of Greenwood, written in 1587 or 1588. It launched the long, written controversy between Greenwood and Gifford. Since there is not much that is new in ideas or arguments, we may summarize the reasons briefly.

Read prayers are apocryphal. They lack the warrant of Scripture. They are not inconsequential, since they convert the spirit into an idol, and they destroy the liberty which Christ purchased for his followers. True prayers involve the heart and the lively voice, but book prayers are tantamount to spiritual ignorance. Set prayers result in idolatrous worship and quenching of the spirit, preclude fervency and steadfastness, and lead to a babbling of vain repetitions without reference to our present necessities. All Christians should abhor stinted services and read prayers, knowing that they are superstitious relics and man-made devices used by an idol ministry serving under a false ecclesiastical government.

Reply to George Gifford

This treatise is an expansion or reaffirmation of the ideas in " Reasons against Read Prayer." We have a perfect rule in the Scripture for knowing the will of God. Since man's wisdom is often foolishness in the sight of God, the devices of man should not be substituted for the procedures prescribed in the Bible. Unless there is Scriptural warrant for an action of worship, it should be carefully avoided, because it may lead to idolatry. Read prayers are a device of men, lacking any warrant from the Scripture, and they are not conducive to a worship of God in spirit.

Greenwood's Examination [March 24, 1588/9]

This examination is the first of which we have any record regarding Greenwood. It is similar to Barrow's fifth examination of March 24, 1588/9. Inasmuch as Barrow had been questioned four previous times, it is likely that Greenwood also had been examined previously, perhaps on October 8, 1587, and May, 1588, and March 18, 1588/9, but we have no record of such occasions.

This examination affords us a little biographical information. We learn that Greenwood had been ordained into the Anglican priesthood, that he had abandoned the ministry in the Church of England, that he had been a prisoner in close confinement, and that he had been transferred from the Clink to the Fleet prison. We discover that he had witnessed the marriage of Christopher Bowman and his wife in the Fleet prison in accordance with the simple Separatist marriage rites without an officiating clergyman. It is clear that he had a son named Abel who was born in the autumn of 1587, and who was still unbaptized. We know that he refused to take an oath before the court, and that he rejected portions of the oath of the queen's supremacy specified in the Act of Supremacy of 1559, so long as it included a promise to give true allegiance to the queen's heirs and lawful successors, whom he did not know, and who perchance might be papists. Furthermore, we perceive the distinction that Greenwood acknowledged the queen as a supreme magistrate, but not as supreme governor of the church. Christ alone was the sole head of the church, and no civil magistrate could alter His laws.

His examination discloses his views on the Lord's Prayer, read prayers, the *Book of Common Prayer*, marriage rites, the Church of England, baptism, Anabaptists, church officers, excommunication, the proper powers of the queen, and the oath of the queen's supremacy.

An Answere to George Gifford's Pretended Defence of Read Praiers

For Greenwood the first principle of religion is to call upon God through the mediation of Christ in spirit and truth, with heart and voice, for our present needs in accordance with the will of the Heavenly Father. This principle is not observed by reading set and stinted petitions from the *Book of Common Prayer*. Reading is helpful for meditation and edification, but it is not true prayer. Only the inward faith of the heart bringeth forth true invocation. Singing psalms is a part of God's service, but it is not prayer. The vain repetition of fifteen *Ave Marias* and five *Pater Nosters* by the papists is not true prayer but a mechanical recitation of words.

There is nothing really new in this treatise. Much of the discussion is a refutation point by point of the arguments set forth by Gifford.

An Intercepted Letter

This letter by John Greenwood, about 1590-1, expresses approval for arguments which had been formulated by an unknown author against the Martin Marprelate pamphlets. It expresses the hope that someone with ability and acumen will examine the major theses in the Martinist writings and then refute them. The Martin Marprelate controversy was of great significance in the years 1588-89, and the authors were unmerciful in attacking bishops and archbishops. Although Barrow and Greenwood were also staunch enemies of the ecclesiastical hierarchy of the Church of England, they did not approve of the arguments or methods of the Martinists. We know from *A Brief Discoverie of the False Church* that Barrow attacked the writer of *M. Some Laid Open in His Coulers*. Inasmuch as it is probable that Job Throkmorton was the author, and since it is also probable that Throkmorton collaborated in the writing of the Martin Marprelate tracts, it seems clear that Barrow and Greenwood were anti-Martin Marprelate.

The True Church and the False Church

This brief treatise is a description of the true church. There is a partial similarity in the language and ideas found in this first paragraph with the attributes presented in the second paragraph of *A True Description out of the Worde of God, of the Visible Church*. The familiar marks of a true church are similar to the ideas suggested in *Four Causes of Separation*, such as true worship, a rightly gathered membership, a ministry selected by the local congregation, and a discipline and government that accords with the ordinance of Christ.

The description of the false church, and the eleven proofs why the Church of England is not the true church, elaborate the same ideas in a more detailed manner. Similar indictments may be seen in *Profes of Aparant Churche*, in *A Brief Discoverie of the False Church*, and in *A Brief Summe of the Causes of Our Seperation, and of Our Purposes in Practise*.

A Collection of Certaine Sclaunderous Articles

This publication was a militant tract which denounced " the

43

bishops' bloudie mandate" and decried their arbitrary and savage treatment of Christians who sought religious reform. The book contains an address to the reader, a copy of Bishop Aylmer's letter to the London clergymen, a summary or " briefe of the [twelve] positions " allegedly held by the Separatists, a list of the forty-two clergymen and fifty-two prisoners, and a reply to the " briefe of the [twelve] positions " ; then follows a summary of two prison conferences with John Greenwood, one with Henry Barrow, and one with Greenwood and Barrow jointly. The final section is " A breif answeare to certayne sclaunderous articles and ungodlie calumniations sparsed abroad by the bishops and their adherents." In this set of twelve articles and replies, seven of them differ from the above-mentioned " briefe of the [twelve] positions."

The first set of articles, entitled a " briefe of the [twelve] positions," is simply a restatement of the replies which Barrow made in his examination of March 24, 1588/9, before a special commission of judges and bishops. The replies here given to these same articles in " A brief answeare to such articles " represent a more expanded form and very likely represent the work not only of Barrow, but also of Greenwood and other Separatists. These Separatist replies in turn are answered about three months later by Richard Alison in *A Plaine Confutation*, pp. 106-113.

The second set of articles is given and then refuted in the section entitled, " A brief answeare to certayne sclaunderous articles and ungodlie calumniations." This Separatist refutation is also answered by Richard Alison in *A Plaine Confutation*, pp. 113-121.

The ideas given in this treatise are not new. The articles or positions, together with their refutation, have been mentioned before. The summary of the four conferences on March 9, 17, 18, and April 13, 1590, is new, but the conferences are mainly polemical in character, with much quibbling, verbal sparring, and arguing about Scriptural interpretations. Much time was spent in discussing John the Baptist, who were baptized, what was the difference between sectories and schismatics, heretics and infidels, bishops and pastors.

A Collection of Certain Letters and Conferences

This work is a sequel to *A Collection of Certain Sclaunderous Articles*. It summarizes the discussions held in three conferences, on March 14, March 20, and April 3, 1590. There are also seven letters written in April and May regarding the issues discussed in the conferences.

The main points in this treatise are that the bishops have usurped civil power, that excommunication by the bishops and their courts is unscriptural, that the English parish churches are not true churches. Unpreaching clergymen are not true ministers of Christ, and their calling by bishops and patrons instead of by the congregation violates the ordinances of Christ. The principle of universal membership without regard to profession of faith and obedience to the will of God constitutes a serious problem, and until the profane are separated from the true believers, the parish assembly remains as an admixture of confused and ungodly persons.

The letters between Barrow, Greenwood, and Egerton constitute a *post-mortem* and recapitulation, with charges of adding, falsifying, and perverting, and with counter-charges of blasphemy, vanity, and vitupery.

Letters to Lord Burghley

On September 13, 1590, Barrow and Greenwood addressed a letter to Lord Burghley, together with a treatise entitled *The First Part of the Platforme*. They sought to prove that in its establishments the Church of England, together with the ecclesiastical courts, merely continued the ministry and orders of the Roman Catholic Church. Therefore, it was not founded upon Christ's ordinances, and consequently was popish and false. " Shall this famous land, then, right honorable, lye still in the knowne dregges of popery under God's wrath for the same ? "

Barrow and Greenwood intended to write *The Second Part of the Platforme*, wherein they would explain how reform should be effected. But Lord Burghley indicated his immediate displeasure, and the second part was never written. In a second letter of September 18, Barrow and Greenwood replied with heavy hearts, appealed for a peaceable and christian conference, and pleaded for freedom from their miserable imprisonment. Their hope of aid from the Lord Treasurer never materialized. The conference was never granted, and the imprisonment continued until death in 1593. To the Separatists Lord Burghley was a broken reed.

THE WRITINGS OF
HENRY   BARROW
1587-1590

I

FOUR CAUSES OF SEPARATION

This writing is a part of the Giles Wiggenton MSS. in the Congregational Library at Memorial Hall, London (I. e. 14). The entire manuscript of seventy-five pages consists of seven treatises, of which the last one, reprinted here, occupies pp. 63-75. The manuscript is first noticed in C. H. Cooper and Thompson Cooper, *Athenae Cantabrigienses*, II, 331, and again by T. G. Crippen, in " A Remarkable Puritan Manuscript," in *Transactions of the Congregational Historical Society*, II, no. 3 (September, 1905), pp. 147-150. It is printed in *ibid.*, II, no. 4 (January, 1906), pp. 292-301, and also issued separately in 1906 as a pamphlet by the Congregational Historical Society, with two other treatises, under the general title, *Relics of the Puritan Martyrs* 1593.

*   *   *   *   *   *

The commonly accepted opinion, based on the judgment of Champlin Burrage and T. G. Crippen, is that in October, 1585, Robert Browne made his recantation before Archbishop Whitgift and became reconciled to the Church of England Barrow and/or Greenwood sent him a letter of remonstrance, to which Browne replied in a treatise called *A Reproofe of Certeine Schismatical Persons*. Barrow in turn replied with his *Four Causes of Separation*, to which Browne made his rejoinder in a treatise of which we know only a fragment quoted by Richard Bancroft.

The difficulties inherent in this explanation cannot be minimized. First, there is no evidence that Barrow or Greenwood sent a letter to Browne, and we must consider that the date of Browne's recantation is 1585, which antedates by two years any of Barrow's known writings. Secondly, it is doubtful that Browne wrote *A Reproofe of Certeine Schismatical*

C

Persons. The author may be Thomas Cartwright, as Dr. Peel believes. Thirdly, it is difficult to see any connection between Barrow's *Four Causes of Separation* and *A Reproofe of Certeine Schismatical Persons*. There is no common basis of ideas, no similar phraseology, no systematic development of arguments, to indicate relationship. The only point which does seem certain is that Browne wrote a treatise against Barrow. The evidence for this may be seen in the fragment quoted by Richard Bancroft and printed in Albert Peel and Leland H. Carlson, *The Writings of Robert Harrison and Robert Browne*, p. 515.

In a sermon preached on February 9, 1588/9, Bancroft quoted from a treatise of Browne. We may conjecture, therefore, that Browne's treatise is dated 1588 or 1587, and that Barrow's *Four Causes of Separation*, from which Browne quotes, precedes Browne's work by a few weeks or months. Since there is no reference to Barrow's imprisonment—a bit of negative evidence—we may hazard a guess that the date of writing is prior to Barrow's arrest on November 19, 1587. Furthermore, the simple direct form of stating the four causes at the beginning of the treatise differs from the more refined amplified phraseology used in 1588, as one may readily see if he will compare the opening paragraphs of *Four Causes of Separation* with those of *A Brief Summe of the Causes of Our Separation*. One other bit of evidence indicating a date prior to November 19, 1587, is that in Barrow's examination on November 27, 1587, he was presented with a bill of objections in which he was accused of saying that the archbishop and the bishops were antichrists, that all ministers in the land were thieves, murderers, secret hypocrites, and hirelings [pp. 57f., *Four Causes of Separation*]. This bill of objections is certainly dependent on the *Four Causes of Separation* for its information, and enables us to say that this is the earliest extant writing of Barrow, and that the date is prior to November—approximately the spring or summer of 1587. It is a clarion call for the people of England to forsake the Church of England. The internal threat of Barrowist Separatism thus begins in 1587,

Four Causes of Separation

one year before the external danger from the Spanish Armada, six years after the Brownists had emigrated to Middelburg, and two years after Robert Browne had made his submission to Archbishop Whitgift.

Two questions remain: what occasioned the treatise, and for whom is it written ?   Barrow's defence of the four causes, his scornful denunciation of the preachers and bishops, and his caustic disagreement with their protests, indicate that he is aware of the arguments of those who disagree with him.   These arguments, used in pulpit, manuscript treatises, and books, Barrow is desirous of refuting.   Furthermore, like Browne, he is desirous of " reformation without tarying for anie."   He is impatient with the " tolerating preachers," the compromisers, the abettors of the bishops, the ecclesiastical politicians, the holders of sinecures ; he condemns men like Giles Wiggenton and Thomas Cartwright, who strained at a gnat and swallowed a camel.   The desire to see his conception of the New Testament model of the primitive church realized in England is the underlying cause, but the occasion of this treatise may have been a letter, a manuscript treatise, a sermon, or a request to have some doubts resolved.   The treatise is a refutation of, a defence against, and a denunciation of, the tolerating preachers—especially the Presbyterians such as Thomas Cartwright, Walter Travers, William Charke, William Floyde [Fludd ?], and Giles Wiggenton.

The other question remains.   To whom is the treatise addressed ?   Since Robert Browne undertook to answer Barrow, the presumption is that Barrow wrote against him. This is a possibility, but it does not necessarily follow that because Browne wrote against Barrow, that the latter wrote against Browne.   Furthermore, there is no reference to Browne, nor to his recantation, nor to his former preaching and writing.   In the treatise Barrow writes as follows: " thus mak[e] they your Christ an idoll and you idolaters."   This would indicate that Barrow is writing to more than one person —perhaps to several, who have asked Barrow's judgment on

the conforming clergy and their stock arguments, or who have submitted a manuscript treatise to be refuted.

There are two other possibilities that should be mentioned. The ideas expressed in this treatise are similar to the arguments which Barrow used as a challenge to the Presbyterian leaders, and which were published in *A Collection of Certain Letters and Conferences* (pp. 67-70), and which are printed in Volume IV as " The True Church and the False Church." The emphasis therein on Christ as king, priest, and prophet has its counterpart in *Four Causes of Separation*, where Barrow discusses the kingdom of Christ, the priesthood of Christ, and the prophecy of Christ. The counter argument seems to have been that the Presbyterians received Christ as king, priest, and prophet. To this argument Barrow explains how they deny Christ in his offices. We know from Gifford, who was regarded as an interloper, that the Separatists " had made chalenge, and looked to be encountred by the learnedest in the land. They take it greevously, and reprehend me [Gifford], as having intercepted this businesse, and taken it from the hands of the learned." Thus, this treatise may have been part of the controversy with the " tolerating preachers," the learned Presbyterians such as Thomas Cartwright, Walter Travers, William Charke, William Floyde [Fludd ?] and Giles Wiggenton. This is perhaps the most likely conclusion we can draw from incomplete evidence.

The other possibility, less likely, is that this treatise represents the earliest phase of Gifford's controversy with Barrow and Greenwood. We know that a schoolmaster in Essex brought to Gifford a copy of " A Breefe Sum of Our Profession," together with diverse arguments against read prayer. The schoolmaster used the argument that " diverse of the people about them were troubled, and did hang in suspense, and for their sakes he did require it." Accordingly, Gifford replied to their arguments, and his answer was brought to the Separatists, who in turn framed " large replies " (Gifford, *A Short Treatise*, signature a 2.). Conceivably, *Four Causes of Separation* was written to refute this reply by Gifford, or to resolve doubts raised in the minds of people who had read Gifford's arguments, who had written to Barrow, and whom Barrow described as persons misled by the tolerating preachers. Since both were manuscript treatises, it is understandable how Gifford's could have disappeared, but it is fortunate that Barrow's treatise has survived.

* * * * * *

FOUR CAUSES OF SEPARATION

By Henry Barrowe

Fower principall and waighty causes whie every on[e] that knoweth God and acknowledgeth the Lord Jesus, or seekethe salvation in him, ought spedelye without any delay to forsack those disordered and ungodlye and unholye sinagogs, and the false teachers of these tymes as they generallye stand in England.

1. The fals maner of worshiping the true God. Esaias 66: 17; Deuteronomy 17: 1.
2. The profane and ungodlie people receved into and retayned in the bozom and bodie of ther churches. Esaias 65: 11, 12.
3. The false and antichristian ministrie imposed upone ther churches. Numbers 16: 21, 35.
4. The false and antichristian government wherwith ther churches ar ruled.

The haynous and fearfull enormities that insue of these are infinitt and cannot be sufyciently expressed ether by word or writing; but sumarylye, you shall find herbye Christ Jesus denied in all his ofices, and so consequently not to be com in the flesh.[1] You shall find herby the last will and testament of our saviour Christ abrogat, his pretious bodie and bloud torne and troden under feette of dogges and swine, Christ Jesus throwne out of his howse and antichrist his enimie exalted above God and rayning in the temple of God as God.

---

[1] This sentence, beginning with the words, "but sumarylye, you shall find," helps to establish the authorship of Barrow. These words were quoted by Richard Bancroft, in his famous sermon of February 9, 1588/9: "Furthermore it may please you brethren to heare the same man's [Robert Browne's] judgement of such, as do labor so busily in this matter: in a treatise of his against one *Barowe*. '*Whereas you charge us* (saith he) *in denieng Christ in his office, and consequently not to be come in the flesh: it shall appeere by your presbyterie or eldermen, that indeede you are and will be the aldermen even to pull the most ancient of all, Christ Jesus himselfe by the beard: yea, and seeke not onely to shake him by the lockes of his haire out of his offices, but also all his ancients under him, I meane the lawfull magistrates and ministers, which have lawfull authoritie from him* '" (Richard Bancroft, *A Sermon Preached at Paule's Crosse*, pp. 76f.).

Four Causes of Separation

The profisie of Christ is denied when anything is aded to or taken from his written word, or wher Christ's woyce [*sic*] onlye is not h[e]ard and obayed in the church. These to be don with them: the apocriphae; worship mad[e] of the invention of man, even that man of sinne, eronious, imposed and thrust upon ther churches;[1] the burdenns and idolatrus inventions with the endles heap of their traditions, approveth; and for mor particular profs of thes things, lett that idolatrus book of the bishops, comonly called the *Boock of Comon Prayer*, be scanned by the word of God.

The presthood of Christ is defiled, yea, denied, when any unlawfull worship is offered to Christ, or in his name. This to be don with them the p[ro]mises [premises?] prove.

The kingdom of Christ is denied wher his lawes and ordernances ar rejected and not obeyed, or anie other thurste [thrust] upon the church, *etc.* This to be with [them] is mor than manifest by ther straung offices, officers, and laws, even the statuts of Omry,[2] never re[a]d of, never h[e]ard of, in the Scriptures.

The testament of Christ is abrogate wher any thing is aded to it or taken from it; or wher it is neckleckted to be performed, yea, rejected as with them. These the promises prove and our dayly complaynts and sufferings manifest.

The body and bloud of Christ Jesus is most haynously torne and troden under fott by dogges and swyne wher the hollye things of God, as the sacraments, etc., ar geven to the aparrant wicked and ungodlye. Thes the second principall cause by dayly experience manifesteth.

Christ is thrown out of his house and antychrist exalted and raineth by his officers and lawes. This the promises and present estate declareth.

Neyther cann all the pretensed titells and decevable gloses, [which] the false profitts [prophets] use, any longer cover or hied these mischefes; for the God that condemneth them is a myghtye God, who discovereth them and consumeth them with the breath of his mouth.

To the first principall cause they comonlye aleadg that this ther worship is not altogether false, but much of it good and godlye; and they ether use not the book at all or but the least part of it, etc. First, I wold know of them whether the worship of God maie

---

[1] This sentence on worship is almost identical with the first transgression. See " A Breefe Sum of Our Profession," p. 84.
[2] The statutes of Omri. See I Kings 16: 27, 28 and Micah 6: 16.

be in part true and in part false.   Then, whether any devise of man or angell may be thrust into the worship of God or imposed upon the church of God the church of God [*sic*].

Now to ther using or not using the boock, we all know and theie cannot denie, howsoever they may desembell, that this idoll is sett upe, and they and all ther peopell stand under it; yea, that no man can by or sell without this mark of the beast, without bowing to this idoll in ther markes [marts?]; so that ther quiet standing under it, ther peac purchased by using part of it, ther joining hands with them that use it and stand under it and justyfy it as brethren; yea, ther joyning with them in the sacraments and reseveing the sacraments at ther hands, even at the hands of the moste dombe idoll and unworthie prests, do manifest what conscience and affection they cary.   Further, the evene joyneng of ther sermons to these abhominations, ether justifieng or tolerating them, showeth bothe what and how they preach.   Can lyght and darknes be isued together?   Can straw remaine in the flaming fyer unconsumed? Suer, thoughe this could be, yeat can the word of God never justifie idolatry, nor Dagon[1] stand up befor the ark of God.   And even that best part of it they use is but Dagon's stump devoted[?], but a pece of swyne's flesh,[2] an abhominable sacrifyse unto the Lord, and so far ar they from withdrawing anie on[e] sowle all this whill with all ther preaching from it, that they becom the most bitter persecutors of such as with draw them selves and keep them selves puer and undefyled from this false worship.

To the second principall cause they have litell to aleag save that it is lawfull to preache the word to all, and for all to hear. From whenc it flowethe [followeth?] not that it is lawfull to receve all into the bozom and bodie of the church, to delyver the most holly and pretious things to God to all, evene the sacraments.   And who is not baptised in Ingland?   Who is not of ther churche? For this ther generall baptisinnge of all I never as yeat co[u]ld hear on[e] reason proveed; but it is as easie to coine som as for the rest.   For the other sacrament [the Lord's Supper] they alleage the

---

[1] Dagon was the god of the Philistines.
[2] This is the earliest use of this phrase. Barrow was later quoted and criticized for this strong language, and especially for using these words. It is discussed in Article 7 in *A Collection of Certaine Sclaunderous Articles*, signature F4 *verso* and G1 *recto*.

power of suspension alowed them by the bishops' book,[1] and how that therby they keep the unworthey from the sup[per], etc. First, I find that [to be] an instrument of the folyshe and idoll sheperd, unknowen to our saviour Christ and his apostels, never used by them. Then I find it of no valew, for nothing is done bie it; and suerlye if ther righte eie wer not utterly darkned, it cowld not be but they must neds perseve how that ther weapone wantethe bothe edg and poynt; for what is don by it? Can they or ther parishe proseed to excommunication otherwise than by the antychristian courts, which lye as open for the party suspended to be asoyled[2] as punished by bribing Mr. Comissary, *etc.*? Nether can they kepe back the partie suspended from the joyning with them in ther prayers or fr[om] being receved into anie other pareshe.

To the third prinsipall cause they aunswear by rayling and blaspheming and persecuting, because it touchethe them nearlye, even to the quick, and uncovereth the fothould of all ther tythes, wages, and living. And som reasons they aleag to prove ther ministrie lawfull. First, for their callyng, they aleag a fine distinction of matter and maner. They have a right calling in matter; that is, they have inward graces as knowledg, learning, and so forthe; how so ever, they have it not in a right maner, that is, after that outward ordeynaunce of the calling and entrannce that Christ hath prescribed. First, therfor, it wold be known of them whether this maner they speak of may be severed from the matter. Then whether he may be estemed and held as a lawfull minister in the church of God, that hathe not a lawfull and trew calling in the church of God, and that standeth by and justifiethe his unlawfull and ungodlye callynge? Then it wold be knowen whether ther be any other treue enteraunce into the shepfould than by our saviour Christ's outward ordinances sett down in his last will and

---

[1] The bishops' book is Barrow's phrase for the *Book of Common Prayer*. The disciplinary Rubrics formed part of the First Reformed Liturgy of 1549 and of 1552. " And if any of those [to be partakers of the holy Communion] be an open and notorious evil liver, or have done any wrong to his neighbours by word or deed, so that the Congregation be thereby offended ; the Curate, having knowledge thereof, shall call him and advertise him, that in any wise he presume not to come to the Lord's Table until he hath openly declared himself to have truly repented and mended his former naughty life . . . " But the problems attendant on brotherly correction, suspension, and excommunication are so difficult, and the habits of individual resistance to authority are so common, that curates, ministers, and priests have rarely been successful in coping with this unpleasant obligation. It is much easier to permit the tares to grow up with the wheat.

[2] Asoyled, or assoiled: to be acquitted, released from ecclesistical penalty.

C*

testament? Then, [if] he that entreth in another way be not a thefe, a hirlyng, and a murtherer? Then, whether all the treu shep of God owght not to fle from such a wolf and hirlyng, etc.

Lett them therfor which willbe h[e]ard and held as treue ministers of Christ aprove them selves such derectly and playnlye by the lawes and ordinaunces of our saviour Christ in that behalf provided, or else we by the same lawes will not dowbt to denounce and pronounce them theves, robers, hirlings, murtherers, wolves, *etc.*,[1] and shunne them our selves, and warne as many as love the Lord Jesus and hould ther own salvation dear to fle from them acording to our savior's comandement. But because it apeareth to all men that they have not his lawfull they [the, that?] true entrans into the shepfould, but ar clymed up another way, and mask disguise and seek to cover ther ravin[2] and intrusion with shep's clothing, and to mak men beleve that they abownd with inward graces, lerning and giftes, and that these may sufice to mak them lawfull ministers, though they be not chosen and apoynted to the ministrye by God, whoe is the gever of all the giftes they have, and best knoweth bothe the measuer, the use, and the end of them. They wold howld it an inderect aunswer to an inditmente of wrong or thefte to aleag that they ar wise or riche, *etc.* Suerlye, nether cane this ther plea of inward graces justifye ther open breach of God's comandements; and evell dothe it bewray any inward grace of the spirit of God when they plead for and justifye by ther utmost indevours open and haynous transgressions. We ar taught by our saviour Christ to judge the tree bye the fruts, and ether to mak the tre good and the frut good or else to mak the tree bad and the frut evell. The graces they bost of indead ar inward indead if they be anye, for they evell appear as yeat ether in love to God, to his truthe, or to his servants. But we will not seacse to besche the Lord for them to bring forthe his own gifts to the service of his own glorye and the use of his church, that thancks may be geven to his holly name for them by manye. But they ar so far from this as yeat that they mak the word of God a clock [cloak] unto ther sinnes. They say they preach the word of God trulye and senserlye [sensibly?], and therfor theye that leve them forsack the ordinarye meanes that God hathe leffte to the begettyng and preserving of

---

[1] These words were cited against Barrow in his examination of November 27, 1587. This citation, therefore, affords some evidence that *Four Causes of Separation* was written prior to Barrow's imprisonment on November 19, 1587.
[2] Rapine, robbery.

faythe; yea, they forsake even the word of life, and therfor they must neds be invaded with daungerus and damnable erores, *etc.*, and such lyke popishe thunderbowlts wherby they afray[1] the simple from hardines so much as to dare to call ther ministrie into question or to examine it by the word of God, much les to judg it by God's word.

In few words, therfor, to discover the falshod and wickednes of this reason, we shall fynd this ther preching as false and as corupt as ther calling and entraunce, and to be as far from that ordeynary blesed meanes lefte by the Lord to his church as they ar from the ordeynary true entraunce. And dowtles even from this false calling and entraunce of thers may a reason be framed, [namely,] they ar not trulye and rightly sent; therfor, they can not trulye and rightlye preach. Ther sending is aparaunt to be of men and not of God. They ar knowen whose servants they ar, bothe by ther lyvery and band and obedience. Ther comission is lymited unto them, and writen and sealed. And mark ther doctrine well: I warrant you they transgrese not ther comission; for behould how they kepe them within ther band, and how they dawbe and undershore[2] that antichristian wall of ther masters, the bishops, and stand under it. For with us they gather not, nay, they opose them selves agaynst us, wrasting and constrayning the word of God agaynst us withe open violence to the Scriptures and injurye to us, slaundering us in the pulpitte[3] against ther own knowledge and conscience with su[n]dry erores devised falsly of ther own brayn; and thus destayne [disdain] they the mouth of God, which they in that place wold seme to posses, with lies. And all to save ther own scines [skins] wholl and purchas peac with the bishops by proclaiming open ware [war] with us, or rather with God, whose we ar and whose cause we defend against them and the bishops. Furder, herby they lyckwise may purchase credit withe the peopell, who ever by the Lord's wonderfull working have bym [byn, been] inclined to the most forward prechers and such as speak the truthe most bowldlye; escaping herby ther m[aste]rs' jealous eies, and that this may be wrought thus, now and then cast out some darke Delphicke words againste ther masters' regiment, and seme to bewayll the lamentabell estat of the church, *etc.*; yeat shall it be so warylie as nether the peopell

---

1 Disturb, frighten, startle.
2 Prop up, strengthen, sustain.
3 The reference may be to George Gifford or Robert Some, or to some of the Presbyterian leaders whom Barrow had condemned, such as Thomas Cartwright or Giles Wiggenton.

shall draw them therby into practic to cast of[f] this antychristyan youk of the bishops, nor ther lords have evident ocasion of wrath, howsever the Lord by his most wyse justice hath kin[d]led an envious hatred betwixt these lords and the courtiers. Furder observe this docktrine they preach, and you shall fynd it not onlie half and unperfecte truths, doubtfull and ambiguous truthes lamley and unfaythfulye utterd; but you shall find this gospell they prech no gospell of lybertie and power, but a gospell framed to the pollysies of the times, and wrested to uphould and serve this haynous idolatrie they use and stand under, and this antichristian government of the bishops and ther oficers. And this I say not that the gospell of Christ Jesus cane this [can thus] be preched or transfygured in it self, for no thing is mor free, mor perfecte, or mor powerfull to consume this chafe and stuble wher it is trulye receved, even in the mowthes of the most simple; but this I say to lett you see the haynous dealying of the tolarating prechers, even those that ar best estemed, and your own fearfull estate that ar misled by them. They, as you see, betray not onlye themselves and you but even Christ Jesus hime self and his gospell into the hands of antichrist. For see howe these deceivers joyn the word of God and idollatrye together, the gospell of Christ and bondage, Christ and antichrist to gether in on[e] temple. See what kynd of gospell and what kind of Christ they geve you: a Christ without power to governe and kep his owne, a gospell without lybertie; or else whie ar you thus intangled with begerlye rudyments, *etc.*; whie ar you thus in subjection to the traditions of men ?[1]

Thus mak[e] they your Christ an idoll and you idolaters. Be therfor no longer deceved; Christ putethe not up these injuryes; his father hathe delyvered into his hands all power in heaven and earth, and he will shortlye show himself with his myghtye angels in flaming fier, rendering vengance unto them that know not God, which ar disobedient to his gospell; alsuche shalbe punished withe ever lasting perdetion from the presence of the Lorde, from the glory of his power. Then shall none of those pretensed titles of graces, word of God, gospell, Christ Jesus, faith, comfort, *etc.*, serve them; for he whos eies ar a flam of fier can not be deceved; no secrett is hiden from his bright eies. Though they byld as highe as Babell and digg as low as hell,[2] *etc.*, he seeith ther hipocrisie and

---

[1] See Galatians 4: 9 and Colossians 2: 8.
[2] See Amos 9: 2 and Psalms 139: 8.

will disclose it, and will judg them by ther fruts, even the bitter and accursed fruts of ther disobedience.[1] This word of God, gospell, and Christ, which they use as a snar and a fayer [fair, beautiful] stall to draw gaynes and ignorant sowles unto them and therby to justify ther wickednes, shall judg and condemn them amongest the devells with all ther knowledg and inward graces, *etc.* Neyther can this fayth [be] wrought by ther ministrie, wherby they subtillie draw the wholl multytud of ther hearers upon us; as who shold saye ye muste ether condemne all these and every on[e] of them to be without faithe or justifye our ministry by the efectts. Alas, we judg not; we with Jerymey wishe even so be it;[2] but ther is on[e] that judgeth them, even that Christ they boste of judgeth them, and his word judgeth them allredye. Ther is no true faythe but that which is builte upon the word and bringethe forthe fruts accordinglye. Allas, the word condemneth them, ther fruts condemn them, yea, them selves, when the boock of ther consciens shalbe opened by the lyght of God's word unto them, shall condemne themselves. The multytud of God's enimies shalbe as one mane [man]; he that spared not the angells, he that spared not the owld world, he that spared not his own people, cannot spar them.

Another false proffe they have depending upon the former of the effectes; and this is the comfort reseved by ther preaching, and herin, lyck Jamnes [Jannes] and Jambres,[3] they apishlie imytate Paull, approving themselves to the consiences of ther auditory because they have beaten down sinne by the power of the word in them, and againe have healed the wounded consience withe the comfortable promises of the gospell. It hath before bin shewed how haynously and wilfulye they transgressee againste the first table, and obstinatly remaine in those transgressions evene against the moste highe and his anoynted son Christ Jesus; so that nowe they cannot geve the frut of ther bodye for the sine of there sowll. Ther is no keping the second table without the first;[4] he that breakethe one commandemant breaketh all; he that breaketh the

---

[1] In the margin, in another hand, are the words: " where shall we fynd such a judgment so peremptorylye uttered by any of God['s] children."
[2] The reference is to Jeremiah 11: 5.
[3] II Timothy 3: 8. " Now as Jannes and Jambres withstood Moses, so do these also resist the truth: men of corrupt minds, reprobate concerning the faith."
[4] The ten commandments were written on two tables of stone. See Exodus 34: 1; Deuteronomy 5: 22; 10: 1-5. The first table related to religious duties, the second to moral obligations.

least commandement and teacheth men so shalbe called the least in the kingdom of heaven.

But to com to ther own efectts, as the beatting down of sinn, *etc.* Do not the heathen so without the lawe? Do not the papists herin exced them? This doen [is done at] Westminster Hall, the Assises generall in every shier, yea, every court barone in every letell town aprovethe:[1] being compared in these our happie dayes to the times of gross popery. Dothe not sin abound, yea, overflow? How is it then beatten down? Nay, mark your mynisters well, you shall find that as they joine and frame the word of God to these haynose transgresyonts against the first table, as idolatrye, *etc.*, so joyne they ther own bodies and becom mynisters to secuer worldly-ings, profane, glutons, covetus, athists, proud, vaine, and carnall epicuers and hipocrits, so that [provided that] these men be rich or have possibillyte and will to plesuer them, feast them and con-tenance them and com to ther sermons. These they uphowld[2] by thus many yeares in ther sinnes, sothing, flattering, and justifieng them, terming them Christians, yea, the pillers of the church. We must bear with them, if these men showld tack offence at the gospell, the peopell wold soner forsack it. And so the gospell should be contemted [scorned] and such lyck stuf. Yea, doubtles these preachers ar very petifull [pitiful] surganes, that mak so foule wounds, and so uncurable. They of ther tender harts may not endur to rannsack to[o] deepe, lest they put ther patients to too gret grefe for ther sinnes. It is easier to mak a wound than to cuer it; therfor, they will not search them to the bottom, but bynd them up quickly with the promyses of the gospell, and power in the oyll of grace.[3] O folysh pittye. Nay, o cruell mersye. Destroye they not herby all ther patients? What wound if it be not searched, or ulcer if it be not launced, and have apte and convenient medy-cines applyed, can be cured? Will they power [pour] the sweett oyll upon dead fleshe, or into stinking and corrupt wounds? Will they laie strong [?] comfortative emplaysters to owld rotten festered soores? So shall they lose bothe ther oyll and ther labor.

Is this the gospell [people?] to whom the gospell belongeth? Is this reppent and " amend your lyves, for the kingdom of God

---

[1] See Jonas Adames, *The Order of Keeping a Court Leete, and Court Baron: with the Charges Appertayning to the Same* (London, 1593).

[2] In the margin, in another hand: " Charitie would have named the offen-dors rather than thus to condemne all."

[3] Another marginal note reads: " O what profe is there of these slaunders."

is at hand,[1] *etc.*" ? Is it not rather that impoysoned playster of peac wher ther is no peac? Can they geve the promises of the gospell to these ignorant, profane, wicked, and open idolaters? Can they geve Christ or the benefits of his deathe and resurrection, as libertye, power, salvation, to a peopell that remayn and will not com out from under the yock of anti-christ? Is not this to bless God's enemies, to justifie the wicked, yea, to curse God's saynts and to condemne the just?

These ar the comforts they geve you; this is the peace, so many spirituall whordoms and wichcraftes remaining in so great number. Ther can be no comforte but such as is grounded on the promyses of God; the promyses of God belongethe not to all unbeleving, disobedient, and obstinat people; "but the foundation of God remaynethe suer, and hathe this seall: The Lord knoweth who ar his, and lett every on[e] that caleth on the name of the Lord depart from iniquitey."[2] This comfort then geven by these ministers and taken by this people, is not withowt blasphemye in the one and presumtion in the other; and God's fearfull vengeance [falleth] upon bothe the one and the other. What promyse of blessing have they from God so long as they remayn in this open wickednes, idolatrie, disorder and rebellyon? But rather a fearfull looking for of judgment. Surlye if they tack comfort to desobey God, God will tack comfort to destroy them. And suerlye I cane but wonder and trembell at the judgment of God upon them, to see them geven over so generaly to so strong delusions and to so great blyndnes, as not having [?] among them any on[e] trew signe of God's presence, any on[e] true profitt [prophet], nor any on[e] that can tell how long these ministers shall last. Yeat they comfort them selves in thes calamities, promising them selves peace with good, yea, great happines, not perseving that they ar wretched and miserabell and poore and blynd and naked. The Lord therfo[re] of his gret mercie draw out such as be his from among them, and anoynt ther eies with eisalve that they may see and fle from this mor than Egipticall darknes and Babilonishe bondage into that most joyus light and libertie of the servants of God. The Lord grant them dezerning spirits to know the true worship of God from

---

1 The reference is to Matthew 4: 17. In the Genevan version for 1560, the words are: " Amend your lives: for the kingdome of heaven is at hand." Evidently Barrow is quoting from memory, or using another version. He did use also the Latin translation by Immanuel Tremellius and Francis Junius, issued in 1585.
2 II Timothy 2: 19.

false, and the true ministers of God from false; that they may save them from the wicked generation and find comfort withe the Lord in his day of refreshing.

To the fourthe principall cause they aleag many slyght and lame excuses, as that the fault is not in them but in the civill majestrat that these disorders and bondages remaine; if it wer in them, it should not [remain]; they wish for reformation and sighe for it daylie, yea, they pray with tears both publycklye and privatlye for it, and as far as it lyethe in them they seek it by all meanes. They sue to the parlyments for it; and seing it cannot be obtayned, they perswad all men to have patienc untill it may please God to torne the prince's harte, and in the mean tyme to rest contented with this measur of God's truthe and fredom they have: ther can be no church withowt some blemishes and defects in this world; suche wer the church of Corinthe, Galatia; thanked be God we have greter measuer of God's grases [graces] than any nation in the world; and such lyck fleshly unfaythfull reasons therby to blear men's eies and hyd ther infidellytye, yea, ther treason to Christ him self, to our prince, and the wholl land. But what is this chaff to the wheat when it cometh to the fane [banner] of the gospell? They have but conseved chaf and brought forthe stubell. First, wher find they that ether our saviour Christ or his apostells sued to parlyments or princes for the planting or practising of the gospell; and whether the word it self if it be faythfullie taught be not of power both to tack princes in the nett and to bind them in chaynes and feters. Then if princes resist or necklect, wher [do] they fynd that the faithfull ought to rest in ther defawlts and disorders untyll God change the prince's hart?[1]

Then, wher [do] they find that our Lord Jesus ever sent owt any without geving them power; or whether the true mynisters and people of God may be without this power of Christ to reforme them selves, and to put in practyce Christ's comandements according to the measuer of faythe and grace the Lord hath geven them? Then, whether he cane be a true mynister that wantethe [lacketh] this power, or neckleckteth it? Then, whether on[e] man can serve t[w]o masters at once, or whether he shall not be judged his servant to whom he yieldeth obedience? Then, whether he be a

---

[1] Barrow's arguments seem very close to those of Harrison and Browne. See Harrison's lament in " Notes Owt of Harryson's Booke " and Browne's arguments in *A Treatise of Reformation without Tarying for Anie,*" in Albert Peel and Leland H. Carlson, *The Writings of Robert Harrison and Robert Browne,* pp. 151-170, 532-537.

faythfull servant that not only faythfulye yeldethe obedience and subjection to his m[aste]r enimie, but unfaythfullye [yieldeth?] the most pretious things of Christ, yea, Christ himself, into the hands of antychrist? Furder, it wold be known of them whether the church of Christ can be without the government and officers that he hath asigned in his last will and testament unto it.

Then, whether his government be not a thing of nesesytye to the church?

Then, whether his government be not a part of Christ's testament?

Then, whether it be a principall part of Christ's kyngdome, and whether Christ can be a kyng and not governe by his own lawes and offycers?

Then, whether the church of Christ can be governed by antychrist, *etc.*?

Then, whether our christian lyberties and the holye order of Christ's governmente be not a thing to be stood for unto the deathe by every servant of Christ Jesus?

To these poynts of doctrine, if they assent not, it is because ther is no lyght in them; if they assent, ther remayneth no mor to do but that they repent and amend withowt any furder allegation of delaye, for certaynlye ther is no subtill distincktion or slye evasion will stand before our God whose lawes these ar. Inward intents will not excuse owtward, yea, obstinat, transgressions; the King of kings will not com in subjection to any king; he yealdeth not his septer to another, nor his sheep to a strainger.

But as they have dealt with Christ Jesus ther Lord, so they have—and with no better fayth—delt with ther prince and ther contry, as shall breflye apeare. Call we not hime by good right a traytor that willingly and wittinglye suffer the[i]r king and sufferayn [sovereign] to fall into undowted destrucktion both of bodye and sowle and geveth hime no warning, no exortation to avoyd, but most wickedly pampereth him up in his sinne, by yealding obedienc unto his ungodlye hestes [behests, commands]? Lyckwise, can any nation or citye tack him for a faythfull wachman who, being plased in the wach tower, not only not discovereth [the] enimie by geving warning, but yealdeth unto hime, conspirythe with hime, openethe hime the gattes, yea, betrayeth into his hands not only the cittie but all the people?

This, and much mor than can be uttered, to be don by theyr wachmen, is mor than maniffest to all suche as eyther slep not to[o]

65

depe in the dreggs of ther securitye, or wilfully shut not ther eies or not beleev ther own eies in those lamentabell desolations; neyther can those fyg leaves of blemishes and coruptions by the exampell of the churches at Corrynthe and Galatiae cuer or cover these wounds.

We may tak a better example from those churches of ther repentance, of ther sorow, of ther amendement; nor yeat have they escaped God's judgments by blessinge them selves and the people in ther sinne. God is a righteous God, and ane holye God, and a jelous God; he cannot justifie sinne, nor blese them remaining in this maner in ther sinne, *etc*. Alas, what a wofull estatte stand they in that ar wrecthed [*sic*] and miserabell and poor and blynd and naked, and yeat thinck them selves riche and incresed with goods, and to have need of nothing. What then is to be done in these confused tymes, save that they buye gold of him that walketh betwen the seven golden candell stickes, gould tried bye the fier that they may be riche, and whit rayment that they may be clothed, and that ther filthie nakedness do not apear, and that they anoynt ther eies with eie saulv that they may see and fle from these un-holye assemblyes, this false and unholye worschip, this false and unholy ministrye, this false and unholye peopell, this false and unholye government, lest they be partakers of ther sinnes and so of ther plages.[1]

---

[1] In this final sentence Barrow summarizes the four causes of separation: a false worship, ministry, membership, and discipline.

II

PROFES OF APARANT CHURCHE

One of the writers who may have been employed by Archbishop Whitgift to refute the works of Barrow and Greenwood was Richard Alison. He is listed as one of the men appointed in February, 1590, by John Aylmer, Bishop of London, to confer with the Barrowists in prison. Alison had obtained a manuscript copy of *A True Description out of the Worde of God, of the Visible Church*, and by the summer of 1590 had also obtained a printed copy of this work. Although the printed work consisted of only eight pages, Alison devoted 104 pages to the refutation of it, in his work, *A Plaine Confutation of a Treatise of Brownisme*. He also used fifteen pages (*ibid.*, pp. 105-120) to refute *A Collection of Certaine Sclaunderous Articles*, and devoted the last nine pages to a refutation of a treatise which was appended to *A Collection of Certain Letters and Conferences* (pp. 67-70). This appended treatise, which has no title, we may describe as " The True Church and the False Church " from its subject matter.

Somewhat related to this treatise, probably antedating it, and very likely written by the same author, is a manuscript (Congregational Library, Memorial Hall, MSS. I. e. 14) entitled " Profes of Aparant Churche." This is a part of the Giles Wiggenton MSS. (ff. 41-52), and was printed in the *Transactions of the Congregational Historical Society*, III, No. 4 (February, 1908), pp. 257-265. There is no suggestion of author or date, but we may give conjectural answers to both problems.

The ideas are consistently Separatist throughout the treatise, and they seem to be Barrowist. Furthermore, Barrow and Greenwood are mentioned by Alison in his book, *A Plaine Confutation of a Treatise of Brownisme*, and in the margin thereof Alison refers seven times to a " Treatise of the Church Apparant," in order to refute a quotation or demolish an idea

of the Barrowists, who are regarded as identical with the author
or authors of *A True Description out of the Worde of God, of
the Visible Church*. The problem, therefore, is to decide which
Separatist or Barrowist is responsible. From the ideas, strong
language, phrases, and style of writing, we may conjecture
that Barrow is the author, but Robert Harrison may have
written it. Similarity of ideas and phrases may be seen in
Barrow's *Four Causes of Separation*, his *Pastoral Letter from
Prison*, his *A True Description out of the Worde of God, of the
Visible Church*, his *The True Church and the False Church*,
and *A Brief Discoverie of the False Church*. Furthermore,
Profes of Aparant Churche is an integral part of the Giles
Wiggenton MSS., and it seems likely that the first three
treatises (1 — 3) are by Giles Wiggenton, that the fourth is
by John Greenwood, and that the last three are all by Barrow:
(5) *Profes of Aparant Churche* ; (6) *A Pastoral Letter from
Prison* ; and (7) *Four Causes of Separation*.

No distinct clue for the date of this treatise is given. It
cannot be later than the summer of 1590 when Alison used
it to write his *A Plaine Confutation of a Treatise of Brownisme*.
From the references to persecution of the church of Christ,
from the absence of any reference to imprisonment, from the
justification of the act of separation from the established
church, and from the promise that the Separatists will return
to the fold and reform themselves if they can be convinced
that they have joined against Christ in any antichristian way,
I conclude that the time of writing is prior to Barrow's imprisonment on November 19, 1587. Perhaps Barrow wrote
Four Causes of Separation and *Profes of Aparant Churche* at
approximately the same time—in the spring or summer of 1587.

Dr. Peel dates " A Treatise of the Church and the Kingdome
of Christ " in 1581. This date may well apply to the letter to
Mr. Fenton (the last eighteen pages of " A Treatise ") but it
does not apply to the first six pages—the treatise itself. If
we assume with Dr. Peel that the first six pages constitute
the treatise which Harrison intended to complete " touching

church government," then the date must be 1583 or 1584, when Harrison was in exile in Middelburg, and not in 1581, when he was in Norfolk. It may be that Harrison's work on church government was never finished, inasmuch as he "let staye that worke." He did write a letter to Thomas Cartwright on church government, church discipline, and English parish assemblies, about 1584. Cartwright replied to this letter (Peel and Carlson, *Cartwrightiana*, pp. 48-58), and Browne replied to Cartwright (Peel and Carlson, *The Writings of Robert Harrison and Robert Browne*, pp. 430-506).

Dr. Albert Peel believes that this treatise was written by Robert Harrison. It is to be found in Dr. Williams's Library, the original manuscript, " Seconde Part of a Register ", (B), pages 441-465. It is also found in the Transcript Volume (C), pp. 533-554. On consulting these, the reader will see that there are two dissimilar treatises. The first six pages constitute " A Treatise of the Church and the Kingdome of Christ," and the last eighteen pages constitute a letter directed against Mr. Fentome [probably Edward Fenton, rector of Booton, Norfolk, from 1564 to 1610]. It seems clear that Robert Harrison wrote the letter, but there is some doubt about the authorship of the treatise.

" A Treatise of the Church and the Kingdome of Christ," is published in Albert Peel and Leland H. Carlson, *The Writings of Robert Harrison and Robert Browne*, pp. 21-41-69. It has also been published separately. See Albert Peel, *The Brownists in Norwich and Norfolk about* 1580 (Cambridge University Press, 1920).

By using either one of two aforementioned identical reprints, and by comparing it with that found in the Congregational Library, " Profes of Aparant Churche," the reader will notice the following differences:

1. The two different titles.
2. The absence of the argument, or the three syllogisms, in the beginning of the Congregational Library version.

3. The phrase " the church aparant " is found about twelve times in the Congregational Library version, but the word " aparant " is missing from the version in Dr. Williams's Library.

4. There are two paragraphs which begin with quotations from David. The order seems to be correct in " Profes of Aparant Churche," and reversed in " A Treatise of the Church and the Kingdome of Christ."

5. In the " Profes of Aparant Churche," one paragraph is missing, which in the other version begins: " In the second of the Revelation "—approximately one printed page.

6. The two conclusions vary completely.

When all the works of Barrow and Greenwood are published, it may be possible to determine if Barrow wrote " Profes of Aparant Churche." When further research is carried on in the ecclesiastical records of the city of Norwich, it may be possible to increase our knowledge of the life and work of Harrison. Until this is done, the attribution of authorship may be regarded as an open question.

*   *   *   *   *

PROFES OF APARANT CHURCHE

1. The churche of Christ is his kingdom; therfor, wher the kyng-dom of Christ is not, his church is not. Wher Christ doth rull and rayne, ther is he kyng; but wher rull and rayngn is taken out of his hand, ther is he disposs[es]ed of his ryght, of his inheritance, which is his kyngdom. But your ministers, or rather tymservors, confes that they have not the true church government; that is as much to say, Christ his regiment and septer; therfor, they have not his kingdom, and therfor not his church aparant.

2. Yf they answer that the whol world is the kyngdom of Christ, and that he ruleth every whair, the question is not of that rulling that he, being God equall with his Father, ruleth and governeth all things; but to him being man, his heavenly Father hath geven him the inhertaunce of Mount Sion, which is his church, as it is written: " I have sett my King upon Sion, my holly mountayn"; also, " the Lord hath chosen Sion, and loved it, and to dwell in it," saing, " this is my rest for ever," " ther will I mak the horne of David to bud, for I have ordeyned a light for myne anoynted."[1] This Sion is the church; this horne of David is the strength of his septer, and of the kyng-dome of Christ.

3. Yf they answer that in som part they have this gover[n]ment, because, as they say, they preach the word, which is the septer of the kyngdom of Christ: first, mark well, they are faine to call back again that which they before have preached, that church government is wanting. Allso I demannd of them yf ther be any partting or halting with the Lord, or if they may yowk an oxe and an asse to gether in the Lord's tillage; or what agreement is betwext God and Belyall. For what peace or felowship hath the scepter of Christ with the septer of anti-christ, that they shold joyn to gether in governing ? The Lord our God is a jelous God, and will not suffer his honour to be geven to another. Lastly, I answer that the word which is his septer of his kingdom as his word of messag preached with power and auctoritye by them which are sentte, which preach

---

1 Psalm 2: 6 and 132: 13, 14, 17.

71

with governing and gov[e]rn with preaching. How they do itt shall apear afterward.

4. When the chifeste and heiest ecleseausticall autoritie is in the hands of antichrist, ther is not the church of Christ; for Christ hath given this auctoryty to his own servants; but in the churches of these mi[n]isters, the lordly byshops, deanes, chaneslors, archdeacons, comisaryes, and such lyck, being the pope's basterds, these have chefer autoritye than his servaunts, and these straunge [?] prelasy execut dominion over them, and they sufer that yoak of bondag; they therfor have not the church of Christ among them aparante.

3. [5]. In the church of Christ every man may executte that which our savior Christ hath commanded, as in the 18 of Mathew, conserning of bringing of dew complaints unto the church, in these words, " tell the church,"[1] but in the churches of these ministers this cannot be executed; no, not when a wolf is thrust upon the people in stead of a shepard, or any other most grose and horryble inequitie is donne among them. They cannot complayn to the church, except they will call the byshop the church; and he is alwayes the chefe workmaster of that messechefe [mischief] of sending of woulfes and dome dogs unto them. Therfor they have not the church of Christ aparant among them. Lett them answer wherever they did know that this commandement of our savior Christ co[u]ld be put in pracktys amonge them, which in the church of Christ may be pracktysed dayly.

4. Also in the church of Christ ther be keyes of the kyngdom of heaven to bynd and to lowsse in outward governmente:[2] but in the churches of these ministers they have not this auctorytie, but they must fetch it from the comisaryes' cortes or other chapell cortes, which ar contrary to Christ and therfor antychristian and against Christ. Therfor they have not the church of Christ among them aparant.

5. They which being put in offyce by a kyng, and they geve over ther offyse and auctorytye into the hands of a straunge kyng, ar becom traytors to ther true kyng; and have not kyngdom amongste them. But these ministers have betrayed the keyes of the kyngdom [of] heaven, which ar committed to them and

---

[1] Matthew 18: 17. Much controversy arose from the interpretation of this verse. See Francis Johnson, *A Short Treatise concerning the Words of Christ*, TELL THE CHURCH.

[2] Matthew 16: 19.

to the church, into the hands of lord byshops, comesaryes, and such lyke, which are strange majestrats; therfore, they ar traytturs to Christ, and have spoylled his kyngdom; therfor they have not his kyngdom nor his church aparant among theme.

6. The church of Christ is sanctyfied and mad[e] glorious without spot of wrinckell [Ephesians 5: 27] or grose pollutions that ar retayned and mayntained when they be ownse [once] many-fested in daungering the statte of the church. But in theyr churches they confes ther be many and gret pollutions, and ar bothe mayntained and retayned. Therfor they have not the church of Christ aparant.

7. We acknowledge ther be many pollutions in the manners of men; but being secrett, and not known openly indangering the statte of the church goverment, ar then left to God. But yf they be manifeste and openly known, in daungering the statt of the church, ar then becom such spottes and wrinckells as declar the church not to be glorious nor santyfied to Christ, and therfor to be none of his.

8. " Know ye not that a letell levene leveneth the wholle lomp," as the apostell Pall [Paul] speaking to have on [one] evel mem-ber cutte of [off].[1] Yf then one wicked man worthie [of] excommunication not being reconsiled tendeth to the savouring [souring ?] of the whole lomp which is the church, how much mor shall so many wicked offyces, and so many wicked men which use them, and so many wicked gyedg [guides ?] which submitt them selves to them, and so many people some ignor-ant and some wilfull that ar holden captyve by these gyudes [*sic*] in those ofyces contynewing after this sorte not onlye mak sower but also mak to stynck the wholl lompe of the church in the nostr[ils] of God. Therfor such churches be not the churches of Christ, seing they ar all corupt and have donne that that is abhominable.

But this is the comendacions of the church by the mouth of the profitts [prophets], " the people shall be all ryghteous, the grafe of my planting shall be the work of myne own hands that I may be glorified ";[2] meaning that outward inyquitey must be fare [far] from the children of the church. And those children which be planted, they be the Lord's plants, and the

---

[1] I Corinthians 5: 6.
[2] Isaiah 60: 21.

profitte [prophet] speaking, saing, " a litell on[e] shalbe a thousand and a small one a strong nation ";[1] as we see this day that the wicked bandes of the Lord's enimies cant not stand agaynst the power which God hath geven to a small on[e] speaking in his name to the confounding of them all.

Also the profytte [prophet] speaketh thus of the church of Christ; that is, " violence shall be no mor h[e]ard of in the land, neather dissolatione nor distruction in the bordars; but thou shalt call salvatione thie walls and peace [praise] thy [9.] gaets."[2] But in these churches whosoever desyreth to live godly in Christ Jesus, and to keep a good contiones [conscience], in the true worship and service of God without bondage of re[a]d prayers in popishe wyse, and a number of other corupt begerlye serimonies, those his people must sufer violence bothe of ther wicked guides themselves and also of the byshops withe others; and those abhomynations of desolations thrust into the people instead of Christ's true worship; and all the mynisters must use them, and the reste of the people must joyne with them and so confyrme them, and so altogether with the lawe add to the bonds of those that suffer for a wittnes against them. Ye [yea], they styll cry for the cevill majestrat's sword, and so crave for more violence against the children of God, unconvinced or uncondemned, and therfor not his church.

10. The harlot which hath not taken away her fornications out of her syght and her adulteryes from between her brests is not the spouse of Christ, yea, though she hath byne the mother church; as yeat is written, " plead with thie mother, plead with her, that she is not my wyf."[3] But to chang the true church offices with false antychristian offices, or spirituall fornications and adult[er]yes, which in the church of these ministers ar not yeat taken away: therefor they be but harlots, and not the churches of Christ.

11. In the church of Christ the horn of David doth bud, and his crown florish upon him.[4] Bute in ther churches the horn of antychrist doth not onlye bud but also florish; and the crownes florish upon her heads of byshops, chaunsslers, comissaryes, plants that the heavenlye Father hath not planted, and must

1 Isaiah 60: 22.
2 Isaiah 60: 18.
3 Hosea 2: 2.
4 Psalm 132: 17, 18.

be pluckt op by the rowtes before the horn of David cane spring. Therfor they have not the church of Christ aparant.

12. In Sion, which is the Lord's church, " the prestes ar clothed with salvation ";[1] but in ther churches the ministers ar clothed with distruction, for most of them ar blynd gydes and dome dogges, destroyers and murderers of sowles; and the rest, which sem to have knowledg, ar malyshsious and envious and obstinat against the Lord's howse building, and will not build them selves nor suffer them that wold: so distruction and not salvation cometh both to them selves and others. Therfor they have not Sion, which is the church of Christ, aparant among them.

13. In the church of Christ they may easilye be deserned who ar within or who ar without; as it is writen, " for what have I to doe to juge those that are without, doye not judge those that ar within."[2] But those churches or p[ar]ishes ar all on[e] felowship; we see not who ar within or who ar without, or who we shold cownt for brethren or whom we shold count for heathen and publycanes by the determynations of the churches' sensors. Therfor these p[ar]ishes ar not the churches of Christe.

14. The psalme speaketh thus: " owt of Sione which is the perfection of bewtye the Lord hath shined."[3] But they that speaketh the best or favourablyest of these churches do confes that in the state of owtward government ther be many imperfections, coruptions and deformities, which darken the face therof; yea, such deformities they be as is fowll and ugllye, as is proved. Therfor they have not Syone which is the church.

15. Also of the people of the church it is written, " lette the highe accts of God be in ther mouthes and a towe [two] edged sword in ther hands, to execut vengance upon the heathen and corrections among the people; such honour have all his saynts."[4] But in ther church ther is no such autorytye; nor any such honour unto the saynts that they should execut vengence and corections upon the wicked, but contrarywise they them selves are smiten of the wicked and dispitfully abused for rightteusnes' sack; yea, the guides them selves lay downe ther neckes willynyly

---

[1] Psalm 132: 16.
[2] I Corinthians 5: 12.
[3] Psalm 50: 2.
[4] Psalm 149: 6, 7, 9.

and slavishlye to antychristian offices, and to be displaced by those courts and such lyck senseurs; so far of[f] ar they from bynding in chaynes and fetters of iron. Therfor they have not the church of Christ aparant amongst them.

16. Paull to the Romans speaketh thus: " we have many members of on[e] bodye, and all members have not on[e] offyce; so we being many ar on[e] bodye in Christ, and every on[e] of us on[e] another's members. Seing then we have gifftes that ar dyvers, according to the graces which is geven unto us, whether we have provesey, [let us prophecy] according to the proporsyon of faythe, or an offyce, lett hime wayt on his offyce, or he that exorteth, on his exortations; he that distributeth, lett him do it with simplisite, and he that ruleth, with diligence, he that sheweth mersye, with chearfulnes."[1] Thus hathe the apostell sett downe the offyces and callings of the church and the menistry of them, namlye of the profyts, pastors, docctors, elders, relevers, and widowes; thus declaring that in the house of God we be mad[e] on[e] another's members by the deversitye of those callynges, gyftes, graces, wherin we sarve on [serve, one] to another's perfection and going foward unto godlynes. But in ther parishes they have not these offices, much les the exercision [executing] of them, nather any gyftes of graces tending therto; for yf any such gifftes spring up in any by the gyfte of God, for want of styring up and not pracktysyng of it, it is quenched. Then, as the tallent head [hid, held?] in the ground. So that the parishners ar not by these gyftes and callings joined together as felowmembers of Christ ar [or?] knite by these as by the synewes and bands of the church. Thefor they have not the church of Christ aparant amongst them.

17. Yf they say they have som of these offyces, as passtors and doctors, we denye that a parson or a vicar plased [placed] by a patron or a lord byshop can be a pastor; but he must fyrst renownce that evell calling, and then to be lawfully called, both by God and bye the consent of godlye Christians to be ruled and guided by hime so fare as the word of God doe lead them; and furder executyng of his dutye not in gathering of the good and bad together, but in separatyng of the good from the bad. And as for the docter, in som fewe places wher he is, he cometh to smale effecte; for most comonlye he is adjoyned

---

[1] Romans 12: 4-8.

with some idoll sheperd or some tym-server, and withdrawethe
not the people from those abhomynactions afornamed, nor do
not plant the church among them; so that the lyght of those
churches is nothing but darknes. O how great is that darcknes!
When the chefest ordars is full of confution, what then is the
disordar offe them. Thes things ar not in the churches of God.

18. Also thosse which persecut the church of Christ ar not the
church of Christ; for Christ is not devided within hime self;
and thei which hate Sione ar not of Sion, but they persecut
those which ar gethered to gether in the name of Christ,
hollding on[e] law and goverment under Christ, and whom
they ar not abell to charg of any abhomynaciones unremoved,
nather in the outward worshipe of God nor in the maner of
lyffe. Therfor they persecut the church of Christ and ar not
his churche.

19. And wheras they say we rend ourselves from the church, it is
childyshe and slaundering of us: for although they wear [were]
the church, we myght leve on [leave one] congregation as many
occasions may fall out, so that we joyne with another which is
the congregation of God's people. Now if they can prove that
we have joyned agaynest Christ in any antychristian [way],
then we will retorne and refforme our selves.[1]

20. David speaketh thus: " be favorable unto Sione for thie good
pleasuer, byld the walls of Jerusaleme; then shalt thow exept
[accept] the sacrifyes of ryghteusnes, the burnt oferings and
oblations; then shall they ofer calves upon thiene alters."[2] So
that the exeptyng [accepting] of our sacrifyses, even all our
prayers and good deds and thancks geving in the true worship
and service of God, dependeth upon God's favor toward Syon
and the building of Jerusaleme, and the place where his honour
dweleth. And his honour dweleth where his ark resteth; and
when his ark departeth, his honor and glory departeth, as
Fineas' wyf speak, saing, " the glorye is departed from Israell, for
the ark of God is taken."[3] But in these churches they have not
brought home the arke of God from the Philystians, which is
Christ bearing his septer; therfor the glory of God is not among
them; and they refuse to bring it home, and that wylfullye:

---

[1] This statement indicates that separation is a new development. The
attitude is more indicative of 1587 than of 1590 or 1593. Later, the
feelings have become militant and hardened.

[2] Psalm 51: 18, 19.

[3] The wife of Phineas speaking — see I Samuel 4: 19-22.

therfor they refuese the Lord's honor. The ark of God is the facce of God and the presence of his grace: therfor they not having it in his resting-place, nor going about to fetche it home, they canot behowld the Lord as he is, nor the facces [*sic*] of his anoynted. And for the walls of Jerusaleme, and the Lord's house, they refeuse to build; not as the Isralytes did in the dayes of Agge the profytt, which pronised [prophesied] unto them from the mouthe of the Lord, that all that they did was uncleane and not exepted [accepted] because the Lord's house was not bylded; for they being admonished speedylye obayed:[1] nether do they as the Isralytes did in the days of Nehemiahe and Annan [Hanani], which sayd it was a tyme of troubullacion and reproche because the walls offe Jerusalyme was not builded; for then thei aplyed them selves carfulye to the work untyll it was fynished.[2] But these mynisters do as the Isralyts did in Meribay, and as in the dayes of Massay in the wyldernes, when they tempted and proved God, and seenne [scanned?] his works, and wold not enter into his reste when they wer comanded; to whom the Lord swar in his wrath that they shold not enter into his rest.[3] Now these which have not the walls of Jerusalem bylded, nor his temple builded, and refeuse obstinatlye to build, being admonished therto, there [their] sacrifyses is not excepted [accepted] of the Lord, and ther relygion but a burden to the Lord, and he werye to bear them; and therfor not his church.[4]

The tabernacell was a figuer of the church of the Lord; and the Lord gave strayght charg that it shold be mad[e] according to the pattern showed to Mosses in the mount.[5] And so our saviour Christ was fortye dayes after his ressurrection conversant with his apostells, teaching them those things which conserneth the byldyng of his church and kyngdom. And the apostels, according as they reseved instructions of hime, so they bylded and have left us a patroun [pattern]. Now these churches are not framed affter this pattron; yea, they fayll not only in a pine [pin] or a curtayn, which want myght not be suffered, but they fayll in the cheffe pillers and walles therof. Therfor they be not the churches of Christ.

[1] Haggai 1: 2, 8, 12 ; 2: 14.
[2] Ezra 6: 14, 15 ; Nehemiah 1: 2, 3 ; 6: 15, 16.
[3] Exodus 17: 7, 16 ; Deuteronomy 33: 8 — Massah and Meribah.
[4] Isaiah 1: 13, 14, 15.
[5] Exodus 25: 8-40 ; 26: 1-37 ; 27: 1-21.

Also David speakethe thus: "Jerusalem is builded as a cittye that is compackte together in it self, wherunto the tribes goo upe, evene the tribs of the Lord goe up, according to the testimonies to Israell, to prays the name of the Lord there: for ther ar trones sett for judgment, even the trones of the house of David."[1]   Jerusalem is a figuer of the church; the trones of David a figure of the holye eldership of the church: but in thes churches they have neyther cowrts nor consystory, counsyll nor synod, holden of our David, Christ Jesus, nor in his name; but only those unlawfull courtts, consistoryes and seann [scenes, synods?] holden by the strength of the canone law, even the sharpest edge of antychrist's sword, and that by the confesshion of them all.   Therfor they have not the church of Christ aparent to be seene.

Thus being so manifestlye proved that they be not the churches of Christ; they which be gathered to gether in his name as he hath apoynted to hear them, neyther cane they have his sacraments, which be seales only to the promyses maed to the church.   For there [their] sacraments ar but dead synes, and pretended sacraments, because they cane prove no church; and the true sacraments aplay [apply] unto the aparant church, and to be grafted into the church of God. Nather have they the word of messag from the mouth of the Lord preched among them, but rezytall [recital] or historycall out of other historyes.   For none can preach the [word] of messag but those that ar sent from the mouth of the Lord onlye and alone.   But they com not only and alone from the mouth of the Lord, but taketh ther warant by antychristian autorytye from the byshope.   So they ronne and ar not sent of God only and alone; and so they speak gracious words, and so minister graces to the hearers, as anye child may doe, or any other man without callyng.   Now lett this reason teach you; yf a man in a town com to the wicked and disobedient, and saye, "I com in the nam of a constable," and say, "I charg you in the prince's name that you leve your wickednes and flowe [follow] me," and is no constable nor have no lawfull autorytye nor callyng; the wicked will not nor hath not to obay hime: but yf the lawfull offiser com that hath his autoritye from the prince, hime they will and must obay, and so do wee.

The callyng of those ministers, and autorytye that they

have, cannot be waranted by the word of God; therfor no autorytey.

Now lett every on[e] xamine hime self by the word of God, and show his obedience; for withowt his obedience ther is no promyse, and without a promise ther is no true fayth. Now, that preaching and governing ar joyned to gethere and can not be separated,[1] the word of God is manifest: Matthew 24, Acts 20: 28, I Timothy 5: 17, I Peter 5: 2, Ezra 3: 9, Zachariah[2] and wheras they mak ther xcuse of doing of ther dutie, for tarieng for the m[a]jestrat's beginning, that is that the majestrat must warant them by lawe, because they dar not do ther dutye for fear of lawe, yea, I say againe for fear of trobell by law in lossing of ther lyvings, as thowgh the majestrats wear [were] against the truth of God, and did lett the buildyng of the church of God, I saye in this they slander the majestrat; for the majestrate is not against the bylding of the house of God and fudarying [furthering] of his glory: for the majestrat being a christian majestrat hath bed [bid] them go forthe and build the church of God; or else lett them challeng the majestrate in that poynt yf ther [they] dare.

Profs for separation upon just cause, being dulye examyned by the word of God. I Corenthians 5: 9, 10, 11, 12, 13; Romans 16: 17; I Corinthians 7: 23; Tessalonians 3: 14; 2 Corinthians 6: 13, 14, 15, 16, 17, 18; Ephessians 5: 6, 7, 8, 9, 10, 11; Acts 19: 8, 9. Christ sayeth, " he that hearethe, lett hime tack head [take heed] what he hearethe; bewar of the leaven of the Pharises."[3]

Yf they aleag the kyngs of Juda and Moses and kings of Isreall for begining of reformation in the church—then, we answer that that they did in ecklesiastical or spiritiuall matters, they did it as they wear [were] sygnes of Christ; and that that they did sivillye in forsyng, they did it bye the sevyll sword, for they had autoritye in bothe cases that our kings and princes want; for the fyguratyve maner was ended in Christe.

---

[1] Matthew 24: 45.
[2] The references to Matthew 24 and Zechariah seem general and inconclusive.
[3] Matthew 16: 6, 11; Luke 12: 1.

III

A BREEFE SUM OF OUR PROFESSION

This brief summary of the views of the Separatists may be entitled a spiritual declaration of independence. It is one of the earliest manifestoes, and represents the position of Henry Barrow, John Greenwood, and the congregation which was meeting in private homes in 1587. If the reader will examine this manifesto closely, he will see that it consists of two main parts: the first portion contains five[1] statements of purposes and intentions, and the second portion consists of four charges or transgressions levelled against the Church of England.

The date may be assigned to the years 1587-1588. In 1585 Greenwood resigned from his benefice in Norfolk, and thereafter came to London. In the spring of 1590, George Gifford said that he had received,

" more than two yeares past . . . certaine articles which the Brownists [Barrowists] doo call, *A Breefe Sum of Their Profession, with Divers Arguments against Read Prayer*. They were brought unto me by a scholemaister in Essex, who of a godly minde, did desire mee to write my judgement of the same, which when I refused, hee urged me with this, that diverse of the people about them were troubled, and did hang in suspense, and for their sakes he did require it ; I did graunt his request, and when they had my writings, they were carried to the cheefe men of that sect. Not long after, I received large replies, where I perceived that which before I did not so much as dreame of, namely, that they had made chalenge, and looked to be encountred by the learnedest in the land."[2]

---

[1] Point number 6 is really a transitional statement which introduces the four principal transgressions.

[2] Gifford, *A Short Treatise against the Donatists of England,* signature a 2 *recto.*

81

D

Gifford is writing against the Barrowists, therefore, at least by March or April, 1588, and probably earlier. How long prior to that time the Separatists' manifesto had been in existence we do not know, but it is reasonable to suppose that it was in existence before October 8, 1587, when twenty-one Barrowists were arrested for holding a conventicle at the home of Henry Martin.[1]

Thus, the summer of 1587 may be assigned as the conjectural date for this (manuscript) writing, but it was not published until 1590, when Gifford first printed it in order to refute it and to reveal to the world the heresies and " frantike opinions " of the Barrowists. I can find no evidence for Powicke's conjecture that it was *published* in 1588, unless he means that the manuscript was in circulation by 1588. I believe Dr. Powicke is correct in thinking that this treatise is one of the earliest manifestoes of the Separatists, although Barrow's *Four Causes of Separation* seems slightly earlier. Therefore, I believe Champlin Burrage is wrong in criticizing Dr. Powicke on this point. It seems that Burrage has confused the one-page " A Breefe Sum of Our Profession " with the longer treatise, *A Brief Summe of the Causes of Our Separation*, which reprints " A Breefe Sum of Our Profession " on the first two pages, and then continues as a reply to Gifford (Burrage, *Early English Dissenters*, I, 133, note ; Powicke, *Henry Barrow Separatist*, Appendix II).

The original title seems to have been, " A Breefe Sum of Our Profession " (Gifford, *A Short Treatise*, p. 2). To the resentment of the Barrowists, Gifford altered the title to " A Breefe Sum of the Profession *of the Brownists*," thereby using a term of opprobrium, and equating the Brownists and Barrowists. He seems unaware that Browne had made his submission to the Archbishop of Canterbury in October, 1585 (Gifford, *A Short Treatise*, signature A 1 *recto*, and A 2 *verso*. See also Albert Peel and Leland H. Carlson, *The Writings of Robert Harrison and Robert Browne*, pp. 507f).

[1] Public Record Office, State Papers, Domestic, Elizabeth, CCIV, no. 10.

A Breefe Sum of Our Profession

Barrow reproduced this one-page manifesto in his longer work entitled, " A Brief Summe of the Causes of Our Separation, and of Our Purposes in Practice, Withstood by G.G. [George Gifford], Defended by H.B. [Henry Barrow] as Followeth," which was written in 1588 and printed in 1591 and 1605 as a part of the book, *A Plaine Refutation*. It is also printed by Powicke in *Henry Barrow Separatist*, Appendix II. I have used the earliest printed form, which appeared in Gifford, *A Short Treatise*, in 1590. The 1591 version, which is in the first edition of *A Plaine Refutation*, may be seen in the section, *A Brief Summe of the Causes of Our Separation, and of Our Purposes in Practice*. The version which was printed in the 1605 edition of *A Plaine Refutation* is reprinted by F. J. Powicke, *Henry Barrow Separatist*, Appendix II, p. 330.

* * * * * *

A BREEFE SUM OF OUR PROFESSION

1. We seeke above all things the peace and protection of the most high, and the kingdome of Christ Jesus our Lord.

2. We seeke and fully purpose to worship God aright, as he hath commaunded in his holy worde.

3. We seeke the fellowship and communion of his faithfull and obedient servants, and together with them to enter covenant with the Lord. And by the direction of his holy spirite to proceed to a godly, free, and right choise of ministers and other officers by him ordained to the service of his church.

4. We seeke to establish and obey the ordinances and lawes of our saviour Christ, left by his last will and testament to the governing and guiding of his church, without altering, changing, innovating, wresting, or leaving out any of them, that the Lord shall give us sight of.

5. We purpose by the assistance of the Holy Ghost in this faith and order to leade our lives. And for this faith and order to leave our lives, if such be the good will and pleasure of our heavenly Father; to whom be all glory and praise for ever. Amen.

6. And now that our forsaking and utter abandoning these disordered assemblies, as they generally stand in England, may not seeme strange or offensive to any man, that will judge or be judged by the worde of God: we alledge and affirme them hainouslye faultie, and wilfullye obstinate, in these foure principall transgressions.

    1. They worship the true God after a false manner, their worship being made of the invention of man, even of that man of sinne, erronious, and imposed upon them.

    2. Then for that the prophane ungodly multitude without the exception of any one person, are with them received into, and retained in the bosome and body of their Church, etc.

    3. Then for that they have a false and antichristian ministery imposed upon them, retained with them, and maintained by them.

A Breefe Sum of Our Profession

4. Then for that their churches are ruled by, and remaine in subjection unto, an antichristian and ungodly government, cleane contrary to the institution of our Saviour Christ.[1]

---

[1] If the reader will compare the first six articles with the following four transgressions, he will see that the latter are the negation of the former. Of the six articles, the first is a general introductory statement; the fifth is a resolution to live and die for their profession ; and the sixth is a transitional statement. In the remaining three articles the Separatists declare their purpose to worship God aright, to fellowship with spiritual members of the church, to select their own minister and officials, and to govern the church by the ordinances of Christ. These four main purposes, and the following four transgressions, may be summarized by the words: worship, membership, ministry, discipline. Throughout the writings of Barrow and Greenwood, these ideas constitute a central core around which they develop their arguments.

IV

BARROW'S FIRST EXAMINATION,
NOVEMBER 19, 1587

This examination is reproduced from the rare tract, *The Examinations of Henry Barrowe, John Grenewood, and John Penrie before the High Commissioners and Lordes of the Counsel. Penned by the Prisoners Themselves before Their Deathes.* It is available in the British Museum, Cambridge University Library, and the Folger Shakespeare Library (*Short-Title Catalogue*, No. 1519). The title-page, preface, and first examination occupy signature A - A iv *recto*. The tract is reprinted in *The Harleian Miscellany*, IV (London, 1745), pp. 326-348, and in *ibid.*, IV (London, 1809), pp. 340-365, and in *ibid.*, II (London, 1809), pp. 10-41. Consisting of thirty-two pages, this tract contains four of Barrow's examinations, one of Greenwood's, and one of Penry's examinations, all written by the examinees and smuggled out of prison. There is a pamphlet issued in 1710, entitled, *A Specimen of the Wholesom Severities, Practis'd in Queen Elizabeth's Reign, against Her Protestant Dissenters; in the Examination of Henry Barrow before the High Commissioners, and Lords of the Council, etc. Recommended by Dr. Henry Sacheverell, as Proper for the Present Times* (London, 1710). This reprints Barrow's examinations of November 19, 1587, of November 27, 1587, and of March 24, 1588/9. It does not reprint the examination of March 18, 1588/9, before a special commission, perhaps because it does not cast reflections upon the archbishop and bishops.

In the *Short-Title Catalogue*, the place of printing is suggested as Dort and the date is conjectured to be 1593. In all likelihood the place of printing is in the Netherlands; inasmuch as Dort was the place where several Separatist tracts were published in 1589-1591, there is a slight presumption in favour of that town. But Amsterdam and Middelburg are also possibilities.

If we could determine who the editor was, and where he was at the time of printing, we could arrive at a clue that would be helpful, though it would not be conclusive. We know that Francis Johnson, minister to the Company of English Merchants of the Staple at Middelburg, had been partly responsible for the confiscation and burning of the entire edition of 1,500-3,000 copies (except two) of Barrow's book, *A Plaine Refutation* (1591). We know also that he read one of the two remaining copies, became deeply interested in the religious position maintained therein, went to London, conferred with the leaders, became a Separatist, and accepted in September, 1592, the position of pastor of the newly-formed Separatist congregation. Arrested in December, 1592, he remained in the Clink prison for the next four and a half years, was exiled to Ramea[1] in the Magdalen Islands, returned to England and escaped to Holland in the autumn of 1597.

During his imprisonment Johnson carried on a written debate with Henry Jacob. In 1596 he prepared two replies and sent them out sheet by sheet. Thus, it is evident that four years of imprisonment had not changed his views. It is further evident that even in prison Johnson was the leader of the Separatists, and that the members of the congregation looked to him for guidance.

Judging from the style and the phrases in the brief introduction, I conclude that Francis Johnson wrote this introduction. One or more of the Separatists helped to see it through the press. The date assigned by librarians is conjecturally given as 1593, a surmise based on the year of the execution of Barrow, Greenwood, and Penry. This is a correct *terminus a quo*, but the possibility exists that 1594-1596 may be the *terminus ad quem*. Writing in 1596, Henry Jacob speaks of

---

[1] F. J. Powicke mistakenly refers to " Rainea," in *Henry Barrow, Separatist*, p. 229.

Penry's examination before Master Fanshaw, "lately published by your selves " [the Separatists]. This slight evidence may point to 1595 or 1596 as a better date, when many of the Separatists had been released from prison.[1]

The *Short-Title Catalogue*, item 1520, lists another edition with the conjectural date of 1594. But this date is an error. The typography is clearly not of the sixteenth century. 1694 would be closer to the true date, since this edition was printed for William Marshall, a bookseller and bookbinder in London, who did business in the period 1676-1725, and who specialized in religious publications.[2] It is possible that this tract was reprinted during the tempestuous days of the Popish Plot, the Exclusion Bill, or the time of the abdication of James II, or the impeachment proceedings against the Earl of Danby in 1678-9. Or, what is more likely, Dean Edward Stillingfleet's famous sermon preached in 1680 before the Lord Mayor on "The Mischief of Separation," and his book, *The Unreasonableness of Separation*, published in 1681, occasioned numerous replies, among which was that of Thomas Wall, *More Work for the Dean* (1681), who most likely reprinted this tract also, about 1681, to expose the bishops' dealings against the Separatists in 1587-1593.[3]

*　*　*　*　*　*　*

---

[1] *A Defence of the Churches and Ministery of Englande* (Middleburgh, 1599), pp. 82, 216. The publishing date is 1599, but the manuscript writing occurred in 1596.

[2] Henry R. Plomer, *A Dictionary of the Printers and Booksellers Who Were At Work in England, Scotland and Ireland from 1668 to 1725* (Oxford University Press, 1922), p. 198.

[3] Thomas Wall's *More Work for the Dean* and [Thomas Wall, ed. ?], *The Examinations of Henry Barrow, John Greenwood, and John Penry*, both contain reprints of Separatist material, both deal with Barrow, Greenwood, Penry, and both were printed by William Marshall, at the Sign of the Bible in Newgate Street.

THE EXAMINATIONS OF
HENRY BARROWE JOHN GRENEWOOD
AND JOHN PENRIE BEFORE THE HIGH
COMMISSIONERS AND LORDES OF THE COUNSEL.
PENNED BY THE PRISONERS THEMSELVES
BEFORE THEIR DEATHES

Ther is nothing covered that shal not
be reviled [revealed]: neither hid that shal not be knowen.
Luke 12: 2

For every worke God himself wil bring
unto judgement, with every secret thing whither
good or evil.   Ecclesiastes 2: [12:] 14.
[Dort ? 1595 ?]

[PREFACE]

[A i *verso*]

The testimonie and sufferings of the prisoners whose examinations here ensue cannot easilie (gentle reader) be forgotten of any whose harte is touched with care of religion and zeale of the truth. How weightie the causes were for which they suffered may appeare partlie by that which foloweth, but [cheefly by other writinges and bookes by themselves set out heretofore].[1]

Here has thow the maner of the prelates' proceding against them, and how they were convicted of theyr Brownisme, Donatisme, Anabaptistrie, schisme, heresie, *etc.*, wherwith they were charged, and for which they were so many yeeres kept in miserable close prisons, and at last bereaved of their lives. Sure whosoever had bene the persons, and whatsoever the errours, it would wel have become the lord arch bishop of the Church of England to have better instructed and informed them by the word of truth and wholsome doctrine, before they had bene adjudged to prison and death. II Timothy 2: 24, 25, and 4: 2; Titus 2: 1. Or if Paul's counsel could not take effect, yet Pilate's example might have stayed such courses, who examined our Lord Christe's accusers

---

[1] The bracketed words are given on the last page, D iv *verso*, under " Faultes escaped."

D*

and found them false, and never sent him to close prison for refusing to sweare to accuse him self, Matthew 27, Luke 23, John 18. Neither yet did the late prelates in Queen Marie's dayes use altogither such severitie. For Bonner[1] him self with the other tyrants of that time had often conference and disputation with the martyrs, and sought by Scriptures to have overthrowen them if they could.

Evil therfore have our bishops provided for their cause and credit, so lightly to deale in matters of such moment, and to proceed to such severe tortures, before more open and orderly conviction of the faultes and errours. Loe, now al posterities shal see their practises: and though they have spilt the blood of those men, which vexed them so sore, yet can they not bereave the world of their testimonie, which by word and writing they have left behinde them. The Lord give these men [the bishops] (if they belong unto him) to advert [take heed] and see their dealinges, and to remember the account which they ere long shalbe called unto, before him who is ready to judge quick and dead.

The publishing of these things can not justly be offensive to any, seyng 1. nothing els is here set downe but that which was then demaunded and answered (as neere as the prisoners could remember); 2. and they, which have themselves set forth the examinations of martyrs heretofore, may not be greeved now when theyr owne turne is come and their proceedings made knowne likewise:[2] they which doe wel need not shunne the light. However it be, the church of God, I doubt not, shal reape some profit hereby, for which, how [smal ?] so ever it be, let him have the praise. Amen.

---

[1] Edmund Bonner, Bishop of London (1540-1559). See *The Life and Defence of the Conduct and Principles of the Venerable and Calumniated Edmund Bonner* (London, 1842), p. 327. This ironical book, by " a Tractarian British Critic," sometimes subtle, sometimes strained in its sarcasm, was the work of George Townsend. See also G. E. Philips, *The Truth about Bishop Bonner*.

[2] Evidently this is a reference to Bishop John Aylmer, who rendered valuable assistance to John Foxe, the martyrologist, by criticizing the Latin translation of the *Acts and Monuments*. See John Strype, *Historical Collections of the Life and Acts . . . John Aylmer* (pp. 8-10). Aylmer's main work, *An Harborowe for Faithfull and Trewe Subjects against the Late Blowne Blaste concerning the Government of Wemen* (Strasborowe [London], 1559), is a reply to John Knox, *The First Blast of the Trumpet against the Monstruous Regiment of Women*) [Geneva], 1558).

Barrow's First Examination

[A ii *recto*]
A BRIEF OF THE EXAMINATION OF ME
HENRY BARROWE
THE 19 OF NOVEMBER, 1586 [1587.]
BEFORE THE ARCH BISHOP,[1] ARCH DEACON,[2]
AND DR. CUSSINS:[3] AS NEERE AS MY MEMORIE
COULD CARY: BEING AT LAMBETH.

This 19 being the Lord's day,[4] betwene 9 and 10 oft [*sic*] the clock in the fore noone, Mr. Hul[5] and I went unto the Clinke[6] to visit Mr. Grenewood and the other brethren there emprisoned:[7] where we had not bene the space of one quarter of an howre, but Mr. Shepherd,[8] the keeper of the prison, came up, rebuked

---

1 Archbishop John Whitgift (1530 ?—1604). For a summary of his work, see George Paule, *The Life of the Most Reverend and Religious Prelate John Whitgift, Lord Archbishop of Canterbury* (London, 1612); see also John Strype, *The Life and Acts of the Most Reverend Father in God, John Whitgift, D.D.* (London, 1718) 3 volumes; also, Oxford, 1822.

2 John Mullyns, Archdeacon of London, 1559-91. His name appears as Mollins, Mollyns, Molyns (so in *D.N.B.*), and Mullins in the records. In St. Paul's Cathedral, there is a statue of him. In the British Museum, Additional MSS. 29,546, f. 55, his signature is J. Mullyns.

3 Richard Cosin (1549-1597), Dean of the Court of Arches, Vicar-General of the Province of Canterbury, and member of the Court of High Commission. He wrote a learned defence of this court, as part of a work entitled, *An Apologie: of, and for Sundrie Proceedings by Jurisdiction Ecclesiasticall* (London, 1591). The work may well have been suggested or requested by Archbishop Whitgift, and directed against Lord Burghley. See G. B. Harrison, "Books and Readers, 1591-4," *Library*, Fourth Series, VIII, no. 3 (December, 1927), in "Transactions of the Bibliographical Society," Second Series, VIII [Oxford, 1928], p. 294.

4 In 1587 Sunday fell on November 19 ; in 1586, on November 20. The correct year is 1587, not 1586, as further proved by references to the length of Barrow's imprisonment scattered through his writings. John Greenwood and the other brethren were arrested on October 8, 1587 (Public Record Office, State Papers, Domestic, CCIV, item 10).

5 Evidently a friend. No further data available.

6 The Clink was a prison in Southwark, on the north side of Clink Street, which runs parallel to the Thames. Nearby were London Bridge and the Globe Theatre.

7 John Greenwood and twenty other Separatists were arrested on October 8, 1587, while holding a conventicle at Henry Martin's house (Public Record Office, State Papers, Domestic, CCIV, item 10). They are listed in Burrage, *Early English Dissenters*, II, 19-20, and also in the Appendix.

8 Mr. Shepherd arrested Barrow without warrant, accompanied him to Lambeth, and remained for the examination before Archbishop Whitgift.

Mr. Grenewood, and stayed me, saying he had commandement from his lord's grace so to doe. I demanded a sight of his warrant: he answered that he would doe it, and I might afterward, if I were wronged, bring mine action. So he locked me up in prison, and forthwith went to his lord's grace to Lambeth. About one of the clock he returned, and brought with him two pursuvantes. I was forthwith put into a boat and caried to Lambeth. By the way one of the pursuvants, called Watson,[1] drew out of his bosome a letter from the court of Lambeth unto me, saying how he had a long time sought me. I told him his paynes deserved thanks neither at God's handes nor mine: I refused his letter, and said that I obeyed neither it nor him, neither would I read it, shewing how I was under the arrest of the keeper of the Clinke, who sate by me. Wel, we arrived at Lambeth, wher after I had perused the B. [Archbishop Whitgift] his state, I was brought into his presence chamber, yet not until this Watson had prevented [anticipated, gone before] me and shewed his maister what had passed in the boat.

Archbishop. Barrowe, is your name Barrowe?

Barrow. Yea.

A. It is told me that yow refuse to receive or obey our letter, know yow what yow doe? It is from the high commissioners, and this man a pursuvant.

B. I refused to receive or obey that letter at that time.

A. Why so?

B. Because I was under arrest, and imprisoned without warrant, and against law; and therefore now it was too late to bring the letter.

A. Why? May not a [Privy] Counsellor commit to prison by his bare commandement? (alledging how the aldermen of London doe daily).

B. That is not the question, what a counsellor may doe; but whither this man may doe it without warrant, by

---

[1] Barrow refers to one Watson. There is a pursuivant whom John Penry denounces, Richard Walton (*The Appellation of I. Penri*, pp. 6, 44, 45), who is depicted as a former blacksmith, a hard, ruthless, and notoriously lewd and roistering individual. There is no mention of the name of the second pursuivant, but in the record of the second examination for November 27, 1587, Barrow mentions "my keeper's man Nicholas," who may have been a guard. Also, in *M. Some Laid Open in His Coulers* [*S. T. C.* no. 12342], not written by Greenwood but most likely by Job Throkmorton, there is a sarcastic reference to Watson, Walton, Haslop, and Munday (p. 42).

the law of the land: (pointing to the keeper of the Clinke).

A. Know yow the law of the land ?

B. Very little, yet was I of Graye's Inne some yeares.[1] (Then his two Doctours[2] and he derided mine unskilfulnes). Let this passe: I look for little help by [A ii *verso*] law against yow. I pray yow, why have yow imprisoned me, and after this manner sent for me ?

A. That yow shal know upon yowr oath: wil yow sweare ?

B. I hold it lawful to sweare, so it be done with due order and circumstances.

A. Reach a book, hold it him.

B. What shal we doe with this ?

A. Lay your hand upon it, man.

B. To what purpose ?

A. To sweare.

B. I use to sweare by no bookes.

A. Yow shal not sweare by the book, but by God onely.

B. So I purpose when I sweare.

Cussins. Did yow never take an oath at an Assise before the judges there ?

B. No.

C. But would yow refuse there to lay yowr hand on a book and sweare ?

B. Yea.

C. Then would your testimonie not be taken.

A. Why man, the book is no part of the oath, it is but a cerimonie.

B. A needlesse and wicked ceremonie.

A. Why, know yow what yow say ? Know you what book it is ? It is the Bible.

B. I wil sweare by no Bible.

---

[1] Barrow became a member of Gray's Inn in 1576 (Gray's Inn Register, Harley MSS. 1912, f. 10). In Joseph Foster, *The Register of Admissions to Gray's Inn, 1521-1889,* together with the *Register of Marriages in Gray's Inn Chapel,* 1695-1754 (London, 1889), p. 49, there is a Henry Barrow of Staple Inn admitted November 21, 1576. The name is listed as Barron, but this seems to be a misprint or a misreading.

[2] Dr. Cosin and Archdeacon Mullins, the latter having received his D.D. in 1565/6.

C. Scismaticks are clamorous alwayes. It is a perpetual note to know them by.

A. Mr. Dr. Cussins saith true, such were the Donatistes alwayes in the counsels, and such art thow and al other scismatiks such as thow art.

B. Say yowr pleasure, God forgive yow: I am neither scismatike nor clamourous: I answer but yowr demandes, if yow wil, I wil be silent.

A. Wel, wil yow lay your hand on the Bible and take an oath?

B. I use to joyne no creatures to the name of God in an oath.

A. Neither shal yow, this is but a custome commanded by law.

B. The law ought not to command a wicked custome.

A. Why, is it not lawful to lay your hand on a book?

B. Yes, but not in an oath.

A. Wil yow lay your hand in my hand and sweare?

B. No.

A. Wil yow lay your hand on the table and sweare?

B. No.

A. Wil yow hold up your hand towards heaven and sweare?

B. That is not amisse: but I wil use my libertie.

A. Why, yow hold it lawful to lay your hand on the table and sweare?

B. Yea, so it be not commanded and made of necessitie.

A. Why, the booke is the like: it is nothing of the oath but a thing indifferent.

B. If it be nothing of the othe, why doe yow so peremptorilie injoyne it? And if it be indifferent, as yow say it is, then doe I wel in not using it.

A. Nay, yow doe not wel in refusing it, for therin yow shew yowr self disobedient to the higher powers set over yow by God.

B. Even now yow said it was a thing indifferent; if it be so, ther is no power can bring me in bondage to my libertie.

A. Where finde yow that?

B. In St. Paul, I Corinthians [6: 12].

The arch bishop, archdeacon [Mullins], Dr. Cussins,

al denied it. I affirmed it. A little Testament in
Greek and Latine was brought me, and a Bible.[1]
I looked foe [for] the place but could not finde it:
great fault was in my memorie, for I looked in the
tenth chapter, neither indeed could I bethinke me
where to find it, they so interrupted me. [A iii *recto*].

A. Your devinitie is like yowr law.

B. The word of God is not the worse for my il memorie.

A. Yow speake not as yow thinck, for yow are prowd.

B. I have smal cause to be prowd of my memorie, yow
see the default of it: but the apostle saith it.
Againe they al denied it.

[B.] Yow then have no cause to condemne my memorie,
seing yow all have utterly forgotten this sayeng.
Then repeated I the words, " Al thinges are lawful
for me, but I wil not be brought in bondage to my
libertie."
Then they recited Romans 14 and I Corinthians 8.
" Al thinges are lawful for me, but al thinges are not
expedient."[2]

[B.] I said I meant not that place.

A. I would like it wel if yow cited your place in Greek
or Latine.[3]

B. Why, yow understand English: is not the word of
God in English ?

[C.] Then Cussin began to speak of *indefinita propositio*, but
wherupon I can not cal to remembranc.

[B.] I told him we were now about the New Testament:
It might be if he had asked me that question when I
knew him in Cambridge, I should then have answered

1 My conjecture is that the little Testament was Beza's first minor edition
of 1565, the second edition of 1567, or the third edition of 1580. Nicholas
Brylinger issued at least fourteen diglot editions in the sixteenth century.
The complete Bible may well have been the Bishops' Bible or the Great
Bible. See T. H. Darlow and H. F. Moule, *Historical Catalogue of the
Printed Editions of Holy Scripture*, vols. I, II.
2 The reference is I. Corinthians 6: 12 or 10: 23. Barrow's mistake in
looking for this statement in the tenth chapter is understandable. Both
I. Corinthians 6: 12 and 10: 23 begin in the same way — " all things are
lawful unto (for) me," but then they diverge.
3 This seems to be a caustic remark, possibly intended to ascertain Barrow's
knowledge of Greek and Latin. It seems ironical that Whitgift himself
has been suspected of being ignorant of Greek — an erroneous suspicion.

him. He forthwith called to remembrance of what howse I was.[1]

A. Were yow then of Cambridge ?

B. Yea, I knew yow there.

[A.] He said he was there before I was borne.

[B.] I said it might be.

[A.] Then he entred into discourse of his antiquititie [*sic*].[2] Then he asked me if I had read books, as Calvin, Beza, *etc.*

[B.] I answered that I had read more than ynough. But yet I know not why I am emprisoned.

A. It is reported that yow come not to church, are disobedient to her majestie, and say that ther is not a true church in England.[3]
What say yow ? Have yow at any time said thus ?

B. These are reportes. When yow produce yowr testimonie I wil answer.

A. But I wil better beleeve yow upon yowr oath than them: how say yow, wil yow sweare ?

B. I wil know what I sweare to before I sweare.

A. First sweare: and then if any thing be unlawfully demaunded, yow shal not answer.

B. I have not learned so to sweare. I wil first know and consider of the matter before I take an oath.

[A.] Thus many thinges being alleaged to and fro by us, the arch bishop commaunded Cussin to recorde, that I refused to sweare upon a book.

1 Barrow matriculated as a fellow-commoner of Clare Hall, Cambridge, on November 22, 1566, and proceeded B.A. in 1569/70. Cosin became a pensioner of Trinity College on November 12, 1561, proceeded B.A. in 1565/6 and M.A. in 1569.

2 Whitgift was born about 1530, and therefore his antiquity amounted to fifty-seven years. He matriculated as a pensioner at Pembroke Hall in May, 1550. Since Barrow was born about 1549-1551, and if Whitgift was at Cambridge before Barrow was born, we may conjecture that Barrow was born about 1551, and was fifteen when he matriculated. Cosin, a precocious lad, was only twelve when he entered Cambridge, but Whitgift was twenty (if his birth occurred in 1530) or seventeen (if born in 1533).

3 This latter charge is very likely true. One of the Barrowists, Margaret Maynerd, made a similar statement when she was examined on October 8, 1587. Barrow's main work, published in 1590, was entitled, *A Brief Discoverie of the False Church*, and in 1589, he had written *A True Description out of the Worde of God, of the Visible Church*. The reference may be to *Profes of Aparant Churche*, wherein Barrow denies that the Church of England is the true church of Christ.

Barrow's First Examination

B. Yea, and set downe also, that I wil not sweare thus at random, but first I wil know and consider of the thinges I sweare unto, whither they require an oath.

A. Wel, when were yow at church?

B. That is nothing to yow.

A. You are a scismatick, a recusant, a seditious person, *etc.*, with many such like.

B. Say what yow list of me, I freelie forgive yow.

A. I care not for yowr forgivenes.

B. But if yow offend me, yow ought to seek it, while yow are in the way[1] with me.

A. When were yow at church?

B. I have answered that in an other place. It belongeth not to yow.

A. Why, are yow indited?[2]

B. I am.

A. Yet belongeth it to ys [us, or this]. I wil not onely medle with yow, but arraigne yow as an heretick before me.

B. Yow [A iii *verso*] shal doe no more than God wil. Erre I may, but hereticke wil I never be.

A. Wil yow come to church hereafter?

B. Future thinges are in the Lord's handes: if I doe not, yow have a law.

A. Have yow spoken these wordes of the Church of England?

B. When yow produce your witnesse I wil answer.

A. But upon your oath I wil beleeve yow.

B. But I wil not accuse my self.

[A.] Then began he againe to charge me with scisme, sedition, heresie.

B. Yow are lawlesse: I had rather yow produced yowr witnesse.

A. Of what occupation are yow?

B. A Christian.

A. So are we al.

B. I deny that.

---

[1] A Pauline phrase, meaning the christian way of life. Compare Acts 9: 2 and 19: 9, 23.

[2] Perhaps Barrow had been presented to the Bishop of Norwich, Edmund Scambler, or to the Bishop of London, John Aylmer, for non-attendance. Evidently he had already made his reply.

Henry Barrow

A. But are yow a minister?

B. No.

A. A scholemaister?

B. No.

A. What then, of no trade of life?

B. In yowr letter, yow know my trade in the superscription.

A. Yow are then a gentleman.

B. After the manner of our countrie, a gentleman.

A. Serve yow any man?

B. No, I am God's freeman.

A. Have yow landes?

B. No, nor fees.

A. How live yow?

B. By God's goodnes, and my friends.

A. Have yow a father alive?

B. Yea.

A. Wher dwelleth he, in Norffolke?

B. Yea.[1]

A. Wher dwel yow—in London?

B. No.

A. Wel, can yow finde sufficient suretie for your good behaviour?

B. Yea, as sufficient as yow can take.

A. What, yow cannot have the queene?

B. Neither can yow take her; she is the judge of her law. Yet for my good behaviour, I suppose I could get her word.

A. Doth she know yow then?

B. I know her.

A. Els were it pitie of your life.

B. Not so.

A. Can yow have any of these that came with yow to be bound for yow?

B. I know not, I thinke I can.

A. What [!] know yow them not?

B. I know one of them.

A. What is he?

---

[1] His father was Thomas Barrow, of Shipdam, Norfolk. There is a brief genealogy in Harley MSS. 1552, folios 43, 47. See Walter Rye (ed.), *The Visitacion of Norffolk*, p. 18.

Barrow's First Examination

B.   A gentleman of Graie's Ynne.

A.   What cal yow him?

B.   Lacie.[1]

A.   But know yow what band [bond] yow should enter?
     Yow are bound hereby to frequent our churches.

B.   I understand yow [that such a bond is a guarantee]
     of my good behaviour.

A.   And in it is this conteyned: and so yow had forfeyted
     your bond at the first.

B.   Wel, now I know yowr minde, I wil enter no such
     bande.

A.   Wil yow enter band to appeare on Tuesday next at
     our court, and so on Thursday if yow be not called,
     and be bound not to depart until yow be dismissed
     by order of our court?

B.   No.[2]

A.   Then I wil send yow to prison.
     Then called he Watson the pursuvant and Dr. Cussins
     a part [aside, apart] into a windowe, where he made
     a warrant to send me to prison.

B.   Yow shal not touch one haire of my head without the
     wil of my heavenly Father.

A.   Nay, I wil doe this to rectifie yow.

B.   Consider what yow doe, yow shal one day answer it.

A.   Yow wil not sweare: yow wil not enter bond for your
     appearance.

B.   I wil put in band for my baile in the prison and for
     my true imprisonment.

A.   Nay, that wil not serve the turne. Mr. Doctor
     [Cosin], enter these thinges.
     Then Cussins wrote that I refused to sweare and enter
     bond.

B.   [sic, A.]   I wil send some to yow to confere.

---

[1] Perhaps " Roberte Lacy of St. Andrewes in Holborne," who was taken
six weeks earlier at a conventicle in Henry Martin's house, October 8,
1587 (Public Record Office, State Papers, Domestic, CCIV, item 10).
Robert Lacy, son and heir of William Lacy, of Stamford, Lincolnshire,
was admitted to Gray's Inn on April 24, 1583 (Joseph Foster, *Register
of Admissions to Gray's Inn,* 1521-1889, p. 63).

[2] This question and answer are not part of the text, but are found in the
last page under " Faultes escaped."

Henry Barrow

A. [*sic*, B.] That were more requisite before my imprisonment.

[B.] So the Arch Bishop delivered me to the pursuant to [A iiii *recto*] carie me to the Gatehouse,[1] where I as yet remayne,[2] neither knowing the cause of my imprisonment, neither have I as yet heard from him.

I was no sooner out of his howse, but I remembred the place in controversie: it is written I. Corinthians 6: 12. " Al thinges are lawful for me, but al thinges are not profitable: I may doe al thinges, but I wil not be brought under the power of any thing."

" The Lord knoweth to deliver the godly out of tentation, and to reserve the unjust unto the day of judgement under punishment."[3]

---

[1] The prison at Westminster, frequently used by the Bishop of London for convicted clergymen and others. Maurice Pickering was the keeper of the Gatehouse. There is an item on " Morrys Pykering " in the Lansdowne MSS. 82, item 63.

[2] This dates the writing between November 19 and his second examination on November 27, 1587.

[3] II Peter 2: 9.

V

BARROW'S SECOND EXAMINATION,
November 27, 1587

Barrow's second examination is printed on signature A iv
recto and *verso* of *The Examinations of Henry Barrowe, John
Grenewood and John Penrie.* In this interrogation before the
Court of High Commission assembled at Lambeth Palace,
Barrow is facing Archbishop John Whitgift, Bishop John
Aylmer and Dean Alexander Nowell, besides other bishops,
deans, lawyers, and clerks. Despite the brevity of the examination, the reader gets an impression of Whitgift's temper,
the disagreement on oaths, the charges made against Barrow,
and the courage of the examinee in replying to Archbishop
Whitgift.

BARROW'S SECOND EXAMINATION
November, 27, 1587

The 27 of November [1587], eight daies after I was commited by [the Archbishop of] Canterbury to the Gatehouse: I was sent for by one of his servantes to make appearance before the high commissioners at Lambeth: whither he and my keeper's man Nicholas caried me.[1] There I found a very great traine without, but within a goodlie synode of bishops, deanes, civilians, etc., beside such an apparance of wel-fedde silken preistes, as I suppose might wel have beseemed the Vaticane.[2] Where after to my no smal greif I had heard a scholemaister[3] deny his maister Christ, I was called.

Canterburie [Archbishop Whitgift], with a grimme and an angrie countenance, beholding me, made discourse how I refused to sweare on a book, *etc.*, as fel out in our first meeting: and demaunded whither I were now better advised, and would sweare. I answered that I would not refuse to sweare upon due occasion and circumstances.

Canterbury. Wil yow then now sweare?

Barrow. I must first know to what.

---

[1] Maurice Pickering was the keeper of the Gatehouse at Westminster. He was regarded as perhaps the most remarkable incumbent of that office. He was a prominent citizen in Westminster, and in an official document was styled " Maurice Pickering, gentleman " (Arthur Penrhyn Stanley, *Historical Memorials of Westminster Abbey*, p. 345). Mr. Nicholas was the underkeeper of the Gatehouse. See Lansdowne MSS. 72, item 39, f. 113.

[2] This description is similar to Barrow's statement that he had been " convented befor the pontyficall corte of bishops, a sort of well feed [sic] and well arayed silken prests " (" A Pastoral Letter from Prison," *Relics of the Puritan Martyrs*, 1593, ed. T. G. Crippen [(London): Congregational Historical Society, 1906], pp. 22-23). Also printed in the *Transactions of the Congregational Historical Society*, II no. 5 (May, 1906), pp. 339-345, and in the present volume, p. 116.

[3] It is just conceivable that this reference might be to Robert Browne, whom Barrow did not know. Although Browne would not " deny his maister Christ," Barrow may mean that this person made his peace with the bishops and recanted his nonconformity. Browne signed articles of submission on October 7, 1585, was presented to the Bishop of Peterborough in April, 1586, for non-attendance at church, was appointed master of St. Olave's School, Southwark, in November, 1586, and was discharged therefrom about 1588.

Barrow's Second Examination

Canterbury. So yow shal afterward.

Barrow. I wil not sweare unlesse I know before.

Canterbury. Wel, I wil thus far satisfie your humour.
[The Bishop of] London[1] began to interrupt, but
Canterbury cut him of[f], and produced a paper of
objections against me, which he delivered to one
Beadle to read. It conteyned much matter and many
suggestions against me, disorderly framed according
to the malitious humour of mine accuser, as, that I
denyed God to have a true church in England:[2]
and to prove this, the four principal causes[3] framed
in way of argument, as, the worship of God with us
is idolatrie: *ergo*, no true church. They have an
antichristian and idolatrous ministerie: *ergo*, no true
church. Further he saith that the reverend father
in God, my lord's grace of Canterbury, and all the
bishops of the land, are antichristes. Further he
saith that al the ministers in the land are theeves and
murtherers and secret hypocrites, and that al the
preachers of the land are hirelinges.[4] That Mr.
Wiggington[5] and Cartwright[6] straine at a gnat and
swollow a camel. [A iiii *verso*] Further, he condemneth al writers, as Calvin, Beza, *etc.*, and saith that
al catechismes are idolatrous and not to be used. The
reasons to these were untrulie and disorderley set

---

1 John Aylmer, Bishop of London. For an account of his career, see John
Strype, *Historical Collections of the Life and Acts of the Right Reverend
Father in God, John Aylmer, Lord Bishop of London in the Reign of Eliza-
beth* (Oxford, 1821).

2 This question was asked of Barrow by the Archbishop on the examination
of November 19, 1587. Whitgift said it was reported that Barrow asserted
there was not a true church in England. Barrow refused to incriminate
himself and challenged the archbishop to produce witnesses.

3 See *A Breefe Sum of Our Profession,* and *Four Causes of Separation,* and
A Brief Summe of the Causes of Our Seperation, in this volume. See also
The True Church and the False Church, which has similar arguments
(in volume IV).

4 These charges against Barrow are taken from his *Four Causes of Separation.*

5 Giles Wigginton, or Wiggenton, minister of a church in Sedbergh, Yorkshire. See *Transactions of the Congregational Historical Society,* II, no. 3
(September, 1905), pp. 147-150, and *ibid.,* II, no. 6 (October, 1906), pp.
379-386. See also Albert Peel (ed.), *The Seconde Parte of a Register,* II,
pp. 238-258.

6 Thomas Cartwright, leader of the Presbyterians. See A. F. Scott Pearson,
Thomas Cartwright and Elizabethan Puritanism, 1535-1603, and also
Albert Peel and Leland H. Carlson, *Cartwrightiana.*

	downe accordingly in the bil, which I cannot rehearse.
London.	How say yow, Mr. Deane of Paul's? Here is for yow. Yow have written a catechisme.[1]
Canterbury.	This fellow deales indifferently, he makes us al alike. Thus far have I satisfied yow: now yow know what yow shal sweare unto: how say yow, wil yow sweare now?
London.	My Lorde's grace doth not shew this favour to many.
Canterbury.	Fetch a book.
Barrow.	It is needles.
Canterbury.	Why, wil yow not sweare now?
Barrow.	An oath is a matter of great importance and requireth great consideration. But I wil answer yow truly. Much of the matter of this bil is true, but the forme is false.
Canterbury.	Goe to, sirra, answer directlie, wil yow sweare? Reach him a book.
Barrow.	Ther is more cause to sweare mine accuser. I wil not sweare.
Canterbury.	Where is his keeper? Yow shalnot prattle here. Away with him: clap him up close, close, let no man come at him: I wil make him tel an other tale, yet I have done with him.[2]

Ther was an article against me in the bil for saying that I thought elders were bisshops and Philippians 1: 1 produced.[3] Here by I plainly discover mine

---

[1] Alexander Nowell, Dean of St. Paul's Cathedral, was well-known for his three catechisms. His first catechism was published in Latin on June 16, 1570. A shorter catechism, and an intermediate catechism, were also issued; an English translation was made by Thomas Norton in 1570, and a Greek version by William Whitaker in 1573. A Hebrew version, by Thomas Ingmethorpe, is said to have been issued in 1633, but I have not seen this version. See Ralph Churton, *The Life of Alexander Nowell*, pp. 151-197. See also William Tite and Richard Thomson, *A Bibliographical and Literary Account of the Volume of Religious Instruction for Children, Usually Denominated CRANMER'S CATECHISM, Printed and Published in A.D.* 1548. William Jacobson issued an edition of the *Catechismus*, with a life of Alexander Nowell, in 1835.

[2] Here is an instance of Whitgift's bad temper. His biographer, Sir George Paule, whose work is highly eulogistic, admits that the archbishop's great fault was "choler."

[3] Paul and Timothy salute the saints at Philippi, with the bishops and deacons. The commentators on this verse vary in their interpretation of the meaning of " bishops." The meaning would seem to be " ministers " or " clergy."

accuser to be Thornelie of Norwich with whom I had communication at Ware[1] as I rode to London, and never talked with any other about this matter.

[1] Ware, in Hertfordshire, almost mid-way between Cambridge and London, is twenty-two miles by road from London. An interesting and detailed road-map is given in John Ogilby, *Britannia Depicta or Ogilby Improved*, ed. J. Owen (London, 1720), p. 12.

VI

A PASTORAL LETTER FROM PRISON

In 1905 T. G. Crippen was fortunate in identifying a manuscript (I.e. 14) in the Congregational Library at Memorial Hall, London. This manuscript had been owned by Dawson Turner, a member of the Society of Friends, by Reverend William Jacobson, D.D., Regius Professor of Divinity at Oxford, and Bishop of Chester, and by Joshua Wilson, of Tunbridge Wells, who presented it to the Congregational Library. It is described somewhat briefly and inadequately in C. H. Cooper and Thompson Cooper, *Athenae Cantabrigienses*, II, 329-331.

The manuscript consists of seven treatises in 75 pages. The first three treatises (ff. 1-26) seem to be in the hand of Giles Wiggenton, the Puritan clergyman from Sedbergh, Yorkshire, are accounts of his experience, and may be safely ascribed to him. The fourth treatise is also in the hand of Wiggenton, but is evidently a copy of a letter by John Greenwood. It is reproduced in the fourth volume, with the title *Fragment of a Letter*. The fifth treatise (ff. 41-52) is entitled, *Profes of Aparent Churche*, and is written by an anonymous Separatist [probably Henry Barrow]. The seventh treatise (ff. 63-75), is entitled *Four Principall and Waighty Causes for Separation*, [or, *Four Causes of Separation*], and is written by Henry Barrow.

The sixth treatise (ff. 53-61), entitled *A Pastoral Letter from Prison*, was described by T. G. Crippen in the *Transactions of the Congregational Historical Society*, II, no. 3 (September, 1905), p. 149, and reprinted in *ibid.*, II, no. 5 (May, 1906), pp. 339-345. Mr. Crippen assigns this letter to John Greenwood, but this is an error. The next to the last paragraph is an exact description of Henry Barrow's appearance on November 27, 1587, before the ecclesiastical commissioners at Lambeth Palace. We are thus enabled to ascribe *A Pastoral Letter from Prison* to Barrow, and we may date this work during his close imprisonment at the Gatehouse in Westminster (November 27, 1587, to about May, 1588, when he was transferred to the Fleet prison). The letter is probably addressed to the incipient Separatist congregation, and contains the words, " sinnce I sawe you I was convented befor the pontyficall corte of bishops." It also refers to his close imprisonment as " a holly use of this his [God's] loving visitation," and speaks of the Lord, " who beginneth to sommone me owt of this world." This implies a date shortly after his examination, and we may conjecture that November 28-30, or December, 1587, is the time of writing. The two references " 28 years " enable us to begin with the Act of Uniformity in May, 1559, and bring us to May, 1587, and to November, 1587, as $28\frac{1}{2}$ years. If the date of writing had been in January-May, 1588, Barrow probably would have written "well-nigh 29 years."

A Pastoral Letter from Prison was first printed in the *Transaction of the Congregational Historical Society*, May, 1906, and was issued in pamphlet form, evidently from the same type, in 1906, together with Barrow's *Four Causes of Separation* and Greenwood's *Fragment of a Letter*, with the general title, *Relics of the Puritan Martyrs*, 1593. The *Relics* are all 1587, and the martyrdom is 1593.

A PASTORAL LETTER FROM PRISON

> The Lord hime self of all comforte and truthe replenish our harts with the knowledge and knowledging of his truth; that wee may both see and taste the heavenly word and salver [healer] of our sowels in the world to come. Amen.[1]

Amos 6: 12 But a lack, my dear brethren, so barren ar the soyls of our harts, so overgrowne with the noysom weds of this world, so unfrutfull or unfaythfull ar our husbandmen and laborers, and so wacthfull that our envious[2] ansient enimey Sathane; and as the hardnes of our harts, with the neclygence of the prechers, and meting with the mallyce of the third, to witt, Satthane, it maks the Lord's feld lye wast. The first canot indever to have the stonye fallowes of ther harts broken up and dewly plowed with the shear of trewe repentance, that is, to 2 Tim. 2: 6 Romysh docktrine; but they will have the gospell, the sacraments, and the promises of sallvation; they will have the harvist without dew tyllag and labor, supposing belyck that ther sowles will bring forthe of it[s] owne accord good frut. They have forgotten for whose sine it remaineth under the curs: and thes tilsmen, thes husbandmen of our dayes, whose sinne cannot be expressed by the pene of a writer, yet ar they ingarven [engraved] with the poynt of a diomond. These idell and desaytfull [deceitful] laborars, these unsavery sault that neyther seasone nor be seasoned, these ether sow the pretious and holy seed among briers and thornes, or else sow such maslyne [mixed grain] and unsownd seed in the Lord's feld that they ned not the offyce of Jere. 4: 4 the third, viz., Sattan, unlesse its be to watter that they

---

[1] This is not a Scriptural quotation, but the language is reminiscent of II Thessalonians 2: 16, 17 and Psalms 34: 8.
[2] And so watchful is that [fallen angel and tempter] our envious [malicious] ancient enemy.

have planted. See howe evene the best ground that
cometh in ther hands yf it becom not and remain not
unfr[u]itfull; yee [yea], and if it wer not that the Lord
hath promised to put out his vinard to other husbandmen, it were next unto cursing. See ther twenty-eight Luke 20: 16
years' labor;[1] they have sowen much and bring in letell, Heb. 6: 8
and he that erneth wages puteth it in a broken bagge. Joel 1
Consider the senseritey of ther mylk by the grouthe and Heb. 5: 12
waxing of ther childrene! Behould the delygent fayth- 1 Pet. 2: 2
fulnes of these builders, which this twenty-eight years
have benne laing the foundatyon, and yeat is not on[e]
ston in order. Nay, in stead of Zion, or rather in dispite
of Zion, they have all with on[e] consent reared up
Babell in the land of Shinar. Geneses 11

Behould what a Christ they prech ether in the habit
of or in subjection to antichrist! The gospell they Zache. 5: 11
prech is withowt lybertye, joyned, and well agreing
with, idollatry and all the synne of the land. What
shall I saye of them, or rather what shall I leave un-
sayd ? I am mor weary and grevyd in reckning the[i]r
sinnes than they in comiting them. Mark for conclusion the good effects of the[i]r preaching, preching: as
thes profytts [prophets] transfygur Christ unto these
tymes, so the people imagine hime to them selves affter
ther own lusts. The greter and polytyck frame hime
to ther lawes, the worldlye to ther insasiety [insatiety,
insatiableness] and covetusnes, the carnall to ther bellye,
all to ther apytitts. See [!] hear [!] [or, see here,] lyke
profitte [prophet], lyck people.[2] See how they ar Mic. 1: 3
wrethed, as the profete sayeth, together, and mak a Nahum. 1: 9
strong cauble [cable] of iniquite; or rather as the profytt
Nahume sayeth, as thornes foulded on[e] within another,
fytte for the fier of the Lord's wrath. Yeat bles they
their selves in this fearfull estat, yea, and ar blesed by
ther profitts [prophets]. They see not, and canot enduer
to hear, that they are naked and poor and miserable,
and near unto distruction. They hatt [hate] them that Mala. 2: 2

---

[1] 1559-1587. Barrow is reckoning from the Act of Uniformity in May,
1559.
[2] Another possible interpretation: " See here an example of the observation
that as the false prophets teach, so the people are."

rebukethe in the gatt [gate], and abhore hime that speaketh uprightly. Every on[e] hopeth to be saved, yeat no on[e] seketh the meanes. Every on[e] promiseth unto hime self salvation, yeat no one beleveth the promises of God. Every on[e] takethe howld of the covenants of God unto them, but no man remembreth his covenant to the Lord. All wold have the gospell still, and hear of comforte stille; but no man goeth to hear John Baptyste sermon in the wildernes: "repent, for the kingdom of God is at hand; prepare yee the waye of the Lord, mak his pathes straight." Such a profitte is not a profitte for this peopell; such a profitte hath a devill, or is a sysmatick, *etc.* But such a people as have such iching eares as canot enduer sound doctrine, whose weack stomacks brouck [brook] not the howlsom fode of the gospell, which can not nor will not learn this leson hear [here], to have repentance goe befo[re] and joyned with the gospell, for [because of] ther fleshly plesuers, and other worldly respets, shall in ane other place rew [rue, regret] this contempt, and for ever have repentance joined to judgment, wher the worm dieth not and the fyer never goeth out. There no pharisycall wall nor hipocritycall mantell can hied them from his eies that are lyck a flamb of fyer, which sercheth the raygnes[1] and seeth the harts, from whom noe secretts are hid, and befor whom all boocks shalbe opened, even the consience of them [who] hear [here] in this world lyved without consience.

But I hoop, dear brethren, yea, I thanck God I am perswaded better things of you, though I thus writ of thes evell tymes. I dowt not your names shalbe found writen in the lamb's book of lyfe to your unspeakabell joy in that day. But then, beloved, in the meane tyme, you must not cast in your lott with the wicked, nor have felowship with the throngue of iniquitie which forgethe [forges] wrong for a lawe. You must as virgines kepe your selves chast to Christ your husband, and undefyled from the idoll temples and false worship, *etc.* You must walk worthie of your hie calling, seing you ar bought from men, and that with a price, and ar becom as first

Amos 5: 10

Tim. 4: 3
Heb. 5: 13

Mark 9

Psal. 94: 16, 20

2 Corinth. 11: 2

Revela. 14: 4

[1] Raines — a kind of fine linen made at Rennes, Brittany. Feelings.

110

fruts unto God and the lambe. Only now lett your conversation be as becommeth the gospell of Christ; for ye ar a chosen generation, a royall presthood, a hollye nation, a people sett at libertye that you showld now shew forthe the vertus of hime which hathe called you owt of darknes into this marvelous lyght. Your candell is not lyghted to be hid under a bushell, but now you ar to hould fo[r]the the lyght and the word of lyf in the midest of this darck and croked generation; and this shall you doe yf you hould faste the proffession of your hoope without wavring. He thate wavreth is lyk a byllow on the sea, tosed of the wind and caried awaye; such a on[e] resevethe not any thing of the Lord. 1 Peter 2: 9

James 1

The Lord above all things abhoreth a dubell minded man; halt not, therfor, betwixt tow [two] opinions; be ether hott or cold; remember the warning geven to the church of Laodicia [Laodicea]. Geve no year [ear] to those haltyng hipocrits which will seek to quench your spirit, zeall, and love unto the Lord, advisyng you to bear those burdens with them for a season, till God's good plesuer be otherwyse; in the mean tym to use prayer and such libertye as you may. Thus cover they ther cowerdesse and covetyie with prayer and the word of God; and betray your lybertye for which Christ dyed into the hands of antichrist. Thus defyll they you bothe sowle and bodie with idolatry and treson doen [done] to the crown and kyngdom of our soverain prince Christ Jesus; thus take they away at on[e] tyme the crown of your suffering, evene of your rejoysing befor him in that great daye. Yea, they tack away that most hollye, blesed, and bewtyfull order of Christ's government, by making it a thing not worthie the suffering. Ah, be not bewiched, I besech you, with the vaien perswasion of these seducers; consider from whom they call you, even from Christ, and from the swett [sweet] sosiettey of hiz faithfull servants, from the benifitt of his suffering, deathe, and resur[e]ction, from his comfortable presenc, his lybertie, and hiz graces. Consider whether [whither] they call you: to antichrist, falc worship, Babylonishe bondag, Egipticall darknes, *etc*. And whie is this? Because they know not the truth, nay, but because they Reve. 3: 16

Mat. 23: 34

Mat. 25: 34

Heb. 12: 22

111

will not suffer for the truthe. Whie do they thus to
Galla. 6: 12
you? Because they love you? Nay, but because they
wold rejoyce in your flesh, and bring you into the sam[e]
snar of the devell with them, and mak you towfould
[twofold] mor the children of hell than them selves ar,
by how much you ar insnared with mor worldlye wealthe,
mor earthlye pleasuers, mor fleshlye delytes, than they
who to make a faier show in the fleshe and to kepe the
Mat. 23: 15
owt syd of the platter cleane refrayn from those things
them selves which they tolerat in you; and so by this
polysie they purchas peace with the world, good will
with men, avoid persecution, yee [yea], even the reprof
of any. By reason of the beames which by ther means
Hosea 5: 12;
6: 9
remaien in the ies of all. The Lord for his Christ's sack
anoynt your eyes with that holye eysalve of his grace
that you may bothe see and fle thos foulers [fowlers] and
ther snares. Thes faier sta [blank space—stales? decoy-
birds], wherwith they bewich you of the knowledg and
Hagg. 19
John 9: 41
comfort you gett by theme, prove nothing as sonne
[soon] as the Lord [looks, frowns?] on them. What
know they that know not the Lord? Yf you say you
Revela. 11
know his will and do it not, your sinne remayneth.
Examyn your comfort by your estate and your estat by
the lyght of God's word; tack the read [reed] in your
hand; measuer your temple, your alter and your wor-
ships; yf you have built upon the true foundation gould,
silver, and presious stones, and that according to our
saviour's last will and testament, your worcks will wittnes
to you; your work will then abyed, and you have good
cause to rejoyce. But yf your building be uppon the
sand, and may not enduer this triall, as you see your
best workmen cannot justifie it to be according to the
Eze. 13
true pattron [pattern], then have you small cause of
comfort, for dowtles you stand in a fearfull estate; for
all the powers and principallytis in the world ar not
able to uphould this ruinous sinagog you stand under;
all the daubers cannot sustain it, for the tempest of the
Lord's wrath shall overthrowe it, to the destructyon of
all them that stand under it; yea, our Samson, Christ
Jesus, doth alredy shak not onlye the pillers but the
foundations of it.

A Pastoral Letter from Prison

Tack warning, therfor, for Christ's sack, and come out [Reve. 18: 4] whilest you may; nay, be warned for your own saks, at the least as manie as howld ther salvation dear. Remember what a fearfull thing it is to fall into the hands of the lyving God; dispise not his gracce ofered in hope of mercie to com. Prefer not the world to your heavenly [Heb. 12: 17] byrthright, lest with Esau lyckwise after ward when you wold inheriï the blessing you be rejected; you know he fownd no place to repentanc, thowghe he sowght it with [John 14: 27, and 15: 18, 19;] teares, *etc*. B[u]y not your worldlye ease at so dear a price; beleve him that have sayd, you cannot together [and 16: 33] have peac with the world and with God. Cast not from you that rare example of the rich glotten in hell torments. I asuer [assure] you as the world goethe withe us at these dayes he had byn an onest man and a right go[o]d Christian. He did no man wrong by violence or oppression; he was a good nyghbor, a good housekep[er], a good felow; he spent that [which] God [Luke 16] sent him, he kept the best company, he was a man of account and estimation, rich, honorable; and what was then his fault? He knew not God. After the common ratt [rate] of Christians he knew him to[o]. He was of the seed of Abrame, an I[s]ralytt, circumsised; and what was then his fault? Surlye he knew not God; he could not brouck [brook] the simple plaine food of the gospell; he co[u]ld not bear Christ's cross. Yeatt read we not that he persecuted Christ's servants with bitternes and rigor.

Well, lose not the benifit of furder aplycation; it was written for our instruction and admonition. We se hime by that most righteus judg condemned, tormented and so fo[r[the. He had but Moses and the profitts [prophets], yeat, no excuse could serve. We have Christ, Moses, the profyts [prophets] and hime. Lett us not deseav our selves; God is notte deceved; yf in our sinnes we exced or equall hime [the rich glutton], in our plags we shall exced or equall hime. Our God is a juste God; so is he a jealous God; we cannote serve hime and mammon; we cannot serve hime affter our own fantasies. We cannot geve Christ our sowle and antichrist our body; Christ died for bothe, he will have

113

E

bothe or nether of bothe. He hath no communion with antichrist, nether can we have communion with hime and Christ. Refuse not Christ for his humillitie, refuse him not for his sufferinges; he was humbled for us, for us he suffered, for us he died, for us he is risen from the dead, and assended into heaven, and sitteth at the right hand of his father in all glory and power even for us— even for us if we co[u]ld but beleve, yf we co[u]ld but be faythfull, yf we co[u]ld but suffer hime that so gratiously worketh in us and for us. Surlye untill we be humbled to hime and with him, we can receve nothing from him and thorow hime. We must be humbled, as new borne babes, even to the eie of an needle, or we cannot enter. Flesh and bloud canot inheritte the kyngdome of heaven. And being thus humble and wained [weaned] from the world, we must daylie tak up his crose and folowe hime, and joyfully goo forthe to him owt of the camp, bering his reproche. We must obedientlye and uncowardlye folow the lambe whither soever he goethe; we must without hallting or excuse folow him that calleth us without delaye, leaving all things, yea, deniing our selves; and we canot love the world or any thing in the world and love the Lord Jesus.

Lett not these false [prophets?] deceve you: he that deniethe Christ hear [here], he will denie hime before his heavenlie Father; he that witnesseth not unto him hear [here] for fear of persecution or other worldlye respects, he will openlye denie such befor his Father and his holye angells. The kingdom of God now is lyckned unto a pearll and a feld of hidden tresuer, which must be purchased, and no part of the pric may be deteyned. And what is that price that is demanded, and whereat we ar so offended and greved? Is it not evene all that we have? And what hath any of us, I pray you, that he hath not reseved, and that of Christ Jesus, which hath geven him self for us, and with himself what [hath He] not [given] unto us? In hime ar all things blesed unto us: without hime all things that we have and so carfully kepe from hime is accursed, yea, and we accursed, and shalbe araynd befor him as unjust owners, violent intruders, and theves! O then our unthankfull

Esa. 53

Mat. 16:24

Heb. 13:13

Luke 17:31;
9:59.

1 John 2:19

Reve. 21:8

Mat. 13:44

dulnes, that grudge at this prise, as though we did give some notabell benifitt! What geve we that we have not receved from him? What geve we that is not his own by duble ryght, both by creation and redemtion? Lett us mark what we gev hime: sinfull wreched bodies, fallen from his excelent creation into a moste miserable forlorne estatte; and our goods, what ar they but accursed for our sinnes? Those exelent jewells we geve him, is it marvell we showld be so lothe to part from them? Is it not rather marvell that he should be so gratious to receve them, to ingrafe them into his own bodye, to redem them with his own body, to purg them with his most precious bloud, to santyfie them with his Holly Spirit, to cloth them with his righteusnes, yea, to crown them with his glory, and for ever to possese them of his heavenly kyngdom? See now what we geve and what we receve. See and receve [?] this happie exchaung, yf by our own inexcusable obstinacy and defaults we depriv not our selves of it, bie depriving our selves of Christ's sufferings. They are irksom and bitter to flesh and blud in the tast, but most healthfull in disgestion and comfortable in operation. Therebie the ashes of worldly securitie and worldlye and fleshlye vanitie, wherein our faythe lay quenched and covered, are blowen away; our faythe kyndled, stired up, and revived. Therby, we aprove our spiritual weapons and our armour. Therby we exercise our love, our corage, and our strenghe. Therby we overcom and ar mor than conquerers over all our enimies, principallyties and 2 Cor. 4: 16 powers. And what ar these momentarye sufferings wherat we ar so agast? The apostell Paull saieth [they are] not worthie [of] that inestimable waight of Psal. 31: 19 that unspeakable glory that remainethe for us. Agayn, yf we wer left unto our selves, we had cause to be dis- Mat. 28: 20 mayd; but we have Christ's promyses, which ar not Luke 21: 15 yea and nay, but yea and amen, that he will never leve John 14: 16 us; that he will geve a mouth and wisdom against the Ephe. 6: 11 which our adversaryes shall not be able to resist; that Revel. 12: 11; no temtation shall tak us above our strenghe, but that 15: 2 he will geve the ishew [the way out] with the temtation. He hath promysed us a comforter to guid us and to govern us; he hath promised us armor, weapons, and victory. Lett not an unbeleving hart deprive us of these promyses, yea, seclude us from these blessings. Ther remaynethe no mor but that we beleve. Lett us not [now] dayllye pray on[e] for another and with another, that the Lord wold increase our faythe, and strengthen us to the ende.

Heb. 3: 12

Sinnce I sawe you I was convented befor the pontyficall corte of bishops,[1] a sort of well feed and well arayed silken prests.[2] Ther found I nether equitie, charitie, nor consience; the Lord forgeve them and amend them yf they be his. Ther h[e]ard I what they can object agaynst me. They wold have had me accordding to ther ungodly wits to tack an othe upon a boock to ansere truly to ther objections. I answered that it wer mor meett that myne acusers should be produced and sworne than that I should be sworne to accuse myself; yeat this I offered by word to awnswer trulye and derectlye. The archbishop very peremttorylye called for my keper, and because I would not swear, comited me very rigoruslye to straight and close prison;[3] wher I remaine till God delyver me.[4] The Lord graunt me a

---

[1] This is the same group before whom Barrow was brought on November 27, 1587. It probably was a session of the Court of High Commission rather than of an episcopal or archiepiscopal court. The dates to be kept in mind are October 8, 1587, when Greenwood was arrested, November 19, when Barrow was arrested and first examined, and November 27, 1587, when Barrow was again interrogated. Although Greenwood's examination is not dated, I conjecture that both he and Barrow were arraigned on November 27, partly on internal evidence and partly on the external evidence from Sir George Paule, who asserts that Barrow and Greenwood " were convente befor the high Commissioners for causes Ecclesiasticall, in November, 1587, for their schismaticall and seditious opinions " (*Life of . . . John Whitgift* [1612], pp. 43-4).

[2] This phrase is similar to Barrow's description, in his second examination, November 27, 1587, of his judges as " a goodlie synode of bishops, deans, civilians, *etc.*, beside such an apparance of wel-fedde silken preistes, as I suppose might wel have beseemed the Vaticane."

[3] These experiences are identical with those of Barrow when he was examined on November 27, 1587: the insistence on taking the *ex officio* oath, the refusal, the demand that witnesses be produced, the bold suggestion that the accuser should be sworn, the display of temper or " choler " by Archbishop Whitgift, and the committing the accused to close imprisonment. Therefore, we may feel certain that Barrow, not Greenwood, is the writer.

[4] A conjectural date for this writing would be November 28-30 or early in December, 1587.

holly use of this his loving visitation; for suerlye this good the enimie dothe me, to separat me from this wicked world—from God's dear children they cannot, to whom thorowghe the vertue and mersies of Christ Jesus I am inseparablye joyned. Pray for me, dear brethren, that I may not resist and hinder this gratious work of the Lord, who begineth to sommone me owt of this world, yea, to prepar my journye, and I hoope will shortlye ackomplyshe it; the rather yf the man of Canterbury [Archbishop Whitgift] may have his will, who is preparing me a fyrye chariot to passe in. But this to the Lord, and all to the Lord, and you to the Lord; pray for me, that the Lord will strengthen me to seall that with my bloud to you that Christ hath sealed with his bloud to me and you. I thanck the Lord of his grace, and I thanck the Lord for you alwayes, being mindfull of you all in my prayers, that the Lord wold establysh your harts in his truth and increase your joye in the practyse thereof; that whether I goe befor you or com affter you, whether we be severred or meett, we may have always to rejoyse befor God our Father in Christ; to whom be withe the Hollye Spiryt inseparablye be all glory and prais for ever. Amen.

"The grac of our Lord Jesus Christ and the love of God, and the communion of the Holly Ghost be with you all." Amen. [II Cor. 13: 14].

Beloved, kepe your sellves from idolls. Amen.   1 John 5: 21

VII

A BRIEF SUMME OF THE CAUSES OF OUR SEPERATION, AND OF OUR PURPOSES IN PRACTISE, WITHSTOOD BY G[EORGE] G[IFFORD], DEFENDED BY H[ENRY] B[ARROW] AS FOLLOWETH.[1]

This treatise occupies pp. 1-20 of *A Plaine Refutation of M. G. Giffarde's Reprochful Booke,* and is reproduced from the extremely rare edition of 1591.[2] It consists of three separate parts. The introductory portion, " A Brief Summe of the Causes of Our Separation, and of Our Purposes in Practise," is a copy, with slight variations, of the Separatists' one-page manifesto, entitled, " A Breefe Sum of Our Profession." The second part, " Withstood by G[eorge] G[ifford]," is the first answer which George Gifford made to the manifesto. The third part, " Defended by H[enry] B[arrow]," constitutes Henry Barrow's first reply to Gifford's first answer. The introductory portion was written (in manuscript) about the summer or autumn of 1587. Gifford's first answer (in manuscript) appeared about November-December, 1587, or possibly in the early months of 1588. Barrow's first reply, which refers to " the bondage and yoake of antichrist 29 yeares," was written at the earliest about December, 1587—March, 1587/8, and at the latest about April—October, 1588.[3] In *Barrow's*

---

[1] Perhaps Barrow should have reversed this title, so as to have it read: " A Brief Summe of Our Purposes in Practise, and of the Causes of Our Seperation." The first five points set forth the purposes of the Separatists ; point six is a transitional statement ; and the last four points establish the causes of separation.

[2] There are two copies of this work. One is in the Huntington Library at San Marino, California. The other copy is in the Lambeth Palace Library, but is not mentioned in the *Short-Title Catalogue.* Some libraries claim to have copies of the 1591 edition, but their editions are 1605 or 1606. Because the date 1591 appears on the title page of the later editions, it is easy to confuse the editions.

[3] Barrow is reckoning from the Act of Supremacy in May, 1559, to May, 1588, a period of 29 years.

118

A Brief Summe of the Causes of Our Seperation

Final Answer to Gifford, written as marginal notes to Gifford's *A Short Reply*, Barrow dates his own first reply as 1587 (p. 83 ; in the margin), which conceivably could include January 1— March 24, 1587/8. But in 1592 Barrow may have erred in giving 1587 instead of 1588.

All three parts were printed, but not completely, by Gifford, plus his rejoinder to Barrow's first reply, in *A Short Treatise against the Donatists of England, Whome We Call Brownists.* This work was published about May, 1590, and caused Barrow to reply a second time, in *A Plaine Refutation of M. G. Giffarde's Reprochful Booke, Intituled, A SHORT TREATISE AGAINST THE DONATISTS OF ENGLAND*, published in 1591, and re-issued in 1605 and 1606. Gifford replied with his *A Short Reply unto the Last Printed Books of Henry Barrow and John Greenwood*, published about December, 1591, to which Barrow wrote a reply in 1592 in a series of marginal notes, now published for the first time. See *Barrow's Final Answer to Gifford — Marginalia.*

*　*　*　*　*　*

[1.] We seeke above all thinges the peace and protection of the most High, and the kingdome of Christ Jesus our Lord.

2. We seeke and fully purpose to worship God aright, according as he hath comma[n]ded in his most holy word.

3. We seeke the fellowship[1] of his faithful and obedient servants, and together with them to enter covenant with the Lord, and by the direction of his Holy Spirit, to proceed to a godly, free, and right choise of ministers and other officers by him ordeyned to the service of his church.

4. We seeke to establish and obey the ordinances and lawes of our saviour Christ left by his last will and testament to the governing and guyding of his

---

[1] The first manuscript " edition " of 1587, as printed in 1590 by Gifford in *A Short Treatise*, (pp. 1 f.), adds " and communion." There are minor variations in spelling and punctuation, which I have not indicated, but all word differences are indicated in the footnotes.

church, without altering, changing, innovating, wresting, or leaving out anie of them that the Lord shall gyve us sight of.

5. We purpose (by the assistance of the Holy Ghost) in this faith and order to leade our lyves, and for this faith and order to leave our lyves, if such be the good will of our heavenly Father, to whom be honor and glorye. Amen.[1]

6. And now that our forsaking and utter abandoning of these disordered assemblies as they generally stand in England, may not seeme strange nor offensive to anie man that will judge or be judged by the word of God, we alledge and affirme them heinously guiltie in these four principall transgressions.[2]

> 1. *They worship the true God after a false maner, their worship being made of the invention of man, even of that man of sinne, erronious and imposed upon them.*
>
> 2. *For that the prophane ungodly multitudes, without exception of anie one person, are with them received into, and reteined in the bozome of the church.*[3]
>
> [2.] 3. *For that they have a false and antichristian ministerie imposed upon them, reteined with them, and maintained by them.*
>
> 4. *For that these churches[4] are ruled by, and remaine in subjection unto, an antichristian and ungodly government, cleane contrarie to the institution of our saviour Christ.*[5]
>
> *When these things stand thus, let him that readeth consider.*

G. G. to the first article The first article is that which all Christians doo seek in

---

1 The 1587 reading is, " if such be the good will and pleasure of our heavenly Father, to whom be all glory and praise for ever. Amen."

2 The 1587 reading is, " faultie, and wilfullye obstinate in these foure principall transgressions." Gifford quotes this reading in his reply.

3 The 1587 reading is, " bosome and body of their churche, *etc.*"

4 The 1587 reading is, " Then for that their churches."

5 It is interesting to note that these causes of separation and purposes in practice are quoted verbatim by two early English Baptists, Hughe and Anne Bromhead, in a letter written about 1609 to William Hammerton (Harley MS. 360, ff. 70, 71. See Burrage, *Early English Dissenters*, II, 172-177).

deed; but the kingdome of Christ, or the kingdome of God (as Christ saith) is within men. It consisteth in righteousness and peace and joye in the Holy Ghost. For the preservation of this, Christ hath ordeined a church government. They sinne against God which do not covet, and according to their calling labour, to have so great a help. But to transport the name of Christ's kingdome which is spirituall, which is in the heart, unto this which is but a part, and as though the kingdome of God could not be in anie unlesse they have this (so they do not wilfully despise it), I say is false, and the contrarie to be proved by the Scriptures.[1]

Our article being by you confessed to be the bounden dutie of al true Christians, we see not with what equitie you can in this maner cavil at our wordes, or with what conscience you can misconstrue and constreine them as you doo; seeking therby to retract by sleight, what you cannot gainesay in truth. And taking occasion to contend about wordes: namely, (the kingdome of Christ). You make it only inward, and use Christ as one of the phisitians' planitarie signes, assigning to him in hipocrisie your heart and soule to rule, whilst in the meane time you yeild your bodies and whole assemblies to the obedience and rule of antichrist; making no conscience to obey his lawes openly, and to transgresse Christ's; thinking belyke Christ's kingdome so inward and spirituall, as that he requireth no bodily or outward obedience; or, because it consisteth of righteousnes, and peace, and joye of the Holy Ghost, that ther may be peace without righteousnes, or joye without peace, or inward righteousnes where is such outward disobedience and wilfull transgression. But all this is covered and cured at once (if so be you covet and labour in your calling to have Christ's outward government, *etc.*). To discusse here how far everie Christian's dutie and calling extendeth herein, were to dismisse all your answers at once, and to pluck away the mantle of shame wherwith you cover your nakednes, [3] your negligence, and all your abhominations. In this place, therefore, we will only ask

marginal notes:
H. B. his replie

No peace to the wicked. They have no way to excuse them selves, but to accuse the state, which notwithstanding they obey in that which they condempne. A kingdome is not devided against itself

---

[1] Gifford, *A Short Treatise,* pp. 90 f.

Henry Barrow

you these two questions. First; whither anie which have their calling of antichrist, or be his marked ministers, or waged servants, can truly and uprightly covet and labour for the sincere government of Christ, which is his whipp wherwith he skourgeth out all thieves, intruders, and idle-bellies out of his house. The next question is: Whither to remaine wittingly and servilely[1] in the bondage and yoake of antichrist 29 yeares, be to seek and labour for the government of Christ faithfully in your callings, or to uphold and undershore [prop up] the kingdome of antichrist rather ?[2]

[G. G.]   But to transport the name of Christ's kingdome which is chiefly spirituall and in the heart, unto that which is but a part, *etc.*

[H. B.]   How diverslie the kingdome of God is read in the Scriptures, we will not contend with you (although it were not hard to shew either your ignorance or forgetfulnes herein). Only this we say; our words can carie no such construction, muchlesse such an erronious opinion, as you (abounding in your owne sense) have not only collect[ed], but confuted. In the first our words being, " that we seeke the kingdome of Christ Jesus our Lord," cannot be thus restreined to Christ's outward orders and government in his church; especially, if you had pondered that which followed, where in the fourth article (after your division) we have expressed this point in perticular. Neither (if we should admit you that interpretation) could you collect from thence (that the kingdome of God could not be in any, unlesse they have this). But as we usually reade in the Olde and New Testament, Christ's kingdome to be taken for his true visible church here in earth; so we acknow ledg his universall church and kingdome to extend to

---

[1] The next nine words are underlined in ink, and in the margin is written: " Her Majestie's goverment the yoak of antichrist." These words were very likely written by Attorney-General Thomas Egerton or one of his collaborators. I am using Egerton's book, which became a part of the Bridgewater Collection, now at the Huntington Library.

[2] This statement helps to date Barrow's reply twenty-nine years after the Act of Uniformity and the Act of Supremacy of May, 1559. Twenty-nine full years would bring us to May, 1588. I believe that the date is about December, 1587—May, 1588, within the twenty-ninth year, or May—October, 1588, just beyond the twenty-nine years. Conceivably, Barrow could be reckoning from Elizabeth's accession in November, 1558.

all such as by a true faith apprehend and confesse Christ, howsoever they be scattered, or wheresoever dispersed upon the face of the earth. Yet both with this interim, without true faith and obedience can be no true church, no true Christian.

The second article ought all men that will please God to approve.[1]

G. G. to the 2 article

This article you say (" ought all that wil please God to approve "). How then seek you to please God, which continue in idolatrie and are a minister therof,[2] which prophecie in Baall and plead for Baall? Or how approve you it, when you condempne us of schisme and heresie because we forsake your false and antichristian worship, and seek to worship Christ according to his word?

H. B. his replie

The third article, if it be taken in this sense, that yee dare set up a societie seperated from all others within this land which make [4] publique profession; then I see not, when you have gon by your selves and set up your officers, how you will cleare your selves from Donatisme. If theirs were a damnable fact [sect?] which God did accurse, then take heed to yours; for if it can be shewed that their heresies are not holden, I will chang my minde.[3]

G. G. to the 3 article

The words of our article being (" that we seek the fellowship and communion of Christ's faithfull and obedient servants ") cleare us of all schisme and heresie. So that if you would convince us of these crimes, it had bene expedient you had first proved your assemblies, as they generally stand, by the evidence of God's word, to be true churches of Christ, rightly entred and keeping

H. B. his replie

---

1 Gifford, *A Short Treatise*, p. 92.
2 The next eight words are underlined, evidently by Egerton or his investigator.
3 *Ibid.*, p. 93. The heresies of the Donatists are less important than their schismatical action in rejecting Caecilian, electing Majorinus instead as Bishop of Carthage, and establishing themselves as a separate church. The schismatical aspect was more serious than their doctrinal views, though they cannot be entirely separated.

covenant with the Lord, continuing in the order and obedience of his word, *etc.*, and that we preposterously have departed from you, and uncharitably have forsaken your fellowship. But as soone as you shal shew us such a church emong you, by the grace of God we wil shew you how free we are of schisme. As likewise, when you shall lay open our errours unto us, how farr we wil be from heresie. In the meane time we will not cease to pray unto God for you, that he will not lay these sinnes unto your charge, which in your ignorant zeale you commyt, but in mercy shew you the fearefull estate you stand in, and give you an heart unfeinedly to repent, and speedely to turne unto him.

G. G. to the 4 article

The fourth article ought all men to practise so far forth as the limitts of their calling doo extend. But let it be shewed that ever privat men did take upon them to reforme when things were amisse in the church; or that anie of the prophetts did wil them to take the matter in hand; or shew your warrant that you be not privat men.[1]

H. B. his replie

This article you first alowe, and after restreyne to we wot [know] not what limits of calling. But if you grant it the dutie of everie true Christian to seek to establish and obey the ordinances and lawes of Christ, left in his Testament to the governing of his church, without altering, *etc.*, it is as much as we indevour or purpose. Otherwise we allowe not that, which the law of God condempneth, either intrusion without lawfull calling, either transgression in calling, or presumption above calling. Our purpose is not to medle with the reformation of the state, otherwise than by our prayers unto God, and refreining from al things that are contrarie to God's lawe. Neither indevour we to reforme your Babilonish deformities, or to repaire the ruines of Hierico [Jericho], or dawbe the wall of antichrist with

Sodom and Babilon reformed by fire

you. This trash we know to be devote to execration by the Lord's owne irrevocable sentence; and therfore we leave the reformation of them to the Lord's visitation

[1] Gifford, *A Short Treatise*, p. 95.

in judgment: holding it our dutie without all delay to
obey the voice of God which calleth us [5] out of all The best way
to reforme
others is first
to reforme
our selves
places where he is not truly worshipped according to
his word, where his lawes are wilfully broken and antichrist's lawes obeyed. And this to be the commandement of God in the law by his prophets, Christ himself
and his apostles, is everie where in the Scripture manifest (without exception of person or restreint of calling)
even unto everie one that wilbe saved. In the rest
(whatsoever you surmise of us) we arrogat no swelling
titles, we are as we professe to be, simple hearted
Christians, which seek to worship and obey Christ as
our only king, priest, and prophet. And to our prince
we are humble and obedient subjects in all things which
are not repugnant to God's lawes.[1]

If a man hath the truth, it is good to stand unto it to G. G. to the
5 article
the death rather than denie it; as our church in the same
estate it is in now, yielded many blessed constant
martirs. But if a man hath not the truth, it is a great
obstinacie to die for it; as sondrie Anabaptists and other
hereticks have shewed. Everie true Christian will rather
die than denie the discipline which Christ hath left.
But you must shew that God commandeth privat men
to set it up.[2]

The word of God and your owne mouth having approved H. B. his
replie
our desires in these articles, we cannot be moved with
Satan's olde tentation, to doubt of the Lord's undoubted
truth, or call his commandements into question, with
(if it be true, *etc.*). Neither can we be removed by that
olde popish reason which you bring, of certeine blessed
martires that died in this estate your church is now in.

[1] This sentence is underlined in ink, and the marginal comment is " in all
things that you fansye." This marginal comment emphasizes an important point that caused much trouble for all who rejected the Elizabethan
Settlement. Who shall determine what are God's laws, and who shall
determine what is repugnant to them ? Anglicans, Catholics, Puritans,
and Separatists held diverse views on the question of whether God's laws
were revealed in Scripture, decisions of church councils, decretals, papal
pronouncements, tradition, or/and nature. Even more diverse were the
views on what was repugnant to God's laws, as the Vestiarian Controversy
revealed.
[2] *Ibid.*, p. 97.

This is not to approve the estate of your church by Christ's Testament. Which untill you doo, though all the men in the world should die both in it and for it, yet could they not justifie that [which] God condempneth. But in deed the holy martires you speak of, neither died in it, nor for it. Not in it, being by God's great mercy deprived and discharged by their enimies. Not for it, but for the truth of Christ they most constantly gave their lyves. Neither can it be shewed where ever they resisted the truth, being shewed them; or denied to heare it at the most simple man's mouth; or ever yeilded to anie corruption or yoake that God gave them sight of, contrarie to their owne consciences, as you doo in these dayes. Therfore so far as they from justifiing you in this your generall apostasie, as that they being found faithfull in that litle in the twilight, shall rise in judgment with this generation in this great light with al the giftes they boast of.

" Everie true Christian " (you say) " will die rather than denie the discipline that Christ hath left." With what conscience then can you esteeme emong the wicked *Anabaptists* and condempned and dampned hereticks that suffer in their obstinacie, us, that cast off the yoak of antichrist, and seek and suffer[1] for the true worship and holy government of Christ ?[2] Or how [6] can you flatter your selves in the fearful estate you stand in, drawing so even by long custome in antichrist's yoake, not only in deed and practise deniing the government of Christ, but (to your utmost indevour) by contumelious reproches, unjust sclanders, and open persecution, seek to resist and suppresse it. But we must shew (" that God commandeth privat men to set it up "). First God commandeth in his law everie one to seek the place where he putteth his name: Christ in the gospel, to seek the kingdome of God, to take his yoake upon them,

---

[1] This reference to suffering is confirmed by the fact that Barrow was in prison as he wrote. Arrested on November 19, 1587, he was confined in the Gatehouse by the Archbishop's order until May 5, 1588, or thereabouts, then transferred to the Fleet prison. Although Barrow does not mention which prison he is in, I believe he is still in the Gatehouse in Westminster. Therefore he would be writing prior to May 5, 1588.

[2] Marginal comment: " a sensles supposing of the matter in question."

etc. Againe, Christ hath left but one forme of government in his last will and testament unto his church, which he hath sealed with his blood; and therfore not left it arbitrable at the pleasures of princes,[1] or pollicies of times to be done or undone, but made it by a double right inviolable, both by his word and his Testament; so that the church of God can neither be governed by anie other lawes or government, neither ought it to be without this; for God holdeth them all in the estate of enimies, which have not his Sonne to reigne over them. *If they have not his scepter of grace, they shall have his yron mace*

Now then the faithfull are commanded to gather togither in Christ his name, with promise of direction and protection, and with authoritie not only to establish his lawes and ordinances emongst them, but faithfully to governe his church therby. For the kingdome of God consisteth not in word but in power. Now this assemblie of the faithfull before they be planted and established in this order, consisteth hitherto but of perticular privat person, none as yet being called to office or function. Therfore we may well conclude, that God commandeth his faithfull servants, being as yet privat men, togither to build his church, according to the true patterne of Christ's Testament (without altering, changing, innovating, *etc.*). And for this we have the example of the primative churches for our patterns and warrant, which sued not to courtes and parliaments, nor wayted upon princes' pleasures, when the stones were in a redines, but presently having received the faith of Christ, received likewise the ordinances of Christ, and continued in the same.[2]

Againe, if they should tarie princes' leisures, where were the persecution you speake of? Princes never punish them that obey their hestes. And thus because you cannot endure the fiery triall of persecution,[3] you utterly (by your perfidious tolleration) abrogate at

---

[1] This sentence is underlined, and the marginal comment is " so, impeaching the prince's supremacy, und[e]r pr[e]tence of Christ's will and Testa[ment]."

[2] Marginal comment: " A miserable collection [assertion ?] to establish their Anabaptisticall pr[o]cedings withall." Compare the same doctrine on courts, parliaments, and princes in " Certen Wicked Sects and Opinions," volume IV.

[3] This sentence suggests a glorying in tribulation and a defiance of those responsible for Barrow's imprisonment.

once the crosse of Christ. And (that you might enjoy this wordly peac and fleshly pleasure for a season) you care not to make Christ attend upon princes, and to be subject to their lawes and government. But (alas) it were fitter with a loude voice to call you out of Babilon, than thus to sing you Hebrue songes in Babilon.

G. G. to the 6 article

This article mentioneth four principall transgressions, wherin the assemblies in England are judged and affirmed to be heinously faultie, and wilfully obstinate. Elias did see outward idolatrie practised, and did see none that did mislike, and therfore complained of all, it [7] was but an error. But wheras God's word is imbraced, and multitudes abhorr idolatry, and labour with sorrowful teares to be purged from their sinnes, it is intollerable pride and presumption of men to set themselves in God's judgment seate, and to condempne all of wilfulnes and obstinacie. Let it be shewed that anie (led by God's Spirit) have dealt in this sort, and especially in chardging them whom they condempne most falslie, as shall appeare.[1]

H. B. his replie

Here you verie vehemently chardge us with intollerable pride, presumption, intrusion into God's judgment seate, to be voide of God's Spirit, to chardge and condempne you most falslie, as you say shall appeare. How justly you chardge us with these crimes, and dischardge your self and these assemblies of these present transgressions, upon the scanne [scrutiny, examination] of your answere shall appeare. In the meane time the Holy Ghost sheweth us what spirit you are led by at the writing therof; and hath foretold how well you shall endure and reforme at the manifestation of your sinnes, and at the powring out of the cuppe of the Lord's indignation, where he saith: " They shall drincke, and be moved, and be madd, because of the sword that shall come upon them."[2] And in another place: " And the fift angel powred forth his viall upon the throne of the beast, and his kingdome waxed darke, and they

[1] Gifford, *A Short Treatise*, pp. 2 f.
[2] Jeremiah 25: 16.

gnawed their tongues for sorowe and blasphemed the God of heaven for their paines and their sores, but repented them not of their workes."[1]   It suffised you not to cavill and spurne against the manifest truth of our former articles; but you must in this not only leave out our words at your pleasure, but abuse them that remaine after your owne lust.

Our article speaketh of the assemblies as they generally stand in England.   You retort our words to God's secret election, which we acknowledg and daily see, and praise God's name for it.   Yet no multitudes, but a litle poore remnant, as the beries of a beaten olive tree, the grapes after the grape-gathering, one of a citie, two of a tribe in respect.   And it is to be doubted, those multitudes you speake of will shrink when they come to his assaye [trial, testing] whose furnace is in Sion, and fire in Hierusalem.   But if it should be so as you say, the heavie wrath of God hangeth over your heades, that have a people so redy and fit for the kingdome of Christ, and suffer them to continue in this confusion, false worship, antichristian bondage, even the snare of the devil; and not only not leade them out of it, but not suffer them that would to depart, and thus slay them that should not dye.   Yea, you smite the phisitian that seeketh to heale you, and are enimies to them that shew you your transgressions, judging them voide of the spirit of God.   But if you had but considered that prophet's zeale, as you remembred his error, you should have found him zealous and fervent against Baall's priests in God's quarrell.   It were long to recite the number of God's faithfull servants which are everie where commended in the Scriptures for their zeale and diligence [8] herein.   Or againe, the Lord's judgements not onlie upon perticular men, but whole contries and nations for the contempt and neglect therof.   So then, if it fall out that the lawe and word of God condempne you of these transgressions, what are we that we should justifie you in your iniquities; nay, rather proude, hawtie, and scornfull is his name that worketh in his arrogancie, wrath, *etc.*

[1] Revelation 16: 10, 11.

Henry Barrow

To blazon your transgressions as they deserve, requireth rather a quire than a shead [sheet] of paper. And (to say the truth) it is an yrksomnes unto anie godly conscience, either to heare or recite them. Yet because ther is no cause so bad which shal not finde as bad a patrone, we will only examine your answeres, and brieflie shew their insufficiencie.

George Gifford his answer to the first principall transgression

The first fault is; that we worship the Lord after a false maner, because our worship is said to be made of the invention of man, yea, of the man of sinne, erronious and imposed upon us. I answere, that our worship is the imbracing of the holy Bible; by the doctrine therof we seeke to believe in God, to call upon him, and to doo all good workes.[1] Manie ministers ther be in England which have not approved the *Booke of Common Praier* further, than they are perswaded it is consonant to God's word, nor used anie thing therin which they judge corrupt. But you say all read prayer is idolatrie. But you must bring better stuffe to prove it than your spiritual fantasies so directly overthrowne by the holy Scriptures, howsoever they may be cavilled against with fond distinctions, as the hereticks have done in other matters.

Henry Barrow his replie

The first transgression we chardge your assemblies with, is: that you worship God after a false maner, your worship being made of the invention of man, even of the man of sinne, erronious, and imposed uppon you. You answere, your worship is the imbracing of the holy Bible. Thus begging the question, you neither prove your worship by the Bible, nor answere one of these four apparant reasons which we bring in our articles, whie it is false and contrarie to the Bible. For the furder manifestation of your worship in perticular, let that great idoll, the *Booke of* your *Common Prayer*[2] (which is so full of errors, blasphemies, and abhominations) be examined by the word of God. See if you can finde in

[1] Gifford, *A Short Treatise*, p. 7. The next three sentences are not printed by Gifford.
[2] Marginal comment: The Coien [Common or Communion] Booke a great idoll.

the New Testament your Romish fastes, your ember dayes, sainctes' eaves, Lent, or your idoll feastes, your Alhallowes, Candlemasse, your severall Lady dayes, saincts' dayes, the dedicating of your churches to saincts, your comminations, rogations, purifications, tithes, offrings, mortuaries, your maner of visiting the sick and housling them with the sacrament, your absolution, your blasphemous dirges and funerall sermons over and for the dead, your corrupt ma-[9]ner of administring the sacraments, your font, crossing in baptisme, your baptising by women, gossippings, the blasphemous collects you use in this sacrament, your bishoppings, with all your hereticall collects in that Booke, which is a wearines to us to repeat, though not in you to use, tollerate, and defend.[1] But all this geare must be swallowed up. This candle may not be lighted, lest the people looke into the abhominable ingredients which you their antichristian ministers give them, or rather sell them in the whore of Babilon's cuppe to the destruction of their soules. But you know some ministers in the land, which neither use nor approve the Booke further, than they are perswaded in conscience it is consonant to God's word. But you know none that use not the Booke. You know never a minister in this land which either is authorized by the state, or standeth in publique place, which standeth not under this idoll, or that hath throwne it out by the power of the word, or withdrawne the people from it with al their preaching these twenty-nine yeares;[2] but joyne their gospel to it, minister to that people that use it, *etc.* Neither can the conningest of you make the best parte of it other than a piece of swyne's flesh, an abhomination to the Lord.[3] Neither can the perswasion of your conscience either justify your worship, cleare you, or satisfie others;

The church-wardens sworne to see the booke used

The gospel of Christ cannot be joyned to this stuffe

---

[1] Gifford defends most of these practices in *A Short Treatise*, pp. 10-17.

[2] From May, 1559, to May, 1588, would be twenty-nine full years. Whether Barrow means 29 full years exactly, or almost 29 years, we cannot be sure. I believe Barrow means this 29th year, and that the month is about December, 1587, or January, 1588.

[3] A marginal comment: "the best part of it, a peece of swine's flesh." Barrow uses similar words in *Four Causes of Separation.* Also, this language is later quoted in "Certen Wicked Sects and Opinions," and in "The Assertions of the Conventicles Lately Apprehended."

especiallie when we see your consciences to tollerat
and submit unto the whole; to use part in respect of
your homage, and to refuse part for shame of the world.

Hitherto appeareth no sclander in our article, your
worship being altogither as ill, and worse than we speake
of; and such indeed as you neither can nor dare abide
by. And therfore to get ridd of this article which pres-
seth you so sore, you chardge us with matter which you
finde not in our article: that we say " all read prayer
is idolatrie," terming it our stuffe, " spirituall fantasies
directly overthrowne by the holy Scriptures," howsoever we may cavill with fond distinctions, as the hereticks have done in other matters. From what spirit
procedeth al this ? Found you this in our article ? If
not, all these blasphemous reproches must returne to
you againe with shame. You want a covert when you
flie into this bush to hide you. When you shall be
better instructed of the Holy Ghost, and have learned
what prayer is, you will not call spirituall prayers
spirituall fantasies, neither thrust your apocripha
prayers to be read in the church of God, where only
God's word ought to be read. But this being beside
our article, in nothing disproving it, nor justifying your
idolatrous worship used in your assemblies, we leave the
further clearing of this to him, to whome it more per-
ticularly belongeth.[1] And we (for everie thing you have
as yet brought) must remaine cleared of all the sclanders
and reproches you have cast out against us; your assemblies still charged and obstinatly guyltie of a popish,
erronious, and idolatrous worship thrust uppon them,
according to our article; and you not a minister, but a
defender of this trumperie, resisting the truth, and blaspheming us for defending the truth. [10][2]

The second fault is: " that all the prophane multitude

---

[1] Barrow means John Greenwood, who wrote extensively on the subject of
true spiritual prayer, and who criticized formal prayers as apocripha
prayers, read prayers, prescript prayers. In the book, *A Short Treatise*,
Gifford presents Greenwood's arguments on pages 17-21 and his own
replies thereto on pp. 21-46. Greenwood made a further reply in his
An Answere to George Gifford's Pretended Defence, about June, 1590.
[2] Wrongly numbered 11 in text.

(without exception of anie person) are admitted and G.G. his answer to the second principall transgression reteined into the bozome of the church." The most churches in England want [lack] godly pastors, and there all are admitted, it may be he that admitteth is the worst in the companie. But ther be manie greater and smaler congregations where the pastor doth keepe back some for ignorance,[1] and some for spotted life, until they amend; as I my self have knowne twenty or thirty repelled from the sacrament in one flocke, and not admitted at all. But you wil say; by what right doth the minister this? I say, that the *Book of Common Prayer* doth expreslie command, that all such as lyve ungodly shal not be admitted. But then you will say, they be admitted to come unto prayers with the rest. Not, if they be excommunicated justly, as sondrie are. Againe, this will hardly be reteined of all that know the truth, that the prayer or worship of the faithfull is poluted if ther be prophane men in companie, especially we that cannot remedie the matter. There were but a few true worshippers frequented the temple emong multitudes of prophane and ungodly men. But what can you aledge more than the Anabaptists did at the first, whie they seperated themselves? Would you have private men reforme the temple, or not come there?

Here you confesse " that the most churches in England H. B. his replie Would you have the faithful joine unto these churches in praier and sacraments? want godly pastors; and that there all are admitted; and that he that admitteth them is the worst of the companie." Thus you make the most churches in England in a verie bad estate, and so far forth you affirme our article. But yet you know some churches, where the pastor hath repelled for ignorance and spotted life to the number of twenty or thirty from the sacrament, *etc.* This verie rare thing being graunted you, what insueth therof? Doth this disprove, that even there, and in the best of your churches, the prophane multitudes are not received into and reteined in the bozome and bodie of your churches? Were there no more prophane, trow yee, but these twenty or thirty

---

[1] Gifford, *A Short Treatise,* p. 47.

you speake of in the parish? Or were not they else
where received to the sacrament? But to take a more
direct course with you, and to prove our article at
once. Know you anie in those parishes you speake of,
or in the realme of England unbaptised? And is not
baptisme a sacrament belonging to the church, wherby
all the faithful and their seede enter into it? Then
all being baptised, it followeth, that all are received into
the bodie of your church. Now being once received in,
they can no way be cast out, but by excommunication.

And it is manifest that the parson with al his parish
have not the power which Christ hath left unto his
church to excommunicate anie offender, be he never so
obstinat or notorious; no, nor to redresse anie enormitie
that is laide upon them by the times. And thus the
other part of our article is confirmed; that all are reteined in the bozome of your church.

And now to your suspension or prohibition from the
sacrament. You wil have us aske you by what right
the mi-[11][1]nister doth this. In deed this would be
knowne; for if it be in the nature of excommunication,
it were no small presumption in the minister to arrogate
such absolute authoritie to himself. But all this your
answere cleareth. The *Book of Common Prayer* (you
say) doth command, *etc.* Here may not be let passe
that even your owne mouth confesseth; that even the
best of your churches and ministers stand under,
observe and uphold this idoll. Whie, is the *Booke of
Common Prayer* Christ's New Testament, that you must
fetch your warrant and direction from that idoll? In
deed it is a fitt portesse[2] for such a priest; and the
suspension you vaunt of, a fitt toole for such workmen,
even the instrument of that foolish sheepheard. If the
judgment of God were not upon your right eie and your
right arme, you might see how your lordes and bishopps
dresse you; and perceive how this weapon they allow
you, wanteth both edge and poinct; it is so reputed by
them, that never a one in the parish setteth a flie by it.

[1] Wrongly numbered 12 in text.
[2] Variant of portas. Other forms are portuary, portuas, portuis, portuos,
and portuous. A portable breviary used by the clergy in the medieval
age.

Againe, one word of Mr. Commissarie's mouth can heale the greatest wound you can make with it.

The next thing that you wil have us to say, is (that they be admitted to come to prayer with the rest). For this you have a cunning solution redie. Not (you say) if they be justly excommunicat, as sondrie are. See how God ensnareth you in your owne words, and how hard a bad cause is to defend, though you make both our questions and your owne answers as it pleaseth you.

First here is to be observed, that you subscribe not in secret, but openly justifie the commissarie's excommunication, for other meanes have your sinagogs none, the parson, church-wardens, sidemen, quest-men being sworne servants, and the whole parish standing in subjection to his antichristian court.

Then is to be observed, what good sheepherds you be, that yield your sheepe to this ravening wolfe to make havocke of them, and excommunicate at his pleasure. But all theis transgressions and enormities whatsoever, you thinke to heale, or hide (at the least) with these two drye wythered fig-leaves: the one, that you cannot remedie the matter; the other, private men may not reforme. In the first you confesse your selves deprived of that powre which Christ unto the world's end hath left unto his church to reforme and redresse things amisse.[1] In the other, deprived of al christian libertie and will, so much as to save your owne soule, and to come forth of this Babilonish bondage you stand in, still dreaming of the reformation of your idolatrous *Private men* sinagogs, and seeking to heale the wounde of the beast, *refraine idolatrie* comparing them to the temple of God, and still begging *though they cannot re-* the question, frame your arguments as though your *forme* people were faithful, and your praier holie. Alas, it were better you toke example by the fearefull judgments of God upon the temples, [*sic*], and learned of the faithfull servants of God which in the idolatrous dayes of Achas, Manasse, Amon, Jehoiakim, *etc.*, refreined from that they could not amend; rather than in this frantick maner to blaspheme the name of Christ wher-

---

[1] Marginal comment: " And whome doth he mean by the church ? "

upon we are called, by comparing us to Anabaptists and heretiks for obeying the voice of God that calleth us from emong you, and for telling you the truth. [12]

G. G. his answer to the third principal transgression

The third fault is: a false and antichristian ministrie imposed and mainteined. Here is no reason rendred whie it is a false and antichristian ministrie which is imposed. If yee be prophetts raised up of God, we must believe that which you say; but they did not lye in anie matter; but everie man may see, that you have in the former article lied. We may not therfore give credit to your imaginations.[1] We have more to prove that ther be manie faithfull ministers of Christ in the land, than that anie shalbe able to overthrow.

This I would wish, that simple men would have thus much wisdome, as to suspend their judgment if they be in doubt, and so enquire if ther be anie churches of Christ under heaven, what they do judge of the ministerie and churches of England. For if ther be no church of Christ nor ministerie, and all the famous men in all the churches say we be (knowing our estate as they doo right well), then be they all guyltie, then where shall we finde the church? Shall we seek it emongst a few uncharitable men, which cannot shew anie church which agreeth with them so nerely as the Anabaptists and Donatists? Let it be set downe what maketh a true minister of Christ, and then if that be not found in manie ministers in England, let them be condemned antichristian. It is the part of everie godly and christian man to have the matter throughly tried, before he pronounce sentence; if it were but against one man, he should sinne grievouslie to doo otherwise, much more when the sentence is against the whole church.

H. B. his replie

Here you say is no reason rendred by us whie it is a false and antichristian ministerie which is imposed. But if you had better weighed these two former transgressions wherwith we charge you; or dulie considered of your owne answere before you had put penne to paper, you might have gayned this labour you have taken, and the

[1] Gifford, *A Short Treatise,* p. 70.

shame you are like to suffer by theis your frivolous and
indirect answers. Or if you had consulted with your
learned brethren upon the matter (to whome this promise which you have intercepted, more nerely by many
rightes apperteined)[1], they would have counselled you
to have used your discretion rather in the pulpit as they
doo, where you may say what you list without controlement, than thus bewray your follie in writing, which
lyeth subject to the censure of all men in all ages. They
consider that an evill and corrupt matter ought rather
to be covered than raked in, lest it become more odious.

They promised
us before the
deliverie of
these articles
to answere or
assent

1. Now we were perswaded by the word of God
that the true minister of Christ could not be
a minister of idolatrous and false worship.
Such in our first cause of our communing
[coming?] out from among you, we proved
the worship in your assemblies to be.[2]

2. Then we were perswaded by the word of God,
that a true pastor could not stand a heard
[shepherd] to the Lord's goates, and swyne,
blessing them with the blessing of the faithfull, and delivering them the holy things of
God, as the sacraments, *etc*. Such in our
second cause we proved both you and your
people, as they generally [13] stand in your
parishes, to be.

[3.] And now in this third cause your self, by but
repeating part of our words, doo give a strong
and sufficient reason, namely: that your

---

1 In the Epistle Dedicatorie to Lord Burghley, Gifford related that a schoolmaster in Essex requested him to answer certain articles, entitled " A
Breefe Sum of Our Profession." When he did so, he received lengthy
replies, which amazed him. He writes: " I perceived that which before
I did not so much as dreame of, namely, that they had made chalenge,
and looked to be encountred by the learnedest in the land. They take it
greevously, and reprehend me, as having intercepted this businesse, and
taken it from the hands of the learned " (*A Short Treatise*, signature a 2
recto). Perhaps the learned men to whom reference is made were Thomas
Cartwright, Walter Travers, William Charke, and William Floyde, to
whom were delivered eleven articles in 1588. In April, 1590, these arguments still remained unanswered (Henry Barrow and John Greenwood,
*A Collection of Certain Letters and Conferences Lately Passed betwixt
Certaine Preachers and Two Prisoners in the Fleet*, pp. 67-70).
2 Marginal note: " Nothing lese than proved."

ministrie is thrust and imposed upon your churches, and not freely chosen by the Lord's faithful people according to Christ his ordinance in his Testament.[1] You know our saviour Christ his judgment of such as come into the shepfolde by intrusion, or ascend up anie other way. So then wee seeke not that you should credit us, or hold us for prophetts. But if this wee speake be that which God by them hath uttered, then you deride not us so much as them, nor them so much as the spirit of God that spake in them.

[But the prophetts of God lied not in anie thing; but everie man may see that we have in the former article lied.][2] The devill is the author of lies, sclaunders, false accusations against the saincts, *etc.*, and therof hath his name. All that make or love lies are his children, and shalbe shut off the Citie of God. This chardge wee have repelled in the second transgression; where wee proved all received into your church by baptisme, and are reteined in your churches, because you have not the powre of Christ to excommunicat anie. Thus still you fall into the pitte you make for us, by God's just judgments, and shall by the same receive the reward of a liar, a false witnesse, a false prophet, if God give you not grace to repent, which wee shall more joye in than in your confusion.

Of the great store of reasons you have to prove your ministrie to be of Christ, and your selves faithfull, you might have bestowed one of your store, either for pitie or for love upon us, who you see are fully perswaded, that ther is not one such minister among you all; at least for saving your self from the blame you layde upon us, one reason would have done wel. But chiefly for confirming your ministerie to be of Christ, one (at the least) had bene more than necessarie. For otherwise wee may not believe your bare affirmation before Christ's negative, in whose Testament wee finde neither the names you carie, the offices you beare, the maner of

---

[1] Marginal note: " where in his Test[ament] doth that appeere ? "
[2] Square brackets as in text.

your entrance, of your administration, neither of your support and maintenance. Your discent and pedegree is within few degrees derived from the pope, you being the children of your antichristian bishops which are the creatures of the pope, who is the eldest sonne of Sathan, and his vicar generall in earth, whose image, marke, powre, and life you beare, and together with him grow, live, reigne, stand and fall, as the branches with the tree. Now wee knowing the plant cannot easilye be deceived in the grafts, especiallie knowing them from their cradles, nourished with the milke of superstition,[1] instructed in the schole of heathen vanitie, brought up in the colledges of more than monkish idlenes and disorder, exercised in vaine and curious artes, whose divinitie is by tradition, and according to their progresse and degrees therin commended to the ordinarie [the bishop], who making probation of them accordingly, doth either initiate or trayne them in this idolatrous office, or els give them their full orders, with his paper licence and popish seale therat. Thus are they either presented to a be-[14]nifice, instituted, inducted, where they ringe their bells, pay the first fruictes, taxes, proxes, and are sworne to their canonicall obedience, to his scenes, courtes, synods, *etc.* Or els (as they terme them) they are become preachers, either waged chaplens, mercenarie curats, or hireling teachers, gaping for promotion. Which being obteined, they change, remove, enterchange, according to their best advantage. In this maner being entred by intrusion, they cannot but lyve by theft, spoile and rapine, as their popish tithes, the goods of the poore, and offrings of the prophane indifferently; and governe, by tyrannie and perfidie:[2] tyrannie in executing the popish injunctions, even the the statutes of Omry:[3] perfidie, in betraiing all into the hands of their lords the bishops.

Marginal notes: The same reasons that overthrow the pope, over-throw their ministerie

Tithing priests, mercenarie Levites, wandring starres

---

[1] Marginal note: "the poyson of aspes is under their lipps."
[2] Marginal note: "our ministers, enter by intrusion, live by theft, governe by tyranye and perfidie."
[3] The statutes of Omri were the evil regulations by which Omri ruled Israel. Omri "did worse than all that were before him," the son Ahab exceeded his father in wickedness, and Ahab's wife, Jezebel, exceeded her husband in evil ways. See I Kings 16: 25-28 ; 19: 2 ; 21: 5-15 ; Micah 6: 16.

Thus fulfil they the Scriptures, by which who so examineth their infinite transgressions in perticular, can want no store of arguments against this ministrie; our purpose being here rather to shew some, than to set downe all, or to confute anie of their odious enormities, which are so grosse, that as sone as they are but manifested by the light, they are reproved. And it could not be (if the Lord had not layde a vaile over their hearts) that where the Scriptures are read, these deformities could be hid, tollerated, or defended.

But in stead of an argument to us, you turne your speach to the simple people, and give them counsell if they doubt of your ministrie [to suspend their judgments, and to inquire if ther be anie churches of God under heaven, and what they do judge of the ministerie and Church of England],[1] *etc.* Is this the best counsell you can give them? Use you thus to appeaze unquiet consciences, and to resolve their doubtes? With what conscience can they which remaine doubtfull of the truth, and lawfulnes of your ministerie, frequent your prayers and preaching in the meane time until they may send over sea and be resolved from thence. You know that what is not of faith, is sinne. But with what conscience can you use poore soules thus that inquire the truth at your mouth, to send them over sea you wot [know] not whether [whither] to be resolved of your ministerie and churches? Is your church built upon the words of men, or upon the word of God? Is this to prove your church and ministerie by the word of God? Or to use the old worne arguments of your mother church of Rome, who was wont to defend her self by universalitie and consent? What if all the churches and learned men in the world should say you are a church: (which wee must tel you by the way they all never did, neither ca[n] anie which knoweth the word of God and your estate aright) but if they should, could they, or all the world justifie, that God condempneth? Should not a people inquire at their God from the living to the dead? Remember yee not that it is written, " to the law: and the testimonies if they speake

---

[1] Square brackets as in text.

not, it is because there is no light in them."[1] "But yee are gone out of the way, yee have caused manie to fall by the lawe, yee have broken the covenant of Levie, saith the Lord of hostes, therfore have I made you also to be despised and vile before all the people, because you kept not my wayes but have bene partiall in the [15] lawe."[2] Yea, the judgments of God are alreadie fallen upon you all (as he speaketh by his prophet) being covered with a spirit of slumber, even stricken with the blindnes of Elimas,[3] groping the way in the noone light, because you have perverted the straight waies of the Lord; and being thus miserable and blinde out of the way, not only perceive it not, but love darknes more than light, refusing the light when it is brought you, yea, despising it, because of the fewenes and basenes of them that bring it you. And in this pharisaicall pride procede, after your accustomed maner of blaspheming, terming us fewe, uncharitable, Anabaptists, Donatists, *etc.*

If the light that is in you be darknes, o how great is that darknes

Thus fulfill you the measure of your forefathers; thus dealt they with all God's faithfull servants that were sent unto them, yea, even with Christ himself, refusing him for his simplicitie, reputing him among thieves, deceivers, *etc.* We looke for no better usage at your hands; the servant is neither greater nor better than his maister; if they have done thus to the greene tree, what shall not you doo to the drie? Yet so far are we from all danger or harme by theis curses, that God turneth them forthwith unto us as a blessing, and to a comfortable assurance both of the fellowship of the faith, and of the suffring of Christ. "Blessed are you when men revile you, and say all maner of evil against you for my name's sake, *etc.*"[4] Againe, through the mercies of our God, all the injuries you can offer unto

God curseth your blessings: therfor he blesseth your cursings.[5]

---

1 Isaiah 8: 20.
2 Malachi 2: 8, 9.
3 Elymas was the sorcerer who lived in the island of Cyprus. Because he withstood the efforts of Saul [Paul] and Barnabas, he was temporarily blinded (Acts 13: 6-11).
4 Matthew 5: 11.
5 This is fallible logic. Barrow's love of absolute statements and his prejudice against "fond distinctions" expose him to fallacies, as well as to folly.

us cannot overcome our charitie, or breake our patience. In the one we possesse our soules; in the other we will not cease to praie for you, even as for our selves, and be redie to doo you anie good we can. Now to those poore soules whome you like miserable phisitians thus cure, we give this advise; (yet not we, but the Lord). That they beware of wolves in sheepe's clothing: that they follow not blind guides too far: that they marke diligentlie and avoide such as transgresse and abide not in the doctrine of Christ, nor walke after the rule of the gospel: that they turne away from such as make a shew of godlines, but denie the power and practize therof, deceiving with faire wordes the hearts of the simple, talking of Christ but deniing him in deedes. Further, we send them not to man's worde, nor over sea, but to God's worde, which is neere them, even in their mouthes and in their hearts: let them therby trie the spirits before thei believe them: let them therby measure their temple, their altar and their worshippers, and especiallie their owne hearts; that thei may be wise to that which is good, and simple concerning evil.

If the latter part of your answere had bene put in the beginning, (to have set downe what maketh a true minister of Christ) and you approved your ministrie accordinglie, we had suffered lesse injurie, and you lesse blame. Notwithstanding, because it is never to[o] late to repent, if this your offer be according to your heart, we most willinglie and gladlie accept of it, and wil refuse no indifferent and godlie conference,[1] which we yer [ere, before] this time expected, and to that end wrote (at certeine of your chief ministers' request) these

---

[1] It is worthy of note that during the years of imprisonment, 1587-1593, Barrow and Greenwood are almost naive in their high hopes of the outcome of any godly impartial conference. Even after their death sentence, while awaiting execution, they plead for a public conference, in a letter addressed to the attorney-general, Thomas Egerton.

articles,[1] which you have taken upon you to answere. In the rest, though you have most rashlie and most un-[16]chari[ta]blie reproched and condempned us alredie, contrarie to all truth, order or equitie, even for telling you the truth; yet if hereafter you can beware of rash judgment, we shall rejoice. Likewise, if you can escape God's judgments for these your heinous transgressions; or make anie better plea for them than as yet we have heard or can perceive, we shall not be sorie, but much glad, if you would prevent the wrath that hangeth over your heads for them by unfeigned repentance and spedie amendement.

The fourth fault is in the subjection to antichristian government. Let it be admitted that ther is some yoake of antichristian government, under which the poore church doth grone, (as it is her lot to be oppressed with outward bondage, to be made to keepe the vineyard which is not her owne, to be beaten of the watchmen, to have her vaile taken from her)[2] is she therfore no longer the spouse of Christ? G. G. his answer to the fourth principal transgression

But o how far are you from this; which winke with your eies, stop your eares, harden your hearts; which cannot endure so much as to heare of your fearefull estate which you see not, no, nor suffer your sores which H. B. his replie

---

1 By "these articles" Barrow probably means the ones under discussion —the six articles plus the four principal transgressions. But there is a set of eleven articles printed in *A Collection of Certain Letters and Conferences*, pp. 67-70, which are substantially the same articles in different words. They were delivered to Thomas Cartwright, Walter Travers, William Charke, and William Floyde [Fluyd, Fludd, Floyd] "more than a yeare and a halfe since." If the time of writing is about March-May, 1590, when the rest of the book was written, then we may date the eleven articles about August or September, 1588. If Barrow is correct in saying he wrote his first reply to Gifford in 1587, we could possibly stretch this to March 24, 1587/8, but Barrow and Greenwood regard January as the first month and date the new year with January 1, not March 25. If we assume that the eleven articles are written about August, 1588, then the first reply of Barrow to Gifford must be after August, 1588, since he alludes to the articles. My tentative conclusion is that Barrow in 1592 erred in remembering 1587 as the date of his first reply and that 1588 is the correct date, but the disturbing fact is that Barrow is accurate in mentioning time despite his references to his own frail memory.
2 Gifford, *A Short Treatise*, p. 82. Gifford is referring to the Song of Solomon 1: 6 and 5: 7.

you see, to be touched; but seeke rather to cloake and
hide them both from God and men; yea, to mitigate,
tollerate and justifie them. Seeke you not here to
mitigate that heavie apparant antichristian yoak your
churches stand under, wherof heretofore you have
complained in parliaments ? Tearming it (some yoake),
being now peradventure through long custome growen
lighter unto you, and more easie than Christ's yoake, at
the least, than Christ's crosse. And yet this (some
yoake) is yeilded but by waie of admition, to be retracted at your pleasure, if either advantage arise to us,
or danger grow to you therby. Further, you have added
to this your hipocrisie, blasphemie; tearming the yoake
of antichrist the lott of the church, which she must beare
by the will of God; wherof in due place.

Now to shew this (some yoake) you speake of according to the indignitie therof in everie perticular, would
make a volume. Yea, onlie to recite the severall enormities therof, would require a discourse; which is neither
our purpose at this time, neither have we skill or experience therin. Only this we see and testifie, that your
churches stand whollie under the yoake of antichrist,
you still reteining his worship, his lawes, his ordinances,
his officers, his courtes, even the whole government that
the pope somtime committed to his faithfull servants
your bishops, which now have taken his power into their
owne hands.[1] What a sort of stagelike antichristian
courtes have you ? As first, that great Court of your
High Commission, the Court (*ex officio*) in everie bishop's
house; the Court of Arches; the Court of Delegates; the
Court of Faculties. Not to speak of your in-[17]feriour
courtes in the contrie; as your commissaries' and officials'
courts, your scenes, and such like.[2] What a rabble of
officers and attendants are unto these belonging ? Ad-

---

[1] Marginal comment: " that o[u]r churches stand whollye under the yoak
of antichrist."

[2] See the article on " courts " in S. L. Ollard and Gordon Crosse, *A Dic-
tionary of English Church History* (1912), pp. 154-161. See also Wilfred
Hooper, " The Court of Faculties," *English Historical Review*, XXV
(October, 1910), 670-686. See also the works of John S. Burn, Richard
Burn, William Stubbs, John T. Tomlinson, and Roland G. Usher.

vocates, doctors, proctors, registers, scribes, pursivants. Who can number all their antichristian canons, lawes, rites, ceremonies, privileges, dispensations, licences of all sortes, probations, inhibitions, *etc.* Which require but the whole age of a man to reade. But now who can recount the perticular mischiefs and enormities that ensue and flow from them, even over the whole land? Or who yeildeth not to this antichristian jurisdiction? Doo not you and your whole parishes without exception of one, bowe downe to this beast, and take the marke of his subjection, or the print of his lawes upon you, even in your foreheads and in your handes? What libertie have you to refreine from these abhominations, without present persecution? Or what powre have you to execute and practize Christ's lawes? Call you this but "some yoake"?

The Holy Ghost hath taught us to call you his servants to whome you obey. So we finding you under the obedience of antichrist, cannot compt you the servants of Christ; unlesse you can prove that you can serve two contrary maisters faithfullie at once. Christ and antichrist are at perpetual war, ther is no communion betwene them. So that it is impossible that the church of Christ can carie the yoake of antichrist, without breach of wedlock, even of the covenant, as appeareth plentifullie in all the prophets, Christ's love being not bound to her anie longer, than shee keepeth faith to him.

The true church never without christian libertie and christian power. Christ divideth not with antichrist

Againe, ther is continuall war betwene the true church, and antichrist; which were at an end, if she should yeild unto him, or carie his yoake, as you suppose. But if you had learned to put difference betwene persecution and bondage, you could not in this matter have runne into this blasphemous error, as to say: (it is the lot of the church to be oppressed with outward bondage, and to be made to keepe the vineyard which is not her owne). Persecution in deed is the lott of the church here in this world; as he that was borne after the flesh persecuted him that was borne after the spirit. But bondage is the badge of antichrist, themarke of the beast, wherby his souldiours are discerned from the

145

F

souldiours of Christ; and the children of Mount Sina[1] from the children of Hierusalem, which is above and free, even the mother of us all, for whome our capitaine Christ hath purchased a full and a perfect libertie at a deare and precious price; which libertie once lost, ther remaineth no more ransoms to make us free. It behooveth therfore all the children of the free woman to stand fast in the libertie wherwith Christ hath made them free, and not to be intangled againe with the yoake of bondage.

Neither can these places of the Songe (which you have falsified and perverted) anie way carie this doctrine you would build upon them, or construction you make. In the first place, though the church confesseth her owne unworthines and deformitie, borne in originall sinne, which conceived and brought out in her manie actuall sinnes, which being kin[d]led in her and against her, often enticed her and provoked her to keepe [18] their vines, wherby she neglected to dresse and keepe her owne vine:[2] yet from hence it followeth not, that because she was sinfull and negligent, that therfore she was obstinate and incorrigible (the contrarie appeareth, in that she thus humblie and modestly confesseth her faultes): or because she kept not her owne vine, as she ought to doo, that therfore she kept antichrist's vine, which she ought not to doo. What a bolde falsifiing of this place in this, to alledge, that the church was made to keepe the vineyeard which is not her owne, in stead of this, that she kept not her owne vine? If you had looked upon the two next verses following, you could never thus groslie have mistaken the matter. In the sixth verse[3] the church prayeth unto Christ that he would shew her where he feedeth, and where he lieth at noone; for (saith she) "why should I be as she that turneth aside to the flockes of thie companions." This is not to grone under antichrist's yoake, nor to remaine with the flockes of these presumptuous sheepheards

Songe 1

The church daily praieth for forgivenes of sinnes

[1] This is the Greek form for Sinai.
[2] The Song of Solomon 1: 6.
[3] Verse seven in the King James Version. Barrow is using the Geneva Bible, which begins the first chapter of the Song of Solomon with what is verse two in the King James Version.

which wilbe Christ's companions, which set their owne lawes over the church, reigne in men's consciences, imposing their heapes of burdenous traditions, *etc.* But here all the faithful are taught to flie unto Christ by fervent and faithful praier, and not to cease untill he shew them the place where he feedeth his flocke, and where he resteth at noone. There shall thei finde a comfortable shadowe in the greatest heate of persecution, and a safe refuge in the greatest storme and tempest that Satan can raise. Againe, if you had considered Christ's answere in the seventh verse,[1] where he instructeth her, yea, and commandeth her and all his faithfull servants with her to come forth, not to stay in the stepps of that flock, but to feede her kyddes above the tentes of other shepherds; you would never have used this place to prove that it is the lot of the church to be oppressed with outward bondage, and to be made to keep the vineyeard which is not her owne, Christ here as you see commanding the expresse contrarie.

Neither have you applied that other place of the fifth Song 5 of the Songe with better successe. For if it be duelie weighed and trulie applied, it will to the life shew forth what church you are, and your behaviours and dealings with the church of God.

First therfore among diverse and sondrie notes set downe here by the Holy Ghost wherby to discerne the true church from the false, we observe especiallie these. Notes of the The true church, though she dailie fall into sondrie true church sinnes, yet lieth not she still in them, nor despiseth the voice and calling of Christ. But (as you see here) awaketh, repenteth and ariseth, openeth, soroweth, seeketh, giveth not over for grievous woundes, persecutions and blasphemies, neither by them is turned backe to the easie bed of worldlie peace and fleshlie quiet from whence she arose, *etc.*, but continueth sorowing and seeking untill she have found the daughters of Hierusalem, the children of the free woman, to whome she communicateth her sorowes and her desires; to them she preacheth and praiseth Christ; to them she recommendeth her estate, chardging them to shew it

---

[1] Verse eight in the King James Version and the Revised Version.

her beloved by praiers, *etc.* On the contrarie, we find here the malignant church fast asleepe in worldlie peace and fleshlie ease, frozen in the [19] dreggs of their sinnes,

such as wil not be wakened, and so far from opening the doores unto Christ, that they barre the doores against him, yea, persecute him from their doores, cast him out of their citie, yea, out of the world if thei could, and with him all such as seeke to serve him with an upright heart according to his word, and will not continue with them in their sinnes and securitie. Now let your church be examined by these workes without partialitie, and it shall easelie appeare of what sort it is (though we saie nothing) whither it be the church persecuting, or the church persecuted, and so in the rest.

Likewise if you and your learned brethren be founde in all poinctes like these wretched watchmen by the description of the Holie Ghost in this place, we doubt not but the most simple by the evidence therof shalbe taught both to discerne and judge you. And the greatest clearke emong you be taught hereafter, how to abuse the Scripture for a cloke to cover your sinnes.

1. First therfore these watchmen were appointed and approved of the secure and wicked citie.
2. Then thei were in all things conformable to these corrupt times, and ministring to those times.
3. Then thei stood pastors and watchmen to the whole citie hand over hand as thei dwelt in the parishes therof (being called the watchmen of the citie).
4. Then these watchmen held the people in diepe peace and securitie (as appeareth by the generall sleep).
5. Then thei held the people in ignorance and blindnes (as appeareth both by the night and their sleep).
6. Then these watchmen gat all the powre into their owne hands (as appeareth by the generall sleep of all others, their watching and persecuting).
7. Then these watchmen not onlie sought not Christ themselves, but suffred not others that would.
8. Then these watchmen not onlie shewed not the

waye to such as sought Christ, but sought with one consent to turne them backe againe, *etc.*, by persecution.

9. Whilest the church continued in the bed of securitie and worldlie ease with the rest, and looked not for these heavenlie things, but trusted the watchmen with all such matters, even with her salvation, she was at good peace with them, and we reade of no violence or force offred unto her. But after she was called and awaked by Christ; after she had risen, opened, sought and called him, but found him not; after she perceived that he was departed thence, and had fullie resolved to give her self no rest, untill she had found him; then these watchmen thought it hie time to bestir them, and to stop this gap. And therfore what thei could not perswade, thei sought by force, persecuted, wounded her, rent away her vaile by railings and reproches, even the name of Christ by which she is called, *etc.*[1]

The watchmen punished not sinne which suffred in the church, but Christ whom they cannot suffer

Stands it not thus in all these poincts with our watchmen? Let the times declare whither thei agree not to them in their entrance and administration, and in their persecutions and sclanders exceed them. Our purpose is not to make perticular application, the matter being so evident. Onlie this litle is said, to redeeme the places from such violence and corruption as is offred unto them; and by the same places to give a glymse to such, as the Lord hath opened the eies of their understan-[20]ding, to discover and search out the false dealing of their watchmen, whom they too long and too far have credited, and to warne al that tender their owne salvation to open their eares and their hearts to Christ's voice in his word, that calleth them out of this sinfull easie couch, wherin their watchmen have held them all too long; and that forsaking the tentes of these presumptuous shepeherds, they seek Christ whilest and where he may be found; and together with the daughters of Hierusalem, the children of the free woman, the heires

---

[1] These nine points are allegorical interpretations of the Song of Solomon 5: 1-7.

of the promises, seek, preach, and praise Christ. Then no doubt they shall finde him, to their unspeakable comfort; then will he be as a roe from the mountaine of Bether,[1] redie to help, succer and susteine them with his flagons; then will he come to his palm tree, and take hold of her boughes; then will he come into his garden, and blowe upon it, and water it, that the spices therof may flowe forth, and that he may eate the pleasant fruictes therof; then shal he descend into the orchard of sweete fruictes and pomegranats, and see whither the fig-tree put forth, and the vine florish and bud her small grapes; then will he prepare and make al things in a readines for that great solemne day of the consummation of his mariage.

The Lord grant we may likewise prepare and be in redines, trimmed and prepared, that we may meete him with joye to our everlasting comfort, Amen. And the Lord shorten that day, and hasten his coming, Amen. " Even so come Lord Jesus, come quicklie, Amen."[2] So be it.

---

[1] Song of Solomon 2: 17.
[2] Revelation 22: 20.

VIII

REPLY TO DR. SOME'S *A Godly Treatise*

One of the men who served well the cause of the Anglican hierarchy was Dr. Robert Some. About May, 1588, his work, *A Godly Treatise Containing and Deciding Certaine Questions*, was published. The date in the preface is May 6, 1588, and on this same day the book was entered in the *Stationers' Register*. The book, which was directed against " popish and Anabaptistical " recusants, contained nine points or theses which Dr. Some supported. Evidently a copy of this book was brought to Barrow in prison, who wrote *marginal* notes on the entire volume of 37 pages. The second edition, issued in September, 1588, has 36 pages, a table of ten points, and 164 additional pages refuting John Penry. Since Barrow used the first edition, which had been annotated by him and then seized by the prison officials before January 1, 1588/9, we may be certain that these marginal notes were written in 1588.

In the examination of January 1, 1588/9, Justice Richard Young produced a copy of Dr. Some's book which contained *marginal* notes. There was a discussion on the subject of Christ as head of the Church of England, to which Barrow had replied that the Church of England had two heads. Since this point is made on page 35 (in a book of 37 pages), in a *marginal* note, it is evident that this is not the same copy which is reproduced here. The book produced by Richard Young was probably seized during the summer or fall of 1588 by the authorities in their periodic rifling, of which Barrow complained bitterly. Thereupon, Barrow set to work again, this time with another copy of Dr. Some's book, *interleaved* with blank pages. Since Barrow was not permitted to have paper or ink in his chamber, I conjecture that this *interleaved* copy was smuggled in to him by Daniel Studley or Cicely, a maid-servant, both of whom had permission to visit Barrow in prison. Barrow proceeded as far as page 12 when again his work was seized by the wary prison officials. It is highly probable that the *interleaved* notes were also written in 1588 or at least before the appearance of Dr. Some's second *A Godly Treatise, Wherein Are Examined and Confuted Many Execrable Fancies Given Out and Holden, Partly by Henry Barrow and John Greenwood.* This *interleaved* annotated volume is in Lambeth Palace Library, and the annotations are now printed for the first time, together with enough of Dr. Some's statements to make intelligible the replies of Barrow.

It is clear that Dr. Some utilized Barrow's arguments, which he obtained from Barrow's marginal and interleaved annotations, and from at least one oral conference in prison. If the reader will consult the January 1, 1588/9, examination, or if he will peruse Dr. Some's book, *A Godly Treatise, Wherein Are Examined and Confuted Many Execrable Fancies Given Out and Holden, Partly by Henry Barrow and John Greenwood*, published about May, 1589 (just a year after the publication of his first *A Godly Treatise*), he will see how Dr. Some has utilized the material obtained from Barrow. For example, statements that "all sortes of wild beasts, as tygres, wolfes, foxes, are received into the bosome of the Church of England," or that "no man without blasphemy can arrogate to himselfe the title of Doctor of Divinity," are taken directly from Barrow's *interleaved* notes, and other of his material is very likely taken from the *marginal* annotations, which unfortunately are not known to exist.[1] Other material which Dr. Some ferreted out is found in Barrow's examinations on March 18 and March 24, 1588/9. That Robert Some was rewarded for his service in combatting the Separatists seems evident from his Epistle Dedicatorie, dated May 12, 1589, in *A Godly Treatise*, where he writes: "I doe owe a particular duetie to your Lordships

---

[1] I have examined numerous copies in many libraries of Dr. Some's 1588 edition of *A Godly Treatise*, in the hope of discovering these marginal annotations. One would expect this volume to be in the Lambeth Palace Library, but it is not there. Dr. Some or Justice Young may have kept it.

[Lord Chancellor Hatton and Lord Treasurer Burghley] for your honourable favour to me." Perhaps Dr. Some had reference to his appointment as Master of Peterhouse, on May 11, probably through the influence of Archbishop Whitgift as well as Lord Burghley, who was Chancellor of the University of Cambridge.

* * * * * *

153

REPLY TO DR. SOME'S *A GODLY TREATISE*

[Title Page]

A Godly[1] Treatise

1. Seinge our saviour Christ hathe fore-warned us, that in the latter dayes shal a multitude of false prophets arise to deceive manye: and that it is not harde for Satan to transfourme himselfe into an angel of light, and with glorious titles to cover his deceipt. Let us holde faste the worde of truthe, that we be not caryed about with winde of doctrine: but be simple concerninge evil, and wise unto that which is good. Romans 16: 19; 2 Corinthians 11: 13, 14. Ephesians 4: 14.

Written by Robert Some Doctor[2] of Divinitie

2. This title can no man without blasphemye arrogate unto himselfe, seinge that we have but one Doctor, even Christ, in whome the devine godheade dwelleth bodelye. Matthew 23: 10. Collosians 2: 9.

[Dr. Some] *Let us follow the trueth in love, and in all thinges growe up into him, which is the head[3] (that is) Christ, etc.*

3. His antichristian titles, and ministerye, shewe to what heade he belongeth; his workes, and life, what love he beareth to Christ and his members. Matthew 7: 16. Revelation 14: 9.

[A iii *recto*] [Dr. Some] — To the Reader.

Two sortes of recusantes are in this land:[1]

1. Two sortes of recuzants are in this lande, the one refuzeth the truthe; the other falshood: refuzers of the truthe be infinit, as Arrians, Anabaptistes, papistes, pontifical prelats, popishe doctors, and preists, tollerators of evil, counterfet professors, atheists, *etc.* Refuzers of al errours, superstition and poperye, are suche as faithfullye profes[s], and patientlye suffer for the trewe practize of the gospell. 2 Peter 2: [1-22]. Revelation 2: 24, 25 and 14: 4.

[Dr. Some] *the one Popish, the other Anabaptis[t]icall[2]*

2. Let it be tryed by the worde of God, what kinde of churche, sacraments, and ministerye you have. Ephesians 5: 13. Revelation 11: 1.

[Dr. Some] *These men labour of two diseases: the one is great pride,[3] the other grosse ignorance.*

154

Reply to Dr. Some's A Godly Treatise

3. The prowde are exalted, pride doeth not patientlye suffer for the truthe, he that thinketh he knoweth any thinge knoweth nothinge as he ought to knowe, we boast of no knowledge, it sufficeth us to knowe Christ Jesus, and him crucifyed. Proverbs 26: 12. I Corinthians 3: 18. 2 Corinthians 10: 18.

[Dr. Some]   *Their pride appeares in their behaviour,*[4] *which is voide of humilitie:*

4. Our behaviour iz suche, as becometh the faithful servants of Christ in al dewe humilitye. 1 Corinthians 4: 3, 4.

[Dr. Some]   *Their ignorance [appeares] in their arguments,*[5] *which hang together like a sicke man's dreame.*

5. Our arguments are drawen from the undoubted truthe of God, against which no cavillers can prevaile. Jeremiah 23: 29. 2 Corinthians 10: 4.

[Dr. Some]   *That her majestie may and ought to compel*[6] *these recusants to frequent our church assemblies, I make no question.*[7]

6. There shal neede no compulsion to us, when you have approved your churche by the rule of the worde. Psalms 110: 3 and 27: 4, 8.

7. None that knoweth the truthe can once suppoze that an unlawful minister can rightlye administer the sacraments. Nombers 17: 8. Matthew 15: 13, 14. John 10: 5.

[Dr. Some]   *There is an other sorte, which either deny or doubt, whether unpreaching ministers doe deliver a sacrament*[1] .... *I will hope*[8] *well of these men: for they erre, onely for want of judgement.*

8. You already enjoye your hope, they stande under your orders, and will nether practize, nor suffer for the truthe. Matthew 6: 24. 2 Peter 2: 19. 2 Timothy 3: 5.

[Dr. Some]   *The holy sacrament is one thing, the minister's ignorance is an other thing: the Lorde's sacrament brings singuler comfort*[9] *to the worthie receiver: ignorance can neither pervert the sacrament, nor pollute the receiver.*

9. A lawful minister iz of necessitye required to a trewe sacrament, nether can there be anye trewe comforte from suche pretended sacraments: but boeth such ignorant be[lie]vers, and receivers,

---

[1] Dr. Some's attitude is that of the medieval church. The office and its incumbent are independent of each other. An ignorant or wicked priest may administer the sacrament, and those who receive the sacrament are not perverted or polluted. Augustine and the Donatists fought over similar issues.

are guiltye of the bodye and blood of Christe; our saviour Christ and his apostles have taught this doctrine; how-soever by your ungodlye slannders you may seeke to deface the truthe. Exodus 28: 1. Leviticus 22: 20. Nombers 16: 40. Proverbs 21: 27. Malachi 1: 7. Romans 10: 15. Hebrews 5: 4.

[Dr. Some]   *The Donatistes taught otherwise in the former time, and the Anabaptistes in our time: but they are notably confuted by two famous men, Augustine[10] and Calvine.*

10. Augustine, and Calvine, never alowed of an unpreachinge minister, or double benefized man, *etc.*

[Dr. Some]   *What account[11] I make of ignorant ministers, appeareth in this treatise.*

11. What greater accompt can you make of them, than to promise a blessinge to thoze sacraments.

[Dr. Some]   *It pleased God to direct[12] my heart and penne in this holy labour: therefore I assure my selfe of his gracious blessing.[1]*

12. How yow were directed, this your worke doeth declare. In the meane tyme after the manner of al false prophets you blesse your selfe in your iniquitye. 1 Kings 22: 11. Zechariah 11: 5. Amos 6: 13. 1 Corinthians 3: 13.

[A iii *verso*]

A TABLE OF SUCH POINTS AS ARE CONTEINED IN THIS TREATISE

[Dr. Some]   1. *A godly prince may and ought to compell his subjects (if any refuse) to the externall service of God.*

1. First ther worship ought to be accordinge to the worde of God. Then thoughe the prophane may be compelled to the hearinge of the worde, and prayer: yet can they not be made members of the churche, without faith and repentance. Deuteronomy 5: 8, 32, 33. Exodus 12: 44, 45. Ezekiel 44: 7, 9. Matthew 15: 9. Acts 2: 38, 41. Hebrews 6: 20.

[Dr. Some]   2. *Able teachers ought to be provided (so much as can be) for the churches.*

2. The choise of theize ought to be accordinge to the worde, and not after men's inventions, and that of necessitye. Exodus 25:

---

[1] For Barrow and others, this claim seems to smack of spiritual pride.

40. Acts 6: 3, 6 and 14: 23. 1 Timothy 6: 13, 14.

[Dr. Some]   3. *The teachers of religion must have maintenance.*

3. They ought to be maintained nether by mercenarye wadges, nor Jewishe tithes, to support them in idlenes, or worldlye pompe. 2 Corinthians 2: 17. Galatians 4: 9. 1 Timothy 6: 8. Hebrews 7: 12. 2 Peter 2: 25.

[Dr. Some]   4. *Almightie God blesseth those kingdomes with peace, which promote and embrace his religion.*

4. God blesseth al such with spiritual peace, az faithfullye embrace, and rightly advance his trewe religion. Deuteronomy 28. John 14. Galatians 6: 16.

[Dr. Some]   5. *The childe of God is not polluted, though he be present at, and partaker of the publique prayers, sacraments, etc., at such time as wicked men are present at, and partakers of them.*

5. If you meane open impenitent offenders, it iz directlye contrarye to the whole course of Scriptures. Exodus 12: 34. Leviticus 13: 45, 46 and 22: 3, 4, 5, 6, 25. Haggai 2: 14, 15. Matthew 18: 17. 1 Corinthians 5: 6 and 10: 17, etc.

[Dr. Some]   6. *They which were baptized in the popish church by popish priests, received true baptisme touching the substance of baptisme.*

6. A false churche cannot have trewe sacraments, nether iz there trewe substance or promise of blessinge to false sacraments. Deuteronomy 32: 17. Isayah 57: 20, 21. Ezekiel 17: 3, 8, and 23. 1 Corinthians 10: 20.

[Dr. Some]   7. *They are the sacraments of Baptisme and the Holy Supper, which are delivered in the Church of England, by unpreaching ministers.*

7. Theye are no ministers, therefore no sacraments. Nombers 16: 10 and 18: 3, 4, 5. Matthew 28: 19. 1 Timothy 3: 10.

[Dr. Some]   8. *The godly are not polluted which receive the sacrament at the hands of an unpreaching minister.*

8. It beinge no sacrament, they are guiltye of the bodye, and blood of Christe. 1 Corinthians 11: 29.

[Dr. Some]   9. *The Church of England is the visible church of Christe.*[1]

---

[1] It is just possible that this claim was the influence which led Barrow to write *A True Description out of the Worde of God, of the Visible Church,* published the next year, 1589. This, in turn, is supplemented by Barrow's major work, *A Brief Discoverie of the False Church,* published with the date 1590, but more likely about March, 1590/1.

9. Here you confownde the common-wealthe, and the churche: then your assemblyes az they generallye stande in Englande, are not the trewe vizible churches of Christ. Ezra 6: 21. 1 Corinthians 5: 10. 2 Corinthians 6: 14.

[p. 1] [Dr. Some] *It is the prince's duetie[1] to provide able men to teach the Lorde's religion in his dominions.*

1. If you make it the magistrat's dewtye to chooze, and provide ministers for the churche, you take awaye the libertye, and the power, that Christ hathe geven unto hiz churche where-of the magistrate iz but a member:[1] but if you meane that the magistrate ought to assist the churche with the civil sworde, we consent, and you falsifye theize places of Scripture, which prove, not that the magistrate choze, but assisted rather the Levites and other preistes, which were lawfullye chozen, and called by God. Deuteronomy 17: 19, 20. Marke 13: 34. Romans 13: 4. 1 Corinthians 12: 18, 19, 20.

[Dr. Some] *Teachers and learners are relatives.[2]*

2. Your reason of your relatives holdes not, for the magistrate can not ordeyne ministers, yet may he compel to heare, *etc.* Acts 6: 3 and 14: 23.

[Dr. Some] *Great[3] outrages were committed against both the tables of the commandements, as appeareth in the booke of Judges: . . . . if a religious prince had bene in place, idolatrie and wicked behaviour had been suppressed, and the Israelites pressed to serve the Lorde.*

3. We graunt the aucthoritye, and office of the kinge, to extende to the advancemente of trewe religion, to the suppressinge of al idolatrye, and wicked behaviour, to compel al his subjectes to the hearinge of Godde's worde, punishinge the deriders, and contemners of the same. For this we have better proofe, than Augustine his reporte. 2 Kings 23. Psalms 101: 8. Proverbs 20: 26.

[p. 2] [Dr. Some] *The prince is bound to sanctifie[4] the Sabboth: so are his subjects:*

4. The Sabbothe iz sanctifyed, where God iz rightlye worshipped, and our lives framed according to Godde's worde; but your

---

[1] Each church should call its own pastor. Barrow contends that the State has no right to usurp this prerogative of the church, that no patron or magistrate may intrude into the calling of Christ's servants. Furthermore, bishops, who are ecclesiastical magistrates, have no right to license clergymen, and even *qua* bishops, may not usurp the function of the congregation.

153

false and supersticious worship, your manyfolde idolatryes, your prophane lossenes of life, after the maner of the Gentiles (especiallye on the Lorde's daye, boeth in courte and cuntrye) your joyninge, your preachinge to al theize abhominations, or rather coveringe them there-with, shewe howe you sanctifye the Sabbothe.

[Dr. Some] *If any[5] refuse, they may and ought to be compelled: for the breach of the Sabboth is a hainous sinne. Jeremiah 17. Nehemiah 13.*

5. Nowe let it be judged by what right, you can compel men to kepe the Sabbothe after your maner. Isayah 10: 1. Acts 4: 19.

[Dr. Some] *Faith[6] commeth by hearing of the word, Romans 10: [17]; therefore refusall to heare, hinders both the beginning and growth of faith.*

6. We graunt this you saye: yet alwayes makinge difference betwixt trewe doctrine, and false, trewe teachers and false,[;] false doctrine, and false teachers, beinge carefullye to be avoyded. Proverbs 19: 27. Matthew 7: 15 and 15: 14 and 16: 6. Romans 16: 17. Galatians 1: 7, 8. 2 John 1: 9, 10, 11.

[p. 3] [Dr. Some] *Asa, Josias, were famous kings of Juda[7] . . . . If it were lawfull for these kings of Juda, to commaunde and compell their subjectes, it is not unlawfull for ours to doe the like.*

7. It iz alreadye graunted, that godlye majestrats ought to abolishe false, and set up trewe religion, and to compel al their subjects to the hearinge of Godde's worde: yet if the majestrate set up false religion, or neglect their dewtye, the faithful must avoyde false worship,[1] and practize the truthe, patientlye under-goeinge, what may be layde upon them for the same. Daniel 3 and 6 chapters. Luke 21: 12. 1 Peter 4: 12 etc.

[Dr. Some] *Ezra[8] was a learned Scribe: he was authorised by the king of Persia, to teach them beyond the river Euphrates the lawe of God, which did not know it, and to punish such as refused to learne.*

8 Yet by Ezra his example iz no popishe, or roveinge ministerye

---

[1] The crucial question here is this: who shall decide what is false worship ? Barrow falls back on the New Testament as an invariable and absolute standard. His opponents allow for expediency and change, especially in areas regarded as indifferent, such as ceremonies, vestments, and even discipline.

maintayned: but al trewe ministers must be ordeyned, and lymitted accordinge to the Testament of Christ. Romans 12: 7. 1 Corinthians 4: 2.

[p. 4] [Dr. Some] [9]*Augustine the Bishop of Hippo in Africke, was a very famous man: he was sometimes of opinion, that heretiks were to be pressed by argument, and not by the magistrate: his reason then was,* ne fictos Catholicos haberemus, quos apertos hereticos noveramus, *that is, least we shoulde have counterfait Catholickes, whom we knewe to be notorious heretikes. But after weightie consideration, he changed his former opinion, and is very resolute, that recusants may and ought to be compelled by the magistrate.* Aug. epist. 48. 204.[1]

9. Your concluzion agreeth not with your tale, we have a rule in the Scriptures for heretickes, how prophane atheists, and ignorant recuzants, are to be compelled, iz above shewed. 1 Timothy [1: 20; 4: 20; 6: 5]. Titus 3: 10.

   [Dr. Some] Si [enim] terrerentur et non docerentur, improba quasi dominatio videretur: Sed rursus, si docerentur, et non terrerentur, etc. August. epist. 48.[2] *that is, to punish and not to teach, were tyrannie: againe, to teach and not to punish, were to harden them in their* [p. 5] *ancient custome, and to make them slowe to enter the path of salvation.*[10]

10. Of your mouthe we judge you, you have punished us by the sworde, before you have either perswaded, or convinced us by the worde.

    [Dr. Some] [11]*Goe out into the high wayes, and hedges, and compell them to come in:*[3]

11. You perverte the place to the power of the seculer sworde, which is spoken of the spiritual power of the worde. Matthew 22: 3, 6.

    [Dr. Some] [12]Ad caenam [cenam] tanti patrisfamilias, si

---

[1] *Augustini Opera* (Basel, 1556). Secundus Tomus, *Epistolarum Liber*, XLVIII, p. 73. This letter may be seen in *Fathers of the Church, A New Translation*, Vol. 18, *Saint Augustine, Letters*, Volume II, translated by Sister Wilfrid Parsons (1953). The letter is addressed to Vincent, and is No. 93, pp. 56-106. In the Benedictine edition this letter is also No. 93 (*Sancti Aurelii Augustini Hipponensis Episcopi Opera Omnia* [Paris, 1836], Tomus Secundus, Pars prior, p. 346).

[2] *Augustini Opera* (Basel, 1556). Secundus Tomus, *Epistolarum Liber*, XLVIII, p. 59.

[3] Luke 14: 23.

sponte non vultis, intrare compellimus. Aug.
contra 2. Gaudentij epist. lib. 2. cap. 28.
that is, to the supper of so great an housholder, if you
wil not of your owne accord, we compell you to enter.[1]

12. The holy man iz dead, if you maintaine this doctrine, that any
ignorant or prophane person iz to be received into the churche,
or to be compelled unto the sacraments: it can-not be helde
with-out dangerous errour, nor practized with-out open sacriledge. Exodus 12: 44, 45. Leviticus 22: 3, 4. John 3: 3.

[Dr. Some] [13]Quod autem vobis videtur, invitos ad veritatem
non esse cogendos, *etc.* Aug. contra 2 Gaudentij
epist. lib. 2. cap. 17. *That is, where as ye think,*
that men are not to bee compelled to the trueth against
their willes, ye erre, not knowing the Scriptures, nor
the power of God, which maketh those willing, though
they be compelled against their willes.[2]

13. It appeareth by this place how you wreste Augustine to the
sacraments, who meaneth of the hearinge of the worde, you
compellinge the whole lande to your sacramentes.

[Dr. Some] [14]Qui phreneticum ligat, and [et qui] lethargicum
excitat, ambobus molestus, ambos amat. Aug.
epist. 48. *that is, he that bindeth a frantike man,*
and awaketh him that hath the lethargie, loveth both,
though he be grievous to both.[3]

14. The faithful servants of God, and our saviour Christe himselfe have alwayes bene thus judged, and bownde (az we are
nowe) by prowde priestes, and false prophets upholden, and
assisted by the civil sworde, who them-selves rage againste
Christ, and hiz truthe, and sleepe in a deadlye liturgye of
sinne, and persecute unto deathe al suche, az either speake
to awaken, or cure them. Matthew 23: 34, 35, and 27: 20.
Luke 23: 14. John 8: 48.

[p. 6] [Dr. Some] *God's*[1] *people are the Lord's sheepe, spouse, citie:*
therefore they must be fedde, garnished, watched over,
with the Lorde's foode, furniture, weapons.

1. Your parishes (az they stande) are nether the Lorde'z shepe,

---

[1] *Septimus Tomus Operum Divi Aurelii Augustini* (Basel, 1556). Contra
secundam Gaudentii Donatistarum Episcopi epistolam, Liber Secundus,
Cap. XXVIII, p. 360.

[2] *Ibid.,* p. 346.

[3] *Augustini Opera,* Secundus Tomus, *Epistolarum Liber,* XLVIII, p. 60.
This is No. 93 in the Benedictine edition (Paris, 1836), p. 346.

spouce [spouse], or citye, nether your ministers suche teachers, az God hathe ordeyned to feede hiz flocke. Isayah 30: 8, 9, 10, 11. Luke 19: 27. John 3: 36.

[Dr. Some] *This cannot be done without able teachers.*[2]

2. Here your owne mouthe casteth out al dumbe ministers, non-residents, and hyrelingez.

[Dr. Some] *The worke[3] of the ministery is a famous worke. Ephesians 4. It passeth Moses' tabernacle, and Salomon's temple: therefore it is to be committed to skilfull and faithful men.*

3. The worke of your ministerye so far digressinge from the trewe patterne, sheweth the unskilfulnes of your buylders, your churchez swarminge with so many idolls, and aboundinge with so grosse ignorance, sheweth your unfaithfulnes; this, everye parishe churche, especiallye your cathredal [*sic*] churches, declare. Jeremiah 23: 14. Ezekiel 23: 8, 9. Malachi 2.

[Dr. Some] *The ambassadors[4] of earthlie princes, either are or should be men of choice: otherwise, they dishonour their princes, and become ridiculous: therfore, the ministers which are the ambassadors of the highest prince, Malachi 2, 2 Corinthians 5, must have some mettall in them.*

4. Az there can be no trewe embassadours with-out the choise, and sendinge of hiz owne prince: so, can there be no lawful minister with-out Christ hiz trewe callinge, and sendinge; this callinge the ministerye of the Churche of Englande wanteth: therfore their mettle [metal] is counterfeit, and they by the juste judgment of God, become vilde [vile] and contemnptible in the eyez of al men. Jeremiah 14: 15. Ezekiel 22: 18, 19. Micah 4: 7. John 10: 1.

[p. 7] [Dr. Some] [5]*A learned teacher is a singular blessing: for hee feedeth God's people with knowledge and understanding. Jeremiah 3.*

5. How unlike your popishe ministerye, wherof you so boaste, iz to theize holye men, who uprightlye walked in the counsells of God: let the godlye judge by the Scripturez.

[Dr. Some] *Therefore an ignorant minister is a grievous plague,[6] for he cannot strengthen the weake, heale the sicke, binde together the broken. Ezechiel 34.*

6. In the tyme of the lawe the plaguye [*sic*], and leaprous were to be removed out of the campe, muche lesse in the tyme of the

gospel are they to be admitted to administer the sacraments: nether iz it safe to receive them at their handez. Nombers 5: 2.

[Dr. Some]   *The popish[7] and Anabaptisticall sorte have done great hurt in this land.*

7. Let it be descided [*sic*] by the worde, whether suche popishe ministers, (az you), which enter in, and rule by the pope's canons, and receive into the bozome of your churche, al fleshlye libertines, atheistes, and hereetikes what-soever, be troublers of the lande, or we that deteste theirs, and al other heresiez. Luke 23: 14. Acts 24.

[Dr. Some]   *Where teaching is not, the people are in a wofull case. Solomon sayeth, Where prophecie (that is, the ex-pounding[8] of God's word) is not, the people perish Proverbs 29: [18].*

8. Then by your owne confession, the bare readinge of the worde, iz not (*verbum aedificans*) an edyfieynge worde, az page 24 you say it [line] 14.[1]

[Dr. Some]   *Where sounde teachers[9] are placed, these commoditities [sic] are apparant: first, Almightie God is notablie served. Secondly, the prince is dutifullie obeyed. Thirdly, the enemie to religion is either wonne or descried.*

9. Where false prophets, and tyme-servers have the dealinge with the worde, a false worship iz advannced. The prince [is] unfaithfullye served. The enimyez to religion, nether des-cryed, nor rezisted: but al theize enormetyez are apparantlye with you, there-fore, even there-by it appeareth, of what sorte your teachers, and teachinge are.

[p. 8] [Dr. Some] *All which love the religion, have and doe desire a greater number of able teachers, that our church[10] may have more beautie, our prince more honour, our people more heavenly comfort.*

10. The trewe churche of Christ hath not more bitter enimyez than suche false prophets az you be, which like grievous wolvez make havocke of Christ hiz poore shepe, by imprizonment and confiscation, make no conscience of Godd his lawez, and had

---

[1] Dr. Some wrote: "The unpreaching ministers doe adde (*verbum aedificans*) that is, an edifying worde, to the administration of the Holy Supper, therefore, *etc.* (*A Godly Treatise* [1588], p. 24). Proverbs 29: 18 may be misinterpreted by Dr. Some. It reads: "Where there is no vision, the people perish."

rather make Christe your cooke: than your kinge.   Nehemiah
4: 3, 12, 13 etc.   Ezekiel 13: 10, *etc.*   Micah 4: 5.

[Dr. Some]   *To provide maintenance[1] for the teachers, is to shew
kindnes to the Lorde's house, Nehemiah 13, verse 14.*

1. The trewe provizion, and maintenance of the churche of
Christe, can neither be bought, nor soulde: becauze, it iz the
free contribution of God hiz faithful people, az neede requireth.
Acts 2: 45, and 4: 34, 35 and 11: 29, 30.   Romans 12: 13. 1
Corinthians 16: 1, 2, 3, 4.   2 Corinthians 8 and 9 chapters.
Galatians 6: 6.   1 Timothy 5: 16.

[Dr. Some]   *What then is their kindenesse, which sell church
livings as Judas did Christ?[2]*

2. You not with-out highe blasphemye can compare your popishe
benefices to the sacred person of Christ.

[p. 9] [Dr. Some]   *The abominable sale and marchandise of church[3]
livings, is cried out against in court, citie, and universities.*

3. Suche popishe livingez, az you pleade, and crye out for, are
fitter for courtes, cityes, and countryes: than for the churche
of God. Luke 22: 25, 26.   2 Timothy 2: 4.

[Dr. Some]   *The polling [plundering] and sale of church[4] livings
is so common that it cannot, and so shamelesse that it
will not, be hidde.*

4. There could be no sellers, if there were no buyers, and thus
before you be aware, you lay open the filthines of your churche,
in pleadinge for your bellye.

[Dr. Some]   *To forsake the house of God, is a heinous sinne: not to
provide[5] for the teachers, is to forsake the house of God,
Nehemiah 10 and 13 chapters.*

5. The faithful servantes of God alwayez carefullye provide for
their faithful teachers, who content them-selvez with foode,
and rayment: but how farre your lordly prelatts, the Romishe
churche-men are degenerate from the simplicitye of the gospel,
theire princelye pallaicez, lardge revenewez, and fat livingez,
declare. 1 Corinthians 9: 7.   1 Thessalonians 5: 12, 13.   1
Timothy 5: 17, 18 and 6: 6, 7, 8, *etc.*

[Dr. Some]   *It is a grosse sinne to spoyle either the souldier or the
merchant adventurer, which in their places are a
singular defence to their countrey by sea and land:
therefore it is a more heinous sinne to robbe churchmen,*

Reply to Dr. Some's A Godly Treatise

> *which (as Elias) are the chariots[6] and horsemen of the common wealth.[1]*

6. You are to the children of God, az the chariots, and horse-men of Egipt, to the commonwealthe, or unsatiable horse-leachez, which ever crye, give give. Exodus 14: 9. Proverbs 30: 15.

[Dr. Some] *The weapons[7] of our warrefare (saith the apostle) are not carnall, but mighty through God . . . 2 Corinthians 10.*

7. You are so whollye disarmed by your lordes the bishopps, az you have not lefte you so muche, az a weedinge-hooke, or pitche-forke, to cast out your Romishe dounge. 1 Samuel 13: 19, 20, 21, 22.

[Dr. Some] *The repairing of churches[8] is to be performed carefully.*

8. The temple of God nowe consisteth not of lyme, and stone: but of faithful men, who are kept, and repayred by the faithful ministerye of the worde. 1 Corinthians 3: 16, 17. Hebrews 3: 6. 1 Peter 2: 4, 5.

[Dr. Some] *The priests' maintenance[9] in Joas' time,[2] neither was nor might be abridged for repairing of the churches.*

9. Your Romishe priesthood iz still mayntained by Jewishe tithes, and offeringez: then, the more sinnes, the more sacrificez, now the more of suche offeringez, the more sinnes, becauze, thoze ceremonyez are abrogate. Ezeckiel 13: 19. Hosea 4: 8. Collossians 2.

[p. 10] [Dr. Some] *Skilfull teachers doe plough the Lord's[10] field, and are the Lord's, both mouth and hands to deliver his blessings and treasure unto us.*

10. The Lorde's fielde lyeth waste, and untilled, ful of bryers, and brambles, thorowe your evil husbandrye, az there-fore, you have sowen: so shal you reape worme-wodd [wood] in stea[d] of bread. Hosea 10: 4. Amos 6: 12.

[Dr. Some] *Therefore they ought to have defence and maintenance, and not to wander[11] as Michas' priest did. Judges 17.*

11. Your rovinge ministerye, and mercenarye chaplaines, are not knowen in the church of Christe, where everye minister hathe his peculier charge to attende upon. Acts 20: 28.

[Dr. Some] *Church[12] pollers [despoilers] shut up the kingdome of heaven before men: for they themselves goe not in, neither suffer they them that woulde enter to come in:*

---

1 1 Kings 18: 44 ; II Kings 2: 11.
2 Joaz, Joash, or Jehoash. See II Kings 12: 4-5.

> *therefore the woe denounced [pronounced] by Christ against the Scribes and Pharisees, seazeth upon them. Matthew 23.*

12. Our teacher Christ Jesus applyed this place to suche prowde Pharisyez, and counterfeit Scribez, az Doctor Some, and hiz compagnyons are. Matthew 23: 13.

[Dr. Some] *Ezechias[13] the king of Juda commanded that the priestes and Levites shoulde have maintenance, and that their wives, children and families shoulde bee provided for. 2 Chronicles 31, verses 4, 18.*

13. Ezechias did neither systayne unlawful priestes, neither compel the people to geve the trewe priestes unlawful mayntenance.

[Dr. Some] *Divers famous princes have had some churchmen to be of their honorable councel: Jehoida was in King Joas' court.[14] 2 Chronicles 24.*

14. The highe priest might not by the lawe, goe out of the precinct of the temple, where-of he tooke the chardge, much lesse not live in the kinge's court. The kinges in matters of doubte were to aske at the prieste's mouthe, who in suche casez, waz to consult, by Urim and Thummim,[1] for him, *etc.* It requireth a lardge discourse, to shewe howe insufferablye you abuze, and perverte theize places. Exodus 28: 30. Leviticus 10: 7 and 22: 12. Nombers 27: 21. 1 Samuel 23: 9.

[Dr. Some] *Zadok and Abiathar [were] in David and Solomon's court.[15] 2 Samuel 20. I Kings 4. Daniel in Darius' court. Daniel 6.*

15. You can-not upholde your antichristian prelacye by the highe priesthood: neither, committ civil majestracye to churche-ministers, with-out abrogatinge the testament of Christe. Matthew 20: 25, 26. Luke 12: 14. Romans 12: 7. Ephesians 4: 10, 11, 12, 13. Hebrews 8: 1, 2, 13. 2 Timothy 2: 4. 1 Peter 5: 2, 3.

[p. 11] [Dr. Some] *It is Queene[16] Elizabeth's pleasure, that the worthiest men shoulde be advanced for the governement and service of the church.*

16. Seinge it iz the queen's pleazure, that trewe religion should be advansed, and the trewe governement of the churche restored: how cometh it to passe, that theize lordlye bishoppes reigne over the churche, by their popishe canons, and traditions,

---

[1] Urim and Thummim. Deuteronomy 33: 8.

persecutinge [them?] and raginge against suche, az stande for
the sinceritye of the gospel?

[Dr. Some] Question. *Whether such things as were given for
the maintenance of idolatry, may, and ought to be
converted to the service of God?*
Answere. *They may, and ought. My reasons are:
If men should convert them to their private[17] use, it
might be justly thought, that in abolishing superstition, private gaine is the marke which is shot at, and
not the advancing of God's religion. August. epist.*
154.[1]

17. If your tithes, and offeringes were restored to the people, who
are the trewe owners of them, [and?] your lordlye revenewes,
with your parson hiz gleabe landes, etc., to the prince, and
realme, to whome they are dewe: then should the churche be
delivered from theize grievous wolvez, and restoared to her
faithful guides, and watche-men, the common wealthe flourishe
in prosperitye, Christ hiz trewe religion be advaunced, and al
idolatrye, and superstition abolished.

[Dr. Some] *Eleazer the priest tooke the brasen[18] censers, which
they that were burnt had offered, and made broad plates
of them for a covering of the altar. Numbers 16.*

18. Korah hiz censers were pronounced holy by God him-selfe.
Nombers 16: 38. And might rather stande a feareful monument to suche presumptuous shepheardez, and intruders, az
Doctor Some, and others; than anye waye geve libertye to
burden the churche with needlesse, and superstitious ceremonyez.

[Dr. Some] *The gold,[19] silver, the vessels of brasse and iron in
Jericho, were brought into the Lorde's treasury.
Joshua 6.*

19. The goulde, silver, *etc.*, of Jericho were by expresse commaundement rezerved: reteyned neither any idolatrous shape,
nor supersticious use, beinge wrought, and applyed to the
holy use of the tabernacle: but the rezervation of your Romishe
trumperye boeth wanteth commaundement from God, retay-
neth an idolatrous fourme, and supersticious use. Exodus 25:
40. Deuteronomy 7: 26 and 13: 17, 18. Joshua 6: 19.

[p. 12] [Dr. Some] *Gedeon did offer unto the Lorde,[20] a bullocke which*

---

[1] *Sancti Aurelii Augustini Hipponensis Episcopi Opera Omnia* (Paris, 1836),
p. 166.

> had bin fed for Baal's service, and did use the wood
> of the grove adjoyning. Judges 6.

20. It waz wel, that Gideon had an especial commaundement from
the mouthe of God: else might you aswel alter the lawe of the
altar, the place, the preist, the sacrifize, the [tyme ?], here-by
al theize in this example disagreeinge from the written worde:
but this with all Jerubbaal waz famous for destroyinge Baal,
[Doctor] Some for pleadinge for Baal. Leviticus 17: 3, 4, 5.
Nombers 3: 10.

[Dr. Some] *If such thinges as were given to the maintenance of*
poperie, may not be converted to the service of God,
then pull downe churches and universities, take away
their landes, etc., and let atheisme be in steade of
God's religion, and Macciavell in the place of the
New Testament.[21]

21. Seinge, theize churche-liveingez, and universityes have the
same popishe original, and retayne the same incurable abuses;
seinge, our soveraigne prince, hathe az good right to them, az
her progenitours to the abbyez, and az expresse commaundement from the Lorde, for the abolishinge theize, with assured
promise of hiz blessinge: she need not feare the vaine divination of false prophets, nor be hindered by any pollitique
impediment of Macchiavel. Deuteronomy 12: 3, 12 and
13: 12 and 18: 22. Judges 2: 2, 3.

[Dr. Some] *The Holy*[1] *Ghost setteth out in lively colours, the*
consequents of teaching and embracing the Lorde's
religion.

1. The comfortable assurance of the Lorde'z promisez may take
awaye al politique, and fleshlye feares of insurrections, and
inwarde tumults, where God hiz religion iz trulye advanced,
because, the lande shal be filled with the knowledge of God,
the people humble to the obedience of hiz will, endevoringe
to kepe the unitye of the spirit, in the bonde of peace. Leviticus
26: 3 *etc.* Deuteronomy 4: 6. 1 Kings 2: 2, 3, 4. Romans
13: 5, 6. Ephesians 4: 2, 3.

[Dr. Some] *Wicked men*[2] *which in cruell affections resemble the*
wolfe, the leoparde, the beare, shall cast off the chaine
of pride, and the garment of crueltie, and shall goe
hand in hand with the godlie, who for their innocencie
are compared to the lambe, the cowe, the kidde.

2. But into the bozome of your churche, are received al sortes of

wilde beastes, az tigers, wolvez, foxez, with al their feirce, and
untamed affections: where-uppon ensuethe continual insurrections, contentions, wronges, suites, and debates, and the
violente oppressinge, and persecutinge of God hiz faithful
servantes, which altogether declare, what kinde of religion
you have.

IX

BARROW'S THIRD EXAMINATION

JANUARY 1, 1588/9

This examination is known to us by a manuscript fragment, in Harley Manuscripts 6848, f. 28 *verso*. It breaks off at the end of the page and in the middle of a sentence. One explanation is that the remainder has been lost. Again, it is possible that Barrow never finished it. One other possibility is that this sheet—not written by Barrow but conceivably by a cellmate—was seized by the authorities in their rifling of the prisoners' cells.

The date of this examination is January 1, 1588/9. It is sometimes difficult to ascertain whether January 1 or March 25 is used as the beginning of the year. Barrow regularly speaks of January as the first month, April as the fourth month, and September as the ninth month. Therefore, we would expect the year to begin with January 1, but dates between January 1 and March 25 are frequently given in Old Style, as in this examination. Since Dr. Some's book was published in May, 1588, the date for discussing it could not be January 1, 1587/8, but must be January 1, 1588/9. Corroborating evidence is obtained from the reference to the Fleet prison. On January 1, 1587/8, Barrow was in the Gatehouse. On January 1, 1588/9, he was in the Fleet. Perhaps the explanation is that since Barrow, in reporting his examinations, gives only the month and the day, the year has been supplied by a scribe, an editor, or a copyist friend, in varying styles of reckoning time.

*　　*　　*　　*　　*　　*

BARROW'S THIRD EXAMINATION

JANUARY 1, 1588/9

The first [of] January. 1588 [1588/9]
" Behold I send yow as sheep in the middest of wolves."[1] Uppon the first day of the first monethe, came into my chamber in the Fleet, being close prysoner ther, Mr. Justice Yonge,[2] Doctor Some,[3] with the Warden of the Fleete;[4] wher Mr. Yonge, makinge knowne unto me that they were sent from the Lordes of the [Privy] Councell unto me, drew out of his bosome a booke writen by Doctor Soame agaynst the recusantes of their English churche:[5] which booke was answered in certaine marginall notes.[6]

---

[1] Matthew 10: 16 and Luke 10: 3.
[2] Richard Young.
[3] Robert Some.
[4] Probably Edward Tirrell, who was Warden of the Fleet in 1581, 1582, 1583, 1587, 1588, and very likely later. Joachim Newton was Deputy Warden in 1587, 1590, 1597, and very likely during the entire period. John Calton (or Cawlton) is mentioned in the State Papers as Warden in 1584 and 1586. See the index for these years in the *Calendar of State Papers, Domestic*; *Acts of the Privy Council*; see also Augustus Jessopp (ed.), *The Oeconomy of the Fleete*, New Series, Vol. XXV of the Camden Society (Westminster, 1879). There is also some relevant material in Lansdowne MSS. 85, items 49, 51, 52, 53, and Lansdowne MSS. 157, item 43, on conditions in the Fleet and complaints of prisoners.
[5] *A Godly Treatise Containing and Deciding Certaine Questions, Moved of Late in London and Other Places, Touching the Ministerie, Sacraments, and Church* (London, 1588). The preface to the reader begins: " Two sortes of recusantes are in this land: the one popish, the other Anabaptisticall. They give out, that wee have no ministery, no sacraments, no visible church."
[6] That is, Barrow had written or dictated his replies in the margin of Dr. Some's book. This annotated book was probably seized by the authorities, but evidently Barrow set to work again. This time he answered Dr. Some on interleaved blank pages, but did not finish his task. Once again, his chamber was rifled of its possessions. I conjecture that when he reached page 12, his interleaved copy was seized. This is the same copy, I believe, which I used at Lambeth Palace Library (30.6.12). We may feel certain that there were two copies of Dr. Some's book seized and two replies, because the first was answered in marginal notes and extended through the entire book of 37 pages, with comments at least as far as the first two lines of page 35, and because the second copy was answered on interleaved pages and only through page 12.

171

Mr. Yonge.	Know you this booke or this hande ?
Barrow.	I know the booke, not the hande.
Yonge.	Will you avouche the booke befor these witnesses ?
Barrowe.	I know not what may be in the booke, but if it be as I suppose, and nothinge added to it by others, I dare avouch it.
Soame.	You may peruse it.
Barrow.	The tyme now suffereth not.
Dr. Soame.	You wrote it, belike.
Barrow.	It may be I was privie to the writinge of it.[1]
Soame.	You will then avouch it.
Barrow.	I know not what may be in the booke, but if you will aske me concerninge anye parte of it, I will tell you.
Soame.	Therfore was my comminge.
	And then he turned to the last leaf[2] concerning the Church of England wheruppon his sainge was that their church had Christ to be their head. It was answered that some of them made their churche to have two heades, which say that the queen's majesty is supreame head in earthe of their church.
Yong.	And Yonge asked me whether I would abyde by it.
Barrow.	I answered yea.
Soame.	Take witnesses.
	And then a great discourse of the majestrate's power, which not framing to his purpose he sayd[3]

---

[1] This may be an evasive answer, or it may suggest that Barrow personally did not write the answers. Perhaps he used an amanuensis—possibly Greenwood or some other fellow-prisoner. Barrow was not permitted to have ink, pen, and paper, but he managed to obtain them despite the vigilance of the prison authorities and the orders of the archbishop.

[2] This reference to the last leaf helps to identify Dr. Some's book as the first edition of *A Godly Treatise Containing and Deciding Certaine Questions, Moved of Late in London and Other Places, Touching the Ministerie, Sacraments, and Church.* There are two editions of this work, the first dated May 6, 1588, and the second dated September 19, 1588 (see signature F ii *verso*). Whereas the first edition has 37 pages, the second (with its long reply to Penry) has 200 pages. Barrow's reference to the " last leaf " should be " next to the last leaf," or otherwise to the last *section*, which is entitled " The Church of England is the Visible Church of Christ." See pages 34-35 of the first edition, pages 33-34 of the second edition.

[3] Here the page ends, and the narrative breaks off.

X

BARROW'S FOURTH EXAMINATION

MARCH 18, 1588/89

There are two versions of this examination. One is printed on signatures B iii *recto*—C *verso* (pp. 13-18) of *The Examinations of Henry Barrowe John Grenewood and John Penrie* [Dort ? —1593-96]. The other is in Harley Manuscripts 6848, ff. 14 *recto*—18 *recto*. It is likely that Barrow wrote the account of his examination within two or three days, and then smuggled out the sheets. Then copies were made for the use of the brethren. One of these, I believe, is Harley Manuscripts 6848, ff. 14 *recto*—18 *recto*, and probably another was used for the printed version which appeared sometime between 1593 and 1596. The two versions vary slightly. Therefore, I have collated them and have reproduced the printed version, together with the manuscript variations. Where there are differences, I have indicated the variants in the manuscript version within round brackets. Any editorial material to clarify or supplement the text is included within square brackets.

The task of ascertaining the correct date of this examination has caused me considerable time and thought. The most probable dates are March 18, 1587/8, July 18, 1588, March 18, 1588/9. Professor Powicke gives March 18, 1587/8, as the date of Barrow's fourth examination, but this is an error. Barrow's first examination occurred on November 19, 1587, not 1586, as Powicke gives it. The second examination fell on November 27, 1587, not 1586. The third examination occurred on January 1, 1588/9, which Powicke omits, and the fourth examination is the present one, as Powicke suggests, but with the wrong year (*Henry Barrow, Separatist*, pp. 16, 19, 20, 24, 34). We may eliminate March 18, 1587/8, as a possibility because at that date Barrow was in the Gatehouse at Westminster, whereas at the time of this examination he is a close prisoner in the Fleet.

The question therefore is whether July 18, 1588, or March 18, 1588/9, is the correct date. The best argument for July 18, 1588, is that this is the date distinctly given in the title of Harley MSS. 6848, folio 14 *recto*. Then follows the first line of the text, which begins: " Uppon the 18th daye of this present monethe." Furthermore, the comptroller of Archbishop Whitgift's household, Sir George Paule (*Life of . . . John Whitgift*, p. 45) says that on July 20, 1588, Barrow and Greenwood, after being free on bond, were recommitted to the Fleet. This at least would suggest that July 18, 1588, could be the true date.

But there are several difficulties in accepting this date. One difficulty is that in July the Spanish Armada was approaching the English shores, and it is unlikely that Lord Burghley, Lord Chancellor Hatton, and Lord Buckhurst would be holding court for Barrow and his followers. Another difficulty is that Lord Burghley was ill on July 16-17, and on the morning of July 18 he was still confined to his bed, though hoping to get out of the house that day (*Calendar of State Papers, Domestic, of the Reign of Elizabeth*, 1581-1590, pp. 503-505). Lord Buckhurst was in Sussex, along the coast, in July. Barrow was never given his liberty, and Greenwood was out of prison in 1592 for a brief time, but not in 1588.

Moreover, the testimony of Sir George Paule is not to be always trusted, since he was an apologist for Archbishop Whitgift. He speaks of John Udall, "whose pardon the Archbishop afterwards obtained," whereas in fact Udall was kept in prison, ladened with irons, and died because of his prison ordeal. Sir George Paule says further that " the fore-said brochers of these opinions [Barrow and Greenwood] at this their first convention [November, 1587, before the High Commissioners] made shew of their conformitie, upon conference with some devines ; and in hope thereof, were enlarged upon bonds ; but all in vaine. For after their libertie, they burst forth into further extremities, and were againe committed to the Fleete, July 20, 1588, where they published their scandalous and seditious writings ; for which they were proceeded with all at Justice-Hall, neere Newgate in London, March 21, 1592 " [March 22-23, 1592/3]. The difficulty here is that Barrow and Greenwood never " made shew of their conformitie," but gloried in their nonconformity. There is evidence that Greenwood may have been free in the summer of 1592, but none whatsoever for Barrow. All the evidence indicates that Barrow remained continuously in prison, from November 19, 1587, until his execution on April 6, 1593. Furthermore, even if we assume the full truth of Paule's statement, it does not necessarily follow that an examination of July 18 preceded the imprisonment of July 20.

What then are the evidences which point toward March 18, 1588/9, as the correct date ? One immediate argument is that the first printed edition [*ca.* 1593-96] of Barrow's examination carried the date March 18, with no year mentioned, in the very first line—" the 18 day of the 3. monethe." The second argument is that the manuscript of Barrow's examination seems to be a copy and not the original. Whether it is earlier or later than the printed copy does not seem to be determinable. Thirdly, Robert Some and Richard Young were present at Barrow's examination. Both men conferred with Barrow on January 1, 1588/9, but there is no mention of a conference prior to that date. Since Barrow's examination includes references to a conference with Dr. Some and Justice Young, it must have been after his conference. In May, 1589, Dr. Some published his book, entitled *A Godly Treatise, Wherein Are Examined and Confuted Many Execrable Fancies.* In the Epistle Dedicatorie, dated May 12, 1589, Dr. Some speaks of the Anabaptistical sort who were "very bold of late. They preassed into her majestie's presence: they complained to her highness of great persecution: how justly, your lordships [Sir Christopher Hatton and Lord Burghley] knowe, which by the queene's commandement did examine and commit them. Henry Barrowe and John Greenewood are the masters of that college."

175

This statement fits in with the supposition that the " Lamentable Petition Delivered to the Queene's Majestye the 13 of March 1588 [1588/9] " is the one intended, and that as a consequence the queen appointed a special commission to examine the Barrowists—an event occurring five days later—March 18. Furthermore, the petition of March 13 requests a hearing before some of the Privy Council—this being granted by the appointment of three councillors—Hatton, Burghley, and Buckhurst. The petition of March 13 has the phrase " to drawe out your sword of Justice,"—an expression which may reveal the pen of Barrow, since we find him replying in the examination of March 18 as follows: " It is a wooful [*sic*] thinge that our prynce's sword shoulde be drawen out against her faythfull subjectes."

Another bit of corroborating evidence supporting the March 18, 1588/89, date instead of the July 18, 1588, date is that Barrow saw twelve of the brethren in a withdrawing chamber. In a petition to Lord Burghley [March, 1589/90], Christopher Bowman states that he and eleven others presented a petition to her majesty in March, that the Privy Council committed them prisoners, and that he has been a prisoner for one year since March 17 [1588/89] in the Wood Street Counter.

Edward Arber has misled students by suggesting that July 18, 1588, is the date on which the manuscripts of the Separatists were *seized* (*An Introductory Sketch to the Martin Marprelate Controversy*, 1588-1590, pp. 35-40). There is no evidence for this assertion and it is obviously an error. He assumes that the " Lamentable Petition " is 1588, but the correct date is 1588/9. He dates a related document in the same collection, which is a list of prisoners, as May or June, 1588, but this is one year too early, as references to nineteen months of imprisonment (from October 8, 1587) prove. He suggests that Barrow's report of his examination was seized on July 18, 1588, but the examination did not occur until eight months later. He dates Barrow's examination as March, 1588, when Barrow was in the Gatehouse, but the examination itself tells us that

Barrow was a close prisoner in the Fleet. The conclusion is that March 18, 1588/9, is the correct date.

This is the most interesting of Barrow's examinations. In one sense, Barrow is before the queen herself, since she was virtually present in her Privy Council. She had received the bitter Barrowist petition of March 13, 1588/9, " A Lamentable Petition Delivered to the Queene's Majestye the 13 of March 1588 [1588/9] " [Harley Manuscripts 6848, ff. 18 *verso*—20 *recto*], which pleaded for " some christian consideration and speedy redresse of the outragious wronges and most extreame injuries " which her true hearted subjects had suffered at the hands of the Archbishop of Canterbury and the Bishop of London. Thereupon, she had ordered a hearing, and five days later, Barrow was hurriedly brought to Whitehall. The hearing was held in the chamber of the Lord Chancellor, Sir Christopher Hatton, who presided. With him were Archbishop Whitgift, Bishop Aylmer, Lord Burghley, Lord Buckhurst, Doctor Robert Some, Justice Richard Young, and others.

This occasion was Barrow's golden opportunity to make a favourable impression upon the privy councillors and to prove that the ecclesiastical commissioners were wrong. Instead, Barrow curbed neither his spirit nor his tongue, and alienated the sympathies of Lord Burghley and Lord Buckhurst. He gave the impression of being dogmatic, fanatic, querulous, and arbitrary. Instead of bridling his tongue, he was needlessly outspoken, and he seemed never to have learned the lesson of Proverbs 15: 1 that " a soft answer turns away wrath, but a harsh word stirs up anger." The result was that Barrow was remanded to prison, there to ponder the stinging admonitions of the privy councillors and to indulge in second thoughts and regrets.

*   *   *   *   *   *

G

[B iii *recto*]   MR. BARROWE HIS EXAMINATION AT
[Folio 14 *recto*]   THE COURTE BY THE COUNSAYLE.
                       JULY 18. ANNO DOMINI 1588.

[MARCH 18, 1588/9].

Upon the 18 day of the 3 (this present)[1] moneth, I, Henry Barrowe, close prisoner in the Fleet, was sent for in al post hast by one Ragland,[2] a gentleman of the Lord Chancellor's, to his lorde's chamber at the court at White-hall: wher being arrived, I found in a withdrawing chamber twelve of the brethren,[3] among a great number of other attendantes with whom I could not have any one word. But after that Ragland had signified my coming, I was forthwith sent for into that chamber, where sate at the boord the Arch Bishop in his pontificalibus, the Lord Chancellor,[4] the Lord Treasurer,[5] the Lord Buckhurst,[6] the Bishop of London[7] in his pontificalibus: at the lower ende of the chamber stood Dr. [Robert] Some, Justice [Richard] Young and others.

Being kneeled downe at the end of the table, the Lord Treasurer began and asked me my name:

---

[1] March 18, 1588/9. The reference to "this present moneth" indicates that Barrow lost no time in recording his statements.

[2] Mr. Raglande seems to be a private employee of Sir Christopher Hatton. His name does not appear in the indices of the State Papers.

[3] These twelve probably included those who were responsible for presenting the "Lamentable Petition" of March 13, 1588/9, to Queen Elizabeth (Harley MSS. 6848, ff. 18 *verso*—20 *recto*). Christopher Bowman was one of the group and was imprisoned on March 17. (See his petition to Lord Burghley, in March, 1589/90, in Lansdowne MS. 109, f. 23). John Sparrow was also one of the petitioners (Ellesmere MS. 2145), and John Nicholas was a third one (Ellesmere MS. 2101). All three were imprisoned for more than three years (Ellesmere MSS. 2101, 2110, 2145).

[4] Sir Christopher Hatton.

[5] Lord Burghley.

[6] Thomas Sackville (1536-1608) was knighted and created Baron Buckhurst in 1567. He served as a privy councillor, and was engaged as a commissioner in state trials. He also served as a commissioner for ecclesiastical causes.

[7] John Aylmer, Bishop of London.

which when I had told him, he asked me if I had not bene sometime of the court: I answered that I had sometime frequented the court: he said he remembred me not.

[B iii *verso.*]

Lord Treasurer. Why are yow in prison, Barrowe?

Barrow. I am in prison, my lord, upon the statute made for recusantes.[1]

Lord Treasurer. Why wil yow (come) not goe to church?

Barrow. My whole desire is to come to the church of God.

Lord Treasurer. Thow art a fantastical fellow I (perceive) see, but why not to our churches?

Barrow. My lord, the causes are great and many; it were too long to shew them in particuler: but breifly [folio 14 *verso*], my lord, I can not come to your church

[1.] Because al the profane and wicked of the lande are received into the body of your church.

2. Yow have a false and antichristian ministery set over your church.

3. Neither worship yow God aright, but after an idolatrous and superstitious manner.

4. And your church is not governed by Christe's Testament (by the word of God), but by the Romish courtes and canons, *etc.*[2]

Lord Treasurer. Here is matter ynough indeed: I perceive thow takest delight to be an author of this new religion.

[Lord Chancellor]. The Lord Chancellor said he never heard such stuffe before in al his life.

Barrow. As I was about to shew that neither I was an author of this religion, and that it was not new,

[Bishop Aylmer]. as they supposed, the Bishop of London interrupted me, and asked me wherin their worship was idolatrous?

---

[1] This is the statute of 23 Elizabeth, *Caput* 1, entitled, " An Acte to Reteine the Queene's Majestie's Subjects in Their Due Obedience." See *Statutes of the Realm,* IV, Part I, 657-8.

[2] Barrow's oft-repeated four accusations or transgressions of the Church of England: false worship, false ministry, false membership, and false discipline or government.

Henry Barrow

[Lord Treasurer]. The Lord Treasurer also demaunded (asked) the same question.

Barrow. Ther is nothing else in that book of your common prayer: being demaunded some particulers, I shewed that their saintes' daies, eves, fastes, (are) idol fastes, *etc.*

London. Stay there: why is it not lawful to keep a memorial
[Bishop Aylmer] of the saintes in the church?

Barrow. Not after your manner: it is idolatrie.

London. How prove yow that?

Barrow. By the first commaundement.

London. Why? That is, thow shalt have no other Gods but me. What of that?

Barrow. The word is, thow shalt have no other Gods before my face. We are (ther) therfore forbidden to give any part of God's worship to any creature.

London. Why? Neither doe we.

Barrow. Yes, yow celebrate a day, and sanctifie an eave, and cal [f. 15 *recto*] them by their names. Yow make a (fast) feast and devise a worship unto them.

Lord Treasurer. Why? May we not cal the day after their names? Is not that in our libertie?

Barrow. No, my Lord.

Lord Treasurer. How prove yow that?

Barrow. In the beginning of the booke it is written that God himselfe (gave names and hathe) named al the dayes, the first, the second, *etc.*

Lord Treasurer. Why, then we may not cal them Sunday, Monday, *etc.*

Barrow. We are otherwise taught to cal them in the booke of God.

Lord Treasurer. Why, thow thy selfe callest it the Lorde's day.

Barrow. And so the Holy Ghost calleth it in the first of the Revelation [1: 10].

London. We have nothing in our saintes' dayes but that which is taken forth of the Scriptures.

Barrow. In that yow say (not) true, for (I can) yow finde no saintes' dayes in the Scriptures.

London. We finde their histories and deedes (dayes) in the Scripture.

Barrow. But not their (sainctes') dayes and festivals in the Scripture.

[Lord Buckhurst]. The Lord Buckhurst then said I was a proud spirit.

[Lord Treasurer]. The Lord Treasurer said I had a hotte braine: and taking into his hande a *Book of Common Prayer*, which lay on the boord, read certaine of the collectes for the [B iiii *recto*] saintes and shewed that the epistles and gospels were part of the Scripture: and asked me what I could mislike therin?

Barrow. I mislike al, for we ought not so to use Scriptures or prayers.

London. May we not make commemoration of the saintes'

Lord Treasurer. lives in the church.

Barrow. Not after yowr manner, to give peculiar dayes, eves, fastes, worship, feastes, unto them.

Lord Treasurer. But what is there idolatrous?

Barrow. Al, for we ought not so to use the Scriptures.

London. What? Not in commemoration of the saintes?

Barrow. As I have said, not after yowr manner.

Lord Treasurer. But what is evil here? [15 *verso*]

Barrow. Al, my lord, for by abusing the Scripture we may make it an idol. The circumstances make evil thinges, of themselves good, as in the massebook from whence this stuffe is fetched, there are sundry good collectes and (good) places of Scripture, which their superstitious abuse make abhominable and evil. Likewise conjurers make many good prayers, which the circumstances also make evil.

[Lord Buckhurst]. Here the Lord Buckhurst said I was out of my wittes.

Barrow. No, my Lord, I speak the wordes of sobernes and truth, as I could make plaine if I might be suffered.

Lord Treasurer. Here we pray that our lives may be such as theirs was (were), void of covetousnes.

Barrow. So ought we to doe, and not to reade or have any

parte of the Scripture without fruite, and to follow and flee that which we finde praised and discommended [censured, disapproved] in them: yet ought we not to use the Scriptures in this manner to dayes and times, neither to be thus restreyned (strayned) or stinted in our prayers, as to be tied to this forme of wordes, place, time, manner, kneele, stand, *etc.*

Lord Buckhurst. This fellow delighteth to heare himselfe speake.

[Lord Chancellor]. The Lord Chancellor also spake some what at that time, which I cannot cal to remembrance as yet.

[Archbishop]. Then the Arch Bishop also spake many thinges against me of smal effect, which I have also forgotten, onely this I remember: he said I was a strower (sower) of errors, and that therfore he committed me.

Barrow. In deed yow committed me halfe a yeare close prisoner in the Gatehowse, and I never until now understood the cause why, neither as yet know I what errors they be; shew them, therfore, I pray yow.[1]

[Lord Buckhurst]. The Lord Buckhurst againe said I was [16 *recto*] a presumptuous spirit.

Barrow. My lord—al spirits must be tried and judged by the word of God: but if I erre, my lord, it is meet I should be shewed wherin.

Lord Chancellor. Ther must be streighter lawes made for such fellowes.

Barrow. Would to God ther were, my lord, our journy should be the shorter.

---

[1] From November 19, 1587, to May, 1588, in the Gatehouse, at Westminster, near the west end of the Abbey. Barrow was committed for refusing to take the oath *ex officio*, and this he certainly knew, but he probably means he knew not why he was first apprehended without warrant and why he was arraigned before the High Commission. The answer is that the Archbishop had known of his "seditious" conversation, of his non-attendance at church, and possibly of some manuscript writings by November, 1587.

Lord Treasurer.	Yow complained to us of injustice.[1] Wherin have yow wrong ?
Barrow.	My lord, in that we are thus imprisoned without due trial.
Lord Treasurer.	Why ? Yow said yow were condemned upon the statute.
Barrow.	Unjustly, my lord, that statute was not made for us.[2]
Lord Treasurer.	Ther must be streighter lawes made for yow.
Barrow.	O my lord, speake more comfortablie, we have sorrowes ynough.
Lord Treasurer.	Indeed, thow lookest as if thow hadst a troubled conscience.
Barrow.	No, I praise God for [B iiii *verso*] it: but it is a woeful thing that our prince's sworde should thus be drawen against her faithful subjectes.[3]
[Lord Treasurer].	The Lord Treasurer answered that the queene's sword was not as yet drawen against us.
[Barrow].	Then in a word or two I complayned of the misery and lingring close imprisonment which we suffer.
[Lord Treasurer].	The Lord Treasurer demaunded if we had had no conference.
[London]. [Bishop Aylmer].	The Bishop of London answered that sundrie had bene with us, as D. [Dr. Robert] Some, Graviat [Gravyate], and others, but we mocked them that came unto us.
Barrow.	That is not true, the Lord knoweth: we mock no creature. Neither doe I know, or have ever

---

[1] The " Lamentable Petition Delivered to the Queene's Majestye the 13 of March, 1588 [1588/9] " prayed for " speedy redresse of the outragious wronges and most extreame injuryes wherewith sundrye of your most faythfull and true harted subjectes have bin a longe tyme and are at this present especially oppressed in all places by the BB. [bishops] of this lande." See the Appendix for this petition, in Volume IV.

[2] Barrow and the Puritans contended that the statute of 23 Elizabeth, *Caput* 1, was designed for papal recusants.

[3] This is suggestive of a similar statement in the " Lamentable Petition " of March 13, 1588/9, and may be an indication that Barrow was a penman, if not the penman, of the petition.

seene, to my remembrance, that Graviat[1] yow speak of. But miserable physitians are yow (they) al, for Mr. Some, he indeed was with me, but never would enter disputation: he said he came not therefore, but in reasoning (questioning) manner to know some what of my minde more cleerly (perfectly).

[Dr. Some]. [Dr.] Some was then by the Arch Bishop called and demaunded whither we had conference or no? Some shewed how that at our last conference [16 *verso*] before Sir A. G. (Sir Henry Goodyeard)[2] ther arose a question betwixt us, whither the prince might make a positive law *de rebus mediis*, of thinges indifferent: I denying it, he asked me whither she might make a statute for the reforming excesse of apparel?[3] I graunted that she might. He then said (that I held) it was a doctrine of divils to forbid meate by a positive law: he shewed me (and shewed him) then that the prince's law did not binde the conscience, and that ther is a difference betwixt (thinges civill and conscientiall) *forum civile* and *forum conscientiae*. Some (So much) to this effect.

[Richard Young]. [4]Mr. Young then uncalled came, and accused me of (arrogant and) unreverend speeches used against his lord's grace at my first conference

---

1 William Gravet was a prebendary of St. Paul's and vicar of St. Sepulchre's. He was mentioned (1582) as suitable to confer with seminary priests, but Martin Marprelate describes him as a drunkard. *Cf.* Peel, *A Seconde Parte of a Register*, II, 161. On June 3, 1588, with eight others, he was appointed by Whitgift as a licenser of books. Arber, in *An Introductory Sketch*, p. 51, and in the *Stationers' Register*, III, 690, is in error in giving June 30 as the date and in listing eight instead of nine licensers. See W. W. Greg and E. Boswell, *Records of the Court of the Stationers' Company, 1576 to 1602 — from Register B*, pp. 28-9.

2 Sir Henry Goodere, father of Anne, who is Drayton's gracious lady. The first conference was an examination on January 1, 1588/9, conducted by Dr. Some and Justice Young.

3 It is interesting to peruse a volume such as Humfrey Dyson's *A Booke Containing All Such Proclamations, as Were Published during the Raigne of the Late Queene Elizabeth* (London, 1618), and see the number of proclamations by the queen forbidding excesses in women's apparel.

4 Richard Young, justice of the peace for the county of Middlesex, and a persecutor of nonconformists. There are frequent references to him in the calendars of State Papers and the *Acts of the Privy Council*. See also Albert Peel, *The Notebook of John Penry*, 1593, xx, 49-52, 55, 69.

	with Some in my chamber:[1] so they were dismissed.
[Barrow].	Then I beseeched the lords to graunt a publicke conference that it might appeare to al men what we held and where we erred.
[Archbishop].	The Arch Bishop in great choller said we should have no publicke conference; we had published to much (inough) already,[2] and therfore he now committed us (I commit you) close prisoners.
Barrow.	But contrary to law.
[Lord Treasurer].	The Lord Treasurer said it might be upon such occasions done by law: and asked whither I had any learning (or no) ?
[Whitgift]. [Aylmer].	Canterbury and London with one consent answered togither that I had no learning.
Barrow.	The Lord knoweth I am ignorant, I have no learning to boast of: but this I know, that yow are voide of al true learning and godlines (good lives).
Lord Buckhurst.	See the spirit of this man.
[Barrow]. [Whitgift].	Then requested I conference againe, and that in writing: which was againe by Canterbury very peremtorilie (princely) denyed. He said that he had matter to cal me before him for an hereticke.[3]
Barrow.	That shal yow never doe: yow know my former answer (well) to that matter: wel, erre I may,

---

[1] There were at least two conferences with Dr. Some. This is very likely the one held January 1, 1588/9. The second one was held sometime between January 1, 1588/9, and March 18, 1588/9, before Sir Henry Goodere and Dr. Some.

[2] No books had been printed by March, 1588/9, but manuscript works by Barrow were evidently in circulation, such as *A Breefe Sum of Our Profession*, and *A Brief Summe of the Causes of Our Seperation*, *Four Causes of Separation*, and *Profes of Aparant Churche*. Perhaps a manuscript of *A True Description out of the Worde of God, of the Visible Church* was already known. Barrow's *A Pastoral Letter from Prison* and Greenwood's *Fragment of a Letter* were already written.

[3] Six days later, on March 24, 1588/9, Barrow was summoned before a special commission of five judges, the archbishop, and two bishops, to answer for his " heresy " by being presented with a formal list of cunningly contrived articles. Barrow spoke with strong feeling to William Hutchinson about this interrogation, and said the bishops had perpetrated the greatest wrong that had ever been done to any Christian in any age (*A Collection of Certaine Sclaunderous Articles Gyven Out by the Bisshops*, signature D 2 *verso*).

185

	but hereticke, by the grace of God, wil I never be.[1] [17 *recto*].
Lord Buckhurst.	That is wel said.
[Lord Treasurer].	The Lord Treasurer then taking up a paper of Some's abstract questions (some of Soame's his abstracted questions), which lay among the bishop's evidence against me, read this: that I held it unlawful (for Parliament) to enacte a law that the ministers shal live by tithes, or the people pay them, and demaunded of me whither I held tithes unlawful (lawfull).
Barrow.	My Lord, they are abrogated and unlawful.
Lord Treasurer.	Why, thou wouldest [C.i *recto*] have the minister live of somewhat; wherof should he live?
Barrow.	*Ex pura eleemosyna,* of clere almes (cleane almesdeedes) as Christ in his Testament hath ordeyned, and as he and his apostles.[2]
Lord Treasurer.	But how if the people wil not give?
Barrow.	Such are not the people of God.
Lord Treasurer.	But what shal the ministers doe (teache) in the meane time?
Barrow.	Not stand a minister to such, neither take the goods of the prophane.
Lord Treasurer.	Where canst thow shew me now in the Scriptures that the ministers now ought not to live upon tithes?
Barrow.	I took the Bible and turned to these two places: Hebrews 7: 12. (Hebrews 12), Galatians 6: 6, in the one where tithes are abrogate: in the other, that an other provision is made for them.
[Aylmer]. [Whitgift].	London began the cavil at the wordes, *pure* and *cleere (cleane) almes*: Canterbury (he began also to cavell) at the place in the Hebrews, saying that the author's intent was to prove an abrogation of the preisthood.

---

[1] Barrow made the same reply to the archbishop in the examination of November 19, 1587.

[2] Dr. Some included this material in his book published in May, 1589, *A Godly Treatise, wherein Are Examined and Confuted Many Execrable Fancies,* pp. 7-9. It is not found in his work, published in May, 1588, *A Godly Treatise Containing and Deciding Certaine Questions,* although the topic is included (pp. 6-12).

186

Barrow. Why, the wordes of the text are these: " If the preisthod be changed, then of necessitie must ther be a change of the law ":[1] and yow cannot deny but that tithes were a part of that law: alleging Numbers 18.

Lord Treasurer. What? Wouldst thow have him to have al my goodes?

Barrow. No, my lord, but I would have yow to withhold none of your goodes from helping him; neither rich nor pore are exempted from this duty. Furder I shewed that if the Minister had thinges necessarie (to this lyef), as food and rayment, he ought to hold him self contented; neither [17 *verso*] ought the church to give him more. Then had we some talke concerning the word " preist ": The Lord Treasurer said that the ministers now were not to be called preistes.

Barrow. If they receive tithes they are preistes. Moreover, they be called preistes in the law.

London. Why, what is the word presbyter, I pray yow?

Barrow. An elder.

London. What, in age onely?

Barrow. No. Timothie was a yong man.

London. Presbyter is Latine for a preist.[2]

Barrow. It is no Latine word, but derived, and signifieth the same which the Greek word doth, which is an elder.

London. What makest thow a preist?

(Lord Chaunccllor). (Why? What make you a preyst?)

Barrow. Him that doth offer sacrifices, for so it is written every where in the law.

[Lord Chancellor]. As we were thus reasoning, the Lord Chancellor asked me if I knew not those two men (pointing to Canterbury and London).

Barrow. Yes, my Lord, I have cause to know them.

---

1 Hebrews 7: 12.

2 Arber has wrongly assigned this error to the Lord Chancellor, Christopher Hatton (*An Introductory Sketch*, p. 47). Evidently following Arber, the latest biographer of Hatton has foisted on him an error of ignorance or misstatement that belongs to Bishop Aylmer (Eric St. John Brooks, *Sir Christopher Hatton, Queen Elizabeth's Favorite*, pp. 341-2). The manuscript reading is Lond. [London, Bishop of], not Lord.

Lord Chancellor. But what [?] Is not this the Bishop of London ?
Barrow. I know him for no bishop, my Lord.
Lord Chancellor. What is he then ?
Barrow. His name is Elmar, my Lord. (The Lord pardon my fault, that I laid him not open for a wolfe, a bloody persecutor and apostate. But by this time the warden's man plucked me up.)
Lord Chancellor. What is that man ? (pointing to Canterbury).
Barrow. The Lord gave me the spirit of boldnes, so that I answered: He is a monster, a miserable compound, I know not what to make (call) him: he is neither ecclesiastical nor civil, even that second beast spoken of in the Revelation.[1]
Lord Treasurer. Wher is that place, shew it. [18 *recto*]
Barrow. So I turned to the thirteenth chapter and began at the eleventh verse, and read a litle. Then I turned to II Thessalonians 2. But the beast arose for anger, gnashing his teeth, and said: wil yow suffer him, my lords ? So I was pluckt up by the warden's man [C. 1 *verso*] from my knees and caried away. As I was departing, I desired the Lord Treasurer that I might have the libertie (benefite) of the aire, but had no answer: and I prayed the Lord to blesse their honours. So I was led forth by an other way than I came in, that I might not see the brethren, nor they me. This is the effect, so neere as my evil memorie could cary away, the very wordes that were used to me and by me in that place. The Lord pardon my unworthines and unsanctified hart and mouth, which can bring no glory to the Lord or benefite to his church: but rather reproch to the one and affliction to the other. " But the Lord knoweth how to deliver the godly out of tentation, and to reserve the unjust until the day of judgment under punishment."[2] The Lord Treasurer admonished me and told me that I took the Lord's name often in vaine: I have forgotten upon what occasion he (I) spake it. But I beseech the Lord

[1] Probably Revelation 13: 15 is meant.
[2] II Peter 2: 9.

that I may not forget this his good admonition, but may set a more careful watch before my lippes: for (sure) no doubt I am greatly guiltie that way and never use his holy name with that reverence I ought.

XI

BARROW'S FIFTH EXAMINATION

MARCH 24, 1588/9

(Barrow's Version)

This examination is taken from *The Examinations of Henry Barrowe, John Grenewood, and John Penrie*, signature A iv *verso*—B iii *recto*.

There are two versions of this examination: one written by Barrow himself, and one manuscript version by the register (or registrar). Both are reproduced, but Barrow's version is printed first because it is longer and more detailed.

It presents Barrow at the Bishop of London's palace before five of the greatest judges of England, two lord chief justices, and three of the highest ecclesiastical officials, including the Archbishop of Canterbury, together with chancellors, lawyers, and clerks. The examination itself consisted of a series of formal questions, based partly at least on material which Dr. Robert Some had gathered in his conference with Barrow or had extracted from Barrow's writings. Other material came from examination of Barrowist prisoners, from the confessions of Clement Gambell, John Dove, and a Mr. Love. Also, some of the material came from manuscript writings confiscated from Quintin Smyth and Roger Jackson. This material may be seen in " Certen Wicked Sects and Opinions," and it is summarized in " The Assertions of the Conventicles Lately Apprehended."

In the printed tract, the examination of March 24 precedes that of March 18, and the implication seems to be, therefore, that it is earlier. Since the March 18 examination occurred in 1588/9, it would follow that the March 24 examination should be dated 1587/8. Unfortunately, this latter date does not accord with internal or external evidence, and must be rejected.

The editor or printer or publisher of the entire tract evidently believed that the March 24 examination came before the March 18 examination, since he placed it first. But at least four, and possibly five to seven, years had elapsed from the examination itself to the publication of it. It is easy to understand, therefore, why a mistake could have been made, especially when Barrow's and Greenwood's summaries of their examinations usually omitted any reference to a year. The first examination of November 19 is erroneously dated 1586, instead of 1587, either by Barrow or more likely by the editor. The second examination—eight days later—is also erroneously regarded as 1586 because of the initial error. The next examination printed is that of March 24 and then that of March 18. This sequence is wrong, and should be corrected.

The best evidence for the year 1589 is to be found in a statement made by William Hutchinson, chaplain to Bishop Aylmer and archdeacon of St. Albans. In a conference on March 18, 1589/90, Hutchinson said: "I was at the great Commission a yeare agoe, where you did set downe with your owne hand your owne answeres." To this Barrow replied:

"Then did you see the bishops offer me the greatest wronge that I suppose was ever offred to anie Christian in anie age. I was brought out of my close pryson and compelled there to answere of the sodaine unto such articles as the bishops in theire secret councell had contrived against us. I could not be admitted anie furder respite or consideration, neither anie present conference with anie of my bretheren, neither yet so much as a copie of myne owne answers, though I most earnestly and humblie besought the same . . . *A Collection of Certaine Sclaunderous Articles Gyven out by the Bishops*, D ii *verso*.

This statement fits the March 24, 1588/9, examination perfectly.

A second argument for placing the March 24 examination after that of March 18 is that in the examination of March 18 Archbishop Whitgift said that he had material indicating that Barrow was a heretic and intimated that he would summon Barrow before him. The March 24 examination six days later is a confirmation of this intention. Thirdly, some of the replies of Barrow are utilized by Dr. Some in his book published in 1589, *A Godly Treatise, wherein Are Examined and Confuted Many Execrable Fancies, Given out and Holden, Partly by Henry Barrow and John Greeenewood : Partly, by Other of the Anabaptistical Order.* The Epistle Dedicatory is dated May 12, 1589. In the previous year Dr. Some issued *A Godly Treatise Containing and Deciding Certaine Questions*, with the preface dated May 6, 1588, but in this earlier work, no mention is made of Barrow's replies.

Another argument is that Greenwood's examination is conducted before the same judges and consists of similar questions. It is a strong presumption that the two examinations occurred the same day or at least the same week. In Greenwood's testimony there is a statement that he had been in prison for one and a half years. Since he was first imprisoned on October 8, 1587, the date of his examination would approximate March, 1588/9, or April, 1589.

One final argument is that the March 24 examination is held " before certeyne commissioners ther unto especially appointed by her majestie." This special commission seems to be a result of the " Lamentable Petition " of March 13, 1588/9, and indicates the determination of the queen to deal effectively and quickly with the growing problems occasioned by the Separatists.

Thus, the conclusion is that March 24, 1588/9, is the correct date, and that this examination is incorrectly placed in the original pamphlet, *The Examinations of Henry Barrowe, John Grenewood, and John Penrie.*

*　　*　　*　　*　　*　　*

BARROW'S FIFTH EXAMINATION

MARCH 24, 1588/9

(Barrow's Version)

The effect, and so neere as my fraile memorie could cary away, the very wordes of such interrogatories and answers as were demanded of and made by me, Henry Barrowe, before certeyne commissioners ther unto especially appointed by her Majestie: namely, the two Lord Cheef Justices,[1] the Maister of the Rolles,[2] the Lord Cheef Baron,[3] and another Baron of the Exchequor, I thinck Baron Gente:[4] togither with the Archbishop of Canterbury, the Bishop of London, the Bishop of Winchester,[5] certaine of their chancellors and civil doctors, with their registers and scribes.[6] The 24 of March [1588/9].

I being brought before the Archbishop of Canterbury, he made knowne unto me that they were authorized by her Majestie to examine me upon my oath upon certaine interrogatories and therfore called for a booke. Ther was brought a great Bible in folio, faire bound, which the Archbishop refused, and called

---

[1] Sir Christopher Wray (1524-1592), Lord Chief Justice of the King's (Queen's) Bench, was appointed justice in 1572 and chief justice in 1574. Sir Edmund Anderson (1530-1605) was appointed Lord Chief Justice of the Common Pleas in 1582. There is an engraved portrait of him in the frontispiece of Les Reports du Treserudite Edmund Anderson (London, 1664), and in G. B. Harrison, An Elizabethan Journal . . . 1591-1594 (London, 1928), p. 144.

[2] Sir Gilbert Gerard (or Gerrard) was appointed Master of the Rolls in 1581. See Lansdowne MSS. 65; item 44, f. 133.

[3] Sir Roger Manwood was created Lord Chief Baron of the Exchequer in 1578.

[4] Probably Thomas Gent, who was one of the commissioners appointed by Elizabeth to go with Sir Edmund Anderson to Ireland in July, 1588 (Lansdowne MS. 57, item 14, folio 50).

[5] John Whitgift, John Aylmer, and Thomas Cooper.

[6] William Hutchinson, chaplain to Bishop Aylmer, archdeacon of St. Albans, prebendary of St. Paul's and licenser of books, was certainly present. Dr. Robert Some, Sir Edward Stanhope, chancellor of the London diocese, Richard Cosin, ecclesiastical commissioner, were probably also present.

193

for an other, which was held to [B. 1 *recto*] me by one of his men, and I commaunded to lay my hand upon it.

Barrow: To what ende?

Canterbury: To sweare.

Barrow: I have not learned to sweare by any creatures.

Canterbury: This is the word of God — the Bible.

Barrow: I began to open the book, and meant indeed to have asked him if the Apocrypha Scripture and notes, which were in it, were the word of God: but Canterbury, belike suspecting some such matter, would not suffer me to look into it; to whom then I answered that that book was not the eternal word of God, that eternal God himselfe, by whom onely I must sweare, and not by any bookes or Bibles.

Canterbury: So yow shal sweare by God.

Barrow: To what purpose then is this booke urged? I may sweare by nothing besides him, nor by nothing with him.

Winchester: How prove yow that?

Barrow: It is so commanded in the book of the law. Deuteronomy 6 and 10 chapters, so expounded by sundrie of the prophets, by Christ himselfe and his apostles.

Canterbury: Wel, wil yow sweare that yow wil answer nothing but the truth, and the whole truth, to such interrogatories as we shal demaund of yow?

Barrow: I have learned to know the matter before I either sweare or answer.

Canterbury: Set downe that he wil not sweare.

Lord Chief Justice [Wray]: You shall onely sweare to answer the truth: if any unlawful thing be demaunded of yow, yow need not answere.

Barrow: My lord, every truth requireth not an oath; ther must great regard and reverence be used in an oath, and an oath for confirmation ought to be the ende of al strife. My lord, if I should erre, and deliver it upon mine oath for truth, it were a double sinne; likewise, if I should eyther not know, not remember, or not utter the whole truth, I were by such a rash oath forsworne: but by God's grace I wil answer nothing but the truth.

194

Canterbury: A christian man's word ought to be as true as his oath. We wil proceed with yow without your oath. (And taking a paper of interrogatories in his hand, said:) What say yow to this? Is it lawful to say the *Pater Noster*[1] publickly in the church, or privatly, as a prayer or no?

Barrow: I know not what yow meane by your *Pater Noster*, unlesse peradventure that forme for prayer which our saviour Christ taught his disciples, commonly called the Lorde's Prayer.

Canterbury: I so meane. Then commanded he the first question to be thus written.

Question 1. Whither he thinketh the Lorde's Prayer may publickly in the church, or privatly, be used as a prayer or no? (When I had expressed my minde, the Arch Bishop commaunded it should be recorded: but I desired the judges that I might with my owne hande write my owne answers, which was graunted me.) My answer then to the first question was:

Answer: It is to be used to that ende for which it was given by our saviour Christ to his disciples, as a summarie groundworke[2] or foundation of al faithful prayers, wherby to instruct and assure their consciences that their petitions are according to the wil and glory of God: but that these prescript wordes are injoyned or that [B 1 *verso*] Christ or his apostles ever used them as or in their prayer, I finde not in the Scripture. Moreover, I see not how it can be used as a prayer, seing that our particular wantes and present occasions and necessities are not therin expressed.[3] And therfore I thinke it [is] not to be used as a prayer. (Heere the Arch Bishop cried out for brevitie, and would not suffer me to answer any more questions at large.)

Question 2. Whither he thinketh that any leitourgies or prescript formes of prayer may be imposed upon the church:

---

[1] There is an article by Charles C. Butterworth, " The Term ' Lord's Prayer ' instead of ' Pater Noster '," in *Library Chronicle*, Winter, 1951-1952.

[2] Robert Some, *A Godly Treatise, wherein Are Examined and Confuted Many Execrable Fancies*, p. 29. In this work Dr. Some uses some of Barrow's answers in order to refute them.

[3] *Ibid.*, p. 30.

Henry Barrow

and whither al read and stinted prayers be mere babling in God's sight?

Answer: I finde in the worde of God no such authoritie given to any man, neither such stinted leitourgies prescribed or used in the primitive churches: and therfore hold it high presumtion to impose any one devised Apocrypha praier upon the church.[1]

Question 3. Whither he thinketh that the common praiers commaunded by the publick authoritie of this land be idolatrous, superstitious, and popish?

Answer: I thinke that this *Book of Common Prayer* publickly injoyned and received in the assemblies of this lande is wel nigh altogither idolatrous, superstitious, and popish.[2]

Question 4. Whither he thinketh that the sacraments which are publikly administered in the Church of England be true sacraments or no?

Answer: I thinke that the sacramentes as they are ministred in these publike assemblies are not true sacramentes: and seale not the favour and blessing of God unto them.

Question 5. Whither he thinketh that the lawes and government of the Church of England now by authoritie established be unlawful and antichristian, or no?

Answer: Because the lawes, decrees, and canons of your church are so many and infinite, I cannot judge of them al, because I know not al: but this I say, that many of them, as also your ecclesiastical courtes and governours, are unlawful and antichristian.

Question 6. Whither he thinketh that such as have bene baptised in the Church of England, since Queen Elizabethe's reign, have bene rightly baptised, or ought to be baptised againe?

Answer: I thinke as before of your sacramentes that they have not bene rightly baptised according to the institution

[1] *Ibid.*, p. 33.
[2] The literature on the *Book of Common Prayer* is vast, but three works deserve mention here: John Henry Blunt, *The Annotated Book of Common Prayer. Being an Historical, Ritual, and Theological Commentary on the Devotional System of the Church of England.* Francis Procter and Walter Frere, *A New History of the Book of Common Prayer.* George Harford, Morley Stevenson, and J. W. Tyrer, *The Prayer Book Dictionary.*

of Christ: yet that they need not, neither ought to be baptised againe. (I doubt least the Arch Bishop, hearing my answer of rebaptising, caused it to be left out of the question and my answer, taking that which might best serve their owne turne to bring us into suspicion of error and hatred.[1] Hereunto many speeches arising of the true and false sacramentes, ministerie, government, as also of the true and false church: I shewed that the false church had also her sacramentes, ministery, government, though not aright. Then Judge Anderson caused this question to be moved to me.

Question 7. Whither the Church of England as it standeth now established be the true established church of Christ: and whither the people therein be the true and faithful people of God, or no.

Answer: I thinke that these parish assemblies as they stand generally in England are not the true established [B ii *recto*] churches of Christ: and that the people as they now stand in this disorder and confusion in them are not to be held the true and faithful people of Christ.

Here the Judge Anderson took exception (as the Bishop of London also) at these wordes (parish assemblies). I answered the judge that I could not for some weightie respectes spare him that word: for I doubted not but that the Lord had many pretious and elect vessels among them, whom he wil in his good time cal forth, whom it became not me absolutely to judge, least I should enter into God's seat: yet I could not in the meane time, whiles they stand members of these assemblies, count them faithful. To the bishops, I said, that when they should better consider of mine answer, they should have lesse cause to finde fault. Much trouble we had before we could agree of the state and wordes of their questions, with putting out and changing, which discourse it is not my purpose here to set downe, so

---

[1] Barrow's suspicions were well-founded. In the registrar's version, Barrow's remarks that rebaptism was unnecessary have been omitted. See *Barrow's Fifth Examination* (Registrar's Version), questions 7, 8.

much as the questions and answers agreed upon and recorded: although for some causes knowne to my selfe, and to some of their consciences, which may hereafter be knowne to al the world, I thought it not impertinent to insert this.

Question 8. Whither he thinketh the queen's majestie be supreme governour of the church: and whither she may make lawes for the church, which are not contrary to the word of God, or no?

Answer: I thinke the queene's majestie supreme governour of the whole land and over the church also, bodies and goods: but I thinke that no prince, neither the whole world, neither the church it self, may make any lawes for the church other than Christ hath already left in his worde. Yet I thinke it the dutie of every Christian, and principally of the prince, to enquire out and renue the lawes of God, and stir up al their subjectes to more diligent and careful keeping of the same.[1] As we had much a doe to come to the state of this question, so the bishops shewed themselves evil satisfied with my answer, and said that the papistes dealt more simply than I did: and surely they very greevouslie interrupted me with slanders, evil speeches, and blasphemies, during the time of my writing these answers, especially the Bishop of London, so that I was even inforced sometime to turne unto him and shew him of his shamelesse untruthes and slanders. The Chief Justice of England [Wray] here saide that he thought I answered very directly and compendiously.[2] Here again, upon some speech that arose, the Judge Anderson asked me whither I thought it lawful to hang a theef or no? I answered that ther were many kinde of theeves, as sacrilegious

---

[1] This answer is quoted by George Gifford, *A Short Treatise against the Donatists of England, Whome We Call Brownists* (London, 1590), pp. 106 f. Gifford writes: " there be certayne Answers which go under the name of Henry Barowe," and he says that this specific answer " goeth also verye currant among manye." Evidently a manuscript version of Barrow's answers had circulated by 1590 and probably by 1589.

[2] See *A Petition Directed to Her Most Excellent Majestie*, p. 74. This work, number 1521 in the *Short-Title Catalogue*, has been ascribed to Henry Barrow, but this is an error. The writer is a Presbyterian in outlook, not a Separatist or Congregationalist.

theeves, men-stealers, *etc.*, that these ought by the lawes of God to die. Then he said, he meant ordinary theeves of goodes and chattels. I said that God in the law had ordeyned an other kinde of punishment for such, wherupon the bishop framed this question.

Question 9. Whither it be lawful for the prince to alter the judical lawe of Moses according to the state of her countrie and policie, or no ?

Answer: I ought to be wise in sobrietie [B ii *verso*] and not to answer more than I know. Great doubt and controversie hath bene about this question a long time, but for my part I can not see that any more of the judicial law was or can be abrogated by any mortal man or countrie, upon what occasion soever, than belonged to the ceremonial law and worship of the temple, for which we have received other lawes and worship in Christe's Testament: but that the judgementes due and set downe by God for the transgression of the moral law cannot be changed or altered, without injury to the moral law and God himselfe. Yet this, as al my other answers, by protestation, that if any man can better instruct me therin by the word of God, I am alwayes ready to change my minde.

Wherupon the Chief Justice of England said I spake wel: and therfore said if I were in doubt, mine answer ought not to be taken.[1]

I said I doubted not, but had set downe my minde.

Yet the bishops, because my answer fitted not their turnes, as I thinke, commaunded the question and answer to be blotted out.[2]

Question 10. Whither he thinketh that any private man may take upon him to reform, if the prince will not or neglect. (I asked whither they meant of a publick reformation of the state, or of a private or personal reformation

---

[1] There is an interesting reference to this by the author [John Penry ?] of *A Petition Directed to Her Most Excellent Majestie* (London,[1591 ?]), p. 74, where we read: " quaere, whether the right honorable and chiefe justice of England, Sir Christopher Wray, Knight, did not at the examination of H. Barrowe in the Bishop of London's pallace, affirme that men should incurre no penaltie for opinions which they held doubtinglie."

[2] This question and answer are omitted from the list recorded by the register.

of himself and his family: it was said, of a public reformation.)

Answer: I thinke that no man may intermedle with the prince's office, without lawful calling therunto: and therfore it is utterly unlawful for any private man to reforme the state without his good liking and license, because the prince shal account for the defaultes of his publick government, and not private men, so they be not guiltie with the prince in his offences, but absteine and keep them selves pure from doing or consenting to any unlawful thing commaunded by the prince, which they must doe as they tender their owne salvation.[1]

Question 11. Whither he thinketh that every parish or particuler church ought to have a presbyterie?

Answer: The holy government of Christ belongeth not to the prophane or unbelieving, neither can it without manifest sacrilege be set over these parishes as they now stande in confusion, no difference made betwixt the faithful and unbeleeving, al being indifferently received into the body of the church: but over every particuler congregation of Christ ther ought to be an eldership, and every such congregation ought to their utter most power to endeavour therunto.

Now was I dismissed, and committed againe to my keeper,[2] with streight charge that no man might speak to me. During this time others of my brethren[3] were examined, which being done, I was called for in unto them, where Canterbury shewed me the Statute of Supremecie, and asked me if I would take an oath according to the same. I said that in that forme I

---

[1] This question is similar to number [13] of the register's list, but the answer is different. Barrow has replied cautiously and well, but this part of his reply is left officially unrecorded. On the other hand, Barrow has omitted his own statement that a church (or private men) need not stay for the prince in reforming ecclesiastical abuses, but the register has included this damaging testimony in his account. Barrow is not evading the point, since he does include it in his concluding statement.

[2] Edward Tirrell was the Warden of the Fleet prison, and Joachim Newton was the Deputy Warden.

[3] These other brethren may have been those who presented the " Lamentable Petition " of March 13, 1588/9, to the queen, or they may be those Barrowists imprisoned on October 8, 1587, and on later dates, as they were caught by the pursuivants. John Greenwood's examination is very likely at this time.

could not, neither could I sweare to such successors as I knew not:[1] but to her Majestie, I acknowledged her authoritie as I had expressed in my article and protested my life in defence of her person, prerogative, and dignitie, loyally against al forreine and domestical ene-[B iii *recto*]mies whither spiritual or temporal. The Arch Bishop said, that the papistes made a better and more dutiful oath than this. I said it was not true, they deneyed not, neither defied the pope: but I was ready to give and performe as much unto my prince as any true subject ought to doe.

Question [12]. He asked me againe whither the church of Christ, if the prince deny or refuse to neglect [correct] abuses, may, without staying for the prince, reforme them? I said that it might and ought, though al the princes of the world should prohibit the same upon paine of death.

[13]. He asked me againe whither the church of Christ might excommunicate the prince, and who should pronounce it? I said that sin obstinatly stood in [continued] did excommunicate, and that the church ought to have judgment ready against every transgression without respect of persons, and that the pastor of the church ought to pronounce it, and alleaged that excommunication was given unto the church as the onely and last remedie for the salvation of the partie in such cases, and that the neglect thereof was both the neglect of God's judgementes, their dutie, and the prince's salvation; and that they might as wel take away al admonitions and reprehensions from princes, and so princes were in a most miserable case.

These my answers were not written with mine owne

---

[1] The Act of Supremacy, Elizabeth, *Cap.* I, section 8, authorizes the queen and her successors to exercise " all manner of jurisdictions, privileges and pre-eminences, in any wise touching or concerning any spiritual or ecclesiastical jurisdiction " (G. W. Prothero, *Select Statutes*, p. 6).

hand, but by the register.[1] And so was I sent againe
with more commaundementes yet to keep me more
streightly. I requested at both times a copy of my
answers, but the archbishop denied it [to] me.

---

[1] This seems to contradict Barrow's earlier statement that he was given
permission to write his own answers. Perhaps he conferred about hur-
riedly-written notes which the register recorded. Or, he may mean that
these last three replies, after he had returned to the examining room,
were not written by himself. Certain it is, that Barrow was denied copies
of his answers, whether recorded by himself or the clerk.

XII

BARROW'S FIFTH EXAMINATION, MARCH 24, 1588/9
(Register's Version)

The register's version of Barrow's fifth examination is of interest because it enables us to check Barrow's own version. By comparing them, we can see that Barrow's memory is remarkably accurate. During the first part of the examination, he was allowed to write out his replies and give them to the register. This privilege seems to have been denied him after his first question or after he had been recalled.

The version before us represents the register's copy of Barrow's written replies. I have used the original manuscript, which is in the Huntington Library, Ellesmere MS. 2100. It was published by J. Payne Collier in *The Egerton Papers* (London: Camden Society, 1840), pp. 167-170.

For the sake of comparison, the following table indicates which questions in the register's version correspond to those in Barrow's version.

Register's Order				Barrow's Order
1	.	.	.	1
2	.	.	.	2
3	.	.	.	3
4	.	.	.	4
5	.	.	.	7
6	.	.	.	5
7	.	.	.	6
8	.	.	.	6
9	.	.	.	8
10	.	.	.	5
11	.	.	.	11
[12]	.	.	.	[13]
[13]	.	.	.	10 and [12]

Thus, it will be apparent that Barrow has included all the register's questions, and he has one question (No. 9), which the register omits. He has varied the order of the questions somewhat, but he has given fuller and more interesting information than the register gave. This test of Barrow's accuracy, honesty, and objectivity in reporting his own examination gives one confidence that he is not guilty of *suppressio veritatis* or *distortio veritatis*.

*   *   *   *   *   *

HENRY BARROWE

1.   INTERROGATORY — Whethether [*sic*] it be lawfull for a christian man to use the Lord's Prayer in the church, publiquely or otherwise ?[1]

Myne aunswhere is, that this prayer is to be used, publiquely or privately, in that sorte as Christ hath geven it and tought it unto his disciples, which is to use [it] for groundworke of all prayers, and the confirmacion of our consciences, that our peticions are to the glory and according to the will of God; but to use all that forme of words of all those peticions, I see it not necessarye, bycause it expresseth not our particuler and private wantes: neither can our faith aryve to all there expressed, neither can I see any warrant or example for it, and therfore I thinke it ought not to be.[2]

2.   INTERROGATORY — Whether all sett and stinted prayers are mere bablinge in the sight of the Lord, and whether it be lawfull to use any such ?

---

[1] This question was evidently designed to embarrass Barrow before his judges. In the public estimation, the Barrowists disapproved of the Lord's Prayer — an attitude that seemed nonsensical. Actually, the Barrowists approved of the Lord's Prayer, especially as a pattern to be followed, but not as a stinted mechanical prayer substituted for individual petition and praise.

[2] Dr. Some quotes four extracts from this paragraph in his *A Godly Treatise, wherein are Examined and Confuted Many Execrable Fancies*, pp. 29-30. It is a strong likelihood that Dr. Some formulated the questions for this examination.

I hould it not lawfull for any man to ympose any forme of lyturgie, or stinted praiers in the churche.[1]

3. INTERROGATORY — Whether he thinketh the publique prayers and worshipp of God, in such sorte, as it is established in the Church of England by lawe, to be false, superstitious, and papishe, or not?

I hould that that *Booke of Common Prayers*, and most of the worshipp therin, is false, superstitious, and popishe.

4. INTERROGATORY — Whether he thinketh that the sacraments of Baptisme and the Lord's Supper, as they are administered in the Churche of England, be true sacraments or noe?

I think that these sacraments, as they are in these publique assemblyes administered, are not true sacraments, neither seale God's favoure unto us.

5. INTERROGATORY — Whether he thinketh the Church of England, as it is now established, to be the churche of Christe or noe?

I think that thes publique parishes, assemblyes, as they are here established, are not the true established churches of Christ, nor the people as they are there assembled.[2]

6. INTERROGATORY — Whether he thinketh the government of the Churche of England, as it is nowe by lawes established, be a lawfull and christian government or noe?

I hould that this publique government, wherewith thes publique assemblies of England are governed, have noe warrant from the word of God, and is unlawfull and antichristian.

7. INTERROGATORY — Whether he thinketh that those which have bene baptised in the Churche of England, sithence the beginning of hir majestie's raigne, have bene lawfully and rightly baptized or no?

I thinke that such as have bene baptised in these publique assemblies, accordinge to the usuall order there established, have not bene rightly baptised accordinge to the institution of Christ.

8. INTERROGATORY — Whether he thinketh that infantes, borne in this Churche of England, ought to be baptized accor-

[1] *Ibid.*, p. 33.
[2] The principle of universal membership required by law makes impossible a church consisting of rightly gathered individuals — the saved, believing, true Christians.

dinge to the order of the Churche of England, or noe?

I thinke that the children of the faithfull ought not to be baptized after that manner.[1]

9. INTERROGATORY — Whether he thinketh that the quene's majestie have supreme aucthorytye to governe the churche in causes and matters eccle[si]asticall, and to make lawes ecclesiasticall, not contrary to the lawes of Christ, or not?

I thinke that the quene's majestie is the supreme governor over the whole land, and over the churche alsoe, boeth of bodyes and goods; yet I am perswaded that she ought not to make or ympose other lawes over them than Christ hath made and left in his Testament, and that the prince ought most carefully, above all other, to revyve [renewe][2] and enquier oute the lawes of God which are commaunded in his word, and cann make noe newe.

10. INTERROGATORY — Whether he thinketh that the lawe eccle[si]asticall, alredy established by aucthoritie, be lawfull or noe?

This beinge a [subject, topic, question] so infinite in your books, decres, and councells, I cannot aunswhere generally, bycause I knowe fewe of them; but of those I knowe, sundrye of them are ungodly and contrary to his word.

11. INTERROGATORY — Whether he thinketh that there ought to be a presbytery in every parishe or congregacion?

I thinke that holy government of Christ belongeth not to thes parishes, as they generally stand, and cannot, withoute sacrilege, be ministered unto them in this estate, but there ought to be a presbetery[3] over everye true assembly of Christ, and the faithfull people of God can receyve noe other government than that of Christ.

[12]. Being asked, whether the congregacion have aucthoritie to excommunicate the quene, saith that, in a reformed

---

[1] Barrow held that those who had been baptised need not and ought not to be rebaptised. His answer was not recorded completely, as he suspected.
[2] The earliest printed version of this examination has " renue." In *A Plaine Refutation*, p. 206, Barrow requotes his reply as being " renewe," and Gifford in *A Short Treatise*, p. 107, has " reuew " — a misprint for " renew."
[3] That is, an eldership, which constitutes a consistory for the particular church. Barrow does not believe in the Presbyterian system of a hierarchy of courts, such as the local classis (or presbytery), provincial synod, and national synod or assembly.

churche, if the quene doe synn, the pastor, in the name of the churche, is to denounce [pronounce] the excommunicacion against the quene which the word of God doeth laye uppon hir for that sinne.

[13].   Beinge asked, whether the congregacion may reforme abuses in the churche, if the quene or magistrate doe refuse or delaye to the same,[1] saith, that the churche need not to staye for the prince in the reforminge of any abuse, but maye reforme it, though the prince saye noe.[2]

---

1 This is a doctrine made famous by Robert Browne in his work, *A Treatise of Reformation without Tarying for Anie,* printed in Albert Peel and Leland H. Carlson, *The Writings of Robert Harrison and Robert Browne,* pp. 150-170.
2 This reply is printed and refuted by Dr. Some in *A Godly Treatise wherein Are Examined and Confuted Many Execrable Fancies,* p. 13.

XIII

A TRUE DESCRIPTION OUT OF THE WORDE OF GOD,
OF THE VISIBLE CHURCH

This tract of eight pages was the first Barrowist publication to be printed. Robert Stokes testified that " he caused a little thyng of one shete of paper to be prynted by their [Barrow and Greenwood's] procurement before all thys, called the Destructyon [Description] of the Vysyble Church."[1] This work carried the date 1589. It may have been printed late in that year, or if it immediately preceded the printing of *A Collection of Certaine Sclaunderous Articles*, the date may be the opening months of 1589/90. But prior to this time there existed a copy in manuscript, which Richard Alison had seen.[2]

It is possible that the idea for the title of this treatise came from Dr. Robert Some. In 1588 his book was published, *A Godly Treatise Containing and Deciding Certaine Questions, Moved of Late in London and Other Places, Touching the Ministerie, Sacraments, and Church*. This book discussed nine points, the last of which was: " The Church of England is the Visible Church of Christ." Dr. Some sought to prove that the Church of England possessed the attributes or essential marks of the church of Christ. Barrow twice refuted this book in his marginal notes and his interleaved annotations, and both of his refutations were seized in prison by the authorities. It is possible that the examination of January 1, 1588/9, which is relevant to this ninth point, and the ensuing argument on whether the Church of England had one head or two heads,

---

[1] *The Egerton Papers*, edited by J. Payne Collier, p. 175. Collier has misread the manuscript. The correct reading is " Description." The original manuscript is Ellesmere MS. 2094 — in the Huntington Library
[2] Richard Alison, *A Plaine Confutation of a Treatise of Brownisme, Entitled*. DESCRIPTION OF A VISIBLE CHURCH, p. 19.

caused Barrow to write *A True Description out of the Worde of God, of the Visible Church* during the year 1589.

There is a great deal of confusion and misinformation about the authorship and editions of this work. It has been ascribed to Henry Barrow, Francis Johnson, John Penry, and others,[1] but the latter two men were not Separatists in 1589, and may be eliminated. Richard Alison sought to refute one particular individual—a Barrowist, and Henoch Clapham says specifically that Barrow drew up a *Description of the True Church* [*A True Description out of the Worde of God, of the Visible Church*].[2] Additional testimony comes from John Darrell.[3]

The problem of the editions is more complicated. According to the *Short-Title Catalogue*, there are two editions, one of 1589 at the Folger Shakespeare Library, and one of [1610 ?] at the British Museum. On comparing these two, I find that they are the same, although the Folger copy is bound separately, and the British Museum copy is bound with [Henry Ainsworth], *An Apologie or Defence of Such True Christians as Are Commonly (but Unjustly) Called Brownists* (1604). In the Henry M. Dexter Collection at the Sterling Memorial Library at Yale, there is another copy (z. d. 937), which is also identical with the above-mentioned copies. All of these copies are without title page, and have the date 1589 printed on page 8, at the conclusion of the tract.

There is a revealing dialogue which Henoch Clapham has included in his book, and which is relevant to this problem. Malcontent and Flyer are talking:

Malcontent: Mr. Henrie Barrow drawing a *Description of the True Church,* when he comes to deliver the canons of discipline, he in that sheete of paper, doth after the excommunication place that canon of the apostle in 2 Thessalonians 3: 15 — *Yet count him not as an enemie, but admonish him as a brother,* because he be-

---

[1] Peter Fairlambe, *The Recantation of a Brownist,* signature C 3 recto.
[2] *Errour on the Right Hand,* pp. 10-12.
[3] In his book, *A Treatise of the Church* (London, 1617), John Darrell [or Dayrell] ascribes the authorship to Barrow (pp. 51 f.).

H

leeved, that excommunication was a power to
edification, not to destruction. Your congregation
then, some yeares after his death, do reprint it,
putting to it the olde date, corrupting his method,
falsifying his will, by placing the sayd canon before
excommunication; because after the casting out you
would rid your handes of all tendernes and compassion, as delighting in nothing more, than in
bitternesse against the soule distressed.   The apostle
can say, [Galatians 3: 15] — *Though it be but a man's
covenant (or will), when it is confirmed, no man doth
abrogate it, or addeth any thing thereto.*   But you have
done that which no man (that is, no honest man)
would doe, in so causing his will to speake contrary
to his meaning.

Flyer: Malcontent, I cannot beleeve that thou sayest.
Malcontent: But I beleeve it, and the copies will proove it.   Besides that, I know him which reprooved that evill,
at the comming foorth of the second edition at
A[msterdam] at the charges of Arthur Billet:
whereas the first was printed at D[ort], where other
writings also of the same man, were then printed.[1]

This dialogue establishes the fact that there was a first
edition printed at Dort and a second edition printed at Amsterdam. It further informs us that there was a change in the
order of the paragraphs.

The earliest refutation of *A True Description* was made by
Richard Alison, who published his *A Plaine Confutation of a
Treatise of Brownisme Entitled*: DESCRIPTION OF A VISIBLE
CHURCH about September, 1590. In this work, the eighth paragraph from the end begins: " All this notwithstanding, the
church is not to holde him as an enemie, but to admonish and
pray for him as a brother." In the Folger, British Museum, and
Yale copies, this paragraph has been placed just before the
preceding two paragraphs, so that it is the tenth paragraph
from the end of the tract. Thus, there is confirmatory evidence
for Malcontent's charge, as set forth by Henoch Clapham.

---

[1] Henoch Clapham, *Errour on the Right Hand*, pp. 10-12.

Fortunately, there are two copies of the first edition of this tract, *A True Description out of the Worde of God, of the Visible Church*, available at Lambeth Palace Library, which have remained unnoticed. In S. R. Maitland's catalogue, *An Index of Such English Books, Printed before the Year MDC., as Are Now in the Archiepiscopal Library at Lambeth* (London, 1845), they are listed not under Barrow's authorship but under the heading "Church," where they are numbered XXX. 6. 9. (4.) and XL. 2. 24. (3.), and renumbered 1590.17 and 1593.13. On the title page of one copy is a note, "Found in Penrie's Chamber," and on the last page is a note, "By me Rechard Malthus [or Walthus]." On the title page of the other copy is a note, "I beseche your honor yf yt maye be lawfull to lycens this booke to Mr. Thomas Purfoote, stacion[er]." Since John Penry was hanged on May 29, 1593, it is certain that this copy cannot be of a later date. Furthermore, the tract is printed with the same type as used to print five other books of Barrow and Greenwood in 1590/1 at Dort. Thus, we may feel certain that the two copies at Lambeth Palace Library are first editions, printed at Dort in 1589. Furthermore, the order of the paragraphs corresponds to the statements of Henoch Clapham and to the order found in Richard Alison's *A Plaine Confutation*.

The problem of establishing the second edition is not immediately solved. From Malcontent's statement, it is clear that the second edition was published at Amsterdam at the expense of Arthur Billet. From the Amsterdam records Henry M. Dexter was able to establish that Sarah Billet remarried in June, 1602, after having been a widow four months. Therefore the second Amsterdam edition would be earlier than 1602. Now, there is at Lambeth Palace Library (L. 2. 29 (2.), renumbered 1595.21) another edition of *A True Description*, unlike any other copy I have examined. It carries the date 1589, but in what appears to be a contemporary hand, the date has been changed to 1599. From this slight evidence I conclude that this is the second edition, printed at Amsterdam in 1599 at Arthur Billet's expense. The order of the paragraphs differs from that of the first edition, as Malcontent charged.

It may be distinguished from other editions by the peculiar syllabication of the first line of the title: A TRUE DESCRIPTI=. There is also on the title page a design including a face with extending curving lines resembling a moustache.

It would follow, therefore, that Dexter is wrong in thinking that the Yale copy (and thus the Folger and British Museum copies) constitutes the second edition. They are all of the third edition, probably printed in Amsterdam, and the most likely date is 1604, (although the date 1589 is retained on page 8), if we may ascribe the same date to it as is given to [Henry Ainsworth's] *An Apologie or Defence of Such True Christians as Are Commonly (but Unjustly) Called Brownists*, with which it is bound. This work is a collection of Separatist material, containing a reply to the Heads and Doctors of the University of Oxford, a reprint of " The Confession of Faith," three petitions to King James I, and Barrow's letter of April 4 or 5, 1593, to an Honorable Lady. It would seem fitting, therefore, in such a collection, to include a reprint of Barrow's *A True Description* in this 1604 work.

In 1603 the Separatists reprinted John Greenwood's *An Answere to George Gifford's Pretended Defence* and also his *A Fewe Observations* ; in 1604 appeared [Ainsworth's] *An Apologie or Defence* ; and in 1605 the reprint of Barrow's *A Plaine Refutation*. Francis Johnson most likely was responsible for the reprinting of the books in 1603 and 1605, and probably collaborated with Ainsworth in 1604.

There is another edition of *A True Description* at the Huntington Library and at the Library of Congress. It carries no date, but on the slight evidence that the Library of Congress copy is bound up with John Robinson's *A Manumission to a Manuduction* (1615) and Henry Ainsworth's *An Animadversion to Mr. Richard Clyfton's Advertisement* (Amsterdam, 1613), I conjecture that it is a later reprint about 1610-1615. It may be distinguished from other editions by a design on page 1. The initial capital letter A is flanked by two half-human or mermaid figures supporting an architrave.

At the Congregational Library, Memorial Hall, London,

there is a 1641 reprint, *A True Description of the Visible Congregation of the Saints under the Gospel, according to the Word of Truth*, with several variants, which F. J. Powicke reproduced in *Henry Barrow, Separatist*, pp. 342-347. Powicke collated the 1641 edition with the " first " edition in the British Museum. Actually, the edition in the British Museum is the third edition, about 1604, which is the same edition as found at Yale and the Folger Shakespeare Library. It is interesting to note the many variants in the 1641 edition. The tract was also reprinted by Thomas Wall, in *More Work for the Dean* (London, 1681), pp. 20-28, as part of a polemic against Edward Stillingfleet, then Dean of St. Paul's and later Bishop of Worcester (1689). In 1839 Benjamin Hanbury reprinted it in his *Historical Memorials*, I, 28-34, and in 1861 John Waddington reprinted it in *Historical Papers (First Series). Congregational Martyrs*, pp. 131-5. It is reproduced by Williston Walker, *The Creeds and Platforms of Congregationalism* (1893), pp. 28-40. There is also a 1953 reprint by the Brownist Press, with an introduction by Hugo R. Pruter, of Berwyn, Illinois.

Besides these various editions and reprints, we may note that after the first edition of eight pages appeared in 1589, it was refuted in 1590 by Richard Alison in *A Plaine Confutation*, wherein he reprints the entire tract section by section, and utilizes 104 pages for his refutation of the eight-page tract. Alison's reprint is the only one to retain the same correct order of paragraphs as in the 1589 edition. Again in 1613, *A True Description* is reprinted and refuted by Christopher Lawne, in *Brownisme Turned the In-side Out-ward*. The book is printed throughout in two parallel columns, the left side containing *A True Description* and the right side unmercifully attacking and ridiculing the Separatist manifesto.

Despite these numerous editions, reprints, and refutations, the only ones which are accurate and in the correct order of paragraphs are the first edition of 1589 and the reprint of it by Richard Alison in 1590, in his *A Plaine Confutation*. It is this first edition which is here reproduced, and the few minor variations of Alison are included in the notes.

*　　*　　*　　*　　*　　*

[A 1 *recto* title page]
[A 1 *verso* blank]
[A 2 *recto*]   A TRUE DESCRIPTION
OUT OF THE WORDE OF GOD,
OF THE VISIBLE CHURCH

As there is but one God[1] and father of all, one Lorde over all, and one spirit: so is there but one trueth,[2] one faith, one salvation, one church, called in one hope, joyned in one profession, guided by one rule,[3] even the worde of the most high.

This church as it is universallie understood, conteyneth in it all the elect[4] of God that have bin, are, or shalbe. But being considered more particularlie, as it is seene in this present worlde, it consisteth of a companie and fellowship of faithful[5] and holie[6] people gathered (togither) in the name of Christ Jesus, their only king,[7] priest,[8] and prophet,[9] worshipping[10] him aright, being peaceablie[11] and quietlie[12] governed by his officers and lawes, keeping[13] the unitie of faith in the bonde of peace and love[14] unfained.

Most joyfull,[15] excellent, and glorious things are everie where in the Scriptures spoken of this church. It is called the citie,[16] house,[17], temple,[18] and mountaine[19] of the eternall God: the chosen[20] generation, the holie nation, the peculiar people, the vine-

---

[1] Genesis 1: 1. Exodus 20: 3.
[2] I Timothy 2: 4. Philippians 1: 27 (2: 25). Ephesians 2: 18. John 8: 41.
[3] Deuteronomy 6: 25. Romans 10: 8. II Timothy 3: 15. John 8: 51. I John 2: 3, 4.
[4] Genesis 17. I Peter 1: 2. Revelation 7: 9. I Corinthians 10: 3. John 17: 20.
[5] Psalms 111: 1 and 149: 1. Isaiah 62: 12. Ephesians 1: 1. I Corinthians 1: 2. Deuteronomy 14: 2.
[6] Deuteronomy 12: 5. John 6: 37 and 3: 14 and 12: 32. Luke 17: 3.
[7] Genesis 44: 10. Psalms 45: 6. Zechariah 9: 9. Hebrews 1: 8.
[8] Romans 8: 34. John 17. Hebrews 5: 9 and 8: 1 and 4: 14.
[9] Deuteronomy 18: 15. Matthew 17: 15. Hebrews 1: 1. Genesis 14: 18.
[10] Exodus 20: 7, 8. Leviticus 10: 5. John 4: 23.
[11] Matthew 11: 29. I Corinthians 11: 16. Mark 13: 34. Revelation 22: 9.
[12] Alison omits " and quietlie."
[13] Ephesians 4: 3. I Corinthians 1: 13. Mark 9: 50.
[14] John 13: 34. I Corinthians 13: 4. I Peter 1: 22. I John 3: 18.
[15] Psalms 87: 2.
[16] *Ibid.*
[17] I Timothy 3: 15. Hebrews 3: 6.
[18] I Corinthians 3: 17.
[19] Isaiah 2: 2. Micah 4: 1.
[20] Zechariah 8: 3. I Peter 2: 9.

yarde,[1] the garden[2] enclosed, the spring shut up, the sealed
fountaine, the orchyard of pomgranades with sweete fruites, the
heritage,[3] the kingdome[4] of Christ: [2] yea his sister,[5] |his love,
his spouse, his queene,[6] and his bodie,[7] the joye of the whole earth.
To this societie is the covenant[8] and all the promises made [A 2
verso] of peace,[9] of love, and of salvation,[10] of the presense[11] of
God, of his graces, of his power, and of his protection.[12]

And surelie if this church be considered in hir partes, it shall
appeare most beautifull, yea most wonderfull, and even[13] ravish-
ing[14] the senses to conceave, much more to beholde, what then to
enjoy so blessed a communion.[15] For behold[,] her king[16] and
Lord is the king of peace, and Lorde him selfe of all glorie. She
enjoyeth most holy and heavenly lawes,[17] most faithfull and
vigilant pastours,[18] most syncere and pure teachers,[19] most carefull
and upright governours,[20] most diligent and trustie deacons,[21]
most lovinge and sober releevers,[22] and a most humble,[23] meeke,
obedient, faithfull and loving people, everie stone[24] living, elect
and precious, every stone hath his beautie, his burden,[25] and his
order.[26] All bound to edifie[27] one another, exhort, reprove and

---

1 Isaiah 51 [5: 1] and 27: 2.
2 Canticles 4: 12.   Isaiah 51: 3.
3 Isaiah 9: 25.
4 Micah 3: 2.   John 3: 3.
5 Canticles 5: 2.
6 Psalms 45: 9.
7 I Corinthians 12: 27.   Ephesians 1: 23.
8 Galatians 4: 28.
9 Psalms 147: 14.   II Thessalonians 3: 16.
10 Isaiah 46: 13.   Zechariah 14: 17.
11 Isaiah 60.   Ezekiel 47.   Zechariah 4: 12.
12 Ezekiel 48: 35.   Matthew 28: 20.   Isaiah 62.
13 Alison omits " even."
14 Canticles 6: 4, 9.
15 Alison has a question mark here.
16 Isaiah 62: 11.   John 12: 15.   Hebrews 7: 8.
17 Matthew 11: 30.   I John 5: 3.
18 Acts 20.
19 Romans 12: 7.
20 Romans 12: 8.
21 Acts 6.
22 Romans 12: 8.   John 13: 17.   Deuteronomy 13: 17.   Relievers were
widows who gave assistance to families, nursed the sick, and served as
" social workers."
23 Matthew 5: 5.   Deuteronomy 18: 10.   Ezekiel 36: 38.   Isaiah 60: 8.
24 I Kings 7: 9.   Zechariah 14: 21.   I Peter 2: 5.
25 Galatians 6: 2.
26 I Corinthians 12.   Romans 12: 3.
27 Hebrews 10: 24.

comfort one another, lovinglie[1] as to their owne members, faithe-fully[2] as in the eyes of God.

No office[3] here is ambitouslie affected, no law[4] wrongfullie wrested or wilfully[5] neglected, no trueth[6] hid or perverted, everie[7] one here hath freedome and power (not disturbing the peaceable order of the church) to utter his complaintes and griefes, and freely to reproove the transgressions and errours of any without exception of persons.

Here is no intrusion[8] or climing up an other way into the sheepe-folde, than by the holy and free election[9] of the Lorde's holie and free people, and that according to the Lorde's ordinance, humbling them selves by fasting and prayer before the Lorde, craving the direction of his Holy Spirit, for the triall and approving of his giftes, etc. [A 3 *recto*].

Thus they orderlie proceede to ordination by fastinge and prayer, in which action[10] the apostles used layinge on of handes. Thus hath everie one of the people interest in the election and ordination[11] of their officers, as also in the administration of their offices upon transgression, offence, abuse, etc., having an especiall care unto the inviolable order of the church, as is aforesaid.

Likewise in this church they have holy lawes,[12] as limites and bondes, whiche, it is lawful at no hande to transgresse. They have lawes to direct them in the choise of everie officer, what kinde of men[13] the Lorde will have. Their pastour must be apte to teache,[14] no yong scholer, able[15] to divide the worde aright, holding[16] faste that faithfull worde, according to doctrine, that he may be able also to exhorte, rebuke, improove, with wholesome doctrine, and to con-vince them that saye against it: he must be a man[17] that loveth

---

[1] Leviticus 19: 17 (15: 17). I Thessalonians 4: 9.
[2] Colossians 3: 23. I John 3: 20.
[3] II Corinthians 2: 17. III John 9.
[4] I Timothy 4: 2, 3. Galatians 6: 12.
[5] I Corinthians 5.
[6] Jeremiah 23: 28. I Timothy 3: 15.
[7] I Corinthians 6 and 14: 30. Colossians 4: 17.
[8] John 10: 1.
[9] Acts 1: 23 and 6: 3 and 14: 23.
[10] I Timothy 4: 14 and 5: 22.
[11] Luke 17: 3. Romans 16: 17. Colossians 4: 17.
[12] Matthew 5: 17. I Timothy 1: 18.
[13] Alison has " them."
[14] Leviticus 21: 17. Malachi 2: 6. I Timothy 3: 2.
[15] II Timothy 2: 15.
[16] Titus 1: 9. II Timothy 4: 2.
[17] Titus 1: 7, 8.

goodnes: he must be wise, righteous, holie, temperate: he must bee of life unreproveable, as God's stewarde: he must be generallie well reported of, and one that ruleth his owne housholde under obedience with all honestie: he must be modest, humble, meeke, gentle, and loving: he must be a man of great patience,[1] compassion, labour and diligence: hee must alwaies be carefull and watchfull over the flock whereof the Lorde hath made him overseer, with all willingnes and chearefulnes, not holding his office in respect of persons, but doing his duetie to everie soule, as he will aunswer before the chief shephearde, etc.

Their doctor or teacher must be a man apte to teach, able to divide the worde of God aright, and to deliver sounde and whole-some doctrine from the same, still building upon that sounde[2] ground-worke; he must be mightie in the Scriptures, able to con-vince the gainsayers, and carefullie to deliver his doctrine pure, sounde and plaine, not with curiositie or affection [affectation],[3] but so that it may edifie the most simple, approving it to everie man's conscience; he must be of life unreproveable, one that can governe his owne houshold, he must be of maners sober, tem-[A 3 *verso*]perate, modest, gentle and loving, etc.

Their elders must be of wisedome and judgement, endued with the spirit of God, able to discerne betweene cause and cause, be-tweene plea and plea, and accordinglie to prevent and redres evilles, always vigilant and intending to see the statutes, ordin-ances and lawes of God kept in the church, and that not onely by the people in obedience, but to see the officers do their dueties. These men must bee of life likewise unreproveable, governing their owne families orderlie, they must be also of maners sober, gentle, modest, loving, temperate, etc.[4]

Their deacons must be men of honest report, having the misterie of the faith in a pure conscience, endued with the Holy Ghost: they must be grave, temperate, not given to excesse, nor to filthie lucre.[5]

Their releevers or widowes must bee women of sixty yeares of age at the least, for avoyding of inconveniences: they must be well

[1] Numbers 12: 3. Isaiah 50: 4. Jeremiah 3: 15. Ezekiel 34: 18. Zechariah 7: 11. Acts 20. I Peter 5: 1, 2, 3, 4. I Timothy 2: 20.
[2] Alison has " the same."
[3] Later editions have " affectation."
[4] In this and subsequent paragraphs, there are no specific references in the body of the text. Scripture references follow each paragraph. Numbers 11: 24. II Chronicles 19: 8. Acts 15. I Timothy 5.
[5] Acts 6: 2. I Timothy 3: 8, 9.

H*

reported of for good workes, such as have nourished their children, such as have bin harberous to straungers: diligent and serviceable to the saintes, compassionate and helpefull to them in adversitie, given to everie good worke, continuing in supplications and prayers night and daye.[1]

These officers must firste be duelie[2] proved, then if they be founde blameles, [let them] administer, etc.[3]

Nowe as their persons, giftes, conditions, manners, life and proofe of these officers, is [are] set downe by the Holie Ghoste: so are their offices limited, severed, and divers [diverse][4].

The pastour's office is, to feede the sheepe of Christ in greene and wholesome pastures[5] of his worde, and leade them to the still waters, even to the pure fountaine and river of life; hee must guyde and keepe those sheepe by that heavenlie sheepehooke and pastorall staffe of the worde, thereby drawing them to him, thereby lookinge into their soules, even into their most secrete thoughtes: thereby discerning their diseases, and thereby curinge them: applying to everie disease a fit and convenient me-[A 4 *recto*]dicine, according to the qualitie and malladie of the disease, and give warning to the church, that they may orderlie proceede to excommunication. Further, he must by this his sheepehooke watch over and defend his flock from ravenous beastes and the wolfe, and take the litle foxes, etc.[6]

The doctour's office is alreadie sett downe in his[7] description: His speciall care must bee, to builde uppon the onely true groundworke, golde, silver, and pretious stones, that his worke may endure the triall of the fire, and by the light of the same fire, reveale the tymber, hay, and stubble of false teachers: hee must take diligent heede to keepe the church from errours. And, further, hee must deliver his doctrine so playnlie, simplie, and purelie, that the church

---

[1] I Timothy 5: 9, 10.
[2] Alison has " truelie."
[3] I Timothy 3: 10.
[4] I Corinthians 12: 12, 18.
[5] Alison has " pastors."
[6] Leviticus 10: 11. Numbers 18: 1. Ezekiel 44: 23 and [chapters] 33 and 34. Psalm 23. John 21: 15. Acts 20: 28. I Peter 5: 1. Zechariah 11: 7. Revelation 22: 2. Luke 12: 42. II Corinthians 10: 4, 5. Hebrews 8: 12.
[7] Alison has " this."

may increase with the increasing of God, and growe up into him which is the head, Christ Jesus.[1]

The office of the auncientes[2] is expressed in their description: Their especiall care must bee, to see the ordinaunces of God truely taught and practized, aswel by the officers in dooing their duetie uprightlie, as to see that the people obey willinglie and redilie. It is their duetie to see the congregation holilie and quietlie ordered, and no way[3] disturbed, by the contentious and disobedient, frowarde and obstinate: not taking away the libertie of the least, but upholding the right of all, wiselie judginge of times and circumstances. They must bee readie assistauntes to the pastour and teachers, helpinge to beare their burden, but not intruding into their office.[4]

The deacon's office is, faithfullie to gather, and collect by the ordinance of the church, the goodes and benevolence of the faithfull, and by the same direction, diligentlie and trustilie to distribute them according to the necessitie of the saincts. Further, they must enquire and consider of the proportion of the wantes both of the officers and other poore, and accordinglie relate unto the church that provision may be made.[5]

The reliever's and widowe's office is, to minister to the sicke, lame, wearie, and diseased, such helpefull comforts [A 4 *verso*] as they neede, by watching, tending and helping them: further, they must shewe good example to the yonger women, in sober, modest, and godlie conversation, avoyding idlenes, vaine talke, and light behaviour.[6]

These officers, though they bee divers [diverse] and severall, yet are they not severed, least there should bee a division in the body, but they are as members of the body, having the same care one of another, joyntlie doing their severall dueties to the service of the sainctes, and to the edification of the bodie of Christ, till wee all meete togither in the perfect measure of the fulnes of Christe, by whom all the bodye being in the meane whyle thus coupled and

---

[1] Ezekiel 33: 1. I Corinthians 11: 19. John 10: 11, 12. Ezekiel 44: 24. Malachi 2: 6. I Corinthians 3: 11. I Corinthians 1: 7. I Timothy 4: 16 and 6: 20. Ephesians 2: 20. Hebrews 6: 1.

[2] Elders or presbyters.

[3] Alison has " man."

[4] Numbers 11: 16. Deuteronomy 16: 18. II Chronicles 19: 8. Exodus 39: 42. I Timothy 3: 15. II Timothy 1: 13. I Corinthians 11: 16 and 14: 33. Galatians 2: 4, 5. Colossians 1: 16. Acts 20. I Peter 5: 1. Romans 12: 8.

[5] Acts 6. Romans 12: 8.

[6] I Timothy 5: 9. Romans 12: 8.

knit togither by everie joynt for the furniture thereof, according to
the effectuall power which is in the measure of everie part, receyveth
increase of the bodie, unto the edifying of it selfe in love: neither
can anie of these offices be wanting, without grievous lamenes, and
apparant deformitie of the bodye, yea violent injurie to the head,
Christ Jesus.[1]

Thus, this holie armie of sainctes, is marshalled here in earth by
these officers, under the conduct of their glorious emperour Christ,
that victorious Michaell.[2] Thus it marcheth in this most heavenlie
order,[3] and gratious araye, against all enimies both bodilie and
ghostlie. Peaceable in it selfe as Jerusalem, terrible unto them as
an armie with banners, triumphing over their tyrannie with
patience, their crueltie with meekenes,[4] and over death it selfe
with dying. Thus through the blood of that spotles lambe, and
that worde of their testimonie, they are more than conquerours,
brusing the head of the serpent: yea, through the power of his
worde, they have power to cast downe Sathan like lightning: to
treade upon serpents and scorpions: to cast downe strong holds,
and everie thing that exalteth it selfe against God. The gates of
hell and all the principalities and powers of the worlde, shall not
prevayle against it.[5]

Further, he hath given them the keyes of the king-[B 1 *recto*]dome
of heaven, that whatsoever they binde in earth by his worde, shalbe
bounde in heaven: and whatsoever they loose on earth, shalbe
loosed in heaven.[6]

Nowe this power[7] whiche Christe hath given unto his church,

---

[1] Luke 9: 46. John 13: 12. I Corinthians 12: 12, 25, 28. Ephesians 4:
11, 12, 13, 16.

[2] Michael, the archangel, is mentioned twice in the Bible, in Jude 1: 9 and
Revelation 12: 7. The word " archangel " occurs in I Thessalonians 4:
16 and Jude 1: 9.

[3] Alison omits " order."

[4] Alison omits this phrase.

[5] Romans 11, etc. I Corinthians 12. Revelation 14: 12. Canticles 6: 3.
Revelation 12: 11. Luke 10: 18, 19. Matthew 16: 18. Romans 8: 38, 39.

[6] Matthew 16: 19. John 29 [20]: 23. Matthew 18: 18.

[7] The power of discipline and excommunication. To the Church of England,
with its almost national membership, the problem of dealing with the
profane multitudes was a never-ending one which to-day is mostly
relegated to the municipal and county courts. For the Brownists and
Barrowists the problem was less acute because of the principle of the
gathered church, whereby the more notorious sinners were excluded.
Nevertheless, the members believed that if the tree was to stand firmly
rooted and strong, the dead branches needed to be constantly pruned.
This function of passing judgment on conduct caused untold problems
and unsolvable dissensions.

and to everie member of his church, to keepe it in order, hee hath not lefte it to their discretions and lustes to be used or neglected as they will, but in his last will and testament, he hath set downe both an order of proceeding, and an ende to whiche it is used.[1]

And if the fault bee private, private [*sic*], holie and loving admonition and reproofe [is to be used], with an inwarde desire and earnest care to winne their brother: but if he will not heare thee, yet to take two or three other brethren with him, whom he knoweth most meete to that purpose, that by the mouth of two or three witnesses, everie worde may be confirmed: and if he refuse to heare them, then to declare the matter to the church, whiche ought severelie and sharpelie to reprehende, gravelie to admonishe, and lovinglie to perswade the partie offending: shewing him the heynousnes of his offence, and the daunger of his obstinacie, and the fearefull judgements of the Lorde.[2]

If this prevaile not to drawe him to repentance, then are they in the name and power[3] of the Lorde Jesus, with the whole congregation, reverentlie in prayer to proceed to excommunication, casting him out of their congregation and fellowship, that is, out of the covenaunt and protection of the Lord, for his disobedience and obstinacie, and committing him to Sathan for the destruction of the fleshe, that the spirit may bee saved in the day of the Lord Jesus, if such bee his good will and pleasure.[4]

Further, they are to warne the whole congregation and all other faithfull, to holde him as a heathen and a publicane, and to abstaine them selves from his societie, as not to eate or drinke with him, etc., unles it bee [B 1 *verso*] such as of necessitie must needes, as his wife, his children and familie: yet these (if they be members of the church) are not to joyne to him in any spirituall exercise.[5]

All this notwithstanding the church is not to holde him as an enimie, but to admonish him and praye for him as a brother, prooving if at anie time the Lorde will give him repentaunce.[6]

---

[1] John 20: 23. Matthew 16: 19 and 18: 18. Deuteronomy [12: 31, 32].
[2] Leviticus 19: 17, 18. Matthew 18: 15. Deuteronomy 19: 15. Matthew 18: 16.
[3] Alison omits " and power."
[4] Matthew 18: 16. II Thessalonians 3: 15.
[5] II Corinthians 10: 8 and 12: 10. I Timothy 5: 20. Galatians 2: 14.
[6] Based on II Thessalonians 3: 15.

For this power is not given them to the destruction of anie, but to the edification and preservation of all.[1]

If the offence bee publike, the partie is publiquelie to bee reproved, and admonished: if he then repent not, to proceede to excommunication, *ut supra.*

The repentance of the partie must bee proportionable to the offence, *viz.*, if the offence bee publique, [the repentance must be] publique: if private, [the repentance may be] private: humbled, submissive, sorrowfull, unfained, giving glorie to the Lord.[2]

There must great care bee had of admonitions, that they bee not captious, or curious: finding faulte where none is; neither yet in bitternes or reproche, for that were to destroye and not to save our brother: but they must bee carefullie done, with prayer going before: they must bee seazoned with trueth, gravitie, love and peace.[3]

Moreover, in this churche is an especiall care had by everie member thereof, of offences: the strong ought not to offend the weake, nor the weake to judge the stronge: but all graces here are given to the service and edification of eache other in love and longe suffering.[4]

In this church is the trueth purelie taught, and surelie kept: heere is the covenaunte,[5] the sacramentes, and promisses, the graces, the glorie, the presens, the worship of God, etc.[6]

---

[1] II Thessalonians 3: 15. II Corinthians 10: 8 and 13: 10. This paragraph, beginning with the words, " all this notwithstanding," belongs where it is. In subsequent editions, it was placed before the two preceding paragraphs. To the best of my knowledge, the first edition is to be found only in the Lambeth Palace Library, which has two copies. This first edition, and Alison's refutation of it, have the correct order of the paragraphs. The editions in the British Museum, Dr. Williams's Library, the Folger Shakespeare Library, Library of Congress, Huntington Library, and Sterling Memorial Library at Yale are not first editions, and do not have the correct order of paragraphs. Most of them have what is probably the third edition, with the original date of 1589 reprinted on page 8. See Henoch Clapham, *Errour on the Right Hand* (London, 1608), pp. 10-12. See also Henry M. Dexter and Morton Dexter, *The England and Holland of the Pilgrims*, p. 201 note.

[2] Leviticus 19: 18. Proverbs 10: 12. Romans 12: 19 and 13: 10 and 14: 1.

[3] Galatians 6: 1, 2. [II] Timothy 2: 24. Mark 9: 50. Ephesians 4: 29. Matthew 18: 15. James 5: 5, 19, 20.

[4] Luke 17: 1. Proverbs 10: 12. Romans 14: 13, 19. Galatians 6: 2.

[5] Alison has " the covenaunte of the sacraments."

[6] Genesis 17. Leviticus 16: 11. Isaiah 44: 3. Galatians 4: 28, and 6: 16. Isaiah 60: 15. Deuteronomy 4: 12, 13. Isaiah 56: 7. I Timothy 3: 15. Isaiah 52: 8.

A True Description out of the Worde of God

[B 2 *recto*] Into this temple entreth no vncleane thinge, neither what so ever worketh abhominations or lyes, but they which are written in the lambe's booke of life.[1]

But without this church shalbe dogges and enchaunters, and whoremongers, and murderers, and idolatours, and who so ever loveth and maketh lies.[2]

FINIS

---

[1] Isaiah 52: 1.   Ezekiel 44: 9.   Isaiah 35: 8.   Zechariah 14: 21.   Revelation 21: 27.
[2] Romans 2: 9.   Revelation 22: 15.

XIV

THE FIRST PART OF THE PLATFORME

This treatise of Barrow was published in 1611 as a part of a larger apologetic work, *Mr. Henry Barrowe's Platform.* The title-page carries the date, *anno* 1593, but this refers not to the date of publication but to the year of the martyrdom of Barrow and Greenwood and Penry. On the last page appears the date 1611, which is the publication date. The entire book, which is a defence of Separatism and Barrowism, contains: (1) " A Dialogue or Discourse, Passing between Desiderius and Miles Micklebound, by Occasion of Their Old Love and New Meeting " (A2 *recto*—C8 *recto*) ; (2) a letter to Mr. Wood, a Scottish preacher in Ireland, 1594 (C8 *recto*—D2 *recto*) ; (3) " The Humble, Most Earnest, and Lamentable Complaint and Supplication of the Persecuted and Proscribed Church and Servants of Christ, Falsely Called Brownists, unto the High Court of Parliament " (D2 *recto*—D4 *recto*), the draft of which has been ascribed to Barrow, but more likely was written by Penry ; (4) a petition to King James I (D4 *verso*—D5 *verso*) ; (5) a continuation of the " Dialogue " (D5 *verso*—E2 *verso* and I2 *verso*—L4 *verso*), and " The First Part of the Platforme " (E3 *recto*—I2 *recto*), with Barrow and Greenwood's letter of the 13th of the 9th month (1590) appended.

The title of this treatise implies a second part. The compiler of the entire pamphlet made diligent inquiry at Amsterdam and Leiden, but found none. Therefore, he concluded that Barrow's death precluded any continuation. In this conclusion he was correct in believing that there was no second part, but he was incorrect in thinking that Barrow's death was the reason for the non-continuation of *The First Part of the Platforme.*

After analyzing the ideas in Barrow's treatise, and after

searching for similar ideas or counter-arguments in the literature of the period 1570-1600, I noticed in Hatfield House among
the Cecil Papers, Volume 167, ff. 100, 102, that Barrow and
Greenwood had addressed two letters on September 13 and 18,
1590, to Lord Burghley. In this first letter they said that they
had " drawen an unperfect discourse of such weightie causes,
as we were desirous (when God should call us thereunto) to
make knowne unto her majestie or some of her honourable
counsell." Later in the same letter, they write: " the other
part of our treatise, how this should be effected, what the true
ministry of Christ is, how it should be erected, and brought in,
we have purposely reserved till we know your honour's pleasure,
for the discussing of these which must be agreed upon, before
we can procede to the other." Lord Burghley quickly made
known his pleasure, by expressing his strong displeasure and
absolute refusal to have any dealings with them, as is seen in
the second letter of September 18, and thus the project was
dropped.

The First Part of the Platforme, fortunately, turns out to
be the " unperfect discourse " or treatise submitted to Lord
Burghley, together with a letter dated September 13, 1590.
By comparing the ideas in the treatise and letter, the reader
will see that they belong together. Thus it becomes possible
to fit this work into the chronological framework of Barrow's
work.

It is a possibility that Barrow obtained the idea for his
title from Thomas Cooper, his opponent and judge, the Bishop
of Winchester, who wrote *An Admonition to the People of
England* (1589). In this work Bishop Cooper warns the
people of England that a new platform of government, as
suggested by ecclesiastical reformers, would bring disastrous
results, and that alterations and innovations were dangerous
to the state (signature A ii *verso*, pp. 85-87, 143). Barrow had
read Bishop Cooper's *Admonition* and replied to some of his
arguments in his *A Brief Discoverie of the False Church*.

The main theme of *The First Part of the Platforme* is

that the false ministry of archbishops and bishops, together with deans, sub-deans, prebendaries, and vicars, should be eradicated. Likewise, the courts of the archbishops, bishops, and archdeacons should be abolished. The queen should disendow the church, confiscate the lands, and—if she so desire—give her subjects a portion thereof. The clergy should be supported by contributions and the benevolence of God's people. Such ideas were indeed radical for the Elizabethan clergy and laity ; and to Lord Burghley, himself a possessor of vast holdings, such doctrines seemed fantastic.

*   *   *   *   *   *

THE FIRST PART OF THE PLATFORME, PENNED BY THAT WORTHY SERVANT OF JESUS CHRIST, AND BLESSED WITNES OF HIS MOST HOLY ORDINANCES, TO THE LOSSE OF LIFE: MR. HENRY BARROWE.

1. That the offices of archbishops, lord bishops, arch-deacons, *etc.*, with all their courts and under officers, ought by the commandement of God to be suppressed by the prince's authoritie: and the persons usurping the same, hereafter to be compelled to walke in some lawfull calling eyther in the church or commune wealth, as God shall make them fit and call them thereunto.

2. That this whole ministery and offices of deane, sub-deane, prebends, *etc.*, parson, vicar, curates, stypendarie lectorers, as the taile of the dragon, ought by the prince to be suppressed and abolished. And the persons usurping the same to be compelled from henceforth to walk orderly in some lawfull calling or office, in church or common wealth. [E 3 *verso*] as God maketh them fit and calleth them lawfully thereunto, using the gifts that God hath given them aright to the glorie of the giver and the good of the church.

3. That the landes and lordly revenues of these arch-bishops, lord bishops, deanes, *etc.*, togither with the gleabes, temporalities, etc., ought to be resumed by the prince, and wholly converted to civil uses.

4. That the prince may give unto her subjects [to be ?] the owners of them, their severall tithes aswel open as privie, or reserve so much by way of tribute therof as shall seeme good unto her majestie.

5. That the true ministerie ought not to be mainteyned by such gleabes, tithes, set stipends, or by the rated wages of the profane, but by the free contribution and dutifull benevolence of the faithful, especially of that congregation unto which they administer.

6. That the prince ought to proclaime and publish the gospel of Christ, with the true preaching and sincere

practise thereof in all things that God shal give knowledge of. And to forbid and exterminate all other religions, worship and ministeries within her dominions.

[E 4 *recto*]

Exod. 20: 2, 3, 4, 5
Mat. 15: 9
Num. 3: 10
Rom. 12: 7, 8

Seeing that holy and mighty God of heaven and earth will onely be worshiped and served in his church according to his own prescript will in his word, and not by any devises of men, how holy or expedient soever they may seem to themselves, and by that ministerie onely which his sonne the Lord of the house hath instituted in his last will and testament, and not by any other or strange ministerie: seeing so great bleseings and promises both of this life and of the life to come are made to those people and churches that thus worship and serve the Lord according to his owne holy wil, as we most

Deut. 28, 29, 30, 31, 32 ch.
Zech. 11.
Ezek. 14.
Jer. 23: 21, 22

plentifully and comfortably read in the Scriptures, and on the contrary such dreadfull plagues and fearfull judgments denounced against and executed upon those nations and people that make a shew otherwise to worship and serve God according to their owne desires or policies: seeing God always [E 4 *verso*] speaketh by his owne ministerie to his owne people, and never by any false Sinistery,[1] but always sendeth the one in his espetial mercie to prepare and make fit unto his heaveny [*sic*] kingdome,

Prov. 2: 10, 11, 12, etc.
Prov. 16: 17 and 14: 12
16 Mat. 7:[2]

the other in his wrath and displeasure to seduce and prepare al degrees unto judgement; it behooveth every soule in what estate soever to look diligently unto and to be well assured of their wayes wherein they walk and are led. Espetially and above all, it is the office and dutie of princes and rulers to whom

Deut. 17: 18, 19
1 King. 2: 3
2 Chron. 15 & 17. & 29. & 30. & 34 chap.

the word and sword of God is therefore committed, most carefully to advance and establish in their dominions the true worship and ministerie of God and to suppresse and roote out all contrary, as they tender their owne salvation at that day of all ac-

---

[1] Very likely this is a genuine misprint and not a play upon words.

[2] The reference is to 16 Matthew 7. I believe the previous reference should be Proverbs 16: 17 and 14: 12, 16, and the following reference should be to Matthew, chapter 7.

compts and the salvation of that people under their
charge. Private members howsoever they ought to
refraine and to keep their soules and bodies undefiled
from al [F 1 *recto*] false worship which is imposed,
suffering rather in all patient and christian manner,
whatsoever may be inflicted upon them for the same
(as they that feare more to offend God than men),
yet ought they not to stretch forth their hand by
force to the reformation of any publick enormities,
which are by the magistrate's authoritie set up. For
that were to transgresse the limits of their owne
place and calling, to usurpe and intrude into the
prince's royall throne and dignitie. Which heynous
presumption escapeth not due vengeance either in
his life or in the world to come. But now, howsoever, no private subject ought to intermeddle with
the execution of any thing, that belongeth to the
prince's and magistrate's office, without the prince's
speciall commandement and deputation therunto.
Yet is it the bounden dutie of every true hearted
subject and faithfull servant of God, to witnes and
crie out against all things [F 1 *verso*] that ar exalted
against the knowledg of God, to pray for and by all
humble, peaceable and godly meanes, to advertise,
exhort, and excite, their prince and magistrates to
remove, and depose all false worship and false
ministers in the land.[1]

For this cause have we, the Lord Jesus Christ's
most unworthy servants and witnesses, hitherto en-
dured in all meeke and pacient manner, the great
outrage and tyranny which this antichristian
Romish prelacie and clergy have long exercised over
our poore bodies, rather than to stoope downe eyther
to that patched traditionall worship which they devise and impose, or unto that unlawfull power which
they usurp and exercise over all men's consciences:
yea, at this present (especially upon your honour's so
gracious acceptation) we are bould (yet in all reverence and humilitie) to declare our loyall heartes and

Marginal references:
Amos 5: 4, 5
Dan. 3: 10
Reve. 14: 4, 9, 10, 11, 12
Luke 12: 4, 5

1 Cor. 7: 20
Tit. 3: 1
1 Pet. 2: 13, 16

Ezek. 4: 4 & 22: 30, 31
Amos 3: 7, 8
Mic. 3: 8
2 Cor. 10: 4, 5, 6

---

[1] Barrow's views about the ecclesiastical powers of the prince are conveniently summarized in Powicke, *Henry Barrow Separatist*, pp. 128-9.

intire affections as in the sight of Christ, unto our most gratious soveraigne [F 2 *recto*] Queene Elizabeth, and unto this whole state, by discovering these deceivers, and manifesting these heinous abuses and intollerable inormities which remaine in the land by their meanes to the high displeasure of God, though it be with the present perill and danger of our lives, which those antichristian bishops, armed with such power and hostilitie, will soone, upon the knowledge that we have revealed these matters, dispatch one way or another. But we make no reckning nor speach of these things, neyther are our lives deare unto our selves, so wee may finish up our testimony and course with joy, and by giving warning (if God's will be) to prevent the heavie wrath and judgements of God that hangs over this whole land, for the hainous prophanation of God's name, contempt of his word, and generall impietie even of all degrees. All which enormities here to discuss in particular as they flow from them [F 2 *verso*] into all estates of the land would require a larger discourse than this present time or purpose will permit. Onely in this place it may suffice that we engage our mortall lives and undertake upon the losse of the same to make manifest proof unto all men by the undoubted word of God in any free and christian conference either publike or private, or to make evident demonstration in writing by the Scriptures (if we may be permitted), that this whole ministery and publike ministration, which is by them exercised in the Church of England is false and antichristian, such as cannot be joyned to the gospell of Christ, nor used in the church of Christ, which being proved such, then is it the prince's duetie as she tendereth the salvation of her owne soule, and the safety of all this people, which the Lord hath committed unto her charge, to abolish and depose the same.

Neyther is there cause why her [F 3 *recto*] majesty should make more scruple or delay herein, than her most royal auncestor of famous memorie King Henry the Eight did in much lesse light and assurance, when he expelled the pope[1] and suppressed the abbies,[2] *etc*. Especially when it shall be proved that the whole ministerie which now remayneth, even from the primate archbishop to the lowest sommoner, togither with their courtes, canons, offices, officers, *etc*., are of the same birth, belonged to the same apostaticall throne, have as litle mention, place or use in the Testament and church of Christ as they, and therfore ought in like maner togither with their foresayd father and brethren be cast out, and not to be suffered in the church or common wealth. Neyther can this matter and motion now seeme strange, seeing all forreign churches in all other places have cast out and changed this ministerie,[3] howsoever eyther of ignorance or fleshly policie [F 3 *verso*] they might for a tyme give handes thereunto, yet except they can shew that Christ hath instituted divers and sundry kindes of ministeries and governments unto his church, one in one age and place, another in an other, or that the ministerie of the New Testament is not certaine, permanent and unchangeable, the same in all churches,[4] then doubtlesse these so divers ministeries, in name, office, entrance, administration, as theirs and this are, cannot both of them be of God. Againe, even at home the forward preachers of these present times (not to speak of such motions unto the kings of this land at sundry other times) have a long time sought and sued unto her majestie

Ephes. 4: 4, 5, 6, 10, 11, 12, 13
Heb. 3: 6 & 12: 27, 28 & 13: 8

---

1 The Acts of 1534 for the restraint of annates, for the stopping of payments of Peter's pence and other fees, for the submission of the clergy to the king's majesty, and for clarifying the succession to the crown, completed the main work.

2 In 1536 the smaller monasteries were dissolved and by 1539 the larger ones had been abolished.

3 In the Netherlands, Denmark, Norway and Sweden, and Scotland; also, in parts of France, Germany ,and Switzerland. Barrowmeans by " forreign churches " the reformed churches.

4 See Thomas Cooper, *An Admonition to the People of England*, p. 81. There are three issues or editions of this work, all issued in 1589, one of 252 pages, one of 244 pages and one of 245 pages. The latter is the edition cited. I believe that the first edition of 252 pages, used by Barrow, was withdrawn and corrected.

and to the parliaments for a reformation,[1] *viz.*, that these archbishops, bishops, arch deacons, deanes, *etc.*, with all their courts, colleages [colleges], government and administration, might be removed and taken away, their ample and great li-[F 4 *recto*]vings converted to the maintenance of sundry poore preachers, and that the church might be restored to that auncient order and governement which Christ hath instituted (by them called discipline): which

2 Chron. 29. & 35. ch.

matter they neither could nor durst have moved or attempted if the office, ministerie, goverment of these lord bishops, *etc.*, had not beene wholly antichristian, and directly contrary to the Testament of Christ. For if the office, ministery, and governement of these lord bishops and their accomplices had been of God, they ought still of necessitie with all reverence to have been reserved, the corruptions and abuses that had grown therin to be corrected and purged. But if their offices, ministery and governement were the institution and ordinance of Christ, what a dangerous and execrable motion had it been to perswade the prince and parliament to reject and cast out the true offices, ministery and government

John 13: 20
Luke 10: 16

[F 4 *verso*] of Christ out of the church? They that should thus reject Christ's ministerie, ordinances, or any part thereof, reject Christ himselfe, doe violence to his members, spoile and ruinate the church, and cannot be of God. But these men sought not the reformation or correction of the persons, or abuses of these lordly bishops, their courts, *etc.*, but the utter remooving and abolishing of their offices, ministery and government for ever out of the land; wherby it is manifest these men (howsoever they have since changed their copie), tooke them to be antichristian

[1] See especially *A Briefe and Plaine Declaration, concerning the Desires of All Those Faithfull Ministers That Seeke Reformation of the Church of England* (1584), and *A Petition Made to the Convocation House, 1586, by the Ministers* (1588). See also John Penry, *A Treatise Containing the Aequity of an Humble Supplication* (1587) and John Penry, *The Appellation of I. Penri unto the Highe Court of Parliament* (1589). Earlier, John Field and Thomas Wilcox published their work, *An Admonition to the Parliament* (1572).

and such as ought not to be used or suffered in the church of Christ.

And now that these bishops and their traine, their offices, ministery, government, are thus found, even by the preachers themselves, not to be of God, (as to any that will further examine them by the rules of Christ's Testament cannot be hid or doubt-[F 5 *recto*]full), we see not how even these Reformists themselves [—] this choice reserved remnant, or this rable of parsons, vicars, vagrant hireling preachers, without certaine place, office, or charge (which are but the very taile of the dragon), should be exempt from the same judgment, seing they all are derived John 10: 1 and proceeded from the same apostaticall throne that the bishops, yea, even from the throne of the bishops. So that if the bishops be not the true ministery of Christ, but false and antichristian, then 2 Cor. 6: 15 can they not make and ordeyne true ministers, or in Ps. 94: 20 that office and estate have any thing to doe in the church of Christ. But all these most forward preachers themselves, with all the rest of these parsons, vicars, curates, were all ordeyned and made ministers by these bishops, and execute their ministerie under them, according to their decrees, receiving their licence, swearing their canonicall obedience, *etc.* Therefore, if [F 5 *verso*] the one be antichristian and to be cast out, so must the other of necessity, especially seeing the names, offices, entrance, administration, and maintenance of these, are as false and contrary to the rules of Christ's Testament, as those of the bishops, and have no more place or mention in the Testament and church of Christ than their lords and bishops and their assistants have. Neyther can we see with what conscience they could both denounce the bishops [to be] antichristian and to be abolished, and yet both receive their ministery from them and execute it under them, and that even when and since they labored this Reformation: whose corrupt covetous minde yet further appeareth in that they sought the fatte livings and lordly revenewes of these bishops,

deanes, *etc.*, which they erewhile blamed in those possessors, and so but laboured to doe as much for their lords the bishops, as the bishops did to their lord the pope: [F 6 *recto*] which is but to cast out their name and persons, yet to reserve all their livings and privileges, even all the fat and gainfull ware of Amalek unto themselves. Thus howsoever they be divided amongst themselves (which is no strength to their kingdome), yet is it evident they came all of a broode, even of that swarme of locusts that came out of the smoke of the bottomlesse pit, when that key thereof was given to that fallen starr antichrist: which locusts devoured all the fruites of the earth, and had the power of scorpions to sting and invenome the consciences of their hearers. But now being discovered they shal together with the beast (before whose throne they wrought their miracles with the east winde of God's judgements) be blowne into the lake that is prepared for the beast and for the false prophet, and not in this estate be allowed any place in the church of Christ for ever.
[F 6 *verso*]

And now that this whole ministery, both lord bishops and their assistants, collegiate deanes and their associates, tithing parsons and their curates, togither with all these mercenarie vagrant preachers, are found to be strange and antichristian, such as are not to be used, suffred or mainteyned in the church of Christ, it remaineth that wee entreat [consider] of their fat portion and large livings, to whom of right they now belong, whether to the church or common wealth, to the ministery or to the prince. To this or any false ministery they cannot belong, because a false ministery is not to be suffered much less to be endowed or mainteined in any christian common wealth. Neyther can the true church or ministery prescribe or challenge any present right or interest in these lands or endowments of this false ministery. [It is] Christ that provided and instituted for his ministerie an other kinde of maintenance than such royalties, lordships, gleabe lands, tithes, or [F 7

Margin notes:
Mat. 6: 24

1 Thes. 2: 3, 4, 5
1 Sam. 15: 21
Luke 11: 17
Rev. 9

Rev. 19: 20

Psal. 16: 4
2 Chron. 13: 9, 10

1 Cor. 9: 7, etc.

recto] set stipends. The true ministery is to live and to be mainteyned of the flock to which they attend and administer, and that not by tenthes or thirds, by stints or rates, by bargain, law, or imposition, but by the loving, free, yet dutifull contribution of the flock, as the abilitie of the one extendeth, and the needs of the other require, each one most willingly, not by constraint, imparting even of all their goods unto them to releeve their wants, not to nourish them in superfluitie, idlenes, *etc.* These worldly promotions, tithes, set stipends, *etc.*, belong rather to idle bellies and hirelings, than to the true ministerie of Christ, wherof they are and always have been rather the corruption than the maintenance. These would but hinder and extinguish the continuall love, care, benevolence and duetie of the flock unto their ministery; as also the labour, diligence, and watchfulnes and faithfulnes of the ministerie to their [F 7 *verso*] flock, as we have lamentable experience in the present estate of this ministery and people generally. Again, the number, estate, and needs of the ministery are so uncertaine, there sometimes being more, sometimes fewer to be mainteyned, according to the greatnes and variable estate of each congregation (and not in each parish one onely, as here), the ministery also some of them having families greater or lesse, and sundry necessary occasions so uncertainly as they cannot be provided for, rated, and limited by any better or other lawes and orders than those Christ hath set downe in his Testament.

To conclude, this alotting of landes, tithes, *etc.*, to the ministerie in every parish both is preposterous, seing as yet there is not in every such parish, no, not in any one parish, a people rightly gathered unto, and joyned in the faith orderly togither, fit for a ministery, much lesse any true ministery, rightly chosen and esta-[F 8 *recto*]blished amongst them, and also it presupposeth, yea, maketh a necessity, that there must be and always shal be unto the worlde's end (so long as there be any inhabitants) a true

Marginal references: Gal. 6: 6; 2 Cor. 9; 1 Cor. 16: 1, 2; Phil. 3: 18, 19; 1 Pet. 5: 2, 3; Rom. 12: 7, 8; 1 Cor. 12: 29; Ephes. 4: 11

church and ministery in every parish, and so confirmeth that popish errour of local and personal succession, besides sundry other inconveniences that would insue therof. This litle that hath been sayd may suffice to shew that the true church and ministerie of Christ have no claim, interest, nor right unto, neyther use of, these lordships, gleabes, tithes, set stipends, *etc.*, which erewhile were possessed by these prelates and prowling preists; then must they of necessity belong and returne unto the prince and commune wealth from whence they first proceeded.

Now whether unto the king as supreme lord, or unto the lordes patrons that owe [own] the advousons,[1] may some question arise, which controversie being a matter in lawe, shall much [F 8 *verso*] better be pleaded and decided by her majestie's sergeants and judges than by us that are ignorant of these matters. Onely this concerning the office of these patrones we say, that we finde no mention therof in the Testament of Christ (where all the offices of his church are perfectly described[)], nor any use therof in the church of Christ, but rather finde it greatly prejudiciall and contrary unto the libertie and holy order of the church. For Christ hath appointed that every particular church, all the members thereof gathered togither as well learned as other, with one accord should make choice of their ministerie after due proofe according to the rules prescribed.[2] Which choice can not be made or order kept when one man (were he never so wise) taketh away the power and dutie of the whole church to make the choice, how much lesse when the patron that oweth [owneth] the advouson, is many tymes [G 1 *recto*] a stranger both to the priest and people, ignorant, and

Acts 6: 2, 5, &
14
& 14: 23
Titus 1: 5
1 Tim. 3: 10

[1] The right of presentation to a living, not infrequently belonging to a secular patron. In Anglo-Saxon times the bishop or feudal lord usually possessed the right, but in succeeding centuries, as laymen built chapels, churches, and monasteries, they obtained the right of nominating incumbents. The right was subject not to canon law but to English civil law, since the Constitutions of Clarendon (1164), and still exists.

[2] This is a clear-cut Congregational principle, differing from the presbyterian system which vested the right in a committee or court — the presbytery, or in one person — the bishop, as in the episcopalian and papal system.

unable to discern or judge of the gifts, fitnes, life of
the person chosen and presented, the patron many
times being a child, a woman, yea, peradventure a
profane or wicked person, a papist, an atheist, an
heretick, *etc.*, which choice the miserable people rue
that are subject to these woefull orders, and must
endure whatsoever these lords their patron and
Ordinary do, be the priest never so bad. Neyther
can all the learning and wisdome these bishops have
or want [lack], their orders, laying on their handes,
or breathing their unholighoste upon them, make
either this trust and callinge of these patrones good,
or the parsons thus called true ministers of Christ.
All that God hath appointed to the ministry he
calleth lawfullie to the ministerie, neither can any
that want this lawful callinge be lawful ministers.

Now then the office of these patrones being found
thus contrarie to the word [G 1 *verso*] of God, thus Num. 16: 5, 40
prejudicial and pernicious to the churche, ought also Num. 17: 8
Heb. 5: 4
by the prince to be abolished: which office being
taken away wee see not how any man can challenge
the revenues belonging thereunto as to their private
use. When in the best consideration these patrones
were but a deputies or feffees of trust to see the
towne furnished of a convenient priest in due time,
and might not at any time deteine any parte of the
revenues to their own privat use. Suche as chalenge
by impropriation[1] claime by a new title and advance
the prince's right from whom they received the
same. Which sheweth that the prince hath power
to change the use and bestow the landes as pleaseth
her onely to civile use. But as to these tithes which Num. 18: 21,
etc.
these ravenous priests extort from all her majestie's 1 Sam. 2: 14,
15, 16
subjects, thrusting in their sickle into everie field, Mat. 23: 14,
23
their fleshhooke into every poore bodie's kettle, without regard of faithfull or unfaithfull, [G 2 *recto*] riche
or poore, devouring widowes' houses, and poore
succourlesse children under colour of long prayers,

---

[1] An impropriation was the lay possession of tithes, or the transference of
the revenues of a benefice to a lay proprietor or corporation. The pro-
prietorship in medieval times was often held by religious houses, which
lost their holdings during the English Reformation.

tithing even to the mint and anyse, though the prince ought to take them out of these greedie harpies' hands, and may of her royall authority assume not onely them, but even what part of her subjects' goods it shall please her, in way of tribute: yet if her majestie of her bounteous disposition shall vouchsafe to give back and restore these tithes to their peculiar owners, especially to the poore, or to reserve what portion therof shee please to her owne use, she shal both inriche and highly content all her subjects, and binde them most firmly unto her: and far surpasse in bounty, not onely all her roiall progenitours, but even rather all the kings and emperours that ever were in the world, and relieve more poore hungrie soules every day, than the King Assuerosh [Ahasuerus] did at his long lasting sumptuous feast,[1] which shal no doubt [G 2 *verso*] be more acceptable and be held more pure religion and undefiled before God, thus to visite the widow and fatherlesse in their tribulation, to smite off this more heavie yoke than ever was imposed by any king of this land, and let the oppressed goe free, and to keepe her self unspotted of the world, than to make sumptuous feasts unto the rich, or to offer store of burnt offrings unto God.

And as her majestie shall hereby release the bodies of her oppressed subjects, from daily grievous exactions of these greedy priests; so much more shall she relieve many a sorowfull distressed soule: yea, even the whole land that long have beene misled and held under these more than Babylonish yoke and Egyptian bondage[2] of their antichristian power, ministery, and traditions, by proclaiming unto al her subjects the joyous heavenly pure gospell of Christ, calling all

Rom. 13: 6
Mat. 17: 25, 27

Est. 1: 3, 4, 5
Esa. 58: 6. & 1: 17
Jam. 1: 27

[1] King Ahasuerus, who reigned over 127 provinces from India to Ethiopa, gave a banquet in the third year of his reign [519/18 or 483/482 B.C.] for his princes, nobles, governors, and army chiefs. This sumptuous feasting lasted 180 days, and was followed by a second banquet, lasting seven days, for the inhabitants of the capital, Shusan, or Susa, in Elam (or Shush, Persia). (Esther 1: 1-9). King Ahasuerus has been identified with Darius I (521—486 B.C.) or Xerxes (485—465 B.C.).

[2] In *Four Causes of Separation*, Barrow speaks of " this mor than Egipticall darknes and Babilonishe bondage."

men by all meanes to the holy free and sincere prac- 2 Chron. 17:
tice therof in [G 3 *recto*] all things as God shal give 7, 8, 9
sight, prohibiting, restreininge, and abolishing all Esa. 2: 2, 3
Joh. 12: 32
contrarie religions and practice, and by seeing the 2 Chron. 19:
law of God in both the tables daily observed by all 5, 6, 7
estates and degrees within her highnes' dominions. Deu. 1: 15, 16,
17
And loe, how the Lord inviteth and inciteth her
highnes hereunto, preferring her and giving her the
preeminence of this glorious work before all the kings
of the world, as also how richly he rewardeth all that
furder this high service both by putting into their
handes the riche spoile of this confused Babylon, and
by bringing them to Sion the citie of his solemne
feasts. O what a joy, what a jubile, what a happie
day were this to the whole land, far surpassing that
at Machanajjm,[1] to see our heavenly king, Christ
Jesus, thus with one accord received and welcomed
into his kingdom, his church? How should God's
name and our queene's praise be celebrated for this
by every [G 3 *verso*] mouth even with a generall
applausion and celeusme?[2] The sound wherof
should not onely fill this land, but be heard into all
others to the giving them example and stirring them
up unto the like extirpation of all idolatrie, and unto
the true practice of the gospel. What Christian,
yea, what stony heart, would hinder God from this
glorie, the prince from this fame, the people from
this comfort, themselves and all others from this
salvation ?

How hainous then is the sinne and impietie of the
divines and prophets of these tymes, against God,
their prince, and the whole land, that by their uttermost power and endevours seeke to stoppe and turne
back her majestie, her most honorable councellors
and nobles from this holy streight course, by speaking

---

1 Machanajjm, or Mahanaim, meaning a double camp, or two armies, is
mentioned in Genesis 32: 2 ; Joshua 13: 26, 30 ; 21: 38 ; II Samuel 2: 8,
12, 29 ; 17: 24, 27 ; 19: 32 ; I Kings 2: 8 and 4: 14, and I Chronicles
6: 80. It was a place in Palestine, north of the Jabbok stream and east
of the Jordan. It was captured by Shishak, the Egyptian king, during
the reign of Rehoboam. It was here that Jacob encountered the angels
of God.
2 Celeusme, or Celeusma, a watchword, battlecry ; [from Keleusma].

Acts 13: 8
2 Tim. 3: 8

evill of the gospell and ordinances of Christ, and perverting the streight wayes of God, by leading and
houlding captive them and the whole land un-[G 4
recto]der their false worship and antichristian ministery to the seducing and destruction of all their soules,

Rev. 13: 6, 7,
15

and by accusing, reproching, slandering, persecuting, false imprisoning, and, if they could, hanging
and burning all such as either in all humble and
christian manner stand and plead for the sincere

Jude 3
Gal. 5: 1

and true practise of the gospel, or by the light thereof discover and eschew the popish corruptions and
abominations which they impose and mainteyne
contrary to the truth of the gospel. These are the
onely meanes wherby these prelates defend themselves or convince their adversaries, which if they
were but even a little while plucked out of their
hands by her majestie, and the honourable governours, and called to the spiritual sword to defend
their doings by the direct rule of God's word, then
were they disarmed, discovered, and confounded at

1 Cor. 3: 13
Eph. 5: 13
Jer. 5: 14
Rev. 11: 5

once, then should it soon be seen how wel these
timber, straw, and stubble buil-[G 4 *verso*]dings of
theirs would endure that fiery trial of God's word,
then should all these controversies soon be at an end.
Yet because they bring certaine delusions, calumniations, and impediments, in humane wisdome,
worldly policie, and divillish deceit, which may
deter, trouble and keep back the weak and simple
from this holy reformation and sincere conversion
to the gospell of Christ, wee will in the meane time
addresse our selves in all brevitie to remove some of
their chiefest stumbling blocks out of the way, that

Esa. 62: 10

an aggest[1] and streight causie [causeway] may be
shewed unto all men, leading into the church of God,
and holy practise of the gospel of Christ.

They object and publish,

That to abolish this present ministerie, worship,
traditions, government of their church, would be
an intollerable innovation and most dangerous

---

[1] Aggest and streight causie — a heaped up, built up, and straight causeway
or highway.

alteration, to the subvertion of the state, both in regard that these bishops are [G 5 recto] *peares* [*peers*] *of the same, and their power, courts, and ordinances have been a long time established and confirmed by sundry parliaments and so all that speak against them and their proceedings, are enemies unto, and speake against the peaceable estate of this land.*[1]

To these politick objections and carnal reasons, we Rom. 8: 6, 7 answer with the apostle, " that the wisdome of the flesh is death, but the wisedome of the spirit [is] life and peace, for that the wisdom of the flesh is an enemie against God, for it is not subject to the law of God, neyther indeed can be." They therefore Mat. 21: 44 that thus stumble at the word of God shalbe broken, and they upon whom it thus falleth shal be ground to poulder.[2] They that call all men unto the law of God and to the Testament of Christ, doe not Jer. 6: 16 innovate: but they that depart in any jote and Deut. 4: 6 Esa. 8: 20 swerve from the same, they innovate. The word 2 Pet. 1: 19 2 Tim. 1: 13 of God is the archtype and ground work of all states, degrees, action, [G 5 verso] both ecclesiasticall and Rom. 2: 16 civil, whereunto they must be framed, whereby they shall be judged, no other thing standing before the face of that great judge than his owne revealed will in his word: whatsoever then is agreeable unto the word of God is agreeable unto the state, and whatsoever is contrary unto the word of God, is contrary unto the state.

If then the estate of these prelates, clergymen, ministery and their proceedings, can not be approved by, but shalbe found repugnant unto the Testament of Christ, then are they pernicious and contrary to the state, drawing into the heavie wrath of God unto utter subversion and destruction. Then are they for the safety of the state, to be abolished, and they, whosoever they be, enemies to God, to their

---

[1] Thomas Cooper, *An Admonition to the People of England*, pp. 85-88, 143, 144, 187. There are three editions of this work, issued in 1589, one of 252 pages, one of 244 pages and one of 245 pages. The latter is the edition cited here.
[2] Obsolete form of powder.

I

prince and unto the whole state that perswade the contrary upon any earthly respect or worldly policy, upon any pretext of expediencie, profite, peace, *etc.* Alas, there is no peace [G 6 *recto*] to the wicked and disobedient. That nation and that kingdome that wil not obey unto the gospel of our Lord Jesus Christ shall perish, and those nations shalbe utterly destroyed as the Lord hath not vainely threatned in his word. And as to the persons of these lordly prelates and pieres [peers, equal] to nobles (or rather some of them without pieres and above all the nobles in the land)[1] wee abash not to affirme them to be no members of this state, eyther civile or ecclesiasticall, as in regard of their offices, functions, and dignities, *etc.* Civile they cannot be, because they pretend to be archbishops, bishops, *etc.* These are no civil honours nor offices, neither may be executed by any civile persons. Truely ecclesiasticall they are not, because we finde no mention in Christ's Testament of any such arch or lord bishops, save our saviour Christ himself only, who is the chiefe bishop and lord of the house. He hath often and earnestly forbid-[G 6 *verso*]den all other bishops, yea, himselfe whilest he was here in the flesh refused such civile dignities, titles, offices, and jurisdictions, which these men or rather monsters are not ashamed, notwithstanding Christ's express inhibition, to receive and carry, colouring their pride under the prince's commandement, as though eyther the prince might give or they receive that which Christ forbiddeth them. Or as though their holy father the pope might not so justifie all his blasphemous titles and fastuous[2] pompe by princes and councels. Thus commingle and confound they these distinct ordinances and callings of God, the civil and ecclesiasticall offices and functions in their own persons, and blasphemously usurpe the very peculiar names, offices and honours proper to Christ alone, wherby it is apparant by all these concurring notes, that they are the very

Esa. 57: 21
2 Thes. 1: 8
Esa. 60: 12
Num. 18: 7
2 Chron. 27: 18.

1 Pet. 5: 4
Phil. 2: 11
John 13: 13

Luke 12: 13, 14
Joh. 8: 11
2 Tim. 2: 4
Mat. 20: 25
Luke 22: 25, 26
John 13: 15
Mark 9: 35, 36

---

[1] The two archbishops. Barrow probably also has in mind John Aylmer, Bishop of London, and Thomas Cooper, Bishop of Winchester.
[2] Haughty, arrogant.

antichrist, that beast, that confound all the orders 2 Thes. 2: 4
and ordinances [G 7 *recto*] both of church and com- Mat. 24: 15
mune wealth, and are the very bane, poison, and
ruine of both church and commune wealth, as if wee Rev. 13
should search out and bring to light the havock and
misrule they keep both in church and commune
wealth, wee could make evident to all men.

But to our purpose! They and al their traine are
strangers in this commune wealth. This kingdom
stoode and florished before any lord bishops were,
and shall much more when they are gone. What
misse hath this state or commune wealth of their
elder bretheren the lord abbats and the munks,
friers and those vermine? Yet were they rooted to
seeming as deepely in this state both in the church
and commune wealth as they, their cleargie and
ministry now are, and carried as great a semblance
of holines, religion, antiquitie, utility, as these doo,
and might as well have bene reserved and reformed
as any of these. They are all brethren, of a birth
they sprang all [G 7 *verso*] of one head, and togither
with their head to one end they shall, for the Lord
hath spoken it. As to the lawes wherewith they Esa 32: 25
would fortifie themselves and bind others so long as Mic. 6: 16
they are but the lawes of men, and not the lawes of
God, yea, contrarie to the lawes of God, they are
but as the new cordes of the Philistimes [*sic*], not
able to strengthen their mast, they shall neyther
avayle them nor yet binde our soveraigne queen
and this whole state. The king of this land, togither with the assent of the nobles and commons,
have alwayes taken absolute power to correct or
abrogate any lawes that are found contrary to the
word of God. There is no cause they should now Deu. 18: 22
fear the false prophets' threats, whilst they have the
warrant of God his word for what they doe. For
God shall bless them in the deed.

> Further they suggest, *that this Reformation*
> *would extinguish all learning, take away the studie*
> *of all* [G 8 *recto*] *liberal artes, and so would draw*
> *the people and whole land into ignorance, atheisme,*

barbaritie, dissolutenes, and in the end change the government from a monarchie to democratie or anarchie.[1]

These calumniations tending to the hie contumelie and reproch of that ministerie, order, and government which Christ hath prescribed in his Testament, yea, even of the gospel and sacred person of Christ himself, deserve rather censure than answer. The untruth therof is evident in that such effects were never found to follow the sincere practise of the gospel, to which whoso consenteth not, is puft up and knoweth nothing, how wise or learned soever he seem in his own eyes; where the gospel is purely taught and faithfully obeyed, there, sayth the prophet, shall the earth overflow with knowledge as the sea with waters.[2] And as to the church of God, it is sayd the piller and sure keeper of truth, the nourserie of all [G 8 *verso*] good education, the schoole of all holy knowledge, no enemy but a favourer of all lawfull artes and science; where the glorie of God and the Lambe are the light thereof; where the lively graces of God's spirite are ever burning and never quenched. There are all men of all degrees instructed in their dueties from the hiest to the lowest. And whose [whoso] walketh not in the light as Christ is in the light can have no fellowship or place there. Into the church of Christ entereth no profane, ignorant, or ungodly person: the leopard must leave his fiercenes, and the cockatrice his poyzon, so that the yong kid may feed with the one, and the weyned childe play at the hole of the other, before they can be received as members.

And being entred, there can [be] no inordinate walking, no dissolute or unruly person [can] be there suffered. The church hath always vengeance ready against all disobedience by the spirituall weapons and [H 1 *recto*] judgements of God's word. The governement therof (as the prophet, ravished in the con-

Marginal references:
I Cor. 16: 22
I Tim. 6: 3, 4
Esa. 2: 9
Hab. 2: 14
John 6: 45
I Tim. 3: 15
Esa. 66: 11, 12 & 24: 23, & 60: 19, 20
Zech. 14: 6, 7
Rev. 21: 23
Mic. 4: 2, 3
Esa. 2: 3
I John 1: 6, 7
Esa. 35: 8
Joel 3: 17
Zech. 14: 21
I Pet. 2: 9
Esa. 11: 6, 7, 8, 9
2 Thes. 3: 6, 14
Cor. 11: 16
Mat. 18: 17

---

[1] Cooper, *An Admonition*, pp. 92, 161, 162, 223.
[2] The reference is to Habakkuk 2: 14. The prophet, however, does not speak of the gospel and its teaching and obedience.

templation thereof, sayth) shalbe of peace and
exactors of righteousnes; violence shall no more be
heard in the land, neyther desolation nor destruction
in the borders.   They shall there break their speares
into sithes and their swords into mattocks.[1] Christ's
servants are an humble, meeke, peaceable, and
obedient people, loyally subject and assuredly faithful to any civil government the Lord setteth over
them.   They reverence and willingly obey even
their heathen tyrannous magistrates, without resistance even to the death, how much more their
christian, faithful, loving magistrates, partakers with
them of the same comforts and hope ?   All power
here is yeelded and rendred to the civill magistrate,
every soule being subject, and no part thereof taken
away, or taken togither with the civil magistrate as
these princely prelates with their palatine royall
[H 1 *verso*] privileges and these lordly bishops with
their courtes and civill jurisdiction.   Neyther can
Satan himself without impudent slaunder accuse the
servants of Christ of sedition or disobedience, much
lesse of such dissolutenes, violence, atheisme, barbaritie.   No, these with infinite other enormities
flow from the false church, from Babylon, the mother
of all the abominations, dissolutenes, confusion,
impietie, where all are received, feasted, blessed,
even every uncleane byrd, and hatefull spirite.
Their ungodly throne, their false and deceitfull
ministery which sheweth them not the counsels of
God, which discovereth not their transgressions,
'neither hath any spirituall weapons or power against
any syn be it never so haynouse, but war togither
in most desperate manner and oppose themselves
against the ordinances of Christ his gospel, are the
very cause of this impietie, prophanenes, ignorance,
and atheisme that aboundeth.   And [H 2 *recto*] this
wee say that if God's ordinance, even the prince's
lawes and sword (which yet punisheth some offences),
kept not out barbaritie, and dissolutenes, more than

Margin references:
2 Cor. 10: 4, 5, 6
Esa. 16: 17, 18
Mic. 4: 3, 4, 5
1 Cor. 14: 33

Tit. 3: 1
1 Pet. 2: 13, 14
Rom. 13: 1, 2
Eccles. 8: 2
etc.

Rev. 17: 5 & 18: 2
Prov. 5: 3, 4, 5 & 7: 10 etc. & 9: 14, 15

Psal. 94: 20
Rev. 13: 2, 6, 7
Dan. 7: 8, 25

---

[1] An agricultural tool, a kind of pick-axe to loosen hard ground or to dig out stumps.

their ministery, there should be no peace nor order, neyther might one live by an other in their church. So that, this their pseudohierarchie is the most pestilent anarchie that Satan and all his instruments

2 Thes. 2: 9

shall ever be able to raise up, as wherein he hath bestowed his uttermost power, delusions, and deceits to suppresse the holy practise of the gospel, and to keep Christ out of his kingdome.

There now remaine certain difficulties and impediments which are propounded by way of question, and being of no great moment are as soon answered as propounded.

They demaund; *if these spiritual courts of theirs were taken away, what order then should be taken for matrimonies, adulteries, testaments, with which* [H 2 *verso*] *the common lawes of this land meddle not? And also how the civilians should then live?*[1]

Luke 12: 13, 14
John 8: 11

Wee answer, that the triall, judgements, punishments of these causes and offences belong unto the civil magistrate's office, and neither to the church nor to any private men. God shall give our magis-

Deut. 4: 5, 6, 7, 8

trates wisdome if they take counsell at his word, to provide for the reformation of these and many other abuses. And as to the officers of these courts, they are to be compelled to walk orderly in some lawful

2 Thes. 3: 10, 12
Ephes. 4: 28
Prov. 20: 17

calling. There are many godly meanes for them to live by their diligent indeavours in this common wealth; but howsoever they may not be suffered to live or to continue in their ungodly trade. Neither

Mat. 10: 33

ought the prince to stay upon their wordly provision from executing the wil of God which so nearly concerneth her own salvation, and the salvation of all her people.

They furder demaund; *if these* [H 3 *recto*] *livings, and revenewes of this present ministery should be quite taken away, how then the true*

---

[1] Cooper, *An Admonition,* p. 86.

*ministery should be mainteyned, or these bishops
and priests hereafter live ?*[1]

To the first we have alreadie answered, that the
true ministerie should be mainteyned of the free, yet
dutifull benevolence of the faithful, especially of
that flock unto which they attend and administer,
according to the present abilitie of the one and
needes of the other. If they here object that if the
ministery should have no more certaine or other
maintenance, they should then famish, the people
now generally being so worldly, covetous, and uncharitable, as they will hardly pay that which is by
law injoyned, much lesse give of their own accord.
Wee answer, that this no way hindereth the main- 1 Thes. 5: 12,
tenance of the true ministery, but bewrayeth rather 13
the unfaithfulnes and impietie both of the people
and the present ministerie: of the people, in that 1 Tim. 5: 17
they no more regard, [H 3 *verso*] love and reverence Heb. 13: 7
to their ministery, if so be it were of God: of the Mat. 7: 6
ministery in that they so evill instruct this people, Jer. 4: 4
standing ministers and hierders [shepherds] unto Amos 6: 12
Hos. 4: 8, 9
the prophane, worldly, irreligious multitudes, ad- Eze. 13: 4, 8,
9
ministring or rather sacrilegiously prostituting and Mal. 1
selling the most holy things of God, as the sacra- Zech. 11: 4, 5
ments, *etc.*, unto them all in this estate for their tithes 2 Cor. 6: 14,
15
and wages, which no true minister of Christ may doe.

The ministery of Christ belongeth not unto,
neyther will take charge over, such prophane world- Gal. 6: 6 & 4:
lings, there can be no spiritual band or communion 14, 15
betwixt them. The true sheep and faithfull people
of Christ will not onely bestow their earthly goods,
but even their lives for those that bring unto them 1 Cor. 4: 11
these heavenly treasures, that tred out the corne and Rom. 15: 27
divide the portion unto them, that labour for, and
watch over their soules, *etc.* Unpossible then it is
that the true ministers of Christ should want meanes
[H 4 *recto*] to live whilest they execute their office

---

[1] Barrow is seeking to refute the views of Richard Alison, Thomas Cooper,
Robert Some, Bishop Aylmer, and Archbishop Whitgift. See his replies
given during his fourth examination, March 18, 1588/9, especially to the
questions of Lord Burghley.

2 Thes. 3: 6,
10, 14
Rom. 16: 17,
18

faithfully (especially where the state receiveth and favoureth the gospell). Neyther are they any longer to be mainteyned than they execute their office faithfully, or they any longer bound to the flock or any member thereof than they remaine in the faith and obedience of the word of God. Thus still breaketh out the corrupt minde and coloured covetousnes of these tithing and hireling priests that thus let out their tongues to hire, make merchandise of the word and portsale [public auction] of their sacraments, making their bargain sure beforehand, which bindeth them togither howsoever they doe the worke, or the people bring fruites of faith. These things are not regarded or looked to amongst them either of the priest or people. Yet these things prove that there can nor may be no such set permanent livings allotted to the ministerie of the gospell.

And now to the other part of their question, *how these bishops and* [H 4 *verso*] *priests should live, if their livings bee taken from them*? We answer as above. They may for no wordly cause bee suffered to continue in so unlawfull and ungodly, yea, so pernicious a course to themselves and to the whole land, but must be compelled to walk orderly in some lawfull calling or other. God giveth much to the diligent, when the sluggard suffereth want worthily. Such as have faith and gifts unto edification never had greater cause to use them, to call the people to faith and to instruct them in the wayes of the Lord. The more they thus labour the more they shal deserve to be cherished and esteemed. The labourer is worthy of and shal not want his hire both with God and man. The others of them that have not these gifts may apply themselves in civill things, as to teach the tongues, to instruct children, *etc.*

Prov. 13: 4 &
14: 23

Mat. 20
1 Cor. 9: 10

Psal. 37: 25

They have yet an other question; *how the people should be taught if al this ministery should be deposed*? To which [H 5 *recto*] we answer: the people ought at no hand to be taught by a false ministery. And further, though they be deposed from their antichristian ministery, which they exercised to the

248

destruction of their owne soules, and of as many
as heard and followed them; yet such of them to Rom. 12: 6
whom God hath given fit gifts and graces to teach, 1 Pet. 4: 10, 11
ought from henceforth to imploy the same to the
glory of God, the benefit of others, and the building
up of Christ's decayed church. Thus shall the
people have all the help they had before. To
whom if you ad such of the faithful as God hath 1 Cor. 14: 29, 30, 31, 32
given the gift of prophecie, and interpretation of Rom. 12: 3
the Scriptures unto, who must and will labour in
this work according to the measure of faith in all
holy order and sobrietie, as also those that the Lord
shall daily raise up and send unto his vineyard, the
people shall want no meanes of instruction, neyther
be destitute of any good gift, but have them much
more plentifully and ex-[H 5 *verso*]cellently than ever Ezek. 4: 7
they had without comparison. Yea, so shall God
blesse his own ordinances and their diligence and
zeale, as they shall in short time be throughly [*sic*]
furnished of teachers every where, and the work in
all places be orderly set up. Onely let no man
despise the day of these small things, for they shall Zech. 4: 10
rejoyce and see the stone of tinne[1] in the hand of
Zerubbabel.

> Your Honour's humbly
> in all duety bounden,
> HENRY BARROWE.

---

[1] The translation from the Hebrew in the King James Version and Revised Standard Version is plummet.

XV

LETTER TO MR. FISHER

This letter to Mr. Fisher has been collated from the original in the Lansdowne Manuscripts, volume 65, item 65, ff. 182 *recto* — 182 *verso*. It is also reproduced with notes by F. J. Powicke, " A Letter of Henry Barrow's to Mr. Fisher from the Fleet Prison, December, 1590," in *Transactions of the Congregational Historical Society*, II, no. 4 (January, 1906), pp. 266-271. Powicke states that this letter is printed in the Separatists' *Apology* (*Henry Barrowe, Separatist*, p. 339), but this is an error. The letter printed in [Henry Ainsworth and Francis Johnson?], *An Apologie or Defence of Such True Christians as Are Commonly (But Unjustly) Called Brownists* (n.p. [Amsterdam?], 1604), is Barrow's " Letter to an Honorable Lady and Countesse of His Kindred Yet Living," which was written April 4-5, 1593. John Strype printed portions of the 1590 letter in *Life and Acts of John Whitgift, D.D.* (Oxford, 1822), vol. II, book IV, chapter XI, section 416, pp. 189-190. John Waddington printed it in *John Penry, the Pilgrim Martyr*, 1559-1593 (London, 1854), pp. 248-252. Unfortunately, Waddington has carelessly read the manuscript, and has made at least seventeen errors. He has " taught " for " stonge," " warning " for " winning," " except " for " but," " began " for " begunne," " these " for " their," " straits " for " sute," " starved " for " sik," " are " for " remaine," " John Pardy " for " Jhon Purdy," " six poor men " for " some poore men," " fleece " for " fleshe," " so now " for " suer," " pent " for " shut," " recording " for " according," " next " for " meete," " fast " for " fiste." He also omits one phrase—" at the civile magistrate."

The letter is undated, but it carries the endorsement—December, 1590, and internal evidence is sufficient to substantiate the correctness of the date. The manuscript has some corrections, especially near the end of the letter (f. 182 *verso*).

It would be interesting to discover the identification of Mr. Fisher, but we do not know anything about him. There was a Mr. Fisher who accompanied Dr. Robert Some and Richard Young when they interrogated Barrow in the Fleet Prison, January 1, 1588/9. There is an Edward Fisher, who had been a prisoner in the Fleet since 1583 (*State Papers, Domestic, Elizabeth*, vol. 163, no. 45 ; vol. 206, no. 88 ; vol. 233, no. 29). There is also a John Fisher or Fissher, who is listed as a Separatist prisoner in the lists for February, 1589/90, and April, 1590. Powicke conjectures that Edward Fisher is intended, but I believe that John Fisher may be a better guess. Barrow is writing to a friend, not an enemy or interrogator, and this fact would seem to exclude the Mr. Fisher who accompanied Dr. Robert Some and Richard Young. Barrow seeks to inform his friend about the condition of himself and fellow-prisoners, and he seeks his counsel and advice as to what may be done in the dire circumstances confronting the Separatists.

*   *   *   *   *   *

LETTER TO MR. FISHER

Sir,

(182 *recto*) I understand that the prisoners lately exhibited a Supplication to her majestie,[1] and how through the great providence of God it was delivered to her own hands, and most graciously received of her and indeed escaped the hands of her Master of Requests[2] for that time, whose custome it is to suppresse all such complaints from her highnes' eyes. Yet, howsoever, it is come abought, I certainly thinck, that either it or the report therof is brought to the arch bishop, who wanteth not his intelligencers in all places.

He, belike being stonge [stung] in his guiltie conscience and fearing his barbarous and lawles procedings should now be brought to light, seeketh, as you by this scedule here inclosed[3] shall perceive, to suppresse the same by all secret and subtile meanes: making and winning his gaolers by extraordinary favour and interteinment and to give up a favorable, if not a parcial, certificat of the prisoners living and dead.[4] And so peradventure thincketh to disprove the Supplication unto her majestie, and through his false informations and suggestions, according to his evil custome and conscience, to abuse

---

[1] There is a " Lamentable Petition " of March 13, 1588/89, which was delivered to the queen, and there is a petition to Lord Burghley, delivered about April, 1590. Also, there is a petition of August 27, 1590, to the Privy Council. Conceivably, there was another petition delivered about November, 1590, but I have found no trace of such a document. I conjecture that a copy of the petition of April, 1590, to Lord Burghley, or that of August 27, 1590, to the Privy Council, was " exhibited " to the queen in November, 1590, or otherwise that there was another supplication to the queen about October-November, 1590. But I have found no trace of such a further appeal in the Harley and Lansdowne manuscripts. In all likelihood, the petition of April or of August 27, 1590, is intended, because of the coincidence of above sixty prisoners mentioned, but there remains unreconciled the fact that the April and August petitions are to Lord Burghley and the Privy Council, whereas Barrow says the supplication was exhibited to the queen.

[2] Probably Ralph Rokeby, but John Herbert and Dr. William Aubrey also were Masters of Requests.

[3] No such schedule has been preserved in the Lansdowne MSS.

[4] That is, to make a report mitigating the harsh treatment accorded prisoners.

and incence her most excellent majestie and stir her up
against us, her harmles subjects. But that God who
hath brought our cause before her shall also bring
forth our innocency as the none [noon] light, and he
that hath thus wonderfully begunne to discover their
tyrannous practises, shall not cease to lay them open
and make them odious to every eye and harte. God
shall and hath given unto her majestie's royal harte
wisdom to search out the truth of this matter. Only
the Lord vouchsafe we be not condempned unheard
upon their accusations and informations. There was,
we heare, an article in their Supplication of above sixty
soules emprisoned by the bishops. Here peradventure
thei will catch hould [take issue, quibble] because there
be not now I suppose fifty in prison. But thei have
committed above eighty.[1] Wherof many through their
tyranny have revoulted and denied their faith and so
were discharged. Sondry through great sute, being sik
to the death or otherwise, obtained baile at the civile
magistrate until times prefixed, who yet are prisoners.
And sondry have died in their prisons of famine, could,
noyse, winds [noysomnes, noisomes ?] of the place beat-
ing in their prison, etc.[2]

The rest, as you may perceive, remaine in most extreame misery, want, and penury in all the prisons, as
the gaolers can not deny. We here [hear] also the arch
bishop maketh inquiry at the Gatehouse, Clinck, and
Katherine,[3] how many of them have died. There being,
I weane, a clause in the Supplication that the Coroner
sate not upon such of us as died in prison. Which is very

---

[1] These two sentences constitute a clue which strongly suggests the petition
of April, 1590, because therein is mentioned the number of " three-skore
persons and upwarde " who have been imprisoned. The petition of April,
1590, included 59 suppliants, and listed ten more who had died in prison.
Between April and December, 1590, probably nine persons were liberated
or bailed, so that Barrow's figure of 50 is close to the truth. Eighty-two
persons had been arrested up to this time.

[2] There is a list of twenty-four who died either in prison or shortly after
they were carried out, in [Henry Ainsworth ?], *A True Confession of the
Faith*, signature A iii, *recto*. Compare F. J. Powicke, " Lists of the Early
Separatists," *Transactions of the Congregational Historical Society*, I,
no. 3, p. 141. At least ten had died before December, 1590.

[3] The Gatehouse prison was at Westminster, the Clink stood on the south
side of the Thames in Southwark, and the Katherine was a part of the
Tower of London.

true. Myselfe being in Nugate[1] [Newgate], there was no jury or inquest soffred to sit upon that rare yong man, Rychard Jacson, who there died.[2] I demanded the cause. As I thinck, M. Deux[3] himself tould me that the Bishop of London commanded the contrary. The like was of the two aged poore widowes that died there,[4] as also upon ould Mr. Crane,[5] there was no inquest called or soffred to sit and pass upon their bodies, though it were required. This there are many credible witnesses to verifie. The coroner's boke, if it be searched, will make all plaine.

Furder, thei would not soffer the body of this antient grave preacher and father, Mr. Crane, to be caried to burial into the city through Nugate, leste the people who knew his vertue and godliness should espie and abhor their cruelty. There likewise died in Bridwell a very godly person called Jhon Purdie,[6] committed

---

1 Barrow may have been called to Newgate prison or Session Hall to testify for the coroner. Since Barrow testified in his March 20, 1592/3, examination that he wrote *A Brief Discoverie of the False Church* in the Fleet, which occurred in the fall and winter of 1590, I conclude that he was not imprisoned in Newgate, but remained in the Fleet prison from about May, 1588, until his execution in April, 1593. It is quite possible that Barrow was temporarily transferred from the Gatehouse to Newgate before or after his trial about May, 1588, at Newgate Sessions.

2 Richard Jackson died in Newgate prison sometime prior to May, 1589. Barrow's statement that he was himself at Newgate may indicate May or June, 1588, as the date. This is the period when Nicholas Crane died, and this is also the period when Barrow was transferred from the Gatehouse [to Newgate awaiting trial ?], indicted, found guilty, and then sent to the Fleet.

3 Unidentified. Probably an official in Newgate ; perhaps the coroner.

4 Margaret Maynerd [Mainard, Meynard ?] and Alice Roe [Row ?] were apprehended on October 8, 1587, committed to prison by John Aylmer, Bishop of London, and indicted. They died in Newgate prison prior to May, 1589.

5 Nicholas Crane, a presbyterian minister, had been imprisoned first in 1568 for his Genevan views, and again on October 8, 1587. He died before June, 1588, at the age of 66.

6 John Purdye was imprisoned about 1588, was living in May, 1589, but had died prior to April, 1590. In prison he was treated with extreme barbarity for his refusal to attend the prison chapel services conducted by a priest according to the Anglican rites. He was compelled to grind in the " mill " and was cast into " Little Ease," the latter being a kind of punishing hole, a cell " of so small dimensions and so constructed that the prisoner could neither stand, walk, sit, or lie at length. He was compelled to draw himself upon a squatting posture and so remained several days" (Lingard, *History of England* (1825), VII, 522. Martin Marprelate suggested " it were good for the Bishop to lie a day and a night in Little Ease in the Counter " (*Epistle*, p. 28). Barrow says that there was a Little Ease in Bridewell to which Purdye was committed.

by the arch bishop, whom thei there put into their Litle Ease and beate with a great codgel very extreamly because he would not come to their chappel in their house.[1] The man was grave, sober, and very godly and honest, as is to be well testified of all that knew him.

If law might be loked upon, these cases are foule. I omit to relate here how many Doctor Stanhope[2] hath caste into yrons in Nuegate and of the boy of fifteen yeares ould he there kept in a dongeon in yrons a whole yeare for this cause, which boy is yet there prisoner.[3] But the arch bishop dealeth wisely and sendeth not to Bridwell, Nugate, the two Counters, the White Lion, nor the Fleet.[4] He mindeth to post all these things over to the civile magistrates. Yet even in the Clincke and the Gatehous will upon due examination be found some poore men whome the Bishop of London hath held in the holes of those prisons now more than three whole yeares and three monethes without so much as sending for them forth to any triall or examination to (182 *verso*)

---

1 In the margin the manuscript is torn, but the words seem to be: " . . . ere with . . . [such ?] unlawful usage made him away."

2 Dr. Edward Stanhope, chancellor to the Bishop of London, was referred to contemptuously by Martin Marprelate as " Tarquinius Superbus Doctor Stanop." Martin further says: " I tell you Doctor Stannop (for all you are so proude) a premunire will take you by the back one day (for oppressing and tyrannizing over her majestie's subjects as you doe " (*Epistle*, pp. 10, 22, 23).

3 This is Roger Waterer, who evidently refused to attend chapel services in prison conducted by an Anglican priest. In the list of prisoners for April, 1590, there were three listed for Newgate: William Dentford, Widow Borrough [Edith Burroughs] and Roger Waterer. Since the former was 50 years old in 1593, he could not have been 15 years old in 1590. He was imprisoned about January or February, 1589/90, and therefore had been in prison less than a year. Barrow states that the boy had been in the dungeon a full year and was still in Newgate prison. Barrow is in error in saying the boy was fifteen. Waterer gave his age as twenty-two in his examination of April 3, 1593 (Ellesmere MS. 2105). He could have been eighteen at this time and seventeen when first imprisoned in 1589.

4 For a brief survey of prisons about 1590, see William Pierce, *An Historical Introduction to the Marprelate Tracts*, pp. 131-4. See also John Stow, *Survey of London*, II, 473. See further the Appendix, in volume IV.

any place all this while.[1] The cause whie he committed them and sondry others, some of whom died
in the Counter Poultry, others there sickened to the
death, was for hearing a piece of the Nue Testament
read and truly expounded in one of their houses upon
a Lord's day.[2]

Well, notwithstanding all these injuries you see the
arch bishop is inraged and hath set a day of Pur,[3] if
God by our Noble Hester [Esther, Queen Elizabeth]
prevent him not. He hath destinat my brother Gren-
wood and me to the death against his holy feaste
[Christmas ?]. All the others both at liberty and elce
where to close prison. Their poore wives and children
to be cast out of the city, their few goods to be confiscat.
Is not this a christian bishop ? Are these the vertues
of him that taketh upon him the care and government
of all the churches of the land, thus to teare and devoure
Christe's poore sheepe, to rend of the fleshe and breake
their bones and chop them in pieces as flesh to the
chaldron ? Will he thus instruct and convince the
gainsayers ? Suer he will persuade but few that feare
God to his religion by this dealing. And evil provideth
he for his own credit or the honour of his prince that
maketh this tyranuous havock. Suer for our partes
our lives are not deare unto us so we may finish up our
testimony with joy. We are alwaise ready through
God's grace to be offred up upon that testimony of
our faith which we have made. And purpose to imbrace the chief pillers of their church and cary them
with us to our grave,[4] if there be no remedy but thei

---

[1] Thomas Freeman and Edmond Thompson were arrested on October 8,
1587, and were in the Gatehouse in April, 1590. George Collier was
arrested at the same time and is listed as a prisoner in the Clink in April,
1590. For a list of fifty-two prisoners in February, 1589/90, see *A Collection of Certaine Sclaunderous Articles Gyven out by the Bisshops*, signatures
A iv *verso* — B *recto*. See also Strype, *Annals*, IV, 130. See further
the Appendix, in volume IV.

[2] This reference to the events of Sunday, October 8, 1587, and to " three
whole yeares and three moneths," is supporting evidence for the endorsement of December, 1590.

[3] Esther 3: 7 ; 9: 24, 26.

[4] The figure is that of Samson pulling down the pillars and wrecking the
house of the Philistines (Judges 16: 25-31). For Barrow, the Archbishop
of Canterbury and the Bishop of London were the main pillars of the
ecclesiastical edifice he wished to pull down.

will take this barbarous course, which shall but hasten their own judgments. As the case standeth, we see no remedie, being thus shut up, but to commit our cause and lives unto the Lord. Meanes to send to any we have not, having none but this poore simple creature to come neare us. We dare not sollicite the noble man you know of any furder. Yet he knoweth our cause, godly purpose, and innocency, no man better.[1] The Lord incline his harte to pleade the cause of the children of destruction.

Thus tediously I have scribled unto you our present estate according as I heare, craving your friendly councel and advise what you thincke meete to be doone in these extremities. And that with as much speed as you can.

Committing you as ourselves to the Lord, in whom we salute you.

> Your poor friend whose scribling fiste you
> know and I dout shall hardly read.
> H. Barrowe.

---

[1] Strype suggests that this is Francis Knollys, but Lord Burghley is a more likely suggestion, since he had been solicited for aid previously, in two letters of September 13 and 18, 1590.

A BRIEF DISCOVERIE
OF THE FALSE
CHURCH

Ezekiel 16: 44
As The Mother Such The Daughter Is

1590

XVI

A BRIEF DISCOVERIE OF THE FALSE CHURCH

Barrow's most important book, and the one from which his judges extracted quotations to find him guilty of writing slanderous statements, is *A Brief Discoverie of the False Church*. It was written in the Fleet Prison in the year 1589 and/or 1590, under the most trying circumstances. Barrow managed to write out a sheet at a time, then delivered it to Daniel Studley, who had received permission from Archbishop Whitgift to have access to Barrow. Studley gave the original manuscript to James Forrester, who prepared another copy for the printer [Hanse or Hause—Hans Stell?], then returned the original to Studley, who at least began to make another copy for himself, but probably never completed the task.

The book was printed at Dort [Dordrecht], in the Netherlands, beginning about December, 1590, and continuing into January and February, 1590/1, with the financial assistance of Robert Stokes (who later deserted the Separatists, and was excommunicated). The book is printed in the same type as used for *A True Description out of the Worde of God, of the Visible Church*, for *A Collection of Certain Sclaunderous Articles*, for *A Collection of Certain Letters and Conferences*, for the first edition (1590) of Greenwood's *An Answere to George Gifford's Pretended Defence of Read Prayers and Devised Litourgies*, and for the first edition (1591) of Barrow's *A Plaine Refutation*. Since there is independent testimony from Robert Stokes that some of these works were printed at Dort, it is almost certain that all six were printed at the same place.

The testimony of Robert Stokes (Ellesmere MS. 2094 and *Egerton Papers*, p. 174) would imply that the entire edition of *A Brief Discoverie* was confiscated at Flushing and Brill, when *A Plaine Refutation* was also seized by Francis Johnson's connivance. But some copies must have circulated, because several prisoners read them. Arthur Billett delivered two copies to Daniel Studley in the Bridewell, about March, 1590/1, and Studley gave one copy to John Gwalter (*Egerton Papers*, p. 176). Some of the prisoners testified to having seen the volume, *A Brief Discoverie*, and I have examined copies at six different libraries in England and the United States. The two books were not printed at the same time, and it is unlikely that all were confiscated. Perhaps an early consignment escaped detection, or a few copies were brought in personally by Stokes.

There is a reprinted edition of 1707, in which the editor has made abundant and unnecessary and unwarranted changes. Passages offensive to the editor have been omitted or paraphrased without any indication to the reader.

Gifford replied to this work in his *A Short Reply* (1591), and William Rathband published a refutation of it in *A Most Grave, and Modest Confutation of the Errors of the Sect, Commonly Called Brownists, or Seperatists* (1644). Rathband was the editor but not the author. His work is really a printing of a manuscript treatise, " The Church of England Is a True Church of Christ," which was written about 1592, most likely by a Presbyterian, such as Thomas Cartwright, Walter Travers, William Charke, or William Fludd. This item is listed in the *Short-Title Catalogue*, no. 10,398, but this is an error. The British Museum copy (117 f. 50), which is catalogued as the 1592 item, is Rathband's work of 1644, minus the title page.

*   *   *   *   *   *

[A ii *recto*]

TO THE READER

If the godlie yong king, Joschiiah, when he heard the 2 Kings 22: 11
booke of God's law read, and compared the acts of his
forefathers, and the present estate of his kingdome therunto, rent his clothes in horror of the wrathfull judgments
of God, in that booke denounced, *etc.* If the prophet
Jeremiah in his time so sone after Josiah his death, when
the defection began but to breake out a fresh, and the
whole land to decline from the antient wayes of the
Lord: upon the consideration of God his fearfull judgments to ensue, brake out into such deepe and extreame
lamentations, as he wished unto himself a cottage in the Jer. 9: 1, 2
wildernes, where he might remaine, never to returne to
the land, to behold either the enormities present, or
calamities to come, but there continually to lament,
and shed forth abundance of teares, for the wrath and
desolation that was to fall upon it, wishing his head a
fountaine, and his eies as buckets hereunto, *etc.* What
occasion of sorrow and lamentation have all christian
hearts, in whome is anie compassion or love, in these
dangerous (if not desperate) daies, where the whole
land (that I say not the whole world) hath lien [lain]
so long, and is so deeplie set in defection, sinne and
securitie, where they are so universally departed from
the strait waies of life and peace, and are so far wandred
and straied in their owne bywaies which they have
sought out unto themselves, as they have now utterly
lost all knowledg of the true way, and have no will to
returne: but though they be shewed the way, and
willed to walke in it, yet even the best of them stop their
eares, wink with their eies, and turne away the shoulder, Zach. 7: 11
least they should be converted and be healed. Others,
and those the cheife governors of the church, and guides
of the people, do not only denie Christ to reigne over
them, or to yeild him anie fruite or tribute of his vineyeard, but most bitterlie persecute all Christ's servantes
that are sent to them, to shew them, and call them back
to the right way, rejecting Christ's ordinances, as

intollerable in this common welth. As for the seers, prophets, and watchmen, they do not only not blow the trumpet, not give warning, not discover the pit and the snare, but cover them rather with flowres and greene hearbes; yea, they are become as fowlers to allure and draw men into their snares. The best of them that pretend a kinde of reformation, seeke not to revive the true patterne, or to call men to the testament of Christ, from whence they are so far departed; so much as to renewe the old skarres of the old and first apostacie from the gospell. In the meane while, deteining the people by their shifts and cavills under the yoke of antichrist, corrupting themselves, even in those things which they themselves see and acknowledg to be evill and unlawfull, for the reformation wherof, they are earnest suters unto the [A ii *verso*] parliament. Thus seduce they and deceave the miserable people and themselves, leading them forward, and deteining them in the wrath of God. What heart would not melt and breake to behold this estate, the breach wherof is like the sea, and in the best help that is administred at anie hand, but to cure it with untempered and unseasoned stuffe; the prophets seeking out vaine things, not discovering the iniquitie to turne away the captivitie, but have looked out burthens, and cawses of putting away and banishment. What teares? What sorrow can suffice to deplore and lament this estate? But alas, private sorrow will not helpe publique calamitie. Many mourners there would seeme in these times for Tzion, who (good men) can take no rest for sleeping, ease, and bellie cheare: faine they would have all things well, but they neither refraine from the pollutions, nor cry out against the abhominations of the times: and therfore, as they are not marked on the foreheads by the angel clothed in linnen with the writer's ynckhorne: so shall they not be spared by the avenging angels that carrie the instrumentes of dissipation in their handes.

But now, whiles no man hath courage, or openeth his mouth for the truth, whiles no man standeth up in the gappe, or offreth himself in this service, whiles the auntients keepe silence, and flie as chaced harts before

Jude 10

2 Pet. 2: 18, 19

2 Tim. 2: 13

Lam. 2: 13

Lam. 2: 13, 14

Ezek. 9: 4, 5

Phil. 3: 18, 19

Isa. 59: 4

Ezek. 22: 30

the enemies, whiles the leaders faint, and lie at the head Lam. 1
of all the streetes, as a bullock in a snare, and are full Isa. 51: 18, 20
of the wrath of the Lord, and of the rebuke of God,
what safetie or hope is in this estate ? Yea, what heart
could endure to behold so manie of his naturall coun-
triemen, deare frendes, and neere kinsfolke in the flesh,
to perish before his eies, for want of warning or help,
wherfore behold, even the zeale of the glorie of my God
inforced me, as also the tender love and care of the Rom. 9: 1, 2, 3
safetie of this my countrie constrained me, to breake Micah 3: 8
silence, and to set the trumpet to my mouth, not any
longer enduring the excellencie of the one, or the life
of the other, thus to be troden under foote, and neglected. My self I willinglie acknowledg of all other
the most unmeet, and everie way unfit unto this worke;
but let my zeale of the truth, my love unto you, and the
present necessitie of the time, excuse me of presumption
or vaine glorie, though no way cover or excuse anie
errors or faults escaped me in this present writing;
which I wholy, even in feare and reverence, submit, to
the trial and censure of all men, at all times, by the
word of God. I desire to have no further credit, than
the word of God giveth warrant, neither yet would I
be reprooved for speaking the truth of God plainlie and
simplie, although the same truth have long lyen [lain]
hid and buried, and be now peradventure generally
impugned of all men. Only, let neither the truth of
God be prejudiced, nor the charitable reader offended,
by the unlearnednes and simplicitie of the writer. Let
not the faith of Christ be held in respect of men's persons,
but let the reader rather consider, [A iii *recto*] that God
is not alwaies bound, or the truth tied to the Phariseis'
lippes, and to the Rabbins' [Rabbis'] chaire, God his Mat. 11: 25
glorie is, to reveale at some times unto babes and sucklings, that, which he hideth from the wise and prudent, 1 Cor. 1: 26,
yea even by such despised things, to reproove and con-   *etc.*
found the wisdome and glorie of the world. Let not the
reader then fixe his eies upon the messenger (in whose
mortall bodie he shall find nothing, but the markes and
dying of our Lord Jesus Christ), so much, as upon the
matter, wherin he shall find life and peace unto his owne 2 Cor. 4: 10

soule; neither in the matter let him regard the forme, so much as the truth. The stile and phrase (no doubt) must needes seeme harsh and unpleasant, being utterlie void of al humane artes and learning (wherwith the whole world is now so deeplie delighted, and wholy carried away), nothing els being welcome or acceptable unto their earthly senses, or ytching humorous eares, which cannot brooke wholsome doctrine, or suffer the wordes of exhortation. I have not desired to speake in the wordes taught by humane wisdom, but in the words taught of the Holie Ghost. From which, where I have swerved (as my unsanctified lippes no doubt too often have),[1] or which wherin I have abused (as fooles knowe not to use a parable aright), I humbly crave the christian correction, rather than the pardon of the reader; for it ought to goe before, and shall be more profitable unto me. Great everie way shal the benefite herof be, both to me and to the whole church: I being instructed, shal (through the grace of God) both repent, and learne to amend my faultes; the church shall reape the fruits of God's graces much more plentifullie in others; which if I may any way stir up, I shal not judg my labour wholy lost.

The diffuse and disorderly handling of these points, will also no doubt be yrksonne unto the reader, neither in deed take I anie pleasure therin: but let that be partly imputed to the confuse subject (you know what Babel signifieth), but chieflie, to my want of skill, that knew not how to do it better. I am content to beare that blame, so others may reape anie good by the rest. If some unperfect sentences, or superfluous repetitions, arise in the reading, attribute those to his weakned memorie, that is but a litle cherished, as also, to the inconvenience of the place, through the iniquitie of the times: where such was the rage of the enimie, as he might not keepe one sheade [sheet of paper] by him, whiles he was writinge of an other,[2] havinge also as evill

2 Tim. 4

1 Cor. 2: 13

Prov. 26: 7

---

[1] These words are reminiscent of Barrow's self-criticism after his examination on March 18, 1588/9, before the Privy Council.
[2] Daniel Studley testified on March 20, 1592/3, that he had received " shete by shete at Mr. Henry Barrowe's study in the Flette [Fleet prison]." *Egerton Papers*, ed. J. P. Collier, p.175.

meanes to revise or retract that he had written: so no wonder though manie thinges escaped, which might with more dilligence have beene prevented: let these also be the writer's blame deservedlie, which he for thy good thinketh not much to sustaine.

But now remaineth the verie argument and subject of this booke, which of al other will be most disliked, and held most odious and heinous of all sorts of men, who wil never endure to heare the magnificence of the false church, wherin they have so long beene nourished in so great delight, reprooved and caste downe. So throughlie are they intoxicate [A iii *verso*] with the wine of her abhominations, and all their senses bownd in the fetters of her fornications, that they have no eies to see, eares to heare, or hearts to beleeve the truth: but Acts 19 especiallie, the shipmaisters, the marriners, merchant-men, and all the people that reigne, row, and are caried in this false church, they will never indure to see fire cast into her, they wil never indure to suffer losse of their daintie and pretious merchandise; but rather will raise up no small tumultes and stirres against the servantes of God, seeking their blood by all subtill and violent meanes, as we reade in the Scriptures their predecessors have alwaies donne, accusing them of treason, troubling the state, schisme, heresie, and what not. But unto all the power, learning, deceipt, rage of the false church, we oppose that litle booke of God's worde, which (as the light) shall reveale her, as the fire consume her, as an heavy milstone shall presse her and all her children, lovers, partarkers, and abettors, downe to hell: which booke, we willinglie receive, as the judge of al our controversies, knowing that all men shall one day (and that ere long) be judged by the same: by this booke who so is found in error or transgression, let them have sentence accordinglie.

Neither let the dreadfull, and severe judgments of God be lesse feared or esteemed, because they are pronounced by a frayle and weake man, or that man or messenger be hardlier entreated, or judged too severe, because he doth deliver the message of his Lord. The Lord assuredlie doth ratifie in heaven, whatsoever he pronounceth heere or [on] earth; neither hath anie servant of God power to alter and change his maister's wil; they cannot loose that [which] he bindeth, or lighten his yoke. Let then that state, people, or person, that findeth himself greeved at anie thing heere said, *Amos 3: 6, 7, 8* first inquire the truth therof in the word of God, and so give credit and obedience accordingly; for when the lion roreth, who should not feare when the Lord hath spoken, who should not prophecie. Let him that *Ezek. 3 ultim[o]* heareth therfore heare, and he that leaveth off, let him leave off: yet let all know, the lion roreth not in the forest, if no pray [prey] be present; neither the young lion out of his denne, if he be not about to take. And when the lion of the tribe of Juda is once raised up, who shall then find argumentes to plead, or weapons of defence: it is a most fearfull thing to fall into the handes of the living God. Great is the mercie of God that bloweth the trumpet and giveth warning before he bring the evill upon us, yea, great is his mercie and patience, that yet continueth to speake, knock, and call, we having so long skorned his messengers, and despised his words, *etc.* Only now let all men, in whome is anie feare or love of God, anie care of their owne salvation, tremble at the word of God; let them be warned and feared, let them ponder their owne waies, and depart from evill, least the finall wrath of God prevent them: let them consider, the further they go on in error, the further they depart from the truth, and the harder [A iv *recto*] they shall find it to returne. Let them not be perswaded to continue in evill, by the authoritie, wisdome, pretended *Exo. 23: 2* learning, or holines of anie, neither by the numbers and multitudes, after they have once heard or seene the error of their way: the Lord keepe all his from presumptuous sinne. Long hath that great milstone of the Lorde's fearfull judgementes beene lift up on high, in the eies *Revel. 18* of all men, over the presumptuous confuse Babel wherin they continue: long hath the Lord called, and commaunded all his people to goe, yea, to flee out of her. Many they see by God's mightie hand escaped and delivered, and marching with the banner of the gospell displaied before all the inchanters of Egipt and Pharaoh

his troupes: let the rest no longer tempt God, or be held 1 Cor. 10: 9
under the dint[1] and compasse of this dreadfull milstone,
by anie perswasions; but let them save their soules out
of this accursed false church, with all speed, whiles yet
grace and time is offred, and joine themselves unto the
faithfull servantes of Christ, under his conduct and gospell; that he may lead them out of the howse of this
spirituall bondage, into the glorious libertie of the sonnes
of God, unto that desired Tzion, there together to serve
God, and lead their lives in holines, according to God's Revel. 14: 1
owne wil, to the comfort and assurance of their owne
soules, and the glorie, of his name.   Amen.

> *Let the unjust do unjustlie yet, and the filthie do filthilie*
> *yet, and let the just do justice yet, and let the holie*
> *be sanctified yet.   Behold I come shortlie and my*
> *reward with me, to render unto everie one according*
> *as his worke shalbe.*   Apoc. [Revelation] 22:
> 11, 12.

[1] Seing we have receaved a most sure word of the 2 Pet. 1: 19
Lord our God, it behoveth us to geve heede therunto, Deut. 4: 6
Psal. 119: 105
as unto a light that shineth in darke places, whiles we
travell in the dangerous wildernes of this world.   In
which word, the whole wisdome and conncells of God
for our direction and instruction in all thinges, are fully
revealed unto us.   So that now we are not to say in our Deut. 30: 11,
heartes, who shall goe up for us to heaven, and bring it *etc.*
us ?   Or who shall goe over the sea, and bring it us
and cause us to heare it, that we may obey it; for loe,
it is neere us, even in our mouth and in our heart, and
set before our eies for to do it; the sound of the gospell
having beene long since caried forth through al the
regions of the whole earth: so that no nation shalbe
excused, which will not serve and obey unto the gospell Isa. 60: 12
of our Lord Jesus Christ; which being proclaimed with
his owne blessed mouth, sealed with his owne heart
blood, written with the pen of the Holy Ghost, de- Hebr. 2: 3, 4
livered and incommended [entrusted] by his holy
apostles and prophets unto us and all posterities, as his Heb. 12: 24, 25

---

[1] Threat of assault.

Gal. 3: 15. Deu. 4: 2, & 12: 32
Pro. 30: 6
Revel. 22: 18
Deut. 5: 32

last wil and testament, wherunto nothing may be added, nothing diminished, altered, or changed, violate, or wilfully neglected, according to fleshly wisdome or worldly pollicie, without most heinous transgression, sacriledge, and impietie. For as all degrees of men, without respect or exception of any person, are bound

Psa. 45: 6
Heb. 1: 8
Joh. 12: 48
2 Cor. 5: 10
Rev. 22: 18, 19
Gal. 18
1 Tim. 3: 15
Deut. 31: 26

unto the same, as unto the scepter of our soveraigne Lord, Jesus Christ, who is king over all, blessed for ever. Amen. So shall all men in particular be judged by the same, of all things done in this mortall life. Neither hath any angel in heaven, any mortall man, no, nor the whole church, power or prerogative, to alter or neglect the least jote or title therof.

But God hath especially committed these holy oracles to the careful custody of the church, there to be inviol-

Deut. 17: 8, *etc.*

ably preserved, as in the side of the arke, purely taught,

Mal. 2: 5. Exod. 23: 20, 21. Heb. 12: 28. Deut. 29
Josu. 24. Jude 3

expounded and delivered, without corrupting, mixing, hiding, obscuring, perverting, wresting, there to be precisely observed with all reverence and feare, without any willing or knowen transgression, or swarving,

1 Cor. 6: 15 & 10: 16, 17 & 12: 13

either to the right hand or to the left, of the whole church or any member therof. And heerunto is the whole church, and everie particular member therof,

Eph. 1: 23 & 4: 12. Hebr. 3: 13 & 10: 24. Phil. 2: 4

both jointly and severally bound; both because they have all of them interest in the tree and river of life, all are bound to the maintenance of the faith which is given, and is common to al sainctes, and because they are all of them the members of Christ, and togeather his bodie, and each others members in him. Therefore are they so often by the apostles charged and stirred up, to exhort, edifie, and [2] admonish one an other, to

Rom. 16: 17

stand upon the watch-towre of their faith, to scowte, and observe them diligently which cause divisions and

2 Joh. 10
1 Joh. 4: 1
1 Tim. 6: 3, 4, 5

offences, contrarie to the doctrine which they have learned, to trie the spirites, to examine the doctrine whether any man teach otherwise, and consent not

Math. 6: 22
Luke 11: 34, 35
1 Pet. 2: 2
Joh. 6
Phil. 2: 16
Math. 15: 13 & 16: 12
Gal. 5: 9

unto the wholsome wordes of our Lord Jesus Christ and to the doctrine which is according to godlines. Many waightie and grave reasons are added to induce them to be the more vigilant and careful; the doctrine being likened to the light of the eies, to the food, yea, to the life of the soule; as also, error and corruption resembled to darknes, leaven, poison, *etc.* Moreover, such teachers, to false and deceitful workmen, blind and unfaithful guides, to greevous and ravening wolves, to thieves and murtherers, *etc.* What counterfeit titles and sheepe's clothing soever they take and get ynto them: yet the Holy Ghost speakes evidently, and everie where warneth, that these builders shal destroie the temple of God, whose howse and worke we are, *etc.*, these guides shall seduce and mislead us in the waies of death and destruction, these thieves and wolves shal spoile and murther us.   Now by how much these goods are spiritual, this death of the soule, by so much are they more carefully to be avoided, shunned, eschewed. Therfore our saviour Christ and his apostles, as they were most vigilant and faithful ministers, and did both prevent and foresee divers dangers and great evils to come, so gave they verie earnest and often warnings hereof unto the disciples, unto the churches, commanding the porter, yea, everie servant of the house to watch, to beware and to take heed, shewing them that manie false Christes should arise and many false prophets, shewing great signes and wonders, wherby to deceave (if it were possible) the verie elect. He foretold them of antichriste's original, increase, and exaltation, how he should behave himself, what havock he should keep in the church of God: as also of the general defection, and even of the verie beginning therof. How immediatly after the tribulation of those daies, namely, the destruction and desolation of the earthly and material Jerusalem,[1] the sunne should be darkned, the moone should not give her light, the starrs should fal from heaven and the powers of heaven should be shaken, and the beautie therof wrapped up as a scroule [scroll], that the whole world should be drowned in sensualitie and securitie, as in the daies of Noah, because iniquitie shalbe increased, and faith scarse found upon the earth at his coming. So that if those daies should not be shortned,

Marginal references:
Revel. 8: 11 & 9: 3, 5, 19 & 16: 13
2 Cor. 11: 13
1 Cor. 3
Mat. 23
2. Tim. 3: 6, etc.
Math. 7: 15
Acts 20: 29
John 10
1 Cor. 3: 27

Mark 13
Math. 24
Luke 21

Math. 24: 29

---

[1] Jerusalem was captured in 70 A.D. by the Roman forces of Titus Flavius Vespasianus. It had been previously captured by the Babylonian forces led by Nebuchadnezzar in 586 B.C. See Edwin R. Thiele, *The Mysterious Numbers of the Hebrew Kings,* pp. 159-166.

there shou[l]d no flesh be saved. Yet, that al these things must and should undoubtedly come to pass, he shewed it by the nearer thinges (namely, the destruction of Jerusalem, the temple there, *etc.*) as also confirmed it by the truth and stedfastnes of his word, shewing how the heaven and earth should passe away, but his wordes should not passe away, neither should this generation passe, until al these thinges were fulfilled. Of these things the prophets spake before, though more darkly, and as a far off, and by divers types as Isaiah 14: 13, 14, Nahum 3: 4, 5, 6, 7, Daniel 9: 27; also Isaiah 13: 10 and 34: 4, Ezekiel 32: 7, Joel 2: 31 and 3: 14, 15. But the apostles [3] gave much more evident and plaine warning of these things, chiefly they that lived longest, and came nearest to these times. As the apostle Paul to the elders of Ephesus, Acts 20: 29, 30, 31 and in al his epistles plentifully; the apostle Peter in his second Epistle 2 and 3 chapters. The apostle Jude, and Jhon in al his epistles: but especially in that heavenly book of the Revelation; wherin he most lively describeth these thinges, even from the original, in several visions, according to the several times it should ensue. Wher-

Revel. 4 & 5 chapters

in he sheweth the happy estate of the church, whiles God's glorious throne was in the midst of the elders, and whiles it was inlightned with the burning lamps of God's spirit, and that the book was receaved and opened of the lamb, and whiles Christ sate upon the white horse, his owne holy word, and that they remained togeather in that heavenly order, wherin Christ had

Ephes. 4: 11
Col. 2: 5

placed and bestowed everie member, and the apostles those excellent workmen, had planted and left them, being fitly coupled and joined togeather by everie joint, for the service and help of the whole, according to the effectual power that is in the measure of everie part; until Satan, I say, that aunciant enimie of our happines, had that great sword given him, wherwith he made, and stil shal make bloudye war, and raise up greevous persecution against the woman and her seed without: within whiles they slept and were negligent, sowing his darnel of errors, and tares of discord amongst them,

1 Cor. 3: 3 *etc.* raising up sectes through the ambition and vainglory of

some, drawing others into schisme through pride and ^{Gal. 6: 12 etc.} Col. 2 hypocrisie, others into heresies, through their headstrong and unbridled affections: al into his snare, through the general default of al, who slacked their duties, and kept not their orderly watch one over an other, and jointly over the whole, as they were commanded and prescribed by the apostles. But as the age that arose after Joshua and those elders of his time, Judges 2 was sone corrupted, and forgate the ordinances of their God, and the great thinges the Lord had done for their forefathers: so these sone fell from the apostolike order, and left their primitive diligence and care. The people 2 Cor. 11: 20 upon a superstititious reverence and preposterous estimation unto their teachers and elders, resigned up al thinges, even their dutie, interest, libertie, prerogative, into their handes: suffering them to alter and dispose of all thinges after their owne lustes, without inquirie or controlement, wherupon, the true patterne of Christe's testament, so highly, and with so great charge incommended [entrusted] by the apostles unto the fidelitie of the whole church, was soone neglected and cast aside, especially by these evil workmen, these governours, who some of them affecting the preeminence, sought to draw an absolute power into their owne handes, perverting 3 John 9 those offices of more labour and care, into swelling titles of fleshly pompe and worldly dignitie. Thus wrought the mysterie of iniquitie, yea so far were manie of them 2 Thess. 2: 7 caried with a vaine opinion and ostentation of the excellencie of their giftes, as they under holy pretextes of 2 Cor. 11: 3 doing good unto others, sought also under this cloke a jurisdiction and regencie over other congre-[4]gations also, which was easily obteyned, the people through the just judgmentes of God being now so bewitched and blinded with their sweet tongues, that they easily condiscended. Then were these caled bishops of such a citie, and if they were cities of rule, to which any territories, townes, or hamletes in the countrie belonged, then were they called bishops of such a diocesse, *etc.*, and had under them inferiour or countrie bishops, as also deacons, subdeacons. Thus the whole church growing remisse and negligent, both people and officers, that heavenly patterne left by the apostles was soone violate, and upon new pretence, more and more innovate. For hereby was a wide gap opened to al licenciosnes and disorder, the people growing dissolute, the priestes (as they terme them) proude: so that religion, with [which] was erwhile [formerly] so irksome to flesh and blood, so mightily persecuted by Sathan and all the princes of the world, grew now so plausible to all sortes of men, so pleasing to their affections and appetites, that the great princes of the world, and all their realmes and countries flowed apace to the church in this estate, the gates and entrie being as ill kept without, as the watch within. So that upon this increase there were manie of these citie bishops, wherby the pride of some could not heerwith be satisfied, until they had gotten them a new dignitie; namely, to be archbishops over all the bishops in a province or countrie. Heer were also new deacons, archdeacons erected: yet was not the ambitious thirst of some thus stanched, but they aspired yet to a more high degree and preeminence; so that there must now be picked out fowre principal cities, which must carrie four patriarches.[1] These had yet higher power than the archbishops and were erected to see to the government and discipline (as they call it) of al churches, in respect, or rather in despite of those four beastes, which had so many eies and wings, and stood day and night about the throne of God, but they were rather those four angels which stood upon the four corners of the earth, holding the four windes of the earth, that the windes should not blow upon the earth neither on the sea, nor on any tree.

Revel. 7: 1   But Sathan having yet a further reach, ceased not heere, but even amongst those four he stil contended to set up one chief, which variably fell out, sometimes to one, sometimes to another, until at length the lot rested upon the Sea [see] of Rome, where the papacie being upholden by, and mixed with the empire, and in the

---

[1] The term " patriarch " was at first an honorific designation for the bishops of Antioch, Alexandria, Rome, Constantinople (from the 4th century), and Jerusalem (from the 5th century). In the Orthodox Eastern Church there were four patriarchs (omitting Rome), with Constantinople having the priority.

end swallowing it up, became the very throne of anti- 2 Thess. 2
christ, where he sitteth in his exaltation, to whome the Revel. 13
key of the bottomles pyt was given; which being by
him set wide open, the smoke of his cannons, devises,
trumperies, and abhominations darkned the sunne, Rev. 9. Verses
poisoned the aire: the locustes and scorpions that came ¹ 1, 2, 3, *etc.*
out of this pit, and out of this smoke, the multitudes and
swarmes of monkes, fryers, cannons, vagrant and men-
dicant preachers, parish priestes, *etc.*, so pestered and
prisoned everie tree, so stung and envenomed everie
conscience, as they could beare no fruite, neither brooke
any wholsome doctrine.   [5] Thus antichrist being now
established and fortified in the midst of his strengths, his
councel of cardinals,[1] his metropolitane and archbishops
palatine and lord bishops in everie countrie: he now
receaved the great charter of his prerogative infernal, Revel. 13: 2, 5.
even the dragon his power, throne, and auctoritie. He ⁶ 6, 7
now boldly opened his mouth against God, blaspheming
the tabernacle of Christ, and them that dwel therin:
innovating and changing all thinges after his owne
lustes, the ministerie, government, orders, worship;
thus exalting himself against al that is called God, and Verses ⎱ 15,
sitting in the temple of God as God, shewing himself ⎰ 16, 17.
that he is God, causing all men to worship his image,
to receave his mark, to buy his wares, *etc.*, bringing forth Revel. 17
his harlot upon the stage of the world, stately mounted
upon his beastly power, pompously araied, and gorgi-
ously decked, and adorned, the more to allure and
intise: whose cup of fornications was caried far and
neere, to many nations, people, and tongues, so that Revel. 18: 3
the kings of the earth committed fornication with her,
the inhabitants of the earth were drunken with the wine
of her fornications, which she conveied unto them by
the handes of her merchantmen, who are waxen ritch
with the abundance of her pleasures.

   Yet in al this defection, corruption, apostacie, hath Revel. 7: 4, *etc.*
God stil reserved a seed, a litle poore remnant, who have

---

[1] Cardinal priests functioned as early as the fifth century, but the College
of Cardinals became increasingly important after 1059, when Nicholas II
issued a decree regulating papal elections; and by 1179, at the Third
Lateran Council, the decretal of Alexander III strengthened the elective
and governing powers of the cardinals.

Revel. 9: 4
Revel. 14
Revel. 12: 7
Revel. 15 beene marked with the mark of God on their foreheades, and have been preserved from the sting of these scorpions, the plague of these locustes, which have had light in the midst of these hellish fogs, which have not bought nor sold with the marke of the beast, neither drunke of the whore's cup, neither have beene defiled with her fornications: but have beene the lambes caled, chosen, and Revel. 14: 4 faithful souldiours, following the lamb in white araye Jerem. 50 & 51 wheresoever he goeth, and leadeth them from faith to Isa. 13 faith. These by the light of the word reade the harlot's mysterie written in her forehead, discover her skirts, and all her abhominations, and by that same light make her knowen to be that spiritual Babilon, where Christe's servantes are kept in servitude from the free practise of his word, where the true temple his church and all the vessels and instrumentes therof are utterlie ruinate, defaced, profaned, trodden under foot. These also doe shew by the same light, even from the ancient prophecies, her, and al her synagogs, to become the verie habitation of devils, the hold of all fowle and wicked spirites, and a cage of everie uncleane and hateful bird. Zim[1] and Iim and all harmful beastes shal lodge there, the dragon and the serpent, the harpies, scritchowles and vultures shal there make their nest, and bring up their yong ones. And therfore these shal call al the Lorde's faithful servantes out from amongst them, least they be partakers of her sinns, and receave of her plagues; shewing them that her sinns are at the ful, come up into the sight of God into heaven, and that God now remembreth her iniquities, and is ready to powre downe his plagues Gen. 6
Gen. 19 upon her, as in the daies of Noah and Sodome.

[6] He only now staieth but untill his arke be built, until Lot his houshould be come forth, and the number of his elect be fulfilled, which time we may evidently discerne approcheth apace: our fig tree hath almost budded al our signes. Therfore it is high time for the servantes Luke 21: 28 of God to looke up, and to lift up their heades, for their redemption draweth neere. We have al seene this

---

[1] Zim and Iim. Zim or Ziphim refers to a wilderness, and Iim refers to a place in the desert. See Numbers 33: 44, 45, Joshua 15: 29, I Samuel 23: 14, 19. See also the title to Psalm 54 in the King James Version.

general defection, even in the maner as it was foretold
to be come to pass: we have also seene in the heavens
the tabernacle of testimonie, even that first and aposto- Revel. 15: 5, 8
like patterne, though we have not as yet beene able to
enter into the same, untill the vials of God's wrath be Revel. 16
powred upon the throne of the beast, the whore, this
Babilon, *etc.* We see all the faithful witnesses and martyres of Christ in their severall ages to have powred out
their vials, some upon the earth, some upon the sea,
some upon the fountaines, others upon the sunne, upon
the throne of the beast, upon their Euphrates, *etc.* We
heare this voice round about us sounding in our eares,
Go out of her my people, etc. Save thyself, O Syon that Revel. 18: 4, 5
dwellest with the daughter Babel: flie out of the midst of Babel, Isa. 52: 11
deliver everie man his soule, be not destroied in her in[i]quitie, Zach. 2: 7
for this is the time of the Lord's vengeance, he will render unto Jerem. 51: 6, 45
her a recompence: and againe, flee out of the midst of Babell, Jerem. 50: 8
depart out of the land of the Chaldeans and be ye as the gotes
before the flock.

And our saviour Christ in that forerunning signe and Math. 24: 16,
type of Judea and Jerusalem, warneth them that are in *etc.*
Judea to flee to the mountaines, them that are called on
the house top, not to come downe into their house to
fetch or save any thing they have lost there, they that
are in the fieldes, not to returne back into the citie to
fetch their clothes, shewing the woes that are upon them,
which either are hindred and pressed downe with
worldly affaires, as a woman great with child, or are
deteined and held with the leave [permission] either of
their earthly frendes how neere so ever, or of their owne
flesh, that they cannot flie and deliver their soules, that
cannot give eare or obey unto the commandement and
voice of God whiles he calleth them, and so deferr and
put off their comming out, either until the winter of
God's wrathful judgmentes circumvent and inclose them,
or the saboth of his final indignation fal and rest upon Hebr. 3 and
them, and then there be no space granted them to flie, chapters
or grace to be preserved. Seing then we have so manie
prophecies, so many tipes [hints], so many warnings, so
manie callings, seing all our signes are accomplished,
and that God's final judgmentes approch and steale

upon us: let us not despise his grace, nor harden our hearts whiles he yet speaketh, and it is called to day: seing we are fallen into these last and perilous times, wherin Satan useth his last and uttermost sleightes, wherby the whole world shalbe deluded, yea the verie elect, if it were possible, drawen away; let us not suffer our selves to be any longer deceaved, with the subtil inchantmentes of the false prophets and preachers of the times, neither to be deceaved with the vaine titles and glorious shewes of church, ministerie, sacramentes, gospel, etc., wherof the false church hath alwaies [7] boasted and arrogated unto her self, as well as the true church, wherwith, as with stales[1] she hath allured, and as with snares detained, her guestes. Cayn (we read) as wel as Habel, offred sacrifice: Ismael and Isaac were both circumcised; Hagar and Sarah were two mothers; the two mothers before Solomon pleaded both of them confidently for the living childe; the harlot as wel as wisdome killed sacrifices, sent out her ministers, invited guestes to her house; Israel in their schisme and defection erected a temple, an altar, a ministerie.

Gen. 4: 3, 4 & 17: 23 & 21: 4

Gal. 4: 25, 26 1 King. 3: 16 Prov. 7: 13, 14 etc., & 9 Chap. 1 Kings 12: 28, etc.

It behoveth us therfore, whiles yet God vouchsafeth us time, carefully by the light of Gode's word, to examine our waies, and to ponder our estate, whether we be in that broad way that leadeth to destruction amongst those multitudes over whome the whore sitteth and raineth [reigneth] or in the straight and narrow way which leadeth unto everlasting life, with Christe's litle flock and marked soldiours, whome the lamb leadeth and ruleth: whether we be in that great defection, in that spirituall Babilon under antichrist and that beast, or whether we be in the mount Sion, in the spirituall Jerusalem, where the commandementes of God are kept, and the faith of Jesus.

Lam. 3: 40, etc. Math. 7: 13, 14 Revel. 14: 1 & 17: 15

This being knowen, al controversies shal forthwith cease: for then shall we either be guiltie of our owne destruction through our wilful obstinacie, or els shal we lay hold of eternal life, whiles yet it is offred, by forsaking our evil waies, and yeilding obedience unto Gode's holy word. Neither need we unto this busines

---

[1] A lure, bait, or decoy; a prostitute.

to goe fetch our light out of men's writinges (as sundrie of the chief builders of this corrupt age do) or curiously to enquire or dispute about I wote [know] not what markes of the true church, which whiles some indevored to set downe, endles controversies and vaine striefe about words hath arisen amongst them, without end or edifying. Therefore let us, for the apeasing and assurance of our consciences, give heed to the word of God, and by that golden reed measure our temple, our **Revel. 11: 1, 2** altar, and our worshippers: even by these rules wherby the apostles, those excellent perfect workmen, planted and built the first churches, comparing the synagogues of this land unto them in the people, the ministerie, administration, order, government, *etc.* This way cannot deceave us, for neither can the simplest erre therin, **Isa. 35: 8** neither any polluted (how subtle and cunning soever) passe by it unespied, unreprooved: for as ther is but one truth, so whatsoever is diverse more or less than that truth, is faultie and to be repented.

First therfore, because everie building consisteth of stones, let us examine of what kinde of stones this Church of England (as they terme it) consisteth, and is compact; whether of such elect precious living stones, which are gathered unto and built upon Christ Jesus, and in **1 Pet. 2: 5** him grow unto an holy and spiritual temple unto God, **Jerem. 51: 26** **1 Chron. 29: 2** *etc.*, or of common, Babilonish reprobate stones, wherof **1 Kings 5: 17** the Lord hath sworne, that not one of them shalbe **2 Chron. 2: 8** taken for a corner, or for a foundation in his house. **Ezra 3: 7** [8] The material temple (which was but a type of this) we reade to be built from the verie foundation, of choice, costly, perfect stones, the beames and rafters of choice cedars, algummin trees: no common or vile thing was **Read Leviticus** used towardes it, neither might any profane and pol- **from the 10 to** **the 23 chapter** luted enter into it. But of the incomparable bewtie and unutterable excellencie of this spiritual temple, under the holy ministerie and happy perfect government of Christ, all the prophetes have with great delight **1 Pet. 1: 10, 11,** spoken and fore told, and with extreme desire inquired, **12** and longed to see the revelation of these joies and graces, which they in the spirit foresaw, and foreshewed unto us, to whome they should be performed. The prophet

Isaiah, speaking of the excellencie therof, breaketh forth
into these wordes, *Behold I will lay thy stones with the
carbuncle, and thy foundations with saphirs, and I will make
thy windowes of esmeraldes, and thy gates of shining stones, and
al thy borders of pretious stones, and thy children shalbe taught
of the Lord, and much peace shalbe to thy children.* And in
another place, speaking of the excellent glorie of this
spirituall temple, he useth these wordes: *For brasse I
will bring gold, for yron I will bring silver, for wood brasse,
for stones yron. I will make also thy goverment of peace, and
thine exactors of righteousnes, etc. Thy people also shalbe all
righteous, they shall possesse the land for ever: the graffe of my
planting shalbe the work of mine handes that I may be glorified.*
And againe; *for thornes there shal grow firr trees, for nettles
shal grow the myrrh tree, and it shalbe to the Lord for a name,
and for an everlasting signe that shall not be taken away.* Al
the plantes of this orchard shalbe of the Lorde's planting; they shal all be incense and aloe trees, pomgranates
and fir trees, which shal continually bring forth pleasant,
newe, and fresh fruit, because they grow by the sides of
the river of life, are watered with the dewe of heaven,
and refreshed with the windes of Gode's spirit. They
come not, nor grow not heere, until they be first cut off
from their corrupt natural stock, where they grewe before, and be ingrafted into the true olive tree, the true
vine: yea, and being planted and ingrafted, that plant,
that branch that bringeth not forth good fruit, shalbe
hewen downe, shalbe cut off and cast out, *etc.* Into
this mountaine entereth no venemous or harmfull creature, the cockatrice and aspe, the lion and leopard enter
not and lodge not heere, untill they have left their
poison, their fiercenes, *etc.*, so that the sucking child
may play upon the hole of the aspe, the weaned child
put his hand upon the hole of the cockatrice, the lambe
and the wolfe dwel togither, the kid and the leopard
eat straw together, and a litle child shal lead them.
Ther may none be admitted into the church of Christ,
but such as enter by publike profession of the true
faith. None remayne there, but such as bring forth
the fruites of faith. The forerunner, John the Baptist,
first preached repentance to prepare the way, and make

Marginal references:

Isai. 54: 11, *etc.*
Jerem. 31: 34, *etc.*

Isai. 60: 17, 21
& 35: 8, 10 &
55: 13

Numb. 24: 6

Cant. 4: 13, *etc.*

Ezek. 47: 12

Revel. 22: 1

Rom. 11: 17, 24

1 Cor. 6: 11
Titus 3: 3
1 Pet. 4: 3
Rom. 6: 4
Math. 3: 10 &
7: 19
Luke 13: 6
Math. 15: 13
Joh. 15: 6
Jer. 2: 21

Isai. 11: 6, *etc.*
and 65: 25

Math. 3 & 10: 7

strait, the pathes of the Lord, before he baptised any. Luke 10 & 13: 3
The like did our saviour Christ and his disciples. The
apostles also first gathered a people (by preaching) unto
the faith: then receaved and [9] joyned them to the Act. 2: 41, 42
church, and administred unto them the holy pledges of And everie where
the faith: baptisme as a seale of their ingraffing into through the whole historie
Christ, the holy supper as a symbole of their communion of the acts of the apostles
with Christ and al his faithful servantes.

Thus see we what kinde of stones, what manner of
people the Lord will have built and receaved into his
church. Now it remaineth, that we by these rules
examine the stones and people of the Church of Eng- Exod. 28: 15, 21
land; whether they by such chosen pretious stones, as
we see here described, as the high priest caried in his Revel. 21
broidered brestplate; whether they be such a chosen, Zach. 9: 16
redeemed, faithful, free, holy people, as are called unto,
and walke in the faith of Christ Jesus; or they be rather
of the reffuse, common pibble [pebble] chalke stones,
which cannot be used to any sownd and sure building,
even al the profane and wicked of the land, atheistes,
papistes, anabaptistes and heretikes of al sortes, gluttons, riotours, blasphemers, perjures, covetous, extortioners, thieves, whores, witches, conjurers, *etc.*, and who
not, that dwelleth within this iland, or is within the
queene's dominion.

All without exception or respect of person are received into, and nourished in the bosome of this church,
with the word and sacramentes. None are here refused,
none kept out. This church (as the prophet saith) Mal. 1: 10
openeth her knees to everie passenger, furnisheth a table Ezek. 44: 7 &
to the multitude, and drink offerings to the numbers; 16: 25 & 23: 42, 44
she keepeth open house to all commers, bread and wine Prov. 9: 17
and welcome. Neither is she more dainty of her stollen
waters, than of her hid bread, of her adulterate baptisme,
than of her Sheshak[1] supper, not denying baptisme to
the seed even of whores and witches; she receaveth
them al into her covenant (which is not with God, but
with death and hell), giving them her peace, selling
them her wares, *etc.* This is their communion of saintes,

---

[1] Jeremiah 25: 26 and 51: 41. A supper in which one becomes exposed to
danger or wrong because of drinking and gluttony.

K*

their holy fellowship: thus are they bound and enchained togither in open sacriledge, idolatrie, impietie, even al estates, prince, priestes, and people, and (as the prophet saith) even wreathed togither as in a strong cable of iniquitie, and folded one within an other as thornes in an hedg, or rather wrapped and plighted together, as thornes to the fire of Gode's wrathfull judgmentes.

Micah 7: 3

Nah. 1: 10

Isa. 1: 16

Lamen. 2: 13

For whither we consider the whole estate or any particuler part therof, we shall find it wholy corrupte, and deeply set, as in the daies of Gibbea; not one sownd part from the crowne of the head to the sole of the feet, but all ful of woundes, swellinges, old putrified sores which cannot be bound up or cured, iniquitie having broken in and overflowed the whole land, and everie place therof, even as the raging sea which cannot be stopped. There is no faith, no mercie, no knowledg or feare of God in the land: by swearing, lying, killing, stealing, whoring, they breake out, and blood toucheth blood: they abhor judgment, and pervert all equitie: they turne justice into gall, [10] and the fruit of righteousnes into wormwood: truth falleth in the streetes. and equitie cannot enter; the heades judg for rewardes; the priestes teach for hire; the prophets prophecie for money; the people are incorrigible, such as cannot brooke nor endure wholsome doctrine, but get unto them after their owne lustes an heap of teachers, which may prophecie to them of wine and strong drink, *etc.* They al hate and persecute him that rebuketh in the gate, they abhor him that speaketh uprightly. They prosecute with mortal hatred him that runneth not to the same excesse and sinne with them; and he that refraineth from evil, maketh himself a pray [prey], and is spoiled of all men. All the lawes of God are heere broken and rejected, both of the first and second table, both of the ecclesiasticall and civille estate, and of everie particular person in both, both in the worship of God, and in civile justice and conversation: all things being innovate in both, according to the lustes and pleasures of men, the law and word of God being quite rejected and cast aside, as may appeare, if the estate either of the church or common welth be examined or tried by the word of

Hosea 4: 1, 2

Micah 3: 9

Amos 6: 12
Isa. 59: 14
Micah 3: 11

Hosea 4: 4

2 Tim. 4: 3
Ezek. 33: 31
Amos 5: 10

1 Pet. 4: 4, 5

Isa. 59: 15

Revel. 13: 17

2 Kings 22: 11, 12, 13

God. The particuler defaults wherof in their customes, lawes, trialls, pleadings, jurisdiction, orders, decrees, *etc.*, are well nigh infinite. And what then are the enormities that ensue therof to everie estate, degree, and person. This need no other demonstration, than the general excesse, pride, superfluitie, covetousnes, rapine, crueltie, deceit, malice, debate, inordinate Ezek. 16: 49 affections, unbridled lustes, dissolutnes, disobedience, *etc.*, which are found most rife, even in all estates and degrees amongst them. Neither hath all kind of sinne and wickednes more universally raigned in any nation at any time, than heere at this present in this land; where all are receaved into the church, all made members of Christ.

All these sinnes, and many more abhominations (which a Christian heart abhorreth but to think or speak of) are amongst them winked at, tollerated, excused, covered and cured with the gospel preached, and their holy sacramentes. All this people, with all these manners, were in one daye, with the blast of Queen Elizabeth's trumpet, of ignorant papistes and grosse idolaters, made faithfull Christianes, and true professors:[1] upon whome, these hungrie priestes, like ravening wolves and greedy foxes flew to divide the pray [prey]; some getting them the roomthes of arch-bishops, others caught bishoprickes, others caught deanries, arch-deaconries, fat parsonages, some more, some fewer, as their estimation and frendes were.

They being thus installed, and their mouthes stopped Isa. 56: 10, 11 with these fat morsels, the world by this time was well amended with them. There was no neede to gather a people to the faith by preaching of the gospell, neither to set the holy government of Christ over such as were called to the faith; all was now well enough, [11] after the people had receaved this ministerie, after their portuise was translated from Latine into English,[2] the

---

[1] This is a reference to the Act of Uniformity, which Parliament enacted on April 28, and which obtained the queen's assent on May 8, 1559.
[2] The Book of Common Prayer first appeared in March, 1549. For its dependence on previous Latin sources, see Francis Procter and Walter H. Frere, *A New History of the Book of Common Prayer, with a Rationale of Its Offices*, p. 54 and chapter V.

supremacie, from the Sea [see] of Rome, to the Sea [see] of Canterburie. And after these pseudomartyres and runneaway professors had tasted the sweetnes of this ro[a]st, and pleasantnes of these roomths, and were once warme in their nestes; then forgate they all their former peregrination, and devowred the vowes they then made, seking now to fortifie and establish their owne, and not Christ's kingdome. And to this end they invented, obteined, and erected their blasphemous High Commission, in stead of the Spanish Inquisition;[1] where they gate power over all causes and persons ecclesiasticall, to make or abrogate what lawes they list, and to impose them upon the whole church, which is the whole land, to molest, cite, fetch up, examine, imprison and fyne whome they list, as long as they list, as much as they list, without controlement or any redresse, though their proceedings be expresly contrarie, prejudicial, and repugnant unto the crowne and prerogative royal, unto the great charter and lawes of the land, as were not hard to shew, if any eare might be given therunto.

Thus being enthronized, they shew themselves playnly in their colours, both in establishing most of the pope's cannons, and in adding new as ill of their owne, still retaine further power to make more at their pleasures: which, howsoever they cannot, nor dare not justifie by the word, yet will they maintaine them by the sword; which sword they now draw forth against Christe's most faithfull servantes that will not bow downe nor worship their beastly authoritie, but stand for the maintenance of the faith, once given unto the saintes, and for the free and sincere practise of Christe's holy testament: which faith, testament, and people of God, these

---

[1] The Court of High Commission was "established" in 1556 or 1557 by Letters Patent issued by Mary and confirmed by Elizabeth in the Act of Supremacy of 1559. But commissions for ecclesiastical causes were created by Thomas Cromwell twenty years earlier. See Roland G. Usher, *The Rise and Fall of the High Commission* (Oxford, 1913). Lord Burghley's famous letter of July 1, 1584, denouncing the Court's procedure, describing the twenty-four articles of 1584, as of a " Romish stile," likening them to the wiles of the Spanish Inquisition, is printed in John Strype, *The Life and Acts of John Whitgift*, III (1824), pp. 104-107. Whitgift's twenty-four articles of May, 1584, are printed by Strype, pp. 81-87, and Whitgift's reply to Lord Burghley, July 3, 1584, is given also, pp. 107-112. See also Strype, *Whitgift*, I, 309-317.

accursed apostataes, with most deadlie hatred and
hostilitie persecute, and seeke to suppresse by all exquisite tyrannie, closing and muing up the bodies of
them in the most noisome places of the most vile prisons,
somtimes not without yrons and blowes, in stead of
argumentes and perswasions, railing, blaspheming and
slandering both the holy truth, and the witnesses therof,
with their poisoned heretical lying bookes, pamphlets,
libells, which the dragon like a flood casteth out of the
mouth of his false prophets after the church: yet dare
they not once produce them to any triall or answere,
knowing in their bad consciences, that their ill dealings
may not endure the light: and therfore seeke they by all Jhon 3: 20
subtill and forceible meanes to suppresse the same, Ephes. 5: 13
limiting and prohibiting their priestes, not to meddle
with the reproofe of anie thing by publike authoritye
established, *etc.* And such as will not be thus nurtured
they inclose up by their sole commandement in close
and strait prisons, never [12] letting them to escape out
of their handes, untill they be brought out upon the
beere [bier]: thus fulfil they the measure of their pre- 1 Thess. 2: 15,
decessors, shed the blood of the righteous, make open Math. 23: 32,
war against Christ and his gospel, cast the sonne and *etc.*
heire out of his house, and will not suffer him to reigne Math. 21: 38,
there by his owne officers and lawes, but take his in- 39
heritance unto them, with his scepter and al his roial
rites and prerogatives into their handes, shewing themselves in the temple of God as God, erected newe lawes,
newe ordinances, a newe ministerie, newe worship,
newe orders and forme of government, as shalbe
shewed hereafter.

Now unto this their apostatical and bloody throne Revel. 13: 16,
and antichristian power, and unto al the abhominations 17
proceeding from the same, standeth al the land both
great and small, rich and poore, priest and people, in
most servile subjection, and therfore in this estate can- Gal. 4: 9, 10
not be held or numbred among Christ's faithful ser- Revel. 14: 9,
vantes, which are fully redeemed by the price of his John 8: 37
pretious blood, from all these bondages and intangle- Gal. 5: 1 &
mentes, which they by a shew of voluntarie religion, Col. 2: 6, 7, 8
and counterfeit holines, would impose upon men's con-

sciences. Neither may such be held the servantes of
Christ, which stand subject unto his enimie, antichrist,
beare his yoke, receave his ministerie, wares, *etc.*, or
which contend not for the maintenance of the true faith,
and for the sincere practise of the gospel with freedome,
in al patient maner unto the death: suffring rather anie
thing, than themselves to be defiled with his abhominations. How then should this people, as they generally
stand in the publique estate of this land, in this subjection to antichrist, in this idolatry, sacriledg, al kind of
excesse and sinne, even in al degrees without repentance,
faith, obedience, knowledg, be receaved, held, or esteemed the redeemed, called, faithful, free, obedient,
loving subjects and people of the Lord? Or how may
Christe's true and faithful servantes have any spirituall
communion or fellowship with them in thys estate,
without open sacriledg, most hainous impietie, and
high profanation of the holy things of God? For if
into the material temple, no profane or polluted person
might enter and offer, untill he had imbraced the faith,
and beene clensed from his filthines; how much more
ought this profane, ignorant, unholy, wicked, disobedient rowte,[1] be kept out of the church of Christ, and from
al intermedling with the holy things of God, which in
this estate belong not unto them.

But as these ungodly priestes of these times have
entred, and do administer unto this profane people, for
the lucre of their goodes, tithes, wages, hire; so wat[2]
not these Balaams sundrie divelish shiftes and cavils for
the maintenance of their doinges, least by this doctrine
their portion should be reprooved, their vantage for
divining cease, as also their sinne and shame be made
manifest. Amongst an heape of their forged excuses,
they set this for doctrine in the fore [13] front: that where
a christian prince is, which maintaineth the gospel, and
the whole land or estate not resisting this commande-

Jude 3
Revel. 14: 12
John 15: 14

Calvin, *Instit.*
Lib. 4. Sect. 9

---

[1] Rout, pack, crowd, assemblage.
[2] Past tense of wite or wet. Two possible meanings are: (1) so, defend
not these Balaams' sundrie divelish shiftes ; (2) therefore, these Balaams
observed not, disregarded, such shiftes. The first is ironical ; the second
meaning seems the better one. Perhaps "wat" should be "want," with
the meaning — so lack not.

ment, reverenceth the word and sacramentes, there the whole multitude of such a land or state, are without doubt to be esteemed and judged a true church. This reason they confirme not with any proofes of the Scripture, but by Mr. Calvin's authoritie, who giveth these reasons therof: because (saith he) it is certaine, the word and sacramentes are not without fruit, and that by this meanes unitie is preserved to the universall church.[1]

Touching the person of the author alledged, I gladly acknowledg him a painful and profitable instrument, in the thinges he saw, and times he served in, yet not without his manie errors and ignorances, especially touching the planting, government, and ordering of the church of Christ: and no mervaile, for being so newly escaped out of the smoky fornace of poperie, he could not so sodeinly see or attaine unto the perfect beawtie of Sion. But seeing my hope is, God hath pardoned all his errors, *etc.*, my purpose is not (with these wicked men) to revive and broach them a fresh, or make them presidentes [precedents], and by them take boldnes to commit the like or worse offences, nor yet to discover Noah his shame and nakednes. So also concerning matters of faith, would I be loth to build upon, or be pressed by the doctrines and examples of men, the best wherof we see to be subject to their errors and faults. For as faith Prov. 19: 27 only beleeveth, and resteth upon the holy word of God: 1 John 4: 1 / Math. 7: 24, *etc.* so are we by the same to examine al the doctrines and doinges of men, yea, of the whole church, and accordingly to approve or refuse the same.

Touching this doctrine, then, that a Christian prince which publisheth and maintaineth the gospell, doth forthwith make all that realme (which with open force resisteth not his proceedinges) to be held a church, to whome an holy ministerie and sacramentes belong, without further and more particular and personal trial, examination, confession, *etc.* This doctrine we find by the word of God to be most false, corrupt, uncleane, dangerous and pernicious doctrine, contrarie to the

[1] From John Calvin, *Institutes of the Christian Religion*, trans. Henry Beveridge, vol. II, book IV, chapter I, sections 9, 10, p. 289. See also Ronald S. Wallace, *Calvin's Doctrine of the Word and Sacrament* (Edinburgh, 1953).

whole course, practise, and lawes both of the Old and Newe Testament; breaking at once al christian order, corrupting and poisoning al christian communion and fellowship, and sacrilegiously profaning the holy thinges of God.

1 Tim. 2: 2

First we know that no prince or mortal man can make any a member of the church: they may by their godly government greatly help and further the church, greatly comfort the faithful, and advance the gospel, *etc.* But to chuse or refuse, to cal or harden; that the eternal and almightie ruler of heaven and earth keepeth in his owne handes, and giveth not this power unto any other. This also we know, that whome the Lord hath before al worldes chosen, them he wil in his due time and meanes cal by his word, and whome he calleth, them he sealeth with this seale, to depart from iniquitie, to [14] beleeve and lay hold of Christ Jesus as their alone saviour, to honour and obey him as their annointed king, priest, and prophet, to submit themselves unto him in all thinges, to be reformed, corrected, governed, and directed by his most holy word, vowing their faithful obedience unto the same, as it shalbe revealed unto them. By this faith, confession and profession, everie member of Christ from the greatest unto the least, without respect of persons, entereth into, and standeth in the church. In this faith, have all the faithfull congregations in the world, and true members of the same bodie, fellowship and communion each with other; and out of this faith have the true servantes of God, no fellowship, no communion with any congregation or member, how florishing titles or faire shewes soever they make heere in the flesh.

Rom. 9: 15
Exod. 33: 19
Rom. 8: 39

Jam. 1: 18

2 Tim. 2: 19

Heb. 3: 14

Heb. 12: 25

Deut. 23: 3
Exod. 12: 48
Numb. 9: 14

None (as hath beene prooved) uncircumcised or polluted in flesh, might enter into the temple, or tast of the passover or other sacrifices, how neere soever they were in consanguinitie, affinitie, or subjection. In King David's time the Edomites, Moabites, Ammonites, and Philistims [*sic*] were brought under obedience and subjection: yet were none of them admitted into the temple, *etc.*, but such as imbraced the faith.

King Hezekias and Josiah,[1] two famous godly kings, after they had rightly reformed the corrupt estate, admitted none to the passover, but such as purified and sanctified themselves, according to the law. The like we reade of the children of the captivitie, after they had finished the temple, set the priests in their order, and the Levites in their courses, *etc.* They kept the passover together with all such as had seperated themselves unto them from the filthines of the heathen of the land, to seeke the Lord God of Israel. These were godly kinges, which truly planted religion, and rightly reformed the state, and had everie way as great priviledg and prerogative, as any kings before or since; yet had they not power, neither durst they presume to open the temple dores to the profane or pulluted, or to admit them unto the passover, *etc.*, for this had beene heinous sacriledg and impiety, for which sinnes the wrath of God would have burnt against them. Neither is the like sinne lesse transgression now, either in the prince that commandeth, the priestes that administer, or the people that receave.

2 Chron. 2:9 & 30 & 35 Chapters

Ezra 6: 21

The prince himself entreth by the same dore of faith, into the church: and is bownd to the strait observation and obedience of God's lawes in his calling, as well as any other; and is for any transgression therof, liable and subject to the censures and judgementes of Christ in his Church, which are without partialitie or respect of persons. Which censures and judgementes if the prince contemne, he contemneth them against his owne soule; and is therupon, by the same power of Christ, to be disfranchized out of the church, and to be delivered over unto Satan, as well as any other offendor. Now though by this sinne he loseth his right to be a Christian or member [15] of the church: yet loseth he not his right to be a king or magistrate, and is so to be held and obeid of all faithful Christians, which are his subjectes.

John 10: 7

Deut. 17: 19
Josh. 1: 7, 8

Psalm 141: 5

2 Sam. 12: 7

2 Chron. 16: 7 & 19: 2
2 Kings 20: 17
2 Chron. 26: 16, etc.

Math. 22: 21
Prov. 8: 15
Eccles. 8: 2
Rom. 13: 1

And sure, they litle know what belongeth either to the entrance into, or continuance in the church of God,

---

[1] Hezekiah was king of Judah from 716/715 to 687/686 and Josiah was king of Judah from 640/639 to 608. I have followed the most recent chronology, in Edwin R. Thiele, *The Mysterious Numbers of the Hebrew Kings* (Chicago, 1951), p. 283.

or what belongeth to the administration of the sacramentes, or to the holy communion of the saintes, which revive or defend this doctrine: for is not the whole church, but especially the porter or pastor (who ought to know those well that come in, to know his sheep by name) guiltie of great negligence and sacriledg, that receave such into their fellowship, and administer the holy thinges of God unto them, of whose faith they have no more testimonie and assurance, yea, or rather of whose infidelitie and profanenes they have such apparant proofes ? Can the word and sacrementes (which they say cannot be without fruit) either take away or excuse their sinne in delivering unto, or joyning with the open unworthy in the sacramentes ? Or excuse the unworthy receavers from eating or drinking their owne damnation ? May the temple of the Lord be thus profaned ? The table of the Lord thus contemned and defiled ? Or is not the Lord a God of judgment ? But it is impossible that the word and sacrementes should be without fruit. This is true, yet the fruit is of two sortes; for falling upon good ground, it bringeth herbs and fruit worthy of the dressor, and receaveth blessing of the Lord. On the other side, if it fal upon il ground, which still bringeth thornes and briars, it delivereth it not from, but rather hastneth it unto the curse and judgments of God. Neither can any labour of man, though Paul plant and Apollos water, any thing prevaile, except God give the increase. That which is crooked can no man make straight. No washing, no sope, or nitre,[1] can cleanse the leopard from her spots; horses cannot run upon the rock; neither can any man plow ther with oxen.

The sownd of the gospel is to some the sweete savour of life unto life, unto others, the savor of death unto death. The gospel preached doth not make al the land, or al that heare it straight way members of the church without seene,[2] faith, and obedience. Noah preached a great while (whiles the arke was in making)

Marginal references:
Mark 13: 34, 37
John 10: 3
Ezek. 34
Math. 7: 6
Mal. 1: 10
1 Cor. 10: 17 & 12: 13
1 Cor. 11: 29
Isa. 55: 10, 11
Micah 5: 7
1 Cor. 3: 6
Jerem. 2: 22
Amos 6: 12
2 Cor. 2: 16
2 Pet. 2: 5

---

[1] An agent for cleansing ; potassium nitrate, saltpetre. Also regarded as a mysterious nitrous element in the air.

[2] Seeing, perception, vision ? " Sene " means a synod, a general council of the clergy for deliberation.

unto the old world, but prevailed not. The Lord sent
to Israel and Judah in their defection many prophets,
rising early and sending; yet they gave not eare, but 2 Chron. 36: 15, 16
mocked the messengers of God, despised his word, and
misused his prophets. The law and the prophets were
dayly read in the synagogues of the Jewes, at such time as
Christ came: yet neither they nor their rulers knew or
acknowledged him, but fulfilled them in condemning
him: yea Christ himself, that most livelie, powerful,
excellent teacher, preached the gospell among them
with great vertue and miracles; yet beleeved they not
on him, that the saying of the prophet Isaiah might be Isa. 53: 1
fulfilled; Lord, who hath beleeved our report; or to Isa. 6: 9
whome is the arme of the Lord revealed: therfore they
could not beleeve, because it is said againe; he hath
blinded their eies [16] and hardened their heartes, that
they should not see with their eies, nor understand with
their heartes, and should be converted and I should
heale them. And againe in an other place: and I said Isa. 49: 4
I have laboured in vaine, I have spent my strength in
vaine, and for nothing: but my judgment is with the
Lord, and my work with my God. Then neither this
doctrine followeth: that where a christian prince maintaineth the gospel, and the people by the same authoritie
are compelled to heare the same; that the whole multitude, without further proofe of their christian obedience,
are hereupon to be receaved into the church, and made
partakers of the bread of the children, and the holy
thinges of God: neither yet this strange opinion which
is generally taught by the learned preachers of these
times; that where there is a preaching minister, there
that parish is undoubtedly (how profane and wicked
soever the people be) to be held and accounted a true
church of Christ: except these presumptuous shepheardes, these companions have greater vertue and
prerogative than Christ himself had, who could not
bring this to passe in the places where he taught. Yea
the folie of some, even of the chief Rabbines amongst
them, hath yet proceeded further; namely, that where
there is one parish that hath (as he termeth him) a
burning lamp, *viz.*, a preaching priest amongst sixe or

seven other parishes having smoking lampes, *viz.*, dumb priestes that cannot preach, there the light of this burning lamp (or star called wormwood) shall enlighten the other candlestickes also, and give them the estimation and dignitie of true churches lik[e]wise. But my purpose is not heer to intreate of the excellencie of these preachers, and how powerfully and purely they preach the gospell: therof in due place. It now remaineth to see, whether the vertue of the sacramentes thus administred unto the whole multitude of a land or state, can sanctifie and make holy, or be availeable to this people or no.

It hath beene above shewed to be great sinne, sham[e]-ful negligence, high contempt, unsufferable profanation and sacriledg in the whole church to admit, administer unto, or communicate with such; neither can the holines of the sacramentes any way excuse, but rather greatly augment their sinne and judgment, which deliver such holy things to such knowen unworthy receavers which discerne not the Lorde's bodie, neither can the holines of the sacramentes sanctifie the receavers, especially the unworthy receavers; whose filthines defileth the sacrament, even as leven the lump. The sacramentes confer not so much, as seale God's grace unto us, they give not faith to any so much, as confirme the faith of all the worthy receavers. But where they are thus prostituted and sacrilegiously profaned, they bring no such joy, they seale no such comfort, but rather God's assured wrath for the abuse of his ordinances, the people, sacramentes and all, being hereby uncleane and polluted in Gode's sight. Neither preserve they unto the church hereby her unitie and power, but [17] rather take away al communion, and so corrupt and poison it, that now their fellowship is not in the faith, but in sacriledg and sinne. And for the power of the church, it is not given them to receave and admit, but to drive away and keep out the profane and open unworthy, from the table of the Lord.

The next shiftes these Balaamites have, for the administring unto, the communicating with, and retayning the prophane in the bozome of their church: are certayne

Marginal references:

1 Cor. 11: 29

1 Cor. 5: 6
Hag. 2: 14
1 Cor. 10: 3, 4, 5

Rom. 4: 11

Ephe. 4: 4, 5
John 1: 6, 7
2 Cor. 13: 8
Deut. 4: 6 & the whole booke
Num. 5: 2, 3

Calvin, *Instit. lib. 4. cap. 1,* sect. 13

argumentes, drawn by Mr. Calvin from the 13 and of
Mathew,[1] against the Anabaptistes, to proove that the
church heer on earth shal never be without sinne, and
is not to be left for sinne, *etc.*, comparing the church to _{Math. 13: 24}
a corne field, which being sowen with good graine, is
by the enimies' fraud scattered with tares: of which it
is not clensed, untill the crop be brought into the barne-
floore: and unto a net, in which all kind of the fishes _{Math. 13: 47}
are gathered together, and are not chosen out, until
they be laid out upon the shore, *etc.*, and unto a floore,
wherin the wheate is so gathered, that it lieth hidden
under the chaffe, until by fanne and syve it be at _{Math. 3: 12}
length layd up in the grainer.

The doctrine which Mr. Calvine heer indevoreth to
proove, as it may be understood, is true; for no doubt
while the church consisteth of mortal men, so long is
it subject to sinne and ignorance; els had we no need
of Christ to be our mediator, our advocate, our high priest,
our prophet, to make our peace, to intercede for us, to _{Heb. 12: 24}
offer up our praiers, to instruct us, *etc.* Therfore such _{1 John 2: 1}
as shall for sinne leave the communion of the church, _{Heb. 4: 15, 16}
must seeke the societie of angels, and not of men. Much _{Deut. 18: 15}
better should they doe, according to the apostle's coun-
cel, to admonish them that are out of order, to comfort
the feeble minded, to beare with the weake, to be patient _{1 Thess. 5: 14}
towardes all men; yea, if the sinne be publike and of _{Heb. 10: 24, 25}
the whole church, gravelie, in the name of the Lord,
to reprehend and reproove the same, and lovingly to
exhort them to repentance and amendment; rather
than preposterously to leave them, and rashly to for-
sake the fellowship, as the maner of some is.[2] And _{Exod. 23: 21, 22}
doubtles, if it be the true spouse of Christ, it wil give _{Deut. 29: 9}
eare to the voice of the bridegroome, and not continue _{Heb. 2: 2, ?}
obstinate in presumptuous sinne; for therfore were they
not receaved to grace. Faith doth not abrogate the _{Rom. 6: 1 & 10: 31 &}
law, neither came Christ to take away the law, so much _{12: 25}
as the curse of the law from the church: and heerunto _{Lam. 1: 25}

---

[1] Calvin, *Institutes*, vol. II, book IV, chapter I, section 13, p. 292. See
also Matthew 13: 24.

[2] This attitude of Barrow reinforces his views about excommunication.
See the last twelve paragraphs of *A True Description out of the Worde of
God, of the Visible Church.* See also Robert Some, *A Godly Treatise,
wherein Are Examined and Confuted Many Execrable Fancies*, p. 36.

Henry Barrow

James 1: 23, 24 serveth that great base and sea of Christe's blood, which
1 Kings 7: 23 is placed in the church to purge and wash away through
faith and repentance those deformities and blots of
sinne, which the glasse of the law sheweth: and not upon
the priviledg of Christe's death to take bouldnes to
sinne, or to continue in any knowen sinne, or to neglect
or despise the word, or to thinke lightly of the least
sinne, or not with all possible speed to redresse it rather,
and remoove it out of the church; wherunto the true
church never wanteth either wil or power: neither ought
any faithfull servant of [18] God to communicate with
that assembly, which wanteth either wil or power to
reforme and amend any default which is committed
amongst them, after it is made knowen unto them; as
shal apear in the further handling of these and other
their places, and argumentes, which they have corruptly sucked from Mr. Calvin in this discourse; who
no doubt hath unsufferably perverted and wrested these
places and other places of Scripture, and drawen verie
foule and corrupt doctrine from them, touching the
estate and order of a planted church, and more dangerous and damnable conclusions from the same: as
that it is lawfull for the church to receive and reteine
the ignorant prophane multitude, to administer the
sacramentes unto, and communicate in the same with
them; that the sacrament is not defiled with such open
unworthy receavers, neither the faithful of the church
with this action, or their fellowship: also that we ought
to abhor and withdraw from the wicked in common
bread and conversation, but not in the worship of God,
and the sacraments, *etc.*, that the people and our saviour
Christ did communicate with the polluted priestes,
corrupted sacrifices and people, *etc.* These and such
other fearful and false doctrines and conclusions, contrarie to the whole course of Scripture, his disciples have
drawen from him. And in deed his abuse of these and
other places; as the epistles to the churches of Corinth,
Galatia, Asia, *etc.*, and his discourse therof, seeme to
import: which that it may more plainly apeare, let us
come to the more particular consideration of his places,
and examine whether any such doctrines, applications

and conclusions may be drawn from them, and that
breefly.

To his first place, where he resembleth the planted
church to that sowen field, or rather confidently affirmeth that sowen field to be the planted church, *etc.*,
and from thence draweth, that seene and knowen tares
shall grow and remaine in the planted church, untill
God root them out; and therupon concludeth, that none
ought to refraine the communion of the church for such
offendors, especially, where the word is purely taught,
and the sacramentes rightly administred; which he
maketh his two infallible markes of the church, leaving
out obedience unto and practise of the word, which he
and his disciples, under the name of discipline, make
an hangby: wherof in due place.

First heer against Mr. Calvin's writinges and his
disciples, I oppose the interpretation of our saviour
himself, who opening this parable upon his disciples'
requests unto our good, saith, that he which sowed the Math. 13: 24
good seed is the sonne of man, and the field is the world,
and the good seed are the children of the kingdom, and
the tares are the children of that wicked one, and the
enimie that soweth them is the devil, and the harvest
is the end of the world, and the reapers are the angels,
etc. What interpretation can be more excellently consonant in everie point unto the parable, than this?
Or what other interpretation can be sufferable? Is
not everie part of it most lively opened? Did not
[19] God at the first make the world, and all things in Gen. 1: 31
the same, good? Was it not corrupted through the Gen. 3
fraude and mallice of the devil? Hath not God stil
in it his church visible and universal, here and there
gathered and scattered in the world? Hath not the
devil also, that prince of this dark world, his children
and servantes, which as tares overgrow and grieve the
wheate, and cover the face of the whole field? Is not
this the condition and estate of the world, and shalbe to
the end? Now here though Gode's children by the
light of his word espie, and grieve at these wicked tares,
so see this world, which is in deed the Lorde's field, and Luke 9: 54
belongeth to the good seed, and not unto the evil, thus

pestered and overgrowne with the wicked: yet may they not by a rash and inordinate zeale be caried away, either peremptorily to judge and condemne, or utterlie to extirpate these tares, as reprobates; both because the

Rom. 9: 24
Jerem. 18: 6
Acts 5: 1, 7
Isa. 40: 13, 14
Rom. 11: 33, 34

Lord hath reserved this final judgment and execution unto himself (who knoweth to what he hath predestinate everie vessel that he hath made, whether unto honour or to dishonour) and reserveth the seasons and oportunities when to cal or cut off in his owne handes; and hath neither committed these things to man, nor need to be councelled or advised in them by man. But Christ in this parable rather teacheth his disciples patience and sobrietie, to be patient towardes al men, as their heavenly Father is patient; rather suffring and

2 Tim. 2: 25

instructing the evil with meeknes, proving if God at any time will give them repentance that they may acknowledg the truth, and come to amendment out of the snare of the devil, of whome they are taken prisoners to do his wil; rather pitying in their soules

1 Tim. 2: 1
Rom. 12: 19
Rom. 14: 4

and praying for al men, than judging and finally condemning any, or calling for fire and vengeance upon them, *etc.* This were a preposterous zeale, and greatly

Jam. 4: 12

against Gode's glorie (who willeth al men to be saved,

2 Pet. 3: 9
Ezek. 18: 32
Ezek. 33: 11

calleth them to his Sone's mariage feast, and therefore causeth the gospell to be preached and proclaimed for us) after we are once entred, to shut the dore of Gode's grace against others. We were not for this cause re-

1 Tim. 1: 16

ceaved to mercy, but rather to provoke others to tast of God's goodnes also, and be examples to them that shal in time to come beleeve unto eternal life. If Paul, Mary Magdalene and others, nay if we our selves (by whome of al others we know most evil) had beene plucked up by the rootes, whiles we grewe amongst the rankest of the weedes and tares in the field of the world, had it not beene much ruth ?[1] Had not much good wheate beene spilt ? But he that chose and called us out of this dark

Titus 3: 3

world, unto the glorious inheritance of the saintes in

Coloss. 1: 13

light, shal shew the like mercie unto them also, if they abide not in unbeliefe. Our saviour Christ whiles he

Rom. 11: 23

was here emongst us, came not into the world as the

[1] An occasion of sorrow or regret.

[judge or critic, seeking] to judge or condemne the world, but that the world through him might be saved. Let not us then take that upon us, which belongeth not unto us, neither judge before the time; seing God hath not given to his church to censure or judge them without, but to attend upon, and judg them which are within: God judgeth them that are without.[20]

Joh. 3: 17 & 12: 47

1 Corin. 5: 13
Jude 14: 15

But now, how may this place of the sowen field (without unsufferable wrasting and falsifying) be understood of, or applied unto the planted church of Christ? Shall these stinking weedes and noisome tares grow there unweeded out? Or hath not God therfore given unto his church and everie member therof, the weeding hooke of his word, and the power of our Lord Jesus Christ, wherby to censure and cut off everie obstinate offendor, to cast downe everie high thing that is exalted against the knowledg of God, and to have vengeance ready against all disobedience and every transgression that ariseth amongst them? Is not the whole church, and everie member therof, often and almost everie where in the Scriptures commanded and stirred up to keep this watch diligently? And for the neglect and contempt therof reade we not of sundrie churches sharply reprooved, yea, utterly cut off? And is it then likely that our saviour Christ would here utterly forbid his apostles and disciples, to intermedle with the weeding out of these tares out of the church, his garden? Doth not this place, thus understood of the planted church, utterly subvert and overthrow all ecclesiastical censures? And condemne the apostles of presumption for stirring up the churches to excommunicate and cast out their obstinate offenders, inordinate walkers, heretikes, etc., from amongst them? Yea, for so sharply reprooving whole churches, and threatning to come against them with the judgmentes of God for their defalts herein? Which way can all the learning these men have, reconcile these places; but that by this their interpretation there must needes be expresse contrarietie. But as they thus pervert this place, so the application of it, and their collection from it, is much more pernicious and unsufferable, as shall afterward appeare.

Math. 16: 19 & 18: 17, 18
Psal. 149

Cant. 6: 9
1 Cor. 5: 2
2 Cor. 10: 4, 5, 6
Heb. 12: 15

2 Cor. 5: 2
2 Cor. 12: 20, 21
Revel. 2 & 3

2 Thes. 3: 6, 14

The next place that is brought for the receaving and reteining their profane sinfull multitudes in their church, is the parable of the draw-net, wherein fishes of all sorts are gathered, and not severed untill the Lorde's finall judgmentes. This is granted them to be understood of the planted church, where, by the power of the word, all degrees and sorts of men are gathered, and amongst them diverse false and wicked hypocrites, which shall continue and remaine in the church, untill the Lord pluck off their visors and pull them out, whether by death or by his finall judgment. This is no new thing, this is not denied, this alwaies hath beene, and alwaies shalbe unto the end of the world. Many shall enter without the wedding garment, without that white stone, that inward testimonie and assurance, which no man knoweth save he that receaveth it, and God giveth unto none, but unto his chosen. Many glorious hypocrites shal there be, which make a faire shew in the flesh, which shal have prophecied, cast out devils, and done great workes by Christ's name, which in that day shall call, and not be heard. But what of all this ? May it from hence be concluded, that the profane multitude, without due [21] testimonie and proof of their faith by publike profession, *etc.*, may be admitted into, or any open wicked which remaineth obstinate and impenitent may be reteined in this church of Christ ? Surelie this ground will beare no such doctrine, this place no such construction.

1 Tim. 5: 24

Math. 22: 11
Revel. 2: 17

Math. 7: 21
1 John 2: 19

There yet remaineth an other maine place to uphold their confused profane assemblies, drawen from the third chapter of Mathew 12 verse; where they liken the gathered and established church of Christ unto a barneflore, in which the wheate is so gathered togeather, that it lieth hidden under the chaffe, untill being clensed with fanne and sive, it be at length layd up in the grainer, *etc.* Yea, Mr. Calvine in an other peculiar treatise against the Anabaptists, using this place of Mathew, saith, that the faithful shalbe in the planted church of Christ hidden amongst the open wicked and ungodly, as a few graines of wheate lie in a great heape of chaffe, *etc.*[1] Than which doctrine nothing can be devised more uncleane and corrupt, or more unworthy the church of Christ, as breaking all the ordinances and lawes of God at once, and utterly subverting and defiling all christian communion, *etc.*, which doctrine, as it is directly contrarie unto the whole course of Scriptures, both for the entrance into the church, and for the order and conversation in the church, so can no place of Scripture be applied to the upholding and confirmation therof, without unsufferable falsifying and violent wrasting the same.

As for this place Mathew 3: 12, it no more prooveth this doctrine, than the others out of Mathew 13, for here Mathew rather recordeth the conclusion of Jhon the Baptiste's sermon and doctrine, than any way describeth the estate of the established church of Christ, in the eleventh and twelfth verses shewing the incomparable excellencie of Christe's person and ministerie, in respect of his; and also in the same shewing the divers effectes of Christe's comming unto such as looked for him, who as they were of two sortes, so had they severall success. The one sort he baptised, the other he consumed with fire, the one sort he fanned, sifted, purged, sined [sived ?], and preserved as wheat and silver; the other with same fanne and fornace he scattered and burnt up as chaffe and drosse. The humble poore of the flock, which gave eare to the voice in the wildernes, which confessed and repented their sinnes, and made strait his pathes, and received Jhon's baptisme; those he received, fed and kept, *etc.*, but those proud Pharisies, learned Scribes, and carnal Saduceis, which thought themselves in a perfect estate, and despised the councel of God against themselves, and would not be baptised of Jhon; those when the Messiah also came, despised and contemned him, and therfore he cut them off in one day, yea, his day was unto them darknes and not light, *etc.*

Mal. 3: 1, 2, 3
Isa. 65: 5
Mal. 4: 1, 2

Zach. 11

Mal. 4: 6

Isa. 8: 14, 15

Luke 2: 34
Luke 7: 29, 30

Amos 5: 18, 19, 20

But now which way should this fowle uncleane barnfloore, thus [22] pestered and overspred with chaffe, be likened almost (without blasphemie) unto the holy

[1] Calvin, *Institutes*, vol. II, book II, chapter I, section 13, p. 292.

church of Christ rightly planted, established and governed according to his holy will and testament? Where (as hath beene said) all the people that enter and are receaved there, are chosen, redeemed, called out of the world from amongst the heathen, saintes by calling, partakers of the same pretious faith and glorious hope, humble, obedient, loving sheepe. And therfore is the church likened to a sheepfold, which is both watched and defended to keepe out the wild beastes, the wolfe and litle foxes; unto a garden shut up, and welspring inclosed; an orchyeard and vineyard walled, where al the plantes are natural sweet incense trees, pomgranate and al sweet fruit trees, myrrhe, aloes, cynnamon, with trees of chief spices. Heere entereth no Cananite, or profane person, but everie vessel shalbe cleane and holy, as bowles before the altar, *etc.* Furthermore even in the material temple there were ashpannes and besoms [brooms], to sweep and carry out al dust and filth. And even in everie barn-flore the husbandman hath his flayle, his fanne, his syve, to tresh his wheat out of the eare, to purge it from the chaffe, to sever it from darnel and tares, *etc.* Which labour if he should slack, he should have no use of his wheat, he should have no cleane nor wholsome bread. And how much more shal our heavenlie husbandman purge his seed his wheat from such reprobate chaffe and giddy darnel, before he receave them into one loafe, and set them at his heavenly table. They cannot be a newe lump unto him, except they be purged from the old leven of maliciousnes and wickednes. The servantes of God can neither build the church, nor joine in any spiritual action with the profane, nor with such counterfeit professors as the Samaritanes, nor with such bastardy false seede as that of Moab and Ashdod, *etc.* There may be no misseline[1] or seedes of divers kinds sowen in the Lorde's field. The God of heaven and earth requireth unto himself a holy seed, he will be sanctified of all that draw neere unto him, for even our God is a consuming fire. How then dare any admit those the Lord shutteth out of his Church? Or how

Marginal references:
John 15: 19
Rom. 1: 7
1 Pet. 4: 3
1 Cor. 1: 2
2 Cor. 6: 17, 18
2 Pet. 1: 1
Numb. 24: 6
Cant. 4: 12, 13, 14
Isa. 35: 8
Joel 3: 17
Zach. 14: 20, 21
2 Chron. 4: 16
Exod. 38: 3
1 Cor. 10: 17
1 Cor. 5: 7, 8
Ezra 4: 3
2 Cor. 6: 14
Nehem. 13: 23, 24
Levit. 19: 19
Exod. 19: 5, 6
Mal. 2: 15
Heb. 12: 28, 29
Ezek. 44: 7, *etc.*

---

[1] Misselin or misseling or missellane — obsolete forms of maslin, meaning mixed grain, such as rye and wheat.

dare they mingle and joyneth such reprobate knowen Jer. 23: 28
chaffe, cockle, tares and darnel with the Lorde's wheate,
wittingly and wittingly [*sic*], which the Lord with fanne
and syve purgeth, and severeth, and casteth out of his
barn-flore, much lesse receaveth not into his granarie.

But how far is their ignorant rashnes, or rather presumptuous boldnes, proceeded ? Which not only
receave into and retaine in their church and fellowship
these heapes of the wicked and open unworthy, even
all the profane multitude, and al sortes of people that
are found within their territories and jurisdiction, without respect of person; but even thrust them upon Christ 2 Cor. 6
whether he will or no, and make him an high priest and
prophet unto them, administring unto them and their
seed the holy thinges of God; as baptisme, and the
Lorde's supper. Is not this to mingle heaven and
earth, ligh[t] and darknes ? Or [23] what higher
sacriledge can be committed ? Shal these places, thus 1 Pet. 2: 8
wrasted and falsified, hide and diminish their sinns ?
Or rather not agravate and make manifest their error 2 Pet. 3: 16
and wickednes ? By what sober construction, or almost
common sense, can this place Mathew 3. be understood
of the planted and rightly ordered church of Christ ?
Or how may such a church be compared to a flore,
where in a great heape of chaffe, a few graines of wheate
lie hid and buried ? We read in the Scriptures, that
the righteous shall shine as starrs in the church of God
(yet I willingly acknowledge that there can in this life
be no wheate so pure, which hath not both chaffe and
branne, *etc.*) but that in an other sense; only I would
know of these men that thus grossly liken the church of
God, what difference we may put betwixt the world
and their church ? In the world in deed the children
of God shal for a season be mingled and remayn amongst
the profane and wicked, until the time of their visitation
and calling; but after they have once given obedience
unto the voice of Christ, then forget they and forsake
their old conversation and companie, and have no
longer fellowship with the unfruitful workes of darknes:
but are renned[1] in righteousnes and holines and true know-

---

[1] Past participle of run. To be active in, to be continued in.

ledg, after the image of him that called them out of darknes into his merveilous light, *etc*.

But to cover and cure al this confusion and disorder, al this sacrilegious profanation and portsale[1] of the holy thinges of God, and al other mischeifes and enormities amongst them, as also to stop the mouthes, and to terrifie al such as find fault with, and reproove these thinges or depart from amongst them, where the same are incurable and without redresse; these Balaamites, these crooked disciples of Mr. Calvin bring from him the examples of the churches of Corinth, Galatia and Asia, where were open wicked men;[2] as the incestuous person, drunkardes, gluttons, extortioners, wranglers, wrong-doers, prowd and ambitious persons, sectaries, heretikes, *etc*., as also sundrie abuses and corruptions in doctrine, and in the administration of the sacrament, *etc*. Yet they were by the judgment of the Holy Ghost notwithstanding al these sinners and sinnes, adjudged the holy churches of God, neither were the faithfull commanded to refraine their communion. Furthermore, the prophets and our saviour Christ, at such time as the estate of the Jewe's temple was wholy corrupted, forsooke not the temple, but resorted and communicated with the wicked people, at their feastes and sacrifices; yea, when the pollution and contagion was generall and incurable, both in the people and priestes: because (saith their author) a godly conscience is not hurt by the unworthines of any, either minister or people, nor yet their ministerie being the ordinance of God (as their ceremonies, sacrifices, and praier with them, *etc*., the word and sacramentes with us) defiled; but are pure and wholsome unto the upright and faithfull receavers, who may lift up pure handes in a wicked [24] assemblie, neither ought for the wickednes of men to refuse the holy ordinances of God; seing it is only Christe's office to purge the barne-floore, and sever the tares, *etc*., and belongeth to no private men to examine others, or the whole church, so much as for everie one

---

[1] Public auction.
[2] Calvin, *Institutes*, vol. II, book IV, chapter I, sections 14, 15, 16, pp. 293-295. Some, *A Godly Treatise Containing and Deciding Certaine Questions*, pp. 18, 34.

to examine his owne self, and to see that he be good wheat, least otherwise he eate unto his owne judgment. For the bread of the Lord, and the faithfull receavers therof, are not made worse with the sinnes of others. It is one thing in common bread and conversation, to flee the companie of wicked men; and an other thing for the hatred of them, to forsake the fellowship of the church. 1 Cor. 11: 28, and 1 Cor. 11: 29

These and such other poisoned blasphemous cavils they bring, to justifie and uphold their confused Babylonish synagogues and al the abhominations they commit in them. Which windshaken figleaves, although I could in a word pluck from them, and so lay their filthines naked; namly by shewing that there can be no comparison betwixt the church of Christ, and their whorish idolatrous church, which hath not one part of a true church, not one pinne, naile, nor hooke, according to the true patterne, or in due frame, and so could set this their author (upon whome they so much relie) most sharply against them; who in all these treatises is alwaies to be understood of a church rightly established and planted according to the testament of Christ, with such ministers, such sacramentes, as there are apointed, *etc.*, than which here amongst these his followers is nothing lesse, as shall not be hard to shew in due place. And therfore the argumentes, drawen from the churches of Corinth, Galatia, *etc.*, even by their author's owne judgment, nothing serve their turne, who are more like to Dan and Bethel in the schismatical estate of the kingdome of Israel, remaining stil in that great defection of antichrist fortold of, *etc.*,[1] yet seing they have taken the paines to fetch these argumentes from over the sea, and so ernestly urge them, let us do them the favour even so far as we may with christian patience, to give them the hearing.

Their first argument seemeth to be this. There were in the churches of Corinth, Galatia, *etc.*, not only wicked persons, but also sundrie errors, abuses and corruptions in doctrine and administration: yet they were stil judged the churches of God, and the faithful refrained not their

[1] II Chronicles 10: 19.

communion, therfore we ought not to leave these their assemblies, though the open wicked and many other enormities be there committed and suffered.

First (as hath beene noted) there is no comparison betweene these holy churches of God, which were truly gathered, planted and ordered, and these their confused idolatrous assemblies. Then here must be observed, that they in nothing can be compared unto these churches, but in sinne and error; moreover that the faultes of these churches, which were but of ignorance and frailty, cannot be compared to the sinnes of these unchristian assemblies, which are in pre-[25]sumption and obstinacie disproved by others, confessed, and yet continued of themselves. Lastly here must be noted, how corruptly they understand, and unsufferably pervert those Scriptures, where the apostle reprehendeth these sinnes in those churches, *etc.*, exhorteth the whole church to repentance, and to redresse the thinges amisse, and that with sundrie severe and apostolike threats, upon their neglect or default therin.

But these men take these places, where the sinnes of these churches are thus sharply reprehended and censured, and would justifie therby, the receaving, reteining and nourishing al this profane rowt of people in the bosome of their churches: as also al the abhomination, idolatrie, open and wilful breach of God's lawes, setting up their owne antichristian divises [devises] and popish cannons in stead therof, *etc.*, and would from hence conclude it, to be no more lawful for true Christians to remove out of these assemblies in this estate than it was for the faithful in the churches of Corinth, Galatia, *etc.*, to forsake those churches, before their sinnes and errors were either reproved or censured. What more unsufferable abuse of Scriptures can there be than this, to take those examples which were written to terrifie, admodish [admonish] and stir up all churches and posterities to eschew, watch against, and redresse such sinnes and transgressions, to colour and cloke al sinne and iniquitie, yea, to take away from al Christians their libertie, and prower [power], either to reprove, censure, or refraine the same.

These churches (say they) were judged and pronounced by the Holy Ghost, the churches of God,
notwithstanding these hainous sinnes amongst them.
Wel, what then? These and al other churches whiles
they remaine in this life, shal commit sundrie and daily
sinnes of ignorance, frailtie, *etc.*, therfore they may also
commit presumtuous sinne, yea, remaine incorrigible
and obstinate in their sinnes, and yet of us be esteemed
and reverenced as the true churches of God: this they
must prove, or els they say nothing: this, these examples
of these churches prove not. For they cannot shew
that ever they despised the apostle's admonition, or
refused to redresse the thinges they were blamed of:
which if they should have done, houw could they be
esteemed the church of God, whiles they reject the
word, breake the law, despise correction, yea, even
Gode's grace and mercie offred, by stopping their
eares and hardening their heart, refusing to repent,
etc.? What can the heathen doe more? Nay, what
doe they so much? For they sinne in their ignorance,
these in the presumtion of their heart, and contempt.
And now in this estate, what communion is to be held
with them? What fellowship may the children of God
have with such rebels, apostataes? Can any glorious
titles or name of a church, hide or diminish these
sinnes? Or how rather can the name of a church
(without blasphemie unto Christ) be given them in
these sinnes? How can Christ be said to stand a king
and Lord unto them that breake and reject his lawes,
and set up in stead therof their owne devises and inventions? Or how can Christ be [26] said a saviour
unto them that despise his grace and mercie offred,
refuse to repent and turne from their evil waies? They
then not being under Christe's protection, nor in state
of grace, while they continue obstinate in their sinne,
etc. I have often wondered, how anye man of sound
judgment, could give them the name of a church?
Or be so terrified with this vaine and false title, that
they durst not leave the communion of those wicked
assemblies and adulterous churches, which have broken Exod. 19: 5
the covenant, and forsaken the faith. God plighteth

305

Levit. 26   not his favour and protection unto us, longer than we vowe our obedience, and keep our faith unto him. At

Deut. 28   what time the most righteous turneth from his right-

Ezek. 18 & 33 chap.   eousnes and committeth iniquitie, and wil not be turned therefrom, all his former righteousnes that he hath done shal not be mentioned, but in his transgression that he hath committed, in his sinne that he

2 Pet. 2: 4, 5, 6   hath sinned, in them he shal die. The same judge, by the same law, giveth the same sentence for the same sinnes, against a whole church, nation, world. Neither

Jude 14: 15   is there cause why any of God's servantes should more doubt to censure, judg, and avoid that congregation, which rejecteth Gode's word, presumptuously breaketh Gode's lawes, despiseth his reproofe and mercie, as a wicked assembly, an adulterous church; than to censure, judge and avoid any particular member of the church, fallen into the like degree and height of sinne, to be a withered unfruitfull branch, to be cut off from the vine, to be throwen out of the vineyard.

But here they deceave themselves and others, with certayne infallible markes of the church, which they have fantasied unto themselves; namely, that where the word of God is sincerely taught, and the sacramentes rightly administred, there undoubtedly is still the true church of Christ;[1] although otherwise there be never so many mischeifes abounding, all the wicked receaved and reteined, *etc.*, no use of the power of Christ among them, either to censure sinne, or cast out obstinate offendors. For this holy power to redresse faultes, they put aside by the name of discipline. They call it an accident, or hang-by, and make it not a thing of necessitie: so that it may be a church without it, though it be to be desired, *etc.* The vanitie and falshood of these doctrines partly apeareth, where I shewed that the preaching of the word maketh not a church, except there be by the same a faithfull people gathered unto Christ Jesus, ordered and governed by the rule of his word in all things, so far as shalbe revealed unto them, *etc.*: so that I need not here stand to refute the same, only I would know of these great learned men, how it

[1] Calvin, *Institutes*, vol. II, book IV, chapter I, sections 9—12, pp. 289-292.

is possible for the ministers of the church, either to
preach the word sincerely, or administer the sacramentes rightly, where there is no regard had to the
faithfull practise of the word, no care to redresse thinges
amisse, no power to shut out or excommunicathe [*sic*]
the unworthy: or how they can with all their learning,
whiles they stand pastors or teachers to [27] such an
unbeleeving profane people, or unto such wicked ones   Isa. 57: 21
as hate to be rebuked and reformed of their sinnes,   Jere. 4: 4
preach the word, exercise praier, deliver the sacramentes, blesse and dismisse the profane wicked people   Isa. 48: 22
in the peace and favour of God, without most high
sacriledg, profanation of Gode's name, casting the pre-   Pro. 24: 24
tious bodie, and blood of Christ to hoggs and doggs,   & 17: 15
blessing Gode's enimies, *etc.*   Math. 7: 6

But now if it be not possible to exercise any true
ministerie, to have any true use of the word and sacramentes, to keep any holy communion or Christian order,
without the diligent watch of everie member, but cheefly   Mark 13: 34, 35,
of the rulers and elders, to see the word of God duly   36, 37
practised and observed by all in their callings, to admonish all offenders, to censure all errors and trans-   1 Thes. 5: 14
gressions, to excommunicate the obstinate impenitent,   Ephes. 5: 6, 7,
by the power of our Lord Jesus Christ which he hath   8, 9, 10, 11
given unto his true church unto the world's end, all
which, these men cover and cast aside in the name of
discipline, without which watch and power, this practise cannot be had, without which power and practise,
the word of God is made an idol, the sacramentes   1 Cor. 4: 20
sacriledge unto us, and all thinges we do, odious and
abhominable unto the Lord: with what common sense   Titus 1: 6
(to let passe their deep learning) can these great preachers say, that the church of Christ may want this watch,
care, power and practise; yea, and that the word may
be sincerely taught, and the sacramentes duly administred, though there be open transgression, obstinate
offendors still kept and held amongst them. Is it not
as much as if they said they knew neither what the
church, sacramentes, ministerie of the word, or Christian communion meant? For to what purpose is the
word or the ministerie of the word, where true practise

and obedience is denied ? Or which way can the true
minister of Christ administer the sacramentes to a people
in this estate ? Or the faithfull servants of Christ, partake with such people in such sacramentes, without most
heinous sacriledg and impietie.

We must not (say they) forsake the church, nor the
ordinance of God, for the sinnes of any, either minister
or people: for a godly conscience is not hurt with the
sinnes of an other, neither the ministerie or sacramentes
therwith defiled.[1] If they meane here by the church,
the assemblie and communion of Gode's faithfull obedient servantes, by Gode's ordinance the use of an holy
ministerie of the sacramentes, *etc.*, I graunt that the
church, ministerie, and ordinances of Christ, are not to
be left, or thought the worse of for the sinne of men,
though all the world abuse them, though antichrist
have corrupted them never so much or long. But if
they meane (as al their reasoning importeth) by the
church and ordinances of God, such wicked rebellious
assemblies, as reject the word of God, with an high hand
breake his lawe, despise admonition, hate to be reformed, receave and reteine the open unworthie,
wicked, impenitent to their sacramentes, [28] *etc.*, I
then denie these assemblies to be the true churches of
Christ; seing they have broken the covenant, cast off
Christe's yoke, *etc.* As also I denie their sacramentes
to be the ordinances of God, seing to them in this
estate belong not the sacramentes, and ministerie of
Christ, but the curse and judgmentes of God. And
therfore they that leave them for, and in their sinnes
in this estate, do neither leave the church of God, nor
the ordinances of Christ, but rather fulfil the commandement of God, and preserve the church, in saving
their soules and bodies from such wicked and accursed
assemblies, from such disobedient rebellious people,
and from al the trumperies and deceites of the false
church, *etc.*

Heb. 10: 30

2 Cor. 6: 17, 18

Revel. 18: 4

---

[1] Some, *ibid.*, 29. Dr. Some is quoting Calvin, who said: " a pious conscience is not injured by the unworthiness of another, whether he be a
a pastor or a private individual ; and sacred rites are not less pure and
salutary to a man who is holy and upright, from being at the same time
handled by the impure " (Calvin, *Institutes*, book IV, chapter I, section
19, p. 297).

But let us a litle examine, what kind of doctrine these men draw from Mr. Cálvine, and spread abrode in their pulpites, and publike writinges. They hould that whatsoever congregation keepeth an outward shew of the ministerie of the word and sacramentes, ceaseth not to be a church, neither is to be left for any sinne in maners (as they call it) whatsoever, though they willingly and presumptuously neglect and break the lawes of God, both in their worship and conversation, and remaine incorrigible and obstinate in these transgressions. Now they teach, that neither for such sinnes God is so displeased with the congregation, that he hereupon withdraweth his favor from them, or they cease to be held and reverenced of us, as a church: neither the publike actions of the said congregation, as their praiers, preaching, sacramentes, *etc.*, neither the communicantes with this assemblie in these actions, are with and for these sinnes, defiled.

For (say they) a godly conscience is not defiled with the sinnes of an other.[1]

What fleshly libertine hath or can breath forth more poisoned doctrines than these ? More contrarie to the honour and whole word of God, from which it at once taketh away al reverence, obedience, and practise. What can be more popishly alledged for their church, than to say, that it can blesse these actions and persons, whome God in his word accurseth: or that the church may commit such high sacriledge and presumptuous sinne, without the judgment and punishment due to the same. If God have made one and the same covenant from the beginning of the world with the whole church, that he hath with everie particular private member therof, and hath given no more libertie to the whole church, than to any private man, to breake the least of his lawes: if God, for the transgression of his lawe, unpartially judgeth al, without respect of persons: if presumptuous sinne with obstinacie joined therunto, breaketh the covenant with God; insomuch as it both breaketh Gode's law, and depiseth Gode's mercie and grace, and so depriveth them in that estate

[1] Some, *ibid.*, 17-20.

of any benefite of Christe's death; if they which in this
maner breake Gode's law and despise his grace, to be
judged of al men, as open wicked, *etc.*; if al the actions
of the wicked be accursed of God, and so much the
more accursed and abhominable, by how much they
take shew of ho-[29]lines, and profane Gode's name
and ordinances: if all they which partake in such
actions, praiers, and sacrifices which are an abhomination unto the Lord, be guilty of the altar, and under the
same curse; how should those assemblies, which continue in presumptuous and obstinate sinne, be esteemed
the true churches of Christ; or any that administer unto,
or communicate with them in this estate, in praiers,
sacramentes, *etc.*, avoid the judgment and curse of God,
both for joining unto, and blessing the wicked, and for
so high profanation of his name, and prostituting the
holy mysteries of the bodie and blood of Christ, to such
open unworthy receivers? Rightly then and directly
to reason to the point. As many places of Scripture
as command Gode's faithful servantes, with al their
forces and uttermost indevor to observe, practise, and
obey unto Gode's holy word and everie part therof,
without any willing neglect or breach of the least commandement, to their knowledg: as many places as shew,
that obstinate and presumptuous transgression breaketh
the covenant: as many places as command us to seek
out and resort unto the true church of Christ, namely
the communion and fellowship of the saintes, Gode's
faithful obedient servantes, there to present our soules
and bodies, to be built and bestowed according to God's
wil, there together with them to worship and serve our
God, *etc.* As many places as forbid us all false churches
and assemblies, al spiritual fellowship and communion
with the wicked, or to repair unto, or joine with them
in their praiers and worship, *etc.* So many places forbid us al spirituall fellowship and communion with al
assemblies in this estate, what faire shewes soever they
make unto us, or glorious titles they take unto themselves: so many places evidently proove, that if in this
estate we should communicate with them, we should
be guilty of their sinns, and partakers of their plagues.

Which doctrines, because they are generally received of all, denied of none (though omitted and forgotten by many) and generally taught through the whole Scriptures; I need not here stand to make any more particular proofe or demonstration of them. And so these being granted, all these doctrines of Mr. Calvine and his disciples fall to the ground. Yet that the falshood of them may somwhat more appeare unto all men; let us draw a litle neerer unto them, and consider of their maine proofes, and fundamental doctrines.

The publike actiones (say they) and ministerye of the church, as praiers, sacramentes, *etc.*, neither the godly conscience of anye are defiled with the open sinnes of others, either of ministers or people, *etc.* For why, such publike actions are the ordinance of God, and cannot be defiled or made unavaileable with the sinnes of men, neither are to be left for such sinnes. Therfore the holy prophets and our saviour Christ himself, refrained not the temple, at such times as the estate therof was wholy corrupted, but communicated with the wicked in their feastes and sacrifices, although the pollution and contagion was generall and incurable, both in the people and priestes. For the rest, everie man is to examine himself and not others, when he resorteth to [30] the church, or receiveth the communion of the bodie and blood of Christ: because he eateth to his owne damnation or salvation, and not to an other man's, *etc.*

First, if the open sinne of the minister or people defile not the praiers and sacramentes by, and to them administred, why hath the Lord said, that the sacrifice of the wicked is abhomination unto him; that they might as wel kil a man, as a bullock unto him; that they might as wel offer a dog or swine's blood, as sacrifice *Prov. 15: 8* or burnt offering? What hath the Lord said, that *Isa. 1: 13 &* sacrifice without obedience, is not acceptable unto him; *66: 3* that he will have mercie and not sacrifice, *etc.* Why hath *Jere. 7* the Lord beene alwaies so jelous over his sanctuarie, and *Hos. 6: 6* over them that come neere unto him? Why hath he made so many lawes for the place, altar, sacrifice, *Levit. 10: 3* priestes, people, *etc.*, that no priest with any apparant *Levit. 21 & 22 chap.*

311

blemish, might offer the bread of the Lord, that no
offring with any blemish might be accepted at the

Levit. 11, 12, 13, 14, 15 chap. handes of any, that none with any pollution or uncleannes upon him, might touch the tabernacle, that
no heathen or profane person which was not yet come
unto the faith, might tread in the courtes of the Lord,

Numb. 5 or any offring be accepted at their handes? Why hath
the Lord said, that whatsoever the wicked offer is uncleane, whatsoever the polluted touch is defiled?
Whether it be the couch or seate they sit or lie upon,
or vessels they use, whether it be holy flesh, wine or

Hagg. 2: 13, 14 oile, it is defiled, *etc*. Now then, seing the whole
Scripture is so evident and plentifull in this point: that
the open sinne of the church, defileth all the actions of
the church, maketh them and their offrings abhominable unto the Lord: seing no polluted person may
either administer or offer unto the Lord: seing whatsoever they touch, is also defiled and uncleane; how
can this doctrine of Mr. Calvine and his wretched
followers, stand? That the open sinnes, either of the
minister or people, defile not the publike actions,
praiers, sacramentes, *etc.*, of that church, those ministers,
people, sacrifices, they cannot deny to have beene the
ordinances of God also. Yet even their holiest thinges
were defiled and polluted, with the sinnes, and uncleannes of men.

Now to the other point: whither a godly conscience
can take no hurt, neither need make scruple to communicate with the open wicked priestes and people, in
their praiers and sacramentes, because they are the
ordinances of God, which are not to be left for the sinnes
of men. I have alreadie often denied their praier and
sacramentes in this estate, to be the ordinance of God.
My reasons are: the wicked have nothing to doe to take

Psa. 50: 16, 17 the name of God in their mouthes, or to use that heavenly exercise and blessed benefit of the word and praier,
because they make no conscience to breake Gode's
lawes, and remaine impenitent and hardned in their
sinnes: then in this estate belong no sacramentes or

Math. 26 ministerie unto them, by the ordinance of God, who
hath as well set downe what manner of minister and

people shall deliver and receave the sacramentes, as Mark 14
after what manner the sacra-[31]mentes shalbe de- Luke 22
livered.   So that where such open wicked, impenitent,
and unworthy ministers and people do administer or
receave the sacramentes, so contrarie unto, and without
regard of Christe's institution, such sacramentes can no
way be said [to be] the ordinances of Christ, the blessed
pledges of his bodie and blood, *etc.*: but rather, sure
seales of his wrath, even to as many as so sacrilegiously 1 Cor. 11: 29
profane his holy ordinance, and joine together in that
ungodly and accursed action, untill they repent.   For, 2 Cor. 13
as in the holy symbole of the Lorde's Supper, the com- 1 Cor. 10: 17
municantes be made one bodie with Christ's, and one 1 Cor. 12: 13
another's members in the same bodie; so are these
bound together as a fagot, in the same judgmentes and
wrath, in as much as they joine together in the same
sinne, and sacriledg, and all become alike guilty, even
principals (as we speake in the law) in the action.   How
then should any here plead himself guiltles, when even
the action they commit and boast of, is most heinous
sacriledge.   The matter will not in this case be shifted
off with saying, an other man's sinnes cannot prejudice
or defile them, seing they receive with pure conscience,
etc.[1]   For though this doctrine (as it is here used) be
most corrupt and false; yet here is now no need, that
they should be charged with others' sinnes, seing they
in this action are joyned unto, and become a like guilty
with the worst, and must now beare the burden of their
owne sinnes.

But is this doctrine so hard and strange to them, that
one should be polluted with the knowne and suffered
sinnes of an other? Let them reade in the lawe,
whether he that touched but the garment of a polluted man or woman, much more of a leprous plaguy,
etc., was defiled therby.   If this were but by outward
and bodily touching; how much more is that spirituall
leprosie, that gangrene, these running issues and plaguy
sores of sinne infectious and deadly contagious, especially in so neere commixture, as that spiritual communion
of the soule?   If the word of God will not prevaile, let

---

[1] Some, *ibid.*, 28, 29.

L*

common sense and experience perswade this. Yea, so spreading is this malady of sinne, as being discovered in any one part of the body, if it be not with al speed cured or cut off, it becometh a like dangerous to the whole bodie; they all now, by this their negligence and tolleration, becoming a like guiltie, *etc.* How many stories have we in the Scriptures to confirme [t]his? Not only in particular, as betwixt Ely and his sonnes (for all whose wickednes he was blamed, in that he did not represse and chastice, but only reproove their sinnes)

Josh. 7

but more generally. Was not the whole congregation smitten, for that Achan his sinne lay hidden and un-

Numb. 25

punished amongst them? Was not all the congregation punished for the sinne of some in mount Peor? Was not the like feared, Joshua 22? Doth not the apostle say, that a litle leaven leaveneth the whole lumpe? And that their rejoicing was not good whiles

Exod. 12

they kept the wicked man amongest them? Doth he not prove it by many reasons? That as by the lawe,

1 Cor. 5: 6, 7, 8

the feast of the passover was to be [32] kept with un-leavened bread, and that person that ate or reserved leaven, was to be cut off from the congregation: so much more ought we to see, that there be no leavened or in-

Levit. 20: 4

fectious person amongst us; that no root of bitternes

Deut. 29: 18, 19, 20

spring up, least many thereby be defiled, *etc.* Doth not the apostle (to take away al controversie) shew by this similitude of leaven, that not only sinne, but even the

Heb. 12: 15

sinner is to be removed, both out of the feast (which

Jude 12

belongeth not unto such, neither is to be kept with such) least Gode's wrath for the breach of his law, in keeping the continual feast of our heavenly passover Christ Jesus, burne forth against the whole house, that is, the whole church; and also that such sinne and sinners be removed out of the church, least the whole lump be leavened therby; which we see how sodainly it is done: for (as the wise man saieth), one dead flie

Eccle. 10: 1

causeth the ointmentes of the apotecarie to stinke. Now then, how can these men say, that the sinnes, yea, the many obstinate sinnes, either of ministers or people, do neither defile the publike actions of the church, neither the conscience of the godly receavers, *etc.*: where (as

hath beene by many reasons proved) the verie action
they so incommend,[1] is no lesse than most heinous and
impious sacriledge. So then, until they can prove it
lawful, and no sacriledge, either for that obstinate and
open wicked, to administer and receave the sacramentes, and also for the godly to communicate in such
sacramentes with them; until they can prove these
sacramentes, thus administred and receaved, to be
blessed of God; until they can prove that two divers,
yea, contrary sortes of people, namly the open wicked,
and the godly, such as despise, and such as feare God,
may be admitted unto, yea united in the sacramentes:
these doctrines of theirs cannot stand. But see into what
straites and absurdities they fall, which goe about to
tollerate or plead for the least sinne: yea see how the
further they wade and strive herein, the further they
intangle and ensnare themselves, falsifiing and perverting the Scriptures, to the upholding of their erroneous
and corrupt doctrines.

For their next shift to couller and hide their sacri-
legd, is to hood, wink,[2] and draw a vaile over the eies
of the receaver. A private man (say they) hath not to
meddle with the publike actiones and affaires of the
church: which (if they be amisse) he is patiently to
beare, and to mourne and grone with love, until God
either amend or correct them, whose office it is to roote
out the tares, *etc.*: but he is not for the sinne of others to
forsake the fellowship of the church, which God will
have kept, by al that shalbe partakers of his kingdom.
It sufficeth that everie private man looke to himself,
examin himself, when he eateth of that bread, and
drinketh of that cup; least he eate unto his owne judgment and damnation. Heere the apostle (saith their
author) willeth them, not to enter into the examination
of other men, neither saith that they shalbe judged for
other men's faultes, or that the table of the Lord is to
be left for the wicked, yea, or that the wicked for some

---

[1] The usual meaning is to commit or entrust, but here the meaning is to
commend, to approve.
[2] Possibly a printer's error for hoodwink. Otherwise, the meaning seems
to be to hood, wink at, or shut one's eyes to an impropriety, to neglect
or disregard.

one or fewe sinnes are to be left. In this case charity
is to judg [33] the best, and to thinke, that in so great
an heape of chaffe, there lye many good graines of
wheate, yea, to perswade himself, that even of those
wicked, many do inwardly repent of their sinnes, although they have not power to amend their lives. The
best man of us al is subject to many sinnes; the sinnes
of others cannot take away the vertue of the ministerie,
and of the holy mysteries, which are not to be left for
the sinne of anie; but such wicked rather to be shunned
and avoided, in common bread and conversation: but
the sacramentes are not because of them, to be refused,
etc.[1]

This and such like detestable stuffe, hath Mr. Calvine
in his ignorance, partly to suppresse and confute that
damnable sect of the Anabaptistes, which fantastically
dreame unto themselves a church in this life without
spot, and for everie transgression that ariseth, are ready
to leave and forsake the fellowship of the church, without due and orderly reproofe, *etc.* Partly also is this
stuffe brought, to defend his owne rash and disorderly
proceedinges at Geneva, whiles he at the first dash
made no scruple to receave al the whole state, even al
the profane ignorant people into the bozome of the
church, to administer the sacramentes unto them:
which confuse rowt, could not fit with Christe's heavenly government, neither could it by any meanes agree
unto them in this estate; but that monstrous disorders,
and heinous enormities daily insued therof: wherby this
their church became a just reproch to all men, even to
these wicked heretikes, *etc.*, yea, that which is worse,
and more to be lamented, it became a miserable president [precedent], and pernitious example, even unto
all Europe, to fall into the like transgression: as the
confused estate of all those regions (where the gospel
is thus disorderly taught) declareth. In which sorowful
spectacle, we may lively behold what the wisdome of
the most learned is, where they swerve never so litle
from the heavenly wisdome of God, and what the most
glorious and sure buildings of man are, when they are

[1] Calvin, *Institutes,* vol. II, book IV, chapter I, sections 13—16, pp. 292-295.

not wholy layd upon that firme rock and foundation
of Gode's word. We may heere also cleerly see, what
it is to receave our faith by tradition, to fetch the rules
of our actiones from the examples and practise of men,
and not from the pure word of God. For behold how
these wretched disciples of Calvin, three fold more
corrupted and perverted than he (who as it is to be
thought would never have opened his mouth against
so cleare truth, being brought unto him) oppose with
mayne force and bitternes these his writinges, against
the manifest truth of God; yea, and contend more
for the crooked practise of them (as their suting to
parliamentes for this reformation declareth), than for
that holy perfect patterne of Christe's testament; to
the upright practise wherof, they wil at no hand be
brought.

But let me returne againe to these doctrines of Mr.
Calvine, from which (by reason of these circumstances)
I was a litle digressed. I have already often, and I
hope, sufficiently shewed, how corruptly [34] Mr.
Calvine thought of the church, or rather how ignorant
he was therof, by these his odious simileas and comparisons. I have shewed, that into the church of Christ,
al must enter by the dore, and open profession of the
true faith, and by the same faith and obedience stand
there: how no profane or wicked person may be received or reteined into that fellowship. I have shewed
that the ministerie and sacramentes of Christ belong not
unto this people or congregation, and how such sacramentes and ministerie are sacrilegious and ungodly, yea,
pernitious and damnable to the whole congregation and
all the communicantes, unlesse they repent and redresse
these faultes. I have shewed touching his markes of the
church, that whersoever the word is soundly taught,
there is not by and by a church;[1] but only where a
faithful people are gathered by the same word unto

---

[1] Calvin's words, more generous than Barrow suggests, are: " wherever we
see the word of God sincerely preached and heard, wherever we see the
sacraments administered according to the institution of Christ, there we
cannot have any doubt that the Church of God has some existence, since
his promise cannot fail, ' where two or three are gathered together in my
name, there am I in the midst of them ' (Matthew 18: 20)." *Ibid.*, p. 289.

Christ, submitting themselves in all thinges to be ordered, ruled and governed by his word, as it shall from faith to faith be revealed unto them. Which people, thus gathered, and leading their lives together, are to be esteemed an holy church, and have power both to receave into, and cast out of their fellowship, *etc.*, although they have as yet obteined to have neither a ministerie nor sacramentes among them: alwaies provided, that this be not by any default or negligence in them, they alwaies being ready (as God administreth men and meanes) to proceed unto that holy order, commanded in the word: wherby apeareth, that the church upon some occasions, may be without sacramentes; and that they are not a perpetual marke of the church, so of necessitie, that it should be no church, if upon some occasions, it be for a season without them. I have also shewed, that without this holy power of Christ, to censure and redresse faultes and offendors, there can be no church, no ministerie, no communion; that the word without practise is an idol; praiers and sacramentes delivered in obstinate sinne, are abhomination and sacriledge in God's sight; and that it is unpossible to have the word sincerely taught, and the sacramentes purely administred, where any open sinne or sinner is maintained, or reteined: which must needes be, where the carefull watch against sinne, and power to reforme defaultes is neglected, or left. I have shewed, that the whole church hath no power to dispence with the breach of the least commandement, and that such obstinate sinne in the whole church, breaketh the covenant with God, and maketh it cease to be a church, or to be in God's favor, untill they repent. I have shewed, that al their praiers in this estate are accursed of God, and also all such as participate with them in the same. I have shewed, that the knowne and suffered sinne of any one member, is contagious unto all such as communicate with him in that estate, and maketh them all which communicate in praiers and sacramentes with such an obstinate offendor as guiltie in God's sight, as he himself is. I have shewed, that no faithfull man ought, by any congregation of men or angels, be drawen

Josh. 5

Exod. 23: 2
Gal. 1: 8

into the least knowne transgression of God's law, *etc.*
Which [35] doctrines, although they suffice to scatter
and disperse these smoky errors of Mr. Calvine and his
disciples, yet seing they have so roiled[1] the fountaine,
and (as it were) darkned the sunne with these mystes
and foggs; it shall not be amisse to discusse these pointes
(which remaine) a litle further; and see what power
everie particular member of the church hath in the
church, and in the publike actions of the church; and
also to see wherin, and how long they are to keepe
communion; and for what, and when to leave the same.

It is manifest, that all the members of the church have
a like interest in Christ, in his word, in the faith; that
they altogether make one bodie unto him; that all the
affaires of the church belong to that bodie together. 1 Cor. 12
All the actions of the church, as praiers, censures, sacra- Rom. 12: 6, *etc.*
mentes, faith, *etc.*, be the actions of them all jointly,
and of everie one of them severally; although the bodie,
unto diverse actions, use such members as it knoweth
most fit to the same.   Al the members are jointly bound
unto edification, and unto all other helpes or service
they may do unto the whole.   All are charged to
watch, exhort, admonish, stir up, reprove, *etc.*, and
hereunto have the power of our Lord Jesus, the keies
of the kingdom of heaven, even the word of the most Psa. 149: 6, *etc.*
high; therby to bind their rulers in chaines, and their
nobles in fetters; therby to cast downe everie strong
hold and high thing, that is exalted against God; therby
to defend and maintaine the faith, and everie iode [jot,
iota] of the word, to stand fast in their libertie, to trie Mat. 18: 20
the spirites, to avoid such as teach contrary doctrine,
and consent not to the wholsome wordes of our Lord Mat. 16: 19
Jesus, or denie the power and practise thereof, to ad- 1 Jhon 4: 1
monish the greatest, even Archippus,[2] to looke to his Rom. 16: 17
ministerie, and (if need be) to plead with their mother,
etc., yea, no further to follow her or an angell of light, 1 Tim. 6: 3, *etc.*
than they walke with God, and have the word for their
warrant.   Our communion must be in the faith, and
not in error or transgression; we are not to follow a 2 Tim. 3: 5

---

[1] To render water turbid, to muddy, to disturb.
[2] See Colossians 4: 17 and Philemon 1: 2.

Henry Barrow

Coloss. 4: 17
Hos. 2: 1
1 Joh. 1: 6, 7
Heb. 10: 39

multitude to do evill, but in all thinges to follow faith to the conservation of our soules, and to grow up into him which is our head, Christ Jesus, whome, whiles we hold fast, and whose word, whiles we have for the thinges we do, or refuse to doe, we need not feare the threates of anie vaine men; neither be amazed at any vaine titles of church, sacramentes, *etc.* For this we know, that there is no church can excuse us for the breach of God's law, before that great judge. Now then, seeing everie member hath interest in the publike actions of the church, and together shall beare blame for the defaltes of the same; and seeing all our communion must be in the truth, and that we are not to be drawen by anie into anie willinge or knowen transgression of God's law; who can denie, but everie particular member hath power, yea, and ought to examine the manner of administring the sacramentes, as also the estate, disorder, or transgressions of the whole church; yea, and not to [36] joine in any knowen transgression with them, but rather to call them all to repentance, *etc.*, and if he find them obstinate and hardened in their sinne, rather to leave their fellowship, than to partake with them in wickednes.

Neither doth the place 1 Corinthians 11: 28, 29, that everie one ought to examine himself, *etc.*, hinder either their christian libertie, or publike dutie; for these rules are generall, the wordes are general and alike given to everie member, and unto all the members of the church, without respect or exception of any, either pastor or others. So that by this reason, neither pastor nor any, were to look unto the life, conversation, and estate of an other: neither can these rules or wordes any way be restrained to one, more than an other; much lesse may such corrupt doctrines, and false conclusions, be drawen from them: that because everie man is to examine himself, therfore no man is to looke to an other. Everie man eateth either to his owne salvation or damnation; therfore the open sinnes of minister or people, do neither hurt the sacramentes there administred, nor the godly conscience of the receivers. What sense or sequele is in these reasons ? What can be devised more false or foolish? Because everie one is to looke to his owne private estate, therfore no man may meddle with an other man's, or with the publike, estate. Were he not as foolish that could be led or caried with these reasons as they that made them?

But being granted them, what kind of church? What communion? What duty? What law or feare of God, would there remaine? If the second were granted; that the open, yea, the obstinate sinnes of others, do hurt neither the sacrament, nor godly receivers; what doth it then skil[1] who they be that administer, or receave them, or where they be administred, whether in the popish or Turkish assemblies? A godly man (as they count him) may resort to what idolatrous or sacrilegious assemblies he will; so he in his heart go to worship God, it skilleth [mattereth] not what outward sinn there be committed, or he joineth unto, that hurteth him nothing. What blasphemous hellish doctrines are these, which take away at once the whole testament of Christ, and word of God, or tollerate the open breach of them, which take away all christian libertie, dutie, and communion. May we joine to open sacriledge, and most heinous profanation of Gode's ordinances, and that with the open wicked and impenitent, and not be guiltie? Call they this to examine our selves, or to eate to our owne salvation? They make a faire interpretation of, and collection from these places.

But might it not better be comprised within the examination of our selves, to examine and looke how we dischardge both our publike and private duties towardes God and our brethren, *etc.*, which, how can I think I any way discharge unto them, that suffer my brethren, even before my face wittingly and willingly, to runne headlong into assured destruction, to eate their bane and damnation, yea and give consent therunto. O what a cruel and unmerciful part were this? Call they this to [37] keepe the unitie of the church, not to breake the fellowship, *etc.* Indeed they say true. In thus doing in this communion, I should not break the fellowship, but even for companie goe to hell with them. For

---

[1] To be of importance, to matter, to make a difference.

(as the apostle saith) " we which are manie make one bodie and one bread, because we are together partakers of one bread."[1]

But o how much better should we provide both for them and our selves, to examine wel, and declare unto them what this action is, and how our saviour Christ hath not only instituted after what maner it is to be delivered and received, but also who should deliver and receave it: and so shew them, how in this estate they remaining impenitent and obstinate, there belong no sacramentes or blessing unto them, but rather a fearful looking for of judgment, seing they both breake Gode's lawes, and despise Gode's grace: and therfore the sacramentes seale unto them, and unto as many as either deliver the same unto them, or participate with them in the same, the assured wrath of God; both for that they blesse and joine unto the wicked, and so become guiltie of all their sinnes together with them: and also commit most heinous sacriledge, in breaking the institution of Christ, in delivering the sacramentes (as they pretend) unto the open unworthy, and joining together with them therin. I hope they are not so grosly popish, to suppose that the sacrament can sanctifie the unworthy receavers, and givers: that in deed were no smal miracle, that it should do more than Christ doth (whome it representeth) especially where the institution is so wilfully and impiously broken, as with them; where it is delivered to the open unworthy, who (as the prophet saith) defile that holy thing whatsoever they touch.

But, say they, charitie must thinke and judge the best; it must think, that in this heape of chaffe are many graines of wheat. Well it doth think so; what of this? Can those graines either justifie this sacriledge, to set a loafe of filthie chaffe upon the Lorde's holy table, or sanctifie the wicked, this heape of chaffe, *etc.*? Surely, well ought charitie to border in it self within the compace of sobrietie, and not peremptorily to judge or determine of any, who belong to Gode's election, and who be reprobates (which God hath kept secret to

[1] I Corinthians 10: 17.

himself) unlesse they see these damnable signes of the ^{1 Jhon. 5: 10} sinne against the Holy Ghost, upon them: yet cannot charity judge or pronounce any to be graines of wheate, whiles they lie together hidden and unseperated from this filthy chaffe, these apparant wicked and wickednes; for charitie must be directed and judged by faith, and faith by the word of God.

But charitie ought to judge (say they) that even the worst, when they come to that table, are inwardly sory, and secretly repent. But doth charitie see this sorrow and repentance? If not, how should it judge, and perwade it self it is so? Yea, and presume therupon to communicate with them, and receave them unto the table of the Lord? Charitie had need have a good ground in these high matters, and not walke by rote, least it destroy both them and it self. Charitie may not breake Gode's lawes: their sinnes are seene, knowne and publike, their repentance must be answe-[38]rable: secret repentance suffiseth not the church for open sinne; they must see and witnesse the repentance, or els they must proceed without delay to excommunication. Charitie for no respect, can either linger, lighten, or take away God's judgmentes. It alwaies, even in all causes, saith: *Right and true are thy judgmentes, King of Saintes.*[1] The judgmentes of the church and of al the faithful, are the judgmentes of the Lord, which must be uprightly (without al earthly affection or inclination any way) executed, least God's wrath burne likewise against them, as we have plentiful examples in the Scriptures. How then say these blind guides, that the faithful ought not to meddle with the judging of the wicked in the church? It is only God's office to root out the tares. Their final judgment, we with al humblenes remit unto the Lord, the judge of al. Their temporal judgmentes the Lord hath comitted to his ^{Deut. 29: 29} church, and to everie member of his church, who are to pronounce upon them the judgmentes that are ^{Deut. 17: 7} written, and everie member of the congregation throw upon them the stone of his judgment and consent. Therfore hath the Lord raised up the thrones of David

---

[1] Revelation 16: 7.

in his church; and set his saintes upon seates round about his throne.

Yet for al this, the beginning and end of their song is: that the church and table of the Lord, is not to be forsaken and left, because of the wicked. True, for the wicked are to be chased and driven from thence, where none may enter or stand, without his seene wedding garment upon him. But (as I have beene often driven to say) they that abandon these wicked perverted assemblies, which will not be withdrawen from their sinnes, but remayne hardned and obstinate, leave not the church or table of God, but preserve the church and table of God. They make not the schisme which keep the faith, but they that forsake the faith: yea, and the faithful, thus seperate, ought not for the sinnes of these or any, to neglect or intermit these holy exercises of the church, but to indevor to have them in al holy and pure maner, according unto Christe's ordinance, *etc*.

The last shift and help they have for receaving the prophane and wicked to the sacramentes is: that we ought to detest and abhor their conversation in common bread, because that is in their power and wil; but not for their sakes to refuse the sacramentes, because that is not in their wil. What can be more grosse and foolish? Know these men what belongeth to the communion of saintes? Is it in our power to refuse him in conversation, to whome we joine in the faith, and in communion? Or may I abhor and drive him from my table, whome our saviour Christ receaveth and admitteth to his table? Am I or my table holier than he or his? What a pharisaical pride were this? Even the same they exercised unto the publicanes: where is now this charitie they erwhile spake of? Love covereth the multitude of sinnes and wantes; let not him that is strong despise them that are weake, but receave them unto him, *etc*., instructing them with meeknes, bearing their burden, *etc*. May they [39] then despise and abhor any that is held a brother, or avoid his companie before he be excommunicate, or have forsaken the faith, and remaine hardned or impenitent, *etc*.?

What a preposterous dealing is this, to receave the 1 Cor. 5: 11, 12, wicked unto the Lorde's table, and to drive them from 13 their owne table. This is cleane contrary to the apostle's doctrine, which place[1] Mr. Calvine thought to escape and put away with his botche. He there teacheth, that if any which is called a brother, be a fornicator, or covetous, or a railer, *etc.*, such one is both to be purged as leaven out of the lampe [lump ?], and also eschued in civil meates. But such prophane or wicked, which have not yet imbraced the faith, such are to be kept out of the church, and from the table of the Lord, though otherwise we are not so to abhor their civil conversation, seeing we may have so many occasions therunto, whiles we remayne in this world. Whether now shall we beleeve Mr. Calvine or the apostle, they being so directly contrarie. For the other point of forsaking the table of the Lord, I insist in that which is already said, still saying, they ought in everie true church to be kept from it, especially upon obstinacie, after admonition.

But yet Mr. Calvine thus giveth not over the matter, but indevoreth to prove (that the godly may, and ought to communicate with the open wicked, and yet shall not be defiled therby) by the examples of the prophets, in the corrupt times before the captivity; and of our saviour Christ while he lived heere, who in the most corrupt times refrained not the sacrifices, prayers, or publike ministery of the temple, for the wickednes either of priestes or people: but having regard to the unitie of the church, and unto the ordinances of God, they held up pure hands in a wicked assembly.[2]

First I cannot perceave that in all this Mr. Calvine hath proved that the prophets, or our saviour Christ, have at any time joined, unto, or with, any unlawfull or pulluted priestes or people, such as by the law of God ought not to administer or offer in the temple: neither yet to any unlawful praiers or sacrifices, which ought not to be

---

[1] That is, which doctrines or Scriptural verse as set forth by Paul in I Corinthians 5: 11, 12, 13, where he urges the Corinthians to put away the wicked person, and not to keep company with evil-doers.

[2] Calvin, *Institutes*, book IV, chapter I, sections 18, 19, 20, pp. 296-298.

offered there. And so all these examples are to no purpose alledged, and make nothing for him. For we still, by
the rules of Christ's testament, hold it utterly unlawfull
to receave or reteine any profane or wicked person, to
administer unto, or communicate with such in the
sacramentes. And that all, and whosoever so doth,
most heinously breake God's law, and are all guiltie of
high sacriledg, *etc.* Into which manifest wilfull transgressions, neither the vaine titles of the church, neither
the false flag of the gospel and sacramentes, ought to
draw or allure us.

As for these times under the law (wherof he speaketh),
the worship of God then consisted in outward legall
ceremonies concerning the time, place, priestes, people,
sacrifices, altar, *etc.*, with prescript lawes for everie
thing: which outward ordinances, if they diligently
kept and observed, there was then no cause why such
sacrifices should be left, [40] insomuch as they were in
that outward worshipp altogeather unreproveable.
Other faultes of maners, except such as outwardly
defiled the bodie, or were contrarie to the lawes of the
temple, as bastardy, whordome, idolatrie, *etc.*, the
priestes or ecclesiastical estate then medled not with.
They belonged to the civil magistrates, whose office it
was then, both to censure and punish such offendors
according to the law. Whiles then the ecclesiasticall
lawes which God in that estate apointed, were duly
observed, there was no cause why the prophets or any
should refraine that worship: yet were the prophets
(which were apointed of God to instruct both the
ecclesiastical and civil estate) to admonish and reprove
the civil magistrates, and to cry out against them, and
to denounce God's judgmentes against the one and the
other, and to shew them, that neither temple nor sacrifice, neither fathers nor covenant, could excuse or
deliver them from the wrath and curse of God, whiles
they continued in these sinnes, and deferred to repent.

Revel. 21: 5 But now under the gospel, where al things are become
new and spiritual, where Christ hath given unto his
2 Cor. 5: 17 church, and unto all his faithfull servantes his power
and authoritie spiritually, to censure al manner of sinne

and sinners; he hath given them his holy word, and made them all kings and priestes therunto; he hath commanded them to watch, and diligently to take heed, that no profane or wicked impenitent person be admitted unto, or kept in his church: but diligently to watch both without and within, that the one sort be kept out, the other cast out of his church. The legal pollutions, leprosies, ulcers, running issues, infections, and uncleane diseases, for which then the people were seperated from the temple and the congregation; are now in this church all manner knowen sinnes, obstinatly held and maintained, which are far more infectious and contagious unto the soules of the whole church, than those filthy diseases were unto the bodie. Neither is the Lord our God lesse jelous, or will be lesse offended, for keeping such in his church, and admitting them unto his table now, than he was in those daies, when the leprous, plaguy, or polluted were kept in the congregation, and admitted to the altar: especially seing he hath now given as great charge, as prescript lawes, both whome, when, and how to cast out, as he did then. So that, as abhominable should our worship and offring now be unto the Lord, and all we in as great blame: (seing unto all his servantes this charge, this watch, this power, these lawes are given) as they in the former times, for the transgressions aforesaid. Exod. 19: 6

1 Pet. 2: 5

Heb. 12: 15

But now peradventure, these disciples of Mr. Calvine will from their maister's mouth affirme (for so in deed his wordes and writings apparantly import, els as we have shewed these examples are brought to no purpose) that the prophetes and our saviour Christ, in those most sinful times, where al estates and persons were throughly and wholy corrupt, al the lawes of God, both concerning the church and common welth, the worship of God and civil conversation boldly broken by al, without any regard or conscience: that yet in these times the prophets [41] and our saviour Christ communicated with these priestes and people in these sinnes, and were not defiled with their sinnes, but held up pure handes amongst them. Before I shew the manifest untruth, the pestilent errors and unsufferable blasphemie of these doctrines, I demaund of them how they prove, that the prophets and our saviour Christ communicated in these times with these priestes and people thus defiled and corrupted, thus openly breaking God's lawes and ordinances, both concerning his worship in the temple, and the government of the common welth. I see no proof alledged, except it be this: they built not other churches, they erected not other altars where they might have their several sacrifices. What of all this? They built not other temples and altars, therfore they communicated with the abhominations in the temple; they had no private sacrifices, therfore they resorted unto the polluted and corrupt sacrifices, used at these times in the temple. Are these their best reasons? That because they did not one sinne, therfore they did an other. Can these men find no meane course? What if the prophets in these times did neither of both? Shall not the ignorance, falshood and boldnes of these men then apeare, which thus slander the prophetes, falsifie and pervert the Scriptures, to maintaine these damnable errors, and wicked dealinge? The first they themselves confess and alledge: the second (though they bring no one place of Scripture to approve) I thus by evident testimonies, both of the stories and of the prophetts themselves, disprove. In the time of King Achas,[1]

2 Kings 16
Ezek. 44

when the Lord's brazen altar was removed and set aside, a new altar, after the forme of that at Damascus was brought in, and used in the place of the other. The priestes that served therunto, offred also upon other altars which were set up by that wicked king to other goddes, *etc.* Likewise in the time of Manasses

2 Chron. 33
2 Chron. 36

and Amon,[2] when altars, groves, and high places were built unto idols, the priestes attended them, and other altars (which the Lord had forbidden) brought in and

Ezek. 8

set up in the courtes of the Lord. In the times of

---

[1] Ahaz, king of Judah, as co-regent from 735—732/731, and as king from 732/731 to 716/715.

[2] Manasseh, king of Judah, as co-regent from 696/695—687/686, and as king from 687/686 to 642/641. Amon followed, 642/641—640/639.

Jehoachas, Jehoiakim and Zedekyah,[1] when the idoll of indignation was againe set up in the utter court of the people, in the next court of the Levites were painted upon the wall the similitude of all creeping and abhominable things, as also all the idols of the house of Israel, and the seventy antientes burning incense unto the them: yea where the women wove hangings for the Egiptian goddes, and mourned for Tammuz,:[2] yea, yet neerer the presence of the Lord, in the court of the priests, even at the verie dore of temple of God, they turned their backes upon God, and with their faces towardes the east worshipped the sunne. I would here demand of the learnedest of these priestes, whether they thinke that in these times the prophets communicated with these priestes? Or how they can prove it?

The contrarie is to be proved, both by the lawes of God, which forbad them to touch any polluted thing, especially to keep themselves undefiled with the filthines of idols, *etc.*, and also in the stories of Hezekiah, and Josiah; Hezekiah in the beginning of his raign, finding all [42] thinges thus defiled and corrupted, called such godly priests and Levites, as had in his father's time refrained the temple, and left off to administer, and exhorteth them to loke [look] and addresse themselves unto their charge which was committed unto them by the Lord, to sanctifie themselves, to purge the temple, and cast out the abhominations his father had brought in, *etc.*, which we reade by them to be done, and the whole house and land purged by solemne sacrifice. And after that, the feastes which had before bene intermitted, were againe renued and orderly kept. Josiah also, after he had purged the temple, cast out and defaced the idols, placed and restored the priests and Levites in their due orders, strook [struck] and renued a covenant with the Lord, summoneth the priestes, Levites, and people againe to the due keeping of the feastes commanded in the lawe. And II Chronicles

---

1 Jehoahaz, king of Judah, 608; Jehoiakim, 608—597; Jehoiachin, 597; and Zedekiah, 597—586.
2 Ezekiel 8: 14.

35: 3. (according to Tremelius[1] his translation) he saith thus unto them. *But he saied unto the Levites preparing the holy thinges of the Lord for all Israel, set, or put them before the holy Arke, in this house which Solomon, the sonne of David, king of Israel, hath built. It lieth no more upon you a burden to be caried upon your shoulder: now serve Jehovah your God and his people Israel.* In which wordes he calleth the priestes, Levites, and people to the law and institution of God, Deuteronomy 12: 5, *etc.*, Leviticus 17: 3, *etc.*, that now all their feastes and sacrifices ought to be brought and kept before the Lord in his temple, orderly according to his law, and not as when the ark might be removed, to be kept in sundrie places, neither yet as in private houses, as in the time of the corruptions where the Lord bare with them, as if they had beene in Egipt in private houses.

Now for the third time of Joziah his successors, let the ninth chapter of Ezekiel be considered: where we find al judged and damned to destruction, which were defiled with these abhominations; and only those marked by the angel with the writer's ynckhorne, and saved, which kept themselves pure from, and cried out against, those abhominations: likewise his sixteenth and twenty-third chapters, where the Lord pleadeth against them as against an harlot which had forsaken her husband, and left, yea, murdered her children; and therfore that his faithful servantes should judg them not as the church of God (as the false prophets then and now do) but as harlots and as murtherers, *etc.* His whole prophecie is plentiful in this argument, shewing all to be defiled and abhominable by these sinnes, and that the glory of the Lord utterly abandoned both the temple and the citie. All the prophets in all their writinges abundantly shew, that the faithfull refrained in these corrupt times, and infinite reasones might be drawen from thence, to prove the same: but I hope, that which hath beene already alledged, sufficeth in this point. Now I would only know of these learned

---

[1] Immanuel Tremellius and Francis Junius issued their Latin translation of the Old Testament from the Hebrew in 1580. The edition of 1585 also contained the New Testament.

disputers, which bring these examples of the prophets
and our saviour Christ, thinking therby fully to conclude the matter, and to drive the naile to the head:
whether if they should have communicated with these
wicked and defiled priestes and people, they should not
also have sinned, and beene polluted? If [43] they
denie that it had beene no sinne in them, and that they
should not therby be defiled (as Mr. Calvine in his
writinges doth), then I bring the manifest lawes of God
against them; where it is written, that no polluted person
might either administer, or offer in the temple. This
then being unlawful for the priestes or people to doe,
must needes also be unlawfull in the prophetts which
were not ignorant of this law, to suffer or consent unto,
etc. It is also written in their law, that whoso touched
any uncleane thing or polluted person, was also defiled
therby: yea, what holy thing soever such polluted person
touched, whether flesh or oile, was defiled and abhominable. How then can these men say, the prophets
willingly joining to such open breach of the lawes and
ordinances of the temple, touching and mingling themselves with such uncleane and unlawfull priestes, people,
and offrings, were not both defiled herein, and transgressed God's lawes?

If they say the prophets communicated not in any
unlawful action, or with any polluted person, then to
what end do they bring and urge their examples, to
draw us to joine with them in open and knowen transgression? If they say they communicated with the
priestes that administred in the temple in these corrupt
times, then could it not be, but both the priestes and
they, must needes be defiled with the idolatry and
abhominations that there were set up, as above is
shewed. Now nothing can be a greater transgression,
or more filthy and contagious defilement, than to joyne
to idolatry, or idolatours. Neither can any be a greater
allowance of joyning unto them, than to make them our
mouth or ministers unto God, or together with such,
to joyne in any action concerning the worship of God.
Thus then it must needes be: that the prophets (if they
communicated or offred, by, or with such corrupt

331

priestes and people) grievously with them transgressed,
and were together with them defiled, neither could they
judge or cry out against the sines of the time, when
they themselves were alike guiltie and partakers with
them in these sinnes. With what conscience then or
feare of God, can they perswade us to sinne, by the
prophetts' examples ? May they not as well by the
examples of the patrirches, David *etc.*, perswade us to
incest, adulterye, murther ? If it were sinne in them,
shal it be lesse in us ? Are these Scriptures and examples
well used or applied by them ?

But how wil they now doe, when even that stone
which they had set us as a triumphant monument of
their victorie, is rouled upon their head, and shall grind
them to dust, except they retire and repent ? For
whiles they affirme our saviour Christ to have communicated with the wicked polluted priestes and people
in feastes and their sacrifices, and that at such a time
(saith their author) as al estates were throughly corrupt
and desperatly incurable; how shal they in this case
cleare him of grievous sinne and pollution, or themselves rather of most accursed and unsufferable blasphemy ? Great corruption there was no doubt in [44]
the civil estate, by reason that the civil goverment was
in the Gentiles' handes, the prophane Romaines that
knew not God; and therby also great slacknes and
defaultes even amongst the priestes and rulers of
the temple, as apeared by the sectes and errors
amongst them, by the many traditions brought in,
and the great and more waighty things of the law,
as mercy and judgment, neglected. Great also was
their blindnes, hardnes of heart and obstinacie, which
not only did not acknowledg, but refused and murthered the Lord of life himself, that flourishing tree
of all righteousnes, that innocent, in whome was found
no sinne. Yet notwithstanding al this, I cannot find
by the hystories of the evangelistes, but that the outward ordinances of the temple were indifferently well
kept and observed, especially about the time of Christe's
birth, when were found divers godly priestes and holy,

just men and women, that administred and offred in the temple.

To take all doubt and controversie away, the Holy Ghost recordeth, that all thinges about him, were done according to the law. We reade also that his parentes accustomably resorted up to Jerusalem, at the feastes; Luke 2: 39 which, they being godly, would not have done, if they had not beene kept according to the law. So that heere was no apparant or lawful cause, to drive away the godly from the temple and sacrifices: neither any comparison betwixt the outward estate of the temple, and the outward estate of those congregations which receave and admit the open wicked and unworthy to the sacramentes, and wil not be admonished or redresse the same. But to come to our saviour Christe's person: I reade not any where, that he communicated or offred with the priestes and people in the temple; neither bringeth Mr. Calvine any proof therof, save that he went up unto the feastes. But we reade not that he went up to offer or communicate with them according to the law, but rather to teach and instruct them, and to call them to repentance and amendment of life. We Joh. 5: 16, 18 everie where reade, how sharply he reproved both priestes and people; insomuch as they, even at the Joh. 7, 8, 9, 10, beginning of his ministerie, sought to kill him; which 11, 12 chap-
ters they would not have done, if he had consented or communicated with them. We reade not that either he or his disciples, no, nor John the Baptist, receaved or baptised any, but such as repented and beleved. We see, that neither he nor his disciples kept the traditions or customes of the Jewes, of washing, fasting, *etc.* We see, that he receaved such as the Jewes had excommunicate, namely, the blind man; and after their obstinacie was apparant, both seperated his disciples from them, and openly everie where denounced against them. We reade againe, that they sought to kill him, because so many went from them after him. As for his going up to their feastes, it is apparant, that it was not to offer and communicate with them, so much as to teach the people, there having the fittest oportunitie, and greatest conc[o]urse. He went not according to the order of the law, but sometime at the midfeast, somtime not at all. We may see in that discourse, John 7, betwixt his kinsfolk and him [45] both by their speach, and his answere, that his custome was not to goe to offer, so much as to teach. When he came there, he reproved and reformed some things amisse, as the tables of the mony changers, and them that sold doves, *etc*. In the great day of their feast of tabernacles, he called them from their superstitious drawing water in their well of Siloam, unto himself, that lively spring of living waters, *etc*. As for their feast of the passover, he kept it not with them, but a part by himself with his disciples, in a private place. To which reasons if we add the continual debate and hostilitie betwixt him, the priestes, Phariseis, and their proselites, and all sortes of ministers and rulers of the temple, with the maner of their reasoning, their spurning against him with envie, he confuting their errors, and convincing their wickednes with power, yea, judging and condemning them for their wickednes, obstinacie, crueltie, and contempt of God and his word, as in the 21, 22, and 23 chapters of Mathew apeare. By all which reasons and circumstances, and many other that may be drawen out of the evangelie, I thinke we may rather deeme, yea conclude, that Christ did not communicate with those wicked priestes and people at their feastes and sacrifices, rather than upon Mr. Calvin's bare report, to beleeve he did. But whether he did, or did not, it were blasphemie to thinke or affirme, that he ever joyned unto them in any action, where they brake the least iode [jod, jot] of his Father's law: for then should he be with them guilty of transgression and sinne, as is above proved; and then the monstrous doctrines that would insue hereof, no christian eares can endure to heare. And sure their sinne is not much lesse, which goe about to draw such poisoned doctrines and divelish conclusions from him, to make him an author of sinn, yea, of most impious sacriledge and profanation of God's name, and all maner headstrong wickednes and abhomination, which these wretches would couller and tollerate, under his name and examples.

Thus having dispatched these foraine cavils, of these our English Romish priestes, not so much for their sakes (to whome by Mr. Calvin's owne judgment they apertaine not) as for the truthe's sake, which by such false and smoky reasons is grievously obscured; it is now high time wee looke homeward unto the present matter in hand: namly, by the rules of the word, to examine this their Church of England. Which as we have found to consist of al the prophane and wicked people of the land; all, without any choice or difference, being alike receaved and nourished in the bozome of their church, *etc*, so if we by the rules of Christ's testament duly examine this their slanting ministerie, wherof their church so boasteth; I doubt not but that we shal find them as counterfeit, prodigious, antichristian, and rightly fitting to this monstrous confuse bodie of the multitudes, this harlot, their church sitteth on. Which ministerie to describe in their coullers, were a fitter argument for a stage play, to bring forth these hypocrits out of their dennes, and to make them play their partes in the light; than for any sober and christian discourse (who abhor to rave in their uncleane cages [46] and filthy kennels). Yet that they may the sodainlyer apeare of what sort they are, and we the soner have done with them: let us first consider what maner of officers Christ hath apointed in the church of God; then, how these ought to enter; then how to administer: and so briefly by these rules examine the ministerie of their Church of England.

The ministerie apointed unto the government and service of the church of Christ we find to be of two sortes, elders and deacons: the elders, some of them, to give attendance unto the publike ministerie of the word and sacramentes, as the pastor and teacher: the other elders together with them, to give attendance to the publike order and government of the church: the deacons, to attend the gathering and distributing the goodes of the church. Now these officers are first duly proved, examined, and compared by, and to these rules set downe in the testament of Christ, both in apparant graces, by the manifestation of the spirit; as also in al

Philip. 1: 1

1 Tim. 3

Titus 1
Rom. 12: 7, 8
Act. 6: 1

Tim. 5: 17
Acts 20: 28
1 Thes. 5: 12
1 Cor. 12: 7
1 Tim. 3
Acts 6. Act.
[*sic*]

unreproveable conversation, witnessed, and wel aproved unto that flock, of which they are chosen to serve and attend. This done with praier and fasting, they are chosen and ordeined in the same congregation, by

1 Cor. 4: 2 publike consent. They being thus chosen and or-
2 Cor. 10: 8 deined by all, are now diligently and faithfully to
Acts 20 execute their office unto all, not prejudicing the libertie of any, ambitiously assuming any inordinate authoritie,
1 Pet. 5: 2, 3, 4 or abusing or neglecting their office, neither holding or executing it, in regard or in respect of person: but up-
2 Cor. 13: 8 rightly and indifferently performing it unto all men,
John 9 as in the eies of God, whose word they purely and
1 Cor. 11: 1 sincerely teach, faithfully and precisely observe, to their uttermost knowledg and power. If in any thing
Phil. 3: 17 they transgresse or offend; they are, as well as any other
1 Tim. 5: 21, members, liable to the censure of the church: which is,
etc. to reprove, depose, or excommunicate them, according
1 Tim. 5: 20 to the qualitie of the sinne, and estate of the offenders,
Col. 4: 17 *etc.*

1 Thes. 5: 14 Now to come to the ministerie of the Church of England, which is so manifold and divers, as I know
Rom. 16: 17, 18 not how to begin to describe it. But let it first be
1 Tim. 6: 3, 4, 5 divided into these three sorts: 1. *Reigning* or *Governing.* 2. *Serving* and 3. *Collegiate.* 1. Of the reigning and
2 Tim. 3: 5 governing ministers, are arch-bishops, lord bishops,
Titus 3: 10 arch-deacons, chancellers, commissaries, all of the High Commission, as likewise such civil doctors, proctors, registers, scribes, pursuivantes, sumners as attend upon their Courtes of Faculties, Prerogative, Archies, Delegates, *etc.*[1] 2. Of the serving sort, are parsons,

---

[1] The Court of Faculties, the Prerogative Court of Canterbury, the Court of Arches, and the Court of Delegates. There is an article on the spiritual courts in S. L. Ollard and Gordon Crosse, *A Dictionary of English Church History.* See further Great Britain. Ecclesiastical Courts Commission. *Report of the Commissioners Appointed to Inquire into the Constitution and Working of the Ecclesiastical Courts, with Minutes of Proceedings, Evidence, Returns, Abstracts, Historical and Other Appendices, etc.* This is in *Parliamentary Papers* (London, 1883), volume XXIV, Command Paper no. 3760. 2 volumes. The contribution of Canon Stubbs, "An Account of the Courts Which Have Exercised Ecclesiastical Jurisdiction in England up to the year 1834," is in volume I, 21-51, and 21-162. See also Wilfrid Hooper, "The Court of Faculties," *English Historical Review,* October, 1910, pp. 670-686. See further, Lewis Dibdin, "On the Report (1883) of the Royal Commission on Ecclesiastical Courts," in *Quarterly Review,* October, 1883.

vickars, curates, hireling lecturers, vagrant and mercenarie preachers, house priestes, chaplens, half-priestes
or catechisers, church-wardens, sidemen, questmen,
parish clarkes. 3. Of the ministerie collegiate, are lord
bishops, deanes, sub-deanes, prebendaries, canons, petie
channons, gospellers, pistellers, singing men, singing
boies, vergiers, sextines. This division, I suppose, wil
wel neere suffice for their officers. But now, how to
divide or distinguish their offices, I know not; I am so
unlearned and ignorant of such great secrets, and high
misteries. Neither yet have I skil to marshial them in
their degrees of honour, which (I have heard say) they
have, both in the common welth, and in their schooles;
as [47] their primate, their metropolitane graces, their
palatine lord bishops and their barony lordships: al
which I weene be peeres of the realme, and estates of
the land. Now there are also certayne doctors of divinitie, and bachelors of divinitie, which have many
great privileges and pr[er]ogatives, of the cappe, the
skarlet gowne, the hood, the habbite, the tippet, *etc.*,
the ring, the chaire: the one of them, being a kinght's
[knight's] fellow, the other an esquire's in any ground in
England. Also how capable these are by statute of
how many benefices, I cannot tell.

Neither have I the cunning to derive their genealogies
and pedegries, as they tooke beginning in the ages
succeeding the apostles, in the first 400 or 500 yeres:
only because I want [lack] that deep learning, I must
content my self to goe to that old book of God's word.
There in deed I remember Revelation 9 that I read of
a s[t]ar that fell from heaven unto the earth, which had
the key of the bottomles pyt given unto him; who when
he had opened that bottomles pyt, there arose the
smoke of the pyt, as the smoke of a great fornace,
wherwith the sunne and the aire were darkned. Out
of which smoke of the said pyt, I read, that al these
monstrous, armed, crowned, poisoned locustes and
scorpions issued, *etc.* Now as they tooke beginning
with antichrist, under their king Apolluon:[1] so

[1] Revelation 9: 11 — " And they had a king over them, which is the angel
of the bottomless pit, whose name in the Hebrew tongue is Abaddon,
but in the Greek tongue hath his name Apollyon."

M

tooke they increase together with him. For when Sathan had enthronized him, given him his high commission, and made him his lieftenant general in earth, *etc.*, then these his peeres and captaines compassed about and guarded his throne, and did miracles before the beast, deceaving with the effectual power of their errors, all such as receaved the beaste's marke, or worshipped his image, and caried forth his image far and neere, and set it up in al places where his person could not be, and compelled al both smal and great, rich and poore, to receive the beaste's mark and worship his image: this I read in the 13 of the Revelation. Now in the sixteenth chapter of the said booke, after that the vials of God's wrathful judgmentes had beene powred out upon the earth, upon the sea, upon the rivers and fountaines of waters, upon the sunne, upon the throne of the beast, upon their great river Euphrates; I read, that these uncleane spirites that came out of the mouth of the dragon, and out of the mouth of that beast, and out of the mouth of that false prophet, which are the spirites of devils, working miracles; should goe forth unto the kings of the earth, and of the whole world, to gather them unto the battel of that g[r]eat day of God almightie: yea, and in the 17 of the Revelation, that they should cause these kings, those ten hornes, to hate the whore, to make her desolate and naked, to burne the whore with fire, even that faire harlot, of whose cup they had drunke, and with whome they had committed fornication so many yeares before, and to give their kingdomes, power, and authoritie unto the beast, until the wordes of God be accomplished. In the 19 and 20 chapters of this said booke, I read; that they, together with all the hostes of these kings that thus make warre against the lamb, and beseege the beloved citie and the tentes of the saintes round about, shalbe taken and [48] cast into a lake of fire and brymstone, and there to be tormented together with that dragon, and that beast, and that false prophet, day and night for evermore. And loe, thus have we brought these fellowes home againe, even to the place where we found them. For out of the bottomles pyt they came, and into that fierie fornace they shal [go, return]. Let them that list more curiously to search, inquire after them in their *Centuaries* and *Annalles*:[1] it sufficeth me to know, that they came out of the bottomles pyt, that they belong not to Christe's kingdom, that they are strangers there, and have there neither name, place, nor office. We find in the church of Christ no mention of these rufflers,[2] they are not members of his bodie, they are neither pastors, teachers, elders nor deacons: but even of late before our eies, these self same officers, courtes, attendantes, even from their primate arch-bishop to the parish priest, and so to the sumner [summoner], administred unto the whore of Rome, and had their originall from the apostatical seate of Antichrist. How then should they thus sodenly become the members of Christ, yea, rulers of his house whether he will or no? Who not only thrust in their parsons by intrusion, but these monstrous offices, courtes, and cannons, never read of, never heard of in the testament and church of Christ.

For there we find no mention of any other arch-bishop or lord bishop, than that chief shepheard and lord of life, Christ Jesus; unto whome everie knee ought to bowe, and everie tongue confesse. But these blasphemous beastes, or rather heades of that beast, are not ashamed to arrogate unto them Christe's names and titles, which are written upon them as names of blasphemie, that the Scripture might be fulfilled: which titles and honors, they blasphemously would Revel. 13 defend, with this Scripture, which is spoken of the Revel. 17: 3

1 Between 1559 and 1574 a group of Lutheran scholars, under the leadership of Matthias Vlacich (Latinized, Flacius), issued a series of thirteen folio volumes on church history, *Ecclesiastica Historia . . . . secundum singulas centurias.* Because each volume dealt with one century, and because the first five volumes were written at Magdeburg, the authors became known as the " Centuriators of Magdeburg." Caesar Baronius, cardinal and librarian of the Vatican, wrote twelve folio volumes, 1588—1607, from the Catholic point of view, on the first twelve centuries of the Christian era, *Annales Ecclesiastici.* Volume I was issued in 1588 and volume II in 1590.

Barrow may have seen Volume I and possibly the second volume at the time he was writing.

Volume IV of the " Centuries of Magdeburg " was dedicated to Queen Elizabeth.

2 A vagabond, a swaggering, arrogant individual.

office and person of the civil magistrate: *I have saied, ye are goddes, and ye all are the children of the most high,* Psalms 82: 6, although our saviour Christ hath expresly, with his owne mouth, said to his apostles (than whome I am sure these are neither greater nor better): *the kinges of the Gentiles reigne over them, and they that beare* Luke 22: 24 *rule over them are called bountifull, but be ye not so: but let* John 13: 12, *etc. the greatest among you, be as the least, and the chiefest, as he that serveth.*

Now when they cannot defend their pride and blasphemie by the word (which glasse most lively sheweth, even to their owne eies and consciences the ouglines and heinousnes of their sinne), they then runne to their last shote anker,[1] to uphold their tottering states by the prince's donation. Which if it were so, were but weake defence for them, against the wrath and judgment of God that condemneth them, and a mightie sinne (and yet no noveltie) for the kings of the earth to give their crownes unto the beast, *etc.* But I would heere know of them, whether any prince may lawfully give that unto them, or they receave that, which Christ hath denied them, yea, and carefully avoided in his owne person, leaving them an example, *etc.,* and why by the donation of the Emperour Constantine, the pope's supremacie may not be as well justified:[2] then I would heere know, how they can avoide the crime of slandering the [49] prince, which lay this charge upon her: which in deed is due to their holy father the pope, who when he received of his father the divel his authoritie and great power, magnificently dealt these honorable titles and offices to these his natural sonnes proceeded from his owne mouth and throne, many hundred yeres before Queene Elizabeth was born.

Now as we find their names and titles blasphemous, so if we looke wel into their offices, we shal find them

---

[1] Variant of sheet-anchor, a large emergency anchor ; that which is used as a last resort.

[2] Barrow was probably aware of the work of Lorenzo Valla, Nicholas of Cusa, and Reginald Pecocke, who had concluded that the Donation of Constantine was a forged document, written about 450 years after the time of Constantine (died 337) and Pope Sylvester I (314—335).

no better. Of the ordinarie established permanent
offices, pastour, teacher, elder, which are to oversee, Acts 20: 26
and administer unto that flock, of which they are
orderly chosen, *etc.*, these are not; who some of them 1 Pet. 5: 2
standes a primate or pope unto the whole land, some Rom. 12: 7, 8
other a metropolitane over half the land, the least of
these Anakims[1] over many hundreth steeples, churches
(as they say). Therfore they have none of these
ordinarie offices, which only now remaine. As for
the extraordinarie offices of apostles, prophetes, evan- Ephe. 4: 11
gelistes, which God at the first used to the cariing forth
of his truth, the gathering together and setting in order
of his saintes and we find them (apostles I meane and
evangelistes) altogether ceased, and now needles; insomuch as the foundation is already fully and soundly 1 Cor. 3: 10, 11,
layde, as also al ordinances and orders which the *etc.*
church is to receave, expressly set downe and mani- 2 Tim. 3: 16, 17
fested in the testament of Christ; to which al churches
are now, for their direction in al thinges, wholy referred.

As for prophets, their office was neither definite nor Acts 20: 32
permanent, but by peculiar and extraordinarie revela-
tions, according to some especial occasions of the church; Acts 14: 23
wherof I suppose these men (who are so ionorant of,
and rebellious against the revealed wil of God) have
final occasion to boast. But if their madnes should
proceed so far, we leave their discoverie and judgment
to the law of God, written Deuteronomy 13: 1, *etc.* Gal. 1: 1
Apostles, I suppose, they are not; having neither any Acts 1: 24
immediate calling from God unto their apostleship
(unles as they in their inscription of their titles and
stile doe write: John[2] *by the permission of God and power*
of the divill bishop of such a place) and so as the apostle
saith are false apostles, laying not the true foundation, 2 Cor. 11: 13 *etc.*
but a new foundation, even their holy father the pope's
cannons, and the devilish injunctions of their blas- Gal. 2, 4, 5, and
phemous High Commission: wherupon and wherby, 6 chap.

---

[1] The Anakims were the children of Anak. They were a people great and
tall, and feared by their enemies. In the areas of Hebron, Debir, Anab,
and the hill country of Judah, Joshua utterly destroyed the Anakims
and their fortified cities. See Deuteronomy 2: 10, 11; Numbers 13:
22, 28, 33; Joshua 11: 21, 22.

[2] Both John Aylmer, Bishop of London, and John Whitgift, Archbishop
of Canterbury, were probably intended.

their church is built and ruled in all thinges. Now
to their office of evangelistes, they want their apostolical
sending, also their worke and building declareth, that
false evangelistes and deceitful workmen they are, that
keep not that true patterne, which the apostles practised
and left to all the churches; but according to their owne
fancies set up and pluck downe, what and when it
pleaseth them, as all their actions declare, having no
one pynne, naile, or hooke according to the true patterne in Christ's testament, or in right frame; which if
I should here indevour in particular to declare, it were
to goe about to emptie that foule sinke, even the bottomles pyt, from whence they came: sufficeth it heere
to have shewed their names, offices, authoritie, not to
be of God, neither to belong to Christ's church. Therfore [50] we need not be further inquisitive, either of
their callings or doings, seeing they belong not unto us,
were it not to cal them, or so many of them as belong
to God's election, unto repentance, to leave their
accursed trade and offices, *etc.*, as also to call such of
the people, as belong to the kingdom of Christ, from
their apostatical and antichristian throne.

What hath beene said of the names and offices of
these magnificent prelates these great lords; the same
(for avoiding tedious repetition) is to be judged of al
the crue of their associates, assistantes, attendants,
inferior priestes and officers: of whose names or offices,
we find no mention in Christ's testament, no use or
place in Christ's church. Yet because some of them
make a fairer shew in the flesh, and under counterfait
shew of holines deceave the simple, and leade captive
many a stule;[1] I wil leave for a while these great peeres
and mightie estates, with all their collegues and followers in their grosse wickednes, which is apparant and
odious unto all men, in whome is any sparck of light or
grace; and wil now addresse my self to pul of[f] the
visardes of these disguised hypochrites, these ravening
wolves which come to us in sheepe's clothing, under
glorious and swelling titles of pastors, teachers, preachers

1 Cor. 4: 17
Phil. 2: 19 *etc.*
1 Thes. 3: 2

1 Tim. 1: 3
Titus 1: 5

1 Tim. 5: 21
2 Tim. 1: 13
2 Tim. 4: 5

---

[1] A variant of stool. The only meaning in the *New English Dictionary*
that seems a possibility is, a gang of workmen employed in one shed.

and ministers of the gospel, men of great learning, of very holy life, and of great sinceritie, seekers and sighers for reformation, such as abhor and cry out against the bishops and their proceedinges, *etc.*

These Phariseis, these sectaries are they, which mislead the people in their crooked and bye pathes of death, and wil neither lead them nor suffer them to enter into the peaceable and strait waies of the Lord, but keep them alwaies learning, and never bring them to the sight or acknowledging of the truth, *etc.*, as when we come to examine their manner of teaching, shal appeare. In the meane while, let us a litle goe back againe (as it were) that we may the more orderly proceed, and consider in a word or two, of these Rabbines' persons, education, learning, training, wherby they are made fit to these great offices; then of the offices themselves, and of their calling and entrance therunto; last of al, of their administration, how they behave themselves therin. And this, but by way of a summarie and most brief recital; for if I should stand to lay open their dealing at large, though it were without either proving or disproving (for this in matters so manifest need not) it would make in it self a most large discourse, and were a subject too great for any man's capacitie to handle, to set downe their monstrous transgressiones and disorders in particular, much more in their heinousnes and indignity, which do even fil the great flying boke of God's curse,[1] the prophet speaketh of. But to give you a blush of some of them, and to open you a way the better at your further leasure, by your further and more diligent search, to looke into their dealings; I wil (God so willing) of many, set you downe a few.

[51] First, for their persons, we find them all generally the seed and offspring of the unbeleevers, of men without the faith, without the church, of these confuse idolatrous multitudes above spoken of, and as the unchristian education of these ympes maketh manifest; who, even from their cradles, are nourished in al maner of prophanenes, heathenisme, vaine and ungodly sciences and literature, ostentation, pride, more than monkish

---

[1] Zechariah 5: 1-4.

(that I say not) Sodomitish idlenes, superstition, idolatrie, *etc.* This, their ungodly nurture in their common
scholes (where they must learne the Latine or Greeke
tongue from lascivious poets and heathenish philosophers)
sheweth evidently. With this liquor are their pitchers
at the first seasoned: when they have beene well nouseled
in these, and have orderly passed to the highest forme;
then are they fit for one of the universities, where they
being placed in some one colledg (as they tearme them)
or other, after they have beene solemnely matriculate
and sworne upon the proctor's booke to their mother
the universitie, to conceale and keepe close her secretes
and mysteries, as also to be obedient to her statutes and
orders; there are they trained up in logick, rhetorick,
and philosophy: which learning they draw from Aristotle and Cicero, and such like. There they learne to
reason and speake by art, by sylogismes and tropes;
which artes when they have gotten (or at the least,
spent some apointed time in the universites), then they
commence bachelors or maisters of art. Now if they
continue still with their mother, and give their minde
to the studie of divinitie (as they cal it), which is as
much to say as the rearding [reading] of men's writinges,
such as are best esteemed of in these times, with those
feathers they flie, and with those eies they see: which
bookes being taken from them, they are as mute as
fishes, as blind as moles.

But when once they are growen skilful in this traditional
divinitie, that they dare undertake upon some moneths'
warning, to speake an howre upon some text, and that
they dare trust their memories to deliver no worse stuffe
than they have read in the commentaries and common
places of these authors: then upon a litle practise they
grow bould to set up their bylles of chalenge upon the
schole dores, that they purpose to dispute for their degree,
and to maintaine certaine hard pointes of divinitie,
generally consented unto, and receaved of all men:
which questions, as also the whole Scriptures, must in
these their schooles and disputations, be unsufferably
corrupted, abused, wrested, perverted, blasphemed
according to the lustes of these philosophical and

heathen disputers; which heer must handle, divide, utter and discusse, according to their vaine affected artes of logick and rhetorick.[1]

Wel, when they have thus performed their artes, either *in luce* or *in tenebris*,[2] and that their solemne day of their commencement draweth neere; there some worthy chaplen or other, to winne the spurres, or a deanry at the least when it falleth, undertaketh to defend non-[52]residencie, or pluralitie of benefices; or some other, to confirme the faith of the Church of England, undertaketh to defend, that the apostolicall discipline (as they tearme it) or government and order which is set downe in Christe's testament for his church unto the worlde's end, is not perpetuall or of necessite; but may be altered according to the will of princes, estates,[3] *etc.*, and also that Christ descended into hell, during that time his body laye in the grave.[4] These and such like damnable heresies and blasphemies, are confirmed in the eies of the whole land, who resort thither to see this stage play, where the fencers fight bootie, the persons that shall dispute being purposely apointed, the time set how long they shall dispute; the dogs being to be puld off, either by masse vicechancellor or Mr. Proctor, as the arguments by any thing strong or the disputers distressed. Now here must also

---

[1] Robert Browne was also caustic in his denunciation of logic and rhetoric at Cambridge University. See Albert Peel and Leland H. Carlson, *The Writings of Robert Harrison and Robert Browne*, pp. 173-193.

[2] In the light or in the darkness.

[3] Thomas Cooper in 1589 challenged his opponents in these words: " Onely this I desire, that they will lay downe out of the worde of God some just proofes, and a direct commaundement, that there should bee in all ages and states of the Church of Christ, one onely forme of outwarde government (*An Admonition to the People of England*, p. 81). Thomas Bilson issued in 1593 his work, *The Perpetual Governement of Christe's Church*, and in 1594—1597, Richard Hooker's famous work appeared, *Of the Lawes of Ecclesiasticall Politie*. Cooper, Bilson, Hooker, and other Anglican writers allowed for change and development as circumstances and historical need dictated, but the Presbyterians, Reformists, and Separatists contended that the pattern of the first-century church was perfect and unalterable.

[4] Barrow, Henry Jacob, Francis Johnson and others denied the doctrine that Christ descended into hell. Bishop Thomas Bilson was commanded by Elizabeth to answer Henry Jacob's *A Treatise of the Sufferings and Victories of Christ*. This he did in a work entitled, *Survey of Christ's Sufferings for Man's Redemption*. The learned Hebraist, Hugh Broughton, wrote *An Explication of the Article* [He descended into Hell].

345

be considered, that al these prizes are plaied in Latine, that the learning may the more, and their folly the lesse appeare, least even the common people should hisse them of[f] the stage, if they spake English. But why doe I thus reveale their mother Osyris' secretes: some of them will say I am an unnatural child, an ill bird, *etc.*, when I come there mine intertainement shalbe accordingly for this geare. Well, I am content heere to cease, it neither being my purpose, nor to the purpose heere, to set downe all their magical ceremonial rites, used and due unto such several degree, *etc.*

To returne therfor againe to these our commenced divines, who when they have once gotten this degree upon them, there is now never a benefice in a shire, but if it be ready for them, they are fit for it. There is now no question to be made before any ordinarie in England of their learning. They need not now be posed by the doctors, by masse chancelor or masse commissarie, how many sonnes Noah had, or whether they can reade distinctly the homilies, injunctions and service booke; all this they could do whiles they were Bible clarkes and fellowes in the colledge; everie morning next their heartes, they said over this geare. Neither shal they be injoined to conne certayne chapters of the testament without booke, their hood and tippet sheweth they have learning inough; and together with their mother the universities' licence to preach, excuseth them of all this stirre, which other poore priestes do passe, but unto them it could not, without the dishonour of the universitie and shame of their degree, be offred. They therfore now (if before this time they have not had the ful order of priest-hood) easily obteine it without any difficultie. Only they must now kneele downe at their holy father the bishop's feet, who solemnely sitting in a chaire, layeth his simoniacal handes upon him, delivereth him the Bible into his handes, breatheth upon him, and giveth or rather selleth him his unholy ghost, as he shal know by the price of his boxe and writinges, ere he goe. I had like to have forgotten the cheefe matter of al (without which it could have beene no bargaine) namely, his solemne and corporal othe upon

the cover of the Bible or service booke, to be buxome
and obedient to his ordinarie and his substitutes, and
to vow his ca[53]nonicall obedience to all such ecclesiasticall orders, injunctions and degrees, as either are by
publike authoritie established and set forth, or hereafter
shalbe by the said authoritie made and set forth; that he
shal not preach any seditious or contentious doctrines,
neither any thing in reproofe of the proceedinges, orders
and injunctiones, by publike authoritie allowed; but shal
exhort al men unto the obedience of the same, *etc*. These
thinges being done, and his dimissaries[1] paied for, he
riseth up a ful priest in any ground of England, get him
now a benefice or a cure where he can.

He is now a priest sufficiently capable of any kind of
office, in any church or churches whatsoever, whether
to be a deane or an archdeacon of many hundred
churches, whether to be a parson of one or moe parishes,
whether to be an hired preacher comonly called a
Geneva doctor, for from thence this new office is (un-
witting to his Grace of Canterburie) stollen into the
Church of England, except peradventure they stand
before him but for mungrel curates still. Wel, if they
will have a personage [parsonage], they must either now
become chaplaines to some great Baal or other, that
hath store in his gift, or els make friendship, for love or
mony, to some inferior Baal, that is such a lord of some
towne or townes, or els enter in chaffaire[2] with some
other priest, for his roomth. And somwhat here would
be said of these Baal or lord patrones, what kind of
office they have in the Church of England, least hereafter I forget, as I doe sundrie other thinges.

It is not needfull heere, to dispute of these lord
patrons, when or how they tooke beginning: whither
at the beginning of the defection when the people first
slacted[3] and neglected their dutie, and gave up their
christian libertie, power, and interest in al the church
affaires, the choice, censuring, and deposing their

---

[1] A letter dimissory was one by a bishop recommending a candidate to
another diocese. Since "dimissaries" mean testicles, one wonders if
Barrow is purposely misspelling to ridicule the new priests.
[2] Chaffer — traffic, barter, buying and selling.
[3] Left undone, failed to pursue and complete, allowed to slip by.

officers, *etc.*, into the handes of their presbitry, as is
above declared: or at the flowing in of the deluge of
the Gentiles, when the provincial bishops, archbishops
and metropolitanes sprang up: or when the pope was
by the general consent of al princes, made supreme
head of the church, and the great tributes out of al
lands paied unto him, *etc.*, that then peradventure, he,
to gratifie these princes and lordes, of his meere be-
nignitie granted unto them the nomination unto
bishoprickes and personages, *etc.* But how or when
they sprang up it skilleth [mattereth] not, we finding
them as antichristian as any of the other. No such
office we ever read of, to belong to the church of Christ,
neither any such lord there, to take away all the libertie
and interest of the people in the choice of their pastor.
Christ's servantes are now no longer wardes, neither are
in this maner to be bought and sold, as open and sheep
in a faire or market. But see, when the lorde's beautiful staffe of his holy government and order is broken,
how he dissanulleth his covenant with those people, and
delivereth them up to the destroiers, to these greedy
wolves and hungrie foxes, as a pray [prey]. For these
lordes patrons, to whome these advowsens belong, are
to apoint and present their clarkes unto these benefices:
who being admitted and instituted by the [54] bishop,
etc., the people have no more power in the negative, to
refuse or depose him (be he never so unable or unworthy) than they had before in the affirmative, to
chuse or elect their minister. But these lord patrons
may alien or sell their advowsons by the law of the land,
even as any other part of their inheritance or possessions: yea, be these patrons never so infamously and
notoriously wicked, gluttons, covetous, prophane atheistes, *etc.* Yea, if he have forty of these advowsons, and
those distant many hundred miles, even to the uttermost boundes of the land: yet is he to all these townes
to present their priestes, except he make lapse, and then
falleth it into the bishop of that diocesse his handes.
Thus must the greatest doctor and clerke of them that
wil have a benefice enter, and be presented therunto by
some of these Baals or other, unto the Ordinarie or

bishop of that diocesse, by whose letters of institution
he is inducted, ringeth his belles, *etc.*, payeth his first
fruites (after the Jewish, or rather popish maner), his
proxes' procurations, *etc.*

Now the parsonage or vicarage to which they enter,
is to be townepriest or parson, or vickar of a certaine
parish, to reade them their service, according to the
times and maner apointed, to marrie, to burie, to
christen, to deliver their other sacrament of their communion, to visit and housel[1] their sick with the said
booke and sacrament, to receave their tithes, offringes,
mortuaries,[2] *etc.* Then (if he be so cunning, and as he
can intend and afford it) to preach them a sermon of
an hower long: but that is in his libertie how seldome
he wil, except his benefice be a certayne [number] of
poundes in the queene's booke, and then in deed is he
bound to bestow a sermon on his parish fower times in
the yeare, either by himself, or by his learned substitute.[3] By this we may also see these their parsonages
and vicarages to be in name, office, and function as
antichristian and popish, as any of the other: no such
office or officer mentioned in the testament of Christ.
For the men that possesse them, and those by common
estimation even the best, most holy, and learned of
them; I have breefly, but verie truly shewed, what
maner persons they are; noseled [nuzzled, nurtured]
even from their mother's breastes in profanenes, heathenisme, vaine philosophy, ungodly artes; how they
are trained up in idolatrie, superstition, and most filthie Phil. 3: 18 *etc.*
abhominations, perjurie, blasphemie, pride, vainglorie,
ambition, studiing these vaine artes, and even divinitye
(which they number among these artes) for filthy lucre,
ostentation, and their bellies' sake, making not only
an art, but a stage play and an occupation of religion;

---

[1] Administer the communion to the sick.
[2] A mortuary was a fine due to the archdeacon or bishop upon the death
of a beneficed clergyman within the archdeaconry or diocese. But the
meaning as Barrow uses it seems to be funeral fees.
[3] See *Injunctions Given by the Queene's Majestie. The First Yere of the
Raigne of Our Soveraigne Lady Queene Elizabeth* ([London], 1559), A ii
recto and *verso*, A iii *recto*. The earliest regulations of Elizabeth prescribed a sermon a month, and required preachers " in their owne persons "
to preach once each quarter at least, or else to read a prescribed homily
every Sunday.

1 Tim. 1: 3, 4

1 Tim. 6: 3, 4, 5,
20, 21 with their traditionall and philosophicall glosses, corrupting, obscuring, and perverting the pure text with their logicall conclusions and rhetorical figures; give libertie to their wittes in their learning to deface, strive, and dispute against the holy knowne truth of God, making and tossing it as a tennise ball amongst them, both publikly in the schooles and privatly in their colledges at their problemes. In which munkish dennes they lurke and lead their lives, in all manner [55] of idlenes and pride; not to speake of those secret sinnes and abhominations, which are commonly committed amongst these Sodomites, which live in such fellowships and fraternities, where God's pure religion and holy ordinance of matrimonie are banished, as amongst them. The particular abuses of which societies and colleges, yea, even of their universitie in general, with all that more than heathenish disorder, popish abhominations, which are there without shame injoined and committed, wherwith the youth, yea, almost all estates, of the land are leavened and poisoned, would in it self require a long and peculiar treatise, but summarily to recken up and bring to light.

I hope, by this litle which hath beene said, concerning the education and training of these our great divines, it apeareth unto all men (that will judg by the word of God and are endued with the spirit of God) what kind of fellowships these universitie colleges are, what kind of cages full of uncleane birdes, of foule and hateful spirites, *etc.* Let these learned clarkes daube them with their untempered morter, whiles yet the time serveth them, yet is their judgment of the Lord: the word is gone out from his mouth, it hasteneth apace, and cannot be called back: even the same judgment and end, which are in their sight executed upon their elder brethren and sisters the templars, the monkes, and knightes of their St. Jhon of Jerusalem, the abbies, fririers, nunneries, they had one and the self same popish original with these: they still retaine the same damnable and incurable abuses: therfore the same, or greater judgmentes remayne them. Let us see if the

Master of Peter-house[1] be now able to ward this blow:
sure I doubt Ely minster wil not defend him from the
haile of God's wrath, in that day. He hath hitherto
taken but half his tale with him, therfore his reckoning
is behind. It is but an easie point of learning, both
to frame and answere other men's, or rather his owne
argumentes: we in the countrie which are not acquainted with such figures, count such but to skirmish
with their owne shadow, and deeme them not the wisest
men in a shire. But this learned doctor by the figure
of omission, in an evill conscience, tooke no more of the
argument, than he was able to deal withall, namely
thus much. The universities of Oxford and Cambridg
have a popish original. Therfore Queene Elisabeth
ought to abolish them.[2] Let him now take the rest of
the argument, as it was made in a marginal note[3] in
the side of a blasphemous booke of his, and put it together thus. The universities of Cambridg and Oxford
have the same popish and idolatrous beginning that
the colleges of monkes, freers, nunnes, and those vermine had, and stil retaine the same unsufferable and
incurable abuses, *etc.* Therfore Queene Elisabeth hath,
and ought by as good right to abolish them, as her
progenitor did the abbaies. Thus was it made before
unto him: but of his doctorlie authoritie, writing with
privilege, he tought [thought, taught] he might take
and leave at his pleasure; especially, having to do with
poore prisoners, which can have [56] no place given to
defend their wrongs, nor to answere unto his lies and
slaunders. But let him yet upon better advise, make
a better answere to this one argument; til then, we will
not trouble him with more. I doubt upon a better
view, he shall scarse find them so like those floorishing
vines in the Lorde's garden, as unto the vine of Sodome,
and the vines of Gomorrahii: their grapes are poisoned

[1] Robert Some was appointed Master of Peterhouse on May 11, 1589.
[2] Robert Some, *A Godly Treatise, wherein Are Examined and Confuted
Many Execrable Fancies* (1589), p. 2.
[3] Barrow's *marginal* notes and then his *interleaved* notes were seized. We
do not have these marginal notes, but we have twelve pages of interleaved notes. See Barrow's "Reply to Dr. Some's *A Godly Treatise
Containing and Deciding Certaine Questions*," interleaved note on p. 12,
reproduced in this volume.

grapes, their clusters bitter clusters: their wine is the poison of dragons, and the cruel gall of aspes. Neither shall he find them so like to the scholes of the prophets he speaketh of, which purely kept and taught the word of God amongst them, in those corrupt times; as unto the pope's seminaries, being as ready upon the least change of the wheather [*sic*] now to serve him, as ever they were; being not unlike the Turke's seraglia in Constantinople, in which place his Janetsaries which are the guard of his person, are first trained and instituted in the discipline of his war, before they serve him either abroade, or in his court. And sure these universitie knightes are the very guard of antichriste's throne, the strength of his battel, his instrumentes to carry forth his wares, to subdue the people unto him and keep them in his obedience, as bitter enemies of the church and servantes of God, and of all righteousnes, as these Turkish Janetzaries unto these christened regions, with whome they have to doe.

But it is time now to returne to these our universitie divines and their ministerie againe, being somwhat overlong staied by this frivolous doctor in the way. I have already shewed their education, learning, degrees, and also in what maner, and upon what conditions the best of them come by and hold their priesthood: that is to say, how they first blaspheme God's holy name, in swearing after that idolatrous maner: how they solemnely and advisedlie forswere and abjure the Lord Jesus Christ, in swearing their canonical obedience to the antichristian throne of these bishops, their courtes, and cannons: for two so contrarie maisters they cannot serve, as Christ and antichrist, neither have communion with both. And how they now remaine the marked soldiers of the beast, even in the forehead, having taken his licence and seales; and how by this their othe and subscription to their Romish trumperie and devilish devises, they have resolutely forsworne Gode's truth, made shipwrack of faith and a good conscience (if any they had before) and how by taking this licence with this limitation, they have emancipate the whole word of God (as much as in them lieth) unto these bishops or

Deut. 6: 13

Amos 8: 14

Zephan. 5

Math. 5: 34

Revel. 13: 16 & 14: 9 etc.

Psa. 94: 20

2 Cor. 6: 15

Gal. 2: 5

rather the pope's cannons. And yet (to make their sinne the more odious and inexcusable) these slaves to sinne, are not only sworne unto such decrees as are already made (although nothing can almost be added to the wickednes and blasphemie of them) but even have bound themselves by othe to such decrees, as they hereafter shal make, being by publike authoritie of the land enjoined, *etc.* Also how they hereby become the vowed servantes and bondmen, the marked ministers and waged soldiours of antichrist. I have also shewed their ministerie to be antichristian, adulterate and vagrant, without place, people, chardge, [57] office, government: and how they must come by it by as unlawful meanes, even by symonical compactes, open bribery and extortion, as the excessive price of their boxe and writinges unto the bishop and his clerke, their first fruites (not to speake of other secret bargaines how they come by the patrone's good wil, *etc.*) declare.

Moreover I have shewed, how their office of parson or vickar is as popish, strange, antichristian: and how their entrance and induction is as popish and Jewish, as the rest: and how the function of, and their behaviour in this office is yet worst of all, most corrupt, blasphemous, and abhominable: which now but by as slight a running over their administration, wil even with detestation appeare unto al men. Whose infinite and odious sinnes heerin to set downe in particuler, according to their hainousnes, no tongue or pen of any mortal man is able; for that were to nomber the haires of the beast, or to divide the droppes of a running river. If I therfore set downe some such principal and especial heades, from whence these mischeves and their particular transgressions flowe, as I remember them (who know of many, but a few) leaving the further search of the rest, and consideration of these, to the further labour and judgment of the godly, by the Scriptures: as also, the more particular remorse and repentance of them, to their consciences which have committed, and shal accompt before the Lord for the same. I hope (I say) by that time, the delusions of these Babilonish divines and Egiptian inchanters, wil apeare unto al men, save unto

them that perish; and their madnes be made so manifest,
as both chey and their proselites shalbe left naked,
without one excuse or figleafe to cover their shame.

Now then as the education, training, learning, degrees
ministerie, maner and conditions of receaving that office
and maner of comming by, and entrance into the same,
have beene partly described; so was the endes and function of their ministerie and office, a litle touched in a
word or two: namly, how they al are, by othe and office
bound, to reade and observe the injunctions, *etc.*, to
reade their service book at their apointed times, places
and maner, according to the same to administer their
sacramentes, church women, visit the sick, burie the
dead, *etc.*, and only for this ministerie they receave the
offringes, tithes, mortuaries and wages of the people.
Also it hath beene shewed, that preaching is no part of
their office or ministerie, but only in certaine special
cases (where that benefice is at a certaine rate in the
queene's book) required, and that not necessarily laid
upon the person of such a parson, but only quarterly
injoined at four solemne feastes of the yeare, as at their
Christmas, Easter, *etc.* [Whit Sunday and Michaelmas],
and may be performed or supplied by ther substitute.[1]

Heere also must be observed, that a person or vickar,
is not by law nor office injoined to be resident and give
attendance in person unto his charge and flock, but
may be absent at his wil, and where he will, so he find
the parish a jornay man [a vicar] to reade their service,
administer their sacramentes, *etc.* Yea, and as he commeth unto them without the [58] people's privitie, wil,
or consent, so may he stand a parson or (as these learned
preachers would have him termed) a pastor unto them,
though he never see his flock, nor his flock him. So
may he also by law (as the best of them usually do) upon
their owne liking or disliking (but especially upon the

---

[1] In the *Advertisements* (London, [1565]), which stemmed from the Queen's
letters of January 25, 1564/5, preachers were required to preach " in
theyr owne persons, or by a learned substitute, once in every three moneths
of the yere " (sig. A iiii *recto*). This alteration from a sermon a month to
a sermon each quarter, as seen in the *Injunctions* of 1559, evidently was
included because too many pastors were "dumb dogs " — non-preaching
clergy. The phrase " yf the Parson be able " indicates that many were
not able to preach.

offer of a better living) depart from them, change or sell his office, without the people's knowledge or privitie. For as their ministery is not tied to any office, so is not their office tied to any charge. Are not these miserable 2. Cor. 11: 20 pastors, trow we ? Or are not the people more miserable, that have such shepheardes and guides set over them, whome they must (wil they nil they)[1] nourish with their goodes, *etc.*, to the gathering up wherof, these priestes wil looke wel enough, without regard or respect of persons, whether they be rich or poore, old or young, widowe or fatherles, that is al one to them, they wil not spare their due: they take up al with the angle, they catch it in their net, and gather it in their yarne. It 1. Sam. 2: 12 skilleth not to them whose it be, whether the goodes of *etc.* the infidel or of the beleever. It skilleth not them Ezec. 34: 2 *etc.* whome they spoile, whether the poore, the widow, or the fatherles, if they fall within the boundes, and pre- Mic. 3: 2 *etc.* cinctes of their parish: they regard not by what right, or after what maner they have it, whither by Jewish tithes and offringes, or popish chrismatories[2] and mortuaries. They regard not, so [long as] the princes and Pro. 30: 20 their lord bishop's lawes allowe them, though God's Zach. 11: 5 lawes expressly forbid. That day of accompt they put far off, and think to do wel inough then: yea, they in the meane while bless themselves in the name of the Lord, though they commit all this wickednes. Of al that groweth or increaseth within the compasse of their parish, whither corne, wood, grasse, or cattel, the priest wil have his part; yea, for whom soever is borne or dieth in his parish, he wil have a fee; and for this geare he standeth a priest to the whole parish and al the inhabitantes therof indifferently. If the devil of hel would come and dwel in his parish, he were a priest for him, and would for his goodes administer the sacramentes, *etc.*, unto him also.

But heere, before I begin to deale with their maner of administration, it were not amisse, in few wordes, to shew the damnable filthines of their maintenance for their ministerie. Christ having abrogate the Leviticall

---

[1] Willy-nilly ; if they are willing or if they are unwilling.
[2] Vessels containing the chrism or oil for anointing.

priesthood and law, instituted for the gospel an other
ministerie, and for the ministerie an other maintenance.
He ordeined in his testament, that the minister of the
gospel should live of the gospel, the shepheard of the
1. Cor. 9: 7 *etc.* flock he feedeth, the husbandman of the vineyard he
dresseth and keepeth.   Now this flock consisted not of
gotes, swine, doggs, wolves, *etc.*, neither is this shepheard
limited, or sheepe constrained to a tenth, or any stinted
part or portion; but according to the present want of
the one, and estate of the other, this matter is otherwise
provided; they together releeving him according to his
present need; he together with them, bearing the bur-
then of their present and common povertie, everie one
2. Cor. 8: 13 that is taught in the [59] word, freely contributing and
Gal. 6: 6 & 4: 15 imparting, even of al their goodes, to the competent
maintenance of such as instruct them in the word, and
1 Thes. 5: 12, 13 have the oversight of them, not unto riot and excesse,
but unto sufficiencie.   Which contribution, as it is a
2 Thes. 3: 9 dutie of the saintes, so is it also, in the maner of it, a free
Exo. 25: 2 offring of their benevolence, and an holy almes unto
the Lord: by which almes and contribution, our saviour
2 Cor. 9: 4 Christ himself, his apostles, and al the ministers or
Phil. 4: 18 officers of the church of Christ, which live or receave
any thing of the church, were, and are to be maintained.
Heb. 13: 16 Within the boundes of which sober mediocritie and
Luke 8: 3 christian modestie, whiles these prowd prelates and
John 13: 6 greedy priestes wil not be held, the one sort breaketh
out into al excesse and riot, the other into miserable
1 Cor. 16: 1, 2 rapine and extortion, thrusting their fleshhook into
everie poore bodie's kettle, and (as it were) plucking
the bread from them and their children's mouthes,
wherwith they should be sustained; besides the heinous
unlawfulnes of the very action it self, and high sacriledge
they commit therin: which, whiles a certaine doctor of
theirs [Dr. Some] hath of late labored to approve; the
wicked man hath termed this blessed almes, and holy
contribution of the saintes (in contempt therof and of
them which are or have beene sustained therby) the
Almes Basket:[1] yea, to disgrace the truth, and to hide the

---

[1] Robert Some, *A Godly Treatise, wherein Are Examined and Confuted
Many Execrable Fancies,* pp. 6, 9.

superfluitie, excesse pride, and unsatiate covetise [covetousness] of the English clergie; he maketh it a common custome in his slanderous pamphlet, to leave out, or take inn at his pleasure, or mistake, where and what seemeth good unto him: as heere he hath done the ninth chapter of the II Corinthians for the ninth chapter of the I Corinthians, and so still fighteth with himself, and confuteth his owne idle fantacies.[1] The one place speaketh of the general charitie we ought to carrie towardes al saintes, even to them of other congregations and countries: the other, of the peculier maintenance of the minister of Christ, how he ought to be maintained by that flock, to which he administreth, and not by infidels or wicked persons, to whome his ministerie belongeth not. Likewise that place Gallatians 6, verse 6, where they that are taught in the word, are commanded to impart of al their goodes unto them that instruct them in the word: which place evidently sheweth, what kind of maintenance belongeth to the ministers of the gospell, who ought to contribute, in what maner, and how far. Namely al such faithful to whome this ministerie belongeth, and they not by any rated proportions, as tenthes, or thyrdes, *etc.*, but even in love, to make him partaker of that litle or much the Lord sendeth, according to his present wantes and necessary uses, who if he have [sufficiency in respect] to food and rayment, ought to be therwith content. This place, this Chemarim[2] would put away, with a marvailing at our folly in quoting it in the side of his former booke, against the stinted tithes and accursed goodes and offringes of the prophane and wicked, wherof he and his fellow priests are maintained. 1 Tim. 6: 8

[60] Wherby it is evident, that these priestes, which thus are maintained, either by these Jewish tithes and offringes, as at the baptisme of children, and purification of women, or by the goodes and wages of the profane and wicked, are not the ministers of Christ. For (saith the Holy Ghost) if there be a change of the Numb. 18

Levi. 22: 25

Ezec. 44: 7

---

1 *Ibid.*, p. 8.
2 Zephaniah, 1: 4 — " I will cut off the remnants of Baal from this place, and the name of the Chemarims with the priests."

Heb. 7: 12   priesthood, then of necessitie must there be a change
of the law. But these men, both priestes and people,
which either pay or receave these tithes and offringes,
still keepe these Levitical lawes for the maintenance of
the ministerie: therfore they not having made a change
Acts 15   of those lawes, belong not to the ministerie and kingdom
of Christ. For (as I have shewed) these are not the
Gal. 4: 9 & 5: 2, lawes which Christ hath instituted for the maintenance
3, 4
Col. 2: 20   of the ministerie of the gospel: neither can these lawes
now be joined unto, or made to accord with the gospell.
For in reteining the gospel, we abrogate the ceremonial
law, in renuing the ceremonial law, or any part therof,
we revive the Levitical ministerie, and therby abolish
the gospel and ministerie of Christ: yea, in retaining
and cleaving unto the shadow, we loose the substance,
and so are left and shut up under the law, and are
abolished from Christ, whome we denie to be either
come, dead, risen againe or ascended, whiles we stil
retaine the ceremonie and shadow. Now it is apparant,
that tithes and offringes were meerly ceremonial, and
instituted for the maintenance of the Levitical ministerie,
and belong not to the ministerie of Christ, neither have
any reservation in the testament of Christ, but sundrie
Num. 18: 3, 28 expresse places there are against them: and in place
therof, we have (as hath been said) the free contribution
of al the faithful, not limited or stinted, but extending
to the communication of al the goodes they have. But
these priestes and people stil retaine the Levitical
decimations in the same forme, to the same endes, *etc.*
Therefore must they needes be under that dangerous
estate above declared. Neither wil their doctor's popish
distinction help the matter. Saieth he: the Church of
England reteineth, not tithes, as any part of the ceremonial law, but as a stipend for the ministers.[1] Why,
I besech him, how did the Jewes reteine and use them?
Was it not as a stipend likewise for their ministers?
And may this law, this stipend now, fit the ministerie
of Christ? Why hath Christ then made new? Or
how is the old law changed with the old ministerie, if

---

[1] See Robert Some, *A Godly Treatise, wherein Are Examined and Confuted
Many Execrable Fancies,* p. 9.

the law of tithes be stil kept? Might not this doctor
as wel bring in the cities and suburbs which were given
to the Levites and priestes, for them and their families
to dwel in, or any other Levitical ceremonie, by the
same excuse? And I doubt not but they would do so
also, were it not that they have already much more
ample allowance in the stead therof in everie citie and
towne of the land: where the parson (yea some where,
both parson and vickar) is indowed with houses and
gleab landes besides their tythes, not to speake of the
whole lordships and townes, that the collegiate priesthood possesse: and yet these cormorantes are never
satisfied, these horsleaches stil suck, though blood in
abundance runne out of their wide mouthes. [61] And
heere also by the way, the unlawfulnes of their gleebes
would be noted; both in that they have no warrant in
the testament of Christ, being so fixed and certaine, he
having there set downe an other kind of maintenance,
not fixed, not certaine, but according to the present
wantes and occasiones, *etc.*, as also that that tying of
land in a parish to the ministerie there, doth presuppose
and necessarily presume of a church alwaies in that
parish; where as the prophet saith: they that were my
people yesterday, are risen up on the other side, as
against an enemie, *etc.*[1] How many famous churches
see we removed and fallen? How many godly fathers
have had wicked children? Godly ages, wicked successors? Many other reasons might be brought against
these gleabes, for which these belly priestes so crie out,
as concerning their idolatrous originall and abuse, being
given to the maintenance of a popish ministerie, and
therfore ought rather to be put to civill uses, and not
to the maintenance of the ministerie of Christ.

But to returne to their tythes againe: wherin as yet
I could never see any difference betwixt the Jewes and
them, save that these swineheardes tythe piggs, geese,
etc., and al such uncleane beastes and fowles for gaine,
which were an abhomination unto the Jewes. But some
of them would hide this, by the prince's commandement.
We have in many places shewed, that the prince hath no

---

[1] Micah 2: 8.

power to breake Gode's lawes, or innovate or alter Christ's testament. Heere I would know of them, whither the due paiment of tithes, *etc.*, was not often commanded by the godly kinges of Juda also. Let them reade the stories of Ezechiah, Joziah, Nehemiah, *etc.*, let them reade the prophecies of Joel, Haggai, Zacharie, Malachie. Why then, we see the commandement of the prince makes no difference betweene them and the Jewes herein: the commandement of the prince cannot alter the propertie of God's lawes: the commandement of the prince can be no warrant or excuse, for the altering of Christ's testament. But what excuse can they now forge for their offringes at the baptisme of children, at their purifying of women ? Is not this also manifest Judaisme ? I wil not heere speake of the superstition of the action, but of the oblation only: what difference is there betwixt them and the Jewes herein ? They wil say the Jewes offred pigeons, *etc.*, not money. But they must understand, the Jewes had a law also of redeeming their sacrifices for mony, and so offred mony also when the sacrifice would not be had, and in sundry other cases. This then wilbe no sufficient difference. I doubt therfore they must be driven to Doctor Robert Some his catholike and universal distruction [distinction] abovenamed. They retaine them not as any part of the ceremoniall law, but as the minister's stipend. Wel, let this distinction be authenticall, because it goes with priviledge: yet let a poore Christian aske them this question; where they find in the New Testament, that Christians may make such offringes, or the minister of Christ live of such offrings ? I suppose they will take day to answere: and I (because I will not too far overchardge them at once) wil forbeare here to [62] call them to accompt for their mortuaries, or portion which they take of the goodes of the dead, for their oblations at their Easter sacrament, at the mariing, and at the buriing of any in their parish. This I think would prove a combersome peece of work for them to approve and justifie by Christe's testament, to belong to the maintenance or office of his ministerie. And sure, I take no great pleasure to rave more than needes I must, in this their

Levit. 12: 6

Levit. 27

doung, which is so grosse, as even with the reciting, it is refuted. So that I hope, by this litle which hath beene said, concerning their Leviticall tythinges, their Jewish oblations, their heathenish and popish customes, *etc.*, it evidently may apeare to all men (in whome is any light) that neither this their ministerie, or these their ministers, which are thus maintained, are of Christ, or belong to his church. Yf this yet be not plaine inough, let such as doubt, give eare to their administration, which now followeth to be examined.

Which administration of theirs, because it is so ample (for the help of my memorie, and that the matter may be the better understood) I will for this time divide it into necessarie and voluntarie. By necessarie, I meane that publike administration, wherunto by law, office, and othe they are bound: by voluntarie, I meane their extraordinarie paines taking in preaching, reading lectures on the weeke daies, catechising families, *etc.* And first (as order requireth) I wil deale with the more general, with that of necessity, which law requireth of all priestes: wherunto, both they, their church-wardens and side-men are bound by othe, the one to observe, the other to see it observed, and to present the defaltes. And this (because it is so infinite, and extendeth so largely, almost to the practise and execution of all the injunctions and orders of their church, *etc.*), I will only (or chiefly at the least) here meddle with their publike administration in their church, in their worship of God, *etc.*, and that but with some few (I will not say chief) thinges: for yet the subject is too large for my capacitie.

Unto this ministration, for their better instruction and direction in all thinges, as also that there might be found one uniforme order amongst them in all places, they have one service book, commonly called *The Book of Common Praier*: unto this are all the priestes of the land sworne, to use it in maner and forme prescribed. Now in this book is included the whole forme and substance of their ministerie. Heere are their praires made to their hand, and prescribed what praiers to say in the morning, and likewise what at evensong: as also what psalmes, chapters, pistles and gospels to read in their due seasons, what in the winter, what in the sommer, what in the Lent, what in the Advent. Heere are set downe their praiers, chapters, *etc.*, for their fastes, their solemne feastes and saintes' daies, yea, and for everie other day of the yeare. [63]

For the Sonday is a governing day, and is written in their calender with red letters, and ruleth all the daies of the week, save certaine unruly daies and their eaves, which will not be governed by it, but chalenge to themselves a peculiar worship also: they having their daies in the same calender written with great letters too, and that which more is, their eaves written with red letters. And because they are but strangers and come but once in the yeare, they looke for the more solemne intertainment, that the priest should diligently watch, and the people wait for their comming, and make preparation accordingly: if they come on a cluster, or at some solemne and double feast, then to intertaine them with new clothes, cleane houses, garnished with greene bowghes, or holly and ivye, with good cheare and much pastime, al work on these their idol daies, laid aside. Yea, though they come but one alone, and that on the week day, yet that week is not S. [Saint] Sonday, Lord of the Ascendent, it is a part of his service to give warning unto the people of the others comming, that they keep his or her eave with fasting and praier; that upon their day they keep an holy feast, abstaine from labour, *etc.* Moreover, by this book are the priests to administer their sacramentes, by this book to church their women, by this book to marry, by this book to visit and housle the sick, by this book to burie the dead, by this book to keep their rogation,[1] to say certaine psalmes and praiers over the corne and grasse, certayne gospels at crosswaies, *etc.* This booke is good at al assaies;[2] it is the only book of the world. He that can but orderly and distinctly reade this booke, may get a living by it. It is no marvaile though they be sworne to and by this

---

[1] A rogation was the chanting of the litany of the saints on Monday, Tuesday, and Wednesday preceding Ascension Day.
[2] In every crisis, on every occasion, in any attempt.

booke. Many great thinges might be said of this book,
how it was made by certayne learned bishops, afterward
godly martyres, and how some of the martyres used
part of it (as the letany) the night before they suffered,
etc. Well, who translated it we will not contend. For
the thing it self, it is evident to be abstracted out of the
pope's blasphemous masse-book, and how consonant it
is unto the word of God, remaineth to be examined;
and shall, through God's grace, by the discussing of
some particular pointes, though not of everie singular
error (for that were an endles labour) apeare: and so
shall neither the martyres' use commend, nor our dislike condemne, but God's word be judge of all.

To let passe therfore what in times past this book
hath beene, and how it hath beene used, either by the
pope or those bishops; we find it now to be the very
groundworcke of their faith, church and ministerie, in
place to them of the word of God, as from whence they
fetch all their direction for all thinges; yea, herein above
the word of God, in that from hence they fetch not only
their rules wherby to doe thinges, but even the verie
things themselves that they do, as their leitourgies, *etc.*
So far is this book from being subject to the word of
God, as it in al things overruleth the word of God,
dismembreth, rendeth, corrupteth, perverteth, abuseth
it to their stinted mattens and evensong, to their idol
[64] dayes, fastes, feastes, *etc.* Yea, the word of God
may not be taught, but where this book hath first beene
read, and hath had the preeminence. This booke in
their churches must have the soveraintie, it may not be
gainsaied or controld, or if it be, the word of God must
give place, that priest called *coram nobis*,[1] lessoned, and
scholed; if he wil not be conformable, deprived of his
priestdome: if he be found stout or contumacious, then
is he cast into prison to coole him, until his stomake
come downe, that he make sute unto his grace or some
other lord bishop his ordinarie, and enter bonde to be
conformable, or silent.

Moreover this booke, in that it standeth a publike

---

[1] Before us — that is, the Archbishop, Bishop, or Chancellor. A play on
the words used in royal writs.

prescript continued leiturgy (not as yet to come to the particulars or meddle with the blasphemous contentes therof but to speake generally of it) as if it were the best that ever was devised by mortal man: yet in this place and use, being brought into the church, yea, or into any private house, it becometh a detestable idol, standing for that it is not in the church of God and consciences of men: namely, for holy, spirituall, and faithfull prayer,

Lev. 1, 2, 3, 4 chapters

it being nothing lesse, but rather abhominable and lothsome sacrifice in the sight of God, even as a dead dogg. Now under the law, might neither any corrupt or any unlawful sacrifice, with any seene blemish, be offred at the altar, nether any part of any beast (though whiles it lived never so sufficient) being slayne before it be brought unto the altar, it was abhomination unto the Lord. Everie sacrifice must be brought quick and new unto the altar, and there be slayne everie morning

1 Cor. 6: 19

and evening: how much more in this spiritual temple of God, where the offringes are spiritual, and God hath

1 Pet. 2: 5
Revel. 21: 10
Rom. 12: 1

made al his servantes kings, and priestes, to offer up acceptable sacrifices unto him, through Jesus Christ, who hath therunto given them his holy spirit into their hearts, to helpe their infirmities, and teach them to crie,

Rom. 8: 26, 15
Ephe. 4: 7, 8
etc.

Abba Father. How much more hath he which ascended, given graces to those his servantes (whome he useth in such high services) to the repairing of the saintes, the worke of the ministerie, and the edification of the church ? Unto whome God useth them, as his mouth, the church againe on the other side, useth them as their mouth unto the Lord. Shall we think that God hath any time left these his servantes so singly furnished and

Isa. 28: 9, etc.
Heb. 5: 13

destitute of his grace, that they cannot find words according to their necessities and faith, to expresse their wantes and desires, but need thus to be taught line unto line, as children new weaned from the brestes, what and when to say, how much to say, and when to make an end; to say this collect at the beginning, that at the end, that before, the tother [sic] after, this in the morning, that at after noone, etc. How like children, or rather like masking fooles, are these great clarkes dressed ? Shew they not hereby, that either they have no faith,

or els are such infantes, as they have more need to be 1 Cor. 3: 2
fed, than to divide the portion unto others? Know
they, trow we, what praier or the spirit of God meaneth?
Praier I take to be a confident demanding which faith Heb. 4: 16
maketh thorow the Holy Ghost, [65] according to the Ephe. 3: 12
wil of God, for their present wantes, estate, *etc.* How 1 Joh. 2: 1
now? Can any read, prescript, stinted leitourgie, which
was penned many yeares or daies before, be said a Eph. 6: 18
powring forth of the heart unto the Lord? Or those Phil. 4: 6
faithful requestes which are stirred up in them, by the The whole
Holy Ghost, according to their present wantes and estate Psalmes.
of their heartes, or church? Unlesse they can say, that
their heartes and church stand in the same estate now,
and so still to their lives' end shal continue, without Lament. 3: 40,
either further increase or decrease, change or alteration, 41
as they did then: yea, that their childer's[1] children shal
also so continue, to whome they leave and incommend Joel 2: 14
[entrust] this leitourgie, unto the worlde's end. What
a strange estate is this, that alwaies thus standeth at a Hose. 14: 2
stay? The way of the righteous (Solomon saith) shineth Pro. 4: 18, 19
as the light, that shineth more and more unto the per- Luk. 11: 23
fect day: as on the contrarie, the way of the wicked is
as the darknes, they know not wherin they shall fall.
Our saviour Christ saith, that if we gather not, we
scatter. The apostle Peter willeth the new borne babes 1. Pet. 2: 2
to desire the sincere milke of the word, that they may Eph. 4: 13
grow therby; until they come to the measure of the age
of the fulnes of Christ, saith the apostle Paul. Now
then, if they and their church increase not in the measure
of knowledg, grace, holines, *etc.*, it is an infallible signe
that they have not the spirit of God. If they do increase,
why then is not God served with his owne best giftes?
Is not the judgment of the prophet then upon them; Mal. 1: 14
which saith, cursed be the deceiver, which hath in his
flock a male, yet voweth and sacrificeth unto the Lord
a corrupt thing.

Is this old rotten leitourgis [*sic*] their new songs they
sing unto the Lord with and for his graces? May
such old written rotten stuffe be called praier, the odours
of the saintes, burnt with that heavenly fire of the altar,

---

[1] Childer is the obsolete plural of child.

the lively graces of the spirit, *etc.* May reading be said praying? May such apocrypha trumperie be brought into the church of God, and there be read, reverenced and receaved, as the sacred word of God? Thrust upon men's consciences, yea upon God himself whether he wil or no? Is not this presumptuously to undertake to teach the Spirit of God? And to take away his office, which (as hath beene said) instructeth al the children of God to pray, even with inward sighes and grones inexpressable, and giveth both wordes and utterance, yea, and (as the apostle Jhon saieth) we need no other teacher to these thinges, than that annointing which we have receaved, and dwelleth in us. Is not this (if they wil have their written stuffe to be held and used as praier) to bind the Holy Ghost to the froth and leaven of their lips, as it were to the holy word of God? Is it not utterly to quench and extinguish the Spirit of God, both in the ministerie and people, whiles they tye both them and God to their stinted numbred praiers?

Is this the unitie and uniformitie that ought to be in al churches? And is amongst al Christe's servantes, to make them agree in a stinking patcherie divised apocrypha leiturgie, good for nothing but for cushsions and pillowes for the idle priestes, and profane carnal atheistes to [66] rock them a sleepe and keep them in securitie, wherby the conscience is no way either touched, edified, or bettered? Truly I am ashamed to think, much more to write of so grosse and filthie abhominacion, so generally received, even of al estates, of these partes of the world, who have by a popish custom and tradition received it one of, and from an other, without any warrant from the word. For the apostles (I am sure), these maister builders, have left no such president [precedent] in, or commandement unto the churches, neither given them any such power to bring in or set up any such apocrypha lyturgie in the church of God. They alwaies used spiritual praiers according to their present wantes and occasions, and so taught all churches to pray, alwaies, with all maner of praier and supplication in the spirit, and therby to make knowen their wantes, and shew their requestes in al thinges unto God their heaven-

Rom. 8: 26, 27

1 Joh. 2: 27

1. Tim. 2: 1
Heb. 13: 15

Eph. 6: 18
Phil. 4: 6

ly Father. Our saviour Christ also, he taught his 1 Cor. 14: 15
disciples, that God is a Spirit, and wil be worshipped in Joh. 4: 24
spirit and truth. He hath likewise set downe most
excellent rules, and a most absolute forme for al praiers
in that part of Scripture Mathew 6: 9, 10, 11, 12, 13,
commonly (but falsly) called the Lord's Praier:[1] wherin
he hath most notably instructed, directed, and restrained
our ignorant and inordinate desires, to those excellent
heades. In which, whatsoever is needful for us to desire,
or lawful for us to pray, is in some one or other of those
branches included: everie one of them being a base and
foundation, wherupon and wherby to frame many mil-
lions of several peticions, according to the several wantes
and occasions, at such several times as the saintes have
cause to pray. They are all of them, so many ever-
running fountaines, from which Gode's servantes by the
Holy Ghost, derive and draw continually fresh and new
graces; and are al together such an abisme[2] and unmeasured sea of wisdome, from which al Christe's servantes thorough the world, have alwaies fetched all their
knowledg, graces, comfort, and assurance of and in their
praiers (according to the capatitie of the vessel of their
faith) some more, some lesse, al some. Yet have not al
of them together, much lesse any one of them is able in
the litle dish of his shallow understanding, to comprise
the unmeasurable depth and greatnes of this ocean of
al wisdome and grace. Wherby it is evident, as also by
the circumstances and maner of delivering the same by
our saviour Christ; by his apostles', disciples' and churches' spiritual use of praier according to their present estate
and wantes, that these prescript wordes were not given
or injoyned as a prescript praier, so to be used by any,
even the wisest, much lesse the simpler, unbroken up,
unexpounded, *etc.*, so much as a compendious summarie

---

1 The Barrowists believed that the Lord's Prayer did not represent Christ's
own personal prayer, since he did not need to pray that he should not be
led into temptation; the Lord's Prayer was a pattern, a guide, for all
who wished to learn to pray by the Spirit. To Barrow the rote repetition
of prescribed words was not prayer. For Barrow, prayer was an out-
pouring of the Spirit, a confident demanding which faith made through
the Holy Ghost.
2 Abisme, or abysm, was a bottomless gulf, an immeasureable space, or
the reservoir of waters underneath the earth.

of all necessarie knowledg, and rules for al praier, gathered (by the author of all wisdome) into a brief, for the direction and instruction of our weaknes and ignorance.

Of which endes and uses, whiles some are ignorant, or rather (as their grosse idolatrie, carnal dulnes, and superstitious presumption sheweth) are ignorant either what faithful praier, or the Spirit of God is: whiles they both popishly abuse this Scripture as a principal collect [67] in their publike leitourgie, with their often and idle repetition therof, five times in their morrow masse, *etc.*, and also through this abuse they grow further bold to mould a new calfe, a new leitourgie of their owne, and set that up also in the church of God, as they count it.

Yf it were granted them, that this Scripture, and sundry psalmes, and other Scriptures they alledg out of the prophetts, were commanded and enjoyned to be read and used, as, and for the very praiers of the church and of the saintes (than which nothing can be more false or grossly fond[1] to conceave), yet which way (if this were granted them) can they hereby prove it lawful for them to bring in their owne apocrypha divises, and set them yp [up] in the church, as and with the holy canonical word of God ? May their stinking filth be compared or placed with the heavenly lively word of God, without unsufferable blasphemie ? May the froth of their lips, and follie of their heartes be thrust upon men's consciences, yea, even upon the Spirit of God himself in this maner ? In the church of God may nothing come, or be heard, but the canonical Scriptures and lively graces of Gode's Spirit, according to the same. But these their apocrypha leitourgies, can neither be said the word of God, neither the lively graces of God's Spirit according to the same word, seing they were made and conceived long before, and are wholy thus used, without warrant, example or commandement in the word of God; yea are contrary to al the rules of and for praier, to the exercise and use of God's Spirit, and directly set against al the lawes of the first table, by worshipping God in vaine, after their owne traditions,

---

[1] Fond means foolish, silly, idiotic.

preceptes, and devises, and not according to his holy _{Math. 15: 9}
wil, and commandement.

Can these men think, that because God commandeth
his lively word to be read or sung in the church, and
promiseth a blessing therunto, whiles it is used according _{Ezech. 47}
to his ordinance, it never being so opened, touched or _{Revel. 22: 12}
heard without great fruit, it being the verie tree and
river of life, with the abundant fruites and flowing graces
wherof, the whole church is nourished and watered;
that therfore the like commandement or blessing is of
their leavened leitourgies? Or because God, in the
infancie of his church, prescribed certaine Scriptures
and psalmes to be read and sung upon their sabath day,
solemne feastes, *etc.*, yea, and at other times of their great
affliction, oppression and calamitie, caused certaine comfortable prophecies to be read in the assemblie, for the
strengthening of the faithful; both that they should not
be dismaied at the greatnes and continuance of these
troubles, or think them strange, or els suppose that God
were either offended with, or unmindful of them, or of
his mercies, *etc.*, that therfore now they may upon such
feastes, sabothes, daies, times, troubles, enjoyne (that
I no more mention their owne leavened leitourgies)
these or any other Scriptures by stint and measure, by
injunction and law upon the church of God now? Is
the church of God stil in wardship and such infancie,
shut up as under a garrison, that it must have such
tutors and rudimentes? Is not Christ now dead, risen,
and ascended, and hath freed his church from such _{Gal. 3: 25}
tutelship, he himself [68] now becoming their lawgiver
and minister in person, and hath now given them his
holy word and Spirit, to administer wisdome unto them,
in al freedome to use the same his word, according to his
wil and their owne occasions, unto his glorie and their
comfortes? And what can now be a greater bondage
to the church, injurie unto Christ and unto the Spirit
of God, than thus to limit, to stint and circumscribe the
church of God, the ministerie of Christ and the Spirit of
God, by apportioning, rating, and enjoyning by way of
subjection and commandement this Scripture in this
number and quantitie for this day, feast, fast, calamitie,

N

etc. ? Where have they any rule for this in the testament of Christ ? They wil say, it sufficeth that they have warrant for it in the Old Testament, where these perscript [prescript] and limited Scriptures at such daies, feastes, times, occasions, were commanded and injoined in the church , *etc.* But I hope they can put difference, betwixt the estate and lawes of the church under Moses, and now under Christ: and that they wil not now reserve, revive, and apply those lawes belonging to the temple and the ministerie therof, now to the church and ministerie of Christ. But they take not these to be ceremonial lawes, but rather morall, which commandeth Scriptures to be read, and praiers to be made in the church of God; these Scriptures which they injoyne, are such: therfore may so be used. True it is, the moral law both commanded the name of God to be called upon, and the word of God to be read, *etc.*, and this to al times, estates, persons, indifferently, as wel to that ministery under the law, as to this under the gospel; leaving the particular maner and order therof, to the wisdom, direction, and revelation of the Holy Ghost from time to time, as seemed good unto him. Now, it pleased God to give those rudimentes of the use of certaine Scriptures, psalmes, *etc.*, to the ministerie of that church, command-

1 Chron. 25   ing such Scriptures to be there read upon such daies, occasiones, *etc.*, such psalmes to be sung by such Levites of such an order, of Asaph, Heman, or Jeduthun,[1] to be sung in such a time, with such musickes, such instrumentes, *etc.* Al which I am sure they cannot deny to be inseperably joyned and used to those Scriptures, in that temple and ministerie, and were meerly ceremonial, now utterly abrogate, with that temple and ministerie, and no way belong to the ministerie or church of Christ. Those stinted lawes and customes, I say, I would not be understood of the precious word of God, wherof everie iode [jot] and title abideth for ever, and is of use and fruite in the church of God, which Scriptures and figures are not without their especial profite in their spiritual

---

[1] For Asaph, see Psalms 50, 73-83.
For Heman, see Psalms 88.
For Jeduthun, see Psalms 39, 62, 77.
For all three, and their sons, see I Chronicles 25: 1-18.

sense and understanding: al and ech of which Scriptures, are now freely to be used without stint or limitation in the church of Christ, as his spirit giveth wisdom, grace, and utterance, and not to be restreined and aportionate by way of prescription and commandement, without the losse of Christian libertie, of the truth of the gospel, and the abusing the word of God unto idolatrie, and making it an idol.

But heere they wil say, that the reading of the Scriptures and [69] singing of psalmes, is also commanded in the church of Christ. This hath beene long since granted, yet no such stinted and limited reading and singing thus and thus much this day, at that time, *etc.*, as they injoine. Well yet, seing they are still commanded, though at our libertie what and when to reade or sing them, many of them being godly praiers; we may yet pray by the booke and by written praiers. As this word (prayer) by a general construction may be understood, I graunt they may be called praiers, in that they conteine fit matter, rules and instructions for praier, and were to that end by the Holy Ghost written: yet can they not be saied our praiers, or my particular praier, because they neither expresse our present wantes, according to the present estate of our heartes, neither can be said the lively graces and work of God's spirit in us, so much as the power of God's word and Spirit unto us. My meaning is; they are not drawen or powred out of our heartes, as out of a fountaine, but rather drawen out of the fountaine of God's word, and powred into our heartes as a vessel: therfore can not be said our praier, which must proceed from the present estate of our heart. They are not our wordes by us offred unto God, but Gode's word by him offred unto us, therfore cannot be said our praiers.

But o how hard a thing is it for carnal men to discerne spiritual thinges? They can by no meanes be made to put difference betwixt the word of God, and their apocrypha leitourgies (which they falsly vaunt to be according to the word of God) betwixt reading, singing, and praying: betwixt the present lively graces of God's Spirit in us, and their old penned dead writinges: be-

1 Cor. 2: 14

1 Cor. 12: 4 & 14: 15

twixt God's word to us, instructing us according to our infirmities by way of petition, and our wordes unto God by faithfull praier. And this vale being layd over their eies and heartes, these blind guides not only affirme, but condemne thinges they know not, the one in setting up their owne rotten leitourgies, abusing the word of God to, and in the same, *etc.*, the other in crying out with open mouth against such as reprove them, and will not partake with them in their idolatrie. Insomuch as Doctor Robert Some confesseth very willingly and freely, that he was amased, when he heard us affirme, that part of Holy Scripture (comonly by them called the Lorde's praier and so highly abused) ought not by Christians to be injoyned or used for, or as a praier, either publiquely or privatly.[1] Our reasons are; it was not to that end instituted by our saviour Christ, so much as to instruct us to pray, and direct and assure us in praier, *etc.* It was never so used by our saviour, his apostles and churches, who ever prayed according to their present wantes, as the Spirit gave utterance. The like rules (beside their examples and practise) they have given unto the churches, no where mentioning nor enjoining this or any other Scripture, to be used for their praier. We cannot arrive nor comprehend the riches and depth of that praier, without more particular explication and application. That prayer expresseth not our particular wantes, or estate of our heartes, neither do we understand those generall doctrines, by the [70] bare saying or reading it over. This Scripture is not the grace of God's Spirit in us; it is not drawen out of the fountaine of our heartes. It is not our wordes to God, but his unto us, *etc.* It edifieth not the whole congregation so that they may al mind one thing, or say, Amen. Therfore, and for all these reasons, it ought not and cannot be used of any Christian, either publiquely or privatly, as their praier: as by many other reasons shall further apeare in the breef answere to this said doctor's argumentes.

---

[1] Robert Some, *A Godly Treatise, wherein Are Examined and Confuted Many Execrable Fancies* (1589), p. 28. Dr. Some had at least two conferences in prison with Barrow in 1588-89.

His first argument is thus from Christ's owne mouth. Christ commandeth Christians to pray thus, Our Father, *etc.* Therfore it is lawful for Christians to pray so.[1]

Wel said: be it so a litle while, be it a commandement Luk. 11 in these wordes, *when ye pray say, etc.* It then being a commandement is of necessitie to be wholy said as it is there set downe, and cannot be in our choice and will, whether we wil say it or no; for the commandement is tied to al the wordes, and no commandement is in our Math. 5: 19 libertie to do, or leave undone: but they that leave it Jam. 2: 10 undone, break that commandement which commandeth it to be done. Moreover, these wordes *when ye pray* are general, and extend to al times of our praier, that whensoever we pray we must say those words there prescribed, and whensoever we faile so to do, we break this commandement. And thus by this doctor his reason, have the apostles and churches, yea, our saviour Christ faulted and broken this commandement, so oft as he hath failed to use these wordes in praier: which wordes, we can never find that either he or they have used at any time in their praiers: but that with other wordes they have praied, we find everie where. By this time you have spunne a fair thred, you have made a goodly reason. But it is peradventure my ignorance and want of learning, that thus wrest that I understand not: for your argument wil beare no such conclusion. Your wordes, I am sure, I misaledg not. Christ (say you) commandeth Christians to pray thus, *Our Father, etc.* Therfore they may pray so. This commandement I trow extendeth to the verie wordes, *Our Father, etc.*, els your argument maketh nothing for you, or against us. And if it be a commandement, and have a relation to the wordes, then I am sure the other conclusions wil follow as wel as this. Therfore it were better for your safety (though not for your fleshly credit) to loose this argument than gaine this blasphemy; and that we consent together in this, that the commandement heere stretcheth not to the wordes, but rather to the doctrine and sense. For if it should at all be understood of those prescript wordes, that the reading or saying of them might be our praier;

[1] *Ibid.*, p. 27.

then must it needes be granted, that this of al other were
the most perfect praier; both in that there is included in
it al other prayers, even whatsoever may lawfully of us
be asked, or can of God be granted; and also avoided al
battologie,[1] vaine repetions, *etc.* Wherfore, it being a
praier to be used, and the best of all praiers, fitting all
times, occasions, *etc.*, it must needes follow of [71] necessitie to be alwaies used, because God is alwaies to be
served with the best. Yea, it must needes follow, to be
solely and only used, and none but that, because all
other praier should be but vaine babling, yea, open
ambition in putting our owne unsufficient stuffe, in the
place of this alsufficient praier. For the best of our
praiers and actions are unsufficient, unperfect, and as
a stained cloth. But this (if it be a praier) cannot be
denied, to be sufficient, perfect, and without staine,

  This doctor's second argument is this. Everie
branch of the Lord's Praier is a petition; therfore
everie branche is a praier. For everie meane scoller
knoweth, that the argument followeth, *a specie ad
genus affirmative.* And if everie branch be a praier,
then must the whole (because they concerne the glorie
of God and our benefite) needs be an excellent praier.[2]
Virtus coniuncta fortior.

  I have before shewed how sundrie psalmes, this and
many other Scriptures may be in some sense called praier
or praiers: because the Lord in them by petition maner
instructeth our weake faith how to pray unto him, how
to frame our requestes, our wordes, how to lay hold of,
and use his promises, *etc.* Yet I have further shewed,
why these Scriptures, thus barely read or said, cannot
be said our praiers, without further explication, application, *etc.*, unto our present needes and estates. So that
Mr. Doctor's learned reason followeth not: for except he
can prove it our praier, he saith nothing. Now in that
I graunt it him, by some construction to be called a
praier, it is to avoide contention about wordes: for els
they would never leave urging the synonimie,[3] betwixt

---

[1] Needless and tiresome repetition.
[2] Some, *A Godly Treatise, wherein Are Examined and Confuted Many
Execrable Fancies,* p. 27.
[3] Synonymousness, or identity of meaning.

a petition and a praier: which in all tongues signifie one thing. Now then Mr. Doctor's reason in his owne sense, is but thus much. Every branche of the Lorde's Prayer is a prayer; therfore everie branch of the Lord's Prayer is a prayer. Need he to have shewed his deep learning and hard logicall rules *a specie ad genus affirmative* for this stout reason? I would have thought he might have learned to have made as good a reason as this at home, and never have travelled to Cambridg for it. For if this reason hould, he may prove himself a learned, a wise, or an honest man, or the falsest and absurdest thing of the world. It is so, therfore it is so. I would here know of his docterhood, whither praier or petition be the *genus*, and which is the *species*, in this his logicall reason? Or if he let it alone and trouble not himself now any further with the matter (seing he hath fethered his nest, and hath got that he al this while waited for[1]) I am content: for I am not greatly desirous to learne away this his cunning.

To the matter in controversie, I denie that Scripture which he calleth the Lord's Praier, or any one particular branch of it, properly to be said a praier, that is, such an exercise or offring, as the saintes (by the worke of the spirit in them) offer unto God through Jesus Christ. Neither followeth it, because everie branch conteineth either a [72] request of some benefite, or the deliverance from some evil, that therfore it is a praier. For this it is as it is written in the booke, though it be never read; therfore I may by Mr. [Robert] Some his reason and logick conclude, that the booke also praieth, because all these branches are in the booke, and all these branches are such praiers. Neither yet doth the reading of these Scriptures make it a praier any more, than the reading of the Scriptures maketh a sermon. There is required a litle more worke of the spirit in both. In the one to the explication and application of the Scripture read; in the other to the powring out and expressing the desires and estate of the heart in faith. For it sufficeth not, that al our wantes, or whatsoever we can aske or stand in

[1] Dr. Some was appointed Master of Peterhouse on May 11, 1589, and became vice-chancellor in 1590.

need of, are there expressed; what booteth that me? I can aske or receave no more, than mine owne faith extendeth unto. An enwrapped faith will not serve or save me: this were to conclude, because in the Bible is all wisdome and Doctor Some hath the Bible: therfore he hath al wisdome. In this Scripture is all praier: therfore when I have said or read this Scripture, I have praied all maner of praier. What pitifull, blind, yea popish and pernicious reasons are these? For (saith this doctor) he is unlearned that knoweth not, that all petitions are contayned within the compasse of, and may be deduced from, the Lorde's Praier. Therfore when we reade or say the Lorde's Praier, we pray for the queene, for the navie, *etc.*, and all other petitions that we need inclusively, and that untill I can prove that all petitions are not therin concluded, I gaine nothing by this reason, in that I alledge, that neither our particular nor present wantes are therein expressed, and therfore it cannot be said our praier. Doth this doctor know what either faith or praier meaneth? Can any thing be devised more popish or idolatrous than this? Popish, in that he maketh praier without faith, understanding, or knowledg of the thing we say? Yea, giveth meed[1] to the verie saiing over these wordes: idolatrous, in that he putteth holines and vertue in the wordes understood. For let me aske of him, which way that can be said a private praier where my wordes expresse not my heart? Were it not rather an idle superstitious or fond [foolish] futilitie? And a taking of the Lorde's name in vaine? I would also understand of him, whether any such publike praier may be used in the congregation, which is not

1 Cor. 14
Act. 8: 31

understood of all? And whither to the simpler sort he might not almost pray in an unknowen tongue as well? Or how should they understand this, without some particuler explication or application? Therfore by these unfallible reasons we may conclude, that this Scripture neither any other can be used either privatly or publikly as our praier, without some further worke of the spirit in us.

But he hath for this an evasion, namely, that our

---

1 Merit, worth, excellence.

knowledg is here but in part, and therfore we may understand in measure, and so have use of this as a praier. If he meane private praier, though I in some measure may by such a speedy reading understand somwhat, yet this understanding nothing expresseth, so much as instructeth my present heart: therfore it cannot be said or used as my praier.   For everie knowledg [73] or understanding maketh not praier: neither doe we heere reason of secret or inward praier, but of pronounced praier. Yf he meane publike praier, it is manifest that whole Math. 24: 45, 46 loaves unbroken up or undevided, may not be set before children; especially in their praiers, which is a publike action of the whole church, and must be understood of the whole church.   But be it granted him to be understod of al the church: yet everie branch being so infinite, from whence spring and are derived so many infinite petitions; how now in this case shal they al with one heart, one mind, and one mouth be said to praise God, Rom. 15: 5 when their mindes ar thus distracted, their thoughts dispersed, one about one thing, an other about an other, even so many several, as there are diversitie of thinges Act. 1: 14 in the world, of conceites, and armies of thoughts in men: & 2: 46 some shal aske private thinges whiles others aske publike. How should this be avoided, though al the church were as learned as this doctor mistaketh himself to be.   And this we know, that publike praiers must so be made, as 1 Cor. 14: 5, 6 they may be with ane [one] accord, that all may be understood, that all may say, Amen.

But (saith this doctor) I then take away the use of this Scripture: no; but the abuse rather.   For how should it now be used as a praier, without these popish errors, grosse absurdities, and heinous idolatrie?   Wherin this popish doctor and al the priestes of the land fal, whiles they use it: some of them saying it for all their wantes at once, that they might soone have done, others five times in a morning next their heart for al the weeke after, or until Wednesday or Friday, that they have service againe. Other more smooth hypocrites (yet as grosse idolaters) use it as a close or supplie (forsooth) to their long and prolixe praiers conceaved before, with this preamble. For these and al other graces necessarie, let us say the

N*

Lord's Praier. What can be more grosse, popish, idolatrous, supersticious than this? Doe they not heerby put holines in the wordes? Why should they els use them after they have praied as God hath given them utterance by his spirit? Doe they not fall into the same errors, abuses, inconveniences, above shewed and confuted?

Heere I had like to have forgotten one of our doctor's maine reasons, which he bringeth to shut up the point, and that is this; it hath *Amen* added in the end; therfore it is a praier.[1] Had it not beene pittie to have lost this reason? Why your A.b.c. before the catechisme of the Church of England hath both the signe of the crosse and *tittle, title est Amen.*[2] Yet I never heard it taken for a praier. Christ himself is called *Amen*, shal I therfore say that he, or the whole written word of God which is called *Amen* also is a praier? Moreover, I find it after Luke without *Amen*, yea, and without *For thine is the kingdome, the power, etc.*[3] Now would I know of you after which evangelist I must say it. And thus being wearied with your frivolous reasons, and nothing refreshed with your unsavorie barren notes, wherwith whiles you would have opened, you have roiled [sullied] and shut up those heavenly pure fountaines; neither yet resting in your interpretation of, much lesse in your collection from this word [74] *Amen*, I betake you (when you shal have recovered your senses from the amazement wherinto you were smitten with this strange doctrine touching praier) to a further consideration of the matter; to see if you can bring any better reasons, or repaire these in your third booke, against the poore persecuted servantes of Christ whome you untruly accuse,

[1] Some, *A Godly Treatise, wherein Are Examined and Confuted Many Execrable Fancies*, p. 27.
[2] In the alphabet in horn-books, a letter or contraction was followed by three dots, which were called a tittle. Then followed "Est Amen." Therefore "tittle est Amen" came to signify the end or conclusion. The horn-book contained the alphabet, ten digits or so, and the Lord's Prayer. See A. W. Tuer, *History of the Horn-Book*, vol. I, 8, 31; II, 81, 125, 126, 203.
[3] The two versions of the Lord's Prayer in Matthew 6: 9-13 and Luke 11: 2-4 vary slightly. In the Revised Standard Version, the *Amen* and the words, "For thine is the kingdom, and the power, and the glory, for ever" are eliminated, but they are in the King James Version.

blaspheme and publish for Anabaptists and what not in these your privileged poisoned writings.[1]

I have sufficiently (as I hope) shewed the unlawfulnes of bringing into, or reading in, the church these stinted numbred praiers, and set service in their written devised leitourgies: both because they want [lack] warrant in the testament of Christ and practise of the apostles, and are contrarie to the same, being apochrypha, and not the lively graces of God's spirit; being contrary to al the rules of praier, yea, to the spirit it self and christian libertie: not being drawen from the spirit of God in us according to the necessities and present estate of the church, or of our heartes as the spirit giveth utterance; but rather teaching the spirit wordes, and usurping the office therof in the consciences of men: yea, setting stintes and lawes upon the spirit and church, prescribing this, and thus much to be said this day in the morning, at afternoone, thus many collectes or *Pater nosters*, heer a Creed, a *Te deum, etc.* I have shewed the superstition, idolatrie, and abhominacion of the best of them, how they are but as a dead stinking carion, and not a lively acceptable sacrifice unto the Lord, and so abhominacion; wil worship, not required at our handes, and so superstition; brought into and standing in the church

---

[1] In Some's first book, against the Separatists, published in May, 1588, entitled, *A Godly Treatise Containing and Deciding Certaine Questions, Moved of Late in London and Other Places, Touching the Ministerie, Sacraments, and Church*, he spoke in his preface of two sorts of recusants: the one popish, the other Anabaptisticall. In September he reissued this book with one additional point and four pages of new material. Added to this book, and bound with it, is *A Defence of Such Points in R. Some's Last Treatise, as M. Penry Hath Dealt against*: *And a Refutation of Many Anabaptistical, Blasphemous and Popish Absurdities, Touching Magistracie, Ministerie, Church, Scripture and Baptisme, etc. Conteined in M. Penry's Treatise, etc.* This is a work of 160 pages, the very length of which indicates the importance attached to Penry's teachings and the need for refuting them. The third book was entitled, *A Godly Treatise, wherein Are Examined and Confuted Many Execrable Fancies, Given out and Holden, Partly by Henry Barrow and John Greenewood*: *Partly, by Other of the Anabaptistical Order.* This book is the most direct attack upon the Separatists, and is the one that Barrow particularly had in mind. Barrow's reference to Some's privileged writings is true, since all three of the books referred to above were printed by G. B. [George Bishop], deputy to Christopher Barker, printer to the Queen, and the third volume not only was dedicated to Lord Chancellor Hatton and Lord Burleigh, but its epistle dedicatory was dated May 12, 1589, " at my Lordes Grace of Canterburie his house in Lambeth."

of God for that they are not, namly, as rules and lawes of the church, as holy praiers and incense of the saintes, as the lively graces and present worke of the spirit, and so idolatrie. I have shewed that those Scriptures used in them, do no way justifie them, no more than they doe the masse-booke, or a conjure[r]'s magical incantations, which have also holy psalmes and Scriptures, and as un-reprooveable praiers: but rather that they make them the more heinous, in that they so rende, mangle, and pervert the Scriptures to such blasphemous abuses. I have shewed that such written stinted stuffe, cannot be said the praiers of the saintes, neither do any good, either instruct or help the weake consciences of any: but are rather the very leaven and poison of their heartes and soules, the very cradles and cushions of these graceles priestes and atheistes, to rock them asleepe in their sinnes and securitie, never touching the heart or conscience, but teaching them to prate over upon the booke or by rote their certayne number of wordes to the Lord, as though the booke were their heart, utterly quenching the spirit of God, and al the light that is in them. They make them beleeve that this prescript praier is good at this time, that at an other time; this when they rise or at dinner, the tother [*sic*] when they goe to supper or to sleepe; this when they are sick, that is special good to be read or saied at the point and hower of death. Thus abuse they and misleade men, keep them wholy from the exercise of the Spirit of God in them, from the searching and powring out theyr heartes [75] before the Lord, from the due confession, sorrow and repentance for theyr sinnes, from the true knowledg or any use or benefite of that blessed benefite, and holy exercise of praier, and wholy from receaving any increase, blessing, or grace from God; as the present estate of their church, their faith and soules sheweth evidently, being by their stinted leitourgie (considered at the best that they can imagine or speake for themselves) kept at a stay, alwaies in one estate, having neither more nor lesse of God's grace, but even the self same stil. Thus are they never led forth one step towardes perfection, until a new leitourgie be made, where they have al things prescribed, both what to doe and how to doe, what to say, how much to say, when to say and when to make an end. Thus juggle they and mock with God, and behold how the Lord deludeth and derideth them, withholdeth the early and latter rayne of his blessinges from them, and the continual spring and harvest of his fruitful graces, they being wholy emptie and destitute therof, deprived of light, true knowledg, yea, common sense and feeling: their consciences being seared as with a hote yron, their heartes paved and hardned in their sinnes, which they commit even with greedines, having left them no sight, judgment or power in themselves, to discerne betwixt good and evil, nether to looke or know what the wil of God is, for any thing they doe or leave undone. Neither have they power to practise it, but depend wholy uppon others for al these things: to them they goe to inquire; as they say, so it is without any doubt: so it must be done without any contradi[c]tion. Thus is their faith, that inwrapped faith of the papistes, to beleeve as the church beleeveth, without knowing what the church beleeveth, to beleeve and doe, as such a preacher, such a Rabbine beleeveth and doeth. O he is a learned, an holy man, he would not doe otherwise than wel for al the world: such a martyre made this, and such a man that, it cannot be but good, say God what he wil. They see with other men's eies, speake with other men's mouthes, pray and beleeve with other men's heartes. Thus doe they al by prescript custome and tradition, without regard to the rules of God's word: thus build they their house and faith upon the sandes: thus are they by their blind guides deluded and led out of the way: thus are they cast into utter darknes, and held in the chaines of sinne unto judgment, their handes, eies, heartes and al their senses and powers being fast bound by these Egiptian inchanters and their delusions.[1]

And now that we have thus largely set out the unlawfulnes and inconveniences of al prescript leitourgies, that all cavilles and pretences may be remooved out of the

---

[1] In critizing the dependence of the laity upon the priest, Barrow is really emphasizing the Lutheran doctrine of the priesthood of every believer. It is a noble ideal, but persons will always have some measure of faith in other people's faith. One cannot be an expert in all areas of life.

way: me thinkes it is now time to returne to this leitourgie of the Church of England, and to consider somwhat
more particularly of it: wherby we shal discerne what
kind of faith they have, professe, and exercise.

And herein to deale with every particular error therof,
or to meddle with the patcheries and innumerable trumperies therin, or al their grosse follies, and more than
childish, even apish triflinges, or their frivolous constitutions and customes wherunto they bind and lesson the
parish priest to say his mattens and evensong in order,
to begin with this com-[76]fession throughout the yeare,
nay, throughout their life. Then cometh the prieste's
general pardon, thorough the power that his lord bishop
hath comitted unto him, and so he proceedeth to his
stinted psalmes and lessons, with his certaine [number]
of *Paternosters* ever and among, and of Creedes, their
forged patcherie commonly caled the Apostles' Creed
or symbole, Athanasius' Creed, the Nicene Creed,[1] sometimes sayde in prose, sometimes songe [sung] in meter on
their festivals: their epistles, their gospels, the one to be
read with the prieste's face toward the weast, the other
with his face toward the east; with their versicles, one
to be said by the priest, the other by the parish clarke or
people; with their times when to kneele, when to sit,
when to stand, when to cur[t]sy at the name of Jesus,
when to glorie their Lord at the beginning of their
gospel, or at the end of their psalmes with their collectes
and anthemes, this in their ordinary journal, that in
their festivals, this at morne, that at even, *etc*. With
these grosseries and follies it is not my purpose to meddle:
the worke is to[o] great for me; if I should begin I should
not know when to make an end. Only here by way of
question, I wold know of them, where they learned thus
to limit and apportion Scripture; this chapter to be read
on this day, that upon their next Sunday, this for the
first lesson, that for the second, these on the morning,
that at evensong. I would moreover know of them,
where they learned to hew out and dismember the
Scriptures in this maner; to pluck them from the con-

---

[1] In the *Articles of Religion,* the eighth article designates the Nicene, Atha-
nasian, and Apostles' Creed as those which " ought thoroughly to be
received and believed."

text with such violence, without al sense, order, or cause; and to make that their gospel of the day more than any other Scripture of the New Testament, or than a whole chapter of one of the evangelistes, commonly read for their second lesson at their mattens; and to give more honor to this shred, al the people being bound to stand up upon their feet, and alowd to glorie God, where they take their ease and sit stil at the other, and say never a word unto it. I would also know of them, how their peeces of the prophecies became epistles? And where they learned to make thus many pistles and gospels? I would also know of them, where they learned to cannonize and reade the apocrypha writinges[1] (which swarme with unsufferable forgeries, lies and errors) in the church, if not of the masse-book? Wherof in deed this their portuise [portas] is a right graffe. In the New Testament I am sure they find none of these customes, they have no president [precedent] there thus to distort, abuse, prophane, dismember and rend the holy Scriptures, or to thrust them by stint and limitation to daies and times in this childish maner, upon the church: neither to reade nor bring in the erroneous devises of men into the church, and set it up as the word of God. Yet are these patches and shreddes, even the very bad, best partes of their service or worship, and even the unsufferable best use they make of the Scriptures: which they not only thus rend, dismember, apportion, stint and limite, this and thus much on this day in the morning, in this or that place of their morow masse, *etc.* But yet see how they abuse it to more accursed idolatry and abhominacion, as to their idol feastes both Jewish and popish, their fastes [77] of all sortes, their holy daies. All which, because they celebrate and solemnize in their church, it shall not be amisse a litle by the light of the word to examine what kind of stuffe they are.

First, therfore, I will begin with the Jewish feastes

---

[1] In fairness to Barrow's opponents, we need to remember that the *Articles of Religion*, and especially the sixth one, designate fourteen books — the Apocrypha — as good to read for example of life and instruction of manners, though not for the establishment of any doctrine. Esdras I, II, were included as canonical, but not III and IV, in the Convocation of 1562 [1562/3].

they stil retaine, as their Easter and Pentecost. Of these solemnities and feastes we reade Exodus 12, Leviticus 23, Numbers 28, Deuteronomy 26, that they belonged and were injoined to the Jewes under the law, were meerly ceremonial and ritual, figuring Christ's person and belonging to the Levitical ministerie, such as appertaine not unto, neither are to be reteined in the church or ministerie of Christ, without the utter losse of Christ, and utter denial of him to be as yet come in the flesh, *etc.* But heer peradventure they will use their doctor's foresaid Catholike distinction, *viz.*, that they keep not these feasts and daies after the Levitical maner, neither unto those endes, but rather in the one to celebrate the resurrection of our saviour Christ, in the other the glorious miracle of the giving the Holy Ghost unto the apostles, *etc.*, and this, their service upon these daies sheweth playnly. Of these endes, uses, and service at and of these feastes and daies (which are a great deale more abhominable than those of the Jewes) hereafter: for with al these floorishes cannot I be satisfied concerning the very feastes and daies of Easter and Whitsontide, which still reteine the same names *Pascha* and *Pentecostes*, the same times, solemnities, cessations, the same solemne Sabothes or Sundaies that the Jewes did, keeping their passover in the first month of the Jewes, the first day more solemne than the rest, numbring seven weekes just after the same unto their Pentecost, whose first day they keep in like maner. Al these ceremonies the lawes and places above alledged, shew evidently to be derived from the Jewes. We find no such customes, no such commandements in the New Testament. We there reade, that if we observe or be brought in bondage of such feastes, daies, *etc.*, we turne from Christ, he profiteth us nothing. But they observe these feastes of Easter and Pentecost as our saviour Christ and his apostles did and so have warrant sufficient inough for that they do. Is it so? Then they observe their Easter wholly after the Jewish maner for so did our saviour Christ being made under the law. But our saviour Christ there instituted this feast to be kept, and that after an other maner, as the institution of the supper

Gal. 4: 9, 10
Gal. 5: 1, *etc.*

Col. 2: 20

declared, how it ought to be kept in the ministerie of
the gospel. I never found any such thing in the text.
Neither did the apostles (who delivered as they had
receaved) ever give any such commandment, or tied the
celebrating the supper to that feast that day as the
Church of England doth: but left the day and time to 1 Cor. 11: 21,
the libertie of the church. If it be to be kept in that _etc._
maner, then is it to be kept in the night after supper.
If the feast and day stil remaine, then doth the passover
still remaine: for both were alike by our saviour observed at that time: but if the passover be abrogate, and Mat. 26: 26
Christ our passover be offred for us, then is that feast
and day also abrogate, and we to keep the feast even 1 Cor. 5: 7, 8
al the daies of our life in sinceritie and truth: other
observation of the day I never found, in all the practise
of the apostles or churches. [78]

For the other feast of their Penticost, they have litle
help from the second of the Acts: for the disciples assembling in that private maner, could not be to keep that
publike feast of their first fruites, where they were to
make publike and solemne offringes, according to the
law, _etc._, so much as according to the commandement
of our saviour Christ, to wait for the promise of the Acts 1: 4
Father, _etc._, which not being as yet performed, they could
not keep that day as in commemoration of the great
wonders the Lord then shewed, and grace he shed upon
them. Now then, if they kept not that day as any feast,
either after the Jewish or this popish maner, how should
these men from thence fetch warrant for their feast; for
after the Jewish maner they will at no hand be said to
keep it, and after their maner it is cleare the apostles
then could not keep it, because the miracle was not as
then done, neither had they as yet those giftes of tongues,
neither knew they at their assembling, in what maner,
or what the Lord would worke that day. For though
it pleased the Lord upon that day to shew these won-
derous workes: yet did not he it, that either we should
keep a superstitious celebration of that day more than
of others after this idolatrous maner, or still reteine the
Jewish feast, _etc._, so much as upon that day, in that
great and solemne conc[o]urse of people, to give publike

witnesse to the gospel of our Lord Jesus Christ, and
furnish up his witnesses according to his promises, *etc.*

For I am sure they cannot shew either commandement
or example in the New Testament, that this or any such
feastes have beene kept or are to be kept in the churches of
Christ. It maketh nothing to their purpose that Paul,
Acts 18, departed from Ephesus to keep the feast ensuing
in Jerusalem: for what he did (no doubt) he did by
revelation of the spirit, unto the more easie winning of
the Jewes, to whome he (for the time) became and
behaved himself as a Jew, and this both by the speciall
revelation of the spirit, and warrant of the word. For
unto the Jewes a time was given of shaking and removing
these ceremonies, from which they could not be so
sodainly or easily removed, because they were given and
delivered unto them by God himself, upon the mount
Sinai, *etc.*, yet seing they never were given nor belonged
to the gentiles, the apostles at no hand would have them
intangled with these ceremonies. Neither did Paul here
injoine the church at Ephesus to keep this feast, but how
sharply he hath dealt with those Jewes or other false
teachers that sought to trouble the churches with them,
appeareth in all his epistles; and how roundly, but for
a litle halting herein, he dealt with the apostle Peter,
appeareth, Galatians 2: 14. And if the apostle then at
the first planting of the churches, when many Jewes
were mingled amongst the gentiles, would not receave
the least ordinance with the ministerie of the gospell,
by way of subjection not for an howre, that the truth
of the gospell might continue amongst them; what
would he now say to these false apostles and counterfait
wretches, which not being Jewes but gentiles by nature,
and having [79] all these examples and documentes
before them; yet dare without any warrant thrust their
Jewish and heathenish traditions upon the churches with
a strong hand; which thus mingle the Jewish ceremonies
with the gospell: which way should the truth of the
gospell remaine with them, when the apostle saith, that
but a litle of such leaven doth leaven the whole lump?

But see, these Phariseis not only reteine the day and
the feast, but joine to the celebration of the one day a

Marginal notes:
1 Cor. 9: 20
Acts 16: 3
Heb. 8: 13

Acts 15

Gal. 2: 4, 5

Gal. 5: 9

principal article of our faith, the resurrection of Christ from the dead: where have they learned (trow we) to make such a set and especial memorial of Christe's resurrection one day above all the daies in the yeare? But here their answere is ready, because forsooth Christ rose as that day of the yeare. Did he so? How shall we know that? Their holy father the pope having in a solemne generall councell corrected his calender saith, he rose ten daies before, and keepeth his feast accordingly.[1] Is it not doubtful they come in the post, and then all their devotions are lost. But be it of their side. Be it that Christ rose just as that day; yet would I faine know the mysterie of the matter, why we should more specially remember and celebrate Christe's resurrection that Lorde's day, than the next Lorde's day, yea, or than any day of the yeare? Or why they should keep such a solemne double feast that Lorde's day more than any other: unlesse peradventure it be, because the sunne daunceth that day when it riseth. I could never as yet find in Christ's Testament any such betternes of one day Rom. 14: 5, 6 than another, neither that Christ's resurrection was to be celebrate with such a stagelike fleshly pompe, in superstition and idolatrie, in fles[h]ly lustes, riote and gluttony; that day making holy two other daies after it, and drawing the whole land both yonge and old, al these daies, to intermit their lawful callings, wherin they are placed of God (upon what necessitie or occasion soever) to give attendance to their popery and idolatrie, so spend the time in idlenes, follie, and vanitie. Is this to celebrate the resurrection of Christ from dead workes? Colos. 3: 10 and to be renewed in knowledg and holines, after the image of him that created them? or is it not amongst Rom. 6: 4 their holy father's superogatorie workes, which God never required or commanded? For I would faine

---

[1] This is a reference to the changes from the Julian to the Gregorian calendar in 1582, when ten days were dropped from the calendar. Thursday, October 4, was followed by Friday, October 15. The Council to which Barrow refers is not an ecumenical council, since the Council of Trent (1545-63) was the nineteenth one and the Vatican Council (1869-70) the twentieth. The task of correcting the calendar was entrusted to a commission, headed by Cardinal Sirleto. Important members were Luigi Giglio, Pedro Chacon, and Christopher Clavio. See Ludwig von Pastor, *The History of the Popes,* ed. R. E. Kerr, XIX (London, 1930), chapter VIII, pp. 282 - 296.

learne of them, where they can likewise shew any commandement or warrant for their solemne White Sonday
and their feast of Pentecost, other than the Jewes' double
Sabaths and feastes, *etc.* But I have now done with this
feast: I would therfore know where in the New Testament they find any president [precedent] or commandement, to solemnise the verie day of the apostles' receaving
those wonderful gifts of the Holy Ghost. That the
apostles did not then keep that day as a feast or gratu-
lation of this matter, is alreadie shewed; because they
had not as then received these giftes, neither knew in
what maner God would work: that ever after they kept
or commanded to be kept any such set solemne memorial
therof upon any one day more than an other, I suppose
cannot be shewed in the New Testament. Paul, they
may alledg, Acts 20: 16, made [80] haste out of Asia, to
be (if it were possible) at Jerusalem at the feast of Pentecost: yet this proveth nothing that the apostles or Christians kept the feast and commemoration of the wonderfull apparition of the Holy Ghost, *etc.*, which until they
can shew, they must be guiltie as forgers and coiners of
a new religion, and so of adding unto, yea abrogating
of the testament of Christ. We doubt not but the Jewes
a long time kept that and many other feastes, but they
may be no example for us in this matter: nor yet these
with their auncient traditions wherin the papistes and
they prescribe, from which forgeries they derive these
and many other trumperies, without some better warrant
from the word of God, than as yet they can shew. Neither
is it my purpose heere to stand to recite their heathenish
maner of keeping those feastes with idlenes, riot and
gluttony, with their maygames, morrice dance, and
sommer lords, *etc.* I now make hast to their popish
feastes.

Which because they are so many, we will keep their
owne division of them in double and single feastes. Of
their double feastes are their Christmasse day, with the
day of his circum[ci]sion and epiphanie, the Annunciation, and purification of their ladie, called *Candlemasse*
day; their day of all the saintes together, called *Hallow-
masse*; their *Michaelmasse* and all angels, besides their

Easter and Whitsontide, wherof we have spoken, also their Assention day, and Trinitie Sonday. Now their single feastes and common holidaies are the saintes' daies in order as they come in their beadrolle, and their common Sundaies. Of which Sundaies, though they have commandement both in the law by the fourth commandement, and in the New Testament by the commandement and practise of the apostles, to keep in the church the first day of the weeke, an holy convocation unto the Lord, spending that day in praiers, hearing the word, and other holy exercises; yet seing they so miserablie profane it to idolatrie, both after the maner of the heathen and papistes, it becommeth an idol feast no lesse accursed than the others. After the maner of the heathen they abuse it, in dedicating it unto, and naming it after the chief idol of the pagans, the sonne, a creature, and in feasting that day after their maner in pride, gluttony, riot, idlenes, sport, play, *etc*. After the maner of the papistes they abuse it, in their stinted, superstitious, idolatrous service, their abuse of Scriptures, of praier at their meeting, which is not to any edifiing or leading forward in the waies of God, their course and direction being set downe both to priestes and people before hand, what they shall doe, say, pray, how much in the forenoone at Mattens, how litle at afternoone at Evensong, *etc*. Further, in that they dedicate one special Sunday above all the rest unto the Holy Trinitye; and yet give lesse honour unto this Sunday and feast, than to their White Sunday going next before. Their other solemne holy feastes, seing they want [lack] warrant in the word of God, and have nothing for their foundation and groundworke, are therby cast utterly out of the church of Christ, which is not to be edified upon the sandes of men's fansies, neither to worship God after the devises of their owne heartes, but according to [81] the prescript rules of his holy word: and therfore I need spend no time in the refutation of them: the bare recital of these their trifling follies and vanities, is inough to scatter them into the wind: for what warrant, commandement, or proofe have these stage players in the word of God, in their maner to solemnize the birth, circumcision, epiphanie, resurrection and assention of Christ upon their several daies, with their set fastes, worship, and feastes? Why do not they celebrate as well his baptisme, temptation and victorie over Sathan in the wildernes, the calling of the woman of Samaria, the receaving the Syrophoenitian, his famous miracles, casting out devils, raising the dead, walking upon the sea, transfiguration upon the mountaine, giving the Holy Ghost unto his apostles, with his commission and mesage, *etc*. These are written in the New Testament, and were done of Him as wel as the other; for our learning and comfort as wel as the other. Why then should not they as well have their peculiar daies, fastes, worship, feastes, as the other? But where have they thus learned Christ, to worship Him by startes and stintes, by daies and eaves, by such idol fastes and feastes? Is not this

Col. 2: 20

Mat. 15: 9

Acts 17: 22

to draw the worship of God (which is perpetual and spiritual) unto carnal commandementes, worldly ordinances and customes againe, and that after so superstitious and profane a maner? Superstititious, in that it is without commandement or president [precedent] in the testament of Christ, wil worship[1] not required or accepted at their handes: prophane, in that they celebrate these feastes in al maner gluttonie, excesse, ryot, prodigalitie, pride, luxurie, vanitie, idle games, and heathen sportes. Thus they celebrate the nativitie, circumcision, epiphanie and resurrection of Christ, with gay clothes, cleane houses, good cheare, the viole in the feast to stir up lust in stead of devotion, eating and drinking and rising up to play and daunce, after the maner of Bacchus in his feastes, with their lords of misrule, commonly called Christmas lordes, games, enterludes, nummeries,[2] Sodomitish maskes, wassal cuppes, with thowsandes of abhominations, which chast and christian heartes and eares abhor to heare or thinke of. This is the fruite of their idolatrie and idlenes: this they learned of their forefathers in the wildernes. Whiles Moses was on the

---

[1] Will — worship is that form of worship imposed by the human will; hence, worship lacking divine authority.

[2] Nummeries. Of or pertaining to money or coinage. Perhaps " mummeries " is intended, with the meaning of ridiculous ceremonial or silly religious rituals.

mount, Exodus 32, their priest cast them a calfe of gold, made of their chiefe jewels that it might be of the more estimation. To this calfe they made an altar, the priest devoutly proclaimed a fast to al the people on the eave, a solemne feast and holy day unto the Lord, yea of the Lord Jehova, as he said. On the day where the people offred burnt offringes, and brought peace offringes on the morning; after sate downe to eate and drink and rose up to play. This is the very mould and patterne of these their idol feastes, fastes, worship, *etc.* In Christe's testament they never learned to divide Christe's actions and life into such a stageplay; making one day a pageant of his birth, an other of his circumcision, an other of his epiphanie, resurrection, *etc.*, though these were distinct things, and done at several times: yet never read I that they ought (in this maner) upon [82] peculiar daies to be celebrate in the church, more than at any other time or day of the yeare; or that they ought to have a set worship with select psalmes, lessons, pistles, gospels, collects, anthemes; or such a devout fast on their eaves, or feast on their daies, with such revels as they keepe.

But that their devotions may yet more appeare, they worship him even in his mother's belly, or rather before she was conceaved with him, they adore the wordes of salutation, even in the angel Gabriel his mouth, and give a solemne fast, worship, and feast day therunto, which they cal the Annunciation of their lady.[1] And least she might be offended, they solemnise also with double feast her purification, comonly called Candlemasse. And heer in this feast I would know of these deep divines, what it is they worship and solemnize; whether this action she did, or the person of their Lady: for needes it must be the one or both of them, heere being nothing either in or joyned with this action besides, worthie of such special veneration and high solemnitie. If then it be the action of her purification; that was but a legal ceremonie, and not now to be brought into the church of Christ. If her person (as it is also

---

[1] The Annunciation of the Blessed Virgin Mary, March 25, commonly called Lady Day in England, in commemoration of the announcement by the angel Gabriel to Mary that she was to be the mother of Christ.

Jer. 44

like) how then wil they escape the breach of the first commandement; unlesse peradventure they hope through her mediation to be dispensed withal, and that she wil speake a good word unto her Sonne for them; and therfore they powre out unto her their drinke off-ringes, and burne incense to the queene of heaven.

And that they might not faile at time of need, see, they make all the saintes, and innocentes in heaven their friendes and on their side, celebrating to the innocentes one day of their solemne Christmas: unto all saintes (because none should be forgotten, and they are many in number) they keep an especial and principal feast day, with a devout fast upon the eave, *etc.*, yet least some of the chief sa[i]ntes, as Jhon the Baptist, and the twelve apostles might be displeased in that they are numbred and passed over with other common saintes, they severally remember them againe in their tourne with their peculiar eaves, daies, fastes, feastes, and wor-ship. Heere is yet also an other saint, whome I had like to have overskipped, the captaine of them al, St. George, their borrowgh,[1] the patrone of the land, a worthy warriour, our ladie's knight I wene. This saint hath heere no smal intertainement, with his solemne procession (and that by no smal states, but even the greatest of the land) with his cornets, trumpets, harpe, shackbutes,[2] psalteries, dulcimer and al instrumentes of musick, *etc.* This saint (besides his noble order of knight-hood) hath also his famous peculiar Chaplain Palatine of the order, who is to weare a goldring on his thomb: and what a famous feast they keep unto this saint, there is none in court or countrie can be ignorant. Because I am no good heralt, I wil not undertake to blazon his armes, the red crosse in white field that he beareth in banner displaied, nor yet his worthy atchivementes: for all those I refer you to his legend.[3] And heere me

[1] Their burrowgh — surety, hostage, deliverer ; to take God or St. George to borrow, that is, as security for one's good faith ; an asseveration as, by St. George.

[2] Shackbutes, or sackbuts — musical instrument, a type of trombone, mentioned in Daniel 3: 5, 7, 10, 15. See Francis W. Galpin, *Old English Instruments of Music* (London, 1932). See also his book, *The Sackbut, Its Evolution and History*.

[3] See *Boutell's Heraldry*, revised by C. W. Scott-Giles (London, 1950), pp. 241-244.

thinkes before we goe any further, we had need enquire
[83] some learned doctor's opinion of this geare, least
we that be silly and looke no further than the word of
God giveth us to see, take it for most grosse idolatrie and
abhomination, because in al the booke of God from the
beginning to the ending, we find no such president [pre-
cedent] or commandement; and therfore (if it please you)
because Doctor Robert Some hath undertaken the matter
we wil heare his learned judgment of this stuffe.

This learned doctor (who hath this wit for the most
part with him, to take no more of a matter than he is
able to deale with) frameth an argument in the name of
an other,[1] thus.   The Church of England maketh mention of saintes deceased, *viz.*, apostles, martyres, *etc.*, in
some of their publike praiers: therfore the Church of
England doth worship saintes deceased.   His answere
is, they are mentioned to stir us up, not to worship them,
but to tread in the steps of their vertue and religion; and
so concludeth the argument very weake and sylly.[2]   But
how if this argument prove his owne, what opinion shal
we then hold of his doctorhood?   Not to speak of his
evil conscience, who (to coullor that he cannot justifie,
and to passe by that he cannot gainesay or disprove) is
not ashamed usually throughout his writings, to father
the forgeries of his owne idle head upon others, thinking
(by depraving the poore professors of the truth) to suppresse it, or (at the least) to get credite and promotion
unto himself.   But I would know of his evil conscience
(which shal ere long be araigned for all these thinges,
before him that is greater than his conscience) whether
he never heard other reasons from some of them, to
prove this their celebration and commemoration of
angels and deceased saintes to be idolatrous, blaspheamous and abhominable, even to the chief authors of this
stuffe, and that in the presence of some verie honorable:
namely [1.] because they dedicate to these angels and
dead saints a peculiar eave and day, caling them after
their names, therby impropriating and giving that to
the creature, which is only due and reserved in the hand

---

[1] Dr. Some is using material from St. Augustine.
[2] Robert Some, *A Godly Treatise, wherein Are Examined and Confuted Many Execrable Fancies,* pp. 37 f.

and possession of the creator. 2. because upon their eaves they enjoyne and bid in their church (upon their Sunday) a publike fast and praier in these angels' and saintes' names. 3. because upon their day (which they cal an holy day) they proclaime a solemne feast to be kept, with general cessation from their labours in their trades, as upon the Lord's day by the fourth commande- ment. 4. and this by a publike law (not to mention al the fleshly and lewd behaviour, idlenes, pride, vanitie, excesse) openly seene and suffered upon these their feastivals and holy daies. 5. because upon these daies they have a peculiar prescript devised worship to each several saint, that they thus celebrate: not heer to men- tion their unsufferable shredding, dismembring, rending and perverting of Scriptures, to clowte[1] up this idolatrie. These reasons if either those two great bishops to whome they were propounded, or this doctor which then heard them, had soundly confuted,[2] and justified this their maner of celebrating and worshipping dead saintes and angels in their church: then had the antichristian tyranny of the one, the reprochful blasphemie of the other, some colour; which now are odious unto God and man.

[84] But now seing these argumentes still remaine with them unanswered, and that they are so loth to meddle with them; I would now only learne of this doctor, where he (in al the Scripture) hath found this idolatrous cus- tome of theirs, to celebrate the memorial of any one deceased saint, and that upon one set day yearly, in this maner: we reade not that the fathers before the flood used it, neither yet after the flood, before the law: yet were they verie godly men, of great vertue, such as in- structed their children in the true worship and waies of God: such as their children honoured and reverenced whilest they lived, and did all filial duties unto them; being dead, decently buried them: but never after kept

---

[1] To patch, mend, or to cover.

[2] This is a reference to Barrow's fourth examination of March 18, 1588/9, when Archbishop Whitgift, Bishop Aylmer, and Dr. Some were present, as well as Lord Burghley, Lord Buckhurst, and Lord Chancellor Hatton. On March 24, 1588/9, Barrow's fifth examination was conducted, and there were three great bishops present, but Dr. Some is unmentioned. Barrow is usually accurate in details, despite his frequent reference to his decayed memory.

any annual or set day in their remembrance. The like under the law we reade of Moses, Samuel, David, *etc.*, men verie famous and renowmed [*sic*] for their vertue and godlines, greatly honored of all whiles they lived, no such matter done to them after they were dead, yet were they presidentes [precedents] by their vertue, even unto all ages unto the worlde's end. The apostles also whome they so especialy above al other saintes prefer and celebrate being dead, yea, taken away as famous martyres, never in this maner upon one special set day celebrated their constancie in the faith and vertue, as we may see by the apostle James and the martyre Steven. Likewise the apostles Paul and Peter being ready to suffer for the gospel, left no such commandementes unto the churches, that any such praiers and festivals should be kept to them or their remembrance, being dead: but rather stirred up and admonished the churches whiles they lived, and disired the churches' prayers for them whiles they lived. So that we seing no ground for this stuffe in the word of God, see not otherwise, but to hold them for detestable idolatries, forgeries and abhominations, for the reasons above recited.

And now, because I have beene somwhat longer even in the bare recital of these trumperies, than I thought; I will passe over the rest of their grosse trash (as their christing their synagogues and belles into the names of sundrie saintes, both men and women saintes, even all in the pope's calender: their solemne visiting their speciall saintes' tombes and monumentes, as their St. Edwine his tombe in St. Paul his church in London by the maior verie solemnely upon Candlemasse night kneeling downe therat, and saying a *Pater Noster*. Likewise the yerely commemoration of the founders and benefactors of colledges in the universities, with their solemne praiers purposely, as also their other idol feastes unto St. Michael and al angels which they adore and celebrate in like maner, with their eave, their fast, their holy day, worship, feast. What wil this learned doctor say to this? Is this also to imm[i]tate their religion and vertue? Where learned he this imm[i]tacion, this religion, if not in the massebooke where they fetch the rest? This is deepe divinitye in deed, and far passing all humane capacitie. No marvaile though he (to whome such misteries be revealed) chaleng to himself to be a doctor of divinitie, advancing himself in the thinges he never sawe, being rashly puffed up with his fleshly mind.

Col. 2: 18

[85] And now having taken a view of their solemne and idol feastes, it remaineth that in a word or two we consider of their hypocritish and pharisaicall fastes, which are in divers sortes: as their saintes' and festivall eaves, their embers or *quatuor tempora*[1], their Lent fast, and their ordinarie Fridaies. Of all which curiously to inquire, by whome and upon what occasions their fastes were first instituted or invented, and how they grew into this abuse, would but minister matter to jangle, and were nothing to the purpose; it is ynough that we find them vaine, ful of hipocrisie, superstition, idolatrie, without ground, and [deviating] from the rules of the Scriptures. Having shewed the feastes to which these eave fastes leade and are a preparation to be heathenish, popish, idolatrous; it sufficeth to prove these fastes which have the same beginning, use, and end, and are of the same conspiracie, to be alike guiltie. Yet I must say, they have more colour and shew of probabilitie, than any of the other: insomuch as in outward pretence they might seeme to humble and prepare the people's heartes to the hearing of God's word, and to withdraw them from worldly encombrances, by attending both to publike and private earnest praier, *etc.* But (as is shewed) the very feast and worship to which they lead being so blasphemous and idolatrous, as also kept and spent in al maner lewdnes, ryote, excesse voluptuousnes, idlenes and sinne: this fast must needes be alike superstitious, abusive, and abhominable. For their embers, they are so grosly popish, as there can nothing be said for them, unles it be Doctor Robert's[2] popeholy excuse, which

---

[1] The *quatuor tempora* were four periods of fasting and prayer during four seasons of the year. Ember days occur on Wednesday, Friday and Saturday, in the weeks following the first Sunday in Lent, Whitsunday, Holy Cross Day (September 14), and St. Lucia's Day (December 13).
[2] Dr. Robert Some.

he maketh for the Lent fast, and al the fasting daies
and eaves that are kept in England at once.

This great clearke saith, they are injoined, not for
religion, but for pollicie, *viz.*, the maintenance of the
navigation, and so referreth unto a statute, made in that
behalf.[1] I perceave now the greatest clarkes are not
alwaies the wisest men. I wil be judged even by any
that never commenced doctor, whether this be a sufficient reason or not. The prince by act commandeth al
these popish fasting daies to be kept, therfore al these
fasting daies, Lent and all, are civil actions. The prince
commandeth all the bishops' ceremonies, government,
injunctions, servicebooke, *etc.*, to be observed, therfore
they are all civill actions, and not to be kept or refused
as in conscience towards God, but as in regard of the
outward court, by Mr. Some his reasons. If he were
not better seene in the statute of nonresidencie than in
the statute of navigation, wel might he be his graceles[2]
chaplen; but never shal he be a true pastor, whilest he
takes this course. It should seeme this popish doctor
either cannot put difference betwixt the first and second
table: or els supposeth that no lay men (as he termeth
them) may medle with the first table; els would he never
be so grosse as to conclude, because the prince commandeth it, therfore it is a civil action: yea, and an
other more blaspheamous conclusion therupon; the
prince commandeth it, therfore it is no matter of conscience, but ought without scruple to be done, for (saith
this doctor) he is a simple divine, that cannot distinguish betwixt the external court and the court of conscience.[3] Might he not [86] thus bring in al maner

1 Barrow is referring to the abstinence from eating meat, which was regarded as a popish error. Dr. Some contends that the encouragement
of eating of fish helps the cause of navigation. See Some, *A Godly Treatise*
(1589), p. 38. By statute, 5 *Eliz.*, C. V, Wednesday, in addition to Friday and Saturday, was declared a Fish Day. This special law for Wed-
nesdays was later repealed, 27 *Eliz.*, C. XI. See "An Acte Touching Certayne Politique Constitutions for the Maintenance of the Navye," in
Great Britain, *The Statutes of the Realm*, IV, Part 1, pp. 422 - 428; 718 f.
See also W. Cunningham, *The Growth of English Industry and Commerce
in Modern Times*, II, Part 1 (1925), pp. 67 - 73.
2 A slur upon His Grace, Archbishop Whitgift. Dr. Some concluded the
Epistle Dedicatorie of his *A Godly Treatise* (1589) with the words: " At
my Lorde's Grace of Canterburie his house in Lambeth. Maii 12, 1589."
3 *Ibid.*, pp. 38 f.

idolatrie and humane traditions, being commanded by the prince? And no man ought to refuse the same, and stand for the maintenance of the faith, because now the action concerneth not the conscience, but the outward obedience to the magistrate. But of that point hereafter.

First let me shew, that publike fasting is an action belonging to the church, to be used upon special occasions, as in time of some publike calamitie, great transgression, *etc.*, with great reverence, preparation of the heart and soule, praier, and other holy exercises. That publike fastes have alwaies belonged to the church and beene exercised therin, plentifully apeareth in the Old and New Testament as Leviticus 16: 29 and 23: 7, Numbers 29: 7, 1 Samuel 7: 6, Ester 4: 16, 17, Nehemiah 9, Ezra 8: 21, Matthew 9: 15, Acts 13: 2, 3, and 14: 23. Besides these examples, we have many doctrines and rules set us downe in the word, how to use, and what thinges to eschew, both in publike and private fastes. Isaiah 58. Joel 1 and 2 chapter. Zachariah 7. Daniel 9. Matthew 6: 16. Luke 5: 35. Matthew 17: 21. 1 Corinthians 7: 5. So that he is a very young Christian, and (in my judgment) not worthy to be a teacher in the church of God, that taketh the publike fastes of the church to be civil actions, and not to concerne the conscience. But let me yet come neerer unto this doctor and use more familiar reasons unto him, wherwith he is better acquainted than with the word of God. Are not al his fasting daies and fasting eaves, as they arise in their calender, solemnely bidden in their church by the priest after his second lesson, on the Sonday? Are not the people commanded there, to fast upon such holy tydes, to resort to church, to pray and heare their divine service? What thinkes he? Are these civil actions?

Well, and now to his Lent fast, which he would put away with abstinence from flesh, and that not for religion, but for maintenance of the navie, *etc.* I would first know of Mr. Doctor, whither he findeth in his bookes, that the Lent was first found out for the maintenance of navigation, and whither it was brought and receaved in England for that purpose. He wil say, that although it hath beene popishly and superstitiously used heretofore in the Church of England, yet now it is used for the maintenance of navigation: this is a thing not denied. So was it also in the most popish and blind time of all, and that much more than it is now; when scarse one in a land durst eate flesh without the pope's especiall dispensation. Men could then no more than now eate fish, except some went to sea to take it. But shall I therfore say that the fast injoyned by, and used in the church, is a civill action? How commeth it to passe then, that it is so solemnly observed in holy church upon the first day therof, commonly called Ash-Wednesday? In stead of the popish shrift, dis[ci]pling, and asshes,[1] they use an especiall communion; wherin the people are invited to do their repentance. Bitter curses and execrations be read and pronounced against certaine sinnes, wherof never a one in the church is free, or ever yet repented of them; and there made to acknowledg and confirme their owne damnation, by ratifying the curse with their owne mouth, saying *Amen* unto [87] them. And this as they most grosly beare themselves and the people in hand, that in the primitive church was used a godly discipline; that at the beginning of Lent, such persons as were notorious sinners were put to open pennance, and punished in this world, *etc.*, that their soules might be saved in the day of the Lord, *etc.* This stuffe by the priest must be read in the pulpet upon their Ash-Wednesday. Where find they this in all the New Testament, in the practise of the primitive churches there? Know they what either the primitive churches or the government of Christ meaneth? That thus popishly dreame of a discipline upon that day especially, of such a corporall pennance of a Lent, *etc.* Where find they this trumperie in Christ's Testament? But

---

[1] Shrift, displing and asshes. Shrift is penance imposed by a priest. Displing refers to disciplining or satisfaction rendered for sin. Asshes probably refers to the practice of sprinkling ashes on the heads of penitents on Ash-Wednesday, with the words: "remember, man, that thou art ashes and to ashes thou shalt return." See John Strype, *Ecclesiastical Memorials*, I, Appendix, CIX, 291.

this wretch that in his conscience knew the idolatrie, and these grosse fooleries wel inough: thought to hide that he could not defend, by saying, the Lent was but abstinence from flesh at the prince's commandement; let him reade the last collect of their commination upon Ash-Wednesday, and see there if they desire not God to be favorable to his people which turne to him in weeping, fasting, and praying. Is this but to abstaine from flesh? Let him looke their epistle and gospell upon the same day, the one taken out of the prophet Joel, chapter 2, verse 12. "Turne you unto me with all your heartes with fasting, weeping, and mourning, *etc.*" The other out of Mathew 6: 16. "When ye fast be not sad, *etc.*" Let him yet further peruse his portuise [portas] upon the first Sunday in Lent: he shall find their collect of the day (as they cal it) to begin thus: "O Lord which for our sakes didst fast forty daies and forty nights: give us grace to use such abstinence, that our flesh being subdued, *etc.*" Their gospell of the same day, taken out of Mathew 4, sheweth the hystorie of Christ's fast and temptation, *etc.* Let him yet turne his portuise [portas], and see if he find not there an especiall communion for everie day in their passion weeke, and upon their Good Friday a trental of collectes.[1] Are all these but civill actions? But abstinence from flesh, for the maintenance of navigation? Doth the statute by him alledged command these things? Or is it the prieste's office to meddle with that statute? Yf all this were, yet could they not help or hide this grosse poperie and heinous idolatrie, which they in these their blasphemous Lent fast, *etc.*, wherof, because this doctor was either ashamed or afeard to meddle which (being such abhominable stuffe as can find no defence or excuse) I also will not meddle with the further discoverie or refutacion therof, as taking no pleasure to rave in their filthy channels.

Yet remaine two pointes of his deep and pestilent

---

[1] A trental is a series of thirty requiem masses. For Good Friday there are three collects, and a reading from the epistle, Hebrews 10, and a reading from the gospel, John 19. Perhaps Barrow is using trental in the sense of a series, but not with the number included. Possibly, Barrow intended the word "trinal," which means threefold, triple.

divinitie to be examined; the one, whether princes may set any permanent possitive lawes, set daies and times, when, what time of the yeare, and how long to fast? The other whither [whether] the prince's lawfull constitutions concerning outward things, bind the conscience. The first Robert Some affirmeth, and therby ratifieth his Lent fast, embers, eve fasts, and Friday fastes. The other he saith toucheth not the conscience, making a [88] subtil distinction betweene the external court and the court of conscience.[1] To follow him so far as the error and wickednes of these two positions would leade, would make of it self too wide a gap in the worke we have in hand. I will therfore handle the first point so far as it maketh to this present matter; and the second very briefly, by way of digression.

Before I come to his divinitie, I would know of this learned doctor, whither if the prince ratifie and command the pope's blasphemous decrees and abhominations; whither this doth either alter the propertie or qualitie of them: or such commandement bindeth not the conscience? I need not here stand to shew these his popeholy fastes of the Church of England to be idolatrous in the first invention, and now more abhominable in the present use, such stuffe as he will not file his hands with the defence of them; and now whether these be bettered in that they are commanded by act of parliament, *etc.*

But to come to the matter in hand, whither the prince or whole church may make permanent lawes for the yearly, monethly, or weekly fastes to be still observed upon this or that day. I have above shewed, that fastes are upon especial and present occasions, actions, calamities, *etc.*, to be exercised, to the humbling and preparing the bodie and soule unto true repentance, praier and other holy exercises. This all the practise of the Jewes in their temple sheweth: who upon especial occasion as war, plague, *etc.*, used fasting. That these set fastes were not perdurable any longer than upon these present occasions, we also find. For the fastes that Ezra

---

[1] Some, *A Godly Treatise* (1589), pp. 38 f. Dr. Some makes his distinction *inter externum forum et conscientiae forum.*

and Nehemiah instituted were not continued from yere to yere unto the posteritie. This very question also the Lord by his prophet Zachary fully resolveth, in the seventh and eighth chapters of his prophecie: where the Jewes sending unto the temple to know whither the fast instituted in the fifth moneth, for the destruction of their temple, were still to be observed, the temple being againe built after their returne out of Babilon; to whome the prophet (after he had reproved their former sinne, obstinacie, and superstitious abuse both of fasting and al the worship of God, which were unavaileable and did but aggravate their judgmentes, so long as they continued in their sinnes) shewed them that it was not their fasting from meat, or eating, that made them more or lesse acceptable to God, but their faithful obedience unto his word, and that his kingdome consisteth not in meates and drinkes, *etc.*, as also instructing them of the true use and endes of fasting and praier; in the end concludeth, chapter 8: 19, *etc.*, that all their former fastes of the fourth, fifth, seventh, and tenth moneth were now to cease, promising unto them in stead therof, a continuall feast, with his abundant blessinges, so long as they walked faithfully with the Lord, comparing in that chapter his former plagues, to their former sinnes, *etc.* So then we see how fasting is upon especial and present occasions to be used, and those or such like occasions ceasing, not to be continued without end or use: for that were not only to make positive lawes, to bind that which God hath left at libertie: [89] but also to put holines in the verie action of fasting, without right end or true use.

Further the practise and use of fasting in the church of Christ under the gospel, sheweth, that there can be no permanent lawes of the time and day made therof. For they (not only upon such present and publike occasions of calamitie) are to use it; but also in some especial and waightie actions, wherof dependeth the good or evil estate of that church or congregation: as upon the choice of the officers and elders of the church. That peculiar congregation in such actions, at such times, is to humble themselves with fasting and praier:

Acts 3: 2

Acts 14: 23

402

and yet this fast neither to be enjoined to others which have not that occasion of such like action; neither to be annually, monethly, *etc.*, continued of them after that action performed. Therfore we may conclude, that neither the magistrate, nor the whole church may set positive lawes of publike fastes, to be holden upon such a day or such a moneth from yeare to yeare; seing they are upon present urgent and especial occasions to be 1 Cor. 7: 5 used. And as for private fastes, seing they are wholy put in everie Christian's libertie and the occasions neither concerning others, nor publikely knowne of them; there can much lesse be any positive lawes made to fast this or that day of necessitie: what gaineth then this learned doctor, by this evasion ? That the prince commandeth these yearly, monethly, and weekly fastes; unles it be to lay that blame and blasphemie, which before was due unto the pope their founder, now upon the prince. Do not these priestes an high piece of service unto her majesty heerin ? But this profound divine, hath yet one trick in his budget, to salve al this matter; and that is, the prince doth not command them to fast, but only upon such daies to abstaime from flesh. How false this is by their especial devotions upon such daies, the priestes' solemne bidding them in open church, *etc.*, hath beene fully already convinced. Moreover, I would know of him (if he can tel me) if the action should be meerly civil as he would have it, what the church hath to doe with it to publish them, to assemble and pray, *etc.*, on those daies. Also, why the very eaves and daies in time and nomber as the pope used and left them, are stil by them so reteined and used ? Were not this to offend the consciences of the faithful ? To nourish others in their foreconceived superstition and idolatrie ? Is not this the verie cause that maketh so manie papistes ? In that so manie popish relikes stil remaine ?

And now further I would know of Mr. Doctor, how he can proove by the law of God, that the prince may forbid his subjectes to eate flesh upon such daies and such times, *etc.* I demaund not now any pollitike reasons, for then he would smite me downe with these two; for the sparing the yong increase of beastes, and

403

for the maintenance of the navie: but my conscience cannot rest upon them: I had rather have one rule or example out of the word of God, where I can find no such president [precedent], unles it be King Saule's: who indeed by solemne curse forbad the Israelites to tast food but for one day, and that upon as urgent occasion as [90] I suppose possibly can be alledged, namly, during the battel and pursuite of the Philistines: but he was reproved for it both by the Holy Ghost in the mouth of Jonathan when he said. My Father hath troubled the land, see now how mine eies are made cleere by tasting a title of this hony; and also by Lot from God himself, the matter comming to be tried betwixt him and his sonne, who had made the default, when the Lord answered not by Urim as he had covenanted and accustomed: the hypocrite Saule desired the Lord to give the perfit or upright: and so Jonathan was taken, denounced by God's owne judgment innocent and not guiltie: and the wretch left as the author and cheefe in the trespasse, by making that ungodly law. So then, if it were not lawful for him upon such a waightie occasion, by way of law, to restreine the use of God's creatures for one day; I cannot see how upon any pollitike cause, such restraintes may be made throughout, and from yeare to yeare.

My reasons are, first God hath created these creatures and not man, and given to man soveraignty over them, to use them to food freely; therfore they which by law restraine the sober and free use of them: 1. both cal back the Lord's liberal grant, 2. and deprive the Creator of honour and praise, in and for the use of them, and 3. make a law of that the Lord hath left in libertie. 4. then the apostle calleth such lawes as in this maner command to abstaine from meates, the doctrines of divels. 5. to conclude, the apostle often chargeth us to stand fast in our libertie, and not to be brought in bondage of any thing, which is by God put in our powre. But by such lawes, our free use of such creatures is for these times taken away, *etc*. For which reasons, I am (as yet) in conscience perswaded, that the civil magistrate ought not to make permanent lawes of that the Lord hath left

1 Sam. 14

Verse 29

Verse 41

Gen. 9: 2, 3

1. Tim. 4: 3, 4, 5

1. Cor. 6: 12

404

in our libertie, neither by way of law to restraine them one day, for any civil or pollitike causes whatsoever. I would not now be understood of ecclesiastical and religious fastes; we have both lawes and plentiful examples in the Scriptures, that the prince and church may proclame such general fastes, upon occasions, *etc.* Neither would I heere be suspected to goe about to diminish or pluck away the high sacred power and authoritie the Lord hath given to the civil magistrate, as to his lieftenant over both body, life, and goodes: so much as to shew that the prince's or magistrate's power is yet by God himself limited and circumscribed; for the transgression wherof, they shal (as any other men) accompt unto the Lord; in whome they are to command, as we also readily in the same Lord to obey. Titus 3: 1 Rom. 13 Eccles. 8: 2

The excesse or abuse of these creatures the magestrate may and ought to punish and represse because that is sinne; and therfore is the law and sword of God committed unto him: but by a law of his owne (wherof is no warrant in the word of God) to restraine them for these or these times, I thinke there he exceedeth his commission, though upon never so great colour of pollicie, and that the action were purged of all this Romish superstition and idolatrie, wherwith nowe it is refersed.[1] The prince is to governe, oversee and provide for the common welth, [91] administring and dispensing, gathering and dispersing the creatures and welth therof, as a father and a steward: yet stil with this interim,[2] as the steward and servant of God according to their maister's will, as they that shall accompt. Deuteronomy 71 Psa. 82: 6, 7 Mat. 25: 19

But heere it may be said, that the magistrat and not we shall answere for this sinne, if it be any; that it is our dutie to obey in these outward things without inquirie or questioning, because the reason, charge, nor accompt of the magistrate's office is not committed unto us: neither may we thus enquire into the same, being private men without apparant presumption and secret rebellion. God forbid that any of his servants should be stained with either of these faults: we honour, reverence and

---

[1] Stuffed or crammed.
[2] Provisional arrangement, qualification.

obey the office and person of the magistrate (I say not now worship and adore) as God himself. In that we seek to know the magistrate's dutie, *etc.* We do not therby either intermedle or intrude into his office: unlesse we knew how to obey and how far, how should we obey ? What is not of faith is sinne: and where should we know either his or our owne duty, but in the book of God ? Wherby both he for commanding and making ungoldly decrees, and we for obeiing them, shal be judged. Obedience must alwaies be in the Lord. If the prince demand or command my body or goodes in his service, I am to yeild them both readily without further questioning of his ententes [intents], endes or purposes, those belong not unto me: only I am to looke to the outward thing which I do, that it be lawful and warrantable by the word: as the prince commandeth me to make ready my weapons to serve in the war, I may not refuse: but if this war be apparantly unlawful, as against God's servantes, *etc.*, I may not obey. The prince maketh me an officer or under magistrate; I am in this place to serve him, but not to execute any of his unlawfull decrees, *etc.* The prince demandeth my goodes; I am readily and willingly to depart with them al unto him, without inquirie: but if the prince command me to give my goodes to such an idol, or after such a wicked maner, as by way of tithes to a minister, or by way of pension to an antichristian minister, I may not obey, but rather suffer his indignation, yea, death, because now I make my self a trespasser, in doing that which God forbiddeth, at the prince's commandement. So in like maner, if the prince should command all the goodes, victuals or cattell I have, I most willingly would obey; knowing that for this he, and not I, should accompt. For I am commanded to pay tribute, and not to set the portion how much or when, my self. But if the prince make a law, that no man shal eate flesh during the Lent, but such as have special licence from him; I say this law is unjust, contrarie to the bountiful liberalitie of God, who hath given al men at al times a free use of these creatures to food. It is contrarie to the order of God's creation, who hath therfore created

Rom. 14: 22, 23

Hos. 5: 11

Mica. 6: 16

Rom. 13: 6
Mat. 17: 27

1 Pet. 2: 13
1 Sam. 22: 17

Dan. 3: 18

and ordeined them. It is contrarie to God's honour, who wil have praise and thankes for the holy and pure use of them. It is contrarie to God's wisdome, who hath seene no such law of restraint expedient. It is contrarie to the libertie and freedome God hath given us in Christ: God having at al times put al his creatures [92] for our sustenance in our choice and power, even as the greene herbe of the field. Therfore I see not why the servantes of God should any more by this comandement be restrained or forbeare, than Daniel did for the decree of the king of Persia for the thirty daies inhibition, to make sute or petition to any, save the king only. We need not feare the indignation of man, when God approveth the thinges we doe. Pollicie must take, and Gen. 1: 28 not give lawes unto religion. The Lord hath by his word given a blessing to all the creatures, that they Levit. 26 should increase and multiplie by vertue therof to the Deut. 28 use and sustenance of mankind, even of everie living soule that he bringeth into the world. Yea, before he made man, he provided food for him. This goodnes he stil extendeth to the good and bad generally to all. So Isa. 28: 18 that to make such pollitike lawes for the restraint of this the Lorde's bountie, is not only to distrust the Lorde's Joel 1: 55 providence, and not to depend therof for the future time, using the bread of the day with thanckfulnes in sobrietie; but to ascribe to our owne pollicie and councel that, which is due to the Lord of life, the gyver of increase. Famine and scarcitie are not kept away with humane pollicie: they are the messengers and punishments of God for sinne. Yet speak I not heer against godly providence, christian parcimonie, or sober and modest use of God his creatures: al this may be done without either breach of God's lawes, or restraining that by law, which God hath left at libertie.

Now commeth to be considered that learned probleme of Doctor Some, wherin he thinketh himself as safe, as if he had got a castle on his back, trusting more to the fame and toomb of his Mr. Calvine for the defence therof, than unto his owne learning or the truth of the matter: namly, that the conscience of man is not bound by this law, but [only] the outward action: and he is a simple

divine that cannot distinguish betweene the external
court and the court of conscience.[1] For the author of
this doctrine, though I cannot assent unto him in this
very point, for such reasons as I shall by and by shew:
yet is he no patrone or maister for such schollers as this
popish doctor, yea, and other divines of these our miserable daies, who doe but seek out shiftes and evasions out
of his writinges, to cover and defend their shameful
transgressions, which they without conscience or feare
of God commit. For by this subtil distinction (being
understood in the best sense) hath D. R. S.[2] both ani-
mated and confirmed princes in their wicked decrees,
by enjoyning obedience unto such lawes, and taken
away al feare of Gode's wrath and judgments from such
as obey these lawes; making them beleeve, that the
conscience is not heerby bound, burdened or charged,
but only the outward action, *etc.*, and therfore they need
to make no scruple of conscience to obey such hestes
[commands].

Wel, that I may at once pluck from him Ajax' shield
(this is his owne profane phrase)[3] and set this his author
most sharply against him, who hath especially excepted
all lawes, which either bind that [which] God hath left
in our libertie, and al traditions whatsoever, that are
brought into the church: he inveigheth most gravely
and worthely against [93] all such lawes and traditions,
and exempteth all Christians from the obedience or
receaving of such lawes or traditions. How will Doctor
Some do now for his Lent? We have shewed it (in
the best construction) to be an humane law, restraining
and inhibiting the sober and holy use of those creatures
which God hath put in our libertie. But as the truth
in deed is, and as their present practise without all contradiction declareth: it is (as it is used with them) a
burdenous idolatrous tradition, a papisticall and
Romish custome, being used after that superstitious

[1] Some, *A Godly Treatise* (1589), pp. 38 f.
[2] Doctor Robert Some.
[3] In 1588 Dr. Some had written, *A Godly Treatise*, p. 26: " If any shall
gather of this I have set down, that I undertake the defence of ignorant
ministers: my answer is, that my writings and sermons are not Ajax'
shielde to cover them, but the Lorde's sword to cutte them."

abhominable manner that I have above declared, a speciall and solemne part of their worship, a great and principall action of their church; as the solemne bidding and keeping of that, sheweth. How can this doctor then say, it concerneth not the conscience? Do not the publike actions of the church, the worship and service of God, praier and fasting, concerne the conscience? Or may such trumperie traditions be brought into the church? Or laid upon the conscience? He learneth no such doctrine of Mr. Calvine: who alloweth no humane divises, no apocrypha traditions, to be brought into the church of God, how holy, pregnant or necessarie soever they may seeme to be.

Yet in handling this point, he hath unhappily stumbled at I wote not what old prescriptions and auncient erronious customes, of keeping a solemne memoriall of the birth, death, and resurrection of Christ upon their peculiar daies yerely; as also the feast of Pentecost, when the apostles received the Holy Ghost, *etc.* He also alloweth of apocrypha leitourgies, viz., a set and stinted forme of numbred publike praiers to be brought into and used in the church, and this as it should seeme, because he would not be thought a Novatian,[1] or an author of new religion, *etc.* But see, how he hath therby both insnared himself, and opened a gap for other like trumperie to be brought into the church, which may easily carrie both as great shew of antiquitie and of godlines, as these. He hath therby also given a verie pernitious president [precedent] unto other ages, as apeareth in the miserable estate of our common welth; who are a great deale more ready to follow him in his errors and transgressions, than to imitate him in his godly vertues, laborious and holy life. Me thinkes also, that Mr. Calvine in the other part of this point (concerning such lawes as pluck away any part of our christian libertie, or inhibit and restraine that which God hath put in our power) hath greatly departed from himself therin. For having very truly set downe, that it is heinous presumption in any mortall man to restraine

---

[1] Novatian, a third century priest, schismatic, antipope, rival of Pope Cornelius, and founder of the sect of Cathari or Puritans.

O*

or make lawes of such things as the Lord hath left in libertie; he straightway (least he should offend, or keepe back civil magistrates from receaving the gospel) inventeth a pollitike distinction, betwixt the outward or civil court, and the court of conscience; saying that this outward court respecteth men only, and bindeth not the conscience of the doer, but the outward actions only: the other concerneth matters belonging unto God, and therfore bindeth the conscience. Thus hath he both lost and intangled himself, and utterly overthrowen all his former doctrine.

[94] Conscience he defineth from the second of the Romanes, verse 15, to be a certaine feeling or remorse within our selves, according to the knowledg of God's wil, which doth continually present us, and accuse or acquit us before the judgment seat of God. Although this definition be somwhat of the scantest, as making the conscience of man extend no further than his present knowledg, which yet we read in the Scriptures stretched much further, namly, to the whole life of man (wherin God as in a book writeth al the thinges done in this mortal life), which booke he often openeth not until the final judgment, but suffereth men to run on, and die in their sinne without feeling, untill then he plucking away all vailes and lets, set al their sinnes that ever they have committed in thought, word or deed in order, according to their indignitie before them: wherupon, in horror of conscience, the Scripture setteth out and describeth their fearfull desperate estate unto our capacitie, shewing, that in that day, they shall even desire the rockes to fall upon them and the seas to hide them from the wrath of the Lamb, *etc.* If our consciences were only charged but with the sinnes which we commit against our knowledg, then ignorance of God's lawe excuseth the breach therof, then were the ignorant in far most best estate, and had the cleerest conscience, then needed we not to pray for pardon for our ignorant sinnes, *etc.* But because our conscience in this life cannot be touched with, or accuse us here of more than we know to be sinne (for as the apostle saith, without the law we lived, but when the commandement came, sinne

Margin references:
Rev. 20: 12
Math. 16: 27

Rom. 2: 3, 4, 5, *etc.*

Eccles. 8: 11, 12, 13

Isa. 57: 11

Revel. 6: 16

Rom. 2: 12
2 Thes. 1: 8
Levit. 5: 17, 18

revived, but we died), therfore to avoide further controversie, I rest in this his description, which me thinkes
also maketh verie fully against himself: for we see how
the knowledg of the law reviveth sinne, and maketh it Rom. 7
out of measure sinful.

But to come to the point: Mr. Calvine saith that by
the civil lawes the conscience is not bound, but the outward action only. If he meane thus, that the conscience
is not subject to the civil magistrate, but the bodie only,
he saith true. If he meane that the civill magistrate
can but looke upon the outward action in the keeping
or breach of his law, he saith true. For man, no, not
the whole church, can enter into God's seat, to search
and judge the conscience, the inward affections of the Jer. 17: 9
heart, *etc.* Man can but behould and judge the out- 1 Cor. 2: 11
ward actions, according to the law of God; for if they
could, then should no hipocrites creep into, or remaine
in the church. The heart and conscience (untill by
outward actions it be revealed) is not only liable unto,
but searched by, and judged of God. And this we see
as well in the lawes of the first table as in the lawes of
the second. Whiles I resort and walket [*sic*] together
with the church, and worship God to all outward seeming unreprovablie: though I be inwardly never so great
an hypocrite: untill my sinne apparantly breake out,
the church can no more censure me, than the civill
magistrate can punish me before I have broken the law.
So then we see the secret conscience is as far out of the
reach, censure and judgment of the church, as it is out
of the [95] magistrate's hand, untill some fault or offence
be made.

But if Mr. Calvine meane (as his wordes and whole
scope intend) that the conscience is not charged with
the law of the outward court, but with the outward
action only, then surely he greatly erred. For this
doctrine is most dangerous and false, as discharging the
conscience from the whole second table, unto which it
is as much bound, as unto the first. Neither can we
keep or please God in the first, that walke not with a
good conscience towardes all men in the second. Our
praiers are abhominable that are offred with handes ful Isa. 1 & 76
[26 ?] chapters

411

Prov. 15: 8 &
21: 27

of blood, or with our heartes abounding with lustes, or set upon the world. We are not to offer our offring upon the altar, untill we have satisfied our injuried or offended brother, and made agreement with our con-

Math. 5: 23, *etc.* science, while we are in the way: we cannot love God whome we have not seene, if we love not our brother, *etc.* Thus we see how God himself hath joined the

1 Joh. 4: 20 tables together, and injoined them upon the consciences of all men; as wherby they shalbe judged before him. I speake not now concerning the heavie waight of God's law, which none of our fathers were able to beare, or the strait exaction of the perimplishment[1] therof; the best of us not being able to answere him one of a thowsand, from both which the death of Jesus Christ hath set us free. Yet hath not our Lord Jesus Christ abrogate one title of his Father's law, neither exempt the consciences of men from the second table, and bound them with, and unto the first table only.[2] If the transgression of the least of God's lawes be death, and this death extend both unto the bodie and soule; who can deliver and exempt our consciences from a carefull and most strict observation of all God's lawes, even with all our strength and the utmost God hath given us, daily examining our consciences even to every idle word or vaine thought, powring out and unfolding our hearts before the Lord, indighting, arraigning and judging our owne heartes before him the knower and searcher of them, that so we may have our debt-book cancelled,

1 Cor. 11: 31 and all our sinnes blotted out through the blood and mediation of that immaculate lamb that taketh away the sinnes of the world.

Moreover, there is no consequent, because the civill court or outward action concerneth men only, and is

Rom. 13: 5 done unto them, that therfore those lawes and actions

1 Pet. 2: 13 bind not the conscience. For both we are bidden to

Act. 24: 14, 15. obey the magistrate for conscience sake, and from the
16 heart; and to behave our selves towardes al men, that we may have the testimonie of a cleere conscience. It

---

[1] Perimplishment implies thorough fulfillment, completion, accomplishment.
[2] The first and second table refer to the two divisions of the Decalogue, the religious and moral commandments, respectively.

sufficeth not to do the thing we are commanded, but we must doe it cheerfully and with a good heart: we must not only doe that which is good, but doe it wel and as we ought to doe. The civil magistrate in punishing an offendor, may yet do it with such affections, as he may before God murther him. We also in all duties of charitie, must do them with a single heart and eie, for els it availeth us not. If we doe them grudgingly, as of constreint, or to be seene or [96] praised of men, or of custome with others, and not of conscience towards God and our neighbour, they profit us nothing. And this holdeth as wel in the first, as in the second table. Our religion is vaine (though it be outwardly never so unreproveable) if our heart stand not sound and upright. Col. 3: 22, 23, 24 Eph. 6: 5, 6

A strange doctrine it is, to sever the conscience, and the law; the conscience, and the outward action; they may aswel heere whiles we live sever the bodie and the soule, which though they are distinct thinges, yet can they not be heere seperate. The bodie shall rue the thoughtes of the soule; the soule shal rue the sinnes of the bodie: the bodie and soule together make a man, and the man both body and soule, are liable unto al God's lawes, and shalbe judged for the breach of the least. Hath God commanded it? We must obey and do his commandement with all our soule, and that with such circumstances and affections as the Lord requireth, be the action never so sleight and bodily in our seeming, yet it must be done in singlenes of heart as in the eies and name of God; yea (saith the apostle), as unto God himself, to whome we shall accompt for all thinges done in this mortall flesh. Knowing then this terror of the Lord, it behooveth us to take heed what we put upon the file of that record against that day, to examine our owne heartes and consciences daily, least they be hardened through the deceitfulnes of sinn; to judge our selves heere how we doe the wil of God in al thinges, and not to put off through securitie, until we be judged of God. And sure if this doctrine were sincerely and soundly taught, it would stay the rage of sinne, which now breaketh out (as the baker's oven whiles it is not Collos. 3: 17 2 Cor. 5: 10 Hos. 7: 4, 6

413

tended) both in magistrates and people. The magistrate would be wel advised what lawes he maketh, the people how they obey; knowing, that both shal answere unto the great Judge: wheras now by this deepe learning of Doctor Some, the conscience not being bound by the prince's law, but the outward and temporal action only; the prince may make what lawes he lust for civill pollicie: the people ought without all scruple to obey, seing their lawes bind not the conscience, *etc*. But if the prince's lawes be contrary or divers to the lawes of God, then is not our conscience or body bound by or unto them, then are we not to obey such lawes, but stand for our Christian libertie and the maintenance of the faith in all patient maner, rather induring the wrath of man, than procuring the wrath of God. The vaine pretence of civil pollicie, wil neither excuse them nor us before God the Judge of al, with whome we have to doe. He will have his lawes, statutes and judgmentes kept and not altered, innovate or neglected, according to humane wisdome, the state and pollicies of times and humors of men, which varie and turne with the wind, making lawes to day and abrogating them to morrow, one prince after one manner, an other quite contrarie. But the statutes and judgmentes of God, which are delivered and expounded unto us by his holy prophetts, endure for ever the pure wisdome, the upright justice, the true exposition and faithful execution of his moral law: which lawes [97] were not made for the Jewes' state only (as Mr. Calvine hath taught) but for all mankind, especially for al the Israel of God: from which lawes, it is not lawful in judgment to varie or decline either to the one hand, or to the other. For what doe we therby, but controle the wisdome and equitie of God's waies, prefer and think our owne more wise and equal, abrogate his, and set up our owne instead therof; frame God to the common welth, and not the common welth to the wil of God. Thus by the neglect of God's lawes, doth the whole world overflow with al maner sinne, plunged deeply and unrecoverably into God's wrath, and even hastneth him unto final judgmentes and vengeance. These are the best fruites that are

Marginal notes:

Deut. 4: 8 & 7: 11 & 11: 1 & 26: 16

Psal. 119 & 106: 106

Mal. 4: 4

Deu. 4: 6

Ezek. 18: 25

reaped by this doctor's deep divinitie, whiles he severeth the conscience from the law, making the law to bind the outward action, but not the conscience.

But see now through this doctor's cavils I have beene drawen from the present purpose: which was, to consider what kind of fastes are used in this their Church of England, which as we have hitherto shewed to be wholly derived from their mother Church of Rome, in the same idolatrous maner, times and seasons: so there now remaineth an other new kind of fast, invented and brought in by the learned ministry of the land, such as sue and seeke for the reformation of the church: and this without the licence or allowance of their lords the bishops. This fast I know not from whence it was brought, whither from Geneva or els where, in despight (it should seeme) of the fastes used by the Jewes and in the primitive churches. Here the learned priestes and preachers lay their heades togither, choose out three or four from amongst them to preach. One of them must play *Sinne*, an other the *Judgments of God*, the third *Repentance*, the fourth the *Gospel.* The people are solemnly bidden from al quarters to this stageplay who (at the first invention of it) flocked in thick and threefold to behold this noveltie. There he that plaieth sinne, frameth himself cunningly to his auditory, that he offend none of his great Cananites nor rich gluttons, but especially having regard unto his first othe at the taking of his antichristian ministerie, when he forsware Christ and the faith, unto his lord the bishop and bound himself not to speake against anie thing by publike authoritie established, *etc.* He hath great regard, not to medle with any of these matters, least he awake the sleepy dogg, and know not how to apease him againe, or recover his credit and estimation with him. Wherfore I warrant you, there is no sinne against the first table in the land, except it be among such as stil remayne papistes, recusantes, *etc.*, and such as will customably blaspheme the name of God, and also such as doe not diligently inough countenance the preaching priestes (I should say as frequent not their sermons), *etc.*, but otherwise for the state of the church, there is nothing amisse,

415

but flourisheth marvailously, abounding with such learned priestes, as no church in the world hath the like: yet
I must say as I have heard, let the audito[98]rie be such
as will back them, and they wil have a fling at the
bishops in some eloquent Delphick darke speaches, such
as may be retracted, or have a double construction (as
shal more apeare when we come to their maner of
preaching). If they were removed, and they had the
discipline of the apostles in their parishes, then all were
wel, there is nothing else wanting amongst them. And
for this all that mourne in the chine,[1] and sigh in secret
for it, (though neither priest nor people know what it
meaneth) yet they must now fast, and then they have
done their duties to the ful; the fault is not in them, but
in God almighty that they have it not. Such a priest
as this is a blazing star, a paragon of a countrie, one of
the new found Martine's saints.[2] And such people are
Puritans or Martinistes praecisians: though both priest
and people for all this glosing and hypocrisie with God
and the world, stand still under the bishop's antichristian yoke, the one adminstring, the other receaving
all their detestable wares and markes. But to returne
againe to this their fast; if you come now to the second
table of the law; o they are severe men, they will make
a conscience to tremble. Yf there be ever an usurer,
or a drunkard, or an whoremaister, they will so bebayt
[bait thoroughly] him, as he will not love a sermon
againe a goodwhile. Yet for all this when they meet
a brode [abroad, outside] they are good frendes, especially when they meet at the sacramentes: then they forgive one another from the bottome of their heartes. Now
here must be noted by the way, that these kind of persons
are not indeed the most beneficiall to these fasting pharisaicall preachers, and lightly will not goe further than
by law he must needes; which is, to pay him his tithes

[1] To mourne in the chine is to suffer from a disease, or to lament, grieve,
bewail. The *Oxford English Dictionary* is uncertain on this point.
[2] Most of the Martin Marprelate pamphlets were published in 1588 and
1589, immediately before Barrow's work. Some of them sarcastically
referred to the saints in heaven, newly knighted as Sir Peter and Sir Paul.
See [Martin Junior], *Theses Martinianae* ; [Thomas Nash ?], *A Counter-
cuffe Given to Martin Junior* ; and [Thomas Nash ?], *The Return of the
the Renowned Cavaliero Pasquill of England.*

and offringes, *etc.* But in their companie they delight
not, neither wil bid them home to their houses or magnifie them: and therfore these men must beare with
them, if in the pulpit (when they are ravished with
zeale of the lord) they have now and then a gird[1] at
them to ease their stomackes, especially now for fashion
sake. As for al the rest of their auditorie, there is no
such sinne amongst them, and therfore they shalbe exhorted to confesse all their sinnes, in thought, word, or
deed unto the Lord, to acknowledg their evill waies, and
powre out their heartes before the Lord, to sorrow and
mourne, and if they have any voluntarie teares, to help
the priest to weep for that present, though neither their
evil waies be shewed them, but (as hath beene said) most
cunningly hid and covered from their eies, least they
should see and avoid them. Neither in their private
conversation, offices, houses, are their sinnes by the
light and power of the word discovered unto them, or
they called to the practise of their duties, least they
indeed should then espie the deceit of these miserable
guides, that have made them beleeve they stood in
God's favour all this time, and detesting their perfidy
and hypocrisie, should returne unto the Lord. And
thus being exhorted to lament and repent their sinnes
they know not, and to returne to the Lord; the priest
that plaieth the last part, will heale them all with the
gospell, dismisse them with the peace and blessing [99]
of God, be they never so many, least they should wound
weak consciences, *etc.* Thus is this solemne fast ended.
When the PP. [Parsons] have said their certaine,[2] the
people dismissed (where I trow for that night is no talke
either by the way as they goe home, or at their supper,
but how excellently such a man and such a man did),
the priestes themselves that tooke this paines are bestowed at some of their hostes, or good dames' houses;
where at night they recompence their fasting and mourning, with good cheare and ease. As for the next day
(by that time they have slept of [off] the matter) al is

---

1 A sharp or biting remark, a gibe or dig.
2 Elliptical — a fixed number of prayers.

Henry Barrow

quite forgotten, everie man upon his ould biace[1] againe even as they were wont to be, they are no changelings: priest and people in the same idolatry, profannes, *etc.*, that before. Thus doe these prophetes, not only not discover the sinne of the land, unto the people by their preachmentes and long pharisaical praiers, but soder them therin, and strengthen their handes therwith, that no man can depart from iniquitie, but dissemble also with God himself, and wearie him with these their abhominable praiers, and hypocritish fastes, counter-faiting a great sorrow and heavines for their sinnes,

Isa. 58
Zach. 7

aflicting their soules for a peece of a day, bowing downe the head as a bulrush, *etc.*, not loosing the bandes of wickednes, nor taking off the heavie burthens and letting the oppressed goe free, or breaking the heavie yokes, nor executing judgment, or releeving the widowe and fatherles; but refusing to hearken, pulling away the shoulder, stopping their eares, making their heartes as an adamant stone, least they should heare the law and the wordes which the Lord of hostes sendeth in his spirit by the ministrie of his servantes, resisting the Holy Ghost as their forefathers have done, persecuting at all handes and smiting with the fist of wickednes such as speake unto them in the name of God, for the redresse and amendment of their lives.

Thus having seene these solemne fastes, what kind of stuffe they are, let us now a litle while turne our eies to the publike sacramentes of this famous Church of England. Which that they may the sooner appeare, let us see in a word or two, what the ordinance of Christ is concerning the outward administration therof. Wee find in his testament unto everie true sacrament required. 1. a lawful minister of the gospel to deliver them. 2. a faithful people or their seed to receave them. 3. the out-ward elementes and forme of wordes which our saviour Christ hath ordeined thereunto: as in baptisme to baptise

Mat. 28: 19

them with cleane water in the name of the Father, of the Sonne, and of the Holy Ghost. Unto the supper of the

Mat. 26: 26
Mat. 14: 22
Luke 22: 19

Lord are required the elements of bread and wine: which bread (after thankes giving) is to be broken and to be

[1] Biace — obsolete form of bias.

418

delivered with such wordes of exhortation as are ther- Cor. 11: 24 unto prescribed, and the cup to be delivered in like manner. Now where any of these wanteth; either a lawful minister of the gospel to deliver them, a faithful people and holy congregation joyned together in [100] the faith and order of Christ, to receave them, or any other forme of administration either in the elementes or order, be used, than our saviour Christ in his testament hath injoined to be used; we may boldly affirme, that such are adulterate and false sacramentes.

And now let us but even as briefly compare these sacramentes of the Church of England, to these rules. They there have (to begin with) an antichristian Romish ministerie, such as the pope left them, as is abovesaid; a profane confuse people and their seed, to receave them. For who with them (that is able to pay for the chrisme [oil]) is not baptised? The seed of heretikes, witches, conjurers, *etc.* Who with them is not admitted to their communion of the supper, that wil pay his offertorie? And to come to their forme of administration, what a sort of fond [foolish] trifling ceremonies are added to their sacramentes? As to their publike baptisme: it must be done in their conjured hallowed font, with a special gospel taken out of the tenth chapter after Mark, the water being wel conjured and hallowed to the mystical washing away of sinne, *etc.*, special gossipes[1] called and chosen which are godfathers and godmothers, which must publikely there undertake for that child, that he shall forsake the devil and al his workes, and constantly beleeve God's holy word, and obediently keep his commandementes. Where, after this pretty dialogue, betwixt the parish priest, the parish clarke, these godfathers and godmothers which answere for the infant: the priest baptiseth it in the name of the Father, of the Sonne, and of the Holy Ghost, and of the holy crosse, and chargeth these godfathers, *etc.*, to teach the infant the creed, Lord's Praier, Tenne Commandementes.

---

[1] A gossip is a sponsor at a baptism, one who contracts a spiritual relationship. It also applied to a woman's female friends invited to be present at a birth. Women who delighted in idle talk and chatter were gossips, and the word came to be applied to the idle talk itself.

All which when he can say, and have learned also some of that worthy catachisme which is set out for that purpose; then must he be brought to the bishop to receave his second baptisme, which they cal bishoping, or confirmation: wherunto also he must have a new godfather, *etc.* Then after he hath beene posed by the bishop, whether he can say his geare above prescribed, the childe kneeling downe, this revered bishop layeth his holy hands upon his head, and saith a certayne collect over him, confirmeth his former baptisme, and giving him his blessing, dismisseth him.

Yet is there a third and fourth kind of baptisme in the Church of England; namely, the hasty baptisme done by the midwife: who if she see the childe in peril and like to dye, before it can be brought to the church; then is she to bestir her, and give the child the christendome [christening], least it never come in heaven: and this baptisme is warranted by their service-boke to be lawful and sufficient baptisme: and the priest finding it orderly done by the cunning midwife, is to publish it in the church to be verie good and allowable, and to commend them that so orderly did it, at that time of necessitie.

But if the priest upon the examination of the matter, find that the midwife was not cunning in this trade; but for haste or feare forgot or left out some of her accomplementes [accomplishments]: then must he (according [101] to the forme prescribed in their publike baptisme), proceed with the godfathers and godmothers, *etc.*, save that when he commeth to dip it, he must say, N. [Name] If thou be not baptised already, I baptise thee, *etc.* And this may be termed baptisme by supposition.

Their other sacrament of the supper also is not free of the like found trifling and superstitious additions: and is by their service-book divided into two sortes: publike, of al together in their synagogue; and private in their houses, called the communion of the sick. In their publike communion, the priest (araied in his ministerial vesture) is placed at the north end of the table, and there is to read his certayne. He is there nurtured, when to turne to the table, when to the people, when to stand, when to kneele; what, and when to say. The people (after they have offred to the priest) are in their place to kneele downe to say and answere the priest at his turnes and times, as is prescribed in their massebook: where (after Sr. priest hath taken a say, and begun to the people) he delivereth unto them (as they kneele) their maker after the old popish manner, altering the wordes and forme of institution delivered by our saviour and his apostles, saying. The body of our Lord Jesus Christ, which was given for thee, *etc*. It were long to set downe their preambles and severall collectes at this their communion, as at their Christ-masse day, their Easter day, Assention day, White-Sunday, Trinitie Sunday, and how the whole queir [choir], priest and people glorie God, with angels and archangels and all the companie of heaven, *etc*., and after they have received the prieste's blessing, they are all dismissed with peace.

But now their private communion or housling of the sick, is after a more cursorie and briefe maner; with a short litle pistle and gospel, and nothing so manie *Pater Nosters*, creedes, collectes, anthemes, nor such solemne exhortations, because the sick desires to have it with him out of the world. He must provide the implementes and some of his frendes (if he may be so much beholding unto them) to take part with him. But if his disease be such, or favor not such, as that he cannot get them unto him, then yet may he and the priest dispatch the matter together; and it shalbe never the lesse wholsome to the sicke man. These are the holy sacramentes, the Church of England boasteth of: which how well they agree to the institution of Christ, I hope by this sleight repetition of some of their popish trumperies and corruptions, apeareth. So that it were but a wearines, either to rip up the rest of their blasphemous leiturgie, in discussing the manifold errors which abound in their collectes and exhortations, and abuse of Scriptures unto the same: or to shew forth their unreasonable profanation and high sacriledg in these thinges which are already shewed. Which be so repugnantly contarie to the institution of Christ, and everie way so popishly grosse, as no pretext or excuse can be forged for them, except it be the prerogative of the apostatical sea [see] of Rome, which by the

high commission of Sathan hath power to forge a new
ministerie, new sacramentes, new [102] lawes and cannons, where in deed this ministerie of theirs, these sacramentes, worship, orders, *etc.*, were minted and stamped.

And so may they draw an argument from thence for
them al, thus. They that were baptised in the church
of Rome, when afterward they came unto the true faith,
were not to be rebaptised. Therfore though this baptisme in the church of Rome, were done by a worse
ministery, and in worse maner than theirs, yet is it of
al men esteemed for a true, and availeable sacrament:
and so if this baptisme be allowable, much more the
baptisme of the Church of England, which is done in
much purer maner than theirs. Well, seing comparisons
be odious, and I might be thought partiall to speake what
I think, and know of the matter: I remit the ful deciding
of this controversie unto the 23. chapter of Ezechiel's
prophecie, where you shall see whither Aholah, or
Aholibah were the honester woman. Only, before I
come to this stout reason, let me a litle turne it upon
themselves. All that were baptised in the church of
Rome, when they come unto the true faith, are not to
be rebaptised, but have reaceaved a true sacrament:

Genes. 17   therfore the church of Rome is the true church of Christ:
Exo. 19: 5, 6   for the seales of the covenant only belongeth to that
& 20: 6
Deut. 4: 7, 8   church or people, to whome the covenant belongeth:
but the covenant only belongeth to the true church, and
Deut. 29 & 30   to them that are in the true faith: therfore now by this
Chap.
Isa. 8: 16   reason, are they all in schisme, by dividing themselves
Song 4: 12   from this their holy mother church of Rome.
Rom. 9: 4
& Ephes. 2:   Doctor Robert Some in his first infamous booke
12   against the Anabaptisticall recusantes (as he of his
charitie calleth them),[1] proveth the sacramentes delivered by the dumb English priestes, to be true sacramentes, because the baptisme in the church of Rome
is true baptisme, for that they baptise, in the name of
the Father, of the Sonne, and of the Holy Ghost. But
in certayne marginal notes added to this great clarke's

---

[1] In *A Godly Treatise Containing and Deciding Certain Questions* (1588),
Dr. Some begins his preface by stating: "Two sortes of recusantes are
in this land: the one popish, the other Anabaptisticall." He then labels
the Brownists and Barrowists as of the latter group.

booke,[1] was this inconvenience among many other, moved unto his further consideration, how he would then ward the blow of flat schisme: but he of his discretion tooke further time in his next booke[2] (which in deed, I suppose was written but in some splene), peradventure in the meane time upon further advise, the wind may blow in such a quarter, as he will be ready (together with his Lorde's Grace),[3] to goe back againe, and so avoide this danger of schisme well inough.

Yet I must say, this doctor was frendly advised when it was (though he of his collerick nature took it not so, but called him ignorant bould Anabaptisticall wrangler for his good will) to spare this deep divinitie derived from Mr. Calvine and other writers of these times, least in deed he opened such a gap to the papistes, as neither the Church of England, nor of Geneva, nor any that hold this opinion shall ever be able to shut.   For see, if this baptisme thus delivered in the church of Rome be a true and an availeable sacrament, then may it be a true sacrament without a lawfull minister to deliver it, unles they allow also [103] popish priestes to be true ministers; then may the seale of the covenant be given to open idolaters, unles they will also make the papistes true and faithfull Christians: then doth God's covenant of peace and love belong unto this apostaticall Babilonish harlot, unles they will make the church of Rome the spowse of Christ.   Then hath Christ many bodies, many spowses, or els cannot three so diverse churches, as the Church of Rome, the Church of England, the Church of Geneva, all or any two (I wil not say any one) of

---

[1] About May, 1588, Dr. Some's book, *A Godly Treatise Containing and Deciding Certaine Questions*, was published. A copy was brought to Barrow, who answered it in *marginal* notations. This copy was seized, and consequently another copy was smuggled in to Barrow, who replied to it on pages *interleaved* in the work. This interleaved work is now printed for the first time in the present volume. The original work is in the Lambeth Palace Library.

[2] Dr. Some's next book would be either the second edition of *A Godly Treatise, Containing and Deciding Certaine Questions*, which was issued in September, 1588, with 200 pages as compared with 37 pages in the first edition, or it would be his book, *A Godly Treatise, wherein Are Examined and Confuted Many Execrable Fancies Given out by H. Barrow and J. Greenewood*, issued in 1589.

[3] A reference to Dr. Some's friend and adviser, Archbishop Whitgift.

them be true churches, or els also must Christ be devided, and stand an head, an husband to all these churches, and so be one in one place, and another in another place: yea, then may Christ be an husband where his wives rule, and set up and pluck downe, bring in and cast out, what and whome they wil without his leave or will. Infinite other absurdities and blasphemies would then insue, even all maner corruptions and abhominations would then prove lawfull. And let me add yet this unto the rest. If the baptisme of the Church of Rome be a true sacrament, then have they one true sacrament, and an other false. For I am sure (or at least I thinke) they are not so grosse and shameles in the Church of England, to hold that breaden God, that magicall conjuration upon their altar, to be a true sacrament.

Good in substance, bad in forme will not salve this sore, for then I may conclude, that by this sophistry, a lawful minister to deliver, a faithful people to receave, the simple and pure element and forme of administration which Christ hath instituted were not necessarily required to a true sacrament or seale of the covenant, or (as they in their logick terme it) of the substance of a sacrament, and so may (nay is) al Christ's testament utterly abrogate at once; and then have mortal men power, both to reject the ministery and lawes of Christ, and to erect new in stead therof in the church. Neither yet will this cavil (good to the faithful receaver, or unto the receaver after he hath faith) help the matter: for first we heere reason not of the persons receaving, but of the thing receaved; not of the time to come, but of the time present: namly, whither this baptisme, thus delivered in that place, be a true sacrament, when and as it is delivered, or no. And sure if then it be not good in that maner, it cannot afterward be made good by any future faith; neither yet can in the present time be receaved of faith: for faith neither alloweth nor justifieth sinne. If the action be evil, a faithful man may neither

Rom. 12: 9 doe it nor joine in the action with, and to them that do it. How then should these false sacramentes be sayde good to the faithfull receiver when the action is evil, and the faithful are utterly forbidden to receave it; neither can they receave it, without most heinous sacriledge. Againe how should faith rejoice in, or justify a wicked and ungodly action ? And then how should this sacrilegious sacrament be availeable, or seale the blessing of God to faith to come ? When God only blesseth his owne ordinance, and curseth al transgression therof: therfore faith is rather to purge it by bitter teares and repentance, than to joy in it and justifie it. [104] But here then wil dangerous conclusions be drawen against us, if popish baptisme be no true sacrement. Then is the prince and all the ancient peeres of the land unbaptised, yea, they wil conclude against our selves, that we also are unbaptised; seing we (for the reasons above said) hold not the sacramentes administred in the Church of England at this present, to be true seales of the covenant and favor of God: and then ought all upon pain of neglect of the holy ordinance of God, to seeke the seale of the covenant: but this now cannot be had, because we have now in all Europe no ministery to deliver it, all the ministerie both of this land, and al these knowen partes of the world, being sprung from and ordained by the Church of Rome. For all the protestantes when they forsook the sea [see] of Rome, yet left not that ministerie they then had, but exercised by vertue of that ministerie, without any new ordination, *etc.* But if we denie the Church of Rome to be a Church, then how should the ministerie made by it, be a true ministerie ? And so is all the ministerie of this land throwne to the earth, both lord bishops and parish priestes, curates, preachers and all. Neither (saith D. S. [Dr. Some]) can this ever be recovered. For if the baptisme in the Church of Rome be not a true sacrament, then are all the people unbaptised. If the people be unbaptised, then can they not chuse a minister; because (saith he) they are not as yet by baptisme ingraffed into the visible church, neither may they (until they be baptised) be admitted to the communion, *etc.*

These reasons (no doubt) are strong and sure, if we find not a better solution than the clerk of Oxenford hath as yet made in the behalf of Mr. Penry.[1] For if the Church of Rome be no true church, then the ministers made therin are no true ministers: for by his owne (and that a true) position; where there is no church, there is no calling: but all the ministers of the Church of England were made either in the Church of Rome, or by vertue of that ministerie fetched from the Church of Rome, and that within the memorie, yea, within half the age of a man; therfore we may by his owne reason conclude all this ministerie, both bishops and priests to be Romish, antichristian and false: and so the sacramentes by them delivered are no true sacramentes. Let him, by all the wit, craft, and sophistrie in his budget avoid this reason.

Againe, if the baptisme of the Church of Rome were not true baptisme, then were all the people upon the change of that religion unbaptised; for ther was no other baptisme then delivered, but that: and being unbaptised, they have neither right nor power to chuse or execute any ministerie, deliver or receave the other sacrament, until they have baptisme. For none un-

Exo. 12: 48 circumcised in flesh might eate the passover, or offer
Lev. 22: 25 any maner of gift in the temple. And thus we see, neither have these ministers of the Church of England, power to deliver sacramentes (they themselves being both unbaptised and also no true ministers, as above is manifestly convinced), neither have the people un-

Mat. 28: 19, 20 baptised, any power to receave the sacraments, or meanes to redresse these mischiefes, until either a third Eliah or second Jhon Baptist [105] came downe from heaven to restore this defection. If Mr. Penrie provide not better stuffe for his owne defence, than his frend of Oxenford hath as yet brought; I can tell him this, that both he and his companions must become Brownistes (as they to the dishonour of Christ terme us) or els this popish doctor wil prevaile against them: for that most

---

[1] This is a reference to *M[aster] Some Laid Open in His Coulers*, pp. 50-62. This book has been erroneously ascribed to John Greenwood, but the style is clearly not that of Greenwood. Nor was Greenwood a "clerk of Oxenford." It is probable that the author is Job Throkmorton, who was a close friend and staunch supporter of Penry. (See F. J. Powicke, *Henry Barrow, Separatist*, pp. 82-85).

odious and unchristian flatterie of her majestie,[1] wil neither cover nor cure this sore.

It wil not suffise to say, that her majestie is perswaded in conscience that she is baptised, therfore she need no other baptisme, though she (as yet) have receaved none. Neither wil it help the matter to say, the bishop or priest which administreth the communion unto her, knoweth not so much; therfore shee may still run on in this course unbaptised. Neither will al the colourable and deceitful argumentes drawen for the assurance of her salvation, help this case; or doe her any good: if she remayne and be found in open and wilful, yea, presumptuous transgression and contempt or neglect of God's ordinance. There is but one common salvation for all men of all degrees, both prince and people: the law of God remaineth sure forever, and can for no estate or person be changed. None can be a member of a planted church, but such as are baptised. This we see by circumcision the common seale to al that were within the covenant, to the church and their seed. This was the practise of Christ and his apostles, they that were baptised were *Act. 2: 38, 41* added and numbred to the church, and not until then receaved into the fellowship: how frendly and wel *Act. 8: 12* affected soever they were unto the church. Now then, *Act. 9: 18 & 10: 48* the state standing thus; that the baptisme delivered in the Church of Rome is no baptisme, the ministerie there given, no ministerie, *etc.*, and this so apparantly prooved *Act. 5: 13* after his syllogistical manner by this scholler of Oxenford;[2] how can her majestie any longer be ignorant, or that congregation to which she joineth (if ther were any such) that she and they all are unbaptised? Seing the matter is published in print, and spread abroad through al partes of the land, and the gloove cast downe with open challenge to maintaine the same against al opponentes: wel, and this being knowen, with what conscience can either that minister deliver, or she and that people

---

1 The Queen had been baptized on September 10, 1533, by a Roman Catholic clergyman, John Stokesley, Bishop of London, with Archbishop Cranmer serving as a godfather. If Catholic baptism was invalid, so was that of Queen Elizabeth. It was embarrassing, for the sake of consistency, to suggest that the supreme governor of the church, the Queen, was not rightly baptized. See *M[aster] Some Laid Open in His Coulers*, pp. 14, 50, 57-59.

2 *M[aster] Some Laid Open in His Coulers*, pp. 57-63.

receave the Lorde's Supper in this estate? Seing none
unbaptised may receave it, but is subject to the same
curse that the uncircumcised were, which were admitted
to the passover: how can they (now that they see thsn
[their] estate) commit further sinne and sacriledge, and
violate the whole order and testament of Christ, by
plunging themselves into further transgression, and
seking no remedie to avoide this? Baptisme, he saith,
is not the cause, but the seale of salvation; and they
may be saved which were never baptised. I graunt
all this, where it can by no meanes to [be] had: but I
hope they wil not so say, that it can not be had with
them, and that the matter is not come to that passe from
the most floorishing estate of a church in Europe, and
that so sodainly with opening but one gap. Then have
Mr. Penrie and D.S. [Dr. Some] spunne a faire thred:
let them take heed, for a [106] few of these argumentes
wil make as many as have sight, grace, or conscience
Brownistes, as this scholler blasphemeth them.[1]

But what remedie for this mischeif? Seing al now
are unbaptised, where shal we come by baptisme?
And that must be had, before either entrance or proceeding to any ministerie or church. It sufficeth not
heere to say, that we may be saved without it, and that
we neither neglect or despise it: for one ynch can we
not stirre in this building and busines of the church,
until we be baptised.

Most pestilent and pernicious is that councel given
unto her majestie: that where she hath receaved comfort to her soule, thither she may stil resort for further
comfort. Is this the best councel and helpe you can
afford her: then (as Job saith) miserable comforters are
you al. Is this sound doctrine to say, that where she
hath receaved or rather supposed comfort, thither she
may stil resort for more? Is this to measure the action
and the comfort by the rules of God's word? What if
the action be unlawful, and she take comfort in unrighteousnes, may she still continue in sinne? May
she not thus justifie any wickednes? For what superstitious papist wil not say, that he hath taken comfort

2 Thes. 2: 12

Isa. 66: 3

Rom. 6: 1

[1] *Ibid.*, pp. 31, 50.

before his shrines and roodes? Yea, how many teares in that conceited superstition wil they shed before them, for very joy imagined? Shal they for this cause not depart from their idolatrie, when it is reproved by the word; because they have receaved comfort?[1]

But me thinkes I see the scholler's solution of this, his meaning and wordes both were, of such a sound inward comfort in Christ her saviour built upon his promises and word, as doth throughly appease her conscience, and acquiet her soule. Wel then, we are agreed of the point, that there is no true comfort, but that which is grounded upon the promises of God; no comfort or blessing promised to any action, but where it is done according to the ordinance and wil of God in his word; God only blessing his owne ordinance. Now then, I hope he can aprove this proceeding without baptisme unto the supper of the Lord, to be warrantable and lawful by the word of God: and that where the want of this baptisme is, not only in the receavers but in the ministers, yea, where he is no minister of the gospel that administreth this sacrament also; or els there is no comfort to her majestie in this action, which is so openly repugnant to al the rules of Christe's testament, which is heere most wittingly and presumptuously 2 Thess. 1: 8 broken: and so nothing from thence to be expected, but a fearful looking for of judgment. I wil not heere urge either the general unlawfulnes of the whole ministerie of England, either the strangenes or unlawfulnes of the office unto which they are called, or of the unlawfulnes of their ordination and entrance, nor of the most abhominable administration of their offices. Neither wil I here urge this want of baptisme both in people and minister: nor yet the open breach of Christ's institution, both in the maner and wordes therof in the deliverance of it. Only I wil come to this scholler in a playne point that he and I shall agree of, least he escape me through his lear-[107]ning, and wind him self away by his sophistrie: for he that so pregnantly defendeth is [his?] frend, I suppose wil do more for himself, when need shal so require.

[1] *Ibid.,* pp. 57, 58.

Henry Barrow

The point then wherin I would be satisfied at his hand is, whether he take the Lord Archbishop of Canterbury his grace, or the lord bishop his brethren to be true ministers of the gospel and church of Christ or no? If he be Mr. Penrie his friend, he wil say no, and surely I wil say Amen unto it: for in the testament of Christ did I never read of any lord bishop but Christ, which is Lord over al, neither of any archbishop but the archbishop of our soules, Christ Jesus; to let passe the unlawfulnes of their office, functions, *etc.* Now then, I would know whether this lord archbishop may deliver the sacrementes? And whither he would advise our soveraigne prince, to receave them at his hand or no? Sure if she may frequent or take comfort in this sacrament, then (to let passe al the other heape of faults, which to lay open would fill a volume) is the lord archbishop a true minister, this a true and holy sacrament, or els he through flatterie perswadeth his prince to sacriledge and transgression, in encouraging her both stil to receave this sacrilegious sacrament in this manner defiled by these Romish bishops and priestes, and also to continue and remaine unbaptised: although that she now know and be persuaded through this man's stronge prooves [proofs]; that she as yet hath received no baptisme.

Phil. 2: 11
1 Pet. 5: 4

Either he is to proove that an unbaptised people (even such a people, where not one of them is baptised, neither can baptisme be administred or held amongst them) may joine together, erect a ministerie, administer and receave the other sacrament, *etc.*, or els that her majestie and this Church of England hath some special imunitie and privilege to proceed without baptisme. Sure, even the two grosse doctors whome he so derideth,[1] wil think

1 Dr. Robert Some and Dr. John Bridges. Dr. Bridges was appointed dean of Salisbury in 1577 and was consecrated Bishop of Oxford, February 12, 1603/4. As a polemicist, he crossed swords with Edmund Campion, Nicholas Sanders and Thomas Stapleton. In seeking to refute the ideas of John Calvin, Thomas Cartwright, Walter Travers, and Theodore de Beze, he wrote *A Defence of the Government Established in the Church of Englande for Ecclesiasticall Matters.* Published in 1587, this hefty volume of 1,402 pages evoked several replies and led to the outbreak of the Martin Marprelate controversy. The first and second Marprelate tracts of 1588 and 1589 in turn evoked a reply from Thomas Cooper, Bishop of Winchester, who wrote his *An Admonition to the People of England* in 1589.

this strange stuffe: there was never any such church or
proceedings read or heard of, in the testament of Christ.
And see how the skornful (by the just judgment of God)
are taken and insnared in their owne delusions.   For
what could Doctor Jhon Bridges, or D. R. S. [Doctor
Robert Some] have devised more corruptly or unfaith-
fully, either towardes God or their prince and the whole
land, for justifiing their open and wilful breach of
Christ's testament; al their poperie and abhominations,
than this ?   Your majestie, saith he (though the playne
evidence of Gode's word be brought into your eares to
the contrarie), yet is perswaded in conscience, that you
in the popish church receaved the true sacrament of
baptisme.   Therfore upon this perswasion your majestie
need not seeke the outward signe, especially seing (God
be thanked) your majestie hath receaved the inward
grace and assured testimonie of your salvation in your
soule: therfore your majestie now hath no need of the
outward signe; for that were a going back againe: yea, Act. 9: 18
a putting necessitie of salvation in the outward element,
which is nothing without the inward grace;[2] that he is
able to make so manie sillogismes for your majestie's
salvation as you need not to be bound to the straight
keeping of Christ's testament, neither feare any danger
that may insue.

[108] For you have done inough alreadie for the assurance of your salvation, in putting downe the Latine
masse, and thrusting the pope out of the land, though
we have an English masse and English popes in stead
therof: you have done inough in publishing and professing the gospel, though al free and sincere practise 1 Cor. 4: 20
therof be utterly debarred out of the land; and could
never by any sute be obtained, that Christ might reigne
in his owne church by his owne ministerie and lawes: Isay. 60: 12
you have done inough in nourishing so many strangers
and preserving their lives under your protection; though
here within the land your owne natural and true hearted
subjectes, and Christ's most faithful servantes, be daily
famished and made away in your prisons by these
murthering bishops, only because they dare not allow

---

[1] M[aster] *Some Laid Open in His Coulers,* pp. 57-59.

or joine unto such abhominations as they thrust upon the whole land: though they daily cry in the eares of your majestie and your honourable councellors for some equal trial, either according to the lawes of the land (which is granted thieves and murtherers) or by the word of God: that if they have made any crime, or hould any error contrarie to the truth of the gospel, they might be censured accordingly, or els delivered from the antichristian tyrannie of these bishops, malitious slanders of these priests, yea, though even these strangers also, whose bodies are heere preserved have lost the freedome of their soules, and are partly by the wretched example of these unfaithfull tollerating subscribing priestes brought into the bondage of these bishops, as sundry of them which have any conscience complayne.[1]

What can these men say? Stand not these thinges thus? Els let their owne complaintes and supplications to the parliamentes, their protestations and new devised scoffing libells be examined: wherin they complaine of these enormities and their wrongs by the bishops, supposing to themselves that they are those servantes of Christ, that are thus oppressed. And how will this geare sort to the assurance of the prince's salvation? Not only to keep out Christ, and not to suffer him to reigne over her, but to set up antichrist his enemie, and to give her power unto the beast, not only to keep out the right and free practise of the gospel, but to set up in stead therof all this heap and dounghil of Romish trumperies, and to ratifie the pope's cannons

Luk. 19: 27
John 3: 37

Revel. 17: 13, 14

[1] This paragraph is an exceedingly forthright statement, full of sarcasm, indignation, bitterness, boldness, and indiscretion, scornful of the slippery, fawning, and obsequious attitude revealed by the author [Job Throkmorton], and damaging to the queen herself, to her Privy Council, and to her priests and bishops.

This paragraph alone would be sufficient evidence that John Greenwood never wrote *M[aster] Some Laid Open in His Coulers*, as suggested by Henry M. Dexter. Although this book is a severe and sarcastic denunciation of his adversary, Robert Some, Barrow denounces it because he feels its arguments are weak and compromising, leading to Anabaptistical phantasies, and providing material for Dr. Some and Dr. Bridges to use in rebuttal. Barrow puts it well: " we poore persecuted Christians (I say) are so far from rejoicing to see you thus ensnared and foiled, that we even grieve and blush for shame, that so glorious a cause should be evil handled of you."

and courtes, not only to exalt Christ's enemies, but to persecute Christ's servantes, and to arme with her sword these wolves against them. What mood or figure will make this geare stand before the face of Christ, when he shall come to judgment with his mightie angels in flaming fire, to render vengeance unto them which do not know God, and which obey not unto the gospel of our Lord Jesus Christ. How can they which submit to these abhominations which they see and condemne, be 2 Thes. 1: 8, 9 held faithful Christians? How can they that thus flatter and dissemble with their prince, and that in such Jude 1: 14, 15 waightie and high matters which concerne her so neere, Ezek. 33: 6 be held true harted and faithful subjectes? How can one mouth blow forth such contrarieties? How can one fountaine send forth at one place such bitter and sweet waters? How can the prince unto us, and in our eies, stand [109] a principall upholder of antichrist, and such a principall member of Christ at one and the same time? I doubt al the logick this scholler hath, or al the learning these renowmed [sic] priestes his abettors (whome he so magnifieth and extolleth) have, can not reconcile this geare, or cover their perfidous flatterie and dissimulation with God and man: which to all men shal even by themselves appeare, if their theses or major propositions, which they use against the Church of Rome, and against these their lord bishops, be duly examined and indifferently applied to this their owne ministerie, administration and practise. And sure it were a worke worthy the labour, to gather and summe their maxims together, and briefly to draw their owne arguments against themselves, that so they may be haltered and judged of their owne mouth:[1] and both their hipocrisie and sinne appeare unto all men. The Lord of his mercie deliver and preserve here [her] majestie from such blind guides as the bishops are, from such unfaithful guides as these counterfaites, these false prophets are.

But what wil Doctor Bridges, and Doctor Some say now to this geare? When their greatest enemies (after

---

[1] This language is similar to that in *An Intercepted Letter* [1590 ?], reproduced in volume iv.

P

all this conflicting and skirmishing with them) have yeilded them the whole cause in open field, and made a more strong and unanswerable argument against themselves, for the maintenance of the archbishop his grace, and all his graceles proceedings, than they all this while have done, with al their studie and lampe-light. How say they by this? Her majestie is here councelled, comforted and assured even by these men themselves, to resort still to that place for the sacra-ment, where she hath found comfort in receaving it. But she hath found comfort in receaving it at the lord archbishop grace's handes, with his rich cope on his shoulders, beraied with al his *pontificalibus*, the English Masse-book in his handes, yea, by your leave with the round wafer. I will not heere speake of attiring the chappel and high altar that day, and other court cere-monies, or whether any receave the said sacrament togither with her majestie or no; or whither these thinges be left. But sure thus hath her majestie receaved it, and either found comfort therin, or els it was not done of faith: but if she found comfort in it, o how wil the arch-bishop then rejoice? For then by these men's full consent and councell, she is still to resort thither, *etc.*, and then need they not be redressed in her daies, and that is the thing he all this while feared, least by the powerfull denouncing of God's judgmentes against these sinnes, God's grace might worke in her majestie's heart, to cast downe all this idolatrie. It is as much as he desireth, that he may remaine in his pallace at Lambeth stil: be his calling, office, ministerie, as repugnant to the word of God, or odious in God's eies as they will, that is no matter.

And see what a subject is heere offred unto his learned doctors to worke upon: for their extravagant learning will not be satisfied with so litle; as his lorde's grace will. But they will replie and come upon you for all olde reckoninges, and not suffer you to depart untill you have [110] fully satisfied. They will thus reason against you: if it be a true sacrament which her majestie hath all this while receaved at the handes of these bishops in this maner, *etc.*, where she hath found comfort; then must

434

the lord archbishop and these lord bishops needs be true ministers of the gospel; for by your owne reason where there is a true sacrament there must needes be a true minister: but here you confesse to be the true sacrament of the supper (for her majestie can take no true comfort in a false sacrament), therfore this archbishop, these bishops that alwaies heere administer it, are true ministers of the gospel of Christ. And if they be true ministers of the gospell and church of Christ, then ought they not, and cannot be put away without open violence to the bodie of Christ, for none of his true members may be either cut off or cast out whiles they abide in his body, without injurie to his body, yea, such injurie as he wil suffer at no mortall man's handes: neither in deed can or will the true church or true Christians commit such outrage against him. So then how high is their sinne against Christ, prince and church, which sue and seeke to the prince and parliament, to have these true natural members of Christ's bodie, these revered lord bishops, cut off and cast away?[1] I speake heere concerning their offices, ministery, jurisdiction and so forth; which these men sue unto the court and parliament to have utterly removed: if they be of Christ, then (without the abrogation of his testament) how should they be taken away? If he have in his testament set downe, that he wil have in and over his church lord archbishops, lord bishops, thus attendend [*sic*] and waited on, to rule and reigne in his absence, to make lawes, to make ministers, *etc.*, then what prince in the world can pluck away these lord archbishops and lord bishops from the church, without they likewise cast Christ out of dores: for Christ wil not be divided nor halfed in this sort. If we will have him, we must take him with all his members: we cannot take one part of him, and refuse an other: he will not abide with them that thus dismember him. What kind of councel then do these men give unto the prince, which thus draw her into battell against God

---

[1] In effect, Barrow is contending that if the arguments used by the author [Job Throkmorton?] of *M[aster] Some Laid Open in His Coulers* are not replaced by more effectual and valid reasons, then the position of the Anglicans is tenable but that of the Presbyterians, Reformists, and Precisians is untenable.

and his Christ, in advising her to cast out of the land the true ministerie of Christ? How can the church of Christ misse these precious members or stand without them? How can she suffer them to be rent from her? How can they rather offer this violence to their naturall mother, so to wound and dismember her? Yea, unto the body of Christ and unto their owne members, if they likewise belong to that bodie? What outrage? What unnaturalnes? What furie? What madnes were this? What high impietie against God and heaven?

Wil not heere be matter ynough for al the pulpets in the land and stationers' shoppes in London? How will they now do with these unmerciful DD. [Doctors] who (now they have them thus bound and fettered) wil lay on loade upon them. They wil now have the popish baptisme and all ere they let them goe, and that thus. Those archbishops and lord bishops and all rable of priestes and ministers which flow from their seate, have no [111] other foundation or warrant for their offices and ordination, than that which they had in the church of Rome: but these archbishops, lord bishops, and priests in these offices with that calling and ordination they had in the Church of Rome administer true sacramentes heere, and so are by them approved for true ministers; therfore there was a true ministery in the church of Rome. This cannot be denied, for that church which hath not a true, but altogether a false ministery in it, cannot in delivering their owne ministerie, deliver a true ministerie: but the church of Rome in delivering their owne ministerie as archbishops, lord bishops, parish priestes and hireling preachers or curates, church wardens, side men, parish clarkes, *etc.*, delivered a true ministerie; els could neither these offices remayne in the church of Christ or these men administer in these offices by vertue of that calling: therfore it may be concluded, there was a true ministerie in the church of Rome. To alledg that these men were called to the true faith, will not help this; for we reason not heere of the men nor of their faith, but of their offices and ordination, both which they found in, and fetched from the church of Rome: and now they administer in the same offices and by vertue of the same ordination; therfore if this ministerie of the church of England, be true, there must needes have beene and be a true ministery in the church of Rome, seeing it is the self same in respect of the offices and ordination; neither can any false minister ordeine a true minister. Well then, having obteined and convinced a true ministerie to be in the church of Rome (for els neither can these bishops or their creatures be true ministers, or the sacramentes by them or any of them administred to the queene and the land, be true sacramentes) now let Doctor Bridges or Doctor Robert [Some] alone with you for all the rest, for they will have both the church and sacramentes of Rome on foot agayne. The true church onlie can ordeine true ministers; but the church of Rome ordeined true ministers, as our lord bishops and al their priestes and ministerie of this land: therfore the church of Rome is a true church. How shal these learned doctors be answered? Againe: such sacraments as are administred in the true church are alwaies true sacraments, sealing the favor and blessing of God unto them: therfore the sacramentes, but especially the baptisme there delivered (for to that above the other, these doctors have an especiall liking) is a true sacrament. What a quandare have you now brought your selves unto? You must either denie all the ministerie of the Church of England, which are not only ordeined by these bishops, but alike with them derived from the church of Rome: or els you must affirme these lord bishops to be the true ministers of the gospell; I speake in respect of their office, which then cannot be taken away: and then are all they seditious persons, disturbers of the peace of the church, and quiet of the common welth, that seeke to disturbe or remove these offices, which Christ hath placed and planted in his church.

For if the parson of [*sic*] or any other learned minister, that you [112] think best of, whither doctor or other, be to be held true ministers, then have they a lawful calling and ordination to a lawful office, *etc.* If their calling and ordination be approved, then are the bishops justified: for no false or unlawful minister

437

can ordeine a true minister, as hath beene proved.

So then if the bishops be allowed for true ministers, needes must the church of Rome, the ministerie and sacramentes therof, be ratified by necessarie consequence, *ut supra.*

No middle course (as you affirme) may heere be taken; we must either make the tree good or evill, these ministers of the Church of England, true, or false: if false, then deliver they no true sacramentes, then is all their administration, sacramentes, sermons, accursed, how holy soever, or neere the truth in outward shew: then are they the ministers of Sathan, of antichrist, sent of God in his wrath to deceave and destroie such as are ordeined to death, then ought al Christ's true sheepe to flee and avoide them: then ought not the prince either to punish such as flee and avoide them for that doing, neither her self to repaire to their sermons or sacramentes for comfort: then is all the comfort she there taketh but delusion, even the deceit of Sathan, to the destruction of all such as take comfort in unrighteousnes, and that which displeaseth the Lord. Then are all they seducers which egge[1] and perswade the queene through their hipocrisie and flatterie, unto them: as wherby they draw her into the wrath of God, and eminent danger, and inevitable destruction, except she forsake them: and this is the sound councell they give her, to betray her soule to these wolves these deceavers.

So long as she is baptised with the inward baptisme of the spirit, though she want the outward and never seek it, it skilleth not. Wil not the two learned doctors judge this to be flat Anabaptistrie, to seperate from and oppose the inward spirit against the revealed word of God? As though they that had that inward grace and earnest of their adoption, need not the outward signe, and ought not to seek it: yea, that which yet is more deeply set, will they not and may they not justly say, that you hould and teach the verie maine groundes of all Anabaptistrie, namly, that (so they be moved by the inward spirit) they may go to any unlawful action, and (so their owne heart condemne them not) they need

Pro. 9: 14, *etc.*

Math. 7: 15
Mat. 24: 24
Joh. 10: 5

2 Thes. 2: 12

Deu. 28: 36

---

[1] Edge — incite, urge, encourage.

not feare though the action be evil, and other men condemne them, for they stand or fall to their owne maister:
els would you never have given the prince councell
(being in your judgment unbaptised) because she hath
receaved inward grace (as you say), therfore not to seeke
the outward seale, which everie member of the established church must receave. Because she hath this inward grace, therfore she may without doubting present
her self to the Lorde's table to receave the holy supper;
though she have beene ingraffed or receaved into the
church by outward baptisme, especially that she will
still perswade her self that she in the popish church
receaved it, for this is in her no sinful ignorance, that
seing she hath receaved great comfort often [113] times,
in the communion in that manner by these ministers
above said, administred unto her in this estate? She
may stil upon the scholler of Oxford his warrant adventure to fetch more there, be the action never so sacrilegious, execrable, and repugnant to God's word. Shal
not these grosse blind doctors (who are in deed the verie
sepulchre of all rottennes) yet explode and detest these
Anabaptistical phantasies? Shal not the glorious cause Prov. 25: 24
of Christ, which you would seeme to affect and plead
(though I never heard of such scoffing divines to help Jere. 1: 17
up Christ's kingdome) through this your hatefull flat- Gal. 1: 10
tery, hypocrisie and dissembling, suffer great blame and
reproch? Because in deed you feare the faces of men 2 Tim. 4: 3
more than you feare God; and dare more bouldly Jer. 23: 17
preach these and manie other apparant lies, than the
truth; which are better accepted of all men in these Ezek. 13: 18, 19
miserable and corrupt times. To their appetites and
humors you transforme and apply Christ, making him Philip 3: 18
a saviour to every rich glutton (live as profanely and Galat. 6: 12
wickedly as he list) for your bellie's sake. You seek to
bring Christ in by the arme of flesh, and not by the Zach. 4: 6, 7
power of his word and vertue of his spirit, into the
heartes and consciences of men: because in deed you Jer. 17: 5
dare not publish that truth you know, and practise it
in a good conscience, enduring cheerfully with patience
what soever may be inflicted upon you for the same
by this evil and sinful generation: wheras now you dare

neither believe nor affirme any more of God's truth,
than either is already publikely receaved, or els confirmed by some of your authentike authors, Mr. Calvine,
Mr. Beza, Doctor Fulke; thus holding and dissembling
the faith of Christ in respect of persons, times, and I
wote not what pollicies. As though the truth of God
were not alwaies in season, alwaies necessarie, alwaies
authentike. And therefore God hath taken you in your
owne pollicies and subtelties, delivered you into the
handes of your enemies whome you so skoffed and
skorned: and certainly unles you repent and turne unto
him, he wil make you even a reproch unto al men, as
unsavorie salt, that can neither season, nor be seasoned
with any thing.

And in deed, we poore persecuted Christians, whome
you so despise and blasphemie, baptising us into the
name of Browne, as though we had either derived or
hold our faith of him, or any mortal man;[1] or els were
detected and convinced of some notorious heresies, thus
adding afflictions unto our bandes, whereas your selves
dare not affirme nor abide by, that Christ is the sonne
of God, if any persecution should arise therfore: we
poore persecuted Christians (I say) are so far from rejoicing to see you thus ensnared and foiled, that we even
grieve and blush for shame, that so glorious a cause
should be so evil handled of you.[2] Why, could not the
sacred Scriptures have given light to the deciding this
doubt and undoing this knot; but that the one side
must runne to Mr. Calvine, and he must be *instar mille*:[3]
the other to Doctor Fulke, and he must be put in the
other ballance as a counterpoise, and these being directly
contrarie the one to the other: the one [114] holding the
church of Rome to be a church though corrupted, defaced (with other such ignorant rotten tearmes that belong not to a true church), the baptisme there delivered
to be a true sacrament, though there were neither lawful

[1] Barrow and Greenwood dislike the name of Brownists, and seek to dis-
associate themselves from Robert Browne, whom they regarded as an
apostate because of his submission to Archbishop Whitgift in 1585.
M[aster] Some Laid Open in His Coulers, pp. 14, 31.
[2] If Greenwood had written this book, instead of Job Throkmorton [?],
it is inconceivable that Barrow could have written this sentence.
[3] Equivalent to or worth a thousand. The representative leader.

440

minister, faithful people, nor the institution of Christ kept in the elementes and manner of delivering.[1] In which opinion, though it be altogether without grownd of the word, or common sense; yet the one he wil rest, because it best fitteth his popish turne and fleshly appetite, to cover al the abhominations which are derived from the church of Rome, and stil as holy relikes kept, reserved, and worshipped in this Church of England. The other side erecteth Doctor Fulke as their patrone and giveth him a garland in his grave, because he hath utterlie denied the church of Rome in any sort to be held a true church:[2] and brought in that famous monument of that pontifical prelate, the dowghtie S. Jhon of Beverlay, that deprived the ignorant doggbolt priest (as he termeth him), disanulled the baptisme that he had delivered, and rebaptised the yongman.[3] Now though no one iote [jot, iota] of this priest of Beverlay his doing be allowable by Gode's word (for there it is not found, that either one man may make or deprive a minister in the church of God, or that the outward signe of baptisme thus given ought to be repeated), yet because this verie wel fitteth their humors, to disgrace the dumb priestes and magnifie the preaching priestes, and for some other

---

[1] Calvin, *Institutes*, book IV, chapter II, pp. 304-314. See especially section 12, pp. 313 f. Calvin's views on baptism under the papacy are given in book IV, chapter XV, section 16, pp. 521 f.

[2] William Fulke (1538—1589), master of Pembroke Hall, vice-chancellor of Cambridge University, staunch Puritan, friend of Cartwright, Field, Wilcox, Chaderton, and Whitaker, chaplain to Leicester, and polemicist. His writings against Gregory Martin, Edmund Campion, Robert Persons, Thomas Stapleton, Richard Bristow, and Cardinal Allen provoked numerous replies from Catholics. His defence of the English translations of the Scripture, and his completion of Cartwright's confutation of the Rhemish translation, brought him great renown.
Since Fulke died on August 28, 1589, and since Barrow refers to the faction which " giveth him a garland in his grave," it is evident that Barrow is writing not earlier than the autumn of 1589.
For the views of Fulke on the Church of Rome, see his books, *A Retentive, to Stay Good Christians, in True Faith and Religion, against the Motives of Richard Bristow* (1580), pp. 38, 72, 140. See also *T. Stapleton and Martiall (Two Popish Heretikes) Confuted, and of Their Particular Heresies Detected* (1580), pp. 30-45.

[3] M[aster] *Some Laid Open in His Coulers*, pp. 54 f. William Fulke, *T. Stapleton and Martiall (Two Popish Heretikes) Confuted, and of Their Particular Heresies Detected*, pp. 11, 21. The story of the rebaptism of Herebald by the bishop, St. John of Beverley, comes from the Venerable Bede. See *Baedae Opera Historica*, trans. J. E. King, volume II, book V, chapter 6, pp. 217-223.

441

private respectes, therfore forsooth this side wil as peremptorily and with as litle truth rest in M. Eulk [Fulke]
his judgment: and he shal want no figures nor flowres,

Cor. 3: 34 that Cambridg or Oxford can afford to deck his hearse
withal. And when think you (if both sides thus con-

[2 Cor. 3: 3, 4] fidently betake them to their captaines) shall they be
accorded, and meet in the truth when they are both so
wilful and thus far from it? Or how shal the poore
people which are led by these miserable guides, ever

Heb. 13: 8 come to the light of the truth? Undoubtedly Christ
is not thus devided, neither is the spirit of God thus
divers and contrary; or the word of God yea and nay.

Eph. 4: 4 There is but one truth, one way, which neither of these
2 Cor. 1: 18 adverse guides have as yet found, and (as it should
seeme) though it were shewed them, they would in this
presumption of their heartes rather run on headlong
unto death in this their headstrong course, than by
repentance turne into the waies of life that they might
be saved. For besides the manifold errors of ech of
these factions, which have beene shewed in part: mark
(I besech you) into what present mischief and inevitable
dangers, ech course leadeth all (that hold the same) unto.

The one side that holdeth with Doctor Robert Some,
that the baptisme delivered in the church of Rome was
a true sacrament, not only therby inclose themselves in
schisme, by such violent deviding in such hostile maner
from the true church, yea, and even therby conclude
against the Church of England, that it is not a true
church, [115] because there is but one true church
through the world as ther is but one God, one Spirit,
one Christ. Christ cannot stand an head to two so
divers and contrarie bodies, as these two church [*sic*]
would seeme to be. Now they confessing the church
of Rome to be a true church, do hereby acknowledge
themselves, both in schisme and a false church. Besides that, they utterlie subvert the whole testament of
Christ, by bringing a new ministrie and new manner
of administration into the church, *etc.* The other side,
that deniing the church of Rome, or any covenant or
seales to belong unto her, doe also deny that any outward baptisme is there delivered, and doe therby affirme,

al the people that now are in our knowen parts of the world to be unbaptised, which receaved none other than that baptisme: and then seing there is no lawfull minister to baptise this people (for none unbaptised may be a minister or baptise, neither have an unbaptised people power to elect, or ordeine a ministerie amongst them. Of this can no rule, president [precedent] or example be shewed in the Scriptures, but all to the expresse contrarie, especially since al extraordinarie offices have ceased) and so must all the building of Christ's church and the worke of the ministrie cease, untill some second Jhon Baptist or new apostles be sent us downe from heaven, except peradventure they after their long travel [travail] bring us forth some new evangelist: and sure if they make a new ministery they must also make a new gospell and confirme it with new miracles. Well thus we see the error and danger of both these waies: neither of which lead unto life; therfore neither to be followed. We may not followe the first sort of guides, least they lead us back againe to Egipt, Sodome, Babilon, Revel. 18: 4 from whence we were escaped, or rather wherin we are Zach. 2: 7 by them still detained. We may not commit our selves to the other guides least we be not led forward toward perfection: but deluded with their doublings and wind- Heb. 1: 6 inges as in a maze: alwaies going, alwaies learning, yet never the further on our way or neerer our journaie's 2 Tim. 3: 5, 6, 7 end, never taught or brought to the acknowlegment and right practise of the truth.

What then is to be done in this distresse? Surely even this; when men are at their wit's endes, to flee unto God for councel and direction: whose word if we Isa. 42: 16 elevate as our lodestar, we shall no doubt by the light therof (God's gracious spirit blowing upon the sailes of our faith) safely saile through all these difficulties, even with a straight course to the free and sincere practise of the gospel; neither striking against the rockes of poperie, nor falling up on the shelves and quicksandes of Anabaptistrie.[1] For he that is ascended upon high,

---

[1] Barrow cannot be classified with the Anabaptists. He regarded Dr. Some's charges of Anabaptism, Brownism, and Donatism as name-calling.

1 Cor. 2: 16 hath not left his house destitute of councel and direction for all affaires and occasions in all times and estates whatsoever: but hath in his word left most perfect rules and absolute lawes for all things. So that though he for the judgment of the world, the trial of his servants 1 Cor. 12: 3 and the manifestation of his owne power, bring his servants into Babilon; yet knoweth [116] he how to Rev. 18: 22, 23 preserve and deliver his servantes, without either justi-fiing of Babilon with Doctor Robert Some and his Jer. 25: 10 disciples, or reforming of Babilon with these learned priestes of the time and their followers: and having Amos 9: 11 brought them forth, to lead them forth to Sion, and Jer. 51: 26 to reare up the decaied tabernacles of David that were fallen downe, without using one stone of Babel in the worke, for a corner or for a foundation. So then we now being fallen into, and found in that general defection and apostacie, wherof we were warned by our saviour Christ, his prophets, and apostles, it remaineth that we search the Scriptures whether we can there find any presidentes [precedents] of any such times, and see wheth-er we can there fetch any better direction, than these learned men abovesaid have given us in this case.

2 Chron. 30: 11, 18   We reade in the time of Ezechiah, that the kingdome of Israel had a long time remained in schisme and apostacie, having forsaken that true temple and erected unto themselves new temples, new altars, new minis-2 Chron. 35: 17 terie, *etc.*, neither could by any warnings, threats or corrections be reclaimed. Yet such of them as left their Ezra 6: 21, 22 false worship and returned to the true temple to worship God there, were receaved and admitted to the passover, without either gathering, correcting, or repeating the circumcision they had receaved in the time of this their schisme and apostacie. The like we reade to be done in the time of Josiah, of Ezra, and of Nehemiah, when they had yet longer continued in their schisme and idolatrie, upon their returne (out of their dispersion and captivitie) unto the Lorde. And yet no doubt to those men, in these times, and in this estate, could the cir-cumcision they there receaved (shal I speake according to the times and say be no true sacrament, or rather leave that traditional word which engendreth strife

444

rather than godly edifying and say) be no true seale of the covenant of God's favour unto them, being added to their false worship, idolatrie, schisme, apostacie, obstinacie, contempt. This I think wil be easily graunted of all handes. For God's covenant is no Rom. 2: 25 longer made or continued with any church or people, than they remaine in his faith and obedience: yet you see this circumcision thus receaved, not to be reiterate when they came unto the true faith. Wherby we are evidently taught, both that such baptisme as is delivered in the false church is no true seale of God's covenant (commonly called a true sacrament) and yet also, that such outward washing or baptisme, delivered after their superstitious maner in that idolatrous place, ought not unto such to be repeted as afterward forsake the false church, and joine unto the church of God. Thus me thinkes this hard difficult knot is (even with a trise[1]) undone; when we take the true light and right way unto it. Which whiles these learned doctors and diep divines (as they in their stile and banner write themselves) have labored by the light of their owne pregnant wittes to unlose, they have the further encombred themselves, and intangled their miserable followers. For what cause hath Doctor Robert Some now to contend, that the baptisme delivered in the false church, should be a true seale [117] of the covenant? Or what occasion hath Mr. Penrie's proctor to denie, that such as there receaved that baptisme, are not (touching the outward action) baptised?[2] They must heere shew some sufficient discrepance betwixt these examples alledged out of the Scriptures, and the estate of the present question; or els with reverence rest in the practise of the Holy Ghost, though neither they nor I be able to arrive to the wisdome therof.

As for Doctor Some, I see not what he can say: unles he either affirme, that circumcision in that apostacie of Israel, to be a true seale of the covenant: which if he doe, then I oppose unto him, not only the through corruption of their estate, but also the publike repudiation

---

[1] Trice — in a moment, with a single pull, forthwith.
[2] M[aster] *Some Laid Open in His Coulers*, pp. 58-68.

Hose. 2 & 4
chapters
and bil of divorce, which the Lord sent them by his
prophets: or els he must in deed shew himself a worthy
champion and prefer his mother church of Rome, to
the defected estate of Israel; which if he doe, then must
we send to Endor to call up Amasiah the priest of Bethel,
Amos 7: 10 to debate the matter with him.   And until they meet,
I leave upon him the seventeenth chapter of the Revelation; where the Holy Ghost (as lively describing the
citie and church of Rome in their scituation and collers
as if he had named them) calleth the one the beast, the
other the harlot or great whore in that vision.   Now if
Revel. 17 she be an whore (as I must beleeve God rather than
Dr. Some), then can she not be the spouse of Christ, the
true church.   Then for the rest let Bethel and Rome
strive in hell for the preeminence: I have nought to do
to judg them that are without.

But now Mr. Penrie's advocate, Dr. Some his adversarie (who hath chosen the much more reasonable
extreme), peradventure wil not be so soone satisfied.   It
is an hard matter to perswade sense where faith is
wanting.   But I for this matter must hold him still
hard to the places of Scripture alledged: so that he
must shew me some sufficient difference betwixt these
cases, or els yeild unto, or reprove the Holy Ghost.   If
he put difference, it must be either in the estate of the
place, of the people, or of the thinges delivered and
compared.   For the place, though Israel were part of
the promised land, yet that could no way sanctifie the
Israelites or better their state, or defend them from the
wrath of God due to their sinnes.   It was also accursed
of God, together with and for them delivered into the
handes of the heathen, as we reade.   Neither was it
ever more holy than Rome, or any place where the
church of God was or is, seing God's blessing is ever
with his church; therfore the place can put no difference.
For the people: as they were sometimes God's chosen
peculiar people, so were somtimes the people of the
church of Rome also: both of them apostate, both in
transgression, though (it may be) not in like depth, yet
both of them out of the favour, and in the wrath of God.
Rev. 22: 15 It were in vaine to plead which of them were worse;

the best place out of the church of God they shal find
ill inough. Though I easilie yeild Rome or the fairest
of her daughters (though it be the Church of England)
to be without all comparison worse. For the things
delivered and compared, both circumcision and baptisme, were seales an[118]nexed to the Lord's covenant,
both signes and markes, which all that were receaved into Gen. 7
the communion of God's servantes ought to have: both
signifiing, a putting away the shame of Egipt, a cutting Math. 3
and washing away our original and natural corruption,
our ingraffing into Christ's death and resurrection both Josh. 5: 9
through and with him, of our diing unto sin, and living Rom. 6: 5
unto righteousnes: as also a verie putting on of Christ,
with the ful benefite of his merits and passion, to the Collos. 2: 11
perfect redemption of our soules and bodies, and ful
appeasing of our consciences from the wrath of God,
the rigour of the law, for all the sinnes that ever we have
committed, as fully and assuredly as we our selves had
fulfilled the law, and satisfied the wrath and justice of
God, *etc.* What then should be the impediment, why
the outward baptisme, delivered in the false and apostaticall church (which I only properly count the false
church) as the outward circumcision delivered in the
false and apostaticall church should now more be denied,
this more than that?

Peradventure it will heere be alledged; that the circumcision there, was much more lawfully done, and
better than this baptisme. I will not stand upon that;
it being nothing to our purpose. I wil not stand upon
tearmes of better and more lawful, in comparing them
one with an other. It sufficeth me, that in comparing
them unto, and judging them by the law of God, neither
of them are found either good or lawful. For unlawful
it was to administer circumcision unto open idolaters,
or apostataes, or unto their seed, until they were renewed by faith and repentance. So is it stil in baptisme;
the lawfulnes of circumcision, or the holines of the word
of God, doth not justifie the action or the people, where
the one or the other are abused. As in the false church
circumcision is good, and the word of God is most holy: Hos. 4: 15,17
but to receave circumcision or to heare the word of God Amos 4: 4 & 5: 5

447

in the false church, is to apostatate from Christ to joine to God's enemies, and to forsake the true church. He cannot have fellowship with both at one time: at what time he joineth to the one he forsaketh the other. Nothing done in the false church (be it never so holy in shew) is justified, either by them or to them; but even the calling upon the name of God, the reading Scriptures, the administring baptisme, *etc.*, is turned into sinne, presumption, and profanation of God's name and ordinance unto them, whiles they remaine in their iniquitie. There was nothing in the false church, either in their maner of doing it, that made this circumcision receaved, allowable, or not to be repeted, neither did the faith subsequent justifie the action past of circumcision done to, and in the false church. It was the meere mercie of God, that pardoned and purged the sinne to the faithful and penitent. It was the wisdom of God (the sin and abuse of the action thus done and receaved in the false church being thus purged) to reserve his owne ordinance, and not to reiterate the action of circumcision. They that give a natural cause therof, as of the impossibility of reiterating circumcision, and so put difference betweene circumcision and baptisme: the one being impossible to be done againe, the other not so, greatly erre in judgment, and misse the point. For both [119] the apostle in expresse words sheweth, and experience in chirurgerie confirmeth the same; that circumcision may be gathered, and so might be iterate or defaced also as baptisme, if that had beene found needful in the wisdome of the Holy Ghost.

What say I then, doe I any way justifie this outward action of circumcision as it is done in the false church? Nothing lesse, but condemne it altogether, as an hainous profanation of God's holy ordinance; yet when it is purged by sincere repentance of al the error therin, and abuse therof; it pleased God in pardoning the faults to reserve and not to repeate the outward action: which because it was wrongly done, yet cannot therfore be said not done at al. For we may, and must put difference betwixt a thing not rightly done and a thing to be done or not done at al. For the errors and faults of

Margin notes:
1 Cor. 10: 20

Isa. 1 & 66 chapters

1 Cor. 7: 18

448

the baptisme being purged by repentance, and done away through the mercie of God; the Lord now beholdeth the rest of the action, and the thing which in pretence before they seemed to do, as his ordinance and commandement: not from henceforth imputing the faults in doing it being now repented, pardoned and done away, either unto the action or them: so that from henceforth they looke more carefully to the doing these holy actions, according to the prescript wil of God, making no willing transgression therin hereafter, neither presenting or willingly suffering their children to be presented in the false church unto their baptisme, for then they cannot be said to have truly repented it. That were to go back againe and wallow them in their former apostasie and sinne, and to bring their old sinnes upon their head.   2 Pet. 2: 20

But now seeing we justifie not the action of baptisme, Ezek. 18: 26 as it is done in the false church by an unlawful minister after an unlawful maner, and yet the error and evill doing therof being repented and purged away doe not reiterate the outward action because it cannot be said no action, *etc.* Peradventure hereupon may be collected that such baptisme as is delivered by an infidel, which never had knowledg of God in Christ, being afterward repented of and sorrowed, that their body hath beene guiltie of such profanation, *etc.* The outward baptisme may in like manner remaine, and not be repeted when they joine unto the true church. This may at no hand be brought to passe, neither in deed doth it herehence follow: for easy it is to put difference betwixt an infidel, which never knew God in Christ, and an apostata which hath had knowledg of, and still outwardly (though corruptly) professeth God and Christ. The one sort know not what the church, worship, and sacramentes meane: the other (though corrupted in their knowledg) yet carrie a shew of church, worship, sacramentes, ministerie; yea, and hath them, though corrupt and adulterate: so there is neither sequele nor comparison betwixt them. For that which the heathen and infidel should so prophane and deliver, can no way be said any kind of sacrament, either true or false; because (as is said) they have no kind of shew of church, ministerie or sacramentes, *etc.*, but the false church hath al these to shew, and seeming true though in deed false.

[120] So is it easie to put a difference betwixt false and adulterate baptisme, and true baptisme; which Dr. Robert Some with all his divinitie hath not as yet learned to do: and also betwixt false and adulterate baptisme, and no baptisme, which these other learned priestes cannot as yet spie out. For els would they never so grossly both denie the baptisme in the church of Rome to be any baptisme, concluding all the people that receaved it altogether without outward baptisme: yet being unbaptised make it a matter of no necessity to seeke outward baptisme, because they (notwithstanding al their writings) still suppose it to be true baptisme they there receaved, and so it is needles that they should seek or receave the outward baptisme; and having the inward baptisme of God's spirit in their heartes, they need not seeke the outward seale, but proceed without it unto the other sacrament. Also they having found comfort in that, then they are safe inough though men and angels, yea, though God himself in his word, say it is unlawful and unsufferable, yea, damnable sacriledg, both to them and the whole church that administreth or joineth unto them in this action. Yet if they have found comfort they may notwithstanding al this, boldly resort thither againe where they have beene thus banquetted; yea, the parties finding this comfort in their soules at the receaving the supper, though (as is said) expressly against God's word, which warranteth no such comfort unto them in that action, but condemneth it flatly, yea, and their estate and sinne being shewed them in the word, wherby their conscience is convinced; yet may they by this great clerke of Oxford his opinion, hang up the law of baptisme as an old cancelled record,[1] yea, as popish traditions that make nothing to salvation, wherof they wil assure themselves, though they wittingly breake God's lawes and remaine in the same transgression.

For (say they) men at the supper are not bidden to

---

[1] *Ibid.,* p. 62.

examine themselves what was done to them being infantes, or what they did ninety or fifty yeres[1] agoe, *etc.* Is this a strong reason to disprove the commandement of God touching the receaving outward baptisme, or to come unto the table and supper of the Lord being unbaptised ? Yea, to count these commandementes as ould worthles concealed recordes, popish traditions, *etc.*, or is it not most high and unsufferable blasphemie rather, against Christ and his ordinance ? Is this the accompt they make of the law of God, or the comfort he taketh and continual use he maketh even of that outward baptisme as an excellent instruction, stay, and assurance of his faith ? Not that I make baptisme the cause of salvation, or think that none can be saved without it. But God hath made it a most comfortable pledg and seale of his love and help to our faith, all the time that we live in this mortal life; even to him most, that hath receaved the greater measure of inward grace. So far is it from being at any time to any man a cancelled record, that it remaineth for ever a sacred and inviolable law, of special use to them that have receaved it, of necessity to al such as wil enter into the established church of Christ, without which they cannot be permitted to enter, much lesse admitted [121] to the table of the Lord. It is no imaginarie comfort of ours can take away, or alter the irrefragable law of God: though we be not bidden to examine what was done to us being infantes, or to particulate everie thing we have done in our life: yet are we to consider our estate before God shewed us this mercie, both of our natural corruption in general, and our particular miserie, being the seed of infidels, idolaters, such as were without the covenant, such as presented and offered us to Sathan in the false church, and we there in that aldulterate baptisme, receaved the pledg of God his assured wrath, and so everie way the children of death and hel, *etc.* These thinges ought not to be forgotten, or as the budget at our back to be cast behind us: but both with griefe to be remembred, that we vile wretches should so highly have profaned God's name, with them of the false church: and also with joy

---

[1] *Ibid.,* p. 60.

that God hath shewed this mercie unto us, to redeeme and deliver us out of these snares of Sathan; but especi-

1 Cor. 11: 29

ally to consider when we come to the supper of the Lord, both what the thing is we do receive, and how, with whome, and in what manner we ought to receave it. Now if we be ignorant of the doctrines of baptisme, but much more, if we have not received baptisme, how should we be held worthy receivers of those high misteries, of the body and blood of our Lord Jesus Christ? The watch and rules of the word are ill kept in that church, which admitteth any, much more many into their communion, without ful assurance of their baptisme.

But what kind of church is that, which consisteth wholy of a people unbaptised? For so (by his argument) are al they that were baptised in the popish churches? And then al the land being such at the first receiving of the gospel (as they imagine to themselves) how should an unbaptised people chuse from among themselves able ministers to baptise? Is it not likely that this famous scholler knew ful litle, what belonged either to the church, ministerie, or sacramentes of Christ, that wrote this learned discourse?[1] Hath not the Church of England gotten a worthy champion, that thus learnedly defendeth her, and her proceedings? And with one word of his mouth pronounceth al such, Brownists, as

Ezek. 16: 44

denie this their Church of England, even the eldest daughter of the church of Rome, together with her mother, to be the true spouse of Christ; and therfore both reproove by the word of God, and refraine according to the same word al their abhominations, suffring in al patient maner whatsoever may be done or said against us for the same by the handes of these Cainites, and mouthes of these Balaamites, rather than defiling our soules with their abhominations. Which, as it were

---

[1] That is, the author of M[aster] *Some Laid Open in His Coulers,* "the scholler of Oxford," "the clerk of Oxenford," Mr. Penry's "proctor" and "advocate." This is very likely Job Throkmorton. A comparison of the style of this work with that of the Job Throkmorton Manuscripts in the Pierpont Morgan Library, with that of the early Marprelate tracts, and with the kind of writing found in Job Throkmorton's *The Defence of Job Throkmorton against the Slaunders of Maister Sutcliffe* (1594) reveals certain similarities but also some dissimilarities.

a wearines for any man but to recite, and bring to light these hellish mistes and fogs, these secret mysteries of their ministerie and worship which they exercise in their temples: so is it an impossibilitie for this learned clerke with al his cunning, or the greatest priest of them, to defend the same, when the light of the word is but once brought unto them: so sodainly are they therby discovered, of what sort they are. Let them therfore that thus contend for their whorish church, approve and [122] justifie hereby the word of God: and then surely I wil yeild them to deserve the garland of a bishoprick, or els let them assure themselves, that it is neither their tyranie, railing or sophistrie, can either cover or excuse their shame from his fierie eies, with whome they have to do, or lay that blame and reproch upon others, which they indevour.

To returne therfore againe to that, from which we have beene somwhat withdrawen by these occurrentes: it remaineth that we proceed in the examination of the publike ministration of this famous Church of England. Of their sacramentes we have heard; but they have besides these certaine half sacramentes or high misteries unto which belong set and prescript communions; which to performe and execute, are no small part of the prieste's office. Not to speake of their orders or injunctions which are fower times in the yeare to be solemnely read,[1] not to repeat their sacrament of peonance, with their bitter curses and comminations going before their Lent fast.[2] They have yet the holy sacrament of marriage, solemnly kept in the holy church (for the most part) upon the Lorde's day: and an especial leitourgie or communion framed to the same. This action is to be done by the priest, *etc.*, who instructing the parties to be joined in wedlock what to say, and when to pray, *etc.*, teacheth the man to wed his wife with a ring, *in the name of the Father, the Sonne, and of the Holy*

---

[1] Section 14 of the *Injunctions Given by the Queenes Majestie. Anno Domini,* 1559, specified that the injunctions shall be read before all the parishioners once every quarter.

[2] Sacrament of penance. Comminations were anathematizings and denunciations, or a recital of divine threatenings appointed to be read after the Litany on Ash Wednesday and at other times.

Ghost, which ring must before by the man be laid upon the service-booke, together with his offring unto the priest and clarke. The booke serveth in stead of holy water to hallow the ring. The ring thus hallowed, serveth in stead of an element to this sacrament, being joined to these wordes, *in the name of the Father, of the Sonne, and of the Holy Ghost*; especialy when al the collectes, special psalme and blessinges are said by the priest, the maried couple devoutly kneeling in the meane while at the communion table, *etc*. But here wil be answered, that the reformed and better sort of priestes, wil not marry with the ring: here must then be noted, that they breake their othe of their cannonical obedience, which they tooke before the bishop when they received their priesthood. Moreover, that for their default herein, they are to be censured and reproved by their church: namly, their commissarie his court, before whome such defaultes are to be presented by the churchwardens and questmen, unles they also will be forsworne for company. Moreover, these reformed and well conscienced priestes, though they reject this ring as an idolatrous relique, yet dare they not by the word pronounce the unlawfulnes therof, that others also might leave and detest the same. That would cost blowes, the bishop would not suffer that: therfore they for the peace of their church, joine to them in the communion, *etc*., that use this execrable idolatrie. But well, let me not discourage them in well doing, least we take them not often in that fault: least if the bishop once heare of it, it then become but a matter indifferent, and then they for the peace of the church, and the saving their benefice, and their skinnes whole, use it againe for companie.

But heere in the meane time I would know of the learnedest of them, [123] where they find in the Old or New Testament, that marriage is an ecclesiastical action, belonging to the worship of God in his church, to be done by the minister as part of his office and function, and that in the church, but especially upon the Lorde's day with such a set leitourgie of collectes, exhortations, psalmes, anthemes and blessings framed to the purpose. I hope they found not this in the fourth chapter of the booke of Ruth: yet I doubt not, but both Booz [Boaz] and Ruth were godly persons, and very lawfully and famously maried. They used no priest in this busines, nor yet made it a matter belonging to the tabernacle or worship of God. I have alwaies found it the parentes' office to provide mariages for their children, whiles they remaine in their charge and government: and that the parties themselves affianced and betrothed ech other in the feare of God, and the presence of such witnesses as were present, and that in their parentes' or other private houses, without running to church to the priest after this manner. I ever tooke marriage for an ordinance and action of the second table, and see not why they might not as well set up the tables of the money changers, or bring in any other civil busines or chaffaire [trade, dealing] as this into their church.[1] But see what these Balaamites wil not doe for gaine; both make God a new divised worship, setting up and bringing in their owne divises, and burning incense therunto, and holding the people in such blindnes and superstition, as they beleeve not themselves to be rightly married, except it be done by a priest, after the prescribed manner, and the [then, that, the same?] in the due seasons also: namely, in the forenoone at morning praier, when mattens is done, next before the communion (as they call it) and this not upon any forbidden tydes,[2] as in the holy time of Lent, *etc.*, when men ought to fast, without an especial licence from the sea [see] of Canterburie, which popedome hath power both to restraine meates and marriage, and againe to permit them upon grave and waighty considerations, to such as wil pay roundly for the same.

Math. 21: 12, 13

1 Tim. 4: 2, 3

---

1 Barrow and his followers believed that marriage was a civil ordinance and not a sacrament. Christopher Bowman, who was elected in 1592 as a deacon in the Separatist congregation, was married in the Fleet prison, about 1588-89, in a service both informal and improvised, without a clergyman. He testified that "mariage in a howse without a mynister, by consent of the parties and frends, is sufficient" (Harley MSS. 6848, f. 70 *verso*, 84 *recto*). He was married a second time, I believe, about 1592, in the home of John Penry, in the presence of two clergymen, Thomas Settle, who offered prayer, and John Greenwood, who had repudiated his clerical status as a priest in the Church of England (Harley MSS. 6848, f. 33 *verso*, ff. 70 *recto* and *verso*. See also Ellesmere MS. 2110).

2 Times or seasons.

455

The priest hath also in this their portuise [portas], a prescript forme of visiting the sicke, with perfect instructions what to say at the first step into the sick man his house, what when he commeth into the sick man's presence, how without any questioning of his estate, whether he be asleepe or awake, alive or dead, without any wordes unto the sick person: the priest must doune [down] upon his mary bones, desire God to forgive the sick man his sinnes, and also to forgive the sinnes of his forefathers, with his due number of *Lord have mercie upon us, Christ have mercie upon us,* his *Pater Noster,* with his versicles and response or aides to this masse for the quick and the dead. Which being ended, he procedeth to his prescript exhortation; which, because it is almost a leafe long, the priest, to make short worke, if the partie be passing away, *etc.,* may cut off two partes of it, and say a creede: then exhort him to remember his debtes, and to make his wil, and to give to the poore: which being done, then by that special authoritie committed to [124] him by his lord bishop, to absolve the sick person of al his sinnes; and so with a special psalme and his certaine of collectes, to conclude the matter. This is the ordinarie visitation over and besides that especial housell or communion of the sick above spoken of.

And heere, before we proceed further, me thinkes there would be somthing said concerning this power of binding and loosing sinnes, which the priestes of the Church of England, and also the Church of Rome, challenge unto themselves as incident to their office, by vertue of some especial graunt and prerogative made unto them above other Christians. Which unlesse they together with their holy father the pope, should fetch from the keyes given to Peter, Mathew 16: 19, or from John 20: 23, I never could heare of any evidence they had to shew. For the first place I think they wil not say, that the promise was made to Peter only; for then it should be contrarie to the second: where the same power is given to more. Besides that, it is an usual doctrine in their pulpets, to confute the pope's false understanding of that place. And for the place of

Jhon, I trow they cannot proove this power there given
only to the apostles, there being many disciples both
men and women in the place. I hope also that they
are not so grosse to suppose this power given to the
persons of men (for then it must have died and ceased
with the apostles, seing we read not in al the Testament of any speciel or personal bequest made by them
to any degree of men one more than another, and so
they challenge it by an old worthles title) so much, as
to the truth and power of the word of God; which word
being beleeved and apprehended by faith, looseth us
from al our sinnes through that blood of Christ our Lord:
which word also being rejected or transgressed, bindeth
our sinnes unto the judgment seate of Christ, without
repentance: which word is bound and sealed up amongst
Christ's disciples. Neither is it given or committed
unto the ministers of the church only, for then none
could have faith but ministers, none ought to professe,
publish or stand for the maintenance of the faith, but
ministers. But we see this power, the word, the faith
committed to the whole church and everie member
therof, all being commanded to watch, to publish,
defend and practise the gospell to the uttermost of their
power, to admonish, reproove one another, *etc.* Now
how should this be done, but by the power of the word?
Moreover, our saviour Christ in sending forth the seventy
gave the self same power unto their word, that he did
unto the twelve to such as receaved the gospel, Mat. 15: 15
peace with remission of sinnes; to such as receaved it Luk. 17: 3
not, the shaking off the dust of the feet against them.
But it wil peradventure be said, that in as much as the Levit. 19: 17
ministerie of the word is chiefly committed unto them, Psa. 149
therfore the power of binding and loosing also. To this 1 Tim. 3: 15
I answere, that I have not learned in the word, so to
tye the power to the person of the man. This power is
not of man but of God. The least in the church hath
as much power by this word of God to bind the sinne
of the pastor, and upon his repentance to pronounce Rom. 16: 17
comfort and peace [125] unto him; as he hath to remit Coloss. 4: 17
or bind the sinne of the least. So that monstrous is
their presumption, that assume unto themselves not

only the power given unto the whole church (as shall be shewed hereafter) but usurpe I wote not what peculiar power above all other, to bind or remit sinnes: yea, to remit for wage the sinnes of everie prophane glutton and wicked atheist, which will send for the priest at the howre of death to reade his masse-booke over him, *etc.*

Likewise also, as these priests visit and housel their sick by this booke; so doe they in like maner burie their dead by the same booke. The priest meeting the corps[e] at the church stile in white aray (his ministring vesture) with a solemne song, or els reading alowde certaine of their fragmentes of Scripture, and so carrie the corps[e] either to the grave, made in their holy cemitery and hallowed churchyard, or els (if he be a rich man) carry his bodie into the church: ech where his dirige and trental[1] is read over him after they have taken off the holy covering cloth, and the linnen crosses wherwith the corps[e] is dressed, untill it come unto the churchyard or church into that holy ground (least sprights in the meane time should carrie it away) the priest there pronounceth, that almightie God hath taken the soule of that their brother or sister unto him, be he heretike, witch, conjurer, and desiring to meete him with joy in the resurrection, *etc.*, who after he hath cast on the first shovel full of earth in his due time with his due wordes, committing earth to earth, ashes to ashes, *etc.*, then may they bouldly proceed to cover him, whiles the priest also proceedeth to reade over his holy geare, and say his *Pater Noster* (which fitteth al assaies) and his other praiers over the corps[e]. That being done, there is for that time no more, but to pay the priest and clarke their hyre. As for the mortuarie, the priest wil come home to the house of the dead for that wel inough.

But now if he be a man of welth, that he make his grave with the rich in the church, he shall then pay accordingly: for that ground is much more precious and holy than the churchyard, having beene consecrate and al to be sprinkled with holy water; there he shal be

---

[1] Dirige or dirge — a song of mourning, a lament. A trental is a series of prayers said.

sure to lie drie, his grave being cut east and west and
he so layed, that he may rise with his face into the east.
Likewise if he have beene any hearer of sermons in his
lifetime, and have loved them well; he will be at cost
to get some learned priest or other to preach over him
at his burial: and that shalbe much more wholsome for
him than a paltrie masse.

But if he be of any great degree, or but stept into the
gentrie; then he hath accordingly his mourners, yea, his
heraldes peradventure, cariing his cote amour [coat-
armour] and streamers before him with solemne adoe
and pitching them over his tombe, as if Duke Hector,
or Ajax, or Sr. Launcelot were buried. Then is the
corps[e] brought in, with singing and many solemne
circumstances that I know not of, and then is masse Ezek. 32: 27
preacher sure of a mourning gowne and a good reward
for his paines.

Besides all the superstition and idolatrie in their
leitourgie, the popish [126] ceremonies and heathenish
pomp and customes, I would here faine know of our
learned priestes, where in all the Bible, they learned to
say prayers or preach over (I wil not though I truly
might say) for the dead. As I take it, they have neither
president [precedent] nor commandement for it in the
word of God. Yet there we read of sundrie christian
burials: as of our saviour Christ, Stephen and others;
where we reade neither of dirgies nor sermons over them, Joh. 19: 38. *etc.*
though there were apostles and sundrie other able men Act. 8: 2
to have done it. And I think it cannot be denied, if any
had deserved such commemoration, these did. But as
they derived this stuffe from the heathens, whether
Persians, Athenians, or Romaines (I will not contend)
which used these pulpit orations for the dead: so to the
heathens I leave them.

The next question is; where I may find in the booke
of God, that it belonged to the minister's office to burie
the dead. It was a pollution to the Leviticall priest- Levit. 21
hood to touch a carcase, or any thing about it. I never
read in all the practise or epistles of the apostles, that
it belonged to any minister of the church, as by office,
to burie the dead.

The next question is; why (of all other places) men must be buried in the church or churchyard? Els they have not christen men's burials; but if they be not buried there and that by the priest, with his booke, then are they buried like dogges, say the common people. Me thinkes those of all other should not be the convenientest places. It was a thing never used until popery began; it is neither comly, convenient, nor wholsome.

Well, now the last question is concerning these solemne mourners araid in black, many of them with hoodes, caps, crosses and other knackes: where they learned thus to bemourne and lament their dead, by I know not how many monteths? They will tell me tis lawfull to mourne and sorrow for the dead; God beareth so far with our

Deu. 14: 1, 2
1 Thes. 4: 13,
etc.

infirmities. True, but yet with this *interim*,[1] as Christians, not as heathens with a black attire outwardly, by set and stinted seasons, untill so many monteths be past: Christians use not to make such outward shew of mourning, and to have it so far from the heart, as for the most part the chief mourners, the wife and the heire have. Neither do Christians use to mourne after such a superstitious and prophane maner, or to have their mourning only in their garmentes, as numbers of serving men, reteiners, mourning boies, and poore men put in mourning weedes, which never got so much by the glutton in all his life time, which are so far from mourning, as they are glad with al their heartes.

Againe how mourne Sr. Priests; either the parish priest that hath his mortuarie and his fee for burying him, or the preacher that hath his mourning liverie and his hire also? Could they not (let them speake of their conscience) find in their heartes to be so set aworke everie day in the weeke. Besides, who be more curious and nicely picked to have their mourneries fitted at an haire breadth, than these mourning women? You shall not have them more choice of any garment [127] that ever they w[e]are, than (for the most part) they are of this: these are signes of a verie sorrowfull heart. To conclude, after al their praiers, preachment, where (I trow) the priest bestoweth some figures in his commen-

---

[1] Proviso, qualification.

dations (though he be with the glutton in the gulfe of hell) to make him by his rhetorick a better Christian in his grave than he was ever in his life, or els he yerneth his money ill. After al is done in church, then are they all gathered together to a costly and sumptuous banquet. Is not this jolly christian mourning? Who would not mourne thus everie day in the yeare?

I wil not here cumber our priestes with over many questions, least they answere me none of these. As how they can prove it now lawful to disbowel and embalme everie rich glutton where his buriing place is hard by, and there is no cause either to keep or remove him, especially seing all figures are long since in Christ performed and now ceased.

Neither wil I trouble them to shew warrant by the word, for the exquisite sculpture and garnishing of their toombes, with ingraving their armes and atcheavements, moulding their images and pictures, and to set these up as monumentes in their church: which church must also (upon the day of such burials) be solemnely arrayed and hanged with blacke, that even the verie stones may mourne also for companie. Is not this christian mourning, thinke you? Els report me to the Church of England.

All this while we have said nothing of the excellent vertues of the partie deceased, for the priest (I trow) hath said inough for him in the pulpet: though he were the veriest prophane atheist, profuse glutton, greedy extortor, covetous scraper in all the parish where he dwelt, though he never had any knowledg, love or feare of God in his life, but lived and died like a wretched worldling: yet if he be rich inough, and his frendes wil be at the cost with him, he shal want none of this funeral furniture to help him to heaven. He shal for his money want neither priest to pray for him, to preach over him, to praise him, to tell the people that his soule is assuredly with God, because in deed ere while upon shrift he forgave him al his sinnes in the name of the Father, the Sonne, and of the Holy Ghost, and peradventure housled him also with the sacrament. Al this, with mourners enough, both men, women and boies, shal he not want for his money in Church of England to be his beades men, and to say a Pater Noster for his soule, and desire God to have mercie upon it, for their liveries and doles which is had at their death: though in his life time the poore might goe naked or starve, for anie help and releife they found of him. He would not then give, least he might need himself ere he died: yea, at his death he shall want no ringers, that will for money ring a soule-peale on all the hallowed belles for his soule, and drink a carrowse for it also. But this you must note, neither rich nor poore, neither young nor old, can get burial without money in the Church of England: no peny, no Pater Noster there: but please the priest, and [128] then he will burie his brother and pray for, and over him whatsoever he be, so far as his booke wil goe. There are all thinges vaenal and venial[1] for money. The priest will for money pardon all his offences, by the authoritie committed unto him: he will for money marrye and burie, both which are become solemne actions of this church, and especial partes of the wor-ship of God; as you may perceave by their several leitourgies and solemnities apointed to the same.

Yet remaineth also an especial part of the prieste's trade and againe; namely, the purification or (as they call it) the churching of women: who, after they have beene safely delivered of childbirth, and have lien in, and beene shut up their moneth of dayes accomplet: then are they to repaire to church, and to kneele downe in some place nigh the communion table (not to speake how she commeth wympeled and muffeled, accompanied with her wives,[2] and dare not look upon the sunne nor skie, until the priest have put her in possession againe of them) unto whome (thus placed in the church) com-meth Sr. Priest, straight waies standeth by her, and readeth over her a certayne psalme, *viz.*, 121, and assureth her that the sunne shal not burne her by day, nor the moone by night,[3] saieth his Pater Noster with the prescribed versicles and response, with his collect.

Levit. 12

---

[1] Things venal are capable of being purchased, available for a price. Things venial are capable of being pardoned.
[2] Women neighbours.
[3] Psalm 121: 6.

And then she having offred her accustomed offringes unto him for his labour, God speed her wel, she is a woman on foot againe, as holy as ever she was; she may now put off her vailing kerchife, and looke her husband and neighbours in the face againe.

Is not this excellent stuffe to be brought into and practised in the church? What can be a more apish imitation, or rather a more ful reviving of the Jewish purification than this? Both in respect of the occasion, as childbirth; the time of her keeping in and seperation from the congregation, namly a ful moneth; the occasion and maner of her comming abroad, vailed, accompanied with her women neighbours, repairing to the church, kneeling downe to the priest until he have said his certaine over her, and then her oblation unto the priest for the same. Is not all this absolutely Jewish? Though in deed the prieste's part savor more of poperie. Seing therfore they will not have it a Jewish purification, let it be a mixt action of Judaisme and poperie. This trumperie is so grosse, as it deserveth no refutation, but a doung forke to cast it out.

If they be ashamed of the action, why doe they use it? If she be not defiled by childbirth, why doe they seperate her? Why doe they clense her? Why may she not returne unto the church (having recovered strength) before her moneth be expired? Why may she not come after her accustomed maner, and give God thankes for all his benefites and mercies, together with others? Why is she injoined to come, and the priest to receave her in this prescript manner? Why are the women held in a superstitious opinion, that this action is necessarie? Why is it a statute and ordinance of their church? An especial part of their worship? Which who so neglect, either priest or people, are for their such defaults pun-[129]ished by the commissarie or ordinarie. To conclude, why should such solemne, yea, publike thankes (to take it at the fairest they can make it) be given openly in the church, more for the safe deliverance of these women, being (though a singuler benefite of God) yet a thing natural, ordinarie, and common, more than for sundrie other strange and marveilous deliverances from sicknes, manie dangers of death, and perilles both by sea and land, shewed by the mighty hand of God towardes men and women daily, if there lay not some high misterie and diepe point of divinitie in the matter? Why should everie private and ordinarie benefite be made a publike action and dutie of the church? Or why should women have this prerogative? If it be but bare thancksgiving (as they when they are called to account for this would beare us in hand) why should (if that be so) the women be more churched upon that occasion, than when they have escaped some great danger of drowning, burning, sword, enemies, or when they are recovered of some extreme sicknes and disease? Yea, why should this solemne publike peculiar thankes be more given for the escaping of evil, than for the receaving many singuler great benefites at God's hand; which they are content (be they as manie as he will) to swallow up in oblivion, and never to trouble him nor themselves with the matter. Thus whiles they seeke to eschew the golph of Judaisme and superstition, they runne themselves upon the shelves of the Massalian heresie.[1]

Thus having summarily runne over the publike worship of the Church of England prescribed in their service booke, rather by way of discoverie than of discourse: I wil now (passing over their superstitious customes in their several churches, some upon this day, some upon that eave, according as they stand affected and devote to this peculiar sainct or that angel, for some special wonders and great miracles shewed in these several places, as largely appeareth in their legend) addresse my self to speake a litle of these their holy synagogues or places of assemblie, commonly called their parish church, wherunto al this rabble of worshippers resort at their apointed seasons to heare this divine booke, together with their learned prieste's sermons, *etc.*

And in the first beginning I feare me we shal fal

---

[1] Massalia is Marseilles. The Messalian practices included an undue emphasis on prayer and fasting on Sunday. Messalian beliefs involved the Arminian view that one could be saved by baptism and faith if he simply desired to be saved. Another belief was that the atmosphere was filled with devils.

into such a controversie, as cannot easily be decided; namely, whether the pagans or papistes where [were] the first founders of them? Some of them which for their fame deserved to be chronicled, are recorded to have beene devote unto the godds of the heathens, like as the days of their weeke stil are,[1] not only into the names of sainctes and angells, but into the names of these heathen godds which they still retaine, having utterly lost the name and order of their creator, as the first, second, third day of the weeke, of the first, second, Gene. 1 third, or such a moneth, *etc.*, and are now quite given away, one day to the sunne *Soli*, another to the Moon, another to Mercurie, another to Mars, another to Jupiter, another to Venus, [130] and the last to Saturne, which they have now so long held by prescription in quiet possession, as it is bonbtfull [doubtfull] when the right owner shall challenge them, his plea wil not be heard in Westminster Hall. In like maner, I have heard, that these their temples have been dedicate unto these gods, who have had their flamins and archflamins[2] therin; but upon the conversion of England to the faith of Rome, they were al then new baptised into the names of holy saintes.

I know heere agine that our learned antiquaries will hardly consent to this: but then I must desire them to shew me, when these their auncient cathedral churches were christened into the saintes' names they now beare. I suppose they shall find some of them to have caried the names they at this day do, a great while. We shal also have much adoe with them concerning the first faith which England received, which they wil confirme by the notable estate of the church the first 500 yeres after the apostles. And here shal be brought upon me a whole cartlode of writers, councils, doctors: unto al which I oppose that litle book of Christ's Testament; Math. 24: 29

---

1 Barrow held to the Hebrew practice, sanctioned by the Scripture and later by the Quakers, that days and months should be referred to by number — the fourth day of the seventh month, rather than Wednesday July 4.

2 Flamen and archflamen were two sacerdotal functionaries in the time of heathen Britain. Their positions were replaced by those of bishop and archbishop.

Henry Barrow

from which they immediatly after the destruction of
Jerusalem, and the decease of the apostles fel away;

Acts 20: 29
changing and innovating all thinges daily more and
more, until they had brought it to this estate: fashioning

2 Thess. 2
religion to the fansies and lustes of men, as it might best

1 John 2: 18
allure, retaine and please the princes and multitudes of
the world, as is above in the beginning of this treatise
more particularlie shewed, and may be these ancient
monumentes of their idolatrie which stil remayne, as
by so many argumentes be evidently convinced.

Exod. 27: 9, etc.
These synagogues are built altogether to the forme of
the old temple of the Jewes, in a long square east and
west, with their holy court walled round about, com-

1 Kings 6
monly called the churchyard, which is holy ground, and
serveth for christen burial, being altogether exempt for
civil use: yet is it lawful for the yong men and maides
to play there together upon their Sundaies and holydaies.
But who so smiteth any in that holy ground, by statute
is to have his hand cut off therfore.[1] These synagogues
have also their battlementes, and their porch adjoining
to their church, not heer to speake of the solemne laying
the foundation; where the first stone must be laid by
the handes of the bishop or his suffragane, with certaine
magical praiers, and holy water, and many other
idolatrous rites. They have unto it their foulding dores
and an especial Levite, the parish clerke, to keep the
key. They have at the west end their hallowed belles,
which are also baptised, sprinkled, etc. They have their
isles, and their bodie of the church: they have also their
selles [cells] to the sides of the walles, their vestery to keep
the priestes' ministerial garmentes, where they are to

1 Chron. 26
attyre and dresse themselves before they goe to their

Ezek. 42
service: they have their treasurie. Al the cathedral or
mother churches also have their cloysters for their deane,
prebendaries, cannons, petty cannons, singing men and

---

[1] The law stated that if one did "maliciouslye stryke anye person," or if
he drew a weapon with the intent to strike another, the offender should
have an ear cut off. If he had no eare, he should be burned in the
cheek with the letter F as a Fraymaker and Fyghter. See "An Acte
agaynste Fightinge and Quarelinge in Churches and Churcheyards," 5
6 Edw. VI, *C.* IV, in Great Britain, *The Statutes of the Realm*, IV, Part 1
pp. 133 f. See also Richard Burn, *Ecclesiastical Law*, I (London, 1809),
pp. 392 f.

singing boies, *etc.*, within their precinct and walles to abide and [131] dwell, that they may keepe the watch of the temple, and their howers of orizons.   Againe they have in the bodie of their church their hallowed fonte, 1 Kings 7: 23 to keepe the holy water wherwith they baptise, al other vessels and waters to the use of baptisme being by expresse law forbidden.   They have also their holiest of al, or chauncel, which peculiarly belongeth to the priest and quire, which help the priest to say and sing his service.   They have their roodloft as a partition betweene their holie and holiest of all.   The priest also hath a peculiar dore into his chancel, through which none might passe but himself.   Now this church thus Numb. 19 reared up, is also throughly hallowed with their sprinkling water, and dedicate and baptised into the name of some especial saint or angel, as to the patrone and Ezek. 41: 17, 18 defendor therof, against al enemies, spirites, stormes, tempestes, *etc.*   Yet hath it within also al the holy armie of saintes and angels in their windowes and walles, to keep it.   Thus I think can be no doubt made, but that the verie erections of these synagogues (whether they were by the heathens or papistes) were idolatrous.

But heere I look to have objected these two reasons against me: the one for the defence of the original, the other for the present estate of them: namly, that many of these superstitions I speake of, were invented long after England receaved the faith, and therfore the original of these churches could not be so evil: the other, that now (thankes be to God) they are quite purged of all these idols in the walles and windowes, and used to the pure worship of God; therfore I doe not wel so to write of them in this estate.

To the first reason (but that I love not to rave in the apocrypha writings as they do with the papistes, and therfore never bring their controversies to end) I could shew most of these idolatrous shapes and customes, to have been very ancient, and indeed by al likelihood, even from the first building of these synagogues, and therfore it skilleth [mattereth] not to inquire whether all these idolatries were invented at the first bringing of their faith into England; seing it is manifest that most

467

of these churches were built many yeres after. For (as hath beene said) they at the first contented themselves with such temples as they ere while worshipped their idols in: so that they that wil object unto me some few of their temples built in a round forme, must both be sure that they were not built by heathens, and that al these Romish relikes of the churchyard, porch, hallowed belles, font, images in the walles and windowes, *etc.*, were added since the building therof. And this I suppose wil be hard for them to doe. The papistes can prescribe a long time for their images and manie other thinges: yet all this if they could doe, what were these few unto all the other so manie thousandes as we see to carrie these idolatrous shapes even from the verie foundation, which we know, and with our eyes have seene thus defiled with idols and idolatrie? So that it shalbe needles for them to trouble themselves with things farther off, when these things stil remaine [132] in this shape before our eies.

And this also may answere their second allegation, where they alledg them now to be quite purged of all the former idols and idolatrie wherwith they were defiled. How then doe they still stand in their old idolatrous shapes, with their aunciont appurtinances, with their courts, cells, isles, chancel, belles, *etc.*? Can these remaine, and al idolatrous shapes and relickes be purged from them? Which are so inseperably inherent unto the whole building, as it can never be clensed of this fretting leprosie, until it be desolate, laid on heapes, as their yonger sisters, the abbaies and monasteries are.

We see now sodainly even in few dayes they may be replenished and garnished with all their idols againe. We had a late proofe therof in Queen Marie's time, which is not yet taken out of the common people's mindes; who in doubt of the like hereafter, partly upon superstition, but generally because they would not be at the like charge to buye new, have reserved the old relikes still: some of them standing up in their church windowes, others kept in their chestes and vesteries; yea, sundry of them are still in use: as their belles, font, organes, copes, surplices, the covering cloth of the altar,

etc., which way can these be purged, so long as they remaine in this shape. Their whole church also, is it not
still a fit shrine to receave all the rest? What letteth
that they might not be set up againe (if the idols were
in readines) in one hower? Seing their very roomths
still remayne as they left them, and want but a litle
sweping: so that everie sainct may know and take his
old place againe. And as it standeth with the whole
frame of their church walles, windowes, and implementes: so standeth it in like maner with the whole
ministerie of this church, from the highest bishop to
the lowest priest, curate, preacher, or half priest. They
may all together within the space of one howre, with a
litle changing of their copye, serve againe in their ould
roomths which they held in the church of Rome, to
which this ministerie of theirs a great deale better fitteth
than unto the church of Christ, which can beare no such
adulterate and antichristian ministerie.

Well, then, you see what good reformation they have
made, and how throughly they have purged their
churches of poperie and idolatrie, and that not only
spiritual idolatry (as in their worship and administration above hath beene shewed) but even this grosse
material idolatrie, which cleaveth to the whole frame
and everie part of those their churches both within and
without, from the verie foundation to the covering stone
therof. So that now they must be driven either absolutely to justifie these their cathedral and parish churches
in this forme, with these appurtenances, furniture and
use, by the word of God; or els we may resolutly by the
same word detest them as abhominable idols; such as by
the law of God are devote to utter destruction, both the
altars, Exodus 34: 13, the very places Deuteronomy 12:
2, and the gold of them, Deuteronomy 7: 25. In such
detestation ought idolatrie to be amongst all God's
servantes, as their eies ought not to spare or covet that
which the Lord rejecteth and de-[133]testeth. Thus the
godly kings of Juda, Asa, Jehoshaphat, Ezekiah, Joshiah,
destroyed all the high places, altars, groves, which were 2 Chron. 17: 6
erected in Juda and Israel contrarie to the law of God. 2 Chron. 29
2 Chron. 3

But here it will be said peradventure, that these

judicial lawes were only made but for the Jewes' common welth, and we now under Christ are not bound unto them. Let such men know, that with as litle sinne and as great reason they may say, the moral lawes of God (as we cal them) were likewise given only to the Jewes, and that we now under Christ are not bound to them. For he that said, *thou shalt have no other Gods before my face, and thou shalt not make unto thy self any graven image*,[1] hath likewise said: Thou shalt utterlie deface and destroie all these synagogues and places where such idols have beene set up and worshipped.[2] Who seeth not that this law hath relation unto, and dependeth upon the other? And is that temporal judgment which God hath set downe, and wil have man execute for the breach of the other. And sure he that will alter or abrogate the one, may by as good warrant alter or abrogate the other. To my seeming, none could better set downe the penalty for transgressing of his law, than he that gave his law: unless now in this learned age some prove wiser than God, and set downe more just judgmentes than he. In the rest I hope no man wil take these commandementes concerning idolatrie to be ceremonial or temporal, or that Christ then hath abrogate or taken these away from any, either Jew or Gentile.

But now (with one consent) they wil all plead it lawful, to convert these idoll places and furniture to the service of God: and this they will confirme with the authoritie of Augustine, Calvine, and many other writers, as also by the practise of Constantinus the bishop of Alexandria,[3] al the churches of Europa at this day: how they from time to time, still have used those temples and places to the true worship of God; which the heathen,

---

[1] Exodus 20: 3 and Deuteronomy 5: 7; Exodus 20: 4 and Deuteronomy 5: 8.

[2] Numbers 33: 52 and Deuteronomy 12: 2, 3.

[3] *The Ecclesiastical History of Sozomen, Comprising a History of the Church, from A.D. 323 to A.D. 425*, book II, chapter 5, for Constantine's practice. See *ibid.*, book VII, chapter 15, for the conversion of the temple of Dionysus into a church by [Alexander], the bishop of Alexandria. See also Robert Some, *A Godly Treatise, wherein Are Examined and Confuted Many Execrable Fancies*, p. 3.

the heretickes, and papistes have before prophaned and
abused to their idoll and false worship.

To these I answere, that they are all but men, but
if they were so many angels, they could not counter-
vaile the authoritie of one of these lawes of God and
places of Scripture alledged: which shew evidently,
that God hath such idol places and al their furniture in
such detestation, that he hath commanded the magistrate utterly to race[1] and deface them. So far is it
that God will be worshipped in them, that he will not Deut. 7: 25, 26
have them so much as reserved, least they defile the Deut. 13: 17
land and draw us to idolatrie: as by experience they
lately have seene in Queen Marie's time, and we now
with griefe behould amongst themselves. And suerly
let them make unto their selves what pretences they
can best devise of this and that holines or end, God
seeth their heartes, how they love the creature more
than the creator; how with the hipocrite Saul they
spare the fat ware of Amalek, the execrable thing, to 1 Sam. 15
sacrifice, to worship God withall. God abhorreth these
thinges, he will not be worshipped with them: and therfore they in reserving them, not only condemne God of
injustice and follie (that belike considered not, that
these [134] things might be sanctifiedly used to his worship) but thrust upon God such abhominations as he
detesteth, and with them they wil worship him whether
he will or no. But they shal one day know the price
of transgression; and that obedience is better than sacrifice and that rebellion is as the sinne of witchcraft, and
transgression as wickednes and idolatrie.

But now D.R. [Doctor Robert (Some)] to fortifie and
back these authors, bringeth also this reason out of
Mr. Calvine: that the use of many things is pure whose
original is impure.[2] As for example; it is lawful to
sweare, though the beginning and occasion of othes was
by reason of man's sinne, who is apt to lie, to deceave,
or not to credit ech other's simple word, *etc.* To this

---

[1] To raise, root out.
[2] Robert Some, *ibid.*, p. 3. Calvin's doctrine is given in *Commentaire de
Jehan Calvin sur le Nouveau Testament* (Paris, 1854), p. 167. He wrote:
" Car il y a beaucoup de choses des desquelles l' origine et la cause vient
de mal, et toutesfois l'usage ne laisse pas d' en estre pur."

example, this in a word: I see not why I should be of Mr. Calvin's mind touching the original of othes. For the like he might say of praier, of the written word of God, yea of Christ himself, the sacraments, and al holy exercises of this life. If man were not in sinne he need not pray, if he were not wrapped in ignorance, he need not the word, *etc.* But shal I conclude hereupon, that the originall of these holy things is impure; sure that were uncleane doctrine. These things no doubt are before all beginnings most holy: laid up with God in the bozome of Christ from whence they spring unto us, and are derived by us through the Holy Ghost to help our infirmities, to instruct our ignorance, and to confirme and assure our heartes. Yea, even amongst our selves an othe for confirmation is an end of strife, given to our infirmities that cannot see things absent or secret thinges, as God doth. And therfore is his holy name which seeth all things, reverently taken for confirmation, and not as it is publikly used in the Church of England. So then an othe hath not the original from man, but from God himself, who is the author of othes. Neither is an othe given to the sinne of any (for so should the name of God be highly prophaned and abused) but it is given to the infirmities of all; that of things uncertaine, unknowne and doubtful unto us, we might rest in that truth which is confirmed unto us in the name of the most high God, *etc.* We may very well put difference betwixt our infirmities and our sinnes: Christ took our infirmities yet without sinne.

And now not any longer insisting upon the doctrine of [Dr.] Some his antecedent, I denie his argument at once: that because the use of many thinges whose original is impure, may be pure: therfore these idol places and temples may be used to the worship of God. He seeth the lawes of God flat to the contrarie, which alloweth them no use at al either civil or ecclesiasticall of such idolatrous places.

But he proveth it thus. The Madianites [Midianites] were grosse idolaters; but the Israelites having vanquished them, offred of their spoiles unto the Lord, *etc.*, Numbers 31. Therfor these idol temples and places

Exod. 22: 11

Num. 5: 19
Heb. 6: 16

Gen. 12: 2
& 15: 18
& 17: 4 &
22: 16, 17

and idolatrous trumperies, may be reserved and used in the worship of God.[1]

I must still denie his argument. First he hath not heere proved, that this gold of the Midianites was either in any idolatrous formes, or had beene dedicate to idols; and therfore from this place can conclude no-[135]thing. It is easie to put difference betwixt the substance of idolaters, as gold, silver, oxen, sheep, cattell: and their idols, and idol places. The one the captaynes of this host of the Israelites offred unto the Lord, for the sinne they had committed in this war in sparing the Midianitish women, even the jewels of gold, bracelets, chaines, rings, eare rings, ornaments of legges (as the text recordeth) and the Lord accepted them. But these I trow he cannot call idols or idolatrous jewels, though they were the jewels of idolaters. The difference is great and easily put betwixt these. The landes, goodes, cattel, of idolaters, we may purchase, inherite, use and injoy: their idols, even of the most pretious mettals, we are to detest and destroie. Yet even here in this example, they were commanded to purge all that might goe through the fire, by the fire and with the water of purification; and all other their utilences[2] which they got in that war, to be purged with water, verse 21, *etc.* [Numbers 31: 21-25]. *Num. 31: 49, etc.* *Verse 23*

But now that second bullock which Gideon offred, is thought and alledged to have belonged to Baal, and brought for an instance to prove that things devote to idols may be used to the worship of God. To this if it were admitted that this bullok had belonged to Baal (which notwithstanding I see not how it may be proved by the text) I answere, that one particular example doth not take away a general law: againe, that Gideon did nothing but by the expresse commandement of God. So that they which will inforce this example against these lawes, may as wel use it against the law of the altar, of the place where to sacrifice, of the priests which ought to offer them: all which were by Gideon much *Judg. 6: 25, etc.*

---

[1] Robert Some, *ibid.*
[2] Utensils, useful articles. This word is not listed in the *New English Dictionary*.

473

Q*

more apparantly to our seeming broken, than this law, which in deed I cannot see that he brake it at all. Further by his example private men might intrude into the magistrate's office to destroie idolatrous places, *etc.*, which is unlawful.

Yet Mr. Some thinking to make the matter more sure bringeth Corah his censors for proof: because of them were made plates for a covering for the altar. But see how the further he goeth, the more he stil mistaketh the matter. For these censors of Corach and his companie, were never offred to any idols, or used to any idolatrie, but are by the testimonie of the Holy Ghost pronounced holy, Numbers 16: 37, and therfore nothing fit his turne. Many other divine reasons he hath to prove this matter, that the churches which idolaters built, the landes which they gave unto the maintenance of their popish ministrie, as archbishops, lord bishops, parish priestes, parsons, vickars, *etc.*, and also to the collegiate priestes, as deanes, prebends, cannons, singing men, *etc.*, ought now to be converted to the maintenance of these persons and collegiate priestes their successors: and (as I heare) he hath gotten himself into one of these colledges, and hath for his good service unto Baal and against Christ, obtained Judas his roomth (I meane not concerning his apostle's but his deacon's office) to carry the bag, and rob the poore.[1]

Wel, howsoever that matter standeth with him, I am sure this his rea-[136]son of Florae's legacie unto the theatre of Rome to maintaine stage plaies, where wicked and filthy persons might meete, deserveth no such recompence. Flora (saith he) was an harlot in Rome and verie welthy: she gave very much for the erection and continuance of a yearly spectacle in Rome. By reason of grosse inconveniences, that absurd shew was abolished. But Florae's legacie was converted to the use and benefite of that common welth.[2]

And what of all this, Mr. Some? Therfore may such thinges as have beene dedicate by idolatours, unto their idol service and the maintenance of their idol ministery,

[1] Probably a reference to Dr. Some's promotion to the mastership of Peterhouse in May, 1589, or possibly to the vice-chancellorship in 1590.
[2] Robert Some, *ibid.*, p. 4.

be now converted to the worship of God, and to the
maintenance of the ministery of Christ? It is already
shewed that God will not be worshipped with such
idolatrous stuffe: and above in the handling the tithes
and gleabes of the Church of England, that Christ hath
in his testament set downe an other kind of maintenance
for the ministerie of the gospell than such popish lega-
cies. But what sequele is in this? Florae's legacie was
converted to a better use, therfore thinges offred by
idolaters to idolatrie may now be converted to the worship of God, *etc.*; you see there is a barre in the way;
the expresse laws of God to the contrarie. Sure it is
doubtfull these profane fables and frivolous reasons
would cost you a laughing at, if you lighted into some
of these new pleasant divines' handling: save that in
deed this subject is as a red whote iron, that would burne
their fingers; and therfore they wil either let it alone,
or with you help to quench it.

But now let me come to that doctorly distinction of
yours, wherwith you most learnedly decide, and judici-
ally conclude the whole point. These founders (say
you), these idolaters, erred not *in genere* but *in specie*.
Not in the general, in that they gave lands to colledges
for God's service; but in the particuler they erred, in
that they gave it to the celebration of the masse, which
they tooke to be God's service.[1]

How shall poore simple Christians that know not
this diepe learning, arrive to this high divinitie, to make
one and the self same action good and evil by logick.
We know not through this divinitie of yours, whether
we should approve or condemne this action of giving
landes to these colledges, to serve God after the popish
maner. For if we condempne it as a maintenance of
idolatrie, then straight he telleth us that it was given to
the service of God *in genere*, wherby what he should meane
I cannot conjecture, except he meane either in name
and outward pretence, or els peradventure in inward
intent, that they gave of a good mind to advance God's

---

[1] *Ibid.* Dr. Some contends that benefactors who aided colleges were doing
God's service. But the *cultus Dei* was confused with the *missae celebratio*.

worship, though the present worship to which they gave it was idolatrous and ungodly.

To the first sense; I find that al idolators have alwaies made profession of the worship of God. So Aaron when he had made the calfe, proclaimed saying: to morrowe shal be the holy day of the Lord: so the harlot said she had peace offrings: the false church maketh pretence to worship Christ, to preach the gospell, *etc.*, therfore the pre-[137]tence of *cultus Dei* cannot justifie their action either *in genere* or *in specie*. We are taught by the apostle, 1 Corinthians 10: 20, that whatsoever the idolaters offer, they offer unto devils and not unto God. This doctrine Moses taught before him, Leviticus 17: 7, where having restrained all offringes, to be brought to the dore of the tabernacle of the congregation, unto the priest, *etc.*, concludeth on this manner: And they shal no more offer their offrings unto devils, after whome they have gone a whoring, *etc.*, shewing there, that all sacrifices offred els where, than in the place apointed of God, by any other than by Gode's lawful ministers, were an abhomination to the Lord, not offred to God but to devils. This also apeareth, Deuteronomy 32: 15, 16, 17, *etc.*, 2 Chronicles 11: 15, wherupon we may conclude, that no outward pretence can justifie an evil action, or make it good *in genere*: as for inward intentes, they can no way justifie outward transgressions: for then who should be found or judged culpable?

But in the particuler he granteth they erred; in that they tooke the popish masse for God's service, and gave their landes for the maintenance and the celebration therof. It is wel yet that this is found an error (though it be a verie faint tearme for such high sacriledge). Let us then see in a word what kind of error it is, that the action may therby be discerned and judged. Is not this masse a most blasphemous and execrable idol, in that it is affirmed to be the verie body and flesh of Christ, and so is adored? Is it not an open and utter deniing of both the natures of Christ? His humanitie, in that they make that his body to be in many thowsand places at one instant, in that they make it now patible,[1]

---

[1] Patible — capable of suffering, passible, susceptible of sensation.

manducable,[1] to be digested and cast out, *etc.*, his deity, in that they pluck him from the right hand of majestie, and now cast him into most filthy places by degestion,[2] in that they offer him up againe, conjure and sacrifice him againe, and seperate his deity from his humanitie, both from his glorie: and is this with Doctor Some but an error, and that *in specie*? I can tel him, a litle of this leaven, will make soure the whole lump. And if he himself were not somwhat tainted with this, he would never for shame of the world cal this *cultus Dei*, or say that they which gave their landes to this purpose, gave them to the worship of God, and erred not *in genere*.

But yet a word or two for the further explanation of this doctor's deep divinitie. Be it they gave their landes *ad missae celebrationem*, to the celebration of the masse, and to these colledges to that end were they given: Revel. 9: 3 which necessarily presupposeth (if we had no other Ezek. 8: 16 proof) that they were such sacrificing priestes as used to say masse, a colledg of these Sodomites, those locustes. Now then they erred in somwhat more, than in giving to that false worship, in that they gave to the maintenance of these idle bellies, these caterpillers, such an ungodly societe and fraternitie. And now, seing the same colleges and dennes remaine and consist of the same wicked idle priestes and their associates, in the same manner that they then did, only the Latine masse removed (and that in what manner, apeareth by that which hath beene above said concerning their service booke), how now can these colledges be said [138] reformed, or these grauntes lawful? When the parties to whome such grauntes are made, are by all lawes, both God's and man's, uncapable of them, yea not to live or be suffred in a christian common welth. And the prince hath as good right to abolish these, as her auncestor hath their brethren the monkes and freeres,[3] and to assume their landes into her handes, and employ

---

[1] Manducable — capable of being chewed, eatable.
[2] Digestion.
[3] And the prince [Queen Elizabeth] hath as good right to abolish these [idle priests and collegiate parasites], as her auncestor [her father, Henry VIII] had [to eradicate] their brethren, the monks and friars [in 1536—1539].

them unto the benefite of the common welth: but
utterly in like maner to dissolve these idle colleges and
to desolate these idol synagogues, that (as it is said by
the prophet) the ravens and owles may make their nestes
there, as they doe in the other.

But heere peradventure it wilbe interjected, that these
synagogues may be purged, or (as our learned priests
say) reformed, and so stil used to the worship of God;
seing al thinges are now made cleane unto us through
the word of God and prayer.

Unto this I say: that idols cannot be clensed with the
blood of Christ, neither by his word which utterly condemneth them, as oft hath bene said. Againe the
idolatrous shape so cleaveth to everie stone, as it by no
meanes can be severed from them whiles there is a
stone left standing upon a stone. So that neither they
can be used to the worship of God, nor we have any
civil use of them, seing they are execrable and devote[d]
to destruction: so that they that use such execrable and
uncleane thinges, cannot be cleane, but must needs be
defiled with the filthines of these idols. And heerin
either the ignorance or wretchednes of these priestes
appeareth, which thus plead for Baal and his temples,
under colour of reformation: which you see appeareth
to be no other thing, than to seeke to repaire and daube
that muddy wall (which the Lord so often commandeth
to be utterly destroied) for their belly, that their portion may be made fat therby.

But it may be heere objected, that an idol is nothing,
and that the worship of God is now spiritual and free
in al places. Though the idol in respect of the inventors
be said to be nothing, because of the vanitie of the invention of man; yet in respect of the thinges offred and
abused to the same, the apostle teacheth that such thinges
are offred to devils, and that they which have any fellowship in these actions, have fellowship with devils.
Now further, the spiritual worship of God doth not take
away the commandements against grosse idolatrie;
neither the freedome which Christ have given to worship him in al places, doth give leave to reserve these
execrable idols, or to worship him in such places: for

Isay. 34

Acts 15: 20

*Levit. 14: 34,
etc.*

*1 Cor. 10: 19,
20*

478

by that reason, we might as well goe to the false church
to the popish synagogues, or Turkish assemblies: but
that we know in a Christian to be an utter apostacie from
God: God will not be worshipped in such places. Wel
yet though they may not be used to the worship of God,
yet why may they not be converted to civil uses, as wel
as the land and dwelling houses of these priestes; seing
it is lawful for us to buy, or to eate flesh offred to idols.

It were reason inough for me to alledg and rest in
the word and wisdome of God, which hath commanded
these idol synagogues and places [139] which have beene
erected and used to idolatrie and false worship, to be
utterly rased and destroied. Yet reserved he the goodes
and landes of the idolators to civil uses, *etc.* So me thinks
there may be great reason rendred, and difference put
betwixt such creatures as are given to idolators to civill
uses (I say not here civil endes) for albeit the end of the
giver be to the maintenance of idolatrie, yet the donees
cannot so use them, but only to civil uses; as houses to
dwell in, landes to til, *etc.* And those creatures which
are wholy seperate from all civil use and consecrate to
idolatrie, as these idol synagogues and al their implements and furniture. The one we see though they have
beene defiled with idolatrie as in respect of the end and
owners ; yet those abuses taken away, the things remaine
cleane and of free use, the other are both accursed by
God's owne mouth, devote to destruction, *etc.*, and therfore can neither be clensed nor reserved. The Lord will
not have any part of the damned thing cleave unto our Deut. 13: 17
hand, neither to reserve the gold and silver therof, least Deut. 7: 25, 26
we be insnared therwith; for it is an abhomination before
the Lord, neither may we bring abhomination unto our
house, lest we be accursed like unto it: but we are commanded utterly to abhor it, and count it most abhominable, for it is accursed. Now then, if the most pretious
mettals be forbidden; the baser, as iron, lead, stone much
more, and that with such vehemencie both with threates
and promises; how great is their danger and sinne both
priestes and people, which spare that which God commandeth to be destroied, which covet that which God
accurseth ? What then in the end shall this doctor get

by his deanrie ?[1] These bishops and priestes by their promotions and fat living ? Yf God be true of his word, there is a fearful reckoning remaineth them; and not only them, but the whole land which is defiled with, and suffreth such abhominations.

But here pollicie maketh an other pollitike doubt: how these collegiate priestes and parsons should doe for livinges, and the people for places to assemble in, if these landes should be taken away, if the idolatrous temples should be puld downe. As to the first part, such unchristian colledges as these dennes of thieves and idle bellies are, ought to be dissolved; they deposed from their priesthood, and turned to some more honest trade of living in the commonwelth: and so is this doubt soone at an end; when their antichristian ministerie ceaseth and ungodly fraternities are dissolved, then there need not any longer landes for the maintenance of such abbay lubbers,[2] and of such locustes.

As for the true ministrie of Christ, they look for no such lordly and setled provision, they depend upon the providence and blessing of God, upon that flock unto which they administer. They are content in the greatest plentie with sufficiencie to necessarie food and raiment for them and their families, as wives and children. And of this also they are neither their owne carvers[3] nor judges, but it is administred unto them from time to time by the church to which they serve and attend, as need re-[140]quireth, and their present abilitie affordeth; which most willingly make their ministers partakers with them even of all their goodes, according to their need, and the others power.

Now for places to assemble in: they have litle love to the gospell which build themselves such stately seeled houses, and allow not to the people of God a house to assemble and worship God in. There were synagogues built in Judea and Israel after the high places were destroied. Great were our blame, if we should suffer

---

[1] Probably a reference to the perquisites which Dr. Some would enjoy from his new position as master of Peterhouse at Cambridge University.
[2] An ill-mannered fellow, a lout, parasite, swindler.
[3] Carvers were those who would choose or take for themselves at their own discretion.

the idolaters so far to exceed and condemne us, which have built such magnificent and sumptuous aedifices to their idols; and we not afford a poore simple house to the Lord Jesus Christ, who now requireth not such sumptuous temples, his true temple being the soules and bodies of his chosen. But I doubt, this worldly pollicie which hath so long borne the sway and ruled religion, wil never in this world yeild her self prostrate as an humble handmaid, to take lawes at God, and suffer him to order and governe all things by his word: I doubt in this last age of the world, there are too many false prophets abrode, which are gone forth unto the kinges of the earth, rather to draw them into battel ^{Revel. 16: 13, 14} against Christ and his saintes, than to bring Christ so generally and absolutely into their kingdomes.

Yet now if I be asked who ought to abolish this idolatrie, to destroy these synagogues, to dissolve these fraternities, and to depose these antichristian priestes: to that I answere, the prince, or state; and that it belongeth not to any private men: for we see they were set up and remained in Israel and Juda, untill God raised up godly princes to pluck them downe and destroy them: yea it were an intrusion into the magistrat's office and seate, for any private man so far to intermeddle.

But hence then it will peradventure be collected; that seing the prince suffreth them, and it is not in any privat man's power to redresse these mischeifes, therfore private men ought likewise to frequent the same idol places and priestes (though with grief of heart) untill God incline the prince to remove these abuses.

I am loth in this place to meddle with the prieste's allegations, for their perfidy and idolatrie; which use this reason with some more colours and faces among many other therunto. Mine answere here is, that this argument followeth not. It is one thing to abolish publike evils, and an other to abstaine from publike evils: only the magistrate may pull downe the publike monuments of idolatre; yet everie private Christian both may, and upon paine of damnation ought to, refraine from ^{Exod. 20: 3} publike idolatry, or from any thing which is evil in ^{Ezek. 9: 4}

Hos. 4: 15
1 Joh. 5: 21
Revel. 14: 4 God's eyes, though it be allowed and commanded by all the princes of the world. The godly Jewes and Israelites, though they could not pull downe the idolatrous places, yet refrayned them; as is above declared.

So that King Asa his example, which is brought by the priestes to couler and tollerate their idolatrie, will not help this matter, or serve their turne. King Asa (say they), though he plucked downe al the altars built unto strange Gods, *etc.*, yet suffred the high places which were [141] built to the God of heaven, to stand; and was commended of the Holy Ghost to have had his heart upright, *etc.* Therfore the prince may suffer these synagogues which were likewise built to the true God (though otherwise abused to idolatrie), and the people frequent them, the idolatrie being removed.

I hope they will not say, that king Asa either did well or was commended for leaving those high places standing, which were expressly forbidden by the law in many
2 Chron. 17: 6 places, and afterward pulled downe by his sonne Jehosaphat. Neither yet can they prove that either Asa, or any godly Jew repaired unto them, or offred
Deut. 16: 21, 22 there [their] sacrifices there, for that had beene expresly against the law of God. So that it nothing maketh either for the suffring of these idoll synagogues, much lesse for the worshipping in the same; which can
Read
Isa. 27: 9 no way be purged of idolatrie and superstition wherwith they are now fraught and highly placed in the people's mindes, untill they be plucked downe and defaced before their eies. Yet even in these abhomin-
Isa. 30: 22 able sties are not the best sort and the most learned of the preachers ashamed to execute their ministerie, and to call the people unto them to the open breach of God's lawes, the feeding and nourishing the prophane and ignorant people in their old foreconceaved superstitious opinion they hold of them; thinking neither the sermons nor sacraments any where els so holy, as they are in these hallowed dedicate churches and chappels: and to the no smal offence, and wounding the heartes of al that have any knowledg of God amongst them, which can no where els come by their sermons and

ministery, but in these forbidden idolatrous accursed places.

And now the publike worship of the Church of England being thus far discovered; me thinkes it due time, and most fit to examine the publike preaching of the Prov. 7: 16 gospell in the said church: seing that therwith, as with a goodly embroidered coverlet and fine sheets of Egipt Revel. 2: 22 they cover Jesabel's bed, and hide al their fornications: seing therwith, as with a sweet whistle they allure, as with a charme they retayne their auditory: seing therwith, as with an angle[1] they take up al, and catch it in Hoze. 9: 8 their net, and gather it in their yarne, wherof they re- Habak. 1: 15, joice and are glad; therfore they sacrifice unto their 16 nets and burne incense unto their yarne, because by them their portion is made fat, and their meate plenteous. But these counterfait ornaments being brought to the trial of God's word, they will straight apeare but whorish skarfes to cover her shame and filthines; and not those goodly broidred coverings, wherwith the Isa. 47: 3 true tabernacle is adorned. These stales[2] being dis- Ezek. 16: 39 closed, I hope they shall in vaine baite their hookes and spread their nets for the birdes that are on wing, and Nah. 3: 5, 6 through the mercie of God espie their grinnes: so that from henceforth these Babilonish marchantmen shalbe driven to waile and lament, because no man buyeth Revel. 18: 11 their ware any more. And sure, if the prophet Jeremie Jere. 23 in his time were so vehemently affected with [142] griefe, that his bowels within him swelled, his bones shooke, and his heart for sorrow and feare even brake, to behold the sinnes of the prophets which drew al the land into transgression, and held them in the wrath of God, *etc.* What would he, or what ought we in these our daies to do? Who find not only all the markes of false prophets which are recorded in the Scriptures upon 2 Cor. 11: 13, them, but even Satan's uttermost deceites and effectual 14, 15 delusions amongst them, suborning and transforming them, as if they were ministers of righteousnes, taking Mark 13: 22 unto them the names and titles of Christ's ministers, 2 Thess. 2: 9, 10 preachers of the gospel, seekers of reformation, *etc.*,

---

1 A fishing hook.
2 Decoy-birds.

2 Pet. 2
2 Pet. 3: 3 wherby he deceaveth the world, draweth them into most heinous sinnes and high profanation of God's name, which can no other way be reformed or purged but by the utter dissolution of the whole frame, when this whole world shall be consumed with fire, unto the which day it hastneth and is reserved. And sure even hereby we may assuredly know, that we are fallen into the last times, inasmuch as in this cleare light of the gospell (wherby the whore of Babilon is not only descried, but consumed and burnt as it were by fire), yet these deceitful workmen not only build their owne timber and stubble devises, but most highly profane that heavenly frame and gracious governement of Christ, in seeking to bring it in, and to plant it over and amongst their confuse prophane multitudes, in these their Babilonish parish assemblies. Yet no doubt, that God that revealed and shewed in the heaven openly, the temple of the tabernacle of testimonie, wil gather in, build, and preserve his elect in the same, even as he did Noah and his family in the arke in the day of the flood.

But to returne to our present purpose, which is to shew after what maner these ministers of the Church of England preach the gospel. Here must be remembred after what order they stand priestes, how they entred, what they vowed by othe at their entrance, what kind of office they are entred unto; likewise unto what maner of people, and how they execute these their offices; not heere to speake of their maner of coming by them. It hath beene above declared, how al the ministerie of the Church of England is derived from and held of these antichristian bishops by the tenure of homage and fealtie at the least, if not of villenage.[1] So that such of them as acknowledg the bishops to be antichristian, do together with the same sword and blow cut off al the ministery springing and proceeding from their apostatical chaire, there is no sence or ward to save them. It hath beene declared likewise, how at the receaving this ministerie, they solemnly upon their knees (by othe) vowed their canonicall obedience to these bishops and

---

[1] Villeinage was a form of tenure, regarded as base or low, and involving or implying complete subjection to a feudal superior.

their substitutes their orders and decrees; and this not only to the observation of the thinges that are or shalbe by these their lordes and superintendents commanded them, but likewise by the same to be disciplined, censured and chasticed for anie thing offensive unto them, which in their ministerie they shal do or say, whither by mulct, suspension, deposition, or prison.[1] Furthermore, from them they [143] fetch their licence to preach, with their lawes of stint, limitation, and praescription, when to preach, what to preach, where and how long to preach, but especially by publike doctrine not to speake against any thing by publike authoritie injoined, or by the same authoritie hereafter to be injoined; as also, to exhort their parishioners unto the due obedience and observation of such injunctions.

And that this be faithfully performed, their lords the bishops have not only the othes of the priestes, to observe, *etc.*, and of the churchwardens and sidemen, to present the defaltes therof; but their severall deputies and officers, as archdeacons, chancelors, commissaries, to keep their courts and scenes[2] to see these things observed and punish the offending; to which substitutes and courts they are al attendant and accomptable.

Their ordinarie offices which they execute are parsons or vickars, not heere to speake of the collegiate priestes, who may and do exercise al the offices of their church in their owne person: for one man may be a person [parson] or pastor, a doctor and a deane or deacon; take D.R.S. [Doctor Robert Some] for example.

As for such as terme themselves ministers or preachers, they are but mercenarie men to helpe an other in his

---

1 At the ordination service, the bishop asks: " Will you reverently obey your Ordinary, and other chief ministers, unto whome the governement and charge is commytted over you, folowing wyth a glade mynde and wil, their godly admonicion, and submitting your selves to their godly judgementes ? " To this the candidate deacon replies: " I wyl so do, the Lorde beying my helper." The promise given by deacons in the ordination service is similar. For both deacons and priests, the oath of the queen's sovereignty was also ministered. See *The Prayer-Book of Queen Elizabeth*, 1559, ed. Edward Benham (Edinburgh, 1909), pp. 165, 166, 172, 173.

2 Scenes are places where business is transacted, where actions are carried on, where performances occur. Barrow may have desired to associate stage plays with court episodes.

office, as the non residents, plurified parsons, or dumb
ministers: they have a roving ministerie, without either
certaine office or place. As for their name of teacher,
which they counterfait and usurpe unto themselves to
hide their wretchednes, and to purchase estimation with
the people: it is knowne their Church of England, nor
yet her mother of Rome, hath no such office, other than
their popish universitie doctors, who have it as an
addition of honour, and not of office; which name you
see they hold together with and far above their office
of a parson. But even thes roving ministers and mercenarie preachers, fetch their ministerie and licence to
preach from the chaire of their lord bishop, upon the
same conditions and covenant that the other, yea, and
execute their charges when they are hired, after the
same maner, both in saing their service injoined them,
etc., in making their apparance and accompt at the
scenes and courts abovesaid.

If some of them heere take exception unto this, and
alledg particular instances to the contrarie, who neither
read the service booke nor yet come at the bishops'
courtes; let these men be more neerly observed, and you
shall find these but meere delusions and jugglings to
bleare the eies of the simple. For mark these men, and
I warrant you this booke must go before or after their
sermon, and be read either by some reading priest, or
els by the roring bulles of their cathedral church: for
there is no church or publike chappell in England, but
is bound unto this booke, and these well conscienced
how learned soever, make no scruple to second this
booke with their sermons by thirty yeres together[1] (if
they have beene priestes so long) and stand ministers to
this people in this idolatrie, idolatrous places, sodomitish
and monkish colledges, *etc.* Is not this all one as if themselves used or read the booke and sung with them for
companie, seing they both joine with them in [144]
praier, stand a minister unto them in these places and
estate: yea and (by their leaves) the wisest of them doe
both administer and receave the sacramentes after the
order of this booke, together with these people, *etc.*

---

[1] 1559—1589. Barrow is writing in 1589 or 1590.

And in that they make not continual apparance unto their scenes and courts; it is by some peculiar priviledge granted by the arch-bishop unto some great man or other, or els by some especial prerogative from the prince: both with this intendement alwaies, that they do nothing contrarie or prejudiciall unto the publike course and proceedinges of the land; for if they doe, there is no privilege or prerogative can defend them from their arch lord bishop: his letters missive and messengers will soone be with them, they must answere the matter before his highnes, and that with due homage and submission, or els they know the price of it, *etc.* And is not this all one in effect as if they made their monethly apparance unto their Ordinaries' substitutes, Revel. 13: 17 when we see they have the open marke of the beast in Revel. 14: 9 their licence, priviledge, *etc.*, and must preach after the same prescription that other priestes do, *etc.* And when we see they do their homage in open court unto the archbeast upon his summons? May I not then justly Revel. 13: 13. conclude, that all the priestes of England have a false 14 & 16: 13 and antichristian ministerie upon them, exercise it in idolatrie and unto idolators, have the markes of, and stand in subjection unto the beast, preach by his licence and limitation, *etc.*, and so joine as the false prophet Revel. 19: 20 unto his throne? And who now can say, that these men preach the gospell truly and sincerely, whiles they remaine in this antichristian ministerie, idolatrie, confusion, subjection?

But that this their preaching may more manifestly appeare unto all men; let the indifferent readers but consider with themselves of the truth of these matters, whiles I but by way of a briefe repetition discover some of their deceites, shiftes, and errors. First, therfore, I must desire them duly to consider of these former circumstances, as of their ministerie and maner of receaving the same; of their office and maner of comming by it, and of their administring in the same: and unto these to joine that which should have beene first remembred, their academicall education and schoole learning wherof they so boast, and wherby they are made fit for the high worke of the ministerie and governement of the church; yea, that most high office of God's dispensor or steward.

These being duly considered, and compared unto the rules in Christ's Testament, concerning the ministerie and ministers of the gospel: see if they find them not peremptory lets,[1] why in this estate they cannot preach the gospel of Christ sincerely, which they have not as yet truly knowne or embraced. Yea, let them examine them neerly by this light, and see if they find them not those noisome Egiptian botches and grievous plague sores, which by the just judgment of God are fallen upon the men that have the mark of the beast, and upon them which worship his image, and are never found upon any of the children of God, much lesse upon the ministers of Christ.

Next let them consider, whether these learned and best reformed prea-[145]chers (for unto them stil as the most pernitious deceavers I bend my speach, the other being so grosse as of themselves they fal to the ground) whether these learned preachers (I say) doe not make merchandise of the word, and open portsale [public auction] of the gospell, offring their cunning, and selling their tongues like the orators and lawyers of the common welth, setting a price of the gospell and compounding for their bellies before hand with the gluttons and profane people to whome they administer: always readie upon the hearing of a better bargaine to remove, as we have above said of their parsonages, deanries, bishopricks, and al other ecclesiastical livings of their Church of England, until they arrive unto the archbishoprick of Canterburie, to be primate and metropolitane of all England. That only office is as their pole-star, fixed, and unmooveable, unto and by which they direct all their course. And now I leave to your judgment whether any such Balaamites and Simoniaks[2] can truly and sincerely preach the gospel.

But all this they wil hide and salve with these two allegations: that the workman is worthy of his hire: and

Math. 6: 24
Rom. 10: 14

Joh. 8: 42, 43, 44
Revel. 16: 2

2 Pet. 2: 15

Jude 11
1 Thess. 2: 5

Phil. 3: 18, 19
Micah 3: 5, 11

Ezek. 13: 19

---

[1] Hindrances, obstructions.

[2] Simoniacs — those who practice simony, or those who buy and sell ecclesiastical preferments. The printing is not clear, and the word may be " Sinioniaks," but this seems meaningless.

that if they should not thus compound, the people are so vircharitable [uncharitable] and covetous, as they should want maintenance for food, raiment, and bookes.

To the former it hath already in a peculiar discourse[1] beene shewed, that the ministers of the gospell should neither be maintained with Jewish tithes, nor Balaam's wages, much lesse bargaine and bartre in this manner, and be their owne carvers.[2]

To the other, if the people want that charitie as not Gal. 6: 6 to administer unto such of their earthly things which tread out the corne, yea, grind, prepare, and divide 1 Cor. 9: 9, 11 unto them their food and portion, and administer unto them spirituall and heavenly things, then are they utterly unworthy of the gospell, then belongeth not the Rom. 15: 27 gospell unto them. Then why doe they administer the Luk. 3: 10, 11 gospell and stand heardes[3] to these Gadarenes?[4] Why cast they their pearles before such swine? Why doe 1 Joh. 3: 17 they sel the gospell and stand ministers, yea, prostitute Mat. 7: 6 the body and blood of Christ for wage, to such open unworthy as have neither faith nor charitie?

As for their apparel, it is either too nice and curious, Zach. 13: 4 or els too affected and framed as the rough garment to Math. 23: 5 deceave.

For their diet, they are so far from suffring these 1 Cor. 4: 1 necessities and distresses, that famine, hunger, cold and nakednes, that labour and painfulnes, etc., which the 2 Cor. 6: 4 apostle susteined; as they are rather of those feasters Jude [1:] 12 the Apostle Jude speaketh of, which feed themselves without all feare.

Yea, these sycophants, these trencher priestes, will Mica. 2: 11 most cunningly insinuate into some great or noble man's house, where they are sure to be wel fed, and safe from all stormes: even the meanest of them will never be without their good hosts and dames where they may lay their knife aboard, and fil their belly of the best. Infinite are their artes both to get and retaine such Judg. 17 & 18 Chap.

---

[1] See page [140] of the present treatise. See also Barrow's views expressed in " Barrow's Fourth Examination, March 18, 1588/89."
[2] Those who determine for themselves their stipends and perquisites.
[3] Heardes — shepherds or pastors.
[4] Gadarenes, or Gerasenes, or Gergesenes. See Mark 5: 1 and Luke 8: 26, 37.

friends; never were there in any age such priests [146] for the welthie sort; but as for the poore, these phariseis will have no medling with them further, then whiles [except when] they bring their offringes or pay their tithes. Sure they will be to have Christ a cooke unto them: as for having him to be their King, that shall be but by way of inscription in a peece of paper, or in the pulpit some time: yet even there medle they as litle with Christ's offices as may be.

Now for their bookes (where in deed lieth all their learning and cunning, without which they are as blind as moles, as mute as fishes),[1] it is no marvaile though they cal for them, for therin consis[t]eth all their glorie: he that can most learnedly fetch out his sermon from them, and preach their notes in manner of discourse, he is the only man, he hitteth the point aright, though the text be never touched or broken up. Neither is it a smal matter that wil furnish one of these learned preachers of bookes: they wil not stick to bestow more welth in their studie, than many a godly christian and good house keeper hath to maintaine his familie, and to relieve his neighbours with.

But they edifie and build up the church heerby, which is much more pretious than earthly sustenance. I beleeve it wel: for upon such sandy foundations is both their owne faith and their whole church built, and not upon the sure rock of Christ's Testament: what good and sound stuffe they pick from thence, partly may appeare by the discussing of sundrie errors, which even the chief and verie best of al their writers have held; partly shall more appeare, when we come to the examination of their pulpet doctrines. Only in this place I set downe my simple judgment, that it were much better for the whole church and themselves also; that for prophecie and doctrine they layd aside all authors, and betake them wholy of all handes to the booke of God. So should that booke be more soundly understood and opened, everie word and leafe of the tree of life have

Marginal references:
Ezek. 34
Mica. 3
Math. 7: 26
Prov. 8: 8
Ezek. 47: 12
Rev. 22: 12

---

[1] "As mute as a fish" and "as blind as a mole" were well known phrases in Barrow's lifetime. See Morris Palmer Tilley, *A Dictionary of the Proverbs in England in the Sixteenth and Seventeenth Centuries* (Ann Arbor, 1950), pp. 217, 467.

his due vertue; so should they see with their owne eies and not with other men's, speake with their owne tongues, *etc.*; so should they and their whole auditorie have greater assurance for the things they doe or leave undone; so should there be many fewer of these blind guides, these traditional preachers. _{Pro. 8: 8} _{Eze. 47: 12} _{Revel. 22: 2} _{Act. 4: 19, 20}

Furthermore heer is to be observed, how these priests or preachers, not only take their licence to preach at their lordes' these antichristian bishops' handes, and againe at their pleasure are deposed and scilenced and submit their doctrine to their censure, the gospell to their limitation and prescription, preaching nothing that may breed either the bishops' dislike or their owne unquiet, *etc.*: but with their sermons deck up and adorne the whore, heale the wound of the beast, curse, reproach and slander Christ's most faithful servantes, blesse Christ's enemies even al the prophane of the land. Finally they therwith dawbe up al the sinne of the land, and joine the gospell to all the abhomination of the time. _{Act. 5: 19} _{Rev. 13: 12, 13, 14} _{Rev. 17: 4} _{Ezek. 13: 10, 11} _{Jer. 6: 14, 20} _{Hos. 5: 10, 11}

The former part of these hath beene often shewed, and need neither proofe nor repetition; their boxe with their paper licence, their othe [147] of canonical obedience, their publike injunctions, *etc.*, declare. _{Mic. 6: 16}

The other part, their present administration and the lamentable estate of the whole land, being through their deceit so deeply set and strongly held in apostacie, transgression and ignorance, manifesteth without further proofe. Let the grosse idolatrie, miserable servitude to the antichristian yoke of these bishops, the more than Babilonish confusion, the Sodomitish pride and excesse, the open perverting of judgment and justice, the through corruption of all estates, the deluge and height of sinne never heard nor read of the like in any nation or time going before, shewe what kind of gospel they preach, or rather how they preach the gospel. There is no man so sinfull and wretched that will come and heare their cunning in the pulpit, whome they send not away with the peace and blessing of God. There is no people within the compace of the whole land that will see and feed them well, to whome they wil not at _{Jer. 6: 28, 29, 30} _{Hos. 4: 1, 2} _{Hos. 7: 4, 10} _{Ezek. 16: 49} _{Hos. 9: 9} _{Amos 6} _{Ezek. 14: 4, 7, 10}

the first sight administer, deliver them the sacraments, *etc.*; yea, be he never so notoriously wicked, impenitent, unworthy, unto and with whome they wil not communicate. Yea, let him be welthie, and one that wil enter-

Ezek. 22: 25, 26 taine and countenance the preacher, receave him unto house, and resort to his sermons, what life may not this man lead, even before Mr. Preacher his face. What

Ezek. 13: 19 gluttony, riot, excesse, idlenes, profannes, pride, what

Micah. 3: 11 crueltie, oppression, wrong, covetousnes, pleasure, vanitie, delight, even al the apples and ripe authumne fruites

Jer. 23: 17
Jer. 8: 11, 12, their soules can lust after or desire, may they not gather
etc. with full hand by Mr. Preacher's permission: yea, so they be riche and of authoritie or noble, then wil he help to reach him downe the boughes, and prepare them to

Revel. 18: 14 his appetite, which way soever his humor stand.

For they are cunning physicians, and wil verie soone espie the constitution and inclination of their patientes;

Hos. 4: 8, 9, 10 which being found, then physick, diet and al shalbe prepared accordingly, which way soever his appetite chiefly tendeth, that shal not be crossed, I warrant you, but finely fed and nourished. If he be ambitious, discontented with his present estate, still aspiring, and climing to further honour, that is imputed to his vertuous and honorable mind, which no meane thing can content or suffice; what soever office or many offices he thus attaineth, they ar al in him the redward of vertue, the especial favour and blessing of God towardes him, wherwith God doth most highly honour, esteeme and advance him before al other men. Let him execute these

Isa. 59: 14 offices as negligently, nay as unjustly and corruptly, with

Micah 3: 3, 12 as great extortion, wrong, violence as apparantly as may be, perverting, yea, selling justice, so that judgment is

Amos 5: 7 turned into gall, and the fruite of righteousnes into wormwood; all this geare belongeth not to Mr. Preacher to

Hos. 10: 4 intermedle with matters too high for them. If they should reproove these thinges, it were the next way to bring him in dislike with the gospell and to bring in poperie againe; and so should the preachers want countenance: so far are they from reproving him by name, or their church from calling these great states to accompt

Levit. 19: 17 for these or any [148] other particular sinne, that so they

might either be turned from their evil waies by repent- Levit. 5: 1
ance, or els receave that publike reproofe and ecclesiastical censure that belongeth to the same, according Jer. 1: 17, 18
to the commandement and power of our Lord Jesus Ezek. 3
Christ for the humbling of his flesh. Ezek. 33: 3

But sure I weene this case is a *Demurrur* in the Church
of England, yea, utterlie denied to be lawful or sufferable, that the magistrate should be excommunicate:
they therfor in stead hereof, receave them in this estate
to their sermons, praiers, and sacramentes, in hope of
secret repentance, as they say: for what though they
have used it al their life and give no outward signe of
amendement, yet repentance may come in the twinkling
of an eie.

Well now if these noble or rich men be given to riote Ezek. 13: 18
and gluttonie, with all manner of delicate fare, pam- 1 Thess. 2: 1, 2,
pering up the flesh, *etc.*, that in them is but good house- 3, 4, 5, 6
keeping: if they and their retinew exceed in monstrous
and vaine apparell, it is but raiment fit to their degree, Isa. 3
age, or sexe. If they keep and nourish troupes of idle
servingmen and followers, this still belongeth to their
degree: if they and their whole houshold spend al their
life time in fleshly and vaine sportes and gaming, so that
numbers of men have no other trade, and be wholy
employed to the keeping of hawkes and doggs to serve
the lust of these men: al this is covered under christian
recreation and pastime, and is tollerable inough so he Math. 12: 34,
wil heare a sermon, and cal his familie to a lecture; yea 35, 36, 37
the priest will not then stick to stay and looke on, until Eph. 5: 3, 4, 5,
the games at tables or set at cardes be done; yea, or at 6
some odd time, to make their exercise give place to an
enterlude. As for their common table talke, they may Col. 3: 5, 6
there be as prophane as Esau, and use there what merri- Eph. 4: 29
mentes, scoffes, jesting and vaine speach they list; al is Isa. 5: 8
in the way of mirth, good fellowship, wrapt up in the
cloth, and sanctified with Mr. Preacher's short grace. Jer. 6: 13
As for most insatiable and greedy covetousnes in pur- 1 Cor. 6: 10
chasing and joining not field unto field, but towne unto
towne, until they be lords of a whole countrie, that is but Col. 3: 5
good husbandrie, wise foresight, and allowable providence for them and their posteritie.

Be the sinne never so odious and apparant, if it be in a man of authoritie, these prophets, these preachers, dare not reproove it, for that were both to transgresse their commission, and forfait their letters pattentes. If these sinnes be found upon any of their patrons, proselites, or hearers, then for love they must winke at them,

Heb. 12: 1
1 Pet. 4: 2 and not find fault: especially if they be any of these inherent or inbred sinnes which cleave close to the soule, and cannot without great strift and dislike unto the flesh,

Rom. 12: 2 be left. With these sinnes these predicantes wil not meddle: as if they be given to pride, to exhort them to

Gal. 5: 19 lowlines and humblenes, to cast away these ornaments which nourish that sinne and wherin the flesh delighteth,

2 Pet. 1: 4, *etc.* and to get unto them the jewels of godly knowledg and christian vertues to deck and garnish their soules therwith: if [149] they be given to riot, fleshly lustes and vanities, spending their time therin, to councel them to redeeme the time whiles it is called to day, to subdue the flesh and bring it into obedience and mortifie the lustes therof, shewing them the end of such pleasures and delights to be bitternes and death, *etc.* If they be given to covetous hoording up treasures, purchasing landes, building sumptuous houses and garnishing them, *etc.*, to shew them that the covetous shall not enter into

Prov. 11: 4
Luk. 12: 17
1 Tim. 6: 17, 18, 19
Luke 16: 9, 10 the kingdome of God, that these uncertaine riches can neither help them, nor establish their posteritie, no not in this world, God having so many meanes to take their welth from them and them from their welth in the twinkling of an eie, much lesse make them the more

James 5: 1 acceptable unto God: shewing them that they are but the Lord's stewards and baylives of them, and shall

Mat. 25: 14, *etc.* accompt unto him for the use of everie farthing: and therfore it behoveth them to be careful that they bestow them according to their master his wil, otherwise the mispence[1] or miskeeping of them shal fret their soule, and rise up in judgment against them: yea even in this life they shal be but snares to them and their posteritie, to bring and hale them to more sure damnation, *etc.* Fie, these were too sowre and unpleasant doctrines,

Luk. 22: 34, 35 especially when they come to be put in practise in all

---

[1] Misspense — wasteful expenditure.

these duties of the second table; I doubt me much, that if they should but once sincerely and faithfully deale with Psal. 69: 22 any one text, the saying would be so hard as they should loose numbers of their disciples, if not the whole multitude of their hearers: and I doubt me, not be halfe so welcome to their gluttons' houses as they are at this day.

But how for such sinnes as either these cheif of their auditorie are not apparantly infected with, or els can endure to be weaned of (for this you must alwayes note, to their appetite must the whole feast be prepared) for such sinnes let their preachers alone, they wil rowze and handle them to the quicke. As if they whome they seeke to please be rather given to prodigalitie, profusion, inordinate wasting in excesse, pride, vanitie: o so they will then be bait [harass] the covetous scraping drudges out of the church. And so of the contrarie, where the cheif of their auditory are more parcimonious and covetous; then wil they as much cry out of wast, excesse, riot in apparel, diet, *etc.*, then may not a great ruffe[1] looke into the church, least they wil do pennance that were it.

Generally els, where they light on gentle and tractable soules, which in deed beare a love to the truth and unto such as most sincerely teach it: here wil they first by their utmost art seek to bring themselves into credit and estimation: for heere wil they take bouldnes to speake (though colourably and but in faint and doubtful tearmes) against many corruptions in their church, as the dumb ministrie, crosse in baptisme, versing and canting their psalmes and anthems from one to an other as tennisballs, against the organs, cappe, tippet, surplesse and such like. They wil also put on such an outside of gravitie and a good conscience, they wil rebuke swearing, and before such as these [they will express their] dislike of vaine apparel;[2] peradventure also

---

1 An article of neck-wear, of starched linen or muslin, with horizontal flutings.
2 See Humfrey Dyson, *A Book Containing All Such Proclamations as Were Published during the Raigne of the Late Queen Elizabeth* (London, 1618). In the volume at the Folger Shakespeare Library, there are eight proclamations against excess of apparel in the period 1558—1588. Other copies of this " unique " volume are at Harvard, British Museum, Bodleian, Queen's College, Oxford, Privy Council Office and Society of Antiquaries. See William A. Jackson, " Humphrey Dyson and His Collections of Elizabethan Proclamations," *Harvard Library Bulletin,* I, no. 1, Winter, 1947.

of idle gaming, exhort to diligent hearing of the [150] word preached, making the poore soules beleeve that even by this outward hearing they are in a straight course and ready way to salvation, though they neither

practise that litle truth they heare, neither understand the word, or be able to know therby when they do well

or evil: yet into such a superstitious feare are they brought, and such a conceit and opinion of these men's

sinceritie, great knowledg and good conscience, that they even depend on their mouthes, beleeve all true that they say, without question or trial therof by the word of God, neither dare they beleeve the expresse Scriptures when they are brought to reprove their doings. In such reverence and estimation have they these good men. Whose counterfet and corrupt dealing as you have somwhat heard it in the second table; so if you now but turne your eie a litle to the first table, you shall see they deale much worse in the worship and service of God.

For stand not they ministers to al this abhominable stuffe that hath beene above recited? It is the verie proper ministration belonging and injoined to their ministerie, unto which by office and othe they stand bound, and not unto preaching of the word of God; for that is a thing voluntarie, supererogatorie: but this is a thing of necessitie, by law, by othe, by presentment, by visitation injoined and seene to be observed, it must always goe before, and take the preeminence of the word of God. And if the word of God happen to follow it (by your leave), it may not be so bould as controwle it, for if it doe, I know who goeth out of dores. And marke the precisest and best of your preachers well, you shall see they will meddle with it as litle as may be. Or if they doe at any time, it shalbe but rather to prune or lop some water boughes that are superfluous, of a tender care to preserve and pollish it, and not to lay the axe to the roote and bulke off the tree. For I tell you if it fall, downe goes ministerie, sacraments, church and altogether: and o what a fall would that be. It standes them upon therfore to take heed how they deale with this geare, least they open such a gap as they be never able to shut with all the learning they wante. No mar-

vaile therfore, though they deale daintily in ambiguous 2 Cor. 2: 17 &
and doubtful termes with such counterfait stuffe; for if 4: 1, 2, 3
Ephes. 5: 13
they should bring it either to the touchstone or to the
light, it would at the first blush bewray it self. In the
meane time what good preaching is this of theirs, that
have had the gospel thus long amongst them daily
taught and preached, and have not in 32 yeres space[1]
as yet discovered this abhominable odious idolatrie,
most grosse and stinking poperie. Must you not needes Mat. 5: 13, 14
now condemne these your preachers, either of ignorance
or perfidy ? Of ignorance if they know or see not these
abhominations: yet you see they dare adventure both
to practise and administer this stuffe unto others, yea, Rom. 2: 17, 18,
to reproch, slander, and revile all such as of conscience 19, 20, 21, 22,
23, 24
unto God refuse to partake with them, and receave at
their handes this trumperie.

Now then if they be thus blind as they cannot discerne
these things, [151] how dare you any longer follow or Math. 15: 14
use them for guides ? If the blind lead the blind, shal
not both fall into the ditch ? But if they say they see,
how heinous then is their sinne, how great their perfidy 2 Cor. 6: 14, 15
and treachery unto God and man ? Unto God, both
in that they thus presumptuously of set purpose with Joh. 8: 12
most high contempt, violate his lawes and tread under 1 Joh. 1: 5, 6
foot his Testament, and also abuse his most sacred word
in joining it to such abhominations; yea, not only not
discover and cast out these idolatries and filthie doung Ezek. 13: 11
therwith, but in stead therof daube and soder up all Jere. 23: 9
the ryftes and leakes therwith. It is most certaine that 2 Cor. 10: 4, 5,
the word of God in the mouthes of all his true ministers 6
and servantes, is as fire and an hammer: as fire, to consume all stubble and trash; as an hammer, to breake in
sunder whatsoever opposeth it self against the truth of
God's word. It is manifest, therfore, that they preach
their owne devises, and not the word of God sincerely:
for the arke of God and Dagon[2] cannot stand up to-

---

[1] From November 17, 1558, to November 17, 1590, would be 32 years.
If Barrow is counting from the Act of Supremacy and the Act of Uniformity in 1559, then the thirty-second year would be from the spring of
1590 to 1591. It is possible that Barrow is writing this portion in the
summer of 1590. Previously [143] and also some seven paragraphs later,
Barrow speaks of 30 years, which may be an approximation.

[2] Dagon — the god of the Philistines.

R

gether, such light and such darknes cannot be mixed. Againe, if they had stood in the councell of the Lord and had declared his word unto his people, they should have turned them from their evil wayes, and from the wickednes of their inventions. But they have fortified and sodered the people therwith in all these sinnes and abhominations, giving them their peace, and blessing, and pardon everie day they come to church, so that none can depart from iniquitie. Therfore the greater is their treason to God and man, in drawing them into the high transgression of God's lawes, and in keeping them in the wrath of God.

Now who is so desperate, as knowing the perfidy and treacherie of these miserable guides both towardes God and man, that would hazard and commit his soule and body to the conduct of such blind and deceitful guydes, as either cannot or will not leade them right? Who

Ezek. 33
1 Cor. 14: 8

would commit the citie to such blind watchmen, as either cannot discerne the enemie; or unto such trecherous watchmen, as wil not blow the trumpet and give warning unto all men to be in a readines; but on the contrarie are in compact with the enemie, have betraied the whole church into their handes, yeilded unto them absolute authoritie, taken their lawes, their peace, their marke, and stand now the sworne waged marked souldiors of antichrist, guarding his verie throne and person,

Revel. 13: 13, 14

Rev. 17: 4 & 18: 12, 13

Ezek. 16: 16, 17, 18, 19
Prov. 9: 14, 15

setting up and burning incense to his image, gylding the harlot the false church, and araying her with all the titles and ornaments, even the gold, silver, precious stones, pearles, fine linnen, purple, scarlet, *etc.*, that belong to the true tabernacle. In her doe they offer the meat, flowre, wine, oile, honie, that God hath given. In her burne they their frankincense and sweetest perfumes. In her they prepare a feast and furnish a table to the multitudes.

These are her chamberlaines, her tapsters, that stand at the doore of her house, of everie high place in the land, and invite and toule[1] in their guests, which flow in unto them at the sownd of their bell. These call and allure such as passe by their way and go right on

[1] Entice, decoy.

their way, take a bayte [152] at their inne, promising
their peace offrings, wisdome and great cheare, and
verie great and good companie of the noble, the rich,
the learned; who will all be readie upon the first blush
of faire weather, as soone as ever it holdeth up over head   Eccle. 11: 4
and these stormes and clowdes are blowen away, to go
with them on that journay whether they are travailing,   Prov. 15: 19
for thither also are they bent; and as soone as ever God   & 22: 5
shall incline the prince's heart, then they wil al forsake   Prov. 23: 13
antichrist and goe unto Christ.   In the meane time they
have all with one consent determined, not to guide
forward one step.

Also these that go before them in the way, and will
not stay for this good companie; such they say marre
all their course, and hinder the discipline they seeke.
And therfore they assay by all meanes to turne them   Amos 5: 10
out of their way: which if it wil not be, then they de-   Isa. 59: 15
Exod. 14: 5
nounce and proclaime them as most bitter enemies,
Brownistes, schismatikes, prowd and ignorant persons,
disobedient to magistrates; whome they in their pulpets
stir up, to send out their horsemen and chariots after
them, to bring them by force back againe into Egipt,
and to hold their bodies in moist [most] noisome, vile
and streight prisons, except they will come to these
fowlers, unto their high places.

For these good men would not have Christ brought in
in that base maner by faith and repentance, leaving all
such thinges as are contrarie to his will, and seeking to   Math. 2: 2, 3,
doe the things that he hath commanded [no matter]   *etc.*
Math. 18: 3
whosoever say nay to it, and whatsoever it cost, whether   Math. 10: 37,
38, 39
imprisonment, confiscation or death, bearing his crosse
in all patient, meek and humble maner, with cheerfulnes   Luke 17: 20
and joy.   Fie, this is all too base, they would bring him   Isa. 42: 2
in with sownd of trumpet by an armie and strength,
by act of Parliament, by consent of all estates of the   Zach. 9: 9
realme, prince, nobles, priestes and people, and that   Math. 21: 9, 15
into these famous synagogues and high places, gor-
geously decked for his majestie; and not in this abject
maner to runne to him into upper chambers, hooles in
woodes, prisons, *etc.*, and that a few poore despised unlearned wretches, and that not with the magistrate's
leave and good will, *etc.*

Thus see you how far these guides are from leading you forward in the straight waies of the Lord, that with this their preaching they keep you and bring you backward. You see how far these watchmen are from ringing the alarme, and sounding the trumpet against the enemie, against any sinne in any person, against antichrist. As you see, they promise peace and blessing to the most wicked, and dare not give warning of or denounce against any sinn either in the state (I meane commonwelth) or church or any great person in the same, be the sinne never so heinous against the first or second table; but rather dawbe up all these abhominations and all the land in their sinne, keeping and houlding them therin bownd as in chaines and fetters, unto the Lord's fearful judgment: yea, by these their sermons, keeping all the people in ignorance, unfurnished of their christian armour and weapons. Neither in deed need they any; for you see in the happy realme of England, there [153] are no enemies, except Sathan draw men to theft, or murther, or treason. If they can keepe themselves from these faults, or keep them secret, why then al is well, there are no other faultes or enemies, Sathan hath no instruments and dare not stir in this estate under a christian prince, where there is such preaching of the gospell, *etc.*, you see how these your learned preachers, your good men, have not with al their sermons and preaching withdrawne one soule all this while from the false church, or the abhominable idolatries therin. But on the contrarie, administer in the false church, dawbing her up and retaining al their auditorie in her, hindering and drawing back by their uttermost artes and indevors, al that seeke to walke in the straight and peaceable waies of the Lord. These, with the infinite enormities that ensue heerof, were inough to discover unto you what manner of ministers these are, and ministery they exercise, and how they preach the gospel.

But yet I must ad this unto the rest; how with all this their preaching, they have not all this while given any increase to the bodie, not leading their hearers one step

Heb. 6: 1

Isa. 56: 10, 11

1 Pet. 2: 2

Heb. 6: 1

towardes perfection: but as they stood 30 yeres agoe,[1] Isa. 48: 17
in the self same estate are they still, in the same confusion,
idolatrie, disorder in their synagogues, as appeareth by
their present estate. And as for other knowledg of God
or his word they have none touching the second table,
as the innumerable multitudes of their sutes, wrongs,
complaintes, in al their courtes of plea declare, which
never were so fraught, not even under the most grosse
poperie, as they are under this light of their gospell, all
these being members of their church. Neither is it
possible that such idolaters as both priestes and people
are, should have anie sound knowledg or judgment of
God's word and truth: for they that know not God
aright, how should they know his word aright. Now
the apostle teacheth us, and our common sense con- Isa. 41: 18, 19,
firmeth, that it is unsound milke that giveth no increase 20
to the bodie in 30 yeres' space, we have to suspect such
milke to be unholsome, I trow: neither would any of
us (in whome is any wit or love) put out our children
to such nourses, much lesse their soules.

But they use to stop the mouthes of their auditorie
that should so say or enter into such discourse with
them, that if they have not gotten knowledg and profited in sanctification by their preaching, then are they
all without faith, and so in a woeful case, in no estate
of salvation, bidding them proove and examine themselves, if Christ be not in them, then are they reprobates, *etc.*

This argument so terrifieth the poore soules' con- 2 Cor. 13: 5
sciences that neither have knowledg to examine their
wayes by Gode's word whether they lead unto life or
unto death, neither have ever seene or beene taught any
better course than that they are in; to which if you add
that general verbal knowledg of Christ, and some few
other doctrines touching faith and manners, somwhat
more pure than the doctrine of the papistes, wherin
they have found comfort, yea, and finding their consciences pricked and convinced of some sinnes they have
[154] blamed in their sermons, have indevored through
the grace of God to leave them, and at length gotten

---

[1] About seven paragraphs previously, Barrow speaks of 32 years.

victorie over them, *etc.* This knowledg, comfort, remorse, so worketh with these poore soules, that they hold the ministers of these things in such veneration, as they are ready with the people of Lystra to sacrifice unto them: not knowing in deed the effectual working of Sathan's delusions, with what shew of light and truth, with what power, signes, and lying wonders he shal, deceave such as have not receaved the love of the truth. They know not that the false church shal have her religion and worship also, her ministers and preachers of the gospel of Christ, *etc.*, and that these ministers shall transforme themselves as though they were ministers of righteousnes, and shall deceave many with their false Christes and gospels that they preach in these latter daies, wherof our saviour Christ and his apostles have warned us, why the false church could not have these thinges without some general knowledg, which general knowledg shall reproove such thinges as are contrarie to the same: and it being spiritual it shal also have spiritual effectes, as to move joy or sorrowe. This the preaching in the popish church also effecteth, who hath taught your preachers this argument, and hath as good right to use it towardes them, as they unto you or unto us. But can this knowledg which you get by them, justifie your waies, your church, ministerie, worship, *etc.*? If not, seing they are so directly against the word of God, what booteth this knowledg to eternal life? Balaam with all the false prophets had, and the devils have this faith and knowledg in as great measure as the learnedst of these ministers; yet the one is damned, the others tremble.

As for the comfort receaved by their preaching, it having no promise of blessing in the word of God (your church and whole ministerie being accursed) is rather a fearefull signe of the effectual working of their delusions, than any reason wherby you may assure your selves, or justifie them in their ungodly proceedings, whome the word of God in al their workes condemneth Looke not to gather grapes of thornes or figs of thistles. or any good fruites of such evil trees as are not of our

2 Thess. 2:9, 10

Mark 13:5, 6, 21, 22, 23

James 2:19

heavenly father's planting, and therfore shalbe plucked
up by the rootes.   You see they have stood teaching you
day unto day, line upon line, line upon line, heere a
litle and there a litle, yet have never brought you to a Isa. 28: 13
cleere sight and acknowledging of the truth.   You see
they lead you in the crooked pathes of death, they Prov. 2: 15, etc.
teach and stand ministers in the false church, of whose
ministerie in this estate is no comfort but assured destruction to be looked for, they being sent of God in his
wrath to deceave the children of death,[1] the reprobate.
You see they are like those inchanters that resisted Moses,
who doe all their miracles both in Egipt and Babilon,
etc., to deteine the people in Egipt and Babilon.   " They
have all gone out of the way, they have beene made
altogether unprofitable, there is none that doth good, [Romans 3: 12-
no, not one, their throte is an open sepulchre, they have   18]
used their tongues to deceit, the poison [155] of aspes is
under their lips; whose mouth is full of cursing and
bitternes, their feet are swift to shed blood, destruction
and calamitye is in their waies, and the way of peace
they have not knowne, the feare of God is not before
their eies."   How then should they profite this people
or guide them right, when they themselves know not the
right way ?

But heere they wil straight be upon me with this
question: where I had my faith and understanding of
the right course, if not from them and their preaching ?
There being no other meanes left in the land to beget
faith, than their ordinarie preaching in this ministery,
[than] this church which we now forsake.   The vanitie
of this argument I have even now shewed, and howe
therby much rather the church and ministerie of Rome
with all the abhominations therin might be justified,
seing they were much more catholike and universal than
these.   But to their question I answere; that God never
leaveth himself without faithful and true witnesses,
which abhor iniquitie, teach and practise the truth so
far as it is revealed unto them; which no doubt instruct

---

[1] Clement Gambell testified that the Separatists believed that the preachers
of England were " false preachers sent in the Lorde's anger to deceyve
his people with lyes " (Harley MSS, 6848, ff. 83 *recto* — 84 *recto*.

Dan. 12: 3

Rev. 5· 6, 7
Joh. 14: 26

Math. 11: 25
John 3: 3

Gal. 1: 8
2 Joh. 10
Phil. 3: 17

1 Cor. 11: 3

Exod. 23: 2

Heb. 10: 39

Joh. 9: 41 &
15: 22

manie and turne them from their evill waies. Further, we have the holy word of God, and the Lambe hath obteined to open the seales therof, who hath given us his spirit to guide us into all truth, and bring all things to our remembrance that he hath taught us. God is not tied to the lippes of these phariseis: yea his glorie is to hide these things from the prowd and prudent, and to reveale them to babes and sucklings. The wind bloweth where it listeth, *etc.* Faith is the only gift of God, who never wanteth meanes to publish his truth, and to save his elect. These popish priests that stand ministers after a false and counterfait order, even after the order of antichrist, not of Christ and the order of his Testament, that stand ministers of idolatrie unto idolaters, that hate to be reformed or reproved, have nought to doe to take God [his] holy word in their mouthes. But if they were as true and famous ministers as ever spake upon the earth, yet, if they should exercise such a ministerie as they do in those places, after that idolatrous and corrupt maner, to al the prophane and wicked; if they had all the giftes of al men and angels; yet were they to be holden accursed, [Galatians 1:8] to be left, and not to be receaved to house, *etc.*, we are to follow the apostles no further than they walke with Christ, no, nor the whole church any further, than they observe the rules of the word: we are not to erre or be drawen into transgression with a multitude or by the mightie. They breake the communion that breake the faith, they breake the faith which transgresse the word. But if these men should know the right course (which in deed I cannot beleeve, because the Scripture speaketh evidently, that God wil blind their eies and bow downe their backes, *etc.*). O how high then were their sinnes which forsake the waies of life, and have in the presumption of their owne heart sought out unto themselves bye waies, and lead the people astray ? With how many stripes are they worthy to be beaten ?

[156] Thus you see how this gospell they teach you is taught in a strange and false ministerie in the false church; is joined to the throne of the beast of antichrist; is joined unto al the abhomination and abhom-

inable of the land; is taught by prescription, limitation
and stint according to the bishops' injunctions, decrees
and traditions; unto which it is, together with the whole
church both ministers and people, in bondage. You
see how it hath neither light nor power in it to discover
and cast out these most grosse and damnable idolatries,
how it utterly wanteth practise in this false church,
where (say Christ what he will) all must be after the
pleasure of antichrist. You see how therby the bodie
hath not beene edified or led forth any one step toward
perfection, but rather (as by Satan's most strong delusions) have beene held therby in this Egiptian bondage
and Babilonish confusion under antichrist. You see the
ministers of these wares, of what liverie they are; how
they are the marked waged servants of antichrist, the
merchantmen of the whore to carrie abroad her abhominable wares.

Now remaineth, that I discover unto you some of the
gall, wherwith their hony is mixed; some of the leaven,
wherwith your milke is poisoned; that you may see how
the Lord in judgment hath mingled amongst them the
spirit of error, and given them up to the spirit of pride
and fornication, and caused them to erre in al their
wayes, and made night unto them for a vision, and Isa. 19: 14, 15
darknes for a divination; how the sunne is gone downe Micah 3: 6
over your prophets, and the day made dark over them. Isa. 59: 8, 10

Now that this may the sooner be brought to passe,
let me verie briefly shew you: first what maner of Christ
they teach you; then some few of the cheif heads of the
infinite errors they teach. And this the rather, because
they say they hould the foundation, and that there is
nothing wanting amongst them but matters of lesse
moment and of no necessitie, making some doctrines
and some part of Christ's Testament fundamental and
substantial, others accidental and such as may be altered
and violate without any prejudice or danger to the
soule. Yea, such may the transgressions and errors be,
as though they be obstinatly continued in, and openly
taught after they be reproved and convinced by the
word of God, yea, and the parties die in that estate
without repentance of these transgressions or errors; yet

may they hold the foundation, and be undoubtedly saved. Of this mind were and still continue five of the verie principall and best esteemed ministers of England,[1] both for learning and conscience: although there were alledged against the same these expresse Scriptures: Numbers 15: 30, 31, where it is written that "that soule that doth anie thing with an outstretched or high hand, whether he be borne in the land or a stranger, the same blasphemeth the Lord: therfore that person shall be cut off from amongst his people, because he hath despised the word of the Lord and made his commandement of none effect, that person shalbe utterly cut off, his iniquitie shall be upon him "; Exodus 23: 21; 1 Samuel 15: 22, 23; Ezekiel 18: 26, where the prophet concludeth, that when a righteous man turneth away from his righteousnes and committeth iniquitie, and dyeth therin, he shall die for his iniquitie that he hath done. Like-[157]wise also our saviour Christ, Matthew 5: 18, 19, teacheth, that one iote or title of his word shall not passe, and that whosoever shall breake one of the least of his commandements and teach men so, shalbe called least in the kingdome of heaven. And the apostle, James 2: 10, teacheth, that whosoever shal keep the whole law, yet faileth in one, becommeth guiltie of all. And how plentiful is the Apostle Paul in this point; that whoso teacheth otherwise, and yeildeth not to the wholsome words of our Lord Jesus Christ, and to the doctrine which is according to godlines, such are of corrupt mindes, destitute of truth, *etc.*, to be seperated, 1 Timothy 6: 3, 4, 5, to be avoided Romans 16: 17, to be rejected, Titus 3: 10. As for offences and transgressions of the word, we have a perpetuall rule, Mathew 18: 17, 2 Thessalonians 3: 14. If he transgresse, he is to be admonished, reproved, censured. If he erre of ignorance, he is to be instructed with meeknes, until God

Phil. 3: 15

Rom. 14

---

[1] Barrow may be referring to the five men who visited him in prison to hold conferences in 1589. These men were Thomas Sperin, John Egerton, Martin or Robert Cooper, William Hutchinson, and Lancelot Andrewes. It is possible that Barrow had in mind five men with whom he contended in print, and who were Reformists or Presbyterians. If so, he probably is referring to George Gifford, Thomas Cartwright, Walter Travers, William Fludd, and William Charke.

reveale the truth also unto him. But if he not only erre, but affirme and teach his error, wherby others are or may be infected; it is time to looke to that gangrene, least it fret further; it is time to purge out such leaven, least it make sowre the whole lumpe. 2 Tim. 2: 17 Gal. 5: 9

But to hold as these men doe, and as they are driven to doe when they plead for their whorish church and antichristian ministerie, is not only to goe expresly contrarie to the whole scope of Scriptures; to infringe and violate all God's lawes and covenant; to hould (as in deed they teach) Christ a saviour without repentance; to make some part of the Scripture more holy, more authentical, more true than other: in summe, to submit the holy Scriptures and Testament of Christ to the wil and lust of man; to ratifie or abrogate them at his pleasure; to make this part of substance, that of forme, this fundamentall, that accidentall, this necessarie to salvation, that needles, *etc.* But if the whole Scripture was given by inspiration of God, and is profitable to teach, to convince, to correct, to instruct in righteousnes: if it be the groundworke and foundation of the church, of our faith: if it be the law and rule of our life, the light of our eies, *etc.*, if everie word of God be holy, pure, perpetuall; then is this diep learning of theirs divelish and blasphemous; that thus to couller and cover their wickednes, make some part of God's word fundamental, substancial, necessarie, other accidentall, superficial, needles; especially where it sheweth, reproveth, and condemneth their doinges; yea, which make some sinnes openly and manifestly convinced, yet obstinatly continued and persisted in, without any repentance in this life, for all this, not to be mortall or deadly, as the papistes say and hould. Yet nevertheless wil these men be said to hold the foundation to salvation, notwithstanding that they disfranchise and reject a great part of Christ's Testament, and hould it not as fundamental and necessarie, and make neither conscience nor care to transgresse the same, and to bring in other lawes into the church in stead therof: yea upon that part which they would seeme to retaine, they build all this stubble, trumperie, and abhominations which have beene recited 2 Tim. 3: 16 Prov. 30: 5 Psal. 19: 8 & 12: 6 Psal. 119 entire Ephe. 2: 20

from the beginning of this treatise. To conclude, though they [158] remaine presumtuously obstinate in all these horrible transgressions, if by any this their shameles assertion (namely that they hold the foundation to salvation) be with never so plaine proof of Scripture denied, and they lovingly admonished and exhorted; against such they whet their viperous tongues, and powre out all the venome of their ralings, reproches, slaunders, and most shameles lies (wherof their owne festered consciences accuse them) in their pulpyts and privie meetings, machinating and devising against them as against open professed enemies, and all because they reprove them of their counterfait walking, which they cannot nor dare not in any Christian and peaceable maner enterprise by the word of God to approve and justifie.

But as you have heard how they generally use and esteeme the word of God, so let me briefly shew you what kind of Christ they preach you. Generally and verbally they hold and confesse him in both his natures verie God and verie man, to the work of their redemtion and salvation as the papistes also doe, though somwhat diversely, stumbling and contending rather about wordes than about any material difference when they are pressed. For Christ they wil confesse their only redeemer, and fully and sufficiently to have wrought their salvation, though by and by stumbling at the phrase of some Scriptures, they will joine unto him their owne beggerie workes and merites, *etc.* Both of them generally and verbally confesse Christ in his three offices, *viz.*, to be their only king, priest, and prophet: but when it commeth to the practise and obedience, then they both with one consent send an embassage after him saying, that we wil not have this man to reigne over us; cause the holy one of Israel to cease from us, let us breake his bandes and cast his cordes from us; this is the heire, come let us kill him, and let us take his inheritance, *etc.*

I know our English priestes wil have many fine floorishes to hide this treacherie: as that they acknowledg him their only priest and mediator, to have with that one oblation of his owne pretious bodie once offred, fully satisfied the justice and appeased the wrath of his Father. Yea, they acknowledg him to be the verie first fruites, and sanctifier of the whole heape, clothing all his with his righteousnes, and that he is entered into the heavens into the verie throne of God, and there offreth up the praiers and maketh intercession for all them. Likewise, that he is heire and king over al both men and angels, that he hath in this his (or rather oure flesh) vanquished al our enemies, Satan, sin, death and hel, and triumphed over them in that his crosse, that he is ascended up on high and sitteth at the right hand of God, from whence he shal come to judge the quick and the dead. And for his prophecie, that he is the end of al prophecies to whome they were directed, the fulnes and fountaine of al wisdome whome we ought to heare; and how by that his heavenly word he begetteth us to life everlasting, *etc.*

These and many other comfortable and true doctrines they can and doe deliver touching the offices of Christ; but all these you must understand, and I pray you observe wel (for so shal you cleerly espie their error [159] and deceit) are still but what Christ hath done in his Psa. 45 owne person for his elect: here is not one word spoken Isa. 9: 7 what he doth in his elect: how he teacheth, sanctifieth and ruleth them by the scepter of his word, how he is a Isa. 33: 22 king, priest, a prophet heere on earth, and exerciseth Deut. 18 the offices here in his church amongst his servantes the saints: how he is their pastour, their teacher, their king; Hebrews entire how he feedeth and reigneth in Sion, yea, and maketh Exod. 19: 6 all his children kings, priests, and prophets. Rev. 1: 6

Kings, in that he hath given them his word into their hearts and mouthes, wherby as with a sharpe two edged sword they cut off sin, and fight against al errors; wherby they reigne over their owne affections, subdue the Heb. 4: 12 flesh, cast downe everie imagination that is exalted against the knowledg of God, and bring into captivitie 1 Cor. 10: 4, 5, everie thought to the obedience of Christ; wherby they 6 unpartially censure, judge and cast out al maner of sin Math. 18: 17 as it ariseth and apeareth amongst them, binding their rulers in chaines and their nobles in fetters of yron, Psal. 149 executing upon them the judgments that are written; Isa. 54: 17

yea, therby condemning everie weapon and tongue that shal arise in judgment against the truth. This is the heritage of the Lord's servants, this honor shalbe to al his saintes. Priestes he maketh them, in that he annointeth them with his owne Holy Spirit, wherby they both offer up their prayers and praises through him unto God, and their owne bodies and soules as living sacrifices unto him daily; which is their reasonable serving of God. Prophets he maketh them, in that he revealeth his truth unto them, and commandeth them to witnesse it and spread it forth in all places to his glorie.

One word of these heavenly effects in and amongst them of their dutie, obedience, love, and faithfulnes they owe and ought againe on their parts to performe unto him, they al this while shew not; and how without this there is no comfort or benefit to be expected or receaved by Christ; without this faith, love, and obedience, none can have him a king unto them to rule and defend them, none can have him a prophet to teach and instructe them, none can have him a priest to sanctifie and blesse them, none can have him a saviour. But al they that either acknowledge not the Lord Jesus Christ, or obey not unto his eternal gospel, but withhold the truth in unrighteousnes, shalbe punished with everlasting perdition from the presence of the Lord, and from the glorie of his power, when he shal come to be glorified in his saintes, and to be made mervailous in al them that beleeve. But alas, how is it possible that they should know or see this beautie of the king in Sion, whiles they remaine in Babilon ? How is it possible that they should teach this submission and obedience unto Christ Jesus, when they themselves remaine the bondservants and sworne soldiours of antichrist in such maner as hath beene rehearsed?

How then in this estate should they stand the faithfull ministers of Christ, or preach him sincerely ? Can there be any accord betwixt Christ and antichrist ? Can they both reigne together in one church; or these men stand ministers unto both at one time ? If Christ be their king, where is then his honour, where is his obedience ?

1 Pet. 2: 5
Rom. 12: 1
Psal. 141: 2

Luk. 19: 27

Isa. 60: 22
Psal. 2
Revel. 19: 15

2 Thes. 1: 8, 9

2 Cor. 6: 15
Mal. 1: 6

Isa. 1: 2, 3, 4
Ezek. 34: 14

Christ reigneth [160] over none but his owne servantes, Zach. 11: 7
and them he ruleth by the scepter of his holy word: but
heere with them his scepter is wrested out of his hand,
and a scepter of reed given him, the canons of the pope,
the bishops' injunctions, and decrees of the High Commission, by which your church is wholy overruled, unto Exod. 23: 21
which your king, Christ himself whiles he is amongst Joh. 14: 21
you, must be subject, or els there is no place for him.
Christ giveth lawes unto his servants, and ordereth al 1 Cor. 2: 16
things in his church according to his owne will: but you Joh. 17: 8
give lawes to your Christ and set strange ordinances over
his church; yea, you have not anie one thing there either Mat. 18: 20
in order or administration, according to his Testament. Joh. 8: 32, 36
Againe, Christ hath given ful power and libertie to all Rom. 8: 15
and everie one of his servantes, to put in practise what- 1 Cor. 5
soever he commandeth, as also to reforme, to reprove,
censure and cast out whatsoever is found to be contrarie Math. 18
and repugnant unto his word, though al the powers in Joh. 20
the earth or in hell withstand it. But the Christ these
men preach you, is utterly without power to put any
thing of his owne will in practise, but is sold as a bond- 1 Cor. 4: 20
slave to these antichristian bishops and preachers, his
enemies. He cannot by vertue of his owne word and 2 Tim. 3: 5
authoritie redresse any thing, be it never so heinous or
enormous: neither can he establish or bring in any thing
that is wanting, be it never so necessarie and important,
without humble sute and attendance unto the high court
of Parliament, or upon the High Court of Commission.
If they reject his sute, though it be by thirty yeres together, and that in these two reasonable requests; that
they would remove their heinous and blasphemous idolatries from before his face, and give him leave to rule
them by his owne officers and lawes: yet must this poore
Christ with all his servants, even the whole church, stil
surcease the practise of the gospel, and continue under
these abhominations; yea (if he anger his lords the
bishops much), he shalbe whipped with scorpions, with
new rods; and this by the universal consent of all his
learned preachers in the land, who are at a ful point and
have set it downe as a resolute decree, not to stir a foot
forward until they have the prince's power and the

consent of Parliament. Then they will bring him in
with horsemen and charets [chariots], with belles and
bonefires. How like you this your worthy king ? Trow
you that ever Pilate arayed him worse when they clad
him in purple, put a scepter of a reed in his hand, a
crowne of thornes upon his head, bowed the knee before
him and hailed him a king, yea, wrytt him one in three
languages, Hebrew, Greek and Latine:[1] or the chief
priestes and phariseis, when they blindfolded him,
buffeted and scourged him, spatt in his face and blasphemed him ? Or the people that with one consent
demanded him unto the death, preferred the seditious
murtherer Barrabas[2] before him, haled him to the crosse,
despighted and reviled him upon the crosse ? A king
he is without power, a king without lawes, a king without officers, a king without subjectes, yea, a slave he is
made to everie slave. He hath strange officers, straunge
lawes that he is not acquainted with set over him and
imposed upon him whether he wil or [161] no, which
not only rule his heritage but overrule him after their
owne lustes. He is fashoned to the common welth,
and not the common welth unto him: and in the church
he is but an idol king, an idol Christ, and hath not there
so much honour given him, as the players doe unto their
kinges upon the stage.

And as for the priestly office he should execute amongst
them, therein they abuse him yet worse: for a new ministerie they erect in stead of his: parsons or mercenarie
roving preachers, in stead of pastors and faithful teachers. As for the other rable that serve in stead of elders
with their multitudes of attendants, as also their other
inferiour new found officers, would fill a booke but to
describe them and their offices. Thus make they him
a minister after an other order than that which he hath
set downe in his Testament, than that wherunto he was
annointed of his Father, and that with an othe, and that
for ever. They impose also upon him a new ministration and strange worship more displeasing unto God
than Nadab's fire, than Uzzah's altar, even al that

[1] Luke 23: 38. John 19: 20.
[2] Matthew 27: 16-26. Mark 15: 7-15.

idolatrous booke of that common service, which he must
(wil he nil he) administer in maner and forme abovesaid. Thus make they him a minister of al their idol- Psal. 110: 4
atries and abhomination; by him they offer up unto Gal. 3: 15
God all this their wil worship, poperie and superstition.
Moreover they make him a mediatour of an other Testament than that of his owne, binding him to this English Heb. 9: 17
masse booke and to al the injunctions of the bishops, the
High Commission, and Convocation House. Finally
they make him a priest, a mediatour, a saviour to all
the prophane atheistes, idolators, miscreantes and wicked
persons, conjurers, witches, heretikes and who not; al
being receaved into the bozome of their church, whome
they blesse in his name with his peace, to whome for
mony they sell and deliver their sacraments: and thus
by all these wayes they most impiously deny, and sacrilegiously defile the holy priesthood of Christ. What kind
of prophecie he exerciseth amongst them, may appeare
by that which is already said. They make him take
upon him the ministerie of antichrist, even that the pope
left in the land: they wil not suffer nor receave his
ministerie, which he hath in his Testament apointed for
his church. They set lawes not only over him in this
ministerie they apoint him, but also over the gospell it
self, both by aportionating how much of his word shalbe
read, in what o[r]der and time, *etc.* And this order
being through the yeere and permanent, they therby
abrogate no small part of the Bible, and take it cleane
away from the church, in that by their law they apoint
what shalbe read for ever, casting the rest quite out of
the church, allowing it no time or place to be publikely Deut. 4: 2 &
read. They bring in also in stead therof divers apocrypha 12: 32
writings, and reade them in their church in the place of Prov. 30: 6
canonical Scriptures. They reade also as part of their
publike ministerie of their church not only their abhom- Reve. 22: 18
inable service booke, but the blasphemous injunctions
of their bishops, and are not ashamed to preach and
publikely to expound in the church their fond [foolish]
aprocri-[162]pha catachismes.[1] To conclude they mus-

---

[1] Probably the best known catechism in England about 1590 was the one
by Alexander Nowell, but others by Martin Luther, John Calvin, and
Bishop John Ponet were also available.

sell and bridle up their Christ's mouth by publike law and power, forbidding him to teach any thing contrarie unto, or to find fault with any thing by publike auth- oritie established or to be established, swearing him daily to execute their injunctions; thus joining the gospel to al the idolatrie, abhomination, blasphemie, and as you see, to all the sinne, iniquitie and mischief of the land, wherby they make Christ a false prophet, an idolater, a blasphemer, and guiltie, yea a ringleader to al this ill.

Thus you see what kind of Christ they teach you, with- out power, holines, truth: what kind of gospel without freedome, without practise, without light. You see how they subject church, gospel and Christ to the apostaticall chaire of antichrist, making Christ both a minister to al their abhominations, and to justifie and dawbe them up with the gospell. Infinite were the labour to reckon up all the forgeries they build upon this founda- tion, this Christ, this gospel; or to shew how these wretches munge,[1] corrupt, pervert, wrast, falsifie and abuse the Scriptures, how they roile, yea poison the pure fountaines; or to recite the sundrie errors they heerby

Ezek. 34: 18, 19 fall into. For whiles they thus blasphemously denie in 2 Cor. 2: 17
& 4: 2 deed and practise the whole annointing of Christ, namely his three offices, his kingdome, priesthood, and prophecie; standing the sworne waged marked servants Gal. 1: 7 of that adversarie, that antichrist, that beast, these 2 Pet. 3: 16 bishops, deriving their forged false ministerie from them, Joh. 5: 23
2 Pet. 2: 1
Mat. 6: 24 propheciing by their licence and limitation, *etc.*, therby they flatly denie the kingdom, priesthood, and pro- phecie of Christ: for two contrarie maisters they can- Deut. 18: 20 not obey, they cannot be subject both to Christ and antichrist: two diverse and contrarie ministeries they cannot execute, the ministerie of Christ and the mini- sterie of antichrist at the same time, neither can they prophecie in both their names, *etc.*

Many are their forged cavillations which they invent unto themselves to hide this their perfidy, all which (as not recking them worthie the reciting) I leave to be refuted by their owne practise, compared to the word of God: as I might also unto their owne alligations and

---

[1] Cheat.

excuses, God having so devided their tongues, and made
them so contrarie one unto an other, as it is an impossible thing to find two of them of one mind; yea or
any one of them constant in that he affirmeth. So are
these accustomed to doe all things without ground or
assurance, following the traditions, writings and examples of others, never looking how consonant they be
unto Gode's word. This maketh them thus ignorant and
blind in all the lawes and ordinances of Christ, touching
the true gathering, building, and governing the Church
of Christ, that they know not the doctrines even of the
beginnings of Christ, of repentance from dead workes,
faith towardes God, of baptisme and laying on of handes.
This maketh them not to know so much, as the stones
wherof Christ's church must be built, nor the true
founda-[163]tion wherupon to build them, as you may
see by that which hath beene said concerning their outward estate and practise; much lesse know they the true
forme and fashion of the house, and least of all the true
administration and ordinances therof; as apeareth evidently by their receaving of, and administring unto this
monstrous confuse bodie of their profane rowtes of
people; by their exercising this their false and antichristian ministerie, and that after such an idolatrous
blasphemous symoniacal maner; as also by receaving
antichrist's yoke, traditions, ordinances; wherby (as Gal. 3: 15
hath beene shewed) they deny Christ in the flesh, by Gal. 2: 5
deniing his offices, his annointing: they denie his ministerie, his ordinances, his whole Testament, by receaving
an other ministerie, other lawes than such as he there
hath prescribed. Or els they must affirme, that earthly
men may admit into and make members of the church
whome they please and wil; that they also may alter,
add to, detract, yea, abrogate and disanul what part
of Christ's Testament they list; that they may erect a
new ministerie, a new forme of administration of sacraments, of worship, of government. Of al which severally to intreat and set downe their particular errors and
enormities, no pen of man sufficeth. I refer heerin the
reader partly to that which heer is already written concerning their ministerie, ordination, ministration, sacra-

ments, worship, *etc.*, but chiefly to his owne more neere view and diligent search of their doings by the light of God's word.

They holde also, that the true church of Christ may be built and established without the outward offices and government he hath prescribed in his Testament: yea, that in stead of them, it may receave a false and adulterate ministerie, be governed by other officers and lawes than he hath appointed in his word. They holde that it may be a true church, though both ministerie, ministration and government be thus wholy corrupted and forged, and though it have never entred or smitten covenant with Christ, but stil and ever have remained in subjection unto antichrist in one false shape or other; whose yoke (they hold) ought not to be cast off, to redresse any sin or abuse among them, or put in practise any more of Christ's Testament, than is by publike authoritie permitted; yea, in this confusion, idolatrie, subjection, though neither the people be called unto nor joined in the faith, though neither ministerie, ministration, nor any thing be aright according to the word amongst them, though their church abound with all manner of sin, abhomination and abhominable persons, though they have neither power to seperate the most uncleane, to censure or cast out anie offendor or offence, to redresse any thing be it never so odious, hateful, and apparantly ill, nor yet have libertie to put in practise any of Christ's heavenly ordinances: notwithstanding all this they hold it with maine force and outcries to be a true established church of Christ, though there be never a true stone nor any one pin or naile of the true tabernacle aright amongst them, as their [164] adulterate ministerie, office, election, ordination, administration, worship, sacramentes, praiers, fasting, abuse of the word read, abuse of the word preached (which they corrupt, roile,[1] distort, pervert, wrast, leaven, falsifie, poison, abuse, prophane, abrogate, exclude at their wils) declare. Of all which what unsound opinions they hold, their present practise compared to the

---

[1] To render turbid or muddy, to perturb, disquiet.

word of God, manifesteth: yea they wil stil be the true church and ministers of Christ, though they reject his word, remaine obstinate in their sinne, defend, plead for, and justifie the same, persecute, blaspheme, and murther Christ's servants that speake unto them in the name of Christ and exhort them to amendement. Thus you may see into what hardnes and blindnes of heart and extreame utter darknes the Lord hath cast these your seers because they have loved darknes more than light, neither have trembled at his word, but walked in the presumption of their owne heart, committing arrogancie in their wrath. O how great is that darknes, when the verie light of your church is such darknes, as it is but that verie smoke of the bottomles pit, when it is duly examined. For as you have heard al their worship, ministerie, prayers, sacraments, fastes, to be but counterfait and abhomination: so yet of all other you may perceave this their preaching of the gospell, to be most detestable and pernitious, even the strongest snare and delusion of Satan, wherby he allureth, deceaveth and holdeth captive the miserable world in the chaines of transgression, error, idolatrie, abhomination and impenitencie, unto judgment.

This preaching of theirs as it is exercised in a false ministerie, a false church, as it proceedeth from the chaire of antichrist: so is it wholy subject therunto, both the person and doctrine of the preacher. Their person either to be still approved and licenciate, or els silenced, suspended, deprived: their doctrine to be allowed or condemned as pleaseth their Lords Ordinaries (in whose pontifical brests and handes standeth the whole doctrine of the Church of England) what they shal receave, what they shal reject, what they shall say, what they shal leave unsaied, *etc*. The word of God, church, ministerie, preaching and al, are wholy in the handes of these lawlesse lordes, to abrogate, estab- Gal. 1: 8 lish, bring in, cast out, depose, suspend without controlement or accompt. A greater power than ever was 1 Cor. 3: 13 given unto or exercised by any of Christ's apostles, who 1 Cor. 11: 1 alwayes submitted their doctrine, practise, persons, unto the trial and censure of the word, and that by any Act. 5: 17, 11

Christian. They never exercised dominion over the faith of any, or layd anie other burden upon the church, than what they either read in the word of God, or acknowledged to be the will of God. But heere in the Church of England it is held a small thing to have a strange ministerye, worship, lawes, orders, government imposed upon them; to have a great part of God's word quite banished the church, the rest that is allowed them but by shredds and patches at starts and braydes; to have their preaching by stint, prescription, limitation; to have the whole doctrine subject not to the wil of God but to the wil of these their Ordinaries, who (they may be [165] sure) wil allow no more and none otherwise, than shal agree to their apostatical throne. The ministers of this church may not preach, the people beleeve, much lesse practise any more of the word of God, than what is confirmed by these their Ordinaries.

The poore parish or congregation where these priestes serve, may not meddle or have to do with the election, administration or deposing of these their ministers: for why, they are lay men and have no skil, neither ought to intermeddle with ecclesiasticall affaires, or with the word of God. Be their minister never so blind, unsufficient or vile a wretch, detected of never so horrible sinnes, yet may not they remove him: their only help is to complayne to their Lord Ordinarie; in the meane while they must joine to the wretch in praiers, in sacramentes, yea, stil and for ever, if it please not their said lord to give eare to their complaint. Let their minister preach never such damnable or hereticall doctrine, wrest, pervert, corrupt, falsifie the Scriptures never so violently and heinously, all the church (no, though there be all the priests in a countrie as at a scene) hath no authoritie, nay is by expresse law forbidden to reprove this doctrine presently or publikely, or yet to forbid him to deale with the Scriptures; their remedy is stil to complaine to their Ordinarie, and until it please him to take order therin, the whole congregation is stil bound to frequent his heretical sermons and ministerie: yea, al the priestes of the land both pontifical and reformistes[1] agree in this point and conclude, that the lay people (as they terme them) ought not to intermedle either with the deposing their minister, or reproof of his doctrine.

The one sort (as you have heard) sendeth them to their lords these bishops, the other referreth them over for these and manie other cases under hand, to a provincial or classical synode or permanent councel of priests, *etc.* Amongst whome all these affaires must be debated: and after they are agreed upon the point, then their decrees to be brought forth, solemnely published and pronounced to the people, who must attend upon, awayte and receave these oracles as most holy and canonical. They have no remedie if they also be contrarie to the truth, but to appeale to a councel, in the meane while still joining to such a wretch, such an hereticke, and that in the high profanation of God's holy name, word and ordinances. But my purpose is not in this place either to refute the popish prelacie of the one sort, or the devilish forgerie of the other (hoping to find a more fit place for both) so much as to shew that everie christian congregation hath power in themselves,[2] and of duty ought presently and publikly to censure any false or unsound doctrine that is publikly delivered or maintained amongst them, if it be known and discerned unto them; yea, anie one member in the church hath this power, whatsoever he be, pastor or prophet, that uttereth it: as also to shew how far this their pulpet preaching differeth from that heavenly blessed exercise of expounding Scriptures or prophecie in the church of Christ. [166] The first me thinkes alreadie verie fully proved in all these places where our saviour Christ hath given unto his church and to everie par- Mat. 18: 17, 18

1 Barrow means by pontifical priests those that support the Elizabethan ecclesiastical settlement and the Book of Common Prayer. By reformistes he means those that would alter the settlement. Since individuals varied in the degree of change advocated, the category of reformers included moderate Anglican reformers, Puritans, Presbyterians, and Precisians, groups which are overlapping in beliefs and nomenclature.

2 This statement illustrates Barrow's conviction that a congregation is the locus of authority, and that an individual member has the right, yea, the duty, of censuring false doctrine. Barrow may not have foreseen how widely men would differ in their " heavenly blessed exercise of expounding Scriptures or prophecie in the church of Christ."

ticular congregation therof himself, his word, his power,
with expresse charge to put in practise whatsoever he
hath commanded them: and threatned his wrath and
displeasure against that whole congregation which neg-
lecteth or breaketh any of his commandements, or
suffreth any seene transgression, or error, or incorrigible
impenitent offendor. Also where he commanded all
men to informe that church wherof they are members.
of such transgressions, offences, enormities, as arise
amongst them. This he in vaine had commanded,
and they in vaine should do this, except he had given
both absolute authority and expresse charge unto the
church to redresse and take order in the same. In as
many places also as he hath commanded the whole
church and everie member therof to watch, to scowte
and observe their teachers, to trie the spirits, to marke
them diligently which cause division and offences
contrarie to the doctrine which they have learned; to
seperate themselves from such as teach after an other
maner, or consent not unto the wholsome wordes of
our Lord Jesus Christ and to the doctrine which is
according unto godlines; to hold them accursed that
pervert the gospell of Christ, or preach any thing besides that hath beene taught by Christ and his apostles;
to reject an hereticke after one and the second admonition to; have in a readines due vengeance against al
disobedience, etc. In al these and sundrie other places
most evidently apeareth, that Christ hath given ful
power, absolute authoritie, and expresse commandement unto his church, even to everie particular congregation, to censure both the persons and doctrines of
their ministers, and of every member of their said congregations. He sendeth them not heere to these popish
Ordinaries, neither yet to a provincial synode or a
classis of priests: there are other uses of synods or
councels, as shal in due place be declared. They can
neither ad to, nor diminish from, the power of the
church, or execute and alter any part of the churche's
dutie.

Moreover, sith everie member hath like interest in
Christ, in his word, the publike doctrine, and minis-

Marginal references:

1 Cor. 5: 4

2 Thes. 3: 6, 14

Zach. 5: 9
Mark 13: 34

Rom. 16: 17
1 Joh. 4: 1
1 Tim. 6: 3, 5
2 Joh. 9: 10
2 Tim. 3: 1, 2,
3, 4, 5

Tit. 3: 10
2 Cor. 10: 4, 5, 6

Cantic. 6: 9

Heb. 12: 22, *etc.*

2 Pet. 1: 1
Rev. 2: 26
Josh. 7: 12, 25

Josh. 22: 18

tration of the church, and shall all be held guiltie and 1 Cor. 5: 6
punished for the publike transgressions and abuses of 1 Cor. 12: 25, 27
the church; seing everie member is bound to the edification, service and utilitie of the bodie; seing everie
member of the church is commanded to watch, to trie Mar. 13: 34, 37
the spirits, to contend for the maintenance of the faith 1 Joh. 4: 1
once indifferently given to all saintes, to avoide false
teachers, false prophets, *etc.*, seing they are commanded Mark 13: 5, 6,
not to follow the multitude or mightie, in evil; seing 21, 23 / Math. 7: 15
they are commanded to reprove their brother playnly,
to bind their sinnes by the word, even their princes in Phil. 3: 2
those chaines and nobles in those fetters, to say to Levit. 19: 17
Archippus, looke to thy ministerie that thou hast receaved in the Lord that thou fulfil it;[1] yea though an Exod. 23: 2
apostle or an angel from heaven should teach either Luk. 17: 3 / Psal. 145
other doctrine or after an other maner, than is in Christ's Col. 4: 17
Testament prescribed, to hold and pronounce him Gal. 1: 8
accursed. To con-[167]clude the point; seing the
praiers, sacraments, sermons, of such wicked or here- Prov. 15: 8, 9
ticall ministers are sacriledg and abhomination in God's 1 Cor. 10: 17, 18, 20
sight, and that all which communicate, joine to, heare
or suffer such ministers are alike guiltie of this sinne
and sacriledg: who can doubt, but that everie Christian
hath power and authoritie in due time and place (not
disturbing Christ's holy order in his church) publikely
to reprove any publike transgression of anie member of
the church, or of the whole church; as also to discover
and refute any error escaped or delivered in publike
doctrine: yet this (as is said) in due time and order, Jude 3: 10
giving leave and place unto the elders and prophets of
the said congregation first: who if they neglect or over-
passe such publike transgression or error, then may any
one of the congregation, or any Christian whosoever;
yea, he ought to reprove such transgression and error,
unles he wilbe guiltie of betraying the faith of Christ,
of the destruction of the whole congregation, knowing
the danger of such leaven, the sodennes of the wrath of
God for such things.

---

[1] Archippus is mentioned in Colossians 4: 17, where he is urged to fulfill the ministry he had received in the Lord. He is also referred to in Philemon 1: 2 as " our fellow soldier."

Heere will be grossly objected, that the common people are ignorant, not able to judg betwixt truth and error, disordered, variable, easie to be devided and led into sects; and therfore they are not to intermedle with the judgment and reproof of faults and errors escaped in the ministerie, or with the censuring their persons.[1]

That their people are blind, ignorant, seditious, headstrong, I readily grant; neither can it be otherwise, having such blind guides and corrupt teachers as all they are. I grant also, that neither the people nor they ought in this estate to meddle with the word of God, or take his blessed name in their mouth, without most high and unsufferable profanation of the same. But for the people of Christ, they are all inlightned with that bright morning star, that sonne of righteousnes. The eye of their faith is single, and the whole bodie is light. They are an humble, meek, obedient people, they will heare and follow the true shepheard, but a stranger they will not heare. They rejoice and love earnestly in the truth, and can by no meanes be drawn to do any thing against the truth. And therfore hath God amongst them bownd up the testimonie and sealed up the law. To them he hath committed the charge and keeping of his holy oracles; to them and everie one of them he hath given his holy sanctifying spirit, to open unto them and to lead them into al truth: to them he hath given his sonne to be ther king, priest and prophet, who hath made them unto him kings and priests. But if they were so blind and ignorant as these men would make them, how could they then discerne truth from error, how could they approve truth, or refute error and transgression.

Happily for all this heere will be saied, that the common sort of Christ's servantes either have not this knowledg, or have it but in small measure; and therfore are unfit to deale in these high matters, and can not doe it orderly and soberly. [168]

To this I answere, that they are to reprove no more

Margin references:
Math. 6: 22
1 Cor. 6: 11
Col. 1: 12, 13

Rom. 12: 9, 10, etc.

Gal. 4: 18
2 Cor. 13: 8

Isa. 8: 16

1 Tim. 3: 15
Rom. 8: 9, 14
Joh. 16: 13

1 Joh. 2: 27
Revel. 1: 6

Rom. 12: 3

[1] Amongst the clerical and lay hierarchy of Elizabethan England there was a deep suspicion and resentful distrust of " popularity." Barrow's advocacy in the following paragraph of " democracy " and " popularity," therefore, is remarkable and courageous.

than their assured knowledg leadeth them unto. If
they transgresse the limits either of their knowledg in 1 Thes. 5: 14
reproving that which deserveth no reproofe, or breake 2 Thes. 3: 14
the established order of the church by rashnes, intem-
perance, *etc.*, then are they for so doing subject to reproofe and censure for abusing their libertie, for break- 1 Cor. 11: 16
ing order: the churches of God have no custome to be 1 Cor. 14: 33
contentious.[1] But if they should be debarred of this
power, libertie, and dutie because they are not so
learned as the priests, and have not beene at the universitie, *etc.*, by that popish reason were the word of God
to be shut up from al lay men (as they cal them) that
no man might reade or speake therof in his house or
family, because they have not knowledg to understand
it and open it after their schoole maner, the word of
God being such an abysme of wisdome and of so great
dignitie and reverence, and that in al places alike. And
should they not by this reason also shut it up from themselves, and from al men in this life? For he that know- 1 Cor. 13: 9
eth most knoweth here but in part, yea, and of that part 1 Cor. 8: 2
he knoweth nothing as he ought to know.   Phil. 3: 13

But they are to understand that God hath not given
us his word that it should be perfected or receave grace
from us, but that it should bring grace unto us, build
up and accomplish our faith, and nourish us unto 1 Cor. 4: 7
eternal life; that it should be milke to the weake and
unexpert, strong meate to them of riper age. According to this word who so speaketh not, it is because there
is no light in them. By this word what so is reproved
or affirmed, the basenes or ignorance of the speaker is
not to be regarded: it no way diminisheth anything from James 2: 1
the dignitie and truth of the word; to which (as the only
object) the church is to cast their eye. As for these
learned divines of our age, I refer them unto, or rather
oppose unto them the wisdome and word of God, who
you see hath given unto al his servantes this libertie and
power; yea rather hath layd upon them this charge and
duty, to reprove and censure any error or transgression

---

[1] In the history of the christian church, this factor of contentiousness has
been the rock on which many councils, denominations, and groups have
foundered. Pride of opinion has been identified with the truth and the
will of God.

which is committed by the whole church or any member of the church contrarie to the word of God, by the same word.

But yet are not our learned Reformists satisfied: for loe, they fetch a reason somwhat more subtilly (though altogether as far from the truth as the other) from 1 Corinthians 14: 32, where it is said, the spirits of the prophets are subject to the prophets, therfore conclude they, that the people are not to reprove, judge, or censure the doctrine of the minister, but only an assembly of ministers, a schoole of prophets, as they call it.[1]

Before I shew their grosse mistaking and perverting this place of Scripture, I dismisse their argument by denying the consequent therof. That because the spirit[s] of the prophets are subject to the prophets; that is, such as have the gift of utterance and expounding Scriptures ought principally and especially to judg of that exercise, and to speake in that exercise as in way of prophecie. Therfore the whole church besides nor any member therof ought not to reprove, and censure such errors as have escaped the prophets and are revealed unto them. And for this [169] I insist in the former reasons and expresse places of Scripture alledged. Very hard it were, that that heavenly and most blessed exercise of prophecie which was instituted of God for

Gal. 5: 9 the singular comfort and general inlightning of the whole church, should through the pride and arrogancie

2. Tim. 2: 17 of a few, be turned to the utter subversion of the faith
Tit. 1: 10 of the whole church, and the desolation therof. For what part can there be pure, where the doctrine is not sound? Or what can be more miserable than to see

Joh. 4: 42 with others men's eies, to beleeve with other men's

---

[1] The classis or the presbytery is better able to judge than the congregation. In normal circumstances this would be true, but the argument turns upon the qualifications of the members of the classis and of the congregation.

hearts,[1] yea, to be brought into that slaverie and sub- Gal. 6: 4
jection, that they must receave and beleeve whatsoever the prophets or ministers speake and agree upon,
be it never so dissonant and repugnant to the word of
God.   This were right after the manner of the atheists
of these daies, to hire into their parish a learned preacher,
though al the rest of the parish be never so blind, prophane, wretched, yet where this burning lampe is, they
are all in happy state and safe inough; because they have
the gospell preached amongst them, they are a famous
church.   But our saviour Christ and his apostles sub- Joh. 5: 39 &
mitted their ministerie and doctrine to the trial, censure $\substack{10:\ 37,\ 38 \\ \&\ 18:\ 20,\ 21}$
and judgment of al, by the Scriptures; yea, and most
commended and rejoiced in these hearers that were most
diligent to examine and try their doctrine.   And I
would faine know what injurie it were unto any, if the
church stil reteined that libertie, not disturbing the holy Act. 17: 11
order therof.   But these priestes, they will not only 1. Thess. 5: 21
submit their persons and doctrine to the censure of the 2. Cor. 1: 13
church where they administer (for they must have a
jurie of clarkes, a classis of priestes to goe upon them),
but they bind their poore church to their lipps, and
build it upon themselves, and with their blazing light
strike al the rest of their hearers and followers starke
blind.

Now let me returne to this place of the Corinths which
they so falsely interpret, miserably misuse, and most
perniciously pervert.[2]   The prophets they give out to
be understood of such ministers only, as have the gift
of preaching (as they call it), holding it lawful for none
els to speake of the Scriptures by way of interpretation
and prophecie, especially to expound them in the

---

[1] This is a plea for the priesthood of all believers, and a hope that in an
ideal situation the members of a gathered church will be genuine students
of the word of God, and will be preservers of sound doctrine.   The principle
seems *de jure* sound, but *de facto* the members of a congregation are occupied
with the practical affairs of life, lack a background of linguistic and historical preparation, are subject to pride and undue love of preconceived
opinions.   Barrow exalts the intellectual and spiritual dignity of the
individual, and believes that such an individual is " inlightened with that
bright morning star, that sonne of righteousness."   Furthermore, he
advocates " giving leave and place unto the elders and prophets of the
said congregation first."
[2] I Corinthians 14: 32.

church or congregation. This exercise spoken of heere by the apostle, they say is understood of such prophet-icall ministers only, is instituted only for such, and be-longeth only unto such. The place of such exercise, they terme a schoole or colledg of prophets.

Heerupon they abuse this heavenly glorious exercise, in that they shut it up amongst a few of them, shut out the people from it utterly, making it like Osyris myst-eries:[1] besides that they heere amongst themselves unsufferably corrupt all the Scriptures they intreate of, by their rhetorical figures, devisions, demonstra-tion, humane and traditional writings, wherin all their universitie learning consisteth.[2] This place they most perniticiously pervert, in that from hence they derive their prophetical conventicles and classical synods, assuming heerby [170] into their owne hands the key of al knowledg, and shutting up the Scripturs, yea all God's graces, even the Holy Ghost it self, amongst them-selves in these their schooles of prophets: as also into their classes of select priests the scepter of Christ and absolute government of al churches, to whome it is left but to receave and execute the reverent decrees of this famous classes [classis] of priestes.

1. Cor. 14

And now let this Scripture wheruopon they build al this stuffe be duly searched and pondered, and you shall find it in all these things direct and flat against them.

Ver. 1
12
13

First, that the prophets there spoken of by the apostle, that are to speake in and judg of this exercise, were not only ministers, is gathered by the whole scope of the chapter, where everie brother is incited to emulate spiritual gifts, the rather that they might prophecie and helpe to edifie the church; this gift by manie reasons being preferred to all other gifts, and prooved far most excellent both in it self and to others, *etc.* Moreover, in this exercise of prophecie which was instituted for the instruction and comfort of all, the apostle saith that

[1] Osirian mysteries. Osyris was an Egyptian deity, associated with fer-tility, with the beneficent power of the Nile, and with the sun. In the latter association, he became identified with Ra.

[2] Compare the sarcasm and denunciation of university learning and logic, as expressed by Robert Browne in " A Treatise upon the 23. of Matthewe." See Albert Peel and Leland H. Carlson, *The Writings of Robert Harrison and Robert Browne*, pp. 173-193.

three prophets may speake in due order, one after Ver. 29
an other at one time, and the others are to judg, *etc.*
Three ministers, I am sure, in any one church there
cannot be, that by office are to attend unto the ministration of the word. The pastor and the teacher are Rom. 12: 7, 8
the only offices that I now know apointed to the ministerie of the word; and therfore even by this place, more
besides the ministers of the church may speake in the
way, yea, in this publike exercise of prophecie. Neither
ought this to seeme strange in the eares of anie that Luk. 10
knowe what belongeth to the exercise of prophecie or
order of the church. It is no other thing than Christ Act. 8: 4 &
hath instituted and the apostles everie where taught, 11: 20
and that by most sensible reasons. For as the bodie
consisteth of manie members, and al the members have
not one office, *etc.*, so the members of the church being Rom. 12: 6
divers and having receaved divers gifts, are (according
unto the grace that is given to everie one) to serve the 1 Pet. 4: 10
church, or rather the Lord with the same, as good dis-
posers of the manifold grace of God. If they have the
gift of prophecie, then are they to exercise it according
to the proportion of faith, speaking as the wordes of God
alwaies, keeping themselves within the bound of sobrietie
and truth: who so doth otherwise is subject to censure
and reproofe. We see the practise heerof not only in
Corinth but in Antiochia and Rome, and no doubt by
the same rule in other churches. In Antiochia we
reade of sundrie prophets and teachers, Barnabas,
Symeon, Lucius, Manahen,[1] Paul. Acts 13:1 and 15:
32, of Judas and Silas, that exhorted and taught in that
church. That there were sundrie also that taught in
Rome, appeareth Philippians 1: 14, 15, *etc.*

Neither hath this beene strange even under the law: Deut. 13: 2 &
we see God chose his prophets of al tribes, whose doctrine 18: 20, *etc.*
was to be tried by God's word. Their prophecies of
future things, by the event: we see our saviour Christ
his apostles and disciples did the like throughout al the
cities and synagogues of the Jewes.

If unto this it be answered that our saviour Christ was
Lord of the [171] law and of the temple, and so might

---

[1] Or Manaem, a member of the court of Herod the tetrarch.

doe his pleasure (for the prophets, apostles and disciples what they did was also by the commandement of God) and so none of these examples to be made presidentes [precedents] unto us without the like warrant. I graunt well, neither would I ground upon these examples if either they were contrarie to any law of God, or that there were not expresse warrant in the Testament of Christ and in the other Scriptures, that such as have the gift of prophecie may and ought to exercise their gift in the church of Christ. To that end I brought these examples, to shew that it was a thing usual amongst the Jewes and not contrarie to anie law, as Doctor Some and almost al the priests of the land very ignorantly and falsly give out.[1] For neither can they proove that it was unlawfull for any besides the priests to reade or expound the Scriptures, or use exhortation and praier in the temple and publike synagogues of the Jewes, neither yet that it only belongeth to the ministers of the church under the gospel, unlesse we wil take their bare affirmation for proof.

1. Kings 8

2. Chron. 34 & 35 chap.

But as under the law I have alledged manie examples to the contrarie, so might I bring more. Solomon prayed, Josiah exhorted in the temple. If they think to evade by saiing they were prophets, and did it by especial warrant; I doubt they cannot proove Josiah a prophet. Againe I would aske them, whither this especial warrant were private and knowen only to themselves, or publike and knowen to the people and state also? Publike they cannot shew it, for then would they never have resisted the message and slaine the prophets, *etc.* If it were only private and knowen to the prophets only, then what was this to the state or people? The priestes would never have suffred them in this maner to have usurped their office. Againe our saviour Christ (if it had beene contrarie to the law) would never have done it, or caused his disciples to doe it; who were no where reprehended for teaching, but for their doctrine only, as apeareth by the examination

---

[1] Robert Some, *A Godly Treatise* (1589), pp. 19-21, 23-26. Barrow's view is that any man who is able may preach without an external calling. Such a practice was Anabaptistical to Dr. Some, who believed that no man, how able soever, might preach without an external calling.

of our saviour Christ before the high priestes: neither were anie of his disciples troubled for teaching in any of the cities and synagogs where he sent them.

After his death also, when the apostles accustomably Acts 4 & 5
chap. taught and praied in the temple, being brought before the councel, they were not reprooved (though they were ignorant and base men of occupation in their eies) because they taught and praied publikly, but because they taught the righteousnes and glorie of that Christ whome they had so unjustly murthered and put to death; and were not forbidden simply not to teach, but not to teach in his name. So you see it was not Christ's warrant that stood them in any stead for the allowance of this action either before magistrates or people who knew or acknowledged not Christ but abhorred him and put him to death. If it had beene contrarie to the law for any but priests publikly to teach, pray, *etc.*, both our saviour Christ and his disciples should have heard of it no doubt at the handes [172] of these carping cavilling phariseis, and of those malicious murtherous priestes. But we see the apostles were everie where permitted to teach through all the synagogs of the Jewes, insomuch as the rulers of the synagogue at Antiochia Act. 13: 15 sent unto Paul and Barnabas, willing them if they had any exhortation for the people, to say. This they would neither have permitted nor done, if it had beene contrarie to their law. By Christ's warrant these rulers did it not; for, for his name sake they persecuted and afterward stoned him. Let this perilous paradoxe then at length be gained, *that others which have the gift of prophecie besides the ministers, may publikly teach or exhort in the church.*

Now remaineth to be shewed, that this exercise of prophecie belongeth to the whole church, and ought not to be shut up in this maner amongst the priests only, the people being shut out either to speake or heare. This the apostle in this fourteenth chapter[1] plentifully proveth by many reasons, and plainly avoweth in direct words. Reason may be drawen from the verie exercise of prophecie it self, which is

[1] I Corinthians 14.

S

nothing els now with the church, than an expounding and interpretation of Scriptures. This light, I am sure they wil grant, ought not to be hid under a bed or bushell; neither to be shut up amongst a few, as these Anabaptistical preachers use in their conventicles at this exercise. There are no eare secrets or hidden mysteries which are to be kept close, but are to be proclaimed and published upon the house top.

The endes also of this exercise of prophecie shew, that it belongeth to the whole church, and none of them ought to be shut out.[1] The endes are the edification, exhortation, and comfort of the whole bodie. What a pride and insolencie, yea, crueltie is it in these men, that would assume unto themselves only this bountiful grace of God, and debarre others from the same, and that the verie church, to whome it belongeth and for whome it was instituted; when the Lord alloweth even strangers and unbeleevers to come unto it, lifting up the sonne of man therby as a standard to other nations. What enemies then are these men unto the glorie of God and contrarie unto all men, that would take from them this most blessed meanes of their salvation.

The apostle also in expresse wordes declareth, that this exercise belongeth to the whole church, verses 23, 24.[2] If (saith he) " when the whole church is come together unto the same, and all speake tongues, there come in also they that are ignorant or unbeleevers, wil they not say that ye are mad ? But if al prophecie and there come in an infidel or idiote, he is convinced of all, he is judged of all," *etc.* The 26 verse also: " what is [it] then brethren ? When ye come together everie one of you hath a psalme, hath doctrine," *etc.* Likewise, verse 31. " For you may all [one] by one, everie one

Mat. 10: 27
Nehem. 8: 8

[1 Cor. 14]
Ver. 3, 5
31
24

Isa. 11: 10
Cant. 8: 13

Joh. 3: 14

[1] During the 1570's, the Puritans utilized " exercises " or " prophesyings " for a deeper knowledge of Scripture and for increasing the number of preachers of the word. When Archbishop Grindal refused to forbid them in 1576, Queen Elizabeth herself ordered the bishops to suppress them. See A. F. Scott Pearson, *Thomas Cartwright and Elizabethan Puritanism,* pp. 155-157. *The Seconde Parte of a Register,* ed. Albert Peel, I, 133-135. Edmund Grindal, *The Remains of Edmund Grindal,* ed. William Nicholson, pp. 376-390. John Strype, *The History of the Life and Acts of the Most Reverend Father in God, Edmund Grindal* (1821), pp. 325-333, 558-574, 574-6, 579-583. Lansdowne MSS. 23, f. 12.
[2] I Corinthians 14: 23, 24.

of you, prophecie, that all may learne and all may be comforted." What can be more manifest and direct than these places, that this exercise of prophecie belongeth to the whole church, and that everie faithful man hath here freedome and power both to be present and to speake also as need requireth, and God revealeth unto him? [173]

Are not also al the carnal reasons of these phariseis taken away, which alledg the ignorance of the most part, or confusion, if al might be suffred to speake? To the one, no man is to speake but as the words of God, according to the proportion of faith within the boundes of sobrietie and truth; his wordes must be to edification, els he faulteth and is judged for them. For the confusion that might hereupon arise if all should have power to speake. It is not here said that everie one which hath power should at al times use this power: 1 Cor. 10: 23 that which is lawful is not alwaies expedient. Christians Gal. 5: 13 are to use their libertie to the edification, and not the 1 Pet. 2: 16 confusion, of the church; for God is not the author of V. 40 [1 Cor. 14] disorder but of peace, as in all the churches of the saintes. They then that thus presumptuously either V. 33 [1 Cor. 14] innovate or abuse this blessed ordinance of Christ, find fault with and controule the commandements of God, and charge God with confusion, who is the author of this exercise, order, libertie.

But Doctor Some hath by the priviledg of the Church of England published it utterly unlawful for any that is not a minister, to deale with the interpretation of Scriptures, what giftes soever God hath given him therunto; and saith, these absurdities would ensue therof: that women may then also preach in the church; that those men that thus speake in way of prophecie usurpe the minister's office with Corath, offer Uzziah's incense, and may also by this meanes enter into the councel chamber, and intrude into the civil magistrate's office; for to give councel also is everie Christian's dutie, *etc.*[1]

What can be more blasphemously and reprochfullie repugnant to the word and order of Christ, who you see is the author of this exercise in this maner, and hath

---

[1] Robert Some, *A Godly Treatise* (1589), p. 25.

for ever left it as a commandement unto al churches. For (saith the apostle, verse 37):[1] " If any man seeme to be a prophet or spiritual, let him acknowledg what I write unto you, because they are the commandements of God, *etc.* But if anie man be ignorant, let him be ignorant. Therfore, my brethren, covet ye to prophecie, and to speake with tongues forbid not. Let al things be done comely, and according to order."

For Doctor Some's first absurditie; women are expresly forbidden to speake by way or in the exercise of this prophecie in the church, verses 34, 35. So then this is but a reproch of his owne absurd brayne, to bring the truth into slaunder.

That such as speake in this exercise of prophecie doe not anie way usurpe the minister's office, hath beene largly shewed by the discourse of this whole chapter. Neither hath he brought any peece of a reason to prove, that only ministers ought to speake of the Scriptures in the church.

For this third impious and odious calumniation; that such as presume to speake in the church not being ministers, may as well intrude into the councel chamber and magistrat's chaire; it is in it self so false, foolish and absurd, as it deserveth none answere. It is but the venome of his serpentine tongue, the adder's poison that is under his lipps, wherby [174] he seeketh to draw the truth of Christ and the professors therof into hatred. He might as wel say, that because Christ hath made us all kings and priests unto him, therfore we will heere usurpe the civill magistrat's and ecclesiastical minister's office. These are but the malicious collections and vaine conclusions of his idle head and graceles heart, thus to blaspheme the holy ordinances of Christ, to call it Anabaptistical, the depraving of the holy Scriptures, abusing of the auditors, disturbing both of church and common welth, calling such christian assemblies as practise this commandement Anabaptistical conventicles, although he never in his life was present at any of their exercises, nor is able to charge any one of them with any one Anabaptistical error, as they by his owne mouth are able to

[1] I Corinthians 14: 37.

charge him and all this antichristian ministerie of England, which exercise a ministerie without a lawfull calling therunto by vertue of their inward calling, which is their learning and sufficiencie; as though Christ did not know the end, use and measure of the gifts he hath given them. In the church of Christ there are none suffered to speake by way of prophecie, but such as have the gift of prophecie: and to forbid such to speake, were to stop up the conductes [conduits] and springs of the church, or rather of God's graces, wherby the church should be watered and refreshed: so far is this exercise from depraving the Scriptures or abusing the auditorie. The rest of his vituperie he hath layd upon Christ the author of this exercise, and to him shall answere for the same at that day of reckoning and accompt.

If none but ministers may speake publikly in the church by way of prophecie, how should the people have trial of the gifts of any? How should any ministers in this generall apostacie and departure, be restored? Yea, how should there ever be any other than now are? For if the people may not heare their gifts, how should they judg them? If they may not utter their gifts, how should the people heare them? Heere I shall by both sorts of our priestes, aswell Pontifical as Reformists, be answered; that the law is not so generall, but that there are exceptions unto the same. The Pontificall will alledg; that their mother the universitie, their father the bishop, have authoritie to give licence to preach in any church whersoever they become before they be either full ministers, or have any office, as the English deacon or half priestes, the cathedral prebends, the common curates or roving preachers. Amongst which you must note a double mysterie. Some of them are full ministers without either certayne charge, place, or office. Others have a certayne, yea a pastor's charge and office, and yet are not full ministers: of which sect are the prebendes and civil doctors, who may have parsonages, and yet be no ministers.

The Reformists they wil likewise answere me; that their mother the universitie she hath power to give leave to preach universally through all churches, and also the select classis:[1] yea, peradventure this schoole of prophets assembled, have power to admit some one picked [175] man to their mysteries which is no priest, and to give him leave to speake amongst them; yet hereof I doubt, and therefore wil not stand; and thus may the people by both sides have triall of their gifts.

Great reason that they which make the law should also make and take exceptions at their pleasure. But wel, what booteth this trial that they allow the people, when neither of them give the people liberty to judg or reprove their doctrine? When both sides, both bishops and this new classis, take upon them to make ministers without the people, without any charge, place, or office certayne? But let this matter rest. I would know of both or any of them, what this their mother they so much boast of is? And where she had this high authority above other women?

Heere they wil with one voice answere, that the universities are the seminaries of religion, of the ministerie of the land; the schooles and colledges of learning, wherin the sonnes of the prophets are trained up, as they were in Naioth, in Bethel, Jericho, Jerusalem and Corinth.

If the tree be knowen by the fruite, the cockatrice by the poisoned egges, the viper by the spawne, the nest by the birdes; then let the religion and priestes of the land shew what kind of seminaries and colledges these universities are. If these be the best fruite and famousest men (that are instructed in nothing but to corrupt and cavill against the truth), then let them take heed, for the axe is laid to the roote of the tree, *etc.* If also these your universities be compared to these cities whither these faithful men repaired (because of these famous prophets) to be instructed in the lawes of God, we shall find them more like to the Sodomitical colledges and fellowships of the idolatrous monkes and

---

[1] For the classis movement, see Roland G. Usher (ed.), *The Presbyterian Movement in the Reign of Queen Elizabeth* (Royal Historical Society, Third Series, Vol. VIII); Edna Bibby, "The Puritan Classical Movement of Elizabeth's Reign," a thesis (1929) at Manchester University (microfilm at Folger Shakespeare Library); Patrick Collinson, "The Puritan Classical Movement in the Reign of Elizabeth I," University of London thesis, 1957.

friars, brethren of a birth, even by both parentes; than unto the holy assemblies of the prophets. And this will appeare if we compare them either in the persons assembled, or in the maner and endes of their education and trayning.

What the sonnes of the prophets were, is alreadie shewed; namly, godly men that repaired to the cities where these famous prophets were most resident, to be instructed in the law of God. But the persons that resort to these universities are the children of all the profane in the land, that repaire thither to be instructed in heathen and vaine artes, wherby they may get their living; or if they studie divinitie (as they call it) they make an occupation of it. It is but for their belly, for worldly promotion, and not for the glory of God, as the greedy seeking after their ecclesiasticall livings by the one sort, the selling of their cunning and letting forth their tongues to hire of the other sort, declareth.

These holy companies of prophets mentioned in the Scriptures, were trayned up in the law of God, lived orderly in the feare of God together with their wives and families. But these universitie colledges are a misseline[1] rowte of very young men for the most part and boies toge-[176]ther, leading their lives in idolatrie, confusion, disorder; spending their lives in vanitie, follie, idlenes, living neither in the feare of God, nor in any well established order of his church, neither in any lawful calling in the common welth. They are forbidden in these societies to live in holy wedlock. If he be maried, he may not there enter: if he being entered marye, he may not there tarye. An endles discourse it were but to recite their severall idolatrous profane usages, mysteries, othes, vowes, ceremonies; all which evidently shew from whence they had their original; namely, from antichrist's chaire, to which they have ever served, and stil in all places doe serve, fighting stowtly under his banner against the faith and church of Christ, suppliing him continually with fresh soldiours to carrie abroad his merchandise, and set abroch[2] the deceits of Satan.

---

1 Miscellaneous, mixed.
2 To broach, diffuse, publish, propagate.

Revel. 18: 2
1 Joh. 1: 7

2 Cor. 6: 14

1 Tim. 1: 4 &
4: 7 & 6: 3,
4, 5,
20. 21

1 Tim. 3

Tit. 1
1 Pet. 5: 2
Act. 20
1 Cor. 4: 2
Math. 23: 7

Act. 14: 23

Act. 20: 28

1 Pet. 5: 2

Col. 2: 9

Neither are they more like unto the churches of Christ, than unto the schooles of the prophets: the church of Christ is no cage of such uncleane and hateful birdes, of their frie[1] and offspring: the churches of Christ have no such colledges, societies, fellowships; the churches of Christ have no such heathenish and idolatrous customes, exercises, usages, othes, vowes, ceremonies; they have no such prophane arts, vaine education and literature; they have no such degrees and ostentation of learning, neither are there found either bachelor or doctors of divinitie. Their pastors and teachers are chosen for their knowledg, gravitie, godlines of life: they have no such fastuous and blasphemous titles, but are called to a labour and a charge; for the faithfull performance wherof, they rather desire to be commended, than to be thus greeted in the market place. As they are by the church wherin they serve, called to this office; so are they orderly and reverently ordeined by and in the same congregation, with fasting and praier, *etc.*, and not araied in scarlet with the habite, hood, tippet, cornered cap, with their maces and beadels proclaiming before them, and such a traine of the pope's clarkes young and old following them through the streetes till they march to the place where they play their prises. Neither are they in this maner dubbed doctors by the delivering a booke unto them, sworne upon a booke to their father's fidelitie and their mother's mysteries, adopted their sonne by a ring and a kisse, or enthronized in a chair with many other ceremonies and made doctors of divinitie, doctors in name and title only, without any certaine office or church wherin and wherunto to administer.

For this title of divinitie,[2] I know not how to give it unto anie mortall man without blasphemie, Christ only excepted, in whome the fulnes of the Godhead dwelleth

---

[1] Fry, progeny.

[2] Dr. Some used this title in both of his books *A Godly Treatise* (1588) and *A Godly Treatise* (1589). See the second article in the " Reply to Dr. Some's *A Godly Treatise*," where Barrow asserts that " this title can no man without blasphemye arrogate unto him-selfe, seinge that we have but one Doctor, even Christ, in whome the devine godheade dwelleth bodelye." For Dr. Some's reply, see his *A Godly Treatise* (1589), pp. 39 f.

bodily. The English of christian religion and profession of the gospell and faith of Christ, I can well away with Revel. 13: 1 and digest: but this English Romish abstract of divinitie, I am assured came from the same forge that their title Revel. 17: 3 of the supreme head of the church did, and cannot with all the glozes, scholions,[1] and learned interpretations they can devise, be made other than most [177] high blasphemie against the sacred person of Christ, who is the only universal Doctor of al his disciples, and of al Math. 23: 8, 10 true religion. And evil may Doctor Some either defend or patterne his doctorhood by St. Paul, who in the same verse by him alledged, 1 Timothy 2: 7, sheweth a lawful calling, a lawful and certaine office, and also a sincere and faithful administration therof. But now as St. Paule's apostolick office is ceased, the church being established and delivered to other certaine offices: so if Paul's apostolike roome or doctorship (as he calleth it) were voide, I suppose Doctor Some not the fittest man in the world for it: although (if it be as I heare) he can be no lesse than an apostle by his offices, he being a pastor, if not a double or plurified nonresident pastor of many churches; a doctor you see by priviledg and stile, and a deacon I meane also at Ely.[2] And what was or could any apostle be more; yet seing al these are but forged stuffe, and that he hath neither anie true office in the church, neither any true calling therunto, *etc.*, we can take him but for a false apostle at the best, if he sit not in an apostatae's chaire, that I say not an apostatae's gowne some where els; and so leave him either to repentance, or to follow his predecessor to his apointed place.

But by following this bird over far, I had almost beene trained from the nest. I was shewing what litle affinitie there is betwixt the churches of Christ and these universities, these colledges of clarkes, these schooles of prophets. In the churches of Christ the names and offices of Chancelor, vice chancelor, commissary, proctors, taskers, bedels, provosts, maisters of colledges, vice

---

[1] Scholia, exegetical or explanatory comments.
[2] Barrow refers to Ely minster on page [55].

Henry Barrow

maisters, bowcers, deanes, fellowes, *etc.*,[1] are all strange and unheard of; as also their several statutes, customes, ceremonies, their manner of degrees and disputing for their degrees and order of teaching, which were no smal labour but to reckon up.

All which as they are strange to the church of Christ, who find not in all Gode's word any of these offices, degrees, statutes, orders, customes, ceremonies, vowes, *etc.*, neither any such universities, colledges, societies of schollers: so (seing they have no ground in the word of God, no fellowship or communion with the church) I see not why they should have any more tolleration than their elder brethren the monks, who everie way had as great shew of holines and couler of utility to the church as they, or these other cathedrall collegiate dennes have, yea, and might both as soone and as well have beene purged of their masse and Latine service, as these are: so that the same end that is befallen the one remaineth the other. The Lord is not pleased with any voluntarie religion. That building that hath not the word of God for the foundation, though it be dawbed with never so great cunning and learning, and undershored with never so great pollicie and power, though it be built as high as Babel, yet shall it assuredly fall, and the greater shalbe the fall therof. As there is no building without the word of God for the foundation; so is there no fellowship or communion out of the church of God. And therfore no such confused colledges, no such idolatrous assemblies as are not gathered [178] unto Christ but unto antichrist, as live not in that christian order and fellowship which Christ hath apointed to all his servants in his church, but leade their lives in antichristian disorder in Babilonish, if not Sodomitish, confusion; no such heathen schooles wherin youth is not trained up in the feare, knowledg, and order of Christ, but in vaine arts, superstition, idolatrie, disorder, *etc.*, have any foundation in the word of God, any fellowship with or allowance in the church of God.

Ezek. 13: 11, *etc.*
Math. 7: 26
1. Joh. 1: 7
Eph. 4: 13, 14, 15, 16
Eph. 5: 8, 9, 10, 11, 12

Eph. 6: 4
Prov. 22: 6

---

[1] Beadles are university officials, with processional duties, such as carrying the mace. Bowcer, or bowser, a bursar, treasurer. Taskers were officials who assessed or regulated prices of food, lodging, and merchandise brought to the market.

But heere wil the universitie knights draw me within the compasse of these two absurdities: first, that I condemne all good arts and literature; then, that I quite drive them out of the world by taking away the schooles of the same, wherin youth might be trained and brought up.[1]

Nothing lesse, I with my whole heart allow of any art or science that is consonant to the word of God, and to the doctrine which is according to godlines: only the curious and heathen artes, prophane and vaine bablings and oppositions of science falsely so caled which they professe and wherwith they poison and corrupt al the youth of the land, I abhorre, because God condemneth.

As for schooles to teach the tongues or any laudable or necessarie art, I wish them in abundance, that if it were possible not only the youth, but even the whole church might be trayned therin: I with my whole heart wish, that al the Lord's people were prophets: such an enemie am I to true knowledg and learning, that I would not have it any longer kept secret in a mysterie, but even proclaimed upon the house top in everie citie and in every street: yet stil and ever with this caution, that these schooles both be in an established church (I meane in such places where the saintes live together in the faith, order, obedience and communion of Christ) and not in such monkish, idolatrous, confused, idle, profane colledges and fellowships as theirs are; likewise that the tongues or sciences be heere taught in an holy, sanctified, reverend, grave maner, and not in such an unsanctified vaine maner as they use. So shal the earth be ful of the knowledg of the Lord as the waters that cover the sea: for in the church of Christ are al his springs inclosed, which by this meanes should runne at everie conduct [conduit], and water the whole land abundantly, whereas now they lie in miserable darknes, wholy overgrowen with brambles and briers.

And surely I even with marvaile wonder, how these men can be so blinded, to compare these wicked idolatrous societies to the assemblies of the prophets, or unto the church of Christ, when you see they have nothing

[1] Compare the comments of Robert Some, *A Godly Treatise* (1589), pp. 1-4.

common with them or like unto them, either in the people assembled, doctrine taught, manner of teaching and learning, or order of life; when they utterlie want warrant in the word of God for such kind of colledges, societies and schooles, these having beene derived either from the heathens, Egyptians, Greekes, Persians, that had their peculiar colledges and schooles to their peculiar sects, or els have is-[179]sued out of the smoke of antichrist's inventions out of the bottomles pit. They alwaies have beene and stil are the verie hyves and nurseries of these armed poisoned locusts and venemous scorpions, I meane either that false ministerie of antichrist, even al the governing and teaching priests as cardinals, archbishops, bishops, suffraganes, archdeacons, chancelors, commissaries, civil Doctors, advocates, proctors, vagrant roving ministers and preachers, parish priests, *etc.*, or those counterfait religious hypocrites, monkes, friers, nunnes, clarkes, or (as we now of late call them) schollers. Al which have in innumerable multitudes from time to time and at all times swarmed and issued out of these hyves into the face of the whole earth, corrupting and destroiing everie greene thing, poisoning the pure fountaines of God's word with their accursed glozes, deepe learning, subtil and figurative interpretations, darkning the sonne and infecting the aire therwith; as also with the blasphemous traditions of their king Apolluon, that angel of the bottomles pyt. They have alwaies most pestilently fought under this their captaine against the lambe his gospell and church, plentifully furnishing and continually suppliing all the offices and roomths belonging to that huge Midianitish host of antichrist: the leaders, captaines, and officers wherof, are and ever have beene wholy taken out of these seraliaes,[1] even from the pope's person to the lowest priest.

How they are reformed by having this English portesse [portas], their service booke in stead of their olde masse-booke, may partly by that which is above written concerning the same, appeare: but more manifestly, by taking a view of some of the blasphemous idolatrous customes which still remaine in practise with them in

---

[1] Seraglios, places of confinement, Turkish polygamous households.

the same maner as they did under the pope: all or any
of which it is not heere my purpose any further to describe. It sufficeth me to have shewed them to be confused, idolatrous, unchristian, unlawful assemblies and
societies; so far from being to be compared unto, or
justified by the assemblies of the prophets or that
heavenlie exercise of prophecie now in the church of
Christ, as they are not to be suffered in a christian
common welth. And therfore heere againe once more
I conclude; that both these ungoldly assemblies, as also
the cathedral dennes and colledges, ought by as good
right to be abolished, as their other brethren and sisters
of a birth the monasteries and nunries are, seing they
all want foundation in the word, had one and the same
hellish original, had and these still reteine the same
blasphemous incurable abuses, which can by no way
be reformed but by their utter dissolution.[1]

Thus have we through the mercie of God by the light
of his word taken a sleight view of the nestes of these
uncleane birdes, and have therby seene both what
maner of schooles, and what kind of prophets these are:
we have seene how evil this 14 of the Corinthians fitteth
either these universitie and cathedral colledges, or these
new devised conventicles of propheticall priests: we
have seene how wickedly they corrupt, pervert, abuse
that Scripture and holy exercise. Now it remai-[180]
neth but in a line or two, compare their publike preaching in their synagogues to this heavenly exercise of
prophecie instituted in the churches of Christ.

First, these parish priests or hired preachers al of
them preach under their Ordinarie's licence, stint, and
limitation, as hath beene shewed. Then they are prescribed their time when to begin. They have a prescript
place like a tube called their pulpyt, for the most part
able to receave no more than one person, except it be

[1] In 1642 a pamphlet was published, *The Pollution of Universitie-Learning*,
by Henry Barrow. This work consists of IV and 12 pages. Pages 1 —
8 are extracted from Barrow, *A Plaine Refutation*, pp. 116-123 of the 1591
edition and pp. 117-124 of the 1605 edition, and pp. 8-12 are taken from
A Brief Discoverie of the False Church, pp. 175-179. Although there is
nothing new in the pamphlet, the views of Barrow on university learning
were deemed of sufficient interest to be reproduced for the readers in the
turbulent days of 1642.

a suggestor or prompter, as in some special places. Neither doe they ordinarily speake any more than one, and he for the most part disputes to the howerglasse, which being runne his sermocination must be at an end. Preach this priest never so unsound, corrupt, or heretical doctrine, there is no present or publike controulement or retractation to be had. Handle he the Scripture never so unsufficiently or unsavorilye, pervert, mistake, or falsifie he it never so grievously, there is no amendes or supplie of others to be looked for, none els being suffred to speake. The church hath no power either to approove or reproove any doctrine delivered them, be it never so consonant to, or dissonant from the word of God.

Here would not be forgotten also the sweete psalmodical harmonie of the vultures, crowes, gleades, owles, geese; of the leopards, beares, wolves, dogs, foxes, swine, goates (pardon me, for thus the Holy Ghost termeth and likeneth the prophane confuse multitudes assembled in the false church).[1] All these together with one accord, sympathie, and harmonie sing some pleasant ballade, or els unto David's melodious harpe some psalme in rime (I say not rithme now or meetre) wel concinnate[2] to the eare (though never a whit to the sense, purpose or true use of the psalme) before the sermon, to stir up the spirit of their worthy priest or preacher. Who being thus rapt or ravished with this harmonie, goes to his geare in forme abovesaid, where his mouth distilles, and his lips drop downe such olde parables, such premeditate and wel studied and chosen sentences, as shal displease no partie, unlesse he be of too suspitious a nature; or howsoever I warrant you he hath his learned priviledged author, and that at his fingers' endes for his discharge. Thus have you briefly seene the usual order of your publike prophecie. If you compare it now to the rules and orders set downe by the apostle for that blessed exercise unto al churches in that 1. Corinthians 14: verses 26, 29, 30, 31, 32, 33: then may you judg of your selves what is right or amisse, and ease me of further

[1] Probably a reference to Matthew 25: 32, 33.
[2] Fitted, arranged, adjusted.

trouble to rave in this filthie doung, and to bring this counterfait stuffe in particular to the triall. Great were the labour and far exceeding my slender capacitie, especially my decayed memorie, but even summarily to recount all the principall and speciall heades of their false doctrines and false practise, from whence flow infinite errors and enormities, even as the innumerable drops of a fountaine: yea, but to prosecute and goe forward in this disordered maner to search out and summe up those which yet are wanting. All which I rather leave to the [181] more diligent and fruitful investigation of such as God hath endued with a greater judgment and more cleare sight, confessing myself both wearied and overcharged with the greatnes of the worke. For whiles I have indevored but to give you as it were a blush of their counterfait and antichristian ministerie, and to shew the error of their education, election, ordination and administration throughout, of the blasphemous and idolatrous worship they use, of their sacrilegious and adulterate sacraments, their prostituting and selling them the gospel themselves, of their profanation of praier, the name and word of God both read and preached, abrogating and excluding part, mankeling,[1] dismembring, distorting, perverting the rest to their idol feasts, sacraments, mariing, buriing, visiting, churching, charming the fields: how they preach the word by stint, limitation, subjection both of themselves and their doctrine to their antichristian Ordinaries, whose apostatical throne they uphold and dawbe therwith, as also gild and adorne the whore-the false church, joining it to all the abhomination and sin of the land, hiding, stealing, concealing, obscuring, wrasting, munging,[2] corrupting, leavening, selling the gospel; as also their abusing, counterfaiting, perverting the holie exercise of prophecie. Al which when I had but lightly touched and discovered according to my purpose, hoping that so I might have made an end of this odious and yrksome argument, these things being so manifest and heinous in themselves that I need not

1 Fettering, manacling.
2 Cheating.

543

stand either to prove or disprove them, or to shew the indignitie, danger and enormities that ensue therof. Even then, lo, is the whole word of God, the law and the gospel, presented unto me, most wretchedly corrupted, abused, violate, and troden under foot by them, by your preachers I say, even your learnedst best good men that you so esteeme of: I still speake and would be understood of the generall and publike errors and transgressions of this church, which if I should goe about to particulate, I could not hope to live until I had made an end.

And that you may not think I speake by the figure hyperbole, as they use: I earnestly beseech any one in whome is any sparke of light, grace, conscience, love or feare of God, to consider and examine by the word of God, or rather to lament and deplore with me the through corruption and universal transgression of al God's lawes both in the church and common welth, as the present estate of ech doth shew. The one I hope this present treatise shal somwhat reveale and discover: the other shal be as manifest, if by this light with a single eye you but peruse the publike lawes, judgments, pleas, trials, customes, orders, trades, estates, degrees (still I speake generally of the whole body which hath not from the crowne of the head to the sole of the feet one sownd parte, but all is full of wounds, swellings, ulcers, corruption), so that he that feareth God cannot in this common welth keepe a good conscience, and live amongst them, whether he buy, sel, lend, borrow, hire, worke for hire, give, take, sue or be sued. The lawes, courts, judges, juries, advocates, generally all estates from the highest to the lowest, are so throughly corrupt.
[182]

Not to speake heere of the particular sinnes, the height, qualitie and universalitie of them, which were infinite; let the idolatrous and blasphemous worship, yea, the idolatrous and blasphemous oathes, publikly admitted, given, required and received of all persons in all causes, so contrarie to the law of God in the maner, and all the circumstances, shew how soundly the first table of the law is taught in the Church of England. Not to speake of the common and usual swearing, forswearing, blaspheming, cursing for everie trifle and cause, yea, without anie cause, used through the whole land without controlement, rebuke, censure, punishment. Let the generall prophannesse, excesse in gluttonie, in apparel; let the idlenes, wantonnes, vanitie, with the idolatrie above spoken of and used upon the Lord's day shew, how well the fourth commandement is taught and observed in the Church of England. Let the common ryot and headstrong disobedience and contempt of al the children and servants, even of al the youth of the land, the due punishment wherof is here neither spoken of, nor executed; let their profane, vaine, idle education shew, how wel the fifth commandement is taught and observed in the Church of England. Let the continual open jarres, fraies, murther, bloodshed in everie corner of the land without either censure or punishment, yea the usual pardons that they give for the same shew, how well the sixth commandement is taught in the Church of England. Not heere to speake of the common contentions, wrangles, jarres, sutes, wrongs; of the wrath, heartburning, malice, envie, cursed speaking, reviling, nicknaming, reproching, blaspheming, that are rife amongst them. Let the general unclennes, whoredome, adulterie, which never abounded more in Sodome (so that almost there is not one amongst them that hath his wife chast or their bed private). Let their maner of punishing and purging this sinne shew, how well they teach and keep this commandement. Not here to speake of their exquisite arts and curiositie in setting out their beautie to the view, their prodigious shapes, whorish atyres, dissolute and immodest behaviours, entising and alluring wordes wherwith they provoke unto lust, all which in this church are made no sinnes but matters of comlines, curtesie, love, *etc*. And that your gravest and best conscienced preachers think not themselves in this case without blame, let them examine their corrupt consciences, how many of their chief hearers and devout proselites they know both men and women, that know such crimes ech by other, and yet for filthie lucre or fleshly respects continue together. Let the publike open

general thefts, violence, robberies, wrongs, and either
their permission, or their corrupt and unlawfull punishing the same shew, how the eyght commandement is
tought. Not here to speake of the privy and more
secret, nay truly of the open falshode, deceit, coven
[coveting] in all trades, offices, callings, estates, degrees,
persons. What should I stand to prosecute the rest.
Let the generall deceit, swearing, forswearing, back-
biting, slaundering; the insatiate coveting, lusting, *etc.*,
shew how well they teach and observe the other lawes.
And as they deale with [183] the lawes and judgmentes,
so handle they in like maner the prophets, which are
the faithful expounders of the lawes: al which to demonstrate in particuler, were an endles and unachev-
able laboure.

And if these general corruptions, errors, transgressions, be so infinite, what is to be thought of their per-
ticuler personal errors which they in their publicke
doctrine and daily ministery sparse abrode, even as
that flood of bitter waters which the dragon casteth
forth of his mouth and the miserable people of the earth
swallow up, partly through their general blindnes, partly
through their servile subjection, which have not the
power or libertie publikely to controule or censure any
error, be it never so blasphemous. Wherupon is come
about, that everie one taketh boldnes to utter in their
pulpyts what him listeth (so he speake not against any
thing by publick authoritie established), he may handle
the word of God after his owne fancie, and abownd in his
owne sense. Wherupon arise such an innumerable
heape of errors, so manie diverse, variable, inconstant
and contrarie opinions amongst them, that (as the
ignorant papistes say) it is impossible to find two of
them in one mind and judgment, yea in any two churches
of the land to heare the same doctrines taught, because
in deed they preach either their owne dreames and
phantasies, or els their lucubrations out of humane
writings, who are almost of as divers and sundrie
opinions as themselves. Yet if any of these authors be
with the bishops' priviledg, then are they authentick,
irrefragable, called by both sides the faith of the Church

of England, and not to be impugned or gainsayed without the censure of most high presumption. Thus hath God in his just judgment devided the tongues and confounded the language of these Babilonish builders, that they almost agree not in or upon any thing, one preaching one thing, an other the quite contrarie; one building after this sort, another after that; one calling for this law, this thing, an other for that. Thus is their kingdome devided, their estate confused, and their house shal shortly be left unto them desolate.

Many and innumerable excuses, shifts, cavils, they daily knit, weave and forge to cover their detestable dealings, and hide their waies from the Lord, both by perverting the Scriptures therunto, and diverting them by their sophistrie and putting them away, be they never so directly against them: with all which their poisoned divises it is not my purpose nor yet in my power here to meddle, they being already so infinite, and their forge daily going to frame new. Only this from the mouth of the Lord I warne al men of. They are but cockatrice egges that they disclose and hatch, Isa. 59 but spiders' webbes that they weave: their egges are full of deadly poison, he that eateth of them dieth, he that is but sprinkled with them or treadeth upon them, is as if he were stung with a viper or scorpion: their webbes shall not be for cloth, neither shal they cover themselves with their deeds: their workes are the works of iniquitie, and the worke of violence in their hands, *etc.* The work and the workmen shalbe consumed together. The wall and the dawbers [184] shall both fal Ezek. 13 and be overthrowne in the storme of the Lord's wrath: all their turning of divises, though they build as high as Amos 9: [2] heaven and dig as deep as hell, shall not cover them from the eies or defend them from the hand of the Lord; but rather as the prophet saith in an other place, they shall pull al downe upon their heads by the same meanes wherby they thought to uphold it.[1] For (saith he) " this iniquitie shalbe unto them as a breach that falleth, as a swelling in an high wall whose breaking

[1] Obadiah 1: 15.

commeth sodainly in a moment ";[1] the sentence is gone
out from the Lord, it hasteneth to be performed. Babilon
shal fall and be utterlie destroied together with al their
substance, people, pleasures: evil commeth upon her,
and she shall not know the morning therof: destruction
shal fall upon her sodainly ere she be aware: the multitude of her divines and inchanters shall neither deliver
her from, nor discover unto her these evils; but they
shalbe as stubble, and the fire shall burne them together
with her.

This is the end of all their cunning and learning;
which you see they employ not to publish and proclaime the Lord's truth, so much as to suppresse and
darken the same; hoping therby to hide their owne
counterfait dealing, which the Lord wil have no longer
covered, but revealeth their wickednes unto all men,
that those which have any feare or love of God, or care
of their owne salvation, might save their soules from
their murtherous mouthes, and follow the deceitful
miserable guides no further in the crooked moovable
pathes of their inventions, nor stay any longer in the
steppes of that flocke, but to come forth from amongst
them unto that true shephard of Israel, which so graciously seeketh and calleth them that he may bring them
to Zion, that citie of joy, that mountaine of holines, that
heavenly inclozed paradise where he feedeth and water-
eth his kiddes with the fruits and water of that tree and
river of life; which so far passeth that earthly garden or
parke where Adam was first placed, as that excelled the
wildernes of Kadesh, or as the heaven passeth the earth,
or in deed as the true substance [is preferable to] the
shadow and type. Which grace that you may find and
apprehend as it is the chiefe end of this my present
writing, so it is my continual praier unto the Lord; herein
resting and being assured of this, that all Christ's sheepe
will heare his voice, but a false prophet or a stranger
they will not heare or follow.

Such are al these your ministers and preachers apparantly proved unto you to be, by all the markes which
God in his word hath set downe to know them by.

---

[1] Isaiah 30: 13.

False prophets they are, in that they perswade unto 1. error 2. transgression 3. idolatrie 4. apostacie, Deuteronomy 13: 2. False prophets they are, in that they prophecie unto this sinfull land in this corrupt estate peace and prosperitie. Jeremiah 28: 8. False prophets they are, in that they cover all the sinne of the land with the name of the Lord, of the church, gospel, sacraments, *etc.*, Jeremiah 7: 4 & 18: 18. Micah 2: 7. False prophets they are, in that they dawbe the muddy wall of this corrupt and apostaticall estate, with their untempered sermons, Ezekiel 13: 10, *etc.* False prophets they are, in [185] that they prophecie in the name of so many Baalims, Baal Bishop, Baal Patron, and those Baalims to whome they stand chaplens, Jeremiah 23:13 False prophets they are, in that they prophecie for hire, and sell their cuning, Ezekiel 13: 4, 19. Micah 2: 11 and 3: 11. Mathew 10: 8. False prophets they are, in that they handle not the word of God sincerely and faithfully, but joine it to all the wickednes of the land, *etc.* Jeremiah 23: 28, 29. 1 Thessalonians 2: 3, 4, 5, 6. Ezekiel 34: 18. False prophets they are in that they blow not the trumpet, but yeild unto the enemie and are scilenced at their commandement, Ezekiel 33: 6, Isaiah 56: 10, Jeremiah 1: 17. False prophets they are, in that they are men pleasers, vailers, pillowsowers,[1] Ezekiel 13: 18, Galatians 1: 10. False prophets they are, in that with their sweet tongues they allure, deceave, nourish and hold all the prophane people in idolatrie and sinne, Jeremiah 23: 17, 31, 32. Strangers they are from the common welth of Israel, in that they are not gathered to Christ their head, but stand members of the false church under antichrist, Ephesians 2: 12, Mathew 12: 30. Strangers they are, in that they execute a strange office, unheard of in the church or Testament of Christ, Romans 12: 7, 8. Strangers in that they are not called of God unto their office, but entred and ascended an other way, John 10: 1, *etc.*, Hebrews 5: 4, Numbers 16: 5, 40. Strangers they are, in that they exercise a counterfait, antichristian, roving, idolatrous ministrie in the false church, Deuteronomy 32: 17, 2 Chronicles

---

[1] People who give a false sense of security to others.

11: 15, Amos 5: 26, Jude [1: 4, 16-19]. Strangers, in that they have their original from the apostatical chaire of antichrist, which they still guard and uphould, fighting under his flag against Christ his gospel and the faithfull witnesses therof, Revelation 9: 3, 12, Revelation 13: 13, 14 and 16: 13. Blind false guides and seducers they are, in that they lead the people in the waies of darknes and death, promising them liberty, reformation, *etc.*, when they themselves stand bondservants of corruption. Proverbs 2: 13, *etc.*, Mathew 15: 14, Hebrews 6: 1, 2 Peter 2: 19, 2 Timothy 3: 6, 7. False builders and deceitfull workmen, in that they neither gather unto nor build upon the true foundation, Christ and his word; but gather unto and build upon antichrist and his traditions, and so destroy the soules of al that are built in this their church, 2 Corinthians 11: 13, 1 Corinthians 3: 9, *etc.*, Ephesians 2: 20, 21, 22. They are powred out in the error of Balaam for wage, in that they sel their divinitie to God's enemies, Jude [1:] 11. The way of Caine they follow in that they murther the faithfull by daily reproches, vituperie and slaunders. Jude [1:] 11, 1 John 3: 12.

The truth of these things you may read and see in the Scriptures: the proof of al these you may see in their standing, doctrines, practise, duly compared unto and truly examined by the rules of God's word. Now it remaineth that you be warned and obey the calling of God, and disterminate[1] your selves from amongst them, least you despise the grace of God against your owne soules, and he give you up to their delusions.

Let such as take offense at my sharpe maner of writing against these their esteemed learned preachers, before they condemne my spirit, trie it, whether these judgments be the Lord's or no. Then let them examine unpartially whither these men be not under the same, in such maner as I have said. As for me, what am I that I should alter, or what [186] is man that should controle the Lord's judgmentes in loosing that which he bindeth, or holding in veneration that which he hath in detestation, or to give titles unto any in their sinne:

---

[1] Separate.

that were to call Christ execrable, yea, to make my self guiltie of the same sin and judgment which the Lord now commandeth me to denounce against them. Of the affection and intent of my heart, I make the searcher of al hearts judg, even whether I desire not their salvation as mine owne. They that judg the medecine too sharpe, and me an austere and unskilful physician, should do well for the first to examine the ingredients by that heavenly herbal, and the whole confection together by the practise of that great physician and his disciples. For the ingredients I have prefixed under everie branche and leafe, the bough and roote where I gathered them. For the composition and confection, I have desired to follow our saviour Christ in his conferences, where he reproved the priests, scribes, and phariseis of his time whiles he lived heere amongst them in the flesh, desiring you to peruse the 21. 22. 23. chapters of Mathew, comparing them to the other evangelistes and unto Zacheriah 11. I have also followed the prophets and apostles, who alwaies dealt most sharply with the false prophets and false teachers of their times, how great estimation or shew of learning soever they caried, and have left unto us perpetuall doctrines to doe the like, both to watch, discover and avoide false prophets which shall arise within the church; as also to bayte the wolfe from the fould, and not to suffer him to enter, much lesse to teach or exercise anie office there, come he never so disguised in sheepe's clothing, wrapped in Samuel's mantel, or in a rough hayrie garment to deceave. If their examples for their incomparable preeminence be not allowed me to follow, yet their doctrines cannot be so taken from the least of Christ's servants. For a particular instance I insist among many other Scriptures upon Zacariah 13: 2, 3 verses: where they may see an expresse warrant for this my maner of dealing with these maner of men, as also the soveraigne vertue and effect of this sharpe medecine; olde corrupt sores must not be cured with skinning plaisters or sweet ointments. If I should obey their ambitious appetite therin, I should destroie both them and myself: their seared consciences must be

wounded, their rough garment and counterfait ministerie which they for gaine and vainglorie so corruptly
execute, must be plucked from them, they shewed the
height of their sinne and the wrath of God due unto
the same for the high profanation of his holy name and
word, and the misleading and murthering so many
soules, *etc.*, that so they may (if they belong to God's
election and to Christ's kingdome) be humbled for their
sinnes, and betake them to some more godly trade of
living, untill Christ thinke them worthy, and call them
to the worke of his ministerie. This grace and effect
with my whole heart I wish them; beseeching them in
the meane while not to fixe their eies upon my basenes
and ignorance which bring the message, so much as
upon their owne miserable estate and the message that
God vouchsafeth even by me to send them, least they
be offended [187] at my basenes and folly (which is
everie way greater than they can imagine or I utter)
and so in the pride of their owne wisdome and presumption of their owne hearts in disdayning me, they stumble
at the words of God, and despise his grace against their
owne soules. The basenes of Christ's choice hath ever
beene no small offence to the learned phariseis and
their proselites, that he should begin his glorious ministry
and kingdome in Galile, and that amongst a sort of the
most despised simple artificers, leaving and rejecting the
great learned phariseis, scribes, and priests who where
[were] the greatest enemies and persecutors of him and
his gospel, *etc.* The Scripture also speaketh evidently
that in these latter daies, when the vialls of God's judgments shalbe poured upon the false church, that the
most part of the men that have receaved the marke of
the beast and worshipped his image shall not repent of
their works, but breake out into noisome and greevous
sores and botches and shalbe so tormented with heate,
that their tongues shalbe smitten with venemous blisters,
that they shal blaspheme the God of heaven for their
paine and sores, *etc.* The truth of this prophecie, and
terror of these judgmentes, I behold (with griefe) executed even upon the cheefest and learnedest of your
ministerie, striken with such blindnes as they grope

their way in the noone light, and reele like drunken men in their pathes: they are hardned with ambition and covetise as they can find no grace, nor place to repentance: yea (that I even tremble to thinke of), possessed which [with] such madnes, as they that sometimes to our seeming sought reformation and the kingdome of Christ Jesus, are now become of al others the most pernicious enemies therof, daily studiing for new cavilles and shiftes to hide their wretchednes, and to keep back and misleade the people, yea, to weaken and discourage the hearts and handes of such as in the love, feare, and truth of God have beginne [*sic*] to build the Lord's temple; despising, accusing, slandering, reproching them worse than ever the Amonites and Samaritanes did the Jewes; yea, even blaspheming the truth of the Lord, when they see they can by no meanes prevaile against it. For all which their impious deeds and hard sayings, they shal shortly give accompt to him that is comming with thowsands of his saints.

Thus having discored[1] unto you the true estate of the people, ministerie, worship and ministration of the Church of England: it remaineth now that we take a litle view of the ecclesiastical government and ordinances of this their church: which though they may partly appeare by that which is already written concerning other pointes, yet if they be brought a litle neerer the light, and compared to these orders and ordinances that our saviour Christ hath set downe in his last wil and Testament, and incommended[2] to his church for ever; then shal they most evidently and easily be discerned of al men; no labor, learning, or power can then any longer justifie, couller, or uphold them.

Great hath beene their craft, and manifold their devises, to cover their [188] antichristian practises, and to uphold this their ruinous and tirannous kingdome (I had need expresse my meaning to be of their false ecclesiasticall regiment, the kingdome of the beast, least they be my interpreters and draw me within danger of

---

[1] Discovered, discoursed.
[2] Entrusted.

treason,[1] so like are they unto their predecessors the priests and phariseis, so apt (as the prophet saith) to lay a snare for him that rebuketh in the gate, and to condemne him as guilty for the word, *etc.*).[2] First they sought to darken the true light, by terming this heavenly government of Christ and holy orders and ordinances of his Testament *the outward discipline used in the primitive churches, especially in the time of Lent, etc.*, then to keepe the magistrates and the people utterlie from all sight and knowledg hereof, both by inhibiting all their priests to preach therof, and not suffring any such places of Scripture as make expresse mention therof to be so much as read in their church, as Romans 12, 1 Corinthians 15 and 12, 2 Corinthians 2, Ephesians 4, 2 Thessalonians 3, 1 Timothy 3 and 5, Titus 1, much lesse to be sincerely expounded and made knowen unto the church, that they can at no hand away with scilencing, suspending, emprizoning such of their forsworne priests as meddle with such matters. Yea, the wretches perswade the magistrates, that it would breed an innovation, if not a subversion of the whole state, hinder the course of the common law, cut off the civil, quite extinguish the cannon law, that it would raise continual schismes, contentions, and unapeaseable troubles and tumultes; that it would innovate and alter the regiment of the common welth, and draw it to an aristocratie or democratie, *etc.*[3]

These things these uncleane devilish spirits that are come and speake out of the mouth of the dragon, blow into the civil magistrates' eares, and breath[e] into their heartes, who being a great deale more pollitike than religious (the Lord knoweth with what truth and sorrow of heart I speake it) are not able to discerne this most impious and high blasphemie against God and his

---

[1] These words were more prophetical than he realized. In speaking of a " ruinous and tirannous kingdome," Barrow means the Church of England and not the commonwealth. Though he is careful to clarify his meaning here, he is less careful elsewhere. More than any other work, *A Brief Discoverie of the False Church* was used by the authorities in finding him guilty of sedition.

[2] Isaiah 29: 21.

[3] Thomas Cooper, *An Admonition to the People of England*, pp. 80-94. (This is the 1589 edition, with 245 pages.)

Christ, from sacred veritie; but because it is plausible
to the flesh, rightly agreeth to the present corrupt estate
both of church and common welth, and in nothing
disturbeth the strong man that holdeth them al in
peace, they readily imbrace it, publish and maintaine
their devilish decrees, give their power unto the beast,
wherby he warreth against Christ his gospel and saints.
And thus are they drawen by them into the great day
of God almightie even against Christ and them that are
of his side, whome they daily persecute and murther in
their prisons; and therfore shalbe slayne with that
sharpe sword of him that rideth upon the white horse;
they shal in the just judgment of God be made a pray
[prey], even a quarry and a feast to these uncleane
spirits, to these greedie ravenous foules [fowls], which
(as that Scripture saith) shall feed and satiate their
ravenous appetites upon them, yea these uncleane
spirits shal draw them together with the beast and the
false prophet into battel against Christ and against his
armie of saints.

These blasphemous wretches (not to darken only but
to reproch the truth yet further) proceed and give out,
that the heavenly order and ordinances which Christ
hath apointed in his Testament, the government of his
[189] church (which they call discipline), are but accidental, and no essential marke of the established church,
but that it may be a church planted without them, yea,
that the true church of Christ may take an other order
of government, other ordinances than Christ hath
apointed in his Testament; that this order of Christ's
government is neither permanent, perpetual, nor necessarie, but that it is in a Christian magistrat's power to
keepe out Christ's government, and to erect and establish an other after their willes.[1]

These hellish and blasphemous doctrines doe al the
priests and preachers of the land give out and publish,
els could they not either esteeme the Church of England in this estate as it receaveth antichriste's yoke, this
popish hierarchie in the true church of Christ, neither
would they exercise any ministerie in this church in this

---

[1] *Ibid.*, pp. 81, 82, 84, 88.

estate, or sue unto and stay for the prince and parliament to bring themselves under Christ's sacred government.

But the pontificals proceed yet further to open their mouthes unto more accursed blasphemie, which would make a christian heart to rend his clothes, to heare that Christ's blessed order wherin the apostles planted and established the first churches, is not only not necessary, but intollerable now under a christian prince, as bringing not only al these publike perturbations and mischiefes unto the common welth which are above recited, and they have suggested unto the magistrates; but also innumerable other inconveniences which would proceed if the people should have election of their owne ministerie and church officers;[1] if the affaires of the church should be directed by a councell or companie of elders; if the doubtes of the churches should be decided by an assembly of other churches (which they cal a synode and a councel); if faults should be censured by excommunication, *etc.* Thus is antichrist exalted and openeth his mouth against God and al his ordinances. Thus are the tongues of the false prophets set on fire of hell.

Many other impossibilities are there brought by the pontificals against the Reformists, why this their course which they seeke to bring in by Parliament ought not and cannot be admitted in this land. Al which because they neither concerne nor hinder the truth, but rather through the mercie of God stoppe and make head to the new devised forgeries of these Reformistes, I willingly passe over in scilence, leaving the devided kingdome to trie out the matter amongst themselves.

Yet now before I proceed further, let me in a word or two give you warning of the other sort of enemies of Christ's kingdome, the phariseis of these times, I meane these your great learned preachers, your good men that sigh and grone for reformation, but their handes with the sluggard denie to worke. These counterfaites would raise up a second error even as a second beast, by so much more dangerous by how much it hath more shew of the truth. These men in stead of this grosse antichristian government which is now manifest and odious unto all

[1] *Ibid.,* pp. 89, 90, 92, 93.

men, would bring in a new adulterate forged government in shew, or rather [190] in despite of Christ's blessed
government, which they in the pride, rashnes, ignorance,
and sensualitie of their fleshly heartes most miserably
innovate, corrupt and pervert, both 1. in the verie thing
they seeke, 2. in their maner of seeking it, 3. in the
people over whome they would set it, 4. and in their
manner of exercising it.

The thing it self they innovate and corrupt, in that
they add new devises of their owne; as their pastoral
suspension from their sacraments, their set continued
synods, their select classes of ministers, their setled
supreame councel.

Their false manner of seeking it is manifest, in that
they seeke to bring Christ in by the arme of flesh, by
suting and supplicating to his vassals and servantes (if
so be they will have them or can imagine them Christians, that have not or will not suffer Christ to reigne
over them by his owne lawes and ordinances) or if they
judg them not Christians, then they seeke, sute unto,
and stay upon his enemies until they wil suffer and
allow Christ to reigne over his church according to his
owne wil and Testament. This is not; kisse the sonne
least he be angrie, and ye perish in the way:[1] repent
for the kingdom of God is at hand;[2] and if they refuse
and speake evil of the way, to shake of[f] the dust of
the feet against them:[3] this is not to bring Christ in by
the power of his owne word and spirit as it hath wrought
in their heartes true repentance and conversion, by
shewing them the error and danger of their waies, and
by calling them unto the right practice of the gospell.
Nay, in stead of this, these men wil not only continew
suting to such despisers where God calleth them away;
but stay the whole land in their idolatrie from receiving
Christ, until these men wil permit them: yea, they wil
so sweeten the matter and so allay it to their fleshly
appetites, as Christ shalbe framed unto the common

[1] Psalms 2: 12, in the older versions. In the Revised Standard Version
the translation is: 11. Serve the Lord with fear, with trembling. 12. Kiss
his feet, lest he be angry, and you perish in the way.
[2] Matthew 4: 17.
[3] Mark 6: 11.

welth and not the common welth unto Christ: they shall still retaine and exercise this their ungodly divelish power to give lawes unto Christ and his church, and to receave or permit no more of his lawes than standeth with their good liking, so they wil but receave this their new devised plattforme, and put downe the bishops.

They also make no other choice, neither seeke further arguments of faith and repentance in the people over whome they would set this their pretended government. These men still would have the whole land to be the church, and everie parrish therin a particular congregation of the same. These men would have all redressed by vertue of one Parliament one day, and not by vertue of the word preached:[1] which, as it hath with them no power to effect any thing, so expect they not any fruites therof, but take in all the common welth, even al the queene's subjectes into this their church under Christ's government and protection, for so would they beare them in hand, that such this reformation which they seeke, is.

Their false maner of exercising this their pretended discipline, may partly appeare by the weake and fearfull practise of some of their for-[191]ward men; who that they might make a faire shew amongst their rude ignorant parishners, in stead of Christ's government set up their counterfait discipline in and over all the parish, making the popish churchwardens and perjured questmen elders. And for Mr. Parson himself, he takes unto him the instrument of that foolish shepeheard, his pastoral staffe or woodden dagger of suspension, wherwith he keepeth such a floorishing, as the flies can have no rest; yea, by your leave, if any poore man in the parish offend him, he may peradventure goe without his bread and wine for that day.

Their permanent synods and councels also which they would erect (not heere to speake of ther new Duch

---

1. Barrow is saying that Presbyterianism would be established, with universal membership in a state church. This type of Erastian Presbyterianism was actually established in England a half-century later — about 1643—1648.

classes, for therin is a secret)[1] should only consist of priests or ministers as they terme them; people of the churches be shut out, and neither be made acquainted with the matters debated there, neither have free voice in those synods and councels, but must receave and obey without contradiction whatsoever those learned priests shall decree. These synods and councels shall have absolute power over all churches, doctrines and ministers, to erect, ratifie or abrogate, to excommunicate or depose at their pleasures. Their decrees are most holy without controulement, unlesse it be by the prince or the High Court of Parliament. Not heere to speake of their solemne orders observed in these councils and synodes, as their choice by suffrage amongst themselves of their *Archisynagogon*,[2] or *Rector Chori*,[3] their president (as they call him), propownder or moderator of their councell; about which their predecessors have had no small stir, until their holy father the pope put an end to the strife by getting the chaire.

This stuffe they would bring in againe under colour of reformation, these and many more their leavened corrupt writings of discipline, and their supplications unto the Parliament, declare. With what pernicious forgeries, what kind of sacrilegious profanation of God's holy ordinances, shal more plainly appeare when we have set downe the truth of Christ's institution, which is the only arch-type and true patterne of all true builders and buildings; which who so at any hand transgresseth, either in matter or maner (as they speake),

---

[1] The Presbyterians established " Dutch " classes, somewhat on the model of reformed churches in the Netherlands, Geneva, and Holland, in the 1580's. These met in London, Oxford, Cambridge, Warwick, Coventry, Northampton, and elsewhere. The Martin Marprelate controversy of 1588-89 strengthened the determination of the Anglican hierarchy to extirpate dissent, and the successful sleuthing activities of chaplain Richard Bancroft made possible the arrest, trial, and conviction of the leading Presbyterians in the Court of Star Chamber by 1590. The best presentation of this story is in an unpublished dissertation at the University of London, by Patrick Collinson, " The Puritan Classical Movement in the Reign of Elizabeth I " (1957). See also chapters V and VI of A. F. Scott Pearson, *Thomas Cartwright and Elizabethan Puritanism*, 1535—1603.

[2] A Greek word, meaning a ruler of the synagogue.

[3] A director of the group, a leader of the band or chorus or group of dancers, a ruler of the multitude.

is to be reproved as an evill workeman, and his work to burne, seeme it to have never so great antiquitie, holines and utilitie in pretence. The auncient waies of the Lord are the only true waies; whatsoever is second or divers, is new and false. This I say, because both these factions of our pontifical and reforming priests have sought rather to the broken pitts and drie cisternes of men's inventions for their direction and groundworke, than unto the pure fountaine of God's word.

The first sort most grosly drawe al their water from that most filthie drayne and poisoned sinke of the papistical corruption, as is to be seene by their whole ministerie, worship, ministration, government, *etc.*, because it in all pointes accordeth to their antichristian prelacie, idolatrie, pride, *etc.*, and only best agreeth to the corrupt estate of this realme, which hath so long beene made dronke with the whore's [192] cuppe, that they can now taste or brooke no other liquor.

The other sort, they fetch their reformation from the primitive defection, when the ministerie began to usurpe and grow into unlawful superioritie and jurisdiction; when they began to decline from the true patterne of Christ's Testament, and grew bold to innovate: as to set up a new and antichristian ministerie, as their provincials, bishops, archbishops, archdeacons, metropolitanes, patriarches, to take the whole regiment of the church into their hands, to gather councils of bishops, to make new decrees, *etc.* All which proceedings, as I find them defected from the rules of Christ's Testament, so far dare I boldly pronownce them (their proceedings, I meane, leaving their persons to the Lord's judgment) wicked and ungodly, not looking unto or respecting the learning or holines of the men, how ancient and how manie soever. From these ancient defections have these learned reforming priests drawen their platforme[1] of reformation, as best suting to the estimation of their persons, the admiration of their learning and holines, and not greatly opposite to the sinfull estate of the land,

[1] Bishop Cooper spoke of his reasons for misliking the Presbyterian " platforme of government " (*An Admonition to the People of England*, p. 85), and Barrow wrote " The First Part of the Platforme " in 1590, which he sent to Lord Burghley.

especially as they in their wisdomes would use the matter; who (I dare undertake for them good men) would not molest or offend anie of welth or authoritie, live as they list; neither need they be so afraid of the thunderbolt of excommunication, they wil, I warrant you, proceed to it with a leaden heele, especially against such men.

And for the rest which seemes so strange in their eares, as their pastors and elders for their parson and questmen, their synodes in stead of their commissaries' courts, their high councels in stead of the High Commission; let them never be afraid, for by that time they are acquainted with the new names, they shall not finde the jurisdiction halfe so strange as it seemes. It wil be troublesome to none but to their lords the bishops, their courts and attendants, and the dombe ministers; in deed their cake is dough if this geare, this sweeping new reformation, come in.

As for these new officers, these elders, they shall be but of the welthiest honest simple men of the parish, that shal sit for ciphers dombe by their pastor and meddle with nothing, neither poore soules shal they know more than they say. As for the ordering of all things, that shalbe in the pastor's hands only, especially in some chiefe men who shall be these presidents and rulers of synodes and councels, and so the people be kept as far from the knowledg and performance of their duties as ever they were: for so long have the priests (for so still I call all false and antichristian ministers) usurped and deteined the sole regiment of the church in their hands, as it wilbe a verie hard matter for the people ever to recover their libertie againe.[1]

You see how the one side (the pontificals I meane) prescribe in their quiet possession and reject al claime

---

[1] This is a thought-provoking statement, and suggestive of the warning: " It is the common fate of the indolent to see their rights become a prey to the active. The condition upon which God hath given liberty to man is eternal vigilance; which condition if he break, servitude is at once the consequence of his crime and the punishment of his guilt." This statement of John Philpot Curran (1750—1817), made in 1790, is usually restated: " eternal vigilance is the price of liberty."
Barrow believed that the people had neglected their vigilance, and thus the transition had been made from the New Testament congregational church to the hierarchical papacy. He feared the same tendency in the Presbyterian discipline.

T

the people can make, refuting them by Machiavel's considerations and Aristotle his *Politikes* in stead of the New Testament, alledging I wote not how many pollitike inconveniences in way of barre. [193] The other sect (or faction rather), these Reformists, howsoever for fashion sake they give the people a litle libertie to sweeten their mouthes, and make them beleeve that they should choose their owne ministers (for further right in the censuring their ministers, or in the ordering the affaires of their churches they allow not, as hath beene sayd), yet even in this pretended choice doe they coozen [deceive] and beguile them also, leaving them nothing but the smoky windy title of election only; injoining them to choose some universitie clarke, one of these colledg birds of their owne brood, or els comes a synode in the necke of them, and adnihilats the election whatsoever it be.[1]

They have also a trick to stoppe it before it come so far; namely, in the ordination, which must (forsooth) needes be done by other priests: for the church that chooseth him hath no power to ordeyne him. And this makes the mother Church of Geneva and the Duch classes (I dare not say the secrete classes in England) to make ministers for us in England.

And these ministers when they are come over, are receaved and esteemed as angels in hell, and shine as bright starrs in these smoky Egyptian fornaces, wherin the miserable people of the land are kept in most harde servitude, daily new taskes laid upon them by this spiritual pharaoh antichrist: so far are these new guides (whome they trust) from leading them freely with the Lorde's banner of the gospell displaied before them, as you see they would be glad of anie of pharaoh's conditions, their suite at the best intendement and uttermost course being but to worship God in Egypt, and to have these tyrannous task-maisters their lord bishops and their attendants taken from them. Most willing they are with al their people to remaine in spiritual

---

[1] Barrow anticipates Milton in his famous line: " New Presbyter is but Old Priest writ Large " (" On the New Forcers of Conscience under the Long Parliament," *The Works of John Milton,* I [New York: Columbia University Press, 1931], p. 71).

bondage to the civil magistrate. (I would not heere be misunderstood of that lawful bodily obedience which al Christians owe in al lawful things unto the civil magistrate.)

But these uncleane spirites are gone out unto the kinges of the earth to gather them into battell against God and his Christ, to make them not only to cast Christ's bandes from them, but to tie him in their bandes; keeping awaie upon their regal authoritie what part of Christ's lawes they lyst from the church, and laying what lawes of their owne they lyst upon the church. Alas what a dangerous and fearful abuse of their authoritie is this? They are not made kinges to reigne over Christ or to give him lawes, but to honour and worship the Sonne, to cast downe their scepters at his feete, not to disturbe or hinder his saintes from the free and sincere practise of his Testament, but to incourage them and goe before them therin, as king David did, daunting and rejoicing before the arke. Princes are Psal. 2 equally bound to the keeping of all Gode's lawes as the meanest or any other, and shal for the breach therof Psal. 105: 14, not escape the judgment of that lion of the tribe of Juda, Deut. 32: 42 who wil tread upon princes (as the prophet saith)[1] as clay when he treadeth the great winepresse without the citie. This is the portion of al the Lorde's [194] enemies, Revel. 14: [20] to this banket [banquet] doe these false prophets with their perfidie and flatterie bring them, that they cannot endure to be reprooved of God himself by his word, to which they can at no hand endure to be made subject. Therfore they hate and persecute him that rebuketh in the gate, they abhor him that speaketh uprightly, and Amos 5: 10 rule all thinges after their owne lustes.

And sure, even this incorrigible pride and wickednes of princes and magistrates which would by no meanes be brought to the obedience of the gospel, first drave the Anabaptistes into their devilish conceites of them, that no prince or magistrate could be saved; afterward, that their verie office and function are utterlie unlawful in the kingdome of Christ: which wicked heresies as they have no ground in the word of God (the civil Rom. 13

[1] Isaiah 41: 25 and Revelation 14: 20.

magistracie being the blessed ordinance of God for the defence of Christ's gospel and sainctes, and therfore al

1. Pet. 2: 13   humble obedience therunto commanded as unto the Lord himself, and this both by our saviour Christ's owne

Tit. 3: 1   example, and the continual exhortations and commandements of his apostles in al their epistles unto the churches), so can these Anabaptistical heresies no way be better refuted and taken out of the hearts of al men at once, than by the humble submission of princes and

Revel. 21: 24   magistrates unto the throne and scepter of Christ, than by bringing their glorie and honour unto the church

Isa. 60: 3, 10, 11   according to the comfortable prophecies of the Scriptures. O what a comfort were this to Christ's poore

Isa. 65: 25   lambes, to see the lion so humbled as to eate hay together with them in the mountaine of the Lord, and not to live of the ravine and spoile of the poore sheepe, so as they dare not come aneere them for their fiercenes. What a joy were it to see God's ordinances thus united, to see Moses and Aaron brethren, and this in the glorious spirituall temple of God, where Christ shalbe Hhimmanuel,[1] God with us, rule, guide, feed, and sanctifie us every one in their callings. O what a heavenlie communion should this be, what a beautie, what a joy to the whole earth.

Revel. 16: 13, 14   But o how far are we from this comfort, our magistrates from this happines, whiles they give their eare to the serpent speaking out of the mouth of the false prophet,

Revel. 17: 17   that blasphemeth Christ and his ordinances, and accuseth his saints unto them; whiles they give their power

Heb. 10: 29   unto the beast that trampleth Christ's Testament under their feete, and counteth the blood therof as a common

2. Thess. 2   thing; that setteth up the image of his owne devises and

Reve. 13   causeth al men of al degrees to worship the same: and

Dan. 7   al such as in feare and faith unto God refuse so to doe,

Rev. 14: 12   those in all hostile manner they confiscate, persecute, imprison, inclose, make away, without anie equal hearing of their cause, or once bringing it to light. This,

---

[1] " Immanuw'el or Emmanuel. God with us. The word " Immanuel " occurs twice in the Bible, in Isaiah 7: 14 and 8: 8. The word " Emmanuel " occurs once, in Matthew 1: 23. In the Latin edition, *Testamenti Veteris Biblia Sacra*, translated by Immanuel Tremellius and Franciscus Iunius (London, 1580), which Barrow is using, the spelling is Hhimmanuel.

their blasphemous writings and sermons, the publike
worship and estate of their church, their prisons generally through London and the land, declare. They have
published in their writings that the orders and ordinances which Christ hath in his Testament left unto his
church, were but temporarie whiles the church was
under heathen tyrants; and that where the gospel is
embraced by a christian prince, they are not onlie not
necessarie but inconvenient, yea, intollerable, as bringing the utter subversion of the land, [195] raising up
tumults, and uprores and withdrawing the people from
obedience unto their magistrates and a number of such
like execrable mandible blasphemies. Reade that most
blasphemous parenthesis of T.C. [Thomas Cooper],
esteemed the Bishop of Winchester, beginning at the
73 page unto the 84 of that his booke which he writ
against the libeller Martin Marprelate.[1] The wickednes
and falshood of whose devilish calumniations that they
may even sodenly appeare, I wil adresse my self to proove
unto him by the undoubted evidence of God's word the
strange proposition which he so confidently condemneth,
and in way of reprochful chalenge to al Christ's servantes
propoundeth: namelie, that there ought throughout al

---

[1] This is a reference to Thomas Cooper, *An Admonition to the People of
England*. Barrow's reference seems to be to a first edition, pp. 73-84.
This edition of 252 pages seems to have been withdrawn or corrected,
because Bishop Cooper erred at three different places. The two copies
in the British Museum are both dated 1589, one with 244 pages and the
other with 245 pages. In these two copies, the section on the government
of the Church of England, to which Barrow is referring, occupies pages
74-84, but pp. 84-94 are also relevant. *An Admonition to the People of
England* was reprinted in 1846 [1847] by John Petheram and in 1881—
1883 by Edward Arber.
The challenge of Bishop Cooper is restated positively by Barrow. Bishop
Cooper's exact words are as follows: " Onely this I desire, that they [the
Martinist Libellers] will lay downe out of the worde of God some just
proofes, and a direct commaundement, that there shoulde bee in all ages
and states of the church of Christ, one onely forme of outwarde governement. Secondly, that they will note and name some certaine particular
churches, either in the apostles' time, or afterward, wherein the whole
governement of the church was practised, onelie by doctours, pastours,
elders, and deacons, and none other, and that in an equalitie, without
superioritie in one above an other."
" If this bee done soundlie and truelie, without any wresting or double
understanding of the places of Scripture: I protest they will shake that
opinion that nowe I have of this present governement of the church of
England. Yet under correction (I will not say, that I know) but I am
surelie perswaded, that they will never be able to doe it " (p. 81).

ages and estates of the world in al places, to be one and the same forme of outward government in al true churches of Christ unto the world's end. *Scilicet*: that apostolike primitive patterne left unto us in Christ's New Testament and none other. And this through the assistance of God's spirit by direct Scriptures, without anie wrasting or perverting the same. Which being done, by that time (I hope) the innocencie of such as seeke this christian order and communion in sinceritie, as also the blasphemie of them that deprave the order and accuse the seekers therof, shalbe evident to al men. I am not ignorant in what a sophistical Saducaical manner this horned bishop hath propounded his questions, quite from the state of the controversie and drift of his reproches subsequent. The deceit and error wherof may be more fitly laid open after this difficult proposition (which he and his associates with such tyrannie impugne) is prooved.

God, we reade, when he first erected his tabernacle amongst the Israelites, set downe in the mountaine the perfect patterne of al things even to the least instrument, hooke, or tape used therin; as also the whole composition and use of everie thing belonging therunto, with all the ordinances therof. He left nothing to the wil or discretion of Moses, whose commendation was, that he was found faithful in al his house as a servant for a testimonie of thinges to be spoken. The like we reade of David in the distribution of the orders and functions of the priests and Levites, of Solomon and Zerubabel in the building the material temple. We see (I say) how perfectlie the Lord set downe the matter and forme, the number, assize,[1] place, order and use of everie thing belonging to his tabernacle and temple. We see what absolute lawes he set downe for everie thing there to be done; how jelous he was over his sanctuarie, and what severe judgmentes he shewed upon them that transgressed the least of his ordinances; as the examples of Nadab, Abihu, Corath, Ely and his sonnes, Uzza and sundrie others, the deportation of both the kingdomes with the destruction of the temple, and at length the utter

Exo. 25: 40

Heb. 8: 5

Heb. 3

1. Chro. 28: 11, *etc.*

[1] Number, measurement.

desolation therof, shew. And may we suppose that
God is lesse carefull, provident, absolute, jelous, over
this his glorious temple, which consisteth of the bodies
and soules of his deare redeemed saintes for the structure, instrumentes, forme, order and ordinances of this
which abideth for ever, than he was of that other which
consisted but of stone and wood, which was to abide
but a [196] time and was but a type and shadow of this?
If we so thinke, let the New Testament of our saviour
Christ convince us; wherin is left unto us a most livelie
and expresse patterne for all things, with the fit mould
wherin everie thing ought to be formed and cast, most
perfect and direct lawes and ordinances for the number,
place, order, use and direction of al things belonging
unto Christ's church. Can anie imagine unto themselves that God is lesse loving unto, delighted in, or
jelous over this temple wherof his owne only deere
Sonne is builder, minister, and head, than he was over
that base earthen temple (for so in respect of the incomparable glorie of this I may call it) wherof Moses
was the builder, *etc.*? Can anie imagine the ministrie,
orders and ordinances of Christ's church delivered by
the Sonne himself, ratified and confirmed by the voice
of God from heaven, by manie miracles and wonders on
earth, of lesse congruence, necessitie, or accompt, than
those of that temple delivered by angels? Or that God
hath given now greater power or priviledg to anie
mortal creature, prince, or minister in this church to
neglect, alter, violate or innovate any of Christ's lawes,
or bring in and set up anie of their owne in this church,
than he did then to Moses, David, Solomon in that
temple? If these lawes be of greater force, estimation,
perpetuitie, both in regard of the dignitie and preeminence of Christ, the minister of the things administred, and of the place, I meane the spiritual temple;
yet if the word spoken by angels was sure, and everie
transgression and disobedience receaved just recompence of reward; if that word might at no hand either
in the building, reformation, or administration, even in
the least and vilest things (as the ashes of the altar which
had their apointed place, instruments, and ministers)

be neglected, broken or innovate by no mortall man of what estate or degree soever, upon what occasion or pollitike respect soever, without some warrant from God's owne mouth that gave the law: how shall they escape, or where shal they stand, that not only neglect and violate, but despise, reproch, and innovate the whole established order and ordinances that Christ hath set downe in his Testament for this his church? Shal not this be to make God more loving, gracious, provident, careful, jelous over that material temple, that shadow, than he is now over this his church the substance, and to prefer the shadow to the substance, that temple to this church? Should not this be to prefer the person and testament of Moses, to the person and Testament of Christ, inasmuch as they make the one to be delivered and confirmed with a great deale more authoritie, majestie, power than the other? Were it not to make Moses more absolute and faithfull in his house, than Christ in his church, inasmuch as Moses left a perfect tabernacle and testament, and did see and gave charge that al the ordinances therof should be most precisely kept and observed? But Christ belike hath left an unperfect church and Testament, in as much as he hath not taken full order for the ministerie, government, orders, and ordinances therof: yea, though he have in his Testament set downe orders and lawes for all [197] these things, yet they are not so authentike or irrefragable as those of Moses. Princes and states may according to their pollicies receave, reject or innovate these, *etc.* Were not this to prefer the ministerie of Levy and those outward ordinances and beggerlie rudiments in dignitie, to the sacred ministerie and ordinances of Christ, inasmuch as they are made more holie, congruent, necessarie and inviolable than Christ's? But the Holie Ghost throughout the whole Epistle to the Hebrewes, handeling this verie subject, convinceth, instructeth, and exhorteth the Jewes to leave al superstitious foreconceaved opinions of their temple, ministerie, and ordinances, and wholy with reverence to embrace and behave themselves in the church, ministerie and ordinances of Christ. Hereunto he perswadeth by the incomparable excellencie, glorie, preeminence, perpetuitie of Christ's person, church, ministerie, Testament, which can never be shaken or removed, compared unto the weakenes, basenes, impotencie, and vanitie of Moses' person, that temple, ministerie and testament which were temporarie, caduke,[1] to be abolished and to give place unto these which they but prefigured whereunto they led and served, this being the beginning and the end of their erection. Manie most grave exhortations and weightie charges doth the Holie Ghost there give unto us concerning the reverence, feare, faithfull, holie, obedient, diligent, orderlie and constant walking and behaviour that we ought to shew in the church of Christ unto his word and Testament, drawing argumentes both from the unspeakeable glorie, majestie, excellencie, beawtie, joy of Christ's church, as also from the terror and severity of God who is the judg and beholder of this church against all inordinate walkers and contumatious offendors therin. From everie word almost of which epistle[2] may an argument be drawen, to prove the inviolable excellencie and perpetual necessitie of Christ's orders and ordinances left in his Testament for the building, direction, and government of his church.

It will not heere helpe them to say that the ministerie and government of Christ are eternall in respect of the covenant and end, in that they lead to the kingdome of heaven, or in respect of the perpetuitie of the doctrine of the gospell, or in respect of the inward rule and worke his Holy Spirit hath in our heartes, and is not understood of the perpetuitie and necessitie of that outward order of government and administration left and practized by Christ's apostles. These ignorant cavils will not helpe them. For this self same covenant of life everlasting touching the end had the Jewes and all the faithful that ever were. They were all saved through faith in Christ seene and apprehended by the eie of faith, though not yet exhibited in the flesh unto them. The difference of the covenant then was not in the end

---

[1] Perishable.
[2] The Epistle to the Hebrews.

T*

to which it tended, so much as in the present church,
ministerie, things administred, orders, ordinances, worship, worshippers, *etc.*, the covenant being made to these
outward ritual figures and ceremonies, but until the
substance should be shewed, and Christ's heavenlie
church and ministerie erected, to which then the Jewes
and al men were called, to which now the covenant is
only made.

[198] As for the truth and perpetuitie of the doctrines
and of the gospel, they were the same from the beginning
that they are now: Christ was before all beginnings that
wisdome and word of God; Christ was the fulfilling of al
the prophets who foreshewed of him.   But if they meane
by doctrine and gospell that heavenly ministerie, sacramentes, exercises, and communion of the church which
are peculiar unto the gospell according to the rules
prescribed in Christ's Testament, then is the question
graunted me; without the due observation of which
rules, they can have no true ministerie, sacraments,
exercises, communion, gospel, as I shall straight way
shew.

Now as for this inward government and sanctification
they speake of, where Christ reigneth in their hearts by
the power of his spirit, *etc.*   I say that the spirit of God
may not and cannot be severed from the word of God.
They that openly and willingly breake the least of God's
lawes, boast of a false gift when they speake of their inward sanctification.   Christ doth not reigne in the heart
of anie that wil not submit all their outward actions to
be ruled by him also.   Christ will have the whole man
both bodie and soule to serve him: he parteth not with
antichrist or Beliall.   This is one of the Anabaptistical
errors, wherby the reforming preachers defend their
popish ministerie.   They say they have Christ's inward
calling to the ministerie, in that they have gifts, learning,
and fitnes; therfore, though they want his outward
calling (which they say is not of the substance of the
ministerie), yea, though they have a false antichristian
outward calling, yet are they to be esteemed as the
ministers of Christ.   Might they not as tollerably, yea,
with lesse offence both to God and man, usurpe the

magistrate's chaire without a calling (inasmuch as it is of no such excellencie or worthines as the heavenlie ministerie of Christ) because they have wisdome and fitnes, *etc.*

But to returne againe to our purpose. This inward government and sanctification of the spirit had the faithful Jewes before Christ came in our flesh, and before they were called to the church and ministerie of Christ. Therfore, either these are no answeres, or els the whole scope of that Epistle to the Hebrues is vaine, for all these things the Jewes enjoyed before: they had the same covenant of salvation, the same perpetuall true doctrines and gospel, the same inward government and santification of the spirit that we have. Only because they wanted the heavenly practise and ministerie of the gospel, the heavenly orders, exercises, and communion of the church of Christ, they were called from those ritual types and figurative shadowes wherby in their infancie and nonage[1] they were trained and shut up, unto the open sight and cleare beholding of the glorie of the Lord with open face, all vailes being taken away, and unto the free and orderlie practise of the same gospel according to Christ's New Testament, al trumperie traditions being abolished. Gal. 3 & 4
chapters
2 Cor. 3

With what extreame desire have all the prophets longed after, and great delight written of, the excellent beawtie, heavenlie government, [199] inviolable order of this church? How often hath David in his psalmes remembred the same? With what admiration hath he expressed the absolute perfect structure of that compact citie? As Salomon also livelie described the beawtie, pretiousnes and juncture of al her parts. How plentifully have the prophets Isaiah, Ezekiel, Zachariah, and others, even with an open eye, described the whole forme of the building of this church? As also all of them given evident testimonie of the perpetuitie of the government and ordinances therof. How oft doth David exhorte the saints to celebrate the excellencie and perpetuitie of Christ's government and throne? By how many testimonies doth he extoll and prove the

---

[1] Not of age ; the period of one's minority, of immaturity.

same, as is everie where found in the psalmes; sundrie wherof, the author to the Hebrewes, as also the other apostles in their sermons and writings have used, both to prove the excellencie, necessitie and eternitie of, and to draw men unto this heavenly government of Christ in his church.

The prophet Isaiah in the 33 of his prophecie, verse 20, *etc.*, willeth the Jewes in al their calamities to " behold Sion that citie of their assemblies, to cause their eies looke upon Jerusalem, that quiet fould, that tent that shall never be dissevered, of whose pins or stakes not one may be taken away, neither shall anie of the coards therof be broken; but there the mightie Jehovah shalbe unto us in place of floods and of broade rivers wherin shal passe no navie with oares, neither shall anie great ship passe through it, for Jehovah is our revenger, Jehovah is our lawgiver, Jehovah is our king, he shall save us."[1] What can be said more plainly for the inviolable perpetuitie both of the order and forme of building, and also for the government, administration and ordinances of Christ's church ? Of al which as God himself is the author, so you see he voweth to be the defendor and revenger against all the power of tyrants or anie mortal man whosoever.

Likewise the prophet Daniel in his seventh chapter after he had beene shewed the calamitie, tyrannie and oppression done unto the saintes by the four beasts, but especially by that presumptuous horne, that livelie figure and foretreader of antichrist, whose mouth spake presumptuous words against the most high, and consumed the saints of the most high, that thought he might change the times and the law into whose handes they were for a season delivered, *etc.* After these visions Daniel was shewed how this presumptuous horne was consumed and destroyed with the fiery streame that proceeded from the ancient of daies, and how this unlawfull dominion was taken from the other beasts and given to him that came from heaven, and having finished the ful redemption of his saints, and being ascended up againe and set at the right hand of his Father, there was given unto

[1] Isaiah 33: 20-24.

him dominion and glorie and a kingdome, that all
people, nations, and tongues should serve him; whose
dominion is a perpetual dominion that passeth not
away, and his kingdome is never corrupted, verse 14.
Also verse 27.[1] What can be more direct for the perpetuity of the government and ordinances that Christ
hath left and apointed in his New Testament for his
church? Which whosoever presumeth to speake [200]
against or violate, much more to innovate or change,
shall he not be under the same sinne, damnation, and
curse with this presumptuous blasphemous horne.

The prophet Zachariah also in the eleventh of his
prophecie sheweth, that all Christ's sheep are governed
and kept under our cheif shepeheards' pastorall staves,
Beawtie and Bands.[2] All other are out of his protection, delivered up in his wrath to be guided by the
instruments of foolish and idol shepheards, whose right
arme shalbe without strength and whithered up, their
right eie shalbe utterlie darkened, there shall be no
light in them. Both these shepheards and their flockes,
even all such as are misled by and with them are given
up of the Lord to utter destruction because they cast
the Lord's coards from them and would not be bound
in his bands, their soule abhorred the Lord, they would
not have him to reigne over them, therfore his soule
abhorred them, he gave them up to their owne lusts and
insnared them in their owne pollicies. For all the wisdome of all flesh without the Lord is madnes, their most
exquisite plattes[3] of government which they can devise
unto themselves, are but the instruments of foolish sheepheards to their owne perdition and of as manie as are
governed by them.

These things are so manifest in that chapter, the true
shepheard, government, and sheepe, as also the false
shephearde, government, and sheepe, with the divers
endes of both being there described, the one in the
person of our saviour and his disciples, the other in the
priests, rulers, phariseis, and people of the Jewes, with

---

[1] Daniel 7: 14, 27.
[2] Zechariah 11: 7. The King James Version has Beauty and Bands, but
the Revised Standard Version has Grace and Union.
[3] Plans, schemes, outlines, platforms.

their verie maner of rejecting and betraiing him so livelie set downe; as none can cavill at these things or mistake them so grosly againe, as one of these foolish shepheardes, Doctor Some, hath done, taking his chapter to be understood of the estate of the Jewes in Zecheriah's time, the 12 and 13 verse of Zachariah's person and wages.[1] Who if he had but compared this chapter in itself, much more to the discourse of the prophet precedent and subsequent, but especially to the evident event and perimplishing[2] in and by our saviour Christ, Mathew 21, 23, 24, 26 chapters, he would never have justified tithes by the 12 and 13 verses of this eleventh chapter of Zechariah. If any doubt of the interpretation of these two staves, Beawtie and Bands, let him consider the allegorie how shepheards use their staves and hookes; or rather let him waigh the seventh verse, where he shall find that Christ with these staves fed, governed, and defended those sheepe his Father gave him, as also verse 14, the interpretation and end of the staffe, Bandes, how there can be no true communion where they are not knit together in the faith, order, government, and love of Christ, But if he compare this prophecie to the event and fulfilling therof by our saviour Christ and his apostles that called al men from the shadowes and figures of the temple unto the kingdome and church of Christ, he shall manifestlie see, that this sense in all things accordeth, and no other can be made to agree to the words and arguments of this prophet in this chapter.

Notes might plentifullie be drawn and manie waightie arguments [201] framed from these allegories, as also from the etymologie of these words, to shew the excellencie, amenitie, pleasantnes, comlines, congruence, utilitie, necessity, perpetuity, of Christ's pastorall government of his church; and how disorderly and unnaturall a thing it were for the sheepe to disobey, especially to controule and teach their shepheard. But I hope the judgments denounced in that chapter for such faultes,

---

[1] Zechariah 11: 12, 13. See also Robert Some, *A Godly Treatise, wherein Are Examined and Confuted Many Execrable Fancies*, p. 5.
[2] Fulfilling.

and the plaine demonstration of the danger, error, folly, horror, of all other governments and instruments whatsoever, may suffice to satisfie the godly in this point, and to restraine them from such presumption and rebellion, either to reject or to innovate or alter Christ's holy government, order and ordinances. As for the unperswaded and disobedient, I leave them to their accompt when they shall see him whome they have perced through come with clowdes: and in the meanewhile will addresse myself to proove by sundry expresse places of the New Testament, that the ordinances the apostles left for the building, administration and government of the church, are the commandements of God, perpetual, inviolable, to be observed, and not to be willingly neglected or changed unto the world's end.

Our Saviour Christ having finished whatsoever was needful here upon earth to be done in his person either for the worke of our redemption, or for the removing and abolishing all the legal shadowes and ceremonial worship, or for the ratifiing his gospel, the gathering, planting and establishing his church, having chosen, apointed, and perfectly instructed his apostles of all things belonging therunto. In the 28 chapter according unto Mathew, verses 18, 19, 20, he used this speach unto them: " And Jesus comming spake unto them saying, all authority in heaven and in earth is given unto me; go therfore, teach ye all the nations, baptising them into the name of the Father, and of the Sonne, and of the Holy Spirit, teaching them to keep all things whatsoever I have commanded you, And loe I am with you all dayes untill the consummation of the world, Amen." Omitting the sundry necessary circumstances and manifold profitable doctrines that might from this Scripture be observed and drawen to hold me to the present purpose, we heere may see not only the apostles' personal power and authority, but the warrant and dignity of all things they taught or did in this brief of their commission and ministery, which we heere see to be derived from and founded upon our saviour Christ's sacred person and soveraigne power. We heere see whome they were to teach, whome to baptise, how to baptise, how and what to teach the baptised, and how to leave such as they had thus taught, gathered, and instructed. In summe, we here see the very maner and order of winning, receaving, gathering, ordering, instructing, building up and establishing the church of Christ. We heere see all the orders and ordinances which the apostles practised in, and left unto the churches by our saviour's owne mouth pronounced to be his commandements, and those perpetuall, such as he will have to continue and be observed of all his [202] servantes unto the world's end. We see them not onlie commanded unto his apostles that they should practise and teach them in their time, or in time of persecution; but he chargeth his apostles to teach all churches, all Christians, to keepe and observe them at all times untill the consummation and end of the world; giving unto al his servantes and churches the same power to practise and observe all these his commandementes, that he gave unto his apostles: plighting upon such their faith and obedience, his presence and protection unto them, in these wordes: " And loe I am with you all dayes untill the consummation of the world "; sealing the truth both of these his commandementes and ordinances and also of this his covenant and protection unto all ages with this his authentike seale, with this word of all truth, *Amen.* So that me thinkes all the blasphemous reproches and cavils of al sortes of enemies unto the sacred inviolable government and order of our saviour Christ delivered and practised by his apostles in his churches, are utterlie by this one place of Scripture (if so be there were no more to the same effect) taken out of the way: both they that denie the continance or necessitie heerof in all ages and places, and they that would make these apostolike ordinances but matters of forme, not matters of faith or of substance (as they speake), they being heere confirmed and commanded by that Lord of all truth of all power in heaven and in earth.

Peradventure that old Saducee that thus sophisticallie hath propounded these questions in that 74 leafe of his answere unto Martin,[1] will stumble (as he ordinarilie doth at the word of God) at these wordes (al things whatsoever I have commanded you), collecting, that because the apostles had not as yet received the expresse rules and commandments for al the things they afterward taught and practised, that therfore this commandement cannot be understood or applied to such things as they afterward taught, and so nothing or litle serveth to the outward forme of government and order of the church.

Although it were not hard from this verie place necessarilie to confirme the intendement and commandement of all the ordinances and rules which the apostles after taught and prescribed unto the churches even by that which is heere expressed concerning the ministerie, baptisme, *etc.*, which heere are commanded al churches to be observed in that manner as the apostles taught them, which ministers, sacraments and ministerie could not in and by these churches be had or practised without the observation of these rules and ordinances, as the election, probation of such ministers by the flockes where they are to administer, *etc.*, which were not al that time set downe by the Holy Ghost or practised by the apostles as yet. Although I could also shew that our saviour Christ had alreadie instructed his apostles that he had chosen and set a part to that worke, of all things belonging to his kingdome, Acts 1: 2, and had given them his Holie Spirit in abundant measure to this their ministerie which should teach them al things and bring al things [203] to their remembrance (John 20: 22), which he had tould them; yet mine awnswere Joh. 20: 22 heere is that if our saviour Christ in these wordes (*Al whatsoever I have commanded you*) had respect onlie unto such precepts as he had then at that time given them, and not unto al other things which he should afterward reveale unto them by his Holy Spirit also; it were both contrarie to their commission and charge they delivered,

---

[1] Thomas Cooper, *An Admonition to the People of England*, p. 74 of the first edition; p. 81 of the reissues with 245 and 244 pages. This book is an answer to Martin Marprelate, whose first two books, the *Epistle* and the *Epitome*, are answered. See William Pierce, *An Historical Introduction to the Marprelate Tracts*, pp. 165-172.

which (as is saied) was that they should win, gather together, build, order, instruct and establish his church according to the rules and commandements of his wil and Testament, which could not at al be done by them if al these lawes and rules were not alike confirmed of, and commanded by him: as also if these words, *Al whatsoever I have commanded, etc.*, should so be restrained, it were to make the other holie lawes and ordinances which he afterward shewed to his apostles, and they by the same spirit both shewed and recorded unto the churches of Christ, of lesse valew and authoritie than those former; to make some part of holie Scripture more true, holy, and authentical than other: yea, it were utterlie to abrogate and disfranchize these latter Scriptures. Furthermore, I suppose it were a hard matter for anie man to discusse and set downe what things Christ had at that time taught these apostles, and what he had as yet concealed. So that this cavil can no way put off this most direct and expresse place, let me therfore proceed to others.

The apostle Paul, 1 Timothy 5: 21, chargeth Timothy before God and the Lord Jesus Christ and the elect angels, that he keepe these things without prejudice, doing nothing according to inclination, *etc.* Also chapter 6, verse 13, he useth these wordes unto him, " I command thee before God that quickneth al things and Christ Jesus that testified before Pontius Pilate that good confession, to keepe the commandement without spot unrebukeable until the appearing of our Lord Jesus Christ, which in due time that blessed and onlie mightie, that King of kings and Lord of lords shal shew, *etc.*" Likewise 1 Corinthians 14: 37, he hath these wordes, " If anie man seeme to be a prophet or spiritual, let him acknowledg the things I write unto you because they are the commandementes of God: but if anie man be ignorant, let him be ignorant." With what greater authoritie or waight of wordes could the apostle either confirme or incommend[1] unto the church in all ages these cannons and ordinances which he in these epistles hath set downe for the building, order, government, of

---

[1] Entrust.

all churches, of al the officers, people, and actions of
the same to be religiously and inviolably kept as the
commandements of that great dreadfull God, as the
lawes of that our Lord and King untill his appearing
in glorie. Who can anie longer doubt (that wil either
rest in the manifest testimonies of the Holy Ghost, give
credite to the resolute affirmations, and eare to the
vehement charges of the apostle, or that will duly
expend either the general scope of these epistles, or
dulie weigh the manifold rules in particular and the
manner of delivering them) that these cannons and
ordinances are the absolute lawes and holie commandements of Christ for the building and government of
his church, so necessarie, inviolable, per-[204]petuall,
as without which or with anie other his church can
neither be built nor kept. Are not all these particular
rules for the several offices, persons, qualities, for their
maner of election, probation, ordination, administration, *etc.*, set downe in way of commandement and law
with as great authoritie, credite and reverence as anie
other part of Christ's Testament or God's word ? So
that the apostles' whole ministerie may with as much
right or reason be called into doubt or question, as these
canons and ordinances which the apostle everie where
confirmeth with the same authoritie that he doth all his
writings, 2 Corinthians 1: 13, 1 Corinthians 11: 1, 2,
2 Thessalonians 2: 15, Colossians 2: 5, and sundrie
other places which were long to recite. Moreover, how
carefully and by how many reasons have the apostles
incommended these orders and statutes unto the whole
church and unto the chief workmen and builders therin ?
What perfect lawes hath he set downe in those his epistles
unto Timothie and Titus, those two excellent workmen,
his trained and exercised children, whome he therfore
calleth his natural and right begotten sonns, and especially commendeth them unto the churches, as to the
Corinthians, epistle 1, chapter 4, verse 17: " For this
cause have I sent unto you Timotheus, which is my
beloved sonne and faithfull in the Lord, who will put
you in remembrance of my waies which in Christ as I
teach everie where in every church." And unto the

Philippians, chapter 2: 22: " But ye know the proofe of him because as a sonne unto his father he hath served with me unto the gospel." Yet notwithstanding al this their promptnes and experience, we see what carefull charges the apostles layd upon them, most precisely and exactly to observe all these rules in al their actions of the church and towards al men; that they keepe that expresse patterne of wholsome words that they had heard of him in the faith and love that is in Christ Jesus, calling these rules the expresse patterne or engraven forme or delineation of all things belonging unto or to be done in the church, charging them of their fidelity and love both unto Christ Jesus and unto those whome they are to build, to keep and alwaies to have this true patterne and forme before their eies in all things they doe, commending it for the soundnes and wholsomes therof both to the builders and the builded therby.

For it being the true patterne, forme, mould, for everie thing, every part, everie member, wherunto they ought to be compared, fashioned and cast, neither can the partes have anie right shape, neither the whole any true forme, if they be not framed and built according to this patterne; and then how should the building either stand or agree unto itself? Much lesse please the lord and owner of the house when he seeth it thus spoiled and destroyed. Therfore it behooveth both the builders, and everie one that is built, to consider diligentlie after what maner and order he buildeth, and is built.

For this cause the apostle Paul, 1 Corinthians 3, having shewed how soundlie the apostles as wise maister builders had laied the foundation, exhorteth all that are to succeed and build upon that foundation, to looke well how they build upon it; for this foundation wil beare nothing but gold, [205] silver, pretious stones, they may not build in this house their hay, timber, stubble. Everie man's worke heere shalbe made manifest, the day shall declare it because it shalbe revealed in the fire, which shall trie every man's worke of what sort it is. If upon this trial by this light it be fownd answerable to that heavenly patterne of Christ's Testament, it then abideth to the praise and comfort of the

workman. But wherin any of these builders shal in
any part of their worke, whether in matter or maner
(as they use to speake to couller their transgressions),
even in the least thing be fownd to have swerved from
the true patterne, by this light; if then upon such discovery made unto them they suffer not these their
workes to burne, acknowledging, forsaking, and repent-
ing their such errors and transgressions, and withdrawing others from the like, they shal not only destroie
themselves by this their presumptuous sin, but al such
as after this discovery and reproof made, remaine with
them and joine unto them in this their presumptuous
sinne. For (saith the apostle) these men corrupt or
destroie the temple of God, which is holy, which temple
ye are, and the Spirit of God dwelleth in you. If any
man corrupt or destroie the temple of God, him shal
God destroie, *etc.*[1]

Wee see with what waightie, grave and plentiful
reasons, exhortations, and proves [proofs] the apostle
affirmeth and confirmeth these things by everie verse
of that chapter, yea, almost by every word of the verse
(which carry a severall consideration and especiall force
in themselves) but especially from the eighth verse unto
the end. He there setteth downe the persons of the
apostles as a perpetuall example unto all builders unto
the world's end. The practise of the apostles as the
true only foundation, the expresse patterne for al buildings, yea for everie thing in every true building unto
the world's end. Which foundation and patterne he
deriveth not from and confirmeth not by the authority
of man, but by the authority of Christ, shewing that
it is not in man's power either to lay any other foundation, or alter this that is laid; calling it but one and the
same in all places, even as Christ is one and the same,
and calling everie part of the word they delivered *fundamental,* as part of the verie foundation of this building,
and maketh not (with the learned pharisies and schoole
divines of our age) some part of Christ's Testament
fundamental and substantiall, other parts therof accidental, formal, not necessary, not of substance or

[1] I Corinthians 3: 11-18.

essence, who thus with the deep learning of Satan abrogate what part of Christ's Testament they please, build their owne stubble divises, destroie the worke of God together with their owne soules and the soules of as many as are built or led by them. And therfore the apostles heere calleth al builders and buildings to this one only foundation of Christ's word and Testament, charging them to make it of all their actions whatsoever the only rule and foundation; and not as these false builders of the Church of England doe, who rejecting the true patterne of Christ's Testament in al things they do or goe about, yet vainly boast that they hould the foundation, preach and practise the gospell of Christ sincerely, *etc.*, although (as is said) they reject what [206] part of Christ's Testament they list as not *fundamental, substantial, necessarie,* abrogate the whole patterne of the apostles' practise, and mowld and lay unto themselves a new patterne, a new foundation, making not only new rules, lawes, orders for the government and whole administration of the church, but a new ministerie, new officers, new actions, which are not read or heard of in the Testament of Christ; it never as yet being agreed amongst them what part of Christ's Testament they allow and hold for the foundation and for the gospel. But in deed to say as it is, the foundation and gospel of their church is not yet layd to either side; for though they all at this present generally embrace the pope's canons and decrees of the High Commission as the foundation, certaine allowed writings and priviledged bookes for the gospell of their church; yet keep the prelates in their hand to coyne and forge new lawes, new doctrines, what and when they please, as also the Reformists, they sue to prince and Parliament that they might be allowed to make and bring in yet other new lawes and doctrines as far from the true patterne as these, as (when they are compared therunto) will appeare. But the apostle heere as he teacheth but one foundation, so teacheth he it the groundworke both of the whole church and of every part therof and action therein, calling al builders hereunto, charging them to take it for the foundation of all their doings, without which whatsoever they doe or enterprize, seeme it never so necessarie or expedient in their eies, yet is it but as an house without a foundation, which not being laid upon the rock but upon the sandes of men's wisdome, wanteth a groundworke, and therfore cannot stand.

He willeth them therfore to be sure of this foundation before they build, yea, and to loke carefully how they build upon it, because their worke shalbe manifested, declared, tryed, revealed, in the day in the fire. This day shal manifest and declare all their whole building both within and without, the whole forme and order therof. Al things when they are reproved of this light are manifest, for it is the light that maketh all things manifest. This fire not only trieth and revealeth al counterfait stuffe, but burneth and consumeth the same: their wood, hay, stubble, cannot be unrevealed in this day, or unconsumed in this fire. To which wood, hay, stubble, he likeneth al the devises and pollecies of man's wit, how prudent or pregnant soever they seeme: and therfore upon the divers ends of such buildings and builders, he exhorteth by the reward and eternitie of the one unto the faithfull and carefull keeping the true patterne; by the terror and losse of the other he dehorteth[1] from all negligent, but especially al wilfull and presumptuous transgressions of the same, shewing God's unpartiall examination and judgment of every man's worke: which by how much it is so deare unto the Lord, so pretious in his sight; by so much it behoveth all men to be the more carefull therof, whose transgressions therin shall be the more hainous.

This worke he calleth the temple of God, which temple we have above shewed in the type to be built in everie thing according to the [207] patterne shewed in the mount. How much more then ought it in the true substance to be built in every thing according to the heavenly perfect patterne of Christ's Testament, wherin we have the whole mind and will of Christ, as the apostle saith in the last words of the second chapter

---

[1] Dissuade, advise against.

of this epistle?[1] Now the Apostle heere saith this temple of the Lord is holy; but even in the figure might no strange or polluted thing enter, it was an abhomination unto the Lord, how much more in this excellent spiritual house ought no fleshly devises of our owne (which are wholy corrupt and altogether defiled) to be brought; but the wisest devises of men being set in the place of the wisdome of God or brought into his temple, are not only foolish, idle, vaine, but abhomination to the Lord, such as corrupt, destroie and deface the temple of God, because the devises of man cannot be joined with the thoughts of God: God needeth not the advise or councell of man. The wisdome of man is alwaies to rest in the wisdome of God; wherin he proceedeth further, it is turned to folly and rebellion, and made a snare unto themselves. Now then (seing the Church of Christ is the temple of God, and the temple of God is holy, and is corrupted and destroied when man presumeth therin to be wise above that he ought, or hath warrant to be wise), the apostle from all these places and every word therof useth reasons and exhortations to exhort all men that enter into this temple to observe their feete, that they be more neere to heare them to offer the sacrifice of fooles: for the Lord is more delighted with obedience than sacrifice; he will be sanctified in all that come neere unto him, and wilbe served in this his temple with reverence and feare, for even the Lord our God is a consuming fire.

But our learned priests treading in the steppes of their predecessors the false prophets, are so far from being moved with reverence and feare because of the Lord's holy temple, that they from hence draw arguments to justifie their transgressions, and embolden themselves therin by the titles of the church and temple of God. Say they the churches of Corinth, Gallatia, Asia had sundrie faultes, yet are they pronounced by the apostle the churches of Christ: therfore much more they that teach not circumcision, denie not the resurrection, *etc.*[2] Though these arguments be largelie answered in an other

[1] I Corinthians 2: 16.
[2] Robert Some, *A Godly Treatise Containing and Deciding Certaine Questions* (1588), pp. 18, 34.

place, yet heere would be observed (besides the poison
that they gather from these examples to tollerate and
commit sin therby) how litle they understand the
estate of these churches, chardging the whole church
with the errors of some few, whome the apostles
there confuted. But if some of these were the
errors of the whole church (as we doubt not but the
church may, doth, and shal, whiles it is in this life,
erre), yet if it shall persist in error after it shall be by
the word of God convinced and reproved, then we may
say with the apostles heere; that such corrupt and
destroie the temple of God, even so manie soules as are
by them and together with them thus misled, wherof
this building consisteth. [208]

Therfore the apostle heere (as in sundrie other places)
admonisheth the whole church and every member therof
carefully to looke to their builders and guides, that they
lead them in the right waies of the Lord, and build them
according to the true patterne of Christ's Testament, to
follow them no further than they follow Christ and have
his word for their warrant: from which when they swerve
or transgresse, and being admonished will not returne,
then is the whole church to excommunicate such a pastor,
leader, builder, whosoever, and to seperate him or as
many as cleave unto him or follow him in this estate.[1]
The argument the apostle useth is of no lesse waight than
the salvation of their owne soules, which otherwise
should be destroied and corrupted by them. He willeth
them neither to be led away with the shew of wisdome,
utilitie, pollicy, holines, nor any pretences wherwith
they shall cover their error, neither with the estimation
of their persons, authority, wisdome, learning, vertue,
etc. For if they teach otherwise and come not to the
wholsome wordes of our Lord Jesus Christ, and to the
doctrine which is according to godlines, they are puft

---

[1] Barrow places the power of excommunication in the whole church. When
T. L. [Thomas Legate or Thomas Lemar or LeMare ?] and others, holding
a private conventicle, excommunicated two of their members, no minister
being present, Barrow disclaimed this particular action (Robert Some, *A
Godly Treatise, wherein Are Examined and Confuted Many Execrable
Fancies*, p. 36 ; Ephraim Pagitt, *Heresiography*, 4th ed. [London, 1648],
p. 77). Nevertheless, Barrow teaches that the church possesses the power
of excommunication " without the pastor, yea, against the pastor [if
necessary] " (*A Brief Discoverie of the False Church*, p. 243).

up, knowing nothing. As for their person and office, they are not to rule over, so much as to build up our faith, for by faith we stand: they are not lords over the heritage, but servants of the church; for Paul, and Apollo, and Cephas are ours, and we Christ's, and Christ God's.

But see, whiles I thought but to have touched the generall argument of this chapter, to prove that the church of Christ ought to be built in all things according to the wil of Christ as he hath set downe in his Testament (otherwise it can neither be said his house, nor the builders therof or builded therin his faithful servantes); see how before I wist or would, I am drawne into particulars as into a whirlepoole and bottomles gulph of knowledg, whiles I thought but to have drawne but a litle water at the brinke in the shallow vessel of my understanding and crazed memory: which though they be no way able to breake up these unmeasured depthes, or orderly to deliver but that litle God giveth me to see in them; yet I doubt not but many infallible arguments may from this chapter be drawn without any violence or wresting to prove the necessity and perpetuity of that forme and order of building and governing Christ's church, which he by his apostles hath set downe in his Testament. Now let me proceed to confirme this proposition by other reasons drawn from other places of Scripture.

As it hath beene shewed that there can be no true building without that only true foundation and expresse patterne of the apostles' practice in Christ's Testament, that all other foundations, formes, buildings, builders, are deceitful and false, and wil not abide the fiery trial or stand in God's sight; so if we consider the manner how the Holy Ghost instructeth us in other places, *vz.*, 1 Corinthians 12, Ephesians, Romans 12, we shall there see the congruence, necessity, perpetuity of the order and government which Christ hath in his Testament prescribed. We there read this his church compared to an humane body, which consisting of divers members, [209] must of necessitie have them duly placed and knit together in their right order and frame. We reade there that as God createth, fashioneth, placeth and knitteth together the members of this our earthly bodie without taking councel of one or another; so in like wisdome and power he createth, prepareth, ordereth, disposeth, commingleth, contempereth al the members of this his heavenlie bodie according to the rules of his Testament by the manifestation of the spirit in everie one.[1] But now even common sense teacheth how far the wisest man upon earth is from being able to make unto man's bodie the least member therof even but one haire white or blacke, much lesse to knit the members together by jointes and sinewes in their due place and function. How then can dust and ashes imagine to make unto the spirituall bodie of Christ new strange members and knit them as strangely together by new jointes and synewes. We reade in these chapters, that the ministers and officers appointed by our saviour Christ in his Testament, are the principal members of this publike bodie of the church; his ordinances and lawes there set downe, the jointes and sinewes wherby the members are fitly knit unto the whole bodie, even as the curtaines of the tabernacle by their strings and hookes.[2]

But now as no mortal man can make, fashion, dispose or knit together these humane members of a naturall bodie, so much lesse can he make anie other members serve in the places of the true natural members, or by anie meanes place, fasten, and knit these as by joints and sinewes unto and in a man's bodie. What use should a man have of an eie of glasse, a nose of waxe, an hand of brasse, a foot of wood? What congruence, coherence, proportion, sympathie, feeling, compassion should these have with the other members? What learning or art can knit these by jointes, sinewes, vaines, artures?[3] Or draw one and the same skin over them as a covering, or fasten it unto them as unto or together with the true and natural members? If man's wisdome cannot effect this in a fraile humane bodie of

---

[1] Romans 12: 4; I Corinthians 12: 12, 14-27; Ephesians 2: 21, 22; 3: 16; 5: 30.
[2] I Corinthians 12: 28-31; Ephesians 4: 11, 12.
[3] Veins, arteries.

earth and clay, what possibilitie then is there to bring
this to passe in the spiritual bodie of Christ? What
communion, what commixture can there be betwixt
heaven and earth, betwixt light and darknes, betwixt
spirituall and carnal things? How then is it possible
to knit or make agree the earthly darke carnal divised
members and lawes of man, to the heavenlie lightsome
spiritual bodie of Christ? Yea, albeit this could be
supposed to be brought to passe (than which nothing
can be more fonde [foolish] than to imagine, more
wicked than to attempt), what kind of strange and
monstrous bodie should they now make unto Christ,
by knytting unto him strange members, such as belong
not to his bodie? If an humane bodie should have
growing unto it anie other than the true members that
belonge unto a man, were not such a creature to be
held a monster and not a man? As for example: if
it had manie heades in steade of one, if it should have
feete like a beare, a mouth as a lion, the rest like a

Revel. 13

leopard, *etc.*, who (that had anie sight or sense) could
take and esteeme this [210] for the natural bodie of
man? Much lesse for the comely beawtiful amiable
bodie of Christ or of his bride: were not this to be liker
unto the bodie of antichrist, that beast, of that whore,
that monster? What then is the presumption, rebellion and furie of those prelates that dare enterprise not
onlie to cast away the true and naturall members, but
in the place of them to plant these adulterate mon-
trous members, and that (as they would make themselves and others beleeve) in the bodie and church of
Christ. Againe, what an astonishment and madnes
hath invaded and possessed these learned reforming
priests, that confesse the want of al Christ's true
members (I meane such officers as he hath ordeined
for the building and governing his church), that complaine likewise of the unlawfulnes and antichristianitie
of these members which now grow upon this bodie and
governe the same; and yet discerne not themselves to
be of these monstrous antichristian members, even the
ministerie and mouth of that beast, having the same
original, shape and forme with them, being all come

out of one smokie forge, *etc.*; yea, and for all this, mistake that beastlie bodie of the harlot their church that beareth, groweth unto, and consisteth of these members, for that heavenlie bodie, that true spouse and established church of Christ; as though Christ's bodie, Christ's church, could grow unto and consist of these false members, or be said built and established without the true members. What strange paradoxes are these, yet are they even the forwardest positions they can be drawen unto.

But we are taught in these Scriptures, that Christ's bodie consisteth not, neither can his church be built with such strange antichristian members, or with anie other than those which he hath there prescribed for the gathering the saints into one, for the worke of the ministerie and for the edification of the bodie of Christ, *etc.* From which Scriptures infinite reasons (if we would enter into particulers) might be drawen to proove the necessitie, congruence and perpetuitie of these officers and ordinances there prescribed to the ministerie, government, and service of his church. But that were to handle the whole platforme and order of Christ's Testament, the excellencie and perfection wherof but slightly to describe, as it far exceedeth my slender capacitie, so not being to this present purpose, I have onlie indevored to use such general reasons as might proove this generall proposition: That the government and ordinances that Christ in his Testament hath set downe and apointed unto his church are necessare, onlie fit and perpetuall, and that the true church of Christ can or may no more receave anie other officers, government and ordinances, than the bodie of a man can receave other members, the members an other order or temperature, than that which God hath assigned.[1]

---

[1] Barrow is strict — constructionist. Bishop Cooper in 1589 and Richard Hooker in 1594—7, more liberal, less literal, more flexible, made allowance for time and place, for novel and special circumstances, for historical evolution and peculiar need, but Barrow contended that differences in various countries during the preceding twelve to fifteen centuries should not alter the fixed prescribed pattern established by the New Testament. It is often true that the specific viewpoint depends on the general point of view, as seen in the differences between Alexander Hamilton and Thomas Jefferson, between Calvinism and Lutheranism, or between Jesuit and Jansenist.

Which I hope by these places is so manifest, as I need stand no longer to inforce the necessitie and onlie fit congruence therof unto the bodie and members of the church; by shewing either the comelines, beautie, features of the church when it is thus furnished of these true members, and the members [211] thus placed, built together, ordered and used. The necessitie of these, let common sense and experience in the base patterne of our owne naturall bodie shew, how ill we could either admit anie other than those members that God hath apointed therunto, or spare anie of those members, or have them kept from their true use and peculiar function, or placed in anie other order or place, or knit together with anie other jointes, sinewes or vaines than God hath disposed for them. But the heavenlie spirituall beautie, order, congruence and use of these members thus commixt and contempered, let the fourth, sixth and seventh chapter of Solomon's Song declare. From all which together and everie member apart, the use, administration, and benefite therof; as also from the disorder, infinite inconveniences and mischeifes that would ensue of the rejecting of this or receaving any other order, government, administration, might infinite and severall arguments be drawen to prove the absolute necessitie of the one, the utter inhibition and unfitnes of any other.

But heere now fitly commeth a certaine objection of the aforesaid D.R.S.[1] to be answered. Saith he, If that outward forme of discipline were of the essence of the church, then where that forme of discipline either was or is not, there was and is no church, which is a grosse absurditie. My reasons are, Samaria had not that forme of discipline, but it was a famous church, Actes 8. Antiochia had not that forme of discipline, yet it was a floorishing church. The greatest part of reformed churches in Christendome have not that forme of discipline, yet they are accompted holie churches of all but of the Papistes and Anabaptistes.[2]

---

[1] Dr. Robert Some.
[2] This paragraph is quoted from Dr. Some's *A Godly Treatise, wherein Are Examined and Confuted Many Execrable Fancies*, p. 34.

A Brief Discoverie of the False Church

What his doctorhood meaneth by these disguised
termes of the discipline and essence of the church I
understand not, and therfore wil leave them where I
find them, eschewing (according to the apostle's rule)
such profane inanitie of words and oppositions of science
falsly so called, which some professing, have erred about
the faith. But if he by these reasons suppose to have
impugned the necessitie and perpetuity of Christ's holie
government and order wherinto the apostles built all
churches, and which they left unto all churches: I shal
then briefely shew how far he faileth of that purpose,
and reasoneth quite to a new and divers question, and
therfore can therby conclude nothing against this. For
our question heere is not, whither the church may not
sometime upon some necessities be without this order
or some part therof for a season, but whither the church
may receave anie other forme of government in stead of
this. So that if he had prooved that the churches of
Samaria and Antiochia had received anie other forme
of government and order than this apostolick; then had
he in deed said somwhat (although a particular instance
or two may not take away or draw us from a generall law
and perpetuall rule). But he trifling about the name
of a church, quite forsaking the question, would infer
from the [212] ambiguitie of the word, that because a
church upon some necessities may for a season be without this established order and government; therfore
they may reject this and take an other according to the
pollicies of the time and place. How diversly the
church is read in the Scriptures (not heere to stand of
the etymologie of the word *ecclesia*) me thinkes this great
divine should not be ignorant: how sometimes it is read
for all the saints in heaven and in earth; sometimes for
all the saints dispersed or gathered heere in the whole
world; sometimes for a companie of faithfull people
joined together in the covenant and communion of the
faith, indevoring to proceed into the order of Christ,
and in the same faithfully to walke together. But
commonly it is taken for a companie of such faithful

thus entered covenant,[1] established and walking in due order according to the rules of God's word; of which kinde of church we al this while reason. For their Church of England is not now unestablished as Samaria and Antiochia were at these times he speaketh of, but it is established into an order, ministerie, and government, though according to the pope's cannons and not according to the Testament of Christ. So that he might as well have reasoned from anie of the other readings of a church, and gained as much; *scilzt*:[2] that because all the saints in heaven are called a church, yet they have not pastors, teachers, *etc.*, therfore the church of Christ may be established without these: as also al the dispersed saints are called a church, yet have not this order and government; therfore, *etc.*, Samaria and Antiochia at their first calling to the faith had not this established order and government, yet were held famous and floorishing churches; therfore the church may be established into an other forme of order and government than that of Christ's Testament: this if he conclude not, he gaineth nothing; this if he conclude, I denie his argument. It followeth not because the church is not alwaies thus established, therfore it ought not to be thus established.

The churches of Samaria and Antiochia neither can be shewed to have received anie other order or government, or to have neglected this; but the contrarie apeareth of Samaria, Acts 9: 31, where Luke recordeth, that the churches throughout al Judea, Galile and Samaria had peace, being built and proceeding in the feare of the Lord, and were replenished with the comfort of the Holy Ghost. What thinketh Dr. Some now? Was not Samaria built and established in this order? Unles he can shew that the apostles built the churches in anie other order; and then from this place may he also conclude, that the churches in Judea and Galile were not thus built, this Scripture not secretly shewing

---

[1] The meaning is not clear. One reading might be: " thus entered [into the] covenant." Another possibility is: " thus entered, covenant[ed], established . . . "

[2] Probably " scilicet " is intended, namely. *Videlicet* is sometimes abbreviated *vidzt.*, *viz.*, and *vz.*

that both they were all built alike, and that there was
but one order of building amongst the apostles in these
wordes (being edified or built). Me thinks this place
also sheweth some letts that sometime may hinder the
churches from this holy order; namely, the tyrannie of
wicked magistrates who persecute the church in such
sort as they cannot safelie meete and assemble to make
choice of ministers, or to exercise anie ministerie. But
wee see the [213] churches here upon the first meanes
neglected not either to attaine unto or exercise this
order (and that without staiing for the magistrate's
permission) and were in so doing replenished with the
comfort of the Holy Ghost. Neither yet appeareth
heere the certaine time when Samaria was thus built.
It is not unlike that it was established into this order,
even Actes 8 (that he speaketh of) when they receaved
the gifts of the Holy Ghost at Peter and John's being
there, who it is to be judged likewise, rather helped to
bestow those gifts in order to the edifiing of the whole,
than left them (having fit gifts for these offices) in disorder, which had beene great sinne both in the apostles
and in the church of Samaria.

The like also is to be thought of the church at
Antiochia, Acts 11, they being called to the faith were
a long time instructed by the apostles Barnabas and
Paule, God so blessed their labours as that church grew
famous, and many prophets resorted thither from
Jerusalem. May we then by Dr. Some's bare affirmation without any proofe affirme that this church being
so long and excellently instructed by these famous men,
having so greatly profited in the faith and knowledg of
Christ above many other churches which had this order,
that they yet should thus long be kept from it more than
any other church, being more fit than many, yea than
any other church at that time, save Jerusalem? This
were not only contrary to the practise of Paul and
Barnabas in al other churches, but contrarie to the rules
of Christ's Testament. But if we would stand upon the
point, it were not hard to prove that Antiochia was then
established into order: we see they were administred
unto the necessities of other churches, and sent Paul and

U

Barnabas upon this their busines, which they having
fulfilled returned back againe to Antiochia; from whence
by the whole church they were at the commandement
of the Holy Ghost sent out with imposition of handes.
Afterward when they had planted and established manie
churches in Asia into this order, they returned thither
againe and there remained a long time until they were
againe sent to Jerusalem about the question of circumcision; which being debated, they with other famous
men returned and abode in the Church of Antiochia,
preaching and teaching the gospell with great joy, comfort, and blessing. Yet in none of these places we find
mentioned that after Acts 11. they were established into
this order; but we see that there and in all these places
they executed the duties, and had the full power of a
church established. Therfore except we wil make the
practise of the Holy Ghost contrary unto it self, we are
not to doubt but this Antiochia also was established in
this order. Doth not Dr. Some then unsufferably both
falsifie and pervert these Scriptures, in affirming that
these churches had not that established order amongst
them, concluding from their example that the christian
order and government of Christ's Testament is neither
necessarie nor perpetuall.

But to conclude and shut up the point at once, he
bringeth the greatest part of the reformed churches of
Christendome which have not this [214] christian order
and government (which he termeth forme of discipline),
yet are accompted holy churches of al but papists, and
Anabaptists.[1] Doth he not heere very learnedly prove
the question by the question: if his church be of God,
let him approve it by God's word, otherwise though he
should fetch the pope's broade seale also (from whome
he borroweth this argument) it would not serve his
turne. With the estate of other churches I am not
acquainted, and therfore will not meddle: but how
well this holy Church of England is reformed, you partly
may perceave by that which is above said; and more
evidently may, if you measure it by the rules of Christ's

[1] Some, *A Godly Treatise, wherein Are Examined and Confuted Many
Execrable Fancies,* p. 34.

Testament, according unto which it hath no one thing in due order or frame. So that why either papists or Anabaptists should denie it, I cannot see; it being an uncleane hould or prison of everie uncleane bird, of everie fowle and hatefull spirit, except it be as that kingdome divided in it self, because it consisteth of such jarring and disagreeing spirits. Neither can I see how any (that knoweth or wil be instructed what a true established church of Christ is) can anie longer mistake that adulterous Church of England that sitteth upon all the confuse people as upon manie waters, that is liker unto Zennacherib's tumultuous campe,[1] than unto the wel ordered and established church of Christ, which hath nothing common with Christ's church but the verie name only. For the true church of Christ, we find upon her all the markes of that harlot and of that beast, whose members, image, yoke, she carieth, and hath cast off Christ's yoke from her necke, despising his word, persecuting and murdering his servants. Wherfore untill she bring us either better arguments or better fruits, we are so far from honoring her with the title of a church, as we are not abashed to render unto her as she hath rendred unto us; and to double unto her double, according to her workes; and in that cup wherin she hath mixed, to mingle to her the double. So far are we from giving that authoritie unto her in this presumptuous sin, as to draw an argument from, or be induced to thinke by her example, that because she casteth off Christ's yoke and beareth antichrist's, therfore the holy order and ordinances of Christ for the building, ministery, and government of his church is not perpetuall, necessarie, or alwaies expedient.

I grant that the true church of Christ may sometimes upon some necessities be without this holy order for a season, as in the first gathering of the saints, especially now when we are not to expect anie such miraculous or extraordinarie giving of God's spirit as was in the primitive times, when we cannot sodenly either be made fit for these high offices, or have such perfect knowledg

---

[1] See Isaiah 37: 36, which records the slaying of 185,000 in Sennacherib' camp by the angel of the Lord.

and probation ech of others' giftes and conversation as is required therunto. Also in time of persecution when the church cannot peaceably meet either to chuse or exercise anie ministerie, or that their chief and principall members be held from them in prisons, or at such time as the chief elders are taken away either by death or otherwise fall away. In these and such like times the church may for a season upon necessitie so inforcing [215] be without this established order: but this is neither willinglie to neglect it, nor presumptuously to reject it. Heerehence it followeth not that this holie order is not alwaies necessarie, because it is not nor cannot be alwaies executed. So they might conclude all God's lawes not always necessarie, perpetuall, or expedient, because they are not or cannot be always practised by us. Should our infirmitie, sinne or default take away the stabilitie or truth of God's ordinances? This would as wel follow of this their reason, as the other: that because the church of Christ may at sometimes be without this established order of Christ and yet be held the true church, therfore that prescribed order of Christ is not perpetuall, alwaies necessarie, or convenient: thus laiing the default upon Christ's sacred ordinances, as though they were not alwaies holy, necessarie, and convenient, which in deed is due to us and our infirmitie and inhabilitie to receave or exercise such a gratious blessed ministerie, or to walke in this heavenly order.

Nothing is more sure than this, the true church can be established into no other order, it can receave none other officers or lawes than are in Christ's Testament prescribed. This hath beene already manifestly proved and yet further might be, by as many places of Scriptures as either the true or false church is spoken of, the true or false ministerie, the true or false ministration; as either Christ's kingdome or anie of his officers are spoken of, or antichrist's presumption and forgerie: as it hath beene proved by the true patterne of the house wherby every part therof ought to be framed and put together according to the will of the Lord of the house, otherwise the house will never hang together or be to the owner's liking or the builder's praise. Likewise it hath by the necessitie, congruence, coherence of the true and natural partes and members of the bodie beene proved, how that no other can be added, without making it a monstrous bodie; neither the true members be otherwise knit together, placed, disposed, used, without the destruction of the whole bodie: and this much more of that spiritual house and bodie of Christ's church; which being so perfect, pretious, comely, excellent, cannot admit to be shaped, fashioned, framed, disposed after the fansies of earthly men, who the best of them that ever was (alwaies excepting the head of the church) in his best consideration, was but a member of the church. Neither was there ever power given to anie of them, whether prince or prophet whosoever or authoritie to alter, neglect, or bring in anie pinne or hooke (even the least thing) or so much as the place therof in the tabernacle, temple, or church of God.

How often doth the church in the Song of Solomon say: " My beloved is mine[3] and I am his "; and how often doth she charge all her freinds to stay without, and not to stir up her welbeloved until he please ? How often doth she vow to keepe her self wholy unto him ? How often doth he againe repeate the amiablenes, comlines, beawty, congruence, features, fruitefulnes, plea-[216]santnes of all her partes even from top to toe ? How greatly he is delighted in her, and how the kings of the earth should be tyed in her rafters, *etc.* Doth not he say that Solomon and earthly princes may put or let out their vineyeards (not being able themselves to till and dresse them) to be dressed and trimmed to their servants, reserving to themselves a rent, *etc.* But his vineyard is always before him, he is able to til, dresse, and keepe it every whit himself, he neither letteth it out to hire, nor suffreth anie to part or possesse the fruite therof with him.

How many arguments then might be drawen either from the perfection, divine order, *etc.*, of the partes of the church, from the faith, love, chastitie, obedience unto Christ as to her husband, lord, king ? Likewise, how

---

2 This phrase occurs twice in the Song of Solomon, 2: 16 and 6: 3. The phrase " my beloved " or " beloved " occurs thirty-two times.

many [arguments] from his absolute power, authority, possession over her wholly by the right of an husband, lord, king. How many reasons might be drawen from the absolutnes and wisdome of his lawes, the graciousnes and peace of his heavenly government and order (which cannot be willingly infringed or broken without rebellion, nor changed and altered without presumptuous treason) to prove the perpetuity, necessity, and fit congruence of those officers and ordinances that he in his Testament hath prescribed for the building, ministery, and government of his church and of every member therof, whither prince or minister over whome Christ

Isa. 60: 12   reigneth by equal right, and even the same jurisdiction that he doth over the least. There is no exception or

Joh. 3: 36   acceptation of persons with God. That nation and

Luke 19: 27   that kingdome that will not serve him shall perish, and those nations shalbe utterly destroied. He that obeieth not the Sonne shall not see life, but the wrath of God abideth upon him. Those that will not have him to reigne over them he judgeth and destroieth as enemies. Christ reigneth by his owne officers, which it is lawfull at no hand for his true subjects either to disobey, alter, or reject. Subjects and servants are not to give, but to take lawes at their king and lord. God hath made his Sonne Lord and heire of al things, and hath given

Phil. 2: 10, *etc.*   him a name above every name, that at the name of Jesus every knee should bow both of heavenly things and earthly things and things under the earth, and every tongue should confesse that Jesus Christ is the Lord unto the glorie of God his Father, because all men should honour the Sonne as they honour the Father.

Joh. 5: 23   He that honoureth not the Sonne honoureth not the Father that sent him.

O how great then is their wickednes, how pernitious their councell, who (for filthy lucre sake) perswade princes that they are not only not subject themselves in person to the lawes and spiritual censures of Christ in his church; but that they are not bownd to admit that order of government prescribed in his Testament (which they shuffle off with the terme of outward discipline) in their landes ? May not, yea, doe not princes

by this meanes bouldly breake all God's lawes, and
disanull anie of them at their pleasures? Breake that
they may follow their owne heart's lusts, fulfilling the
inordinate appetites therof, wallowing [217] and glut-
ting themselves in all fleshlie pleasure, vanitie, and
excesse, committing what wickednes they wil without
admonition, censure or reproofe (I would heere still
be understood of the ecclesiastical spiritual censures by
the word). May they not yet proceed further and
disanul which of God's lawes they list, either in common
welth or church? In the common welth, when they
both abrogate all God's judicial lawes and cut them off
at one blow, as made and belonging to the common
welth of the Jewes onlie (as though God [had] no regard
of the conversation of other Christians his servantes also)
or els had left some other peculiar lawes for the manners
of the Gentiles, or had left them in greater libertie to be
and to make lawes and customes unto themselves.
Heerupon it commeth to passe, that so manie wicked
ungodlie lawes and customes are decreed; that the
whole order and course of judgment and justice is
constuprate[1] and perverted, that so manie capital mischeifes as God punished by death, as blaspheming the
name of God, open idolatrie, disobedience to parents,
are not by law punished at al; incest, adulterie, either
psssed over or punished by some lighter trifling chas-
ticement; wilfull murther often pardoned; theft (if it
be above 13 pence) punished by death:[2] yea, this sin
is punished not only in the person of the theefe (who
that wise king saied if he should steale seven times, may
yet live and satisfie with his body or goodes) but in the
persons of al such as this their unjust law judgeth anie
way accessarie; which extendeth so far, as manie honest
men may for this trifle for buying or receaving part of
these stollen goodes, be also put to death and forfait al
the lands and goodes they have; wherby their wives,

---

[1] Violated.
[2] Barrow is urging that English law be brought into line with Mosaic legis-
lation. Bishop Thomas Cooper took the opposite point of view when he
warned his readers that if the reformers prevailed, the judicial law of the
Jews would apply, and that an English judge would be unable to punish
theft by the death penalty. *An Admonition to the People of England*,
p. 87.

children, and families are punished also and utterlie undone. And thus by this their pollicie are manie theeves made for one; not to speake of al this guiltles blood that is upon the head of the magistrate, judg, officers, jurie, and the whole land by this meanes: what should I stand to particulate their infinite transgressions of God's lawes even in their civil estate, which is in much worse case than manie heathen nations which never knew God or his Christ. Al this ariseth of this immunitie from the order, government, and censure of Christ in his church, and from the inordinate authoritie the apostaticall church giveth unto princes and magistrates, and they assume unto themselves: so that the saying of the prophet concerning the proude kings of Babel is now rightly verified in them. "Thow didst say with thy heart, I will ascend into heaven above the stars of God almightie, I wil exalt my throne and wil sit in the mountaine of the congregation in the sides of the north, I will ascend above the heigth of the clowdes, I wil make myself equall unto the most high."[1]

For see, whiles they take power to reject that holie government, order, officers, lawes, that Christ our King hath ordeined and apointed to his church, they stretch their hand also and presume further, to erect a new government, new orders, lawes, officers, ministry, ministration, *etc*. And what is this but both to reproove Christ's lawes and to reject his yoke from them, and also to take Christ's offices, throne and scepter from [218] him, whome the Lord hath set upon the throne of David to order and stablish it with judgment and justice, and laid the key of government upon his shoulder, that what he openeth no man should shut, and what he shutteth no man should open.

How great then is their pride and presumption that are so far from obeiing and seing Christ's lawes executed, as they utterly abrogate them and take them out of the way, and set up their owne idol divises in the stead of them? So far are they from taking lawes at him as their King and Lord, as they give lawes of him as King and Lord. Is not this to denie, nay, to put an

[1] Isaiah 14: 13, 14.

end to his ministerie and kingdome ? To his ministery,
by taking away that which he established, and bringing
in a new [ordinance] into the church; to his kingdome,
by abrogating his lawes, offices, ordinances, and by
bringing in and establishing their owne. In so much as
through the odious flattery of these their priests, some of
them have suffered themselves to be called the supreme
head of Christ's church in earth,[1] as though Christ's
church had one head in earth and an other in heaven,
or that Christ were not the head of his church here in
earth also. But the wretched priests would excuse this
inaudible blasphemie with this interpretation (which
yet they expresse not) 1. under Christ, as though
Christ's church might have two heades, an upper and
an under head one above an other: were not this to
make her a monster like their church, which hath manie
heads, and upon them written names of blasphemy, as
supreme head of the church, primate bishop, metropolitane bishop, lord archbishop's grace, lord bishop
and archdeacon, *etc.* Al which heads, but especially
that their supreme head of the church, may (they say)
make lawes for the church. And al this execrable
blasphemy they hide under the title and office of the
civil magistrate, who in deed is God's blessed ordinance.

Neither wil these lymmes of the devill be satisfied
with any humble acknowledgment of the civil power,
or with anie christian submission unto the same; but
wil extort by othe an allowance and subscription unto
this their ungodly power, blasphemous titles, antichristian decrees and proceedings, *etc.* It wil not
suffice to confesse that God hath made the civil magistrate the keeper of the booke of the law, to see both

---

[1] The Supremacy Act of 1534 designated Henry VIII, his heirs and successors, as the " only supreme head in earth of the Church of England,
called *Anglicana Ecclesia.*" This Act was repealed in Mary's reign by
Parliament in 1554, and in the first year of Elizabeth's reign, the Supremacy
Act of 1559 continued the repeal. The oath of supremacy of 1559 required ecclesiastical and temporal officials to take a corporal oath, testi-
fying belief that " the queen's highness is the only supreme governor of
this realm, and of all other her highness's dominions and countries, as well
in all spiritual or ecclesiastical things or causes, as temporal, and that no
foreign prince, person, prelate, state, or potentate, has, or ought to have,
any jurisdiction, power, superiority, pre-eminence, or authority ecclesiastical or spiritual, within this realm."

U*

the tables therof observed by al persons both in the church and common welth, and so hath power over both church and common welth; but they must have this indefinite proposition granted them: that a prince hath power to make lawes for the church. By which word *making* is implied, or rather (as the general estate both of church and common welth shew) expressed plainly that they meane that the prince may devise and make new lawes for the church such as are not heard of in that booke of God. By lawes they meane any traditions, ordinances, customes, *etc.*, which are not prescribed in Christ's Testament; otherwise why should they use these words or urge that power of making lawes. A godly prince is bound to God's lawe, made the keeper therof, not the controler; the servant, not the Lord. God hath in that booke made most perfect and necessary lawes both for church and common welth: he requireth of the king and [219] magistrate to see these lawes executed, and not to make new. He that maketh any new lawes taketh unto him the office of God, who is the onlie lawmaker: al men of what estate soever are but God's creatures, servantes, and subjectes to his law. Moses, Joshua, Samuel, David, Hezekiah, made no new lawes, but revived and executed the olde lawes which God had made. These examples that miserable man and high traitor to God and his prince, Robert Some, citeth to proove that princes may make lawes for the church and common welth, therby indevoring to deteine and hold her majestie and the honorable magistrates of this land in this presumptuous breach of al God's lawes in this church and common welth, by causing them to ratifie and publish the ungodlie decrees which that blasphemous High Commission hath made or shal heerafter make, under this pretext, that christian princes have power to make lawes for the church.[1]

Which Commission and al their proceedings, because they can no way be justified by the law of God and Testament of Christ, but are directly contrarie unto the same (as shal straight way be prooved), therfore

---

[1] Some, *A Godly Treatise, wherein Are Examined and Confuted Many Execrable Fancies,* pp. 13-16.

that old lymme of antichrist, that crowned horne of
the beast, that T.C.,[1] breatheth out of the mouth of
the dragon most hellish blasphemie against Christ's
tabernacle and them that dwel in the heaven, accusing
Christ's blessed order and manner of government, of
sedition, tumults, disobedience unto the civil estate, as
giving the raines [reins] to the people's unbrideled and
inordinate appetites which can not be restreined, subverting al magistracie and the whole order of the
common welth.[2]

Had that beast anie religion that thus blesphemed
Christ's ordinance? Have not the heathen at al times
thus reproched and accused the word of God and gospel
of Christ? Yet what is more free of these crimes, than
this order they so accuse, wherof Christ himself is the
author and preserver. Is it not the fellowship and
communion? And have such sinnes anie fellowship
with him? Before anie can enter or be receaved into
this fellowship, he must be renewed by repentance,
deniing all his fleshly conversation concerning the time
past; he must be begotten by that immortall seed; he
must be borne againe of water and the spirit, and enter
as a new borne babe and as a child wained [weaned]
from the brests; he must leave al his venome and fiercenes, and become as a meeke lambe obedient unto his
shepheardes. At what time anie is found disobedient
and headstrong or incorrigible, he forthwith looseth his
place in this communion and fellowship, he is seperate
and cast out.

As for their order of their assemblie, it is not tumul-
tious or contentious, but rather an heavenlie schoole of
all order, sobrietie and modestie, which the angels with
great delight behold, everie one there knowing his
calling, place, and boundes, which he without present
blame may not breake; as free, but not having that
libertie as a cloke of wickednes, but as the servantes of
God; whose law is heere purelie and sincerelie taught,
every estate and degree instructed how they ought to
walke and behave themselves towardes God and men

---

[1] Bishop Thomas Cooper.
[2] *An Admonition to the People of England,* pp. 23-30, 36, 86-89, 92-94, 229.

in al manner con-[220]versation. Nothing more or more often inculcate, than to yeild due honour, obedience, submission, unto all magistrates, parentes, superiors, and that not for fashion sake or ignorantly, but as of knowledg, faith and conscience towardes God. Hereunto, as also unto al other duties they are continuallie instructed, exhorted; whosoever transgresseth is admonished, censured, and (without present repentance and amendment) dulie cast out of this fellowship and communion, where no inordinate walking or contumacious persons are suffered.

Who then but that old Sathan or some sonne of his, could thus accuse the lambes, the babes, these litle ones of Christ, of rebellion, sedition, tumult, *etc.*? What mouth els could reproch and blaspheme that heavenlie gratious blessed order of Christ in his church of subverting common welths, destroiing civil magistracie and government?[1] Without which holie ordinance and magistracie as there can be no church, no assemblie, no execution of law, no callings, no trades, no order, no safetie amongst men; so without this instruction, government, and holie order of the church can no estate, no magistracie, be blessed of God, because without this they can neither know nor execute their duties, neither walke holily or lawfully in their callings, or doe anie thing that may please God. Who then but these uncleane spirits that speake out of the mouth of that dragon, and out of the mouth of that beast, and out of the mouth of that false prophet, could in this manner disjoine those that God hath so neerlie joined? Widowing and spoiling the church of that comfort and assistance she should have of the civil magistrate, depriving the civil magistrates of that instruction and joy they should have in the church.

As we have above alledged, that nation or common welth, prince, magistrate, estate, degree, person, whosoever that submitteth not to our Lord Jesus Christ to be wholy governed by his word both bodie and soule in al things whatsoever without anie exception, reservation, or pollitike respect; that nation, prince, magistrate,

1 *Ibid.,* pp. 85-94, 141-4.

person, soule shall be utterlie destroyed amongst Christ's enemies. So Christ may not neither wil be fashioned or framed to anie common welth, pollicie or pleasure of anie prince: he is Lord of lords and King of kings; al the kingdoms of this world are his, and he shal reigne for evermore: those that are not under his scepter of grace, those he will rule with a red [rod] of yron, those shal be broken as a potter's vessels. So far then is this heavenlie and blessed government of Christ in his church by his word (to which everie soule that will be saved must be subject) from being the overthrow of anie common welth or lawfull estate therof, that you see it is the only foundation of the one, and stablishment of the other, a perfect rule for both, to which all lawes, pollicies, states, degrees, persons, in al actions, must be framed and subject. To which whatsoever is contrarie or transgressing, whither common welth, common, cannon, or civil lawes, their judges, pleaders, courts, must either be reformed or consumed therby. No titles, pollicies, pleas, or prerogatives can ex-[221]cuse them from or before that judge who upholdeth, governeth, and judgeth all things by that his word, and with the same sifteth and fanneth out whatsoever is found contrarie to his will. To which government and trial of his word, because they will not submit their persons and proceedings, therfore with one consent all the estates and degrees of the land, prince, priests and people, hate him, and send by their elders an embassage after him, that they will not have him to reigne over them, accusing his government of innovation, dangerous to their state, pernitious to the whole land, *etc.* Thus take they boldnes to breake his bands and cast his yoke from them, to transgresse his lawes, change his ordinances, and to breake the everlasting covenant, even that Testament purchased for them and sealed unto them with that pretious blood of the giver. Therfore hangeth the wrath of God over them, the day of his vengeance hasteneth, feare and a pit and a snare are upon them. He that flieth from the noise of the feare shall fall into the pit, and he that commeth out of the pit shalbe taken in the snare, for the windowes from on high are open, and the foundations of the earth doe shake. The earth is utterlie broken, the earth is quite burst in sunder, the earth is moved exceedingly, the earth shall reele too and froe like a drunken man and shalbe re-mooved like a tent, and the defection therof shalbe heavy upon it, so that it shall fall and rise no more because the land is defiled under the inhabitants ther-of;[1] for they transgresse the lawes, they change the ordinances, and breake the everlasting covenant.

There remaineth yet an other question of this ould captious Sadducie,[2] wherin he requireth to have noted unto him some particular churches either in the apostles' time or since, wherin the whole govern-ment of the church was practised only by doctors, pastors, elders and deacons and none other, and that in an equalitie without superioritie in one above an other.[3]

To satisfie his demands in this cavilling question (which evidently apeareth to be made rather for a snare than anie godly edifiing) I hold neither lawfull nor expedient, until he have acknowledged and yeilded unto the former: namely, unto the necessity and per-petuity of that order of government and administration which Christ in his Testament hath prescribed, which he hath miserably violated, rejected and blasphemed. That in this estate to shew him the treasures and ordin-ances of this spirituall temple is utterly forbidden and unlawfull, appeareth, Ezekiel 43: 10, 11, in these words: " Thow Sonne of man, shew unto the howse of Israel this house when they shal be ashamed of their wickednes, that they may measure the patterne "; when (I say) they shalbe ashamed of all they have done, make knowen unto them the forme of the howse, and the constitution therof, the goings out therof, and the com-ming in therof, and the whole forme therof, and all the statutes therof, and all the figures [222] therof, and all the lawes therof, and describe them before their eies, that they may keep the whole fashion therof, and al the

---

[1] These three sentences, beginning with " feare and a pit " come from Isaiah 24: 17-20.
[2] Thomas Cooper, Bishop of Winchester.
[3] *An Admonition to the People of England*, p. 81.

ordinances therof, and do them. Therfore until he have repented and forsaken his antichristian ministery, unlawfull lordship and jurisdiction, I hold it not lawfull whilest he remaineth in and will not come out of Babel to reason or jangle with him concerning the heavenly and most holy ordinances of Sion, which he doth but blaspheme and reproch with his ungodly mouth that is opened to all impietie. That it is not expedient untill he have yeilded unto the former question to answere this, is manifest. For to what purpose were it to reason with him how these officers of Christ's church ought to administer and governe, when he utterly denieth that in the Church of England such offices and jurisdiction were tollerable. So that it could no way edifie him, but rather minister matter of cavil unto his blasphemous mouth, who seeketh nothing els in this captious (yet with al most ignorant and fond) vaine question. We ought not to cast our pearles before swine, or to expose the Lord's holy truth to reproch. This is my answere to him concerning his second question.[1]

Yet to remove these stumbling blockes out of the way of others, and to rid them out of the snares which this spider hath woven; I will through God's grace briefly shew them the errors and follie of this cavilling question, cheifly in these three pointes therof. First, in that he requireth some particular churches by name, wherin this whole government of the church was practised, *etc.*; secondly, when it was practised by doctors, elders, pastors, deacons only and none other; thirdly, where these practised it in an equalitie without superioritie in one above an other. In the first point he stumbleth and cavilleth at this, because in deed no church that ever was or shalbe upon earth hath or can fully execute this government of Christ (but have beene and shalbe subject to many defalts, many transgressions), taking here the government of Christ for his whole revealed will in his word and Testament; to the faithfull observation of

---

[1] Bishop Cooper's first question or challenge was, in effect, a denial " that there should bee in all ages and states of the church of Christ, one onely forme of outwarde governement." The second question pertains to doctors, pastors, elders, and deacons, as the true and only officers in the church.

every title wherof the church is by covenant bound (where by the way must be noted, that this carping Pharisey knoweth in his corrupt and festered conscience what Christ's true government is, which he so mainly impugneth, namely, that righteous scepter of his holy word) which in deed because none of the primitive churches that the apostles planted and governed could ever fully keep, but have beene subject to manie faltes and reproofes; therfor this man would conclude this government of Christ to be an unnecessarie and impossible thing, which God neither would command nor we can performe. Wherin his wickednes and impietie yet proceedeth a degree further than that of the tollerating priests; who would excuse and defend their most hainous transgressions by the sinnes and defaltes of other churches; this man therby would utterlie abrogate and disanull the whole law of God, and Testament of Christ, by which the church ought to be governed, unto the faithfull practise and observation wherof the whole church is bownd. Can the infirmity and sin of any mortal creatures take [223] away the truth and stabilitie of God's lawes, of Christ's Testament ? Might he not as wel conclude, no church or member of the church hath at any time put in practise al God's lawes, and to say (as it is) are not able to keepe anie one of them, therfore the lawes of God are not permanent, necessarie, nor now commanded, because no church can keepe them all: such reasons are not worthie the refuting.

The second part of his question, where he demandeth to know where this government of Christ was practised by doctors, pastors, elders and deacons only and none other, is so full of vanitie and follie as it deserveth none answere. For my part, I never read or heard of any such church: I ever thought that everie member of the church without exception or exemption of anie one person, had beene all alike bound to the obedience of God's word, the practise of Christ's government, to be instructed and ruled by him in all things, every one walking within the bounds of his calling. I never thought that the practise of Christ's government belonged only to these officers; I rather thought it had beene their dutie and office to have seene this government faithfully and orderly practised by all the members of the church. Why, we see Christ's ecclesiastical government is not only tied to the publike actions of the whole congregation, but extendeth to everie action of every Christian, wherof Christ is the beholder and judg, yea, and for everie knowne transgression and disobedience hath due vengeance ready, whither by reproof or excommunication. I ever thought that the execution of Christ's government and judgments had belonged to the whole bodie of the church which assigneth the publike ordering therof, as the ministery, *etc.*, to the proper and fit members, ech one in their due functions; not hereby resigning up her power and authority and government wholy into their hands, but still reserving the right in the whole body together, and in every member apart. So that if these officers or anie of them transgresse, the church reserveth power to every member freely (according to the quality of the offence and the rules of the word) to admonish and reprove, the whole to censure and excommunicate such officers so offending. Which officers in execution of their office and function, do rather reserve this liberty and power to the whole church and everie member therof in due order, than any way diminish or pluck away the same from the least. It were a disorderly part and against nature for any member to arrogate the power of the whole body unto itself. Such presumption was not heard of in the church of Christ untill antichrist sprong up, neither wil it be removed until he be abolished. Elders are apointed to see the government and order of Christ observed, not to take it al into their hands. One other grosse error and ignorance in this branch is to be observed, that is, he numbreth the deacons amongst the governing officers of the church: this he never learned in Christ's Testament; well may it be the practise of the Church of Rome and England where are such jolly archdeacons and ruffling deanes. The deacon's office in the church is, to gather and distribute, not to governe. [224]

The third point in this cavilling question[1] is, to know
where these officers abovesaid practised that government in an equalitie without superioritie in one above
an other. It hath beene even now shewed how this
government belongeth and is committed to the whole
bodie, how their office consisteth to teach the church
how to practise it and to see it observed by al in due
order, and not ambitiously to assume it wholy into
their owne hands. For the rest, though there be a
communion in the church, yet there is no equalitie.
The church knoweth how to give honour and reverence
unto their elders, especially to them that labor in the
word and doctrine. The church of Christ is taught to
obey and submit unto their leaders, to acknowledg them
that labour amongst them and that are set over them
in the Lord, and to admonish them, and to hold those
in superabundant love for their worke sake. The elders
also amongst themselves know how to give honour one
unto another by going before; yet al this without prejudice to themselves that give, or detriment to him that
receaveth it, without the losse of the least iote [jot, iota]
of their owne libertie, or puffing him up, or setting him
in anie unlawfull authoritie. They give it to his labor,
diligence, vertue and desert; which ceassing, they
straight withdraw their praise, and in the stead therof
use exhortation, admonition, yea (if need be) censure.
All the parts of man's bodie are not alike esteemed and
used; we have much more care and tendernes over the

---

[1] Barrow accuses Bishop Cooper of caviling, but he is guilty of his own
accusation. Instead of answering the bishop, he has denounced the
questioner, the questions, and the implications thereof. The essential
difference in the views of the two men is that Bishop Cooper believes that
" when God blessed his church with christian princes [beginning with
Constantine], the Scriptures doe not take away that [christian] liberty,
that with the consent of their godly magistrates they [the church] may
have that outwarde forme of jurisdiction, and deciding of ecclesiastical
causes, as to the state of the countery and people shall be most convenient.
And that liberty have divers reformed churches, since the restoring of the
gospell, used" (*An Admonition to the People of England*, pp. 141, 84, 92).
Bishop Cooper believes that the government of the church in the New
Testament is descriptive of the discipline in the first century, and that
Christ allows for change, alteration, improvement, and variety, so long
as the spirit of the law is observed. For Barrow the New Testament
model is " a perfect government and direction for the church," normative,
mandatory, and prescriptive ; therefore the letter of the new ordinances
must be followed.

eies than of the hands or feet, yet may not the eye heerby
refuse to doe service and attend to the hand or foote in
all their busines and affaires, neither may it disturbe
the least member of the bodie in their peculiar office
and function, or intrude into their place.   The eye
guideth and directeth the hand, shewing how it ought
to doe the worke; the hand againe washeth, wipeth, and
doth all loving helpe it may unto the eye.   Both eie and
hand and everie other part of the body are distinct members, yet so knit and joined together in the bodie, as
they do their due service unto the eie, and ech unto
other in the whole, not confounding the order of nature,
nor disturbing ech other in the worke.   The church
hath like care to see that inviolable order and temper
of the members in Christ's bodie dulie preserved; the
honor they give to one member is not the dishonor of
another, or hinderance of the whole bodie.   The church
neither doth, neither may, give immoderate honour
either in fastuous swelling titles of vanitie, or any inordinate authoritie to anie member; that would rather
puffe up the flesh than cheare up the spirit.   All the
gifts God hath given any member, are to the service of
the whole bodie: he that will be greatest must be as
the least, he must wash the feet and not have his feete
kissed of the least; all superioritie is heere comprised
within the bounds of christian order and modestie.
Humilitie goeth before and is the compagnion of honor;
honor is not heere conferred to lift up the hearts of the
greatest above the least, but rather for their counsaile,
care, love, service unto al; it is willingly given unto
such by al.   Ambition and vainglorie are heere carfully avoided both by the givers and receavers: who
so see-[225]keth the primacie with Diotrephes[1] is heere
suggillate[2] and layd open, resisted and rebuked of al, 3 Joh. 9
as that antichrist, that Lucifer; the greatest elder of the
church, the pastor, is but a servant and steward of the Tit. 1: 7
house, not lord of the heritage; but a member, not 1 Pet. 5: 3
lord of the bodie; to be honored for his excellent place
in the bodie and giftes of God; to be reverenced for his

---

[1] III John 1: 9.   " I wrote unto the church: but Diotrophes, who loveth
to have the preeminence among them, receiveth us not."
[2] Beaten, reviled, bruised, marked with livid spots.

faithfulnes, labour, and diligence. Yet this must ever be remembred, his honour consisteth in his service, his service belongeth unto al; so that the least member of the bodie hath like interest in him, as he in the least member: the le[a]st member hath like libertie and freedome with him in Christ, though not like gifts or function of Christ.

And now this strange and troublesome proposition is thus proved, *that Christ's church can be established into no other order, or governed by any other officers or ordinances, than Christ in his Testament hath prescribed*; and that these great impediments and difficulties are also remooved out of the way; me thinckes it time, and heere a fit occasion offred, to goe in hand with the examination of the present established government of the Church of England. And heere to begin with the antichristian authoritie of the chiefe rulers (namelie, the bishops), which they would beare away and hide under this word *superioritie*: of their lineage, petigree, original, you have above heard, as also of their strange manner of offices and consecration; and somwhat also of their power generally, and from whence they derived it: but let us now a litle further consider therof.

First they take upon them ech one of them to sit upon (as they call it) or to governe many hundred churches, others of them many thowsands; one of them as pope, or primate over al: they make and depose ministers by their absolute authoritie; they make and disanul lawes: they ratifie or reject what Scriptures they list; they confirme or refuse what doctrines they list; they make what kind of worship, ministration, they list; they change, innovate, coine, alter, bring in, cast out, what and whome they list, without checke or controulement. The truth of al these need no other proofe than their present estate; the warrant of anie of these I am sure cannot be shewed in Christ's Testament; therfore I doubt not at one word to call them all divelish and antichristian. To confute them severallie were a labour both needles and trobelsome, they being of themselves so apparantlie odious; yet this brieflie in a word.

One man cannot stand a bishop unto divers churches

at one time, no more than one eye can be a (1) member, and (2) doe the function at one time to divers bodies, (3) in divers places; no more than one candle can be put [1.] in two or mo[re] divers candlesticks, (2) in divers howses, (3) and shew light unto them al at one time. Thus are bishops in their office, place, ministerie, called members, yea, the eye of the bodie, lights, and the candle of the howse; the church it self also called the bodie, the can-[226]dlesticke in the Scriptures. No ^{Math. 5: 14}one shepheard can attend, watch, feed, oversee, two or ^{Revel. 2: 1}more flockes at one time in divers places; no watchman ^{Ezek. 34}can keep watch in divers cities at one time. Bishops ^{Acts 20}are called shepheardes, watchmen; the church, a flock, a citie, in the Scriptures. Besides, Christ hath established an other quite contrarie order; not one watchman or shepheard over manie churches, but manie watchmen over one church; and yet hath given power and commanded everie member to watch, and al litle enough. Moreover, it is Christ's only office now to walke in the midst of the seven golden candlesticks, he holdeth the seven stars in his owne right hand, he is the arch-bishop and visiter of all churches and shep- ^{Revel. 1}heardes; Christ is the head over the universall and everie particular bodie of his church; he hath given this office to no mortal man in earth; they are al but members of some one bodie, though divers in function and dignitie, as the eie, hand, foote, *etc.*, yet al but members of the bodie to which they serve; everie member being circumscribed within the limites of their place, office, function. One member cannot place, displace, or cut off an other, this ought to be done by ^{1. Cor. 5}the whole bodie, as in the name and power of their head Christ, unto everie one of which congregations Christ hath given this his power, to be executed according to the rules of his word; Christ is the bridegrome, he only hath the bride; but the frendes of the bride- ^{John 3: 29}grome they stand and heare and rejoice exceedinglie for the bridegrome's voice. Christ is that slaine living ^{Reve. 5}Lambe that hath obtained to take that sealed written booke out of the right hand of him that sitteth on the throne, and to open the same. All elders, angels, and the whole host in heaven and in earth fall downe on their faces and give glorie to the Lambe; Christ is the only lawgiver unto his church, and hath given most heavenlie perfect lawes in his Testament unto his church, and hath sealed his Testament with that his blood, so that nothing may be added unto, or taken there from. He never gave to anie mortal man power to make new lawes, but hath commanded all men faithfullie to keep those lawes which he hath made, within the limits of their calling. It is onlie the office of the Holy Ghost to teach the saints to pray, to give wordes according to the wil of God, to fill their mouthes with new songes, which they, as sweete odors and incense, day and night offer up unto God through Christ.

James 4: 12

Rom. 8: 26, 27
1. Joh. 2: 27

What then and how great is the sinne of these presumptuous shepheardes, these blasphemous antichristian bishops, that climbe up and intrude into the place, office, and roome of Christ? That take his spowse from him, and al his ministers, officers, orders, and ordinances from her: that alter, abrogate, bring in, cast out what and whome they list, *etc.*, that take the office of the Holy Ghost upon them, and not onlie set up in the church of God their moulten Egyptian calfe, cast in the old mould of the masse booke (save a litle new annuled and ingraven with a few of their owne divises) but thrust this filthy idoll upon men's consciences as their praiers, yea, upon God himself, as al the service and [227] worship they wil allow him in his church. See whither these be not the undoubted markes of antichrist, that adversarie? Search the prophecies and the Scriptures whether this be not that verie abhomination of desolation? Lift up your eyes, to the destruction, havock, and wast these adversaries have made in the sanctuarie, how they roare in the midst of the congregation, and have there set up their banners and signes, and lift up their axes upon al the Lorde's plantes, and broken downe with their malles al the beawtiful sieling and carved worke, have cast the Lorde's sanctuarie into the fire, have raced [razed] it to the ground, and have profaned the dwelling place of his name; they are resolved in their hearts to doe violence, and to destroy them altogether, and have

Psal. 74

brought in al ma-[nner] of filthy abhominable thinges into the sanctuarie. When they find these thinges in this estate, then let him that readeth consider; let them that be in the citie, and wil save their soules, flee into the mountaine.

There belongeth no reformation to this estate, even that reformation which these counterfait preachers pretend, is altogether as il. You see what inordinate antichristian power they still retaine in the priests' handes: in al their parishes, the parson or minister (as they cal him) must rule all and be above the whole flocke, who may controwle him or withstand him in nothing, either in doctrine, or practise, be it never so ill. They must complaine to the synode, classes, or councel of priests: which synodes, classes, councels, must consist wholy of ministers, the people shut out, and those have absolute power over al churches, persons, matters, causes, to debate, define, determine, decree, ratifie, disanull what they list, by permission of the High Court of Parliament, which hath supreme power over the church and all councels and causes therof, *ut supra*: otherwise, untill by this court these decrees be taken away, all churches are burdened and must stand subject unto them.[1]

But let us now returne to the execution of this monstrous antichristian power of the bishops. This extendeth even to al the whole practise, worship, ministerie, orders, ordinances, injunctions, decrees, lawes of their church alreadie made, and heerafter to be made, and therfore are infinite, and passe any man or creature whatsoevers [*sic*] setting downe in particular. A great labour it were to recken up all their constitutions and cannons which they have fetched from I wote not what old councels, or rather from their holie father the pope, or the heape of their civil lawes and customes which they have receaved from their mother of Rome; al which are pleaded, judged, sould by these lords bishops, their chancellors, deanes, civil doctors, proctors, advo-

---

[1] In this paragraph Barrow is speaking of Presbyterian government, as advocated by Thomas Cartwright and other reformers.

cates, pleaders, brawlers,[1] archdeacons, commissaries in their courts of Faculties, Arches, Prerogative, Delegates, and in their Commissarie's Court (not heere to spake of the wel head, that ever running spring of al mischief, their Spanish Inquisition or English High Commission, it deserveth especial mention by it self. These lawes they take for the foundation of their church instead of [228] Christ's New Testament: these courts give the whole direction unto, and execute all the censures of and for this church, whether it be excommunication, suspension or mulct, Mr. Archdeacon and masse commissary beare no small sway. It were long and hard to relate the divers orders, processe, and maners of pleading, that belong to these courtes, that is no small secret, it is no easie occupation, many a man's living dependeth theron; it is no small calling to be but a pursuyvant[2] or cursetor[3] of these courtes: (I say not so of the parators[4] and sumners[5] that belong to the Commissarie's Court:) heere are all things pleadable and vendible for money, but without money heere is no man will open his mouth, be the cause never so just. For money you may heere have expedition or delay of judgment, with sundry shifts and evasions which I want skill to utter. For money you may have priviledges, dispensations, licences, to eate flesh, or to marry at forbidden times, as in the holy time of Lent, *etc.*, privatly in the night, in some secret place, sodenly without consent of parents, yea, without banes asking, and by what priest you will; also to have many benefices, and in sundry other cases, wherof these courtes exercise jurisdiction, as of precontractes, adulteries, testaments, and

---

[1] Canon CXXXIII, entitled " Proctors not to be clamorous in Court," speaks of " lowd and confused cries and clamours of Proctors in the courts of the Archbishop." See H. A. Wilson (ed.), *Constitutions and Canons Ecclesiastical*, 1604 (Oxford, 1922). Bishop Cooper felt constrained to defend the bishops against the charge that " they maintayn pilling [plundering] and pouling [fleecing], and (as some in despite terme them) bawdie courtes " (*An Admonition to the People of England*, pp. 135-7).

[2] A pursuivant was a warrant officer.

[3] A cursitor was a clerk in the Court of Chancery who made out writs *de cursu*. More generally, he was a messenger, a courier.

[4] A paritor, or apparitor, was a summoning officer in an ecclesiastical court.

[5] A summoner was a clerk who cited people to appear in court.

sundry other that I know not of.[1] All which and whatsoever, an auncient bishop[2] of this land hath undertaken to defend by Christ's New Testament:[3] wherfore
until we see his profes I dare not give sentence against
them, or pronounce them antichristian. His proofe is
drawn from 1 Timothy 5: 19. "Against a priest or
elder receave no accusation under two or three witnesses." Heere (saith he) "is an accuser, here is a
person accused, heere are witnesses examined, heere
is a judgment and deciding of the matter; therfore,
heere is an exercise of a jurisdiction and a maner of a
court." To make it yet more sure, he takes away an
objection that lay in his way; namely, that it was not
Timothy his court only, but jointly exercised with
the residue of the elders that had the government. This (he saith) cannot be, because the wordes
are directed to Timothy only.[4]

It is pitty Martin his presse was gone before this
reason had an answere,[5] so should he not have lost his
due shame for the same. But was there ever litle
portion of Scripture so violently wrested, distorted,
perverted, and that by an old bishop ? I am deceaved
if he fetched not this reason from the schoole of Sorbon:
for either my memory faileth me, or I have read their
citations also by sumners [summoners], pursivants, *etc.*,
prooved by Genesis 3: 9: "Adam where art thow ? "
Well to the point: I cannot rest either in his translation

1 It is interesting to read Barrow's censure in 1590 of the ecclesiastical
   courts, and then read the judgment of G. W. Prothero, who concluded:
   " It is not too much to say that these [ecclesiastical] courts were among
   the most efficient causes of the quarrel between the monarchy and the
   nation, which culminated in the rebellion of 1642 " (*Select Statutes and
   Other Constitutional Documents Illustrative of the Reigns of Elizabeth and
   James I* [Oxford, 1949] p. xl).
2 Thomas Cooper (1517 ?—1594), was about 73 years old at this time. In
   1570 he became Bishop of Lincoln, and in 1584 was translated to the see
   of Winchester.
3 *An Admonition to the People of England*, pp. 135-9.
4 *Ibid.*, p. 138.
5 The Martin Marprelate press was seized on Thursday, August 14, 1589,
   in a house in Newton Lane, about a mile from Manchester. The printer,
   John Hoskins or Hodgkins, and his two assistants, Valentyne Symmes
   and Arthur Thomlyn, were apprehended, examined by the Earl of Derby,
   and then sent to London. See Ellesmere MS. 2148 and also William
   Pierce, *An Historical Introduction to the Martin Marprelate Tracts.* See
   also Harley MSS. 7042, ff. 9, 10.

or interpretation of this verse, they are both corrupt and popishly false: The text is: " Against an elder receave not accusation except in two or three witnesses." I cannot heere allow the word priest, nor spare the words *except in*: his interpretation is most grosse and false, contrarie to the whole scope and phrase both of that chapter and the whole epistle, prejudicial to the perpetuity and true practise of the commandement.[1] For if this lawe were directed to Timothy only, and that the other elders and the church were shut out in the examination and censuring of such faultes; then how could the church or any member therof now have any use of this [229] commandement? I never heard of any speciall bequest Timothy made to these lord bishops above all other, neither can I see from hence, why they should usurpe this jurisdiction over their superiors; namely, over the parish priests and parsons that stand for pastors, these bishops (if they have any office) being put elders. So then by this rule the parson should keep court over the bishops, and not the bishop over so many parsons. But to say the truth, this reason would much better fit the pope, in whome this supreme jurisdiction over al churches and elders should in one person be bestowed, as by his saiing it was in Timothy, rather than unto so many bishops, who all cannot have that sole peculiar authoritie which belonged unto Timothy alone, from which so many worthy bishops were then shut out.

But why should this commandement belong more to Timothy alone, than all the other commandements in this chapter (that I say not in this epistle), which was wholy written and directed to Timothy; there was bare shift when this was made the only reason: and now further, why should this commandement more than al the rest of this chapter, of the maner of rebuking elder men, and elder women, honoring widowes, *etc.*, be tied

---

[1] Wiclif's Bible and the Rheims version have " priest." In the Tyndale, Cranmer, Geneva, and Authorized versions, the word is " elder." The Authorized Version has " but before two or three witnesses ; " all the others have " but under." Compare Deuteronomy 19: 15. The Bishops' Bible reads: " agaynst an elder receave none accusation, but under two or three witnesses."

more to Timothie's person and office, yea, or to the persons and office of elders? May none reproove an elder, but a lord bishop? Or (as the Reformists would have it) but a synode or councell of priests? It is plentifully above proved, that the whole church hath power to observe, reproove, censure, their greatest teachers and elders, or why should this rule of hearing and receaving yl [ill] reportes so solely belong to Timothy, or to other elders, more than the contrarie commandement going next before, of the honour, care, and love due to elders. I hope they can be content to be honored, provided for, and loved, of the whole flocke, especially for their desert and vertue; surely so must they be contented to be reproved and censured of all, when by evill life they deserve it.

This commandement in deed willeth all Christians to be carefull what reportes and tales they heare or beleeve of their elders, and that they be sure they have good and lawful proofe in two or three witnesses, *etc.*; other Christians had eares, mouthes, and hearts which had need to be governed as well as Timothie. I graunt well that publikely in the church the trial and censuring of elders ought chiefly to be done by the elders of that church, but this neither prejudicing the libertie of anie, even the least, freely to object or speake what he knoweth to be blamed, either in the elder accused, or in the publike action by the other elders that trie and examine; much lesse to the secluding and shutting out the whole church, with these wicked priests, even both these factions, Pontifical and Reformists, who both of them would assume the whole government of the church into their owne hands, at the least utterly debar the congregation, where these things are amisse, to intermeddle. The church must receave what they amongst themselves have decreed, whither in their brawling courtes, whither in their select classes. [230]

The publike censuring of anie member, whither elder or other, is an action of the whole church: wherunto (if it use the most fit members or officers) should such officers and members hereupon arrogate the whole action, interest, and power to themselves, secluding the whole bodie the church, whose officers and members they are? As when the body useth the eye, the mouth, the feete, to see, speake, goe, is not the whole bodie of consent with these actions, and said to see, to speake, to goe, although to these particular actions it useth these particular members? What a dismembring of the bodie, and rending of the church, would these ambitious priests make? Who the one would withdraw all publike actions of the church into their popish courtes, the other into their conventicles and synodes of priests.

As for reproofe by admonition, anie member of the church hath free power also to reprove the greatest elder of the church, according to the quallitie of his offence: if his offence be private, privatly; if publike, publikely.[1] Yea, he is bound by the law of God so to doe, and not to suffer sinne in him; yet this within the bounds of modestie and order; as if there be others present more fit to doe it, to give them time and place, but if they neglect it, or doe it amisse, then to use his power, yea to doe his dutie.

Now then seeing the whole church hath this power to censure faultes in their hands, and that it properly belongeth unto them (as we shall have many occasions hereafter to shew) and that these elders are but ministers and servants of the church, substituted to this and other functions. Seing also every one, even the least member in the church, hath interest, power and freedome in and over this or any action of the church, to approve or orderly to reprove any action or person of the church, and that publikly if need so require; how can any from this place draw, that the reproofe of elders only belongeth to elder; or how could this popish prelate collect, that this power was only given to Timothy, when Timothy and the apostles themselves were subject to the reproofe of the least, where these transgressed from the word and wil of God: how could he from hence derive his absolute power over all churches

---

[1] In *A True Description out of the Worde of God, of the Visible Church*, there is a similar statement: "The repentance of the partie must bee proportionable to the offence, *viz.*, if the offence bee publique, [the repentance must be] publique: if private, [the repentance may be] private."

and priests, when no such thing is heere by this commandement given to Timothy? How could this old dreamer[1] from hence derive, or hereby defend these Romish brawling bawdy courts, with all their popish cannons, customes, pleadings, pleaders, even al that swarme of vermine that live and attend upon the same courts? I hope if we granted him his owne most false interpretation; that Timothy had sole power, and by vertue of this commandement exercised absolute jurisdiction over the whole church and the other elders; that yet he did it not after this antichristian ungodly maner as he and his brethren bishops doe, by such mercenarie Romish doctors, pleaders, proctors, *etc.*, which are to couller and plead the most vile, hatefull causes which a Christian's eare abhorreth to heare of, or by such wicked blasphemous customes, othes, purgations, *etc.* These I suppose he can not prove to be used in Timothie's courte, neither can he [231] derive any of this doung from that holy commandement of God; for then might every Christian keepe such a court over and against bishops, *etc.*, seing they may reprove and rebuke the greatest bishop in the church, that transgresseth against the word of God. No [now] let him looke into the ninth chapter of the Revelation, and there he shall see his owne and al these poisoned armed locusts' original to have come out of the smoke of the bottomles pyt, *etc.* Further to discusse the poperie, wickednes, and folly of this reason, or the unlawfullnes of these antichristian courts, were labour needles: they being so grosse of themselves, as by the first bringing the heavenly light unto them, they are discovered therby, and chased away as the darknes of the night by the sunne rising, the grosse vapours by the wind. They have no foundation of the word, and therfore must needs fall: the word of God wil beare no such rotten stubble and filthy doung, therfore I leave this reason to remaine to his perpetual shame, and the shame of all the brood and houshold of Anak: who if they could be drawen but to any peaceable opening the booke of God, but with the least Christian (I would not now be under-

[1] Bishop Cooper.

stood of any learned priest of the opposite faction, who
having derived all their ministerie and ministration
from them, and exercising the same under them, can
never prevaile against their fathers, as in all their con-
flicts hath beene seene, because in deed they take not
the whole cause and right groundworke, therfore they
cannot further the gospel, or bring glory to God): but
if the least Christian whome both factions so depise and
persecute, might have but free and orderly triall with
either or both sides and factions, I doubt not but God
would give such blessing and power to his word which
he would put in their mouthes, as their counterfait and
wicked dealings should be discovered; yea, albeit both
sides hate the light and flee this christian peaceable
triall (wherby they plainly bewray of what spirit they
are), though they digge as deepe as hel to hide their
devises, yet God will disclose them, and that even by
their owne pennes and tongues, rather than he will
want instruments.

An other fleshly reason he bringeth from the lawfulnes
of these courts, and that is from the prince's authority.
A christian prince that alloweth the free course of the
gospel commandeth them; therfore every godly subject
ought to obey them.[1]

The gospel cannot have free course, whiles these antichristian courts, bishops, ministery, stand; if the gospel
had free course, they should all be abolished. But is
this a bishoply or christian reason ? A godly prince
commandeth them, therfore they ought to be obeyed ?
Why have princes authoritie to command what they
list ? Of if they doe, ought Christians to obey any
ungodly decree ? I had thought that both they ought
to command and we to obey in the Lord alwaies. But
especially may princes bring in any new ordinances at
their pleasure into the church of Christ ? What can
the pope say more for his sackfull of traditions ? Make
you this unlawfull in the person of the pope that maketh
some more shew of learning, knowledg, and religion,
and hath his learned councell of cardinals about him,
and yet make it lawfull in a christian [232] prince to

---

[1] *An Admonition to the People of England,* pp. 138, 143.

innovate or abrogate the Testament of Christ in this maner? To bring in or keep out of the church what ordinances they list? You shew your self a faithfull watchman and bishop over the church and unto your prince's soule, that suffer such rule to be kept in the church without blowing the trumpet of God's word against it, that suffer your prince thus to runne into, and remaine in the wrath of God unadmonished, unreproved. You learned this of no true prophets, no faithful bishops; let it remaine then upon you for an undoubted marke of a false prophet, a Balaamite, a wolfe, a murtherer of soules. And as for your authoritie, know (seing it hath no better ground in the word of God) it shall all fall to the ground; al the princes of the world or powers of hell shall not be able to uphold it; Rev. 18: 17 Babilon shall fall and all her pompe shall vanish, though her princes and shipmasters or bishops, and all her mariners, ministers, and marchandmen howle and wayle therfore; for the God that condemneth her is a strong Lord: as for the King of Egipt, he is a man and not God almightie, and their horses flesh, but not Isa. 31: 3 spirit: wherfore when Jehovah shall stretch forth his hand, the helper shall fall and the helped shall fall, and all these shall faile together.

Let us now proceed to the censures of the Church of England, which wholly consist in the bishop's hand, who executeth them by himself or his commissarie; they are not exercised for obstinacie joined to sin or error, but lightly (if not altogether) for contempt of their courtes, either in not appearing at, or [in not] obeiing their commandements and decrees; or els for some transgressions against their idoll service booke, in speaking against it or against their Ordinarie or his stubstitute [*sic*!] Mr. Commissarie, or the parish priest or such like; or els for not observing their idoll holy daies; or not receaving with their parson; or not having their children baptised, *etc*. For these and such like they shalbe convented and very severely punished either by mulct or excommunication or imprisonment; there are no other sins amongst the people that deserve excommunication, they have other punishments for sin besides excommunication, as to fine them and punish them by the purse. Neither in deed know I many sins that they use to enquire after, except it be adultery and fornication; there are no more sins worthy of ecclesiasticall censure. But these they punish very sore; for if he will not pay for the shooing Mr. Commissarie's mare, he may peradventure do his pennance before al the Sodomites in the parrish in a white sheete, whiles Mr. Parson is reading his service book to them, or els his sermon. But if he speake a word in Mr. Commissarie his eare, and wil stand upon his purgation, then must he get as bad brothels as himself to sweare by Mr. Commissarie's booke, that they think in their corrupt conscience that he is cleare. This done, and cost of the court discharged, then (have he beene never such a whoremaister all his life time, or beene never so manifestly or often detected or taken in this crime) yet is there no credit to be given to anie proofe, in respect of [233] the othes of these his sodomiticall companions that cleare him by othes: and this is called his purgation. I am shamed and abhor, but to thinke in my heart of that proofe of adulterie they require, or els all complaint or suite is unavaileable. Thus doe these holie fathers the bishops make adulterie either a laughing, or els a pecuniarie, matter; purging and expiating it by perjurie or skorne.

They have also a censure of suspension, and this is diversely used; somtimes towardes their priests and preachers, by the bishops; somtimes by these priests towardes their parishioners. It is used towardes the priests when they breake their orders injoined them and wherunto they are sworne, or are contumacious to their Ordinarie or his substitutes or commissarie, *etc.*, when they refuse to weare such garmentes as are enjoined them, or to read their service orderlie, or to administer the sacramentes after anie other manner, or refuse to burie the dead, and to church women[1] with the booke, or if they preach anie doctrine against anie thing by publike authoritie enjoined; then for such

---

[1] Churching was the offering of public prayers for the safe delivery of a child. This ceremony, in keeping with the prescription of the *Book of Common Prayer*, was usually held one month after child-birth.

faultes is his Ordinarie to suspend him from preaching
or ministring for a season, untill he be brought into
order, or become conformable, or els to deprive him
and disanul his orders and ministery. The priests,
they execute this suspension against open offendors,
such as are not in love and charitie with their neighbours, and by vertue hereof keepe them from the
sacrament of the supper, unlesse they get Mr. Chancelor or Mr. Commissarie's commandment unto the
priest to receave them. Yet in the meane while they
are admitted to their publike prayers, *etc.*

To the first kind of suspension al the priests generallie
(except it be some od man in the land) submit, and yet
such a one joineth unto these other priests as brethren,
though he hold the bishops and their power antichristian, and they submit both their ministerie and
the gospel unto the bishops' power and censure. To
the second kind in the hand of the priests they al wholy
consent, insomuch as some of the cheife maisters of this
faction in their bookes of church discipline, have set it
downe for a cannon and rule, to suspend some such
from the sacraments, who have committed some publike
sin and persisteth obstinatlie in the same, after publike
reproofe, whome notwithstanding they still hold as a
member and a brother with them, and joine unto in
their common praiers, exercise of the word, and other
mutual duties as contribution for the poore.

First, this suspension of theirs must needes be held
the instrument and toole of that foolish shepheard, because it is not found nor heard of in all the practise or
writings of the apostles, neither in al the Testament of
Christ, where yet a perfect government and direction
for the church is set downe. Then if it be a censure
of the church, it is a publike censure, because we see
they are openlie kept backe from participation of the
publike communion. If it be a publike censure, it must
be for sin publikelie knowen; but Christ and his apostles
have set downe [234] unto the church one only other
course to be taken for publike sinnes, namelie, when Mat. 18: 17
he refuseth to heare the voice of the church, or rather
of Christ in his church, to proceed forthwith to excom-

V

munication. Therfore in this case of open obstinacie in publike sin, if suspension be used, it not onlie taketh the place of excommunication, but keepeth away that onlie true course which Christ hath instituted; and therfore is a meere forgerie and an idolatrous divise, and hath no place in the church of Christ.

If anie heere object, that excommunication being the extreamest and most severe censure of the church, and an utter cutting off, therfore it ought to be proceeded unto with great pitie, patience, and long suffring, triing al meanes before we cut off a member. In regard wherof they in their wisdome and pitie thinke it expedient, first to trie and use this censure of suspension before they proceed to cast him quite out, prooving if this may draw him to repentance.

My answere is, that we cannot be more wise, patient, loving, tenderlie kind, than our God is, or than God wil have us to be. If we seeke to exceed or goe beyond these rules and boundes that he hath set us downe, we are vainlie puffed up in our fleshlie mind, our wisdome is turned to follie, our pitie into crueltie, our love into hatred, our patience into transgression, wherby we destroie both ourselves, and such as we seeke to save. God looketh for obedience rather than sacrifice at our handes: he needeth no direction or instruction from us: our wisdome is to rest in the wisdome of God, to be wise, patient, and loving as he wil have us wise, patient, and loving. If, or when, he commandeth to smite, it is not in man's power to spare or stay, so should we pull the wrath of God upon our owne heads also: we breake no love whiles we execute God's lawes uprightly: as it is sin to prevent, so is it to foreslowe[1] the Lorde's judgmentes. Excommunication is not man's, but God's judgmentes, though God have committed it unto the church as to his ministers. God hath set downe the whole processe and due time and maner of sentence therof: he hath left nothing therin to the discretion of the church, wherby to make al men the more to stand in awe and tremble at so dreadfull a sentence of so terrible a judge. When the sinne is come to that ripenes

[1] Delay.

prescribed, then is excommunication due, and to be pronounced: but when publike sin is orderly and publikly reproved, and yet still the partie offending remaineth impenitent, and will not confesse and forsake his sin, but despising the exhortation and censure of the church, he harden his heart in his sin; then is sin at that prescribed ripenes apparantly. Therfore then the Church cannot, neither hath in their power to protract or defer the sentence of excommunication anie longer upon anie hope or further trial, because they have already had that triall which God alloweth. They therfore should now sin greevously against the justice and majestie of God, they should draw themselves into God's wrath, harden the heart and destroie the soule of the other, yea, even open a gap and wide doore un-[235]to the whole church to sin, who seing such foreslacking of judgment, would take boldnes, upon hope to find repentance time inough. They that give anie further time upon pitie, or anie other fleshlie reason, condemne the Lord of cruelty and rashnes, who giveth no further time, after publike reproofe and exhortation despised. So that to that leaden rule of proceeding to excommunication with a leaden heele when the sin is thus ripe, I oppose this golden rule, to remoove sinne out of the church with the wings of a storke, and the wind under their wings: yet first that the epha[1] be Zach. 5: [9] lifted up betwixt the earth and the heaven, that the sin be publikly seene, publiklie censured.

Now for this same new found censure of suspension which they (these Reformists) would bring in and exercise in stead of excommunication or (as they pretend) as a preparative to excommunication, wherby they may first be shut out from the holiest of all, out of the chancel, where the priest by sole authoritie raigneth, and so by degrees proceed to excommunication, to shut him out of the church also, if he repent not; what doth this their wisdome and pitie, but condemne the Lord of follie and crueltie, or rather shew forth their owne presumption and follie that thus forsake and condemne the

---

[1] A Hebrew dry measure. *The New English Dictionary* gives a pertinent example: " By your Grace's means, the epha, wherein popish wickedness sitteth, may be lifted up between the earth and the heaven."

waies of the Lord as unequall, by bringing in and following their owne waies, as more equall.

How can these forgers, these coyners of religion, seeme and sue to cast out the heape of humane traditions, as contrarie, and such as cannot be joined unto, or with, the Testament of Christ, and yet bring in these forgeries of their owne? For so I may justlie cal them from whencesoever they have derived them, if not from the booke of God. But least I be noted of prejudice, to find fault with the thing I know not, and to condemne before I have convinced; let us in a word or two see, how this timber of these accordeth to the rest of the building, and upon what socket or foundation it standeth.

This suspension we find to be a publike seperation and putting away of some open offendor and unworthie receaver from the table of the Lord by the pastor before excommunication, he yet being held a member of their church, communicating with them in praiers, contribution, *etc*. Heere I must not be understood of the yonger sort which are not as yet admitted to the table of the Lord, the seed of the faithful of them called *Catechumenoi*;[1] but of such as have beene partakers therof, and are under the censures of the church. Let us now see how lawful it is for the whole church, but especiallie for anie one member, as of his owne sole authoritie, to shut out such members from the table of the Lord, before, or otherwise than by excommunication. That this may be done, let us see what the table of the Lord is.

The apostle thus defineth it: " The cup of blessing which we blesse, is it not the communion of the blood of Christ? The bread which we breake, is it not the communion of the bodie of Christ?[2] Because we manie are one bread, one bodie, for al participate of one bread." Heere we see this table or supper of the Lord, a livelie and most comfortable symbole of our com-[236]munion with Christ, as also ech with other in Christ; excellently shewing unto us the meanes and maner of our redemp-

---

[1] Catechumenoi — passive participle of catēcheō. Those being instructed in the rudiments of the faith, those preparing for confirmation.
[2] I Corinthians 10: 16, 17.

tion, to stir us up unto thankfulnes, to rejoice in our God and praise his name therfore, to the generall strengthning of all our faithes, and to the mutuall binding us together in all holie duties and love, *etc.* Here we see the table of the Lord to be publike, free, open and alike common to all saints, ech one having a like interest, necessity, use, comfort therof, the least as wel and asmuch as the greatest, Christ having alike died and paied one and the same ransome for them all, that they all might have a like interest in him, feed and feast through one and the same spirit, faith, hope, joy in him. Which interest, power, joy, *etc.*, no mortall man, nor the whole church, much lesse any member therof, no, nor hell gates shalbe able to plucke from the least member of Christ, whiles he remaineth and abideth in the body. A most unnaturall part were it in the mother to plucke away the brest from the child, wherby it should be nourished: but though the mother might do this and murther her owne child without blame; yet the whole church cannot drive away or keep out the least of these members from any publike action of the church, much lesse seperate them from this heavenly comfort, free publike communion, whiles they remaine members of Christ, and are not cut off from his body.

Further, seing this table is called " the communion of the body and blood of Christ," as also the communion of the whole church, who can keepe back any such member as still remaineth in the body of Christ, in his church, without depriving him of this communion of Christ and of the church, and so of life: for " except they eate the flesh of the Sonne of man and drinke his blood, they have no life in them."[1] But these men keepe them from the body and blood of Christ, from the communion of Christ and of the church, therfore also from life it self; and so in seeming to correct him lightly, they kill him out right, for more than this can they not do by this orderly excommunication which they hold so rigorous.

Such as shall cavil at these words, " except ye shall eate the flesh of the Sonne of man, *etc.*", saiing that I

[1] John 6: 53.

popishly abuse the place, let them cavil: though I
acknowledg that many thowsands that never attained
the symbole of the Supper, yet do feed of that body
and blood of Christ by faith unto eternall life; yet this
I say, that such as by censure are put backe from the
table of the Lord, are cut from the communion of
Christ and of his church, and so from life. For if he
have not communion with Christ and his church, he
can have no life: he cannot be both thus seperate from
their communion, and have it together. They that
pluck away the seale, cancell the deed; but they pluck
away the seale of the covenant, in that for his sin they
debarre him from this comfortable communion, which
is yet more than the seale, in that it bringeth such
present effect and comfort. Therfore they (as far as
man can doe) cut him from Christ and his covenant,
by this their idol suspension.

Now then, having thus shut him out of their communion, how should they hold him in it; having thus
cut him off from Christ, and the bandes [237] that
should bind him to Christ and to the saints, how can
they hold him a member of Christ, a saint, or admit
him as a brother amongst them in their praiers, ministery, contribution? This is very strange divinity, to
shut him out, and yet to hold him in; to cut him off
from the body, and yet to hold him of the body: this
may by logick be proved, but it never can be proved
by Christ's Testament.

Yet is there an other as strange a mysterie in the
matter, which I never learned in Christ's Testament:
and that is how a member that is publikly convicted
of, and remaineth obstinate in, open sin, should be
shut out from the table of the Lord, and yet be receaved and admitted as a member, unto the other
ministerie of the church; as to praiers, contribution,
etc., belike the other ministery and praiers of the church
are not so holy as this Supper, that such an offendor
is held unworthy to communicate in, and therfore is
shut out from the one; but he is worthy inough for,
and therfore is admitted unto the other: this is a strange
censure, a strange case as ever I heard of. I had

thought that after the sin grew once publike, being knowne and dealt with by the church, if then such offenders remaine obstinate, they had beene forthwith to be cut off, and cast out as dead withered branches, and not to be thus halfe shut out and halfe kept in, halfe cut off and halfe remaine, seperate from the Supper, admitted to the ministery of the word and praiers. This is to make him halfe a brother and halfe no brother, halfe a Christian and halfe no Christian.

But yet further, seing this suspension is a publike censure of the church for publike sin, a seperation from publike exercises and actions, *etc.*, how chance it is thus put in one man's power, who by his absolute authoritie may keep back any one of the flocke from the table of the Lord, without the commandement, yea, the privitie of the whole church; yet this me thinkes is the strangest of al, and never heard of in the church and Testament of Christ. Christ hath given and committed his power to censure faultes and persons, as also the interest, possession, and government of all officers and actions to the whole church (I meane to every such particular congregation) and not unto one particular special man above the rest or more than the rest. Every particular member of the church hath like interest in the publike actions and ministery of the church, like power to censure the offences of the whole church or the greatest minister therof, in due order and time (as hath already in this treatise beene often and plentifully proved) and therfore cannot in this maner be kept backe by any one man, as of his sole authority, any more than they may keep back that man whatsoever he be. I speake not this to raise contention betwixt these where there ought to be love and reverence, so much as to note out the popish pride of these pharisaicall Reformers, that take upon them to be lords over the church and this feast: wherof, if they were as good as they would be taken to be, they were but servants and guests at the best. The church it self can neither receave nor cast out a member as of themselves: they doe it by the power and commandement of Christ; they must see faith and [238] profession therof, before they receave; they must see sin and obstinacie before they cut off: until these be seene, the whole church nor all the men of the world have not power to receave or put by any one; if they doe, the action is voide, and the judgment and wrath of God resteth upon them for that sin, until they repent therof. Likewise also when this profession of faith, or this obstinacie in sinn is found in any, then cannot the whole church or all the men of the world keep out or keep in such, without incurring the judgment and wrath abovesaid. How great then is the sin and judgment of these popish priests, that not only pluck away the power of the church from them, but even the power and office of Christ from him, and assume it into their owne hands? Who thus dare innovate and abrogate Christ's Testament, reject his wholsome excommunication as too rough, bring in their deadly suspension in place therof, and with that idol toole of that foolish shepheard, smite and keep out whome it pleaseth them, and as long as

Zach. 11: 15 they list?

Their olde popish reason that they bring from the power of the keies,[1] hath beene above refuted in the discovery of their absolution, and proved to be tied neither to the person or office of any man, more than to every faithfull member and servant of Christ, by the power of God's word, *etc.*

Yet have I also sometimes read in some of their bookes of church discipline (as they tearme it) some other reasons for it; namely, from the law of seperation for uncleannes: such as were defiled by the dead, by creeping and uncleane things, by issues, *etc.*, were to abstaine from the tabernacle for a season, yea, the priest also upon suspicion of leprie[2] or other fowle disease might seclude such a one for certaine daies, as we read in the bookes of the law plentifully; from whence they derive both this power of the pastor, and the censure of suspension. I have there read also (or els my memorie greatly faileth me) drawn from Matthew 5: 23, 24 verses, because he that had injuried or offended his brother was taught by our Saviour Christ

---

1 Matthew 16: 19.
2 Leprosy.

first to make satisfaction and be reconciled, then to offer his gift, *etc.*, that therfore such as had done wrong unto, or were not in charity with their neighbours, are by the priests to be kept from the altar, wherupon they inchanted and offred their breaden God, and now they popishly apply to the communion table, and from hence draw their suspension. But because I have not their bookes with me, and would be loth any way to injurie them or charge them falsly, I will briefly shew the insufficiencie of these reasons, and so proceed, hasting to an end.

From those Levitical lawes wherby the priests secluded such as they suspected of uncleane diseases, untill proofe were made one way or other, may no conclusion be drawen, that therfore the pastor now may suspend such as he suspecteth, or rather knoweth to be infected with incurable deadly and obstinate sin, from the communion board, *etc.* In the Leviticall tabernacle the priests did nothing without prescript lawes, there was nothing left to his discretion, he had his certaine signes set him downe wherupon to seclude, wherupon to pronounce cleane, as also wherupon to pronounce uncleane. But now under the gospell [239] where that priesthood and those lawes are quite taken away, we have now no such commandements of suspecting or suspending. The causes heere of seperation are not bodily but spirituall, not diseases of the bodie, but diseases of the soule, sinne: which sinne when it publikely appeareth, and obstinacy be added to the same, when it is publikly vewed and censured; then hath the church a prescript law and commandement to excommunicate and to cast out; not the pastor to suspend such an uncleane person: therfore betwixt these suspensions (as they call them) that under the law, and this under their gospel, is no proportion or comparison; that being done according to God's prescript lawes, this altogether without warrant of the word, except peradventure they doe it by warrant of these Leviticall lawes, or els I see no cause they should thus bring them for the maine proofe of this their suspension; which if they do, then are they Levitical priests also, for none els might meddle with the administration of those lawes; then are they also under the shaddow, under the law, not under Christ, grace, the gospell. The lawes of the Leviticall ministery cannot be exercised by the ministery of the gospel, neither any of them now receaved, without the losse of Christ. A dangerous thing it is thus violently to wrest and misapply these Levitical lawes, figures, ceremonies, or to build upon the same such stubble, wooddendivises, as they doe, as their tithes, offrings, purifications, feasts, suspension, not to speake of their ministeriall vestures, holy cemitory[1] synagogues, with all the Jewes' implements therof, wherby they innovate or rather abrogate the Testament of Christ, coine and forge a new ministerie, a new worship, a new gospell; for the gospell of Christ only accordeth to his owne ministerie, and the ministerie of Christ to his owne gospell: the gospell of Christ may neither be added unto, nor diminished from, the legal ceremonies and figures, whiles they are soberly understood and rightly applied, give a good light and gratious instruction: but when they are thus rashly allegorized according to the phantasies of men, and boldly applied to maintaine their divises, then become they unto them a stone to stumble at.

The other reason from Mathew 5: 23, 24, is altogether as false, and yet rather more corrupt. Our Saviour there teacheth, that God requireth mercie and not sacrifice; sacrifice with bloody hands or an evill heart is abhomination unto God. He therfore there exhorteth, that they first make cleane their hands from oppression, and make peace with their neighbour, then purge their heart and make peace with God by sacrifice according to the lawes, Leviticus 6: 5; Numbers 5: 7, 8. This doctrine still remaineth and belongeth to every Christian, even to the pastor himself. The Lord abhorreth all hypocrisie, he looketh not to Caine's sacrifice, neither is pleased with Balaam's altar: he will have all that approch unto him, to draw neere with a true heart, their hearts being sprinkled from an evill conscience,

---

[1] Cemetery. Probably a reference to the churchyard, the consecrated enclosure.

and washed in our body with pure water, *etc.* But what of all this? What place is heere found to suspension? Or what power is here given to the pastor to seperate from the communion [240] table in this maner? Unles (as the papists doe) they take themselves for sacrificing priests, their communion table for the altar: this their priestly power derived from these Leviticall lawes is above answered. I would here know of these allegorisers what the alter in the law signified, and what our saviour Christ here meant by the altar, if not the whole worship of God, and with what sense they can thus popishly understand it of and applie it to their communion table only, shutting them from that, admitting them to their praiers and other exercise. Heere me thinkes their answere is ready; because the sacrifice of Christ's body is there remembred and resembled. It is well; and will they shut such from the communion of the sacrifice of Christ's body, whose praiers they will offer up upon that golden altar? Might the priests under the law receave and burne the odours upon the incense altar, whose sacrifices they refused at the brazen altar for burnt offrings? Whosoever for unclennes, *etc.*, was seperate, was seperate from the whole tabernacle and al the ministerie and exercises therof. How then can these blind and foolish pharisies thus halfe[1] Levit. 22: 3 Christ, to make him a minister, an advocate, an altar for the praiers of such to whome he is no sacrifice, no minister at the brazen altar, whome he driveth from his table from his communion, and will neither give his body unto them, nor suffer them to be knit with his members unto it. What maner of juggling, what kind of fast and loose is this? What shall we thinke of the estate of these men that are thus suspended? They being halfe driven from Christ, halfe received unto Christ, halfe cast out of the church, halfe admitted in. What is this estate like unto, if not to the popish purgatorie? These men being neither wholy Christ's, nor wholy Satan's. And surely seing they wil with the papists from hence take this popish priestly power unto themselves, as also this fond [foolish] toole of suspension,

---

[1] Divide.

I see not why they should dissent from them in the third, namely, in the purgatorie.

By this time I hope you perceave what kind of stuffe this their censure of suspension is, which both the sorts of these priests generally allow of and receive. You see how evill it accordeth to the heavenly frame of Christ's Testament and church: you may also by this which hath generally beene saied touching the most reformed use of it in the hands of these supposed pastors (that should be) judg what kind of toole and weapon it is in the hands of these popish prelates, the bishops. You may see by the exercise of it upon any private member, what an odious and intollerable thing it were to be exercised upon the pastor or other ministers of the church, especially at the pleasure and lust of one man: now let us proceed to their excommunication.

This is executed by one man or his commissary in their courts (as hath been said), never for any sin or error (for such matters they either let passe, or punish by the temporall sword, by fines, imprisonment, or penance, *etc.*). But their excommunication is altogether exercised for contumacie: as for not obeiing their summons, or for not satisfiing the judgment of their courts, namely, for not paying these ravenous voul-[241]tures, these officers, their fees, or not paying the mulcts that are inflicted upon them in their courts, *etc.* And as it most commonly ariseth but about these money matters, so is it in effect but a money matter it self: you shal find Mr. Commissarie, if he see it coming, no unreasonable man, he had as leeve take your money himself as an other should, for this he knowes it shalbe dispensed with for money, either in his court or some where els. The forme of this excommunication I cannot set downe, but I weene it be in manner of a writte in Latine, as also the absolution therof proclaimed in the name of the bishop or archbishop after the order of their mother church of Rome: these their spider webbes of their ecclesiastical lawes and jurisdiction extend not but unto the smaller and common flies, the magistrates and greater personages are wholy exempt from them.

The other sect of these priests, the counterfait Reformists, they also would exclude the church from this and al other ecclesiastical censures, assuming them wholy into their owne hands, either into the priest's hands with his silly presbitery or eldership, which he overruleth at his pleasure in everie particular congregation, or els into their synodes and councels, which have power over al churches and every member and action therof, to excommunicate and absolve, to make and depose, to ordeine and abrogate, without the privitie and consent of the churches, other than of their preachers or priests. Thus both sides subvert the libertie of the church, and pervert the ordinance of Christ, the one sort by corrupting, the other by utterlie rejecting the unpartial use of true excommunication by everie christian congregation according to the rules of Christ's Testament, as intollerable and a mischiefe to this common welth.

We have above larglie prooved, the necessitie, stabilitie, perpetuitie, of that order and government which Christ in his Testament hath set downe for the building and direction of his church. By manie places of Scripture and reasons we have shewed, how that order and government onlie best accordeth and fitteth to the church of Christ, in al places and times whatsoever: and how the church can neither receave other orders and lawes, or change these which Christ hath given, without casting off Christ's yoke, and disanulling his Testament; Christ's Testament and church being for ever in all places one and the same. We have also in manie places of this present writing shewed, how Christ hath given unto his church his spirituall power and authoritie, with the sharpe two edged sword that proceedeth out of his mouth, to cut off all transgression and error, as also all trespassers and heretikes that remaine obstinate and impenitent in their sinne; and hath given them straight commandement vigilantly and unpartially to use the same sword and power unto the worlde's end. The necessitie of which power, though it were not confirmed by so manie direct and expresse places of Scripture; yet might it to al men appeare, in that without the same they can neither receave Christ, who is never severed from his power, neither can they keepe sound anie communion, when they have not [242] the power to cast out and seperate the plaguy and leprous from amongst them.

Moreover, we have shewed how this power of excommunication, election, ordination, *etc.*, is not committed into the hands of one particular person, as the pope and his natural children, our lord bishops, now use it; nor yet into the hands of the eldership only, or of the pastors of many particular congregations (as the reforming preachers would have it) so much as it is given and committed to the whole church, even to every particular congregation, and to every member therof alike. To which holy spiritual power of Christ, every member of the church and servant of Christ must be subject alike, without exception or exemption of person. How contrary then unto God and prejudiciall unto his church, is the blasphemy and pride of those men, which thus presumptuously open their mouthes against heaven and all the ordinances of God, pronouncing this spiritual and heavenly censure of excommunication duly executed by the church according to the wil and comandement of Christ (as the only meanes for the preservation of the whole church and of the parties so excommunicate) to be intollerable in a christian realme, prejudiciall to princes and magistrates; yea, that popishly assume this sword of Christ, this power of his church, into their owne hands, and therwith of their owne sole authority smite some, exempt others as they lust themselves: whose monstrous and enormous abuse of this heavenly ordinance, cannot by the pen or mouth of any be so lively discribed, as it is with great letters to the view of all men ingraved and exposed in the daily practise of their commissaries' courtes, the Court of High Commission, *etc.* But that all the pretextes of this their odious blasphemy and pride may at once be plucked from them, let me in a word or two by expresse Scriptures shew what true excommunication is, by whome, upon whome, and how it is to be executed.

We read 1 Corinthians 5, Titus 3: 10, 1 Timothy 1: 20: excommunication to be an utter disfranchizing; and publike cutting off of all convinced obstinate

offendors from all interest in Christ and all communion
with his church, in the open congregation. We reade
in the said 1 Corinthians 5, as also Mathew 18: 17,
Mathew 28: 20, Romans 16: 17, 2 Thessalonians 3: 6,
14, the power and execution of this censure of excommunication to be committed to the whole church, else
why should the apostle charge and blame the whole
church for the neglect therof, and command the whole
church to execute it? Why should our saviour Christ
command his disciples to admonish their brethren when
they offend, and if they repent not, to complaine unto
the church? He sendeth them not heere unto the
pastor to complaine unto him, nor unto the bishop,
High Commission, presbutry, synode, or councel to
complaine unto them for redresse; neither yet comit-
teth he here or in any other place of Scripture this
action unto them, or commandeth them as by vertue
of their office to do it. But (as may evidently appeare
in these and sundry other places of Scripture) both this
publike casting out and receaving in of any member,
is committed and [243] belongeth unto the whole
church and everie member therof jointly together, and
is not especiallie or solely committed to anie one or
anie some of them anie more than unto al the rest. We
see also the pastor, and al the teachers and other members of the church subject unto this censure; yea, and
the church where these members make such offence,
is to proceed against them, to avoide them, to excommunicate them. Read for further proofe of this Galatians 1: 8, 9, 2 John 9, *etc.*, 1 Timothy 6: 3, 5, 2 Timothy
2: 17, and 3: 5, Colossians 4: 17, Phillippians 3: 2, 17,
18, 19. So that although the church performe this
action by the pastor, as a member most fit therunto;
yet neither the pastor gayneth, nor the church looseth,
anie right or interest in this action heerby, because we
see evidently the church hath power to doe this action
without a pastor, yea, against their pastor.

The maner of this excommunication, we in the said
5 of the 1 Corinthians find to be done in the publike
congregation where the whole church is assembled, and
not in anie courtes or bishops' howses; in the name and

power of our Lord Jesus Christ, and not in the name and power of a lord bishop or archbishop, in the usuall tongue of that congregation as it may best edifie, and not in the Romane tongue after their popish maner in forme of a writ. This censure is not done before the fault be publikely knowne, either in the first committing of it, or els by processe for contemning admonition, neither before the partie offending be duly convinced, admonished and exhorted. But when the sin thus appeareth and becommeth publike, the sinner is thus convinced, admonished, exhorted, and still continueth obstinate and impenitent; then is the church without delay or partialitie to proceed, by the power of our Lord Jesus Christ with one consent to cast out such a one, and deliver him unto Sathan for the humbling of the flesh, that the spirit might be saved in the day of the Lord, yea, to avoid from themselves both the contagion and judgmentes following his sin.

Now then seeing this censure of excommunication is an especiall part of the judgment, power, and scepter of Christ; seing Christ hath committed it unto his church, even unto everie christian congregation, whether it be established in order, or it be indevoring into order, as a most necessarie meanes to preserve and keepe them in the unitie of the faith and godlines, without which power and the due execution therof it is impossible to keepe anie communion, how great is their sin against Christ and his church, that thus presumptuously wrast the sword out of Christ's hand, and take it into their owne furious handes, that utterly deprive the church of all use of it, save that they smite and wound the poore lambes and servantes of Christ with it, or rather with that great sword given unto their father the devil to shew innocent blood.

But especially what injurie doe they unto their princes and magistrates, that thus deprive and exempt them from the heavenlie government of Christ (if so be this their ecclesiasticall discipline and church government be the true government of Christ (as they vaunt and give out), doe [244] they not heerby manifest, that either princes and magistrats are not the servantes and sub-

jectes of Christ, or els that themselves have the great
charter of antichrist as well as their sire the pope, to
dispense with the breach of God's lawes, and to assoile[1]
princes and magistrates from the obedience and reverence of Christ? Or els peradventure with their deepe
learning they are able to proove: that christian princes
and magistrates, either cannot sin in such manner to
deserve excommunication, or els are not liable to the
same judgmentes of God, as other Christians are for the
like transgressions; or els that Christ hath not made one
and the same covenant with al men, but hath apointed
one way for princes and magistrates to be saved, an
other way for inferior Christians of lower callings. But
if the covenant and law of God be one and the same
unto al men; if al men ought to be alike liable to the
law of God, and subject to the sacred person and
scepter of Christ; if rebellion be as the sin of witchcraft, and transgression as idolatrie; if Christ be an
upright and unpartiall judge; if Topheth be prepared
of olde, if it be prepared even for the king deep and
large, *etc.*[2] Then most dangerous and damnable is the
perfidie and flatterie of those prophets that not only
pronounce peace unto wicked magistrates in their sin,
but exempt christian magistrates from subjection and
obedience unto the scepter and government of Christ
in his church, wherby they draw them into battel
against Christ. For if they be not under his scepter
of grace, then are they under his iron rod, wherwith
he wil bruise them to sheardes.[3] If they be his subjects, then doth he reigne over them, and that by his
owne lawes: but if they wil not have him to reigne over
them, then commeth he against them and judgeth them
as his enemies. This is the good service these men
doe unto their magistrates, to bring them into the
wrath of the lion of the tribe of Juda: this is the care
these good shephardes have of the soules of their prince
and magistrats, to suffer them to runne on in their sin

---

[1] Absolve.
[2] Isaiah 30: 33. Topheth is a burial and burning place, in the valley of the
sons of Hinnom; "for the [Assyrian] king it is made ready, its pyre
made deep and wide."
[3] Fragments, pieces. Cf. p. [220].

without coercion or reproofe; yea, to deprive them of the onlie meanes and cure that God in his mercie and wisdome hath provided for al his servants in that estate.

But these pollitike divines make princes beleeve that it is no small injurie and derogation to their persons and office to be subject to the reproofe and censure of Christ in his church. Excommunication of magistrates (say they) was an instrument to bring the neckes of emperors and princes under the pope's girdle, the onlie meane wherby he became so dreadful to al men, and got to himself so great authority: therfore our English pope and lord bishops, though they stil retaine in their handes this popish thunderbolt of excommunication; yet so warily doe they use it, as they wil not affray princes or great personages therewith.[1]

Alas, and cannot these learned bishops in al this light and free passage of the gospel they bost of, as yet discerne or put difference betwixt Christ's most lawfull sacred spiritual power, and the pope's usurped divelish carnall powers? Should not magistrates be subject to the first, because they ought not to endure or suffer the second? Hath not God spoken [245] from heaven; this is my beloved sonne, heare him?[2] And againe; therfore God hath highly exalted him and given him a name above every name, that in the name of Jesus every knee should bow, etc., and every tongue confesse, that Jesus is the Lord?[3] And speaking unto the sonne, he saith, "Thy throne o God to the world of worldes, the scepter of thy kingdome is a rod of righteousnes ";[4] and in an other place, "I have annointed my king upon Zion, mine holy mountaine," etc.[5] "Give heed, therfore, ye kings, be ye disciplined, ye judges of the earth, serve the Lord in feare, rejoice in trembling: kisse the sonne least that he be angrie, and ye perish in the way."[6] It were long to recite the expresse Scriptures which every where shew, that all kings and magis-

---

[1] Thomas Cooper, *An Admonition to the People of England,* pp. 141 f.
[2] Mark 9: 7.   Matthew 17: 5.
[3] Philippians 2: 9.
[4] Psalms 45: 6.
[5] Psalms 2: 6.
[6] Psalms 2: 10-12.

trates ought to be subject to the scepter and censure of Christ in his church, to bring their glorie and honour thither, and cast downe their crownes before him, of whome they receave and hold their crownes, even by homage tenure, from whome they derive al their power, and therfore, with all their power ought to serve him, unto whome they shal accompt. All the godly kings of whome we read in the Scriptures, have beene bownd and subject unto the lawes of God and censures of the church, in their calling, as any other. How earnestly did David beseech the Lord, that he would seek out his servant, when he erreth, as a sheepe? That the righteous might smite him, for that shalbe a benefite; that they might reprove him, for that shalbe as a cheefe oyntment. As kings enter into the church, and are made members of Christ by profession and true practise of the faith; so when they fall and depart from the same faith, and will not be reduced by admonition and reproofe, they are no longer to be held of the faith of the church, but are as any other, to receave the judgment and censure of Christ, to be cut off and cast out as withered branches; and this as the only remedy of their salvation for the humbling of their flesh, *etc.* Yf kings be subject to the instruction and admonition of the church as David, Asa, Jehoshaphat, Ezekiah, *etc.*, were; why should they not also with Uzziah (when the running ulcers of fretting and incurable sinne appeare uppon them) be cut off from the howse of the Lord, and seperate from the communion of the saints, as he was,[1] least they defile more, and make the whole offrings and companie abhominable unto the Lord. Yf in that materiall temple, where the worship consisted in externall ceremonies, no degrees of persons were exempted from the observation of the lawes, the king himself might not enter with his uncleannes upon him, but as you see was cast out according to the law? How much more in this spirituall howse of Christ, ought they to be subject to the lawes and judgments of Christ, as well, yea, and rather more than any other.

To this they object, because the king is the cheefe

---

[1] 2 Chronicles 27: 16-21.

and supreame governor here in earth over all persons and causes as well of the church as of the common welth, unto whome every soule must be subject: therfore cannot the whole church, much lesse any member therof (all being his subjects) censure, judg, or excommunicate the prince, the pla-[246]cing, punishing, and deposing of whome, only belongeth unto God, by whome kings reigne.

O how great is the blindnes of these phariseis, that cannot put difference betweene the spirituall judgments of Christ in his church, and the temporall or rather corporall judgments of the magistrate in the common welth? But most grossely and wickedly oppose the one against the other? Might they not as well reason, and upon the same grounds conclude, that the prince is no member of the church, neither that the church hath any communion with him, because he is supreme governour of the church, and all the church are his subjects? Yea, doe they not as much, when they give unto princes such blasphemous titles, popish prerogatives and dispensations, as SUPREME HEAD OF THE CHURCH,[1] to make lawes for the church concerning the worship, ministery, ministration and whole government of the church, and those such as are not read of in the booke of God, and to be exempt from the jurisdiction and censure of Christ in his church? Now which way in this estate can they make the prince a subject of Christ or member of his church, when both in titles, power, and pre[ro]gative they exalt princes into the chaire of Christ, or (to say as it is) rather into the chaire of antichrist. But to come to this pollitike impediment and intollerable inconvenience that would ensue, if princes should be subject to the excommunication of the church, then say they he should be subject to the church, and so subject to his subjects. I denie the sequele of their argument: for this censure is not the censure of the church, so much as of Christ in his church: so that though Christ use the ministerie of

---

[1] By the Supremacy Act of 1534, Henry VIII became " the only supreme head in earth of the Church of England." By the Supremacy Act of 1559, specifically in the oath of supremacy, Elizabeth was designated as the only supreme governor of this realm . . . ., as well in all spiritual or ecclesiastical things or causes, as temporal.

his church, [though] the church [use] the ministerie of
some most fit member unto this action, yet is it still the
censure and judgment of Christ, unto which every servant of Christ and member of the church must be subject.
So that they might as well reason, that the prince is
subject to the church, *etc.*, because he must be subject
to the gospell; which is also the ministerie of the church.
The least member of the church is not subject to the
church, neither to follow it further than it followeth
Christ. But whiles some, without all feare of God have
indevored to draw, and others not doubted to yeild that
honour which is due unto God, unto the persons of men;
herehence hath al this exaltation of antichrist and pride
of the prelacie arisen; yea, these impious collections and
blasphemous conclusions against Christ's holy ordinances ensued: to such a measure and height is this sin
now growen, that they not only cast off Christ's yoke
themselves, but assoile[1] princes of their allegeance unto
him; yea, proclaime this most peaceable and spiritual
censure of Christ, to be seditious, intollerable, contrary
unto the magistracie, *etc.*

Than which assertion what can be more heathen and
barbarous? Is it not to set their state expressly against
Christ? Yea, Christ against God? Cannot these
carnal men consider, that Christ himself whiles he was
heere on earth, as also his apostles, were subject in al
lawfull things unto the civile magistrate, and taught the
churches so to be unto the world's end? [247] Yet both
Christ and his apostles gave perpetuall and often commandements for the diligent and upright use of this
spiritual censure unto the world's end. Are they so
Anabaptisticall to thinke, that there never were or should
be magistrates of the church? Or thinke they that
these lawes were made for the church, before the magistrates were called to the faith? Were not Nicodemus,
Joseph of Aramathia, Sergius Paulus, Cornelius, Dioni-
sius, Erastus, *etc.*, magistrates,[2] and called to the faith?
Yet in their time was the use of excommunication in-

---

1 Absolve, release.
2 John 3: 1; Mark 15: 43 and Luke 23: 50; Acts 13: 7; Acts 10: 1;
Acts 17: 34; Romans 16: 23.

joined, and practised. No where can they shew in all the Testament of Christ any exception or immunity of any one person from this spirituall censure and government of Christ, which is no way contrary unto the temporal estate and civil degree of the prince or magistrate.[1]

Who though they be excommunicate, yet still retaine their civil estate and dignity wherin God hath placed them, and still are reverenced and obeied of the whole church, as such magistrates whome God hath set over them: only members of the church they cannot be held, whiles they presumptuously transgresse, or obstinately disobey Christ's voice. It is not in the power of the church to receave or cast out any member, before they see faith or transgression accordingly: nor yet hath the church power to keepe in any member, longer than he keepeth the faith and walketh orderly. So then until they can prove that there can be no magistrates but such as are of the church, or that this ecclesiastical excommunication is a depriving and deposing of the civil magistracy, they do but reproch the truth, and seduce the magistrate. As these spirituall judgments extend not unto, so the church that pronounceth and executeth the same, no way medleth with the office or person of the prince, or magistrate. They are taught not to lay violent hands upon the Lord's annointed, but to be obedient unto the death.[2] It alwaies hath beene the custome of the pope and his offspring, to encroch both upon churches and princes, to assume this antichristian

---

[1] Barrow is courageous in teaching plainly that princes, including Queen Elizabeth, are subject to discipline, and even to excommunication, by the church. Barrow certainly knew that the queen would not be disciplined, censured, or excommunicated, but he is concerned with a broad principle and he is willing to draw unpopular conclusions from it. This doctrine must have been galling to Elizabeth, who guarded jealously her ecclesiastical prerogatives, as seen in her harsh treatment of Archbishop Grindal. To the ecclesiastical hierarchy Barrow's doctrine must have seemed presumptuous. To the civil magistrates it would be regarded as illegal, since they took an oath to uphold the queen's temporal and ecclesiastical power by law established.

[2] Barrow is contending that the king's subjects would remain good subjects, even if the king or queen were excommunicated. He seeks to refute Bishop Cooper's argument that abuses and dangers would ensue from such a power of excommunication. In effect, Barrow says that a prince who was *persona non grata* to his church could and would be *persona grata* to temporal subjects.

power over both into their hands, to bind and to loose, to curse and assoile [absolve] whome they list. Neither can I see the sin of these antichristian bishops, these ympes of the pope, to be lesse in discharging princes from this holy censure of Christ; than their sire's [sin] was in tyrannizing and oppressing them therwith: neither yet how these men can beate downe the tyrannous usurped power of the pope, when they assume into their owne hands, and execute the self same power over the whole church and all the ordinances therof without accompt or controlement, as hath beene plentifully shewed in all this discovery, and yet more shall appeare, if we now take a litle view of their [Court of High] Commission, which is the very abisme and golph from whence spring and flow all these innumerable enormities, into every part of this whole land their church.

This indefinite monstrous [Court of High] Commission I (having never seene their letters pattents or any copie therof)[1] cannot otherwise describe, than by certaine apparant circumstances: as the men of [248] whome it consisteth, and that have the chiefe rule therof; the persons and causes over which this Commission is set, and hath jurisdiction; and the maner of using their sayd power.

The commissioners are certayne ecclesiasticall and civile persons; as first the primate of England (the archbishop of Canterburie), then I suppose the metropolitane of Yorke,[2] with certaine other bishops, as London, Winchester, *etc.*, certaine deanes, arch-deacons and chancelors, with sundry especial civile doctors, *etc.* The civil persons of this Commission are now of late dayes some few of her majestie's honorable Councell, the two chiefe judges: certaine courtiers; as the two maisters of her majestie's [Court of] Requests; certaine chosen

---

[1] The commissions of 1559, 1562, 1572, 1576, and 1601 are conveniently available in G. W. Prothero, *Select Statutes and Other Constitutional Documents Illustrative of the Reigns of Elizabeth and James I* (Oxford, 1949), pp. 227-241. See also *Calendar of the Patent Rolls, Elizabeth*, I, 1558—1560, pp. 118 f.; II, 1560—1563, pp. 279-281. There is a manuscript commission of twenty folios (twelve leaves), dated June 20, 1589, entitled "The Highe Commission for Causes Ecclesiasticall," in the Huntington Library, Ellesmere MS. 1988.

[2] The Archbishop of York is not listed as a commissioner in any of the commissions for 1559, 1562, 1572, 1576, 1601.

aldermen, and the recorder of London; certaine other officers about the citie; as the lieftenant of the Tower, the post-master and sundry other that I know not, not heere to recite that rabble of advocates, proctors, scribes, pursuyvants, attending therupon.

These thus joined in this high great Commission, have (or at the least exercise) by vertue therof absolute power and jurisdiction over the whole Church of England and every particular congregation of the same, and over every minister and member of the same, even over al the queen's subjects. They also exercise small jurisdiction and absolute power over all causes ecclesiasticall whatsoever, to handle and determine, to visite, enquire and punish, to make new lawes, orders, decrees, and to injoine the same as authentike upon all churches, as, and before the holy oracles of God. They have power also to assume any cause or plea out of any other of their inferior spiritual courtes (as they call them) into their owne hands, to ratifie or disanul any thing there done. They have power also to erect and to authorise new litle high commissions in any citie of the land, where it pleaseth them: only with this exception; that they alwaies acknowledg the supreme power of their parent at Lambeth.[1] Yet further this great High Commission hath absolute power over sundrie (and what not) civil causes, insomuch as they feare not to meddle with matters belonging to the queen's crowne or prerogative roial, or to any of her courts of plea whatsoever: yea, they have not doubted to intercept causes belonging unto, and depending in the high Court of Parliament, if Mr. Penry in his appeale say true.[2] They have power to cite, summon, or convent by their pursuyvants and cursitors, what person of the land either man or woman at any time when they please: they have power to command all the queen's officers, as maiors of cities, sherifs, etc., to serve and attend, watch and ride, by day

---

[1] See the list of letters patent, general and special, in Roland G. Usher, *The Rise and Fall of the High Commission*, pp. 361-7.

[2] John Penry, *The Appellation of John Penri, unto the Highe Court of Parliament, from the Bad and Injurious Dealing of the Archbishop of Canterbury and Other His Colleagues of the High Commission* ([London ?], 1589), pp. 39-41.

or by night upon their busines whatsoever: also to apprehend, to incarcerate, or to deliver out of prison, what person or persons, how innocent or flagitious[1] soever, upon their barre warrant, without further enquire or delay: yea, they have power to fetch up any of these officers before them from their charge in her majestie's services, and there also to ymprison them, if they so thinke good. They have power to authorize these rakehel[2] robbers, their pursuyvants, to herry, molest or attach any of the queen's [249] faithful subjects they list, to breake open and ransack their houses by day or by night, to spoile and carrie away what and whome they please without controulement, their warrants being made indefinite, without anie certaine perscription [sic] or limitation.

Wel, and being thus furnished with this power, they Revel. 9: 7, 9 come together at their session as charrets [chariots] armed to the battel, a great tayle of officers and court of attendants being assembled, the apparance wherof exceedeth I suppose that of the Vaticane at Rome, no praier used before, neither the booke of God opened in this their ecclesiastical councel. The parties convented are to attend, being called to appeare before them: before whome being come, what affaires soever they have, whither of a whole church, or of manie congregations, what office or degree soever they be of, they must there stand, their heades discovered before them, no place given them with or by these commissioners. Yf they be to propound, speake, or complaine of any thing, they must doe it by the officers of this courte, their advocates, proctors, registers, scribes, *secundum modum et formam*,[3] and that to no small charge by that time all these voultures have their fees: otherwise than by these they may not plead in this courte: the judgments of this court they must receave without contradiction or gainsaiing; there is no appeale, no helpe, no meanes to reverse the same, be they never so unjust. Any others that are blamed and accused unto this courte, have not heere place to answere unto such

---

[1] Extremely wicked, atrociously criminal.
[2] Vile, dissolute, debauched.
[3] According to custom and form, method and plan.

things as shalbe objected against them by their accusers, being brought face to face, or to defend themselves according to equitie: but heere they shall hardly know their accusers, or accusations at anie time, until they have taken an othe to answere truly unto such things as shalbe demanded of them in that court; wherby they are driven to accuse themselves, and so minister matter abundantly unto their adversaries. The othe that is heere administred is, that laying their hand or three fingers upon a booke, they sweare by God and by the contents of the booke, to answere truly unto such things as shalbe demanded of them, and so kissing the booke their othe is accepted, and no further leisure given to consider what they answere unto their demandes.[1] But if anie make conscience, or denie to receave this idolatrous wicked othe (which though it be proved unto them to be never so unlawful, and contrary to the commandement of God, Deuteronomy 6: 13 and Deuteronomy 10: 20, to be never so superstitious in devising and adding, yea, in injoining ceremonies where God in these lawes hath made none, but commanded to sweare without anie ceremonies by the name of God only; though it be proved to be never so idolatrous, in joining any thing unto or with God, in swearing by any thing besides or with God; though the fearful curse of God be shewed to be denounced against such maner of swearing and swearers, by the Lord's prophets in these words: " they that sweare in the sin of Samaria, and that say, thy God, o Dan, liveth and the way of Beerschebah liveth, even they shal fal and never rise up againe ";[2] and in an other place, that the Lord will cut off al that sweare [250] by Jehovah as they sweare by Malcham:[3] be this othe prooved never so unnecessarie, the cause not requiring anie such triall; be it proved never so

[1] See Mary Hume [Maguire], " The History of the *Ex Officio* Oath in England," a Ph.D. thesis (1923) in the library of Radcliffe College, Cambridge, Massachusetts. See also *Cartwrightiana*, ed. Albert Peel and Leland H. Carlson, pp. 21-46. See also Richard Cosin, *An Apologie: of, and for Sundrie Proceedings by Jurisdiction Ecclesiasticall* (1591 and 1593). James Morice, *A Briefe Treatise of Oathes Exacted by Ordinaries and Ecclesiastical Judges*, pp. 45-58. John Penry, *The Appellation*, pp. 41-3.
[2] Amos 8: 14.
[3] Zephaniah 1: 5.

unnatural, it being to accuse themselves; and that unto
their adversaries), yet wil these graceles bishops inforce
this othe; first by way of perswasion, by Abraham's and
Jaacob's examples, who caused the one his servant, the
other his sonne to sweare, putting their hand under
their theigh, *etc.*, and by the angels lifting up his hand
unto heaven to sweare. If unto the first they be answered, that Abraham and Jaacob joined not this
ceremony unto the othe, so much as to exact the fidelitie
and performance of the othe, seeing God himself sware
unto Abraham without this ceremonie, Genesis 15 and
17; as also Ishaac sware, and Jaacob sware without this
ceremonie, Genesis 26: 31 and Genesis 31: 53; so that
there can be no law drawen or example made of Abraham and Jaacob heerin, especially seing this was before
the law was given: but now we have an absolute law
given of God for the forme of othes, from which law we
ought not to swerve.[1] If unto the second, namely, the
angels lifting up the hand unto heaven whiles he sware,
it be likewise answered; that no law can be inforced
from hence, or any new ceremony injoined in swearing,
nothing being done heere, contrarie to the law of God,
neither any example given to breake or alter the law
given of God, seing now both al superstitious ceremonies
and idolatrous othes are forbidden us, by our saviour
Christ and his apostles: Mathew 5: 34, 35; Mathew 23;
Galatians 4: 9; Colossians 2: 20. Their next reason is
drawen from the prince's priviledg; that the prince
hath power to make lawes of indifferent things, and is
therin to be obeied: this maner of othe is shewed to be
no indifferent thing, but altogether unlawful and prohibited for the reasons above alledged. But if it were 1 Cor. 6: 12
a thing indifferent (as they suppose) so to sweare or not
so to sweare, yet were it not lawfull for any mortal man
to bind that by way of law, which God hath left in our
libertie; much lesse to bring in new ceremonies or divises
into the worship of God: for so might al the pope's
traditions be brought in and justified. When these

---

[1] " Do not swear at all, either by heaven, for it is the throne of God, or by
the earth, for it is his footstool, or by Jerusalem, for it is the city of the
great King." Matthew 5: 34, 35.

reasons wil not serve to perswade or assure the conscience, then these holy fathers, these tender hearted christian bishops, are driven to their last argument wherby they uphold their antichristian throne, *viz.*, the civil power and authoritie which is committed into their murtherous handes.

Then are they forthwith committed unto close prison, there to remaine until they either yeild, or die; and this without respect of age, sexe, or degree, especially if they be convented for refusing or speaking against the bishops' popelike authoritie, antichristian decrees, idolatrous injunctions, *etc.*; such with mortall hatred they persecute, much more than they doe the most hainous malefactors and traiterous papists: such they openly publish to be sectaries, scismatikes, heretikes, Anabaptists, disobedient to magistrates, seditious, conventiclers, *etc.*, and al because they will not beare antichriste's yoke, nor carie the beaste's marke, nor bow downe unto and worship his image.   Such therfore they hunt and pursue abrode by their spials[1] and pursyvants, and having caught them, use with al exquisite tyranny, never suffring them to depart out of their [251] hands, until they either deny the faith, or be fetched from them by the Lord's peremptorie messenger, death.   Long it were to relate their fine Spanish arts[2] to molest these constant witnesses and faithfull servants of Christ when they get them in their prisons, by shutting them up long close, by causing them to be produced and indicted at the general sessions upon the statute of recusansy, having made some of the judges on their part; although this statute was made for Christ's and her majestie's enemies, the papists, recusants of all

---

[1] Spies, scouts.
[2] In his letter of July 1, 1584, to Archbishop Whitgift, Lord Burghley complained of the twenty-four articles or interrogatories which Whitgift had devised in May, 1584. He said: "which I have read, and find so curiously penned, so full of branches and circumstances, as I think the inquisitors of Spain use not so many questions to comprehend and to trap their preys." See John Strype, *Whitgift*, III, 81, 104-107.

christian veritie.[1] When upon this statute they have
gotten them indicted, and upon the execution therof
cast into prisons; yet heere their malice ceaseth not, but
although they be the queen's prisoners in her execution,
yet will they (contrarie to all law) assume them back
againe into their handes, and by their sole authoritie
without anie cause alledged, commit them perpetuall
close prisoners, therby to shorten their lives, and to cut
off all meanes either of their owne maintenance from
them, or wherby they might any way satisfie the queene.
Thus play they with poore Christians as the catte doth
with the mouse, boldly committing them unto and
taking them from the secular powers at their owne
pleasure; abusing the queene's lawes and most faithfull
subjectes at their owne lust, without checke or controulement, they being subject and liable to no lawe.
To such a height is this strange Romish Spanish court
now growne, under colour of reforming ecclesiasticall
abuses, that it usurpeth absolute power over al lawes,
causes, persons, estates; yea, and becommeth the very
fountaine or synke rather, from whence flow al errors,
abuses, and disorders into the whole land, it being the
very bane and poyson both of the church and common
welth, that ever going forge of Sathan, wherin he daily
minteth al his antichristian new devises and decrees for
this monstrous harlot the false church, that senate wherin all their affaires are consulted, that councel wherin
all their decrees are concluded, a synode wherin all
causes are debated, a schoole wherin al questions are
disputed, a fayre wherin all their wares are sould. This
monstrous court taketh utterly away the power and
stoppeth the course of God's word, of his church, and
of the godly lawes of the land: prejudicial it is to the

---

[1] Barrow and Greenwood were indicted about May, 1588, at the Newgate
Sessions, found guilty of violating the statute of 23 Elizabeth, *cap.* I.
The Puritans and Separatists insisted that this " Act to Retain the Queen's
Majesty's Subjects in Their Due Obedience " was originally intended for
Catholic recusants, but was misapplied to the Protestants. The first
three sections clearly emphasize the role of Catholics, and section III
specifies that those who say or sing or hear mass shall be fined and suffer
imprisonment. But the other sections contain language which applies
to " all persons whatsoever " and to " every person above the age of
sixteen years, which shall not repair to some church."

prerogative of the prince, to the jurisdiction of her royall courts, to the libertie of her free subjects, and to the Great Charter of England, as their practise evidently sheweth. How contrarie it is unto God, and unto al the rules of his word, even by this summarie recitall and insufficient description of their doings, at the first reading may appear to al men that wil bring them to the light. So barbarous is their power, so odious their proceedings, as no apologie can be made for them, unlesse by the same they wil also justifie the authoritie of the pope, and proceedings of the Spanish Inquisition; both which yet heerin they exceed, in that this court hath power to make lawes and ordinances for al churches without their consent, which the pope cannot doe: as also, in that this court hath power and jurisdiction over many, and almost al civil causes, which the Spanish Inquisition hath not. [252]

Let not my words be wrasted or misconstrued to the reproch of these honorable personages, and such civile magistrates as are of this Commission; whose civil offices and persons we from our hearts unfainedly honour and reverence: yet can the authority of their personages no way justifie, the unlawfulnes of this Commission, or hide the ungodlines of the bishops' proceedings therin; with whose crafty practises we suppose they are not made acquainted, being tised[1] into this Commission by the subtilty of the bishops (who suppose to fortifie their antichristian power and popish regiment, by the authority and countenance of these honorable and reverend men), whome they perswade that they shal do much good herein: before whome they bring none, but the most heinous and fowle causes, as incest, plurality of wives, papistry, *etc.*, never suffring them to looke into the secrets and mysteries of their kingdome, or to heare the just complaints of the queen's oppressed subjects by their tyranny. These (as is abovesaid) they wil not suffer so much as to expose their griefes, utter their wrongs, or to plead and defend their owne cause before these civil magistrates, no, not in this their owne courte, where the archbishop is in his exaltation, and their

---

[1] Enticed, induced.

chiefe adversaries are judges; so fearful are they least the light should breake forth, and all their packing and wickednes be bewraied. But he that discloseth all secrets, will (I doubt not) shortly reveale all their doings, and make them as odious as they are now honorable. At which time, such as now joine to them and uphold them, shall stand far off for feare of their torments, when the wrath of God shalbe reveled from heaven against all the impiety and injustice of these men that withhold the truth in unrighteousnes. For sure, if the prince and magistrats but knew the unlawfulnes of this Commission, either in the persons, power, or practise therof, they would soone withdraw their power from the beast, and would not in this maner uphold or joine unto the throne of antichrist, that forgeth wrong besides law.

The ecclesiasticall persons of this Commission we have by expresse Scriptures shewed, neither to be true ministers of the gospell, neither true members of the church of Christ. Both which though they were, yet could they not receave or exercise such antichristian power and inordinate authority over all, or any one congregation of Christ; much lesse in the estate they stand. For the civill magistrates that are of this Commission, though they may as members together with those congregations wherunto they are joined, jointly with the whole church exercise such spiritual power to censure faltes, discusse matters, and determine of such affaires as belong unto and arise in their congregations, *etc.*, yet can they not (as by vertue of their civil office) exercise these spirituall censures and power, which Christ hath given and belongeth unto the whole church; much lesse assume into their owne hands, and plucke from the whole church this power which Christ hath given them. So then all the persons of this Commission, both ecclesiastical and civil, are utterly uncapable of this inordinate power and jurisdiction; which being [253] so monstrous and heinous over al churches, al ecclesiastical causes, persons and doctrines; to ratifie, or disanul, erect or pull downe, bring in, or cast out of the church, handle and hold plea of many civile causes also, and that after so blasphemous and un-christian a maner, by administring and enforcing their idolatrous booke othe, by prohibiting so much as to speake for themselves or in their owne causes, by in-flicting penalties and fines, by incarcerating whome and for what they list, and there deteining them as close and as long as they list, and that without bayle, mainprise, or trial: which monstrous confused power, belongeth rather unto, and is more fit for that anti-christ, that beast; and unto the false church, than unto any member of Christ, or of his church. God hath put difference (though no disagreement) betwixt the church, and the common welth, betwixt the minister's jurisdiction, and censures of ech of them; having set unto ech sort their due bounds, officers and limits which they ought not after this maner to transgresse or con-found, making I know not what commixture of persons, offices, causes in this monstrous Commission, where the civil magistrate is made a judg and minister of ecclesi-astical causes; their church ministers, of civill and common welth matters, and al under pretext of the commission of the prince: who because he hath power over all causes and persons both of the church and common welth; therfore these men suppose that he may make what new lawes, decrees and orders for both church and common welth that he list, and change the ordinances and decrees of God at his pleasure, especially if he be a christian prince; for then he is no way bownd to the lawes of God or limits of his calling.

But against such devilish doctrines we have often in this treatise proved, that though the prince be placed of God in the most high authority both over the church and common welth here upon earth, yet he is but the servant of God, circumscribed with lawes, as one that shal render an accompt, and be judged before the Lord of all his doings, as any other. Though the prince have the booke of God committed unto him, with charge to see it duly executed by every one in his calling, yet hath he it to keepe and observe, and not to breake or change. We have also proved all the lawes of God to be most

holy, inviolable, and al sufficient both for the church
and common welth, and the perfect instruction of every
officer and member of the same in their several duties
and callings: so that nothing is now left unto any mortal
man, of what high dignity and calling soever, but to
fulfil and execute the will of God in his word, in their
places and callings: which word being now perfected
in the heavenly ministery of Christ, nothing may be
added to, or taken from the same, without most high
sacriledg and impiety, and the utter abrogating of
Christ's Testament: no new devise (how holy or necessary soever to our earthly seeming) is now to be brought
in, or required at our hands, our obedience being more
acceptable unto God than our sacrifice. Which way
then can this strange monstrous Commission, never
read nor heard of in the New Testament of Christ, or
whole word of God, so unlawfull in the [254] persons
that are the commissioners, in the power and authority
they exercise, and in al their proceedings; so pernicious
to the whole church, so directly contrary to the word of
God, and to the utter subversion and taking out of the
way the whole Testament and ordinances of Christ;
how may this Commission (I say) be set over the whole
church, or be justified by the prince's authority?

But to prove that this ecclesiastical High Commission
is no antichristian ungodly or new divise, Mr. Some
hath taken some paines, and bestowed upon us a few
reasons, such as they are.[1] Saith he, this Commission
is derived from our gracious soveraigne Queen Elizabeth,
to whome the antichrist of Rome is a professed enemy,
and is directed to honorable, reverend, and wise men
of the clergie and temporalty: therfore it is not antichristian. Againe sundry branches of this Commission
are godly, as to preserve God's religion whole and sound
from popery, Anabaptistry, *etc.*, to meete with and suppresse notable disorders, as incests, polygamies, oppression of the ministers, *etc.*, and to give defence and
countenance to the good: therfore this Commission is
very godly. Thirdly, high commissions were directed

---

[1] Robert Some, *A Godly Treatise, wherein Are Examined and Confuted Many Execrable Fancies,* pp. 21-23.

W

from Jehoshaphat, king of Juda, and from Artaxerxes, king of Persia; therfore the High Commission of England is no new devise, 2. Chronicles 19, Ezra 7.[1]

By the first reason it should seeme that Mr. Some supposeth that there is no antichrist but the pope of Rome; neither any thing to be antichristian, which commeth not from him: otherwise there wil be litle sequele of this reason; that because the queen's majestie directeth this commission to honorable and reverend men of the clergie and temporalty, therfore the High Commission is not antichristian or unlawfull. Might not by this reason King David's commission or letters mandatory unto Joab, for the murthering of Uriah, be accompted good,[2] because King David was a most godly prince, if so be that the goodnes of any mortal man might make that which is evill good, or justifie any unlawfull action. We heere reason not of the goodnes of any men's persons, so much as of the unlawfulnes of this Commission, which by so many reasons being proved such, can neither be justified by the prince's authority that directeth it, nor by the goodnes of any to whome it is directed, but remaineth altogether unlawful for the one to graunt, for the other to accept. Yet for the persons of these commissioners, we have shewed the civil personages and magistrates to be utterly uncapable of any ecclesiastical functions, whiles they retaine these civil offices, much more of such unlawful and ungodly authority and jurisdiction over so many churches, as they execute in this Commission. As for the honorable, reverend clergie this doctor speaketh of, if we had said nothing concerning their office and ministery before, yet this his popish tearme of clergie (wherby he segregateth the ministery from the rest of the church, or els only would have them to be the Lord's heritage) sufficiently bewraieth from what forge they al came, and plainly sheweth them to have come from their holy father the pope, begotten and borne upon their mother of Rome, such a lordly clergie or clearal [clerical?] prelacy not being before heard

---

[1] 2 Chronicles 19: 8-11.   Ezra 7: 25, 26.
[2] 2 Samuel 11: 14-17.

[255] of, or read in the Testament of Christ: and so by this reason the High Commission is like to prove antichristian, this honorable, reverend clergie which beare al the rule in this Commission, being so immediately derived, and directly discended from that antichrist of Rome. And as for this popish distinction, betwixt the clergie and the laitye; I refer him to reade with due consideration Acts 26: 18 and 1 Peter 5: 3.

There is as litle sequele of his second reason; that because this Commission hath some good branches, as to purge God's religion of popery, anabaptistry, to punish and to suppresse notable disorders, as incests, polygamies, oppression of ministers: therfore this whole High Commission is good and godly. Might not the most ungodly councels that ever were, be thus defended and justified? Because they decreed not some, but many good things? Might not any sect or heresy be thus also defended and justified? Because they hold and teach many good things? Yet judge we such ecclesiasticall councels and assemblies antichristian, which have no warrant from the word of God, where the Holy Ghost is not both the author and ruler. Therfore untill this High Commission be approved either by president [precedent] or rule, we must still hold it antichristian and unlawful. And now touching these faire pretexts wherwith this sepulchre of all rottennes is guilded, this deepe grave is covered, as with flowers and greene grasse; let even these fairest shewes therof be examined and proved by that which hath bene said touching their service-booke, and ministery, what a pure worship and holy ministery this Commission preserveth and maintaineth. Let the commonnes of incests, polygamies, adulteries, fornication and al uncleannes that aboundeth in the land, shew the great good that this Commission doth in the land: yea, let their profane and ungodly order that they take for the suppressing and punishing these crimes, shew what a holy councel this is. The Lord commandeth odious and unnatural incests and al adulteries to be punished with death: the High Commission punisheth the most hatefull incests and poligamies by prisons or by the

purse. As for such incest as is not in marriage and
other adulteries, they are but *peccadilia*,[1] punished by
doing penance in a white sheete, or els by some lesse
mulct without imprisonment. Moreover, this Commission punisheth the most high and execrable idolatries
by prisons and forfaiturs, making it a pecuniary matter,
contrary to the law of God, Deuteronomy 13 and
Deuteronomy 7.

Now let us come to Mr. Some's third argument, where
by Scripture he doth approve this High Commission to
be no new divise. King Jehoshaphat and king Artaxerxes directed high commissions. Jehoshaphat (saith
Mr. Some), in these words. " In Jerushalem did
Jehoshaphat set of the Levites and of the priests and
of the chiefe of the families of Israel, for the judgment
and cause of the Lord. And they returned to Jerushalem, and he charged them, saying, *etc.*"[2]

How ignorantly, if not corruptly, Doctor Some hath
inverted this text, both in the words and distinctions,
may appeare to any that wil compare it to the original.
He hath inverted the wordes thus, in that he saith (" for
the judgment and cause of the Lord "), where [whereas]
the text is (" for the judgment of the Lord, and the
plea, or strife ") Lemischphat Jehovah velarib. He
hath inverted [256] the distinctions in these words:
" And they returned to Jerushalem, and he charged
them, saiing," in which wordes he hath put a periode,
where the text is continued in the verse without distinction, and hath made a litle comma, where should
be an Hebrew periode; beginning the verse where he
should not, rending part of the eighth verse, and giving
it to the ninth:[3] wherby he hath dismembred and confounded the text (as shal by and by appeare) by mis-
placing this word Jehovah, and putting it after both

---

[1] Trifling offences.

[2] Some, *A Godly Treatise, wherein Are Examined and Confuted Many
Execrable Fancies*, p. 20. Also, 2 Chronicles 19: 8-11.

[3] Barrow's observation will be clarified by giving Dr. Some's quotation:
" In Jerusalem did Josophat set of the Levites, and of the priests, and
of the chiefe of the families of Israel, for the judgement and cause of
the Lord. And they returned to Jerusalem, and he charged them, saying,
Thus shall ye doe . . . . " Actually, verse eight ends with " Jerusalem,"
followed by a period. Verse nine begins: " And he charged them, saying, . . . "

the judgment and the plea, he hath given or rather
taken occasion to thinke, that this was but one entire
commission, consisting of ecclesiastical and civil persons
joined together, and that this commission had authority
to handle and decide both ecclesiastical and civil causes;
whereas in deed the word Jehovah is joined to the word
(*Mischpat*) of purpose to put difference betwixt the
ecclesiastical and politicall judgments, which are expressed in the tenth verse; the eleventh verse also
shewing the distinction both of these judgments and
judges: for ecclesiasticall matters sending to the people
Amariah the high priest to the temple and to the
ministers therof, the priests and Levites: for pollitike
and civil causes, sending the people to Zebadia, and
to those heads of the families mencioned in the eighth
verse, here called *Schitrim*, rulers or judges: which verse
he also hath most corruptly delivered, both by mis-
placing the wordes of the text, and conveiing in words
of his owne, especially in these words (" and the Levites
shal be officers before you ") where the words lye in
the next thus (" and judges Levites before you "),
wherby he craftily would collect, that the Levites executed civile functions, and so our bishops and priests
may be lords judges, justices of peace, and hold jurisdiction of civil causes; and this rable of Romish civilians,
advocates, proctors, *etc.*, might be officers in the stead
of Levites.[1] Further, his rash inverting the Hebrew
distinctions in the latter end of the eighth and beginning
of the ninth verse, he hath so roiled[2] and confounded
the text, as no man can understand who they were that
returned to Jerushalem (or rather as the text is *when
they should returne to Jerushalem*) whither these judges
commissioners (as Mr. Smoe [Some] calleth them) or
the other judges and people of the land, that in cases
of doubt should returne to Jerushalem, according to
the law and commandement of God, Deuteronomy 17:
8, 9, to enquire at the priests or at the chief judg, *etc.*
But Doctor Some having thus troubled and roiled [dis-

---

[1] In 2 Chronicles 19: 11, there is a clear distinction ; " And behold, Amariah
the chiefe priest is over you in all matters of the Lord, and Zebadiah the
sonne of Ishmael, the ruler of the house of Judah, for all the king's matters."
[2] Obscured, mixed up.

turbed, muddied] the pure fountaine with his feete, would now give us this muddy water to drinke: that this commission (as he termeth it) at Jerushalem was set over all the cities, judges, *etc.*, of the whole land, and that these commissioners were they that returned to Jerushalem. By which Scripture thus delivered and understood, he would shape and erect this his Lord's Grace High Commission. But let us now even a litle compare them together, and see what likenes there is betwixt Jehoshaphat's proceedings in Jerushalem, and theirs in this High Commission.

verse 5

Jehoshaphat set judges in the land through all the strong cities; he set in Jerushalem of the heads of the families of Israel, appointing amongst them one chiefe judg for al civil affaires, and the king's busines, as the king's substitute. He commanded also, and caused the priests to remaine [257] in their due course at Jerushalem, to studie and teach the law of God diligently: and to see this duly done of them, he set the high priest over them, to be the chiefe in all matters of the Lord. What of al this? What new thing is heere done, or besides law, Exodus 18, Numbers 11, Deuteronomy 1. That the prince also is charged, and of dutie ought to see the ministers of the church to doe their dutie and teach the law of God diligently and sincerely, we reade Deuteronomy 17, 1 Chronicles 28, 2 Chronicles 29 and 30 and 35. This did Jehoshaphat and no other thing. Now in that he placed it at Jerushalem, it was according to the commandment of God, who had chosen that place to put his name there, that the law might proceed out of Zion, and al people flow thither to worship God, and heare his word. But in al this Jehoshaphat hath neither commixt, nor confounded, the civil and ecclesiasticall offices in one commission; neither erected any new ecclesiastical ordinance, besides those which God in his word had prescribed; or perverted or diverted any ordinance that God hath instituted. But in this High Commission of the Church of England is an open commixture and confusion of civil and ecclesiastical offices and causes; a new divised ordinance with new officers, new pro-

stagelike or pontificall maner, as these our prela[...]
are in this Commission; but in this christian coun[...]
or assembly ech one hath free liberty and place [...]
relate or debate his owne cause, without interrupti[...]
or prejudice: neither is any thing heere decreed by t[...]
wil of any man, but only by the wil of God, and th[...]
upon evident demonstration of the word; otherwis[...]
no credite or obedience given to anything they s[...]
downe or determine. During the time of which counce[...]
and at any time after, without any prejudice, an[...]
Christian hath freedome and liberty, in due time an[...]
place, not disturbing the peaceable order of christia[...]
assemblies, to speake according to the word of God[...]
either in approbation or reproofe of any thing to be[...]
done, or done in that councel. Which councel or[...]
synode, as it hath not power to erect or bring in any[...]
new decrees or ordinances into the church, besides[...]
those which are prescribed in the booke of God (which[...]
are alsufficient for al times and occasions unto the[...]
world's end), so hath not this councel any power or[...]
authority over any church, or any member of the[...]
church, to censure, excommunicate, erect or depose[...]
any. This councel or assembly is only ordained for[...]
the help and quiet of churches, to discusse questions[...]
and to decide doubts, as they fall out and arise; that[...]
so all churches in all places might walke by one rule[...]
in the unitie of the spirit. This councel is not per-[...]
manent, or alwaies setled in one place, but to be used[...]
by any churches at any time or place upon due occa-[...]
sions. Neither is this councel so subsisting of the[...]
presbitery, or tied to the persons of any, that the least[...]
member of Christ is therby shut out, not suffred to[...]
heare or to speake, or any way prejudiced: neither is[...]
any church by this councell either deprived of their[...]
high power and authority, which Christ hath given to[...]
every severall congregation alike, or forestalled from[...]
the due execution therof towards any member of their[...]
congregation, or cause that ariseth amongst them. But[...]
(as is said) this councel is only a brotherly and peace-[...]
able meeting of sundry churches, for the better and[...]
more assured deciding and discussing of doubts and

ceedings, and a strange course not heard or read of
in the whole word of God. Yea by this Commission
they pervert and turne away the whole practise of al
the ordinances of Christ in his church.

Neither will that great commission which Artaxerxes
gave unto Hezra the priest,[1] any whit more either
couller or warrant this monstrous High Commission
of theirs, granted unto their chiefe priest and archbishop: which commission, if it should have reached
over far; yet had it rather beene to be imputed unto
the ignorance of the heathen king that knew not the
lawes of God, than to have beene alledged or urged as
an example for us to follow in the same evil, especially
now under Christ's most perfect absolute Testament
and ministery in his church. But what was this commission of Artaxerxes that Doctor Some so enforceth?
Artaxerxes granted unto Hezra leave by commission to
carry up with him unto Jerusalem al such of Israel and
Juda, as were willing to goe, together with al such
vessels, instruments, gold, silver, or free gifts, as should
be given unto the service of God by them in Babilon:
as also that being come to Jerushalem, he should set
judges and arbiters, that might both diligently teach
and see the lawes of God duly executed. What is in
this commission found contrarie to the law of God; or
what did Hezra by this commission contrarie to the
law of God? It wil heere be said, that Hezra being
a priest, had civil and ecclesiastical power committed
unto him, and by vertue of this commission exercised
both civil and ecclesiastical jurisdiction, *etc.* We see
manifestly in the 23 and 25 verses that the king's commission had relation wholy to the law of God, that
Hezra being a man prompt therin, should see al things
done in the temple at Hierusalem and in the kingdome
of Juda and Israel, according to the law of God; yet
heere is no commission given him to execute both civil
and ecclesiastical offices in his owne person, neither
reade we, or may we [258] (without sin) imagine that
ever he did so; for that had beene an heinous breach
of all God's lawes, and unsufferable confusion of al God's

[1] Ezra 7: 25, 26.

ordinances; who as he hath in his word alwaies put difference and distinction betwixt the civil and ecclesiastical estates, so hath he unto ech several office, apointed several ministers to attend. Monstrous therfore and most ungodly is that commission, where both these estates and offices are mingled and confounded in one. Antichristian and beastlike is that person,[1] that sitteth as chiefe of this Commission, and exerciseth both civile and ecclesiastical jurisdiction, by the commandement of any mortal creature, it being so directly repugnant to the lawes of God, and the Testament of Christ, so pernitious to the church of Christ, utterly perverting and diverting al the ordinances therof, and subverting the whole libertie, powers, censures, and duties of the whole church, and of everie member and minister therof. Evil then may this mixt confuse ecclesiastical High Commission be compared unto, or approved, by this godly commission of Artaxerxes; or this popish supremacie, inordinate power, and civil jurisdiction of this high arch-priest or bishop, by the person of Hezra: who most painfully and sincerely taught the law of God, most precisely practised the same within the boundes of his calling, most modestly and faithfully behaved himself in al things, as the Scripture beareth recorde.

The 26 verse, where the disobedient and the offendors are commanded to have due judgment and execution according unto the law of God, and qualitie of their offence, can by no common reason, much lesse by any christian judgment, be said to be commanded to be executed by Ezra his person. The prieste's office (as we have said) was to teach the law, and to exhorte al persons to the obedience of the same; but their office was not to exercise civile jurisdiction, or to execute civil judgmentes: these were to be performed by civil magistrates. Neither may these judgments of death, eradication, mulct of goods, of bandes, by this commandement of Artaxerxes (who no doubt used such words in this commission as agreed to the lawes and judgmentes of Persia, rather than of knowledg in God's law) be

[1] Archbishop Whitgift.

made either ecclesiastical censures, or any way be executed in any christian pollitike regiment, otherwise than they are found to accord with the lawes and judgments of God prescribed in his word. But this new divised High Ecclesiastical Commission doth not only censure and punish al faultes of their churches, by these judgments and penalties, but doth inflict them in what measure and manner they lust upon al persons, for al cawses whatsoever; whether cawses of religion, as open idolatrie, popish masse, *etc.*, or contempt of their injunctions and decrees, in not resorting to their worship and sacraments, or administring them after any other maner, than they have prescribed, *etc.*, whither for civil offences, be they never so hainous and abhominable, as most odious incests, adulteries, polygamies, *etc.* Al these by this Commission are punished by the purse and by the prison; for the law of God for idolatours and adulterers were al to sharpe: therfore this holy councel (guided belike by some better and wiser spirit) have found out this more mitigate course, repressing these sinnes. But if any upon faith and conscience [259] towards God, refraine their idolatrous devises, there can for such be found out no kind of hostility, confiscation, perpetual close imprisonment, sufficient for their faultes.

Thus no way can this High Commission of the Church of England, be justified by these examples of Jehoshaphat and Artaxerxes, neither hath it any more defence in the New Testament, where is no mention of any such councel or court set over all churches and over every member, minister, cause, affaire and censure therof to impose, depose, determine, judge, censure, punish, at their pleasure whome and what they lust, without controlement. We reade in the practise of the apostles, of a synode or councell of sundry churches for the deciding of controversies and doubtes, where certaine chosen elders of the churches are therunto assembled, together with such faithfull of any church as will be present, without shutting out of any of them:[1] neither are these elders here gathered in any such

[1] Acts 15: 2, 3, 4, 6, 22, 30.

X

questions that arise, leaving the whole practise and due execution of al things, to every particular congregation, in that order and maner that Christ hath prescribed in his Testament. [260]

These occasions, rules, and proceedings of synodes, councels, or meetings of divers churches, we find left unto us in that holy patterne, Acts 15, where though the chiefe builders the apostles themselves were, yet even there were al things handled with this order, modesty, sobriety, freedome, *etc.*

But now if we compare their High Ecclesiastical Commission unto this holy councell and meeting, how unlike in al their orders, proceedings and actions shall it be found? Their Commission being made a continuall setled permanent court, having strange judges, advocates, officers, jurisdiction, pleas, processe, *etc.*, usurping and exercising supreme power and absolute authority over al churches, ministers, persons, lawes, doctrines, to ratifie or disanull, to establish or reject, to erect or depose whome and what they lust, executing al the censures and offices of the church, changing, bringing in, and setting up what they please, shutting out the sentence of all churches and Christians, allowing them neither interest, election, voice, or presence in this their councell, thrusting their decrees and constitutions as most holy upon all churches and the consciences of all men with an high and strong hand, to be received without contradiction or question, adjuring, examining, suspending, deposing, fining, emprisoning, persecuting with all hostility all such as receave not their constitutions, and submit not unto their power. Now let any Christian judge, whether this Commission be not more like unto the high court of the beast, than unto an holy peaceable orderly assembly of Christians, met in the feare of God, and guided by his spirit to enquire and search out God's wil, and humbly to rest in the same.

The civill magistrat's power or presence can no way justifie this Commission, or their proceedings, being found so directly contrary to the Testament of Christ, unto which it is now lawfull for no man or angel to superordeine, alter, or pluck away anything, without hainous sacrilege. This monstrous commixture then of these distinct powers in one court or person, together with this confuse practise, barbarous havock and tyranny they make and exercise over God's heritage and Christ's poore servants, doe evidently denote, and, as by the very steppes, trase out unto all men, the person, throne, and power of that antichrist, that adversary, that beast, accordingly as they are described and foreshewed unto us in the Scriptures, Mathew 24: 15, 2 Thessalonians 2. How antichrist should presume into the very place and office of Christ, shewing himself in the church of God as God, by changing the lawes and Testament of Christ, and by bringing in new ordinances, new ministery, worship, *etc.*, Revelation 13 and Revelation 17: 12, 13, 14, 17. How antichrist being thus exalted, the dragon should give him his power, his throne, and his great authority; as also the kings of the earth; yea, such kings as had before burnt the whore with fire, should give unto the beast their power and authority, wherwith he should fight with the lamb, and make war with the saints, opening his mouth unto blasphemy against God, and his tabernacle, [261] and them that dwell therin; setting up his blasphemous image in all places, *etc.*

Now as we have by the light of God's word, in this litle that hath beene saied, evidently found and seene these bishops, their courtes and government, to be wholy antichristian, and utterlie unlawfull, but especially this their High Court of Commission, to be most blasphemous, the very throne of the beast, utterly commingling, confounding, and subverting al God's ordinances, all estates, and offices both of church and common welth, the whole liberty of Christians, the power and duties of the church: so likewise if we by the same rules, but as lightly examine and measure the secret classes, the ordinary set synodes, and councels of ministers (as they terme themselves) which these Reformists now privily bring in; and would openly set up;[1] they shall no doubt be found as new, strange, and antichristian, as prejudicial to the liberty of the saints, and to the power, right, and duties of the whole church, and as contrary to the gospell of our Lord Jesus Christ, as these other, what shew soever of former antiquity, or of present necessity, they may pretend. And this, if they be compared in the persons assembled, and causes for which they are assembled, and which they handle in the set continued times and place of their meeting, in their order and maner of proceeding and judgment in their decrees and power, unto that perfect patterne of all christian councelles, Acts 15, will forthwith appeare.

The persons assembled in these councels are only ministers, al other Christians being shut out, and allowed neither place, voice, or consent among them. The causes for which they are assembled, and which they handle, not being doubtes or questions which arise in the churches, but al the affaires, offices, and duties of the church, and that without making the churches privy wherfore they assemble, or what they will there handle. The time and place of these councels, they (without the wil and privity of the churches) make setled, continual, permanent; not leaving to the church either the liberty when and where to keepe these councels, or whome to use in these councels. The order and maner of their proceeding and judgment, is, first to choose and erect amongst them a prolocutor, moderator, or judg, to governe and order this action, who and when they shall speake, and when they shall cease, *etc.* Where the matters being debated, the greater part prevaileth and carrieth the judgment. Their decrees are peremp-

[1] For the policies and practices of the Presbyterians in the 1580's, see A. F. Scott Pearson, *Thomas Cartwright and Elizabethan Puritanism, 1535—1603*, chapter V; *The Presbyterian Movement in the Reign of Queen Elizabeth as Illustrated by the Minute Book of the Dedham Classis, 1582—1589*, edited by R. G. Usher for the Royal Historical Society. Marshal M. Knappen, *Tudor Puritanism, a Chapter in the History of Idealism*, chapters XII, XIII, XIV. Two unpublished theses, one by Edna Bibby, " The Puritan Classical Movement of Elizabeth's Reign," Manchester University, 1929, and the other by Patrick Collinson, " The Puritan Classical Movement in the Reign of Elizabeth I," London University, 1957, are very good. Microfilm copies of both theses are available at the Folger Shakespeare Library.

tory, irrevocable, most holy, inviolable, to be receaved and embraced of all churches without contradiction or scruple, no power left to any church to examine, refuse, or reverse the same, be they found never so contrary to God's word, but only either by the same councell, or by act of Parliament: in the meane while they all must practise and obey these decrees. The power of these councells is over all churches, persons, causes, doctrines, to give the right hand of fellowship (as they terme it) or to send the bill of divorce, to ratifie or reject, whome and what they will.

This councel also executeth al the censures and duties of the church, [262] as to make or depose ministers, to censure, excommunicate, *etc.* To conclude, as all these councels have and exercise power and jurisdiction over the church, so are they in authority one above an other: as the synode above the classes, the councell above the synode, to confirme, abrogate, or disanul whatsoever constitutions or actions the other hath made. Yea (as some report), upon the enormities and abuses that did arise in these councels and assemblies of bishops, were devised and erected these new strange orders and degrees of bishops, arch-bishops, patriarches, popes, and all their substitutes and courtes. From which strange councels, offices, ministery, courtes, have flowed forth and daily spring, all these strange popish antichristian orders, decrees, innumerable divises and traditions, daily innovations, continuall changes in the worship of God, all the proceedings of the church and of the whole Testament of Christ; whiles men rest not in the wisdome and councels of God, but presume to be wise above that they ought to be wise, some attributing unto their clergie (as they call them), others to the prince, others to the church more than inough, none yeilding unto Christ that which is his due: namely, to suffer him to governe his whole church by such officers and lawes as he hath in his Testament prescribed; but rather in the presumption of their owne hearts they will set over him and his church such lawes and officers, or at the least assigne unto him such lawes and officers, as they thinke best to accord, and judg most meet for their pollicie: as though Christ could be a minister or mediatour of any other Testament, than of his owne; or that any mortal men may alter, change, neglect or reject Christ's Testament, without his fearful wrath and heavy indignation for the same.

Wherfore, seeing the whole church and al the proceedings therof must be built upon Christ's Testament; seing every soule and every action shalbe judged by Christ's Testament; seing nothing is pleasing unto God, or wil stand before the face of Christ, that is found disagreeing to Christ's Testament; seing also even by this litle search and superficiall view we have taken of the present estate, and pretended reformation of this their Church of England, all things appeare to be out of frame, stil in the olde corruption, and (at the best) but enclining to the primitive and ancient defections from Christ's Testament, nothing being aright or according to the will of God amongst them: seing we find all those Scriptures that have foreshewed of antichrist and his proceedings, lively fulfilled amongst them, al the markes of that painted deceitful harlot, the false and malignant church, to be founde upon them; as also all the vials of God's wrathfull judgments to be powred forth upon them, and all their doings. Finally, seing God vouchsafeth both to discover, and to call al men forth out of Babilon, by proclaiming of his glorious gospel, and yet offreth more grace before he let fal the heavy milstone of his finall indignation upon them al to grind them to dust, and to presse them to the bottomme of hel, being ready to receave all that come forth unto him, to esteeme, guide, and defend them as his deare children: it [263] behooveth al such, in whome is any care of their owne salvation, any feare of God, or love of that ^{Revel. 18} appearing of our Lord Jesus Christ, to preserve their soules and bodies pure from the idolatrie and abhominations of the false church, to save themselves from this wicked and perverse generation, by comming out ^{Act. 2: 40} from amongst them, and fleeing out of Babel, and by ^{2 Cor. 6: 17} gathering themselves unto the lambe in mount Sion, there amongst and together with his chosen called ^{Zach. 2: 7} faithful servants under his banner and conduct to ^{Revel. 14}

fight in all patient and constant maner that good fight of faith, holding forth the word of life against al the works and powers of darknes, not abhorring the crosse of Christ, or loving in his service their lives unto the death, but being alwaies ready to do or suffer according to the will of God, following the lamb wheresoever he goeth: that so he may lead them in the waies of life and peace, and at length bring them to the full fruition of that endles happines which he hath prepared for all his in his Father's kingdome, there to rest with him in perfect joy for ever and ever.

Which grace that they may find, as I have not spared my poore endevour (though therby I have exposed my self to present peril and open reproch, by the violent hands and virulent tongues of these malignant adversaries) to blow the trumpet, awaken and admonish all, that yet some might be saved: so shal I not cease, whiles yet God preserveth me alive amongst them, even in my continual praiers, incessantly to beseech the Lord to shew this mercie unto his chosen; who because they are only knowen unto himself, I shal not cease to hope and wish that even the greatest enemies might be of this number: that whereas now they stand the waged marked servants of antichrist, they might by unfained repentance, wash away those stigmatical skarres, be mustered and inrolled in the Lamb's booke of life, having his Father's name written in their foreheads: to whome be praise in the church by Christ Jesus throughout all generations for ever. Amen.

But the foundation of God standeth firme, having this seale: the Lord knoweth who are his; and let every one, naming the name of God depart from iniquitie. 2 Timothy 2: 19.

If thow be wise, thow shalt be wise for thy selfe; but if thow scorne, thow alone shalt suffer. Proverbs 9: 12.

By the Lord's most unworthy servant and witnes in bandes.

HENRY BARROWE.

FINIS

[264]   *The Printer*[1] *to the Reader.*

I must acknowledg verie many faults escaped in the printing of this booke, and therfore do crave the reader's patience, and the author's pardon, having given the one (no doubt) some cause of offence; and done the other (I feare) a greater wrong: but hopinge that both will rest satisfied, and that the reader shall reape the proffit of this fruitfull discourse, I bid them farewell.

[1] The printer was one Hanse, and the place of publication was Dort. Daniel Studley and James Forester aided in copying Barrow's manuscript, Robert Stokes arranged the financial details and Arthur Byllett read the proof. See *The Egerton Papers,* edited by J. Payne Collier for the Camden Society (London, 1840), pp. 166-179. The original documents are in the Huntington Library, Ellesmere MSS. 2094—2096.

INDEX

Act of Supremacy, 19, 21, 42, 118, 122, 200, 201, 497, 601, 644

Act of Uniformity, 107, 109, 122, 283, 497

Additional MSS., 91

Admonition to the People, 36, 225, 231, 241, 244, 246, 534, 565, 577, 603, 622, 642

Ainsworth, Henry, 212, 250, 253

Alison, Richard, 44, 67, 68, 208, 210, 211, 213-222, 247

Anabaptists, 10, 33, 89, 125, 126 133, 136, 151, 154, 163, 171, 175, 293, 316, 438, 443, 532, 563

Anderson, Edmund, 17, 20, 21, 193, 197, 198

Andrewes, Lancelot, 506

Answere to George Gifford's Pretended Defence, 42, 132, 212, 261

Arber, Edward, 176, 187

Arches, Court of, 37, 91, 144, 336, 616

Aristotle, 21, 29, 344, 562

Aubrey, William, 252

Augustine, 12, 21, 155, 156, 158, 160, 161, 167, 393

Aylmer, John, 15, 16, 17, 20, 26, 33, 44, 67, 90, 97, 101, 103, 177-181, 183, 185-187, 193, 197, 242, 247, 341, 394

Bancroft, Richard, 49, 50, 54, 559

Baptism, 1, 13, 20, 31-34, 56, 134, 196, 197, 205, 281, 419-453

Baronius, Caesar, 339

Barrow's First Examination, 5, 86-100

Barrow's Second Examination, 7, 101-105

Barrow's Third Examination, 14, 170-172

Barrow's Fourth Examination, 14, 173-189, 489

Barrow's Fifth Examination, 19, 190-207

Barrow's Final Answer, 119

Barrow, Thomas, 6, 98

Beza, Theodore, 7, 95, 96, 103

Bibby, Edna, 534, 669

Billet or Byllett, Arthur, 210, 211, 262, 673

Billet, Sarah, 211

Bilson, Thomas, 36, 345

Bonner, Edmund, 90

Book of Common Prayer, 1, 10, 15, 16, 18, 30, 34, 39, 42, 55-57, 130, 131, 133, 134, 196, 283, 361, 485, 624

Bowman, Christopher, 41, 176, 178, 455

Breefe Sum of Our Profession, 5, 9, 55, 81-85, 103, 118

Bridewell, 254, 262

Bridges, John, 430-437

Brief Discoverie, viii, 27-38, 43, 68, 96, 157, 225, 254, 261-673

Brief Summe of the Causes, 9, 43, 50, 82, 83, 103, 118-150

Bromhead, Anne, 120

Bromhead, Hughe, 120

Broughton, Hugh, 345

Browne, Robert, 38, 49, 50, 51, 54, 64, 82, 102, 207, 345, 440, 526

Brownists, 82, 89, 224, 452

Brylinger, Nicholas, 95

675

Buckhurst, Lord, 16, 174, 176, 177, 178, 181, 182, 186, 394

Burghley, Lord, 15, 16, 24, 26, 27, 45, 46, 91, 137, 152, 174-189, 224, 226, 247, 252, 257, 284, 379, 394, 560, 652

Burke, Edmund, 13

Burrage, Champlin, 49, 82, 91, 120

Burroughs, Edith, 255

Calendar, x, 30, 170, 362, 387, 465

Calling, 4, 12, 45, 59, 76, 162, 236

Calvin, John, 7, 12, 28, 30, 33, 96, 103, 156, 287, 293-335, 407, 409, 411, 440, 441, 471, 513

Canterbury, Archbishop of, *see* Whitgift

Carlson, Leland H., 50, 64, 69, 82, 103, 207, 345, 526, 650

Cartwright, Thomas, 51, 52, 59, 69, 103, 137, 143, 262, 506, 615

Catechisms, 103, 104, 513

Cecil, William, *see* Burghley

Charke, William, 51, 52, 137, 143, 262, 506

Church Government, *see* Discipline

Cicero, 29, 344

Clapham, Henoch, 209-211, 222

Clare Hall, 96

Classis, 206, 524, 534, 559, 668, 669

Clink, 6, 38, 41, 87, 91, 253, 255, 256

Collection of Certain Letters, 45, 52, 67, 137, 143, 261

Collection of Certaine Sclaunderous Articles, 43-45, 56, 67, 185, 191, 208, 256, 261

Collier, John Payne, 203, 208, 266, 673

Collinson, Patrick, 534, 559, 669

Conscience, 30, 31, 33, 184, 229, 397, 401, 407-415, 427

Cooper, Martin, 506

Cooper, Robert, 506

Cooper, Thomas, 17, 20, 33, 36, 193, 225, 231, 241, 242, 244, 246, 247, 345, 430, 554, 565, 577, 589, 599, 602-612, 616, 617, 621

Cosin, Richard, 6, 91, 93-96, 99, 193, 650

Courts, Ecclesiastical, 4, 24, 37, 144, 226, 246, 336, 616-622, 636

Crane, Nicholas, 26, 254

Cranmer, Thomas, 39, 427

Crippen, T. G., 49, 102, 106

Darrell or Dayrell, John, 209

Deacons, 22, 104, 217, 219, 274, 606-609

Delegates, Court of, 37, 144, 336, 616

Dentford, William, 255

Dexter, Henry M., 209, 211, 212, 222, 432

Discipline, 2, 3, 22, 36, 37, 71, 84, 126, 143-150, 196, 263, 264, 306, 345, 516-525, 553, 606-647

Donation of Constantine, 340, 443

Donatism, 89, 94, 119, 123, 136, 155

Dove, John, 18, 190

Education, 29, 139, 244, 343-346, 350-352, 538-541

Egerton, John (Stephen ?), 506

Egerton, Thomas, 122, 123, 142

Elders, *see* Presbyters

Elizabeth, Queen, 12-14, 18, 30, 39, 98, 166, 192, 198, 256, 339, 345, 351, 427, 432, 477, 530, 644, 646

Ellesmere MSS., 178, 203, 208, 255, 261, 455, 617, 647, 673

Ex-officio Oath, 6, 15, 37, 182

Excommunication, 19, 20, 23, 45, 57, 133, 134, 201, 221, 222, 293, 585, 623-647

Faculties, Court of, 37, 144, 336, 616
Fairlambe, Peter, 209
Fanshawe, Thomas, 88
Fasts, 396-407, 415-418
Feasts, 383-396
Fenton, Edward, 68, 69
Fewe Observations, ix, 212
Field, John, 232
First Part of the Platforme, 24, 25,
    224-249, 560
Fisher, Edward, 251
Fisher, John, 251
Flacius, Matthias, 339
Fleet, 14, 41, 126, 170, 171, 174, 175,
    177, 178, 200, 251, 254, 255,
    261, 266
Fludd or Floyd, William, 51, 52,
    137, 143, 262, 506
Folger Shakespeare Library, ix, x,
    86, 209, 210, 212, 222, 495, 534,
    669
Forrester or Forester, James, 261,
    673
Four Causes of Separation, 1, 49-66,
    68, 82, 103, 106, 107, 238
Foxe, John, 90
Fragment of a Letter, 38, 106, 107
Freeman, Thomas, 256
Fulke, William, 31-33, 440-442

Gambell, Clement, 18, 190, 503
Gatehouse, 7, 15, 100, 102, 107, 126,
    170, 173, 176, 182, 253-256
Gent, Thomas, 17, 193
Gerard, Gilbert, 17, 193
Gifford, George, 9-11, 41, 42, 52, 53,
    59, 81, 82, 118-150, 198, 206,
    262, 506
Godly Treatise Containing (1588),
    14, 151, 169, 171, 172, 186,
    192, 208, 351, 379, 422, 423
*Godly Treatise, Wherein Are Exam-
    ined* (1589), 152, 175, 186, 192,
    195, 207, 293, 351, 372-379,

393, 397, 423, 528, 536, 574,
    590, 602, 657, 660
Goodere, Henry, 184
Gravet, William, 183, 184
Gray's Inn, 6, 93, 99
Greenwood, Abel, 41
Greenwood, John, viii, ix, 5, 14, 24,
    27, 32, 38-46, 67, 81, 85, 91,
    106, 116, 132, 137, 175, 191,
    192, 200, 212, 224, 225, 426,
    432, 440, 455, 653
Greenwood's Examination, 41
Grindal, Edmund, 530
Gwalter, John, 262

Hanbury, Benjamin, 213
Harley MSS., 170, 173, 174, 177,
    178, 252, 455, 503
Harrison, G. B., 91, 193
Harrison, Robert, 64, 68-70
Haslop, 92
Hatton, Christopher, 17, 153, 174-
    179, 182, 187, 379, 394
Henry VIII, 12, 14, 477
Herbert, John, 252
Heresy, 17, 123, 160, 185, 192, 542
High Commission, Court of, 7-9, 37,
    38, 91, 92, 101, 102, 106, 116,
    144, 174, 182, 284, 336, 511,
    582, 602, 616, 647
Hooker, Richard, 36, 345, 589
Hul, 5, 91
Huntington Library, x, 118, 122,
    203, 208, 212, 222, 673
Hutchinson, William, 185, 191, 193,
    506

Intercepted Letter, 42, 433

Jackson, Richard, 26, 254
Jackson, Roger, 18, 190
Jackson, William A., 495
Jacob, Henry, 87, 345
Johnson, Francis, 72, 87, 209, 250,
    262, 345

Junius or Iunius, Francis, 63, 330, 564

Knappen, Marshall M., 669
Knollys, Francis, 257

Lacy, Robert, 99
Lambeth Palace, 6, 7, 107, 116, 118, 152, 171, 211, 222, 397, 423
Lansdowne MSS., 100, 102, 171, 178, 193, 250, 252, 530
Latimer, Hugh, 39
Lawne, Christopher, 213
Letter to Mr. Fisher, 26, 27
London, Bishop of, *see* Aylmer
Lord's Prayer, 13, 195, 204, 367, 372-379
Lord's Supper, 34, 56, 205, 418, 630
Love, Mr., 18, 190

Magistrates, 13, 25, 64, 80, 158, 159, 229, 326, 405, 554, 640-646
Maintenance, 12, 16, 25, 157, 164-168, 186, 227, 234, 247, 286, 355-361
Maitland, S. R., 211
Manwood, Roger, 17, 193
Marriage, 34, 41, 453-455
Marshall, William, 88
Martin, Henry, 82, 99
Martin Marprelate, ix, 43, 176, 184, 254, 416, 430, 452, 559, 565, 577, 617
Master Some Laid Open, ix, 32, 43, 92, 426-453
Maynerd, Margaret, 26, 96, 254
Membership, 1, 45, 56, 132-135, 169, 281, 286, 290, 291, 298-306
Middleburg, 87, 88
Ministry, 2, 11, 12, 29, 57, 136-143, 162, 163, 226, 233, 335-355
Mullins, John, 6, 91, 93, 94
Munday, 92

Newgate, 175, 254, 255
Newton, Joachim, 171, 200
Nicholas, 92, 102
Nicholas, John, 178
Norton, Thomas, 104
Nowell, Alexander, 101, 104, 513

Oaths, 42, 93, 102-104, 116, 194, 601, 650, 651

Pastoral Letter, 8, 68, 106-117
Paule, George, 91, 104, 116, 174
Peel, Albert, ix, 50, 64, 68, 69, 82, 103, 184, 207, 526, 650
Pembroke Hall, 96, 441
Penry, John, 32, 86, 151, 184, 199, 209, 211, 224, 232, 379, 426-453, 648, 650
Peterhouse, 153, 351, 375
Petition Directed, 198, 199
Pickering, Maurice, 100, 102
Plaine Confutation, 44, 67, 68, 208, 210, 211, 213
Plaine Refutation, viii, 24, 87, 118, 119, 261
Polity, *see* Discipline
Powicke, F. J., 82, 83, 87, 173, 213, 229, 250, 251, 253, 426
Prayers, 16, 18, 39, 40, 42, 132, 181, 196, 204, 365
Prerogative Court of Canterbury, 37, 336, 616
Presbyterians, 11, 51, 52, 103, 137, 143, 198, 206, 254, 262, 435, 506, 519, 533, 534, 558-562, 588, 590, 615, 619, 627, 637, 668-670
Presbyters, 22, 37, 187, 217, 219, 525, 606-609, 618
Presbytery, 19, 20, 37, 54, 200, 206, 524
Prisoners, 26, 27, 89, 91, 252-257
Prisons, 38, 41, 87, 91, 100, 126, 170, 171, 252-257
Privy Council, 14, 92, 176-189, 432

Index

Profes of Aparant Churche, 3, 43, 67-80, 96, 106
Prophesying, 524-541
Pruter, Hugo R., 213
Purdye, John, 26, 250, 254

Quakers, 15, 465

Ragland, 178
Rathband, William, 262
Reasons against Read Prayer, 40, 41
Reformists, *see* Presbyterians
Reply to George Gifford, 41
Ridley, Nicholas, 39
Robinson, John, 212
Rokeby, Ralph, 252
Row, Alice, 26, 254

Sackville, Thomas, *see* Buckhurst
Sacraments, 13, 31-34, 131, 155, 157, 196, 287, 292, 308, 418-453
Scambler, Edmund, 97
Separation, 1, 50, 54-66, 68, 77, 84, 88, 120, 503
Settle, Thomas, 455
Shepherd, Mr., 6, 91
Short Reply, 119, 262
Short Treatise, 52, 83, 119, 198, 206
Smith, Quintin, 18, 190
Smyth, *see* Smith
Some, Robert, 11, 12, 14, 15, 18, 30-32, 59, 151-172, 175, 177, 178, 183, 186, 192, 195, 204, 208, 247, 251, 293, 308, 313, 351, 356-358, 372-379, 393-401, 407, 408, 422, 423, 425, 428, 431-433, 442, 445, 471-485, 528, 531-533, 536, 574, 584, 585, 590, 594, 657, 660
Sparrow, John, 178
Sperin, Thomas, 506
Stanhope, Edward, 27, 193, 255
Stillingfleet, Edward, 88, 213
Stokes, Robert, 208, 261

Stokesley, John, 32, 427
Strype, John, 91, 103, 250, 256, 284, 399, 530
Stubbs, William, 144, 336
Studley, Daniel, 151, 261, 262, 266, 673

Thompson, Edmond, 256
Thornelie, 105
Throkmorton or Throckmorton, Job, ix, 32, 33, 43, 92, 425-453
Throkmorton MSS., 452
Tirrell, Edward, 171, 200
Travers, Walter, 51, 52, 137, 143, 262, 506
Tremellius, Immanuel, 63, 330, 564
Trinity College, 96
True Church and the False Church, 67, 68, 103
True Description, viii, 21-23, 43, 67, 68, 96, 157, 208-223, 261, 293, 620

Udall, John, 174
Usher, Roland G., 144, 284, 534, 648, 669

Vestments, 35, 125, 536

Waddington, John, 213, 250
Walker, Williston, 23, 213
Wall, Thomas, 88, 213
Walton, Richard, 92
Waterer, Roger, 27, 255
Watson, 6, 92, 99
Whitaker, William, 104
Whitgift, John, 6, 7, 9, 15-21, 26, 27, 33, 49, 51, 67, 82, 91-100, 101, 103, 116, 117, 153, 174, 177, 178, 185, 192-195, 197, 247, 256, 261, 284, 341, 379, 394, 397, 423, 652, 664
Wiggenton or Wigginton, Giles, 49, 51, 52, 59, 67, 68, 103, 104
Wiggenton MSS., 49, 67, 68, 106

Wilcox, Thomas, 232
Winchester, Bishop of, *see* Thomas
 Cooper
Wood Street Counter, 176
Worship, 10, 15, 41, 55, 84, 130-
 132, 156, 159, 179, 364-382

Wray, Christopher, 17, 18, 20, 21,
 193, 194, 198, 199

Young, Richard, 14, 15, 17, 151,
 171, 172, 175, 177, 178, 184,
 251